Effective Writing

ROBERT HAMILTON MOORE

GEORGE WASHINGTON UNIVERSITY

Effective Writing

THIRD EDITION

8490

HOLT, RINEHART AND WINSTON

New York · Chicago · San Francisco · Toronto · London

March, 1967

PREFACE TO THE
THIRD EDITION

This third edition of *Effective Writing* is at once the same book and a new book. Like the other two it is founded on the belief that students first need to learn to control an idea as distinct from a topic and to work with unity, development, and organization before being able to master precise control over the sentences and words with which their ideas are expressed. Consequently, I have retained the pattern of the whole composition, the paragraph, the sentence, and the word, presenting rhetorical principles applicable to all types of writing, with special attention to exposition and with constant emphasis on the importance of the writer's purpose and of his audience in controlling his choice of methods.

As before, I have tried to produce a book which will be sufficiently flexible to lend itself to different kinds of courses. But I have not, I hope, tried to be all things to all men, since such attempts usually end by pleasing no men at all. In this revision, I have retained much detail which an experienced teacher might regard as obvious and unnecessary, or might prefer to present in his own way. Still, limitations of space have forced me to omit much that I would like to have included, and the experienced teacher will find constant opportunity to supplement the text. If he is willing to assume that his students can and will read with understanding and retention, he may indeed find that a relatively full text provides him with an unaccustomed freedom to range beyond the fundamentals. But now more than ever many of our teachers are not yet experienced enough to know what needs to be said about the problems of writing. For such teachers, and their students, a detailed text is invaluable.

In all of these ways, this third edition closely resembles the first two. Yet in the ten years since *Effective Writing* was first published, college freshmen have changed a great deal. For one thing, students' interests and attitudes and assumptions are not what they were a decade ago. Accordingly, in explanatory detail, in the exercises, and in illustrative examples throughout, I have addressed a somewhat more sophisticated student. Furthermore, as the students have changed, the composition course has changed with them. For a single example, many composition courses now include material on the nature of language itself which ten years ago would have been introduced only incidentally or reserved for later years. To meet these changes, in this complete reworking of the text I have tried not only to tighten the phrasing and provide fresh details, but to adjust the book to the students we now meet in the courses we now offer.

This adjustment has necessitated the addition of new material to provide the approaches and the depth which many freshman courses demand. In the chapter on diction, for example, much has been added on the sources of our vocabulary and on the effects of metaphorical extension on denotative and connotative meaning. The chapter on critical writing now includes discussion of most of the types of critical themes assigned in literature-centered courses. In the chapter on reasoning and persuasion, I have expanded the discussion of implication and inference, have rewritten the section on emotional appeals to suggest the major subtleties introduced by recent motivational research, and have strengthened the section on the problems peculiar to argumentative writing. In the chapter on the research paper, the major changes lie in the adoption almost entirely of the documentation recommended by the Modern Language Association, with its attendant simplification of footnote form, and in the addition of material on the nature of paraphrase and the danger of unintentional plagiarism.

The revised Handbook attempts to apply the insights of linguistic study to its descriptions of written English as the college student usually needs to write. I believe that the usages recommended are realistic within the sometimes contradictory attitudes with which readers—including college teachers in all fields—judge student writing. What readers believe to be the facts of reputable usage cannot be ignored if writing is to be effective, and a student needs to be aware of existing shibboleths even when they are linguistically ill-founded. I have not hesitated to make recommendations which may help a student choose wisely when he is confronted with disputed choices, but I have tried at the same time to make the student aware of the necessity of choice.

Throughout the Handbook, I have reviewed all items and modified most of them in the light of recent linguistic and rhetorical studies. The chapter on grammar has been completely rewritten and the chapter on punctuation has been extensively revised to take eclectic advantage of those elements of the linguistic revolution which seem to me to be most useful in freshman classes. The grammatical terminology I have used, however, is largely traditional, for despite its weaknesses the traditional terminology remains the only one which all freshmen have somewhere met. It is also the one which lends itself best to use by teachers who are not specialists, or by students who consult the Handbook individually for guidance while writing or revising themes. Finally, the Glossary has been extensively revised to adjust it to current needs. Though it will not wholly please the specialists of any school, the Handbook will, I believe, prove more useful than before to both teacher and student.

I continue, of course, to be very grateful to my own teachers, including my students, my colleagues, and the writers of many books. And I am very grateful to all who have helped through the past decade by generous comment on the preceding editions. These include Richard Beal, James McCrimmon, Edward Robbins, and Dorothy Rushing. In addition, I'd like to thank those who reviewed the present edition and made helpful suggestions: William Madden, Nancy Dasher, and Robert Weaver. I am most grateful of all to my wife, whose contributions, both directly and in forebearance, have been so great that I do not understand how a bachelor could ever produce a book.

Robert Hamilton Moore

Washington, D.C.
December 1964

CONTENTS

* Items marked with an asterisk are followed by exercises.

The Handbook

Effective Writing

1

Writing Themes

Because the process of learning to use language efficiently is very complex, your instructor may employ any of widely varying methods. You and your classmates may need more, or less, grammar review; more, or less, reading practice; more, or less, attention to the meanings of words, their origin, and their development. You may be given a great deal of speaking practice, or very little. You may work with movies, and magazines, and newspapers; with literary masterpieces; with the problems that engross students of language; or with your own writing and that of your classmates. But whatever methods or emphases best fit your needs, you are certain to have themes to write.

DEFINITION

What is a theme? How can themes help anyone learn to use language effectively?

A theme is a practice exercise in writing, in the techniques of saying something in a way that will convey it to the reader you want to reach. Themes are accounts of events; explanations of processes, of definitions, of ideas and opinions; arguments presenting opinions persuasively; critical evaluations of what you have experienced or of what you have read. Writing themes and having them criticized by your instructor will help you discover where your weaknesses lie and will help you learn to control your presentation of what

1

you are trying to say. Their length will depend on how much you know about the central idea you are developing and on how much specific detail the reader will need in order to understand exactly what you mean.

We shall consider later in more detail where to go for subjects if the choice is left open to you, and how to limit general subjects to a central idea that can be developed in a unified paper. Usually you will do your best work, get the best grades, and learn most if you write about subjects you are interested in and know from your own experience or from wide and interested reading. Write about yourself, what you have done, what you think, what you honestly and thoughtfully believe. Think over what you want to say and decide what kind of reader you want to reach. Then write, as simply and directly as you can. A theme is not an exercise in embroidery; forget about being "literary." Be honest with yourself and your reader, always.

As the course progresses, you will learn new methods, new writing devices; you will learn how to clarify your own thinking and how to adapt what you are saying to your audience. You will learn new ways to arrange and organize your material and new sentence patterns that will more exactly reflect your thought. When a later need to write occurs, you will know how to say what you want to say.

The way words go together, the arrangement of ideas in logical and effective patterns, the mechanical problems of grammar and syntax—these will be the same in a freshman theme or a scientific report or an address on the state of the nation.

Certain other aspects of writing, of course, will vary from one writing problem to the next, in college and out. The tone you adopt, the details you include or omit, the vocabulary you employ—all of these will change as your purpose in writing or your audience varies. Themes will give you practice in controlling those aspects of writing, too.

You can learn to write only by writing, and themes give you a chance to write for a friendly audience and a friendly, experienced critic who can show you what your weak points are and how to strengthen them, and who can often suggest ways to make your strong points stronger. From one end of the course to the other, and *forever after*, write always as well as you can; then rewrite and polish, until you are sure that your reader will understand what you are saying to him.

WRITING THE THEME

Most of the pages that follow will be concerned with one aspect or another of writing, with particular emphasis on the immediate problem of writing themes for your composition classes. For the moment—to get you started on what may be an unfamiliar task—the writing process may be sketched under three main headings: deciding what you want to say, planning quickly how to say it, and actually writing the first draft of the paper. (For more detailed discussion of these three topics, see Chapters 3 and 4.)

Deciding What You Want to Say

When you have selected a single topic from all the things you know and are interested in, you have arrived at the general subject of your paper. But general subjects, as you will quickly discover, are too big to manage in a theme of a few pages. You must limit yourself to a subdivision of the general topic that is small enough to enable you to present it adequately, in concrete, specific terms that will make it clearly understandable to your reader. Because you have just gone through the confusion of registering for your first classes, your instructor may suggest that you write about something suggested by that experience. But "Registration" is only a topic, about which you could say a thousand things, and so is "What I think about Registration," and "How Registration affected me"; and even "The crowded and confusing Registrar's Office, full of perplexed freshmen, where I picked up my registration papers" is only a topic, not an idea. You need a fully formulated thought to guide your writing, a topic and something to say about that topic, a subject *and* a predicate—a central idea, or *thesis*, to develop into a unified paper. Thinking about the problems of the Registration day, you decide to write about the way you were sent from one place to another and then another, as you tried to learn what was expected of you, and finally you realize that much of the confusion could have been avoided if you had only known how to ask for the specific information you needed. So you phrase for yourself the central idea: "At Registration, as at many other times, getting the right answers often depends on knowing how to ask the right questions." Now, and not before, you know what you want to say. You have arrived at an idea that you can reasonably expect to develop in your theme.

Planning Quickly How to Say It

As soon as you arrive at your central idea, your thesis, write it down on a piece of scratch paper. It is the sentence summarizing the idea you want to develop, and everything that goes into the paper will be subordinate to it. You need not only to know what it is, but to have it before you as you work, to control your selection of detail and the way you express the details you select.

Then decide what audience you are addressing, for we speak and write in different ways for different auditors, according to their knowledge of the material, their relationship to us, and the intimacy or formality of the occasion. Suppose, for example, you were writing your comments on Registration in a letter to your parents, one to a brother who formerly attended your university, one to a friend at another school, or one to the Registrar himself with a suggestion for improvement in the system. Each would differ from the rest in the tone you adopted, the details you would need to include, and the degree of formality of the presentation. The writer can scarcely begin until he knows what reader he hopes to reach.

Usually your instructor is an editor helping you reach the intended reader, not the audience itself. Sometimes a particular audience may be specified in the assignment ("Write a paper describing the wiring of high-fidelity loudspeakers for a trade paper circulating among phonograph repair men. Write a paper on the same topic for a general magazine—say the *Reader's Digest*"). But more often the assigned audience will be the members of your own class, or perhaps the general "educated reader" of the sort addressed by *Harper's Magazine* or the *Atlantic Monthly* or the *New Yorker*. Always, think about your thesis in relation to your intended readers, what they know about the subject and what they do not know.

If, for example, the assigned audience is your own class and you are writing a paper on the importance of asking the right questions in order to get clear and useful answers, you can assume that all your classmates have been through Registration, but you cannot assume that all of them have talked to your own adviser or are familiar with the curriculum you are following, nor can you assume that all of them were sent from pillar to post in registering. You will have to indicate clearly what information you needed, how you asked for it, and why you were misunderstood. Such terms as *section,* *course, curriculum, placement test,* and the names of college buildings, familiar to the Registration clerks but strange to you and to your classmates, might come in as a jumble of double-talk. Certainly the details of your travels from pillar to post will have to come in. And all the time you will select or reject details because of their appropriateness in developing your chosen thesis: "At Registration, as at many other times, getting the right answers often depends on knowing how to ask the right questions."

Jot down rapidly, under your thesis sentence, the details you will have to include to make your experience meaningful to your reader. Do not worry about outline form, but do be sure you get down at least the main points.

Then check over the scratch outline you have made to see in what order those details ought to be handled. If your curriculum, for example, requires preliminary courses that are not required by most curricula, you will have to explain those unusual requirements early, or your reader will be lost. If your regular adviser was absent, and the one you talked to was uncertain about your needs, you will have to say so. If your own confusion grew as you made the rounds, so that your questions became less and less exact, you will need to make that fact clear. Your basic pattern of organization will be chronological, but at every step you will have to be sure that your details are kept in a manageable order.

Writing the First Draft

Having decided what you want to say, and having planned at least roughly how to say it to make the effect you want to make on your audience, write out the theme while the idea is hot. Unless you have had a great deal of practice in writing, you will find it better not to work word by word and sentence by sentence. Do not stop to rephrase, to look up spelling, or to brood over punctuation. Those are problems for revision. Now, while you know where you are going and how you want to get there, put your mind on the journey. If you have fixed your main idea clearly in your mind, visualized your audience, and planned carefully how to develop the idea for that audience, your job now is to get your thoughts down on paper—in the best phrasing you can manage—while the ideas are all vivid to you. You may well produce a fluent, eloquent theme that way; you probably will not if you stop to scrutinize every step you take as you take it.

The first draft will be full of weaknesses. It is by no means your best work, and it should never be your final theme—too many accidents may have happened by the way. But the method thus outlined will ensure, better than any other method, that your theme will be fluent, vivid, and interesting.

REWRITING AND REVISING

In order to produce a good theme, you need to plan what you want to say and to write as well as you are able. But even with a careful plan and considerable skill in writing, you need also to rewrite and revise.

The revision process is not easy, but with practice it will become less difficult, and it can be very rewarding. The paper which you first carefully planned and then wrote out without undue worry about mechanics, transitions, or exact diction will still require polishing. But before you begin to revise it, put it aside, if possible, to cool. Give yourself every opportunity to forget what you meant to say, to make it easier to see what you have actually said and how it will affect the reader. Every writer must be at least two people: himself and the reader he is addressing; and the farther you are from the writing, the better you can read critically what you have written.

A list of ten successive steps in revision follows. Take each step, so far as time allows, separately. Do not, in other words, attempt to catch all kinds of mistakes in even the most careful single revision. Your attention should be directed toward one problem at a time. Only in that way can you be sure you have done the best job you can do. Hard work? Certainly it is hard. But the weaker your writing is, the more vital careful revision will be.

Check the Whole

1. Go back and reconsider your main idea. Was that what you really wanted to say? (The more exactly you have phrased your central idea the better.)

2. Now reread the theme, the whole theme. Have you really developed and presented the central idea? Does some other idea, or some part of the whole, stand out unduly when you read?

3. Check the details in your working plan. Did they all get in, and did they fit? Did any irrelevant details creep in as you wrote?

Check the Parts

4. Look at the main sections of your paper. Do the parts add up to the whole? Are the parts themselves properly developed? Is the emphasis right? Have the parts been given space proportional to their importance, or has enthusiasm or ease of composition led you to give too much space to some parts, too little to others?

5. Check the relation between the parts. Are the transitions between the parts clear, and do they show exactly the right relation between the ideas? Remember that your reader needs clear indications of how each idea is related to the next.

Check the Individual Sentences

6. Look at each sentence. Does it say what you wanted to say? Does its form exactly reflect your thought, with the most important idea in the main clause and the lesser ideas in subordinate constructions? Is the emphasis right in each sentence? Are the transitions between the sentences clear?

Check the Diction

7. Does every word work for you? Could what you are saying be more exactly or more efficiently phrased? Do the words you are using belong in the vocabulary of the audience, so that you can reasonably expect your readers to understand them? Have you explained technical terms? Is the diction appropriate?

Read the Paper Aloud

8. Read your paper aloud and *listen* to it. Are there passages of overelaborate "fine writing"? Are there any awkward passages? Are there any constructions that might be misread by a hasty reader? Are there any unduly harsh sounds, unintended rhymes, or inappropriate rhythms? Such flaws are often more easily detected when you hear the paper as well as see it. Is the tone right? Have you kept the intended audience in mind?

Check for Your Own Weaknesses

9. Go over the paper carefully to find and correct the errors you know you are liable to make. If you have trouble with spelling, make one complete check to look for misspellings alone. If certain sentence patterns lead you into mistakes in punctuation, look for those patterns and correct the mistakes. The more writing you do, the more you will know what weaknesses to look for. Correct those weaknesses carefully before you submit the paper to your instructor.

Reread the Final Draft

10. Finally, after all the revisions have been made and just before you prepare the clean copy you will hand in to your instructor, reread the final draft to be sure that none of your revisions have resulted in new errors. Be sure that a rephrased sentence, for example, fits the sentences before and after it, that no shifts in tense or person or mood have crept in, that the transitions are still clear and smooth, the proportions are still right, and the tone is still harmonious.

This kind of revision is obviously not an easy process. It takes hard, dull labor continuing long after the first flush of inspiration has faded. But it is the only way to make sure you have done the best work you can do. Neither your instructor nor anyone else is much interested in anything less.

REVISING GRADED THEMES

We have now considered two of the three processes necessary in every theme assignment. You have written, and you have revised until the paper you hand in to your instructor represents the best work you can do at the time. After your instructor reads and marks the paper, he will return it to you, and you will go through the third, and in some ways the most important process: As your instructor directs, you will correct, revise, or rewrite the marked paper.

Your earlier revisions put to use all that you had learned up to that point. The marking your instructor does, including his comments on the back of the theme, shows you where your writing is still weak. Perhaps sentences that are too long and too complicated lead you into errors in sentence structure or punctuation. Perhaps you habitually misspell certain types of words. Perhaps your writing is still too general, or still lacks clear organization. Or you lose sight of your intended reader. Or you write awkwardly, even though your grammar is conventional. Only by writing can you find out how you write and learn to write better.

As much as possible, your instructor will use symbols or comments which will send you to the sections of this textbook where certain common weaknesses are discussed and their correction is illustrated. *Use the whole textbook throughout the term.* Classroom discussions must take up one problem at a time, but your own theme revisions enable you to concentrate from the first on the problems that particularly bother you. If you make comma splices, for example, do not wait for the class to get around to discussing them; learn to avoid them when you revise Theme One.

Your instructor may give you special directions for revising, and they, of course, should be scrupulously observed. If he does not, follow this practice: When your marked theme is returned, go over it carefully to be sure you understand all the symbols and all your instructor's comments. Never attempt to correct an error or a weakness unless you are sure what it is. Look at the correction chart or the index to find the section of the textbook that discusses the error. Read that section carefully, comparing the examples with your own writing. When you understand what is wrong, make the correction. If you cannot see your mistake with the help of the book, consult your instructor, but be sure you have done all you can to understand the error by yourself before you take the problem to him. Further, make intelligent use of all the allies at your disposal. If an explanation in the textbook employs a grammatical term you are unfamiliar with, look up the term, in the index or in your dictionary, before you decide that it is beyond you. When you thoroughly understand your mistakes, correct your paper, rewriting any sections that were awkwardly phrased or that need expanding.

A NOTEBOOK RECORD OF ERRORS

One good way to identify your real weaknesses, the problems that turn up in theme after theme, is to keep a notebook to record your errors. There are a thousand mistakes you might make, but as a matter of fact you really do make half a dozen mistakes over and over. A notebook is the best way to identify that half dozen.

Any weaknesses which frequently recur can then be identified and guarded against in revision before submitting your themes.

Keep a spelling list, for example. That way you can find out what words you misspell, or at least what kind of misspelling you make, since spelling errors tend to fall into recognizable groups. (See Chapter 15.) With your instructor's help, diagnose your spelling problems so you can know what to watch out for in revision. Keep a record, too, of the mistakes you make in punctuation or in grammar. If in theme after theme you fail to set off parenthetical elements by commas, you can correct that weakness in revising a new theme before you hand it in. If you often use pronouns without expressed antecedents, you can keep an eye on your pronouns. And if your notebook shows that you never make certain mistakes, you know you need not worry about some of the problems that bother your classmates.

Revise each marked theme *before you write the next one assigned.* Learn your own weaknesses by noting the recurring entries in your notebook. Study those weaknesses, understand them, and try to learn to avoid them before your next theme. Do not be discouraged if you tried something new and fell short of complete success. You are learning to use very complicated tools, and their use must be practiced over and over again before they fit your hand like familiar old tools you can use skillfully. Study your weaknesses and learn to correct them.

THE CHARACTERISTICS OF A GOOD THEME

When you have written a theme and revised it carefully, you naturally hope that your instructor will think it is a good theme and will say so with a good grade. If he does not (and you will sometimes be disappointed), you will wonder where you fell down. "What does he want?" "What is he looking for when he grades a paper?" These are common questions, and they deserve a clear answer.

Within the limits of the assignment, he is looking for and eagerly hoping to find the following characteristics:

1. Clarity, for the intended audience. This is the first essential of good writing, and we shall be concerned with it throughout the book.

2. A central idea which is worth the time and trouble the writer and the reader put into it. (In the next chapter we shall consider what such a worthwhile idea is like.)

3. Unity of idea and harmony of tone. (See Chapter 3: Unity.)

4. Well-selected, concrete, and specific detail to make the paper clear to the intended reader. (Chapter 3: Development.)

5. An honest, thoughtful, and original presentation. (Chapter 3: Originality.)

6. A logical and effective arrangement of the details. (Chapter 4: Organization.)

7. Effective paragraphs, and coherence between the parts. (Chapter 5.)

8. Mature sentences that reflect the writer's thought in the way that will best convey that thought to the audience. (Chapter 6.)

9. Compression, or conciseness. (Chapters 6 and 7.)

10. Diction (word choice) that is exact, and appropriate to the topic, the tone, and the audience. (Chapter 7.)

11. Conventionally accepted spelling, punctuation, grammar, and other mechanics. (The Handbook.)

12. An appropriate title. (Chapter 3.)

At the moment, this must seem a formidable list, but unfortunately there is no way to shorten or simplify it. A theme which possesses all these characteristics will be a good theme; one which falls short will be weaker than it should be. You can take comfort from the fact that, by the end of the English composition course, any intelligent and diligent student should be well on his way toward learning to write themes which possess these qualities.

As the course progresses, use the preceding list of characteristics as a yardstick to measure your themes. Be sure that each theme possesses as many of them as possible. When you write and revise, keep them in mind. And when, after your theme has been graded, you revise it for the final time, check against the list to see where you fell short. Then your next attempt will be more successful.

2

What to Write About

Characteristics of a Good Theme: 2. A central idea worth
the writer's and the reader's time and trouble.

CHOOSING SUBJECTS

Finding the Subject

Freshmen worry too much about finding subjects for themes.
Admittedly, producing a three- or four-page paper every week is
not an easy task, and there is an unavoidable artificiality about
writing something because a theme is due rather than because you
have something you want to say. But that problem is not peculiar
to freshman English. The newspaper columnist must be funny, or
startling, or profound every single morning, Sundays included. The
advertising copy writer knows he must sell that same old bar of
soap. Another copy writer at an adjoining desk must be coy about
corsets no matter how badly his head aches. The businessman must
write a sales letter, the government worker must finish a report, the
boss wants a memorandum, a term paper is due tomorrow, the
examination is scheduled for three o'clock.

The freshman has one tremendous advantage over all these
fellow sufferers: He has not been writing long enough to have
written himself out. All of the vast number of things he is interested
in and knows about are still there, waiting for him to select them
and write about them. The people he knows, the places he has

lived in, his experiences and ideas and plans and hopes and fears are still available. And yet he will sit at his desk and squirm for hours wondering what to write about. Anthony Trollope, who boasted with some reason that he had filled more volumes than any other major English novelist, long ago insisted that inspiration was far less important than sitting resolutely down to work. But it does no good just to sit, or even to sit and "think." What does help is to think purposefully, fasten on a possible subject, and go to work on that.

What subjects are possible? Sometimes the answer will be easy to find. The assignment for the theme may specifically limit you to a particular problem. You may, for example, have just read and discussed an essay which now is to be imitated in subject matter and style, or there may be set questions to answer about a book the whole class has studied, or you may have to write critically about a play or a poem you have read but not discussed. At the other extreme, sometimes the assignment will be so general as to leave the choice of topic entirely up to you, but you may be so overwhelmingly interested in some particular subject that you are burning to discuss it in theme after theme. Whether that overriding interest concerns the weaknesses of the current national administration or merely the dance you went to last Saturday, you will have no trouble finding a subject for the next theme.

The chances are, however, that the assignment will not specifically limit you to a set topic and that you are not greatly excited about any particular subject. Really, that makes it easier, because your choice is wider. Think about yourself, your family, your friends. What is it like to be the oldest of three children and have to give up things you would like to have so the younger ones can have something they want instead? Or if you are the youngest, how did it feel to be always wearing hand-me-downs and never knowing the pride of owning a brand-new bicycle? Did you learn to work efficiently in a summer camp, or are you learning now as a fraternity pledge? What half-dozen types can you fit your friends into? Joe is hearty and healthy, bounding out of bed in the morning and bustling all day, but his sense of humor is a little trying. Dick gets out of a lot of work just by being so inefficient that no one wants to trust him with a job. Mary is snobbish; Joyce is a clinging vine. In short, your friends are people, and in them you can see, and seeing can report, what the human race has been like for a long, long time.

(And which type, by the way, do you yourself belong to? How did you get that way?)

Or think about where you have lived. What was it like to have to cut grass before you could go swimming? What games did you play in the wood lot behind the house? Remember the fire in the apartment house next door? How did you feel on the very first day you went to school? What was the first play you ever saw? Think about your first dance, your first date, your first hay ride. How should a horse or a dog be taken care of? Are cats really cold and aloof? Why do people keep canaries? Do you see how easy it is to find subjects by the dozens, once you start thinking about what you have done and what you know?

Any of the topics in the last two paragraphs—and many, many more like them—would serve for the kind of theme you may be asked to write early in the first semester. They are concerned with your own interests and your own experience, so that you will have a multitude of details to select from and can consequently produce a vivid and interesting paper. Notice that none of them imply unusual experiences. Few students will have had all the experiences suggested, but fewer will have had none of them. You need not have served in the Foreign Legion or shot lions in Africa or fallen off the Empire State Building to have something to write about. An honest and closely observed report on any human experience will furnish a subject worth the trouble it costs to present it effectively. Think of the boredom of waiting for a bus, the pleasure of meeting a friend who seems genuinely glad to see you, the foolish but irrepressible fears that come while you are walking home alone at night, the excitement of a trip to the zoo or to the fair or to a big department store at Christmastime or to the seaside in summer —you have plenty of subjects. The problem is to select one, not to find one.

You may be shy about writing revealingly about yourself, or your instructor may forbid themes of the autobiographic, descriptive-narrative sort which such suggestions imply. Still, your own ideas and opinions and plans, the skills you have acquired, and the things you hope to do will provide you with more than enough material for all the themes of the course. An early theme can explain a process with which you are familiar: How to Groom a Horse, How to Show a Dog or a Steer, How to Make a Model Airplane or a Dress or a

Ventilating Fan, How to Prepare Watercolor Paper for a Painting, How to Enjoy a Vacation, How to Sell Shoes, How to Build a Fire, how to do any of the countless things you know how to do well. Give your readers clear and exact instructions they could successfully follow.

Another theme might present a process in a somewhat different way, showing how something is done that the reader is not likely ever to do. How Steel Is Made, How the Chain Store Produce Buyer Selects Vegetables, How Hotels Handle Reservations, How Forests Reproduce Themselves after a Fire, How Contour Plowing Prevents Soil Erosion, How a Bus Line Handles Rush-Hour Traffic —the possibilities are endless.

Still another type of theme explains the operation of a mechanism. What does a carburetor do? What makes an airplane fly? How does a sewing machine work? a corn picker or a cotton picker? a telephone receiver? a television tube?

A very important type of expository writing is the extended definition, and you will have many occasions—in examinations, term papers, themes, reports of all kinds—to explain in clear and complete detail what you mean by the terms you use. You will do well to practice defining technical or even common terms under your instructor's guidance. It is not as easy as you may think. What, for instance, is "a fair grading system"? What constitutes "a good vacation," "a good job," "a friend"? What do you mean by *happiness?* What is "work"? Or, drawing from other courses you are taking, what was Henry Clay's "American system"? What does the chemist mean by *oxidation?* What is meant by *laissez faire?* What is a lyric? a tragedy? a symbol?

A still more advanced type of expository theme deals with analysis, either breaking down a topic into its parts or grouping and combining isolated items in larger classifications. In an elementary way we have already suggested such papers. A simple exercise in the first type of analysis would be to break down the general topic of playing in the wood lot into the specific games you played there; grouping your friends by types and generalizing about them is an example of the second kind of analysis. As the semester progresses, more mature papers can be tried. What are the study habits of the successful student? What sort of legislation has been passed by the current Congress? What is wrong with the average Hollywood movie? What are the characteristics of the typical congressman or druggist or coed? What are the characteristics of a Hemingway novel? an essay by William Hazlitt? a building by Frank Lloyd Wright? Such topics may tempt you to generalize too hastily, but they present a common writing problem in which you need practice.

Yet another type of paper is the exposition of opinion. What do you think of your college's registration system? Should girls be educated in the same way boys are? Should students have more, or less, freedom to choose their own courses? Is a "practical education" enough for a civilized man? Notice how these types of writing overlap. That last topic calls for at least two definitions in addition to the expression and development of the opinion. Or, to get away from school topics, should parents intefere more, or less, in their daughter's love affairs? Does every man have a right to his own opinion on any topic? If not, who does, or on what topics? Who is right in the latest national controversy, and why? In papers on such subjects, be sure to offer the reasons for your opinion, the evidence rather than mere assertion; and be sure of your facts. (See Chapter 8 on the difference between fact and opinion and on the nature of evidence.) But with those limits carefully observed, there are many argumentative subjects ready at hand.

One final suggestion: It is always wise to write on what you yourself know and are interested in from your own experience. But your reading and your honest and thoughtful responses to your reading form a large part of what you know and an important part of your experience. Your reading in this course is probably designed not only to increase your ability to read and to show you how other writers have solved writing problems, but also to add to your experience by stimulating your thinking about concepts significant to men. Your work in other courses is obviously designed to add to your specific knowledge and your general wisdom. Within the limits of your instructor's assignments, draw on your other courses for theme material. You must, of course, give all due credit to the sources from which you borrow *phrasing, ideas,* or *organizational patterns.* (See Chapter 9 for detailed comments.) And you must, of course, know the material thoroughly. But with those qualifications, feel free to include topics from other courses in "what you yourself know and are interested in."

We could, obviously, go on and on. You have so many things to write about that a lifetime could not exhaust them, even if nothing else were ever to happen to you. If you are even half-conscious of the world you have been moving in for seventeen, eighteen, or even more years, you can never in reason complain that you have nothing to write about. The big problem, it should by now be clear, is selecting from the vast supply of available topics and reducing your selection to a subject small enough that you can say something worthwhile about it in a three- or four-page theme.

Selecting the Subject

Students often complain, "I spent six hours on that theme, and all I got was a *C!*" Frequently they mean that they spent four or five hours the night before the theme was due wondering what to write about, meanwhile fiddling with the radio, wandering down-stairs for a look at television, buffing their nails or examining themselves in the mirror while they considered the advisability of raising a mustache, glancing at the next day's English literature assignment, and just staring at a blank sheet of paper. Only an hour, perhaps, went into the paper itself, from the final desperate choice of a vaguely conceived topic through the planning, writing, and revising. No wonder it was worth no more than a *C*. No one who waits that long for lightning to strike can expect to raise more than a dim glow from the frenzied friction of pencil on paper at one o'clock in the morning.

Let us, parenthetically, notice a few of the overlooked theme topics inherent in the very inactivity they were so busily engaged in: The Folly of Procrastination, The Reluctant Muse, Radio Programs, TV Commercials, The Syrup-Voiced Announcer, Color Television, How to Buy a Good Set, Vanity—All Is Vanity, Chaucer Had an Eye for Folly, What Makes a Good Story? Poets Who Were Not Impractical, If Chaucer's Griselda Were Alive Today, Why Should I Study Literature? The Value of Paper, How Paper Is Made, What Is White?—we could go far beyond those sixteen perfectly good topics our hypothetical students had in front of them all the time they sat staring at the blank paper. But, of course, no students who could see such topics would have sat there stumped for five hours. It will be more profitable to consider how such students could have avoided perplexity in the first place.

You will find at the end of this chapter a list of theme topics grouped according to common experiences and according to gradually increasing complexity. They will offer practice in many of the types of writing you may have occasion to do later in college—and after. If your instructor does not make specific theme assignments, and if you wish to avoid the bother of discovering your own subjects, you might select topics directly from that list, gradually working your way from the simpler subjects to the more complex ones as the course progresses.

A far better practice would be to make up a similar list of your own when you finish reading this chapter, drawing on your own experience for subjects you know and are interested in and can write about. Put down four or five topics under each category. Make the list as long and as full and as exciting as you can.

Then, when a theme is due, go to your list and see how many possible subjects are ready and waiting for you. If the first possible subject, or the second, or the third does not seem wildly exciting, *go back to the first.* Forget about wild excitement and start thinking about that first possible topic. What did you really have in mind as you put that topic on your list? What one central idea would you develop, if you settled on that first possible subject? Could you phrase that thesis more exactly, more specifically than you first phrased it? If you should write on that subject, what main points would you have to develop before your readers knew exactly what you meant? What details would be necessary before each of those main points was clear and vivid?— Do you have answers for those questions? All right, put your list away for another time. You have found your subject, and you are almost ready to write your theme.

Limiting the Subject

Before you can write, however, you must be able to answer Yes to a highly paradoxical question: Is this topic small enough to be worth writing about?

A big subject in the hands of a master of English prose can sometimes be effectively treated in a short paper. Lincoln's Gettysburg Address said a great deal in two hundred and sixty-six words. But few men can write such compact prose, and no college freshmen can manage it. Most early freshman themes are too general, written in vague and cloudy terms that may be clear to the writer but cannot be clear to anyone else. Make a conscious practice of cutting at least in half the early topics you select to write about. If you tend to think of extremely general topics, of course, cut one of the halves in half and then cut again. Phrase a very specific thesis sentence. You can usually take it as a safe rule that your first impulses are too generous. Only experience can tell you how much too optimistic you are likely to be.

A Subject Worth the Trouble

Two plaintive objections are often made to such advice. The first is, "Unless I write on a big subject, I don't have enough to say to fill three or four pages." The answer to that objection is that you have more to say than you think; besides, you need to say more than you may suppose in order to make your meaning clear to your reader and to have the effect you want. Our next chapter, on developing your theses, will attempt to amplify that answer. The other objection is, "If one important characteristic of a good theme is a central idea worth the time and trouble of developing it, why am I told now to write on small subjects instead of big ones?" The obvious answer to that question is that a worthless paper on a big subject is not saved by its subject, and that a vague, general paper —like the usual four-page treatment of a big subject—is of necessity so superficial as to be worthless.

But the question is too important to be brushed off lightly. To get a positive answer, more than the mere advice not to write a worthless paper, we need to consider a larger question: When, exactly, is a central idea worth the trouble? The answer has already been suggested.

A central idea that is worth the trouble is one which, honestly and vividly developed, adds genuine information to the reader's store of knowledge.

The addition to the reader's store of knowledge does not have to be so tremendous as to revolutionize his approach to the problems of life. But a paper which shows a reader what a real human being really thought or did in a real situation adds to the reader's knowledge of mankind. A sincere and thoughtful expression of idea or opinion adds to the reader's knowledge of the topic discussed, stirs his thought, increases his understanding. A process clearly explained adds to the reader's potential skills. A description of a way of life differing from his own—and no two ways of life are identical—broadens his tolerance and strengthens his essential humanity. You have heard the phrase "universal truth" applied to poems in your high school or college literature courses. That universal truth does not have to be, and usually is not, world shaking. The phrase means only that the poet, the artist of any sort, has closely observed and honestly reported a fact which other men can confirm from their own observation. Many a man has been astonished to see that a painter has laid blue shadows on a snow scene, and then been more astonished to see that shadows on snow really are blue on a clear winter day. The fact had been there all along, but until the artist pointed it out, the fact had eluded the lesser man's observation. Chaucer can tell modern men more about men, and women, than most of us are likely to discover for ourselves. The college freshman, looking closely and carefully at his own experience and ideas and then honestly reporting them, can add a very great deal to the understanding of his fellow freshmen, a very great deal to the understanding of his instructor. And a paper so written is emphatically worth all the trouble it costs.

Finally, to go into the problem by the back door, what sort of paper is *not* worth the trouble it costs? Any paper vaguely conceived and hastily written. Any paper which has no central idea at all, but merely makes random remarks about a general topic. Any paper mouthing clichés on a commonplace subject, repeating others' thoughts and representing no thought at all on the writer's part. Any paper which is not developed enough to answer the reader's legitimate questions about the subject, or about passing details or phrases in the writer's treatment of the subject. Any paper in which the details are poured helter-skelter on the page, without organization and without coherence. Any paper in which the diction is inexact, fuzzy, and incomprehensible. In short, any paper in which the writer has not taken the trouble to be sure he really knew what he wanted to say or the trouble to say it in a way that would convey a controlled idea to his reader. None of these papers would be worth the trouble.

THESIS OR STATEMENT OF PURPOSE

The Thesis

Before a writer can be sure he really knows what he wants to say, before he can be sure he is setting out to develop an idea that is worth the trouble, he must know what his central idea is to be. That fact would seem self-evident, but countless freshman writers resist accepting it—and countless writers of letters-to-the-editor resist it, as well as countless writers of letters to insurance companies or to Social Security offices or to mail-order houses, and even countless would-be contributors to magazines. Nor before they set pen to paper or dictaphone to lip are the writers of the replies always as careful as they should be to be sure they know exactly what they hope to say.

There is only one way to be sure. Even the practiced writer takes the step in his mind, and the lesser man must take it with pencil and paper. *To be sure you know what central idea you want to develop, put it clearly and specifically into a sentence.* Phrase it as exactly as you can. Look at it and think about it. If your reader should remember no more than that one sentence you have just written, would he at least understand your main point?

That one sentence—a full sentence, notice, with subject (your topic) and predicate (what you mean to say about the topic)—is your thesis. *A thesis is a one-sentence summary of the whole paper.* It is the central idea, the main idea, the idea you want your reader to understand and realize and remember. Every paper expressing and developing an idea should have a clearly phrased thesis behind it, whether or not that thesis ever appears in the paper itself. The very act of phrasing the thesis will do much to help you limit your paper to an idea which can be effectively developed in a theme.

It is never enough, remember, to have only a topic in mind, since many things could be said about even the smallest topic. Registration is only a topic. Registration Run-around is only a topic. Why I Had to Spend Three Whole Days on the Simple Problems of Registration is only a topic, no matter how long it is. *Registration is complex,* however, because it states a full idea, is a thesis, though too general to be of any use to a writer. *During Registration, I was sent from office to office and from clerk to clerk* is a thesis, but still too general. *During Registration, I was sent from office to office and clerk to clerk because I did not know how to ask for the information I needed* is a thesis, and perhaps a useful one; but for the purpose of controlling your paper, it could be more succinctly phrased. *At Registration, getting the right answers often depends on knowing how to ask the right questions* is a thesis you could use to produce a paper worth the trouble of writing and reading.

Before we leave this point, it would be useful to glance at a few of the many other theses that might stem from the same topic.

> Because I had planned alternative schedules, Registration was no trouble.
>
> Registration would be simplified if old students were allowed to preregister.
>
> Thanks to the Registrar's efficiency, Registration is managed expeditiously.
>
> The Registration procedure is so full of holes that a clever student can get himself enrolled in any class he wants.

And so on. But obviously not all these ideas can be developed at once. Topic alone is not enough.

The Statement of Purpose

The use of a carefully phrased thesis is the best guarantee that any theme expressing an idea (that is, a fully formulated thought) will possess unity. Sometimes, however, your papers are not really expressing ideas, but instead are presenting a picture or are creating a mood or an impression or are recounting events. Early themes of autobiographic reminiscence, descriptions, the narration of incidents, even the explanation of simple processes— in none of these is your purpose likely to be to develop an idea; yet unity remains essential. For such papers, a clear-cut *statement of purpose* may be more useful than a thesis.

Suppose, for example, you have been told to write a theme reproducing the earliest fear you can recall. You could formulate a central idea and phrase a thesis:

> THESIS: The earliest fear I recall came when I lost my mother in the toy department of a big department store my third Christmas.

That bald statement of fact will keep you on the subject, but it will not help very much to make the theme vivid. With such a subject, it is often better to decide as specifically as possible what you want to do in the theme and express that purpose as exactly as you can.

> STATEMENT OF PURPOSE: I want to re-create the experience of being lost in a toy department at Christmas so that my reader will feel like a three-year-old trapped in a jungle of strange legs, in a bewildering chaos of sights and sounds, suddenly cut loose from his mother, deserted and terrified.

Such a statement of purpose will give you a much better sense of direction than the bald thesis would, and will guarantee unity just as well.

Similarly, a paper which is to present a report of fact, rather than an interpretation, may be better controlled by a statement of purpose, if it is specific enough, than by a thesis. For example, Rachel Carson, in *Under the Sea Wind*, developed the purpose:

> To make the reader realize how sea creatures live by presenting vivid accounts of events in the lives of typical members of representative species, chiefly sandpipers, mackerels, and eels.

With that in mind, she could select the details she needed merely by asking herself what probably happened during the lives of most mature members of each species.

Yet even writing that deals largely with fact is usually best controlled by a thesis. The historian, for example, cannot include everything. Both his choice of detail and the interpretation he gives it are likely to be governed by a controlling thesis, whether he is writing a short article or a multivolumed book. And the same is true of the sociologist or the literary critic or the astronomer or anyone else who is dealing basically with ideas.

Whichever you use, thesis or statement of purpose, phrase it as specifically as you can. A vaguely phrased, general statement will do little good, and in fact may do harm if it fools you into thinking you have thought about what you intend to say when really you have no clear intention beyond that of making random remarks about your subject. Such a mock thesis as

Registration is complicated,

or such a mock statement of purpose as

I intend to write about being lost,

will be of no use to you at all.

In deciding whether to use a *thesis* or a *statement of purpose*, ask yourself not, "Which is easier to phrase?" but, "Which will be more helpful in keeping my paper on the track I want it to follow, so that my readers will get the idea I want to convey in the way I want to convey it?"

When you have selected a topic in this way, limited it to manageable size, phrased a clear and specific thesis or statement of purpose, and chosen the details that are to develop it, then you are finally ready to write.

SUGGESTED TOPICS

If your assignment has been deliberately made general or is an "open assignment" and you are stumped, if you really have "nothing to write about," if at the moment of sitting down to a theme you cannot think of a good topic, the following list may be of help. It outlines a sequence of themes dealing with topics of increasing complexity, progressing from descriptive-narrative themes of personal reminiscence or historical re-creation through varied expository problems and argumentative problems to critical papers in which you will pass reasoned judgment on the writing of others. The groupings are by no means exhaustive, and the classifications, like writing problems generally, tend to overlap. But the writing problems are real enough.

The few topics offered are suggestions only. Every one of them could and for your purposes should be modified to fit your own interests and your own knowledge. Let the list suggest merely the sort of thing you might write about. Almost all the suggested topics, for example, are too big for a good theme. They offer points of departure, not definite assignments. Some state theses, but these should not be allowed to restrict you.

Remember that some dozens of topics have already been suggested in the foregoing chapter. They have not been incorporated in the following list.

To make the best use of this list, take it as a possible model and make up a similar list of your own, one which, in increasing complexity, arranges topics you are yourself interested in and could easily write on when papers are due. Then, if inspiration flags later, turn to your list for suggestions.

I. Autobiographic description and narration

A. Family and friends

The people I live with	Men!
What would we do without parents?	A friend in need
	Adopted
Mother had to work	When Father is sick
Our old man	My gal Sal

B. Home and neighborhood

Our house	Our gang
We tried to raise rabbits	The girl who made fun of me
The neighborhood grouch	
The best farmer in the neighborhood	Saturday matinee
	Trick or treat

C. Play

Pirates and buried treasure	Camping, canoeing, and coming home
A bicycle is many things	
The voyages of the *Bouncing Betsy*	Railroads I have run
	Dressing up
Who's for third base?	An attic on a rainy day
My first fight	Cowboy

D. Vacations

The sea and I	A faded summer love
Summer is a time for work	Moonlight on the mesa
Sun worshipers	Ski and sky
The "pool"	Loafing is an art
Mountains are for men	Camp staff

E. Travel

The wayward bus	Cave crawling
We shouldn't have fed the bears	The opera in Munich
	Edinburgh Castle
Williamsburg, colonial	We go to the city
The pine forests of Wisconsin	Dude ranch
	The Golden Gate

F. Family traditions

Picnic	Our family hero
Snowbound	When Daddy trapped a skunk
Family reunions	Rich uncle
We came over in the *Mayflower Annex*	Fire!

G. Hobbies

Fishing is fun	Swinging in a hammock
I do my own sewing	Poolroom
Backyard grill	Football is a man's game
Relaxation? Read	Rifle range
Stereo	Horse and hound
Give a man a horse he can ride	Model building

H. Jobs

Paper boy	Timber!
Dime stores are deadly	Fishing fleet
Scoop!	Round-up
Detasseling corn	Chores must be done

I. Education

Multiplication tables	The value of fraternities
The school I went to	Are examinations fair?
The brightest girl in the class	Campus politics
Grading systems	What is a liberal education?
	Required courses

J. Ambitions

I want to be a farmer	Housewife
The future for the engineer	Stage, screen, radio, and television
If I had a million dollars	I want to write
Missionary zeal	Pro baseball
Missileman	

II. Character sketches

A. Individuals

A real teacher	Eyes in the back of her head
Southern belle	Blabbermouth

A. Individuals (*cont.*)

Sergeant	Queen Elizabeth I
Big shot	Samuel Johnson
Maine guide	

B. Types

A good sport	The modern Babbitt
Tenant farmer	Serf
Shopper	Pilgrim
Poker player	

III. Processes

A. How to do it

Laying out a painting	Throwing a vase on a pot-
How to select good wool	ter's wheel
Dipping a sheep	How to haggle with a
Electroplating	huckster
Paddling a canoe against the wind	Reading a poem

B. How it is done

Planning a balanced meal	Trapping beaver
Altering a suit	Planning a sales campaign
Plotting a course for an air- plane	Plotting a short story
Mitosis	Trawling for cod
	Balancing the books

IV. Mechanisms

A percolator	A drawknife
A turbine generator	Hydraulic brakes
A jet engine	A lever
Electromagnet	A laser device

V. Organizations

A 4-H Club	A chain grocery
The Presbyterian Church	A summer camp
A mining company	A city council
A sorority	Student committee

VI. Definitions

Functional architecture	A useless course
Courtesy	Luxury
A good boss	A short story
Oxidation	A state

VII. Analyses

A. Division (breaking down general topics into their parts)

Student rooms	Student jobs
Dairy cattle	Summer resorts
Seasonal sports	Plants

B. Classification (combining individuals in groups)

The typical politician	The English movie
Texan	Clubwoman

VIII. Opinions   (See also Arguments.)

A cure for the traffic problem	The desert can be friendly
The small college has its advantages	Army life is good for a man
I like a modern house	Laziness is the mother of invention
Engineers are uneducated	The "liberal arts" are a luxury

IX. Arguments   (Remember that assertion is not evidence.)

Students should be allowed to select their own courses	Socialized medicine is inefficient
Nationalism is dangerous	The best government is the least government
Our lives are too specialized	Congressmen should act on their personal convictions

X. Criticisms

Comments on a textbook	My favorite poet
Characterization in a modern novel	The value of realism
What has become of plots?	Do artists communicate ideas?
Twentieth-century romantics	Interpretation of a poem

XI. Research papers

Jackson's attitude toward the Bank of the United States

Where did the Indians come from?

The Fire of London

Who wrote the traditional ballads?

Byron's contribution to Greek independence

The destruction of Pompeii

The case for Richard III

Walter Scott and the American South

The Piers Plowman controversy

Was Longstreet to blame at Gettysburg?

Is radiant heating practicable?

How the horse came back to America

Wordsworth's wild oat

Did McClellan have a chance?

Rainmaking

The birth of the essay

The Norse in Greenland

American dialects

Samuel Sewall and the witchcraft trials

Whatever became of Cro-Magnon man?

Senator Norris and TVA

Henry V, good king or shameless aggressor?

EXERCISES

A. The most difficult concept for beginning writers to grasp concerns the nature and importance of the **thesis:** a single, unified, declarative *sentence* summarizing the central idea of a paper and containing not only a subject (the topic of the paper) but a predicate (a specific assertion of what the paper is to say about the topic). From the following list of items, select those which make complete statements and which might serve as theses for anything from a short theme to a full-length book.

1. Any expository or argumentative paper should develop a specific central idea about its topic.

2. Many of the Spanish names along the Pacific Coast record the visits of the earliest Spanish explorers.

3. How the French names were given to places along the Canadian border of the United States.

4. Because medieval and modern towns occupy the sites of Anglo-Saxon settlements in England and therefore make excavation difficult, archaelogists know very little about the town life of the Anglo-Saxon period.

5. What jurisdiction does the Congress of the United States have in the apportioning of congressional districts within a state?
6. The nature of a people's language influences the nature of that people's thought.
7. Speakers of English cannot express an idea without relating it to time.
8. Saturday night is a poor time to try to study in a fraternity house.
9. The measurement of the tensile strength of cables in relation to their diameters and constituent materials.
10. Shakespeare's *Richard III*, which has done much to fix our opinions of Richard's character, is based on Tudor accounts which may be seriously biased.

B. For ten topics from the list on pages 25–29 prepare clear and specific thesis sentences; then prepare theses stating different central ideas for each of the same ten topics.

C. Select two courses you are now taking and prepare a list of five possible theme topics related to each course. For each topic, state a clear and specific thesis sentence.

3-

The Best Themes

Characteristics of a Good Theme: 3. Unity of idea and harmony of tone. 4. Well-selected, concrete, and specific detail. 5. An honest, thoughtful, and original presentation. 12. An appropriate title.

All twelve of the characteristics of a good theme listed at the end of Chapter 1 are important, but as in any such list, some are more important than others. A reasonable accuracy in the mechanics of grammar, sentence structure, punctuation, and spelling, for example, is basic, and later chapters of this book will be concerned in detail with such mechanics. But a paper may be written with reasonable accuracy and still be a poor or at best a mediocre paper. This chapter will largely ignore errors in mechanics, and will consider instead those further characteristics which must be mastered before you can compete successfully with the most skillful of your classmates—those characteristics of a good theme which lie above and beyond elementary accuracy in mechanics, the elements which characterize the *best* themes.

There may be—there should be—disappointment when themes are graded down because of elementary errors. But there is little need for frustration. Anyone who cares to expend the necessary intelligent energy can learn grammar and sentence structure, can learn to spell and punctuate as the educated writer does. If mechanics are all that prevent your themes from getting A's, you are lucky. More frustrating is the experience of having a paper returned with a C grade, but with few marks or comments to indicate what is wrong with it. Such a C means, usually, that although there is nothing greatly wrong in the theme, there is nothing much good about it, either. The instructor would have to write a full essay on the nature of good writing to make clear how the C theme could have been improved. And since the margins of the theme give him little room, he often cannot say anything very helpful. The student is understandably discouraged.

But the chances are that the instructor, if he had room and time, would say something like this:

> I hope you had a single thesis in mind in writing this. At least, I can see how all the details might be related to what could be your central thought. But your paper is so general that I can't be sure I know exactly what central idea you really meant to express, or just what you meant by some of the general sentences you have written about it. You phrase *them* clearly enough, but by the very nature of generalizations, they might mean any one of several things. I assume that you knew what you meant at each stage of the paper, and I hope that you have relived the experience you were trying to reproduce, or have clearly and fully realized the idea you tried to communicate. But it doesn't come through. *I* can't tell quite how you feel or think about the subject. There aren't any obvious illiteracies I can mark, but your paper is not vivid, or graphic, or clear, or even very interesting. Be concrete. Be specific. Give me illustrative or exemplifying or amplifying or clarifying details. Make me see, feel, think as you do. Let me understand what you are saying. Be as honest as you can in what you say, and originality will follow.

Most unsuccessful freshman papers, in other words, fail to possess three of the essential characteristics of a good theme—characteristics which are so essential that they often account for the difference between merely average grades and high ones: *unity, development,* and *originality.*

Some papers, especially early in the term, lack *unity.* That is, they lack a central thesis or a clearly defined statement of purpose and merely make random remarks about a topic. As we have already seen in Chapters 1 and 2, a unifying central idea is fundamental. Often, however, the writer has decided on such a central idea to begin with, but has failed to keep it in the forefront of his mind as he wrote, so that the reader cannot be sure what it is. Sometimes unity is obscured by failure to maintain *harmony of tone*—a failure resulting from shifts in the writer's attitude toward the subject, from the use of words or phrases that do not fit the overall tone of the paper, from details that contradict what the paper as a whole is trying to say, or even from details that belong in the paper but are introduced in a confusing order or without transitional links to show their connections with each other and with the thesis of the whole paper.

Still more often, many freshman papers lack *development,* that is, they fail to provide *enough concrete and specific details* to make the central idea clear to the reader. The writer, knowing what he means by his generalizations, forgets to expand them so that the reader will interpret them the same way he did. Or perhaps the writer does *not* know very clearly what he means by his generalizations, and neglects to expand them because he has not thought in specific terms himself. The student who says, "If I say any more, I'll just be padding it," is usually a student who does not realize how little a generalization can mean by itself.

Finally, many freshman papers are unified and harmonious in tone and are detailed enough to be clear, but still are not outstanding. They lack the sparkle provided by an *original presentation* of the idea. Such papers frequently are returned with *B* grades. They are better than average, but they are not really good.

Let us consider each of these characteristics of a good theme in turn. The paper may lack *unity,* so that the reader must ask, "What are you talking about?" It may lack *development,* so that questions raised by the thesis or by subsidiary ideas are left unanswered: "What do you mean by that?" or "What about it?" It may be clear, and yet be so commonplace in idea and so trite in phrasing that it seems completely lacking in *originality:* "So what's new about it?" A paper that leads a reader to ask any of these questions is weaker than it should be.

UNITY: "WHAT ARE YOU TALKING ABOUT?"

Unity is oneness. A successful paper must confine itself to making a single point that the reader can summarize in one unified sentence. To write such a paper, the writer must phrase for himself in advance the single unified sentence that expresses his central thought, *and he must keep that sentence, that thesis, before him as he writes.* If you phrase such a thesis and make sure that no irrelevant ideas creep in as you write, your reader should be able, when he has read your paper, to summarize your central idea in a sentence which is not greatly different from the one you wrote down for your own guidance beforehand.

If you have no clear thesis in mind, but write only on a topic, you may merely make random—and fuzzy—remarks about that topic. You may even end by writing nonsense, as the following paper illustrates.

Why Do People Go to Europe?

It has become a recognized fact that one of the best ways to gain prestige is through travel abroad. More and more Americans are following this road to importance every year. The unfortunate side of this is that the returned traveller would much rather tell of his experiences in a French night club than tell of his relations with the people of a foreign country.

It is possible that the American abroad overlooks the value of his experiences because he knows little about foreign countries. He probably does not speak any foreign language and does not really care about the history or culture of the people that he has imposed himself on. His only purpose is to see as much as he can in his two or three week jet tour.

Because he is sure that everything is better at home, he creates ill-feeling wherever he goes, but he has no intention of creating ill-feeling, or of doing anything wrong. They are "Ugly Americans." Their ignorance of socially acceptable European customs has a very important effect upon the people they come in contact with. This rudeness to and lack of understanding of foreign peoples should be stopped. We Americans are blessed to have the opportunity to see other parts of the world. We should try to appreciate the real beauty in things.

There is no thesis behind that paper, at all—not even a vaguely conceived answer to the title question, which is abandoned after the second sentence. There is not even a consistent tone or a unified point of view to help hold these aimless comments together. Sometimes the writer sees the tourist from an American vantage point,

sometimes from a European one. And the American viewing the
virtues of travel in the last paragraph is certainly not the cynic
of the first paragraph and the last sentence of the second one. The
paper raises many questions, but the most important is, "What are
you talking about?"

Remember, too, that the reader cannot know what central
idea you are trying to express until he has read your paper; and if,
as you write, you yourself lose sight of the exact relation between
each detail and the central idea, that central idea may be so obscured by your phrasing that the reader will have trouble deciding
what you meant to say. In the following theme, for example, every
detail is relevant to the student's thesis, as that thesis was expressed
in the outline that accompanied the paper; but the total effect
is very confusing.

A Dirge

The fourth Thursday in November has been designated by law
as Thanksgiving Day—a day on which everyone gives thanks not
only for tangible belongings, such as homes and automobiles, but
also for such intangibles as happiness and freedom, and for the gift
of the future. It is truly a day on which to thank God, a day to
gather together with others and share the blessings we enjoy. And
yet it is becoming a day which children remember only as one on
which Mother serves turkey. Christmas and Thanksgiving are losing
their true meaning because of the importance which retail stores are
imposing upon Christmas.

By the first week in November, cities and towns across this
country begin to prepare for Christmas, the focal point of the retailers' year. Not just by increasing inventories, but by displaying
Yuletide decorations and adorning both the inside and the outside
of their establishments, do stores announce the coming season. What
the downtown businessman feels like after hearing two months of
Christmas carols and music must be very difficult to express. With all
the emphasis placed upon attracting and selling to the public, the
important and traditional day of Thanksgiving is completely overlooked. On the other hand, if department stores and other retailers
insist on the premature opening of the Christmas season, they will
feel serious effects.

If Christmas loses its true religious meaning, and the public
becomes aware that it has become solely a time for money making,

the reaction will be immediate and fatal to the retailer. Where there is no worthy reason for buying, purchasing is bound to slacken. People have always discovered when they were being mulcted, and though the process of rebelling has often taken a long time, eventually the rebellion has come.

There is no reason why man cannot give full respect to the tradition of Thanksgiving, but with his God-given brain and ingenuity, he should be capable of retaining a full realization of the true religious meaning of the great festival of Christmas and still increase his selling records.

There are numerous weaknesses in that theme, but the greatest is that the reader cannot help asking, "What are you talking about?" Christmas and Thanksgiving, the meanings of the holidays, and the retailers' sales charts are all so confusingly intermingled that it is impossible to tell what the writer really meant to say. No less than seven conflicting possible statements of thesis were suggested by the members of the class to which that puzzle was presented. (The reader will try desperately to make sense out of your themes. Your job is to be sure that the idea he gets is the idea you wanted to give him.) Not one of the seven guesses agreed with the thesis the writer had confidently phrased at the head of the outline he handed in with the theme. What he meant to say was, "The spirit of Thanksgiving—and perhaps even of Christmas itself— is being lost because of the retailers' shortsighted greed for Christmas sales." There is one central idea, and nearly every detail can be interpreted to support it. But the writer forgot to keep that thesis before him as he wrote, and as a result the reader becomes hopelessly lost. Even though the paper is reasonably accurate in mechanics, it is not a good theme. In fact, it is a very bad one.

Unity may also be obscured by a failure to maintain *harmony of tone*. A paper on a serious subject may be flawed by an inappropriately flippant remark; a paper may suddenly introduce a confusingly ironic note, so that the reader is forced unexpectedly to realize that the writer does not literally mean what he is saying; a paper may present both sides of an argument without ever making clear which side the writer regards as the stronger, so that the writer's attitude toward the subject seems to change in mid-flight, and the reader cannot be sure exactly where the writer stands. Or perhaps words or phrases that do not fit the overall tone of the paper are allowed to creep in and are not removed in revision. Or details which contradict what the paper as a whole is trying to say are allowed to stand in the final paper. Or sometimes details which really do belong are brought in out of their easiest, most logical order.

We will later (Chapter 7) consider in detail the various levels of language and the way in which words may be appropriate in one context and completely inappropriate in another. Here, a single illustration may suffice to suggest how a flaw in the harmony of tone resulting from inappropriate diction may spoil the unity of effect that a more careful writer might have secured. Consider, for example, this sentence:

> In addition to a well-rounded education and sound specialized training, the college graduate who is to succeed in life must have persistence, good fortune, and the gumption to exploit such opportunities as come his way.

Gumption simply does not fit. The colloquial word is out of harmony with the tone of the rest of the sentence, and unity is destroyed.

Details which contradict what the paper as a whole is trying to say may be as obvious as the inappropriate detail in the following description:

> He was a masterful-looking man—tall, broad-shouldered, and burly, with a mass of black hair, piercing eyes, a foolish grin, and an air of firm determination.

Or confusion may result more subtly as a writer unexpectedly changes his attitude toward his topic, perhaps by suddenly injecting irony into what had seemed to be straightforward statement:

> New methods of teaching foreign languages—such as listening carefully to the teacher's pronunciation, using tape recorders to let students hear their own speech, and developing a knowledge of grammar as a child does, by observation rather than direct instruction —have greatly increased the speed and efficiency of learning. Students now learn to speak fluent French, for example, with a pure Paris, Kentucky, accent in less time than students once learned to read and write it. Developed during the crash programs of the Second World War, these new methods are almost completely successful, although today's students can rarely read or write in French,

or speak intelligibly in France. The schools which cling to older methods of teaching are making a great mistake, and their students may suffer for it.

Which side is that paragraph supporting?

To secure unity, to avoid the fatal question, "What are you talking about?" get a clearly defined thesis or statement of purpose in mind and keep it there all the time you are writing, so that you can check each paragraph, each sentence, each detail against it. In no other way can you be sure that your paper will be unified.

DEVELOPMENT

The problems of unity we have been considering are less common than problems more directly concerned with the full development of your ideas.

Detail: "What do you mean by that?"

After the first few papers, most students write unified themes. But a great many students have trouble learning to use enough details for clarity. They know what they mean; they do not realize that the reader cannot be sure what is meant until he has been given enough concrete, specific detail to restrict a generalization to the one meaning the writer had in mind. The overall thesis may be plain, but the reader may still ask, "What do you mean by that?"

Sometimes, such an undeveloped theme provides little more than a bare statement of the central idea.

Generals as Presidents

The wisdom of a military man's entering a presidential race rests entirely on his individual qualifications, not on the fact that his training has been restricted to filling a position of command. Presidential material cannot lie only in certain set vocations.

We as a nation should have progressed beyond the point where a mere personal and military popularity can sway our selection of the national executive. If our national intelligence, considered as a unit, selects a man not because of his outstanding military achievements, but because he is found to be sufficiently endowed with that dignity of mind and honesty of purpose which characterize a capable executive, then, whatever his previous vocation, there is no question but that we shall have chosen well.

The reader feels that there should have been more. Perhaps pages two and three were lost, and only page one was turned in. But page one is all that there is to judge by, and it cannot be called a good theme. In most composition courses, it would clearly be a failing paper.

Many other freshman themes are so general and therefore vague that they can only impress the reader as flabby. Often, as has been suggested before, the overgeneral theme is simply trying to cover too much ground. One student launched himself on a twenty thousand mile trip.

A Trip to Hawaii

Our family was living at West Point, New York. Dad was stationed away, and we were to go to Hawaii. We left upstate New York in our small grey Ford and began our trip halfway around the world.

Arriving in New York City, we were lucky enough to spend several days. The crowds and the bright lights were amazing. After our all too short visit we proceeded across the country.

Our drive was uneventful until we were about halfway across. It had been raining slightly, and then all of a sudden the skies let loose. We had to cross a most unstable bridge or else turn back and lose several hours. It was finally decided that the best thing to do was to cross. Safely on the other side, we felt fine until we heard a crash. We looked back and there was no bridge. Fortunately, there was no one on the bridge at the time of its collapse. Westward bound out of the flood area, we were again calm and cool.

We crossed the Rockies at dusk, and our welcoming party was of course an old grizzly bear looking for a hand-out. We spent the night in a cabin without heat. There was no need for heat in the middle of July. But by the time midnight came, the weather must have been freezing, and the whole family had on almost all the clothes we had brought along.

We left the United States on a ship that was sunk during the war. Probably that was a good thing, because the ship was falling to pieces. The little ship plugged right along without too much occurring. Reaching Hawaii, we were met by girls who presented us with leis. We had leis up to our noses and were led off to the hotel. After living several weeks in the hotel, we moved to a house in a valley. We had only lived in the house a week or so when we experienced our first earthquake. The dishes rattled and fell off the shelves, the lights went off, and then it was all over.

Driving around the island is quite an experience. It takes only a few hours, and the scenery is marvelous. There is an upside-down waterfall, which is caused by wind coming around the mountain so swiftly. There is also Diamond Head, and a Devil's Pit. In the Devil's Pit the water is purple and it looks vicious.

Our two years away from the States were terminated by a wonderful trip through the Panama Canal and shopping in Panama. Then we came back to New York.

There is material in that paper for a dozen themes—narrative, descriptive, and expository. It has a unified purpose behind it: The student is telling about the most interesting trip he has ever taken. But what good is it to the reader? He sees none of the things the student saw, feels none of his excitement, learns none of all the writer must have learned in all of that travel, gets no sharp effect of any sort. A paper on the bridge that collapsed or an explanation of why even well-built bridges let go once in a while could have been well worth doing. The bears in the parks, the Park Service, a night in a cold cabin, life aboard ship, the operation of the ship or its engines, the duties of the purser—there are plenty of subjects implied by that theme. But the paper that was actually written might better have never been written at all.

Here is another paper which depends too much on unsupported generalizations. The reader feels that he is being given undigested notes from a half-understood lecture course.

Modern Architecture

Modern architecture is based on two things new to men in this modern day and age. There are new materials and new construction methods the architect can use, and there are new ways in which men and women and their families live which the traditional architect, building the old-style house, doesn't take into account as the modern architect does.

The old-style architect who still designs traditional houses may use the new materials and the new gadgets, but he just sticks them on to the same old house. If he uses the new construction methods, he doesn't know what to do with them. But in the hands of a really modern architect the new methods and materials lead to new proportions and new textures.

The modern architect tries to fit the house to the family.

Good architecture provides for man's six needs. It provides for a man's (and his family's) health. It provides also for his safety at home, for his convenience, and for his comfort, privacy, and desire for beauty. It does all this as economically as it can.

The modern architect fits the house that he is designing to the family that is to live in it, as efficiently as he can.

Even the lot the house is to be built on is taken into consideration, and both house and lot are fitted to the family.

The goal of housing should be unhampered and gracious living. It is the modern architect who knows this and tries to achieve it, not the old-fashioned architect building Tudor mansions.

The reader at every point needs concrete, specific detail to clarify the general ideas the writer is presenting. He needs *concrete* detail that presents tangible, solid, "real" figures to his mind. He needs *specific* detail that will pin those concretions down to individual items he can visualize. In narrative, a single incident, presented in concrete, specific detail, can come through to the reader. But an incident or an exposition of idea which is vaguely presented in general terms will make only a vague and general impression.

Perhaps a student who could write "A Trip to Hawaii" would be equally general even when treating a single incident. But a student who realizes how the use of well-chosen detail can draw the reader into sharing the experience will be as specific as he can. He will use names for people and places. He will amplify the details of setting. He will tell how he feels, what he feels, and even why he feels it. He will choose vivid and exact words—*shuffled, sidled, strode, strutted, minced,* not *walked* or *moved.* He will give the reader sharp and graphic pictures, not nebulous sketches.

Consider the following theme. Reduced to its barest idea, it says merely, "One day I caught a fish." That experience is surely common, even commonplace. Yet the student who takes the trouble to remember the experience can reproduce it vividly for a reader.

A Summer Experience[1]

I straddled the narrow cockpit, bracing my legs against the short, sharp, pitching motion of the deck. Behind me in the cockpit, Murphy shifted his bulk in the fishing chair, heaved himself from it, and

[1] From *The Green Caldron: A Magazine of Freshman Writing,* published at the University of Illinois. Reprinted by permission.

handed the big rod to me. "Here, you take it a while. I gotta stretch my legs." So, I sat down and fitted the butt of the rod into the socket of his fishing belt. I tested the drag and reset it, but I didn't really expect anything.

Unexpectedly, the rod tip jerked. I waited cautiously, then set it hard and began to reel. The line sang out, wheeling, screaming, looping freely across the water. The big one had hit! Tightening up on the drag, I began to get a little line back between lunges by raising the rod tip and reeling fast as I let it down again. Each time it was like lifting a horse. Suddenly, the line started coming up, leveling off. Not more than twenty or thirty yards behind the boat, the big fish surfaced. A barracuda doesn't jump much; instead it mostly stays down and pulls like a mule, but this one jumped. He shot straight up out of the water, tall and solid, in a shower of spray. In the split second he stood there, I could see him trying to spit the lure, his gill plates standing out like elephant ears.

The three in the cockpit held their breaths, waiting for the big, viciously-barbed jig to come slamming back into the boat, but the hooks held. The barracuda hit the water with a sound like the crack of a pistol. He dived deeply and swam straight for the boat. Reeling as fast as I could, I struggled to my feet and moved to the gunwale. Please, God, I was thinking, don't let him foul up the line. Please let it be all right.

And it was all right, and Diego, our boatman, was there with a gaff and got the big fish in the cockpit. With a short lead pipe, Diego tapped the barracuda twice at the base of the skull. Then he disengaged the hooks from between the needle-studded jaws. Murphy tossed his dead cigarette into the water and nudged me with his elbow. "Gimme a hand with this tiger. I'll show you how to clean 'em."

Ben Watson

There are weaknesses in that theme. It is not professional writing, but freshman writing, the kind you can hope to do and the kind at least some of your classmates will do. But any instructor would call it a good theme. And the chief difference between it and the paper on "A Trip to Hawaii" is that the writer looked, and saw, and remembered, and reported, concretely and specifically, so that the reader has a chance, if he wants to, to relive the experience with him.

The inept theme on modern architecture could have been clear and effective, like the one that follows.

Modern Residential Architecture[2]

Modern residential architecture justifies its drastic changes from conventional styles by two facts: first of all, radical changes in modes of living require equally radical changes in house planning; and secondly, the ever-increasing inventions of this highly industrial age make possible radical changes in the modes of construction. These factors, which receive little attention in recent homes of traditional type, become primary in the new architecture.

Although the designers of traditionally styled homes may use the products of recent invention such as equipment, prefabricated parts, and new materials, these tend to be mere accessories, leaving the standardized form almost unchanged. To modern architects, however, each of these offers opportunity for new expression. The mode of use may translate the characteristic of the material in question. The materials and fixtures derived from modern technology lose value when enclosed in traditional forms. Modernists consider it absurd that concrete should be made to look like natural stone, or electric light fixtures like candlesticks. Each in its use may honestly reveal its peculiar nature and purpose. The new materials make possible thinner walls, lighter construction, new proportions, and new textures. Again and in quite another sense, it is seen that "form follows function."

Modern architects, then, seek not style but substance, not ornament but simplicity, not standardized plans but proficiency in exposition, not fitting the family to the house but the house to the family, not imitation but creation. Ideally, they strive to give a fresh approach to the problem of design by the study of the latest findings concerning the nature of man and of social trends. They seek fresh achievement in construction by thorough understanding and mastery of new materials and processes and their potentials. They study intensively the client and the members of the household, the site and its neighborhood, the available local organizations and materials for construction. In short, they attempt to develop a home to fit the purpose. The result is a house, not a machine for living. The products of machines, however, facilitate and even inspire each process of daily living for each member of the family.

It is characteristic of good residential architecture that it should provide for man's six fundamental housing needs: health, safety, convenience, comfort, privacy, beauty, and each of these with refer-

[2] From *The Green Caldron: A Magazine of Freshman Writing*, published at the University of Illinois. Reprinted by permission.

ence to economy. Modern architects have, however, made a fresh analysis of these needs and have not been forced into the compromise so frequently dictated by other architectural forms. Since they are free to develop their plans from a close study of the interest of each member of the household, instead of first considering what architectural style to apply, the plan may become the logical solution of the family's needs. Just as plants develop from seed, modern architecture seeks to be the organic expression of the interests of the family for which the house is to be built. The house develops outwardly from the core or center of the family life.

Specifically, needs may run the gamut of work and play, domestic life and social life, chores and hobbies, love and worship, and the obvious routines of sleeping, eating, bathing, and dressing. Thus, consideration is given to areas of family life under such groupings as service areas, sleeping areas, living areas and recreation areas. Each of these, though requiring many sub-divisions, is planned as an operative unit for its specific purpose and is carefully interrelated with the other areas within the house. This is a wide departure from earlier types of planning in which each room tended to serve one purpose alone. Though there are obvious needs for efficiency in all household operations, there remains a greater requirement, that the home should as far as possible unite or coordinate the lives of the people within.

Peculiarly characteristic of modern architecture is the adaptation of both the house and the lot to the man. Attention is paid to the orientation of the warming rays of winter sunshine and for protection against the intense rays of the summer. Windows, doors, decks, and terraces are placed to take advantage of the things which nature offers while protecting the family from the curiosity or intrusion of neighbors and passersby. In warm and temperate climates there has also been a high development of the "indoor-outdoor house"; the indoor space is "enlarged" by the view of the outside offered by large glazed areas which can be thrown open. The sense of confinement is all but eliminated.

Thus does architecture seek to fulfill the goal of housing, which is not mere shelter, but the opportunity for unhampered and gracious living.

Robert Poggi

There is enough detail in this theme for the reader to understand what the writer is trying to say.

Here is another in which, brief as it is, the details are full enough to build up a clear picture for the reader.

The Mill[3]

It is old, very old, that mill with its moss-covered water wheel. A century or more its wheels turned, turned, turned, grinding the grain of the country folk for miles around. The miller and his sons toiled from dawn to dark and went to their humble home at night in ghostlike dustiness. But the miller is gone, and his sons and their sons, and all of the millers.

Now the wheels go round no more, the castings are gone to rust, the great millstones have fallen from their sockets. Cobwebs glut the feed chute and fill the space above the beams with filmy grayness. Bright rays of light stream through the sagging clapboard roof and lose themselves in dusty corners. Everywhere is dust; thick, heavy, gray dust that rises in dense clouds as I walk across the creaking floor. The floor, which once bore up the heavy millstones and loads of grain, now groans and gives beneath my weight. In the cracks of the worn oak sill of the door stand slim, sear stalks of wheat rustling in the breeze. They have been there, seeding and reseeding themselves since last the mill was run. . . .

Only the water in the mill race remains the same, sparkling, singing, happy, unaware of any change.

S. J. Ewald

The themes we have just considered are based on personal experience or course work, and represent the kind of writing you may be called upon to do early in the year. As you shift from early themes of reminiscence to simple exposition, calling on your own experience for subjects, you will still need to use specific detail at every point to make your generalizations clear. For example, examine the following process theme, which is even more specific than "Modern Residential Architecture."

The Smell of Greasepaint[4]

It's a half-hour until curtain time, and the house seats have begun to fill. The props and costume crews are making final checks, and the directors are still arguing about the blue lights in the death scenes. People with unknown destinations are scurrying everywhere, and the whole set is alive with anticipation. Now is the time for the most exciting preparation of all—making up.

[3] From *The Green Caldron: A Magazine of Freshman Writing,* published at the University of Illinois. Reprinted by permission.
[4] From *The Green Caldron: A Magazine of Freshman Writing,* published at the University of Illinois. Reprinted by permission.

A make-up kit is set out. In it are the basic materials of theatrical cosmetics. There are bases, rouges, liners, powders, false hair, and nearby, and just as necessary, lots of cold cream and Kleenex. Ready? Then let's start.

First a base is applied. It may be the old standby, greasepaint, or it may be a liquid with an oil base. Whatever its form, the base must cover all visible skin. It looks a trifle strange to see an actor whose face and neck are different shades, no matter how well they look together. The base must also be applied sparingly lest the face look pasty onstage.

Next comes rouge. Wet rouge is used for the lips, wet or dry for the cheeks, although dry rouge usually assures a more even job. Eye-shadow should be applied in dabs to the centers of the eyelids and gently smoothed outward to make the eyes appear wider. Eyelashes, if pencilled, are extended slightly beyond the outer corners of the eyes. Lashes, brows, and wrinkles follow the natural lines. Smile-wrinkles are the easiest to trace. White liner, used to accent wrinkles, is tricky, and the more miserly the amount the better. The whole painted surface is finally doused with powder, the excess dusted off, and the lips repainted and blotted.

The final complexion of the subject depends on the number of base, powder, and rouge used. These are numbered in order of lightness from one to eight. Lighter shades are used by blonds and redheads, while brunets take a darker shade, one ranging from four to six. Boys take darker make-up than girls with the same skin and hair tones. In liners, blonds take blue eyeshadow and brown pencil, while brunets take brown shadow and black pencil.

The age and physical state to be portrayed are also factors to be considered. Darker bases make the skin look more faded. Deeper hollows in the eyes, less rouge or even a touch of blue on the cheeks, less lip-rouge, and lined wrinkles all give an older look, while a ruddier or lighter base, few wrinkles, pinker cheeks, and red dots on the inside corners of the eyes tend to accent youth. To make cheekbones and nose more prominent, a touch of white liner gives the needed emphasis.

False hair is applied with spirit gum. Liberal amounts of hair are glued lightly to the skin, then trimmed to fit the specifications.

These, of course, are the most basic of rules, but they can produce an unlimited variety of effects. Make-up, however, is a dangerous thing. Too little is no good at all; too much is worse than none. The effect must be subtle but unmistakable. Skillfully applied make-up gives new meaning to a character portrayal by allowing the actor to make the fullest use of facial expressions. A skillful job will eradicate certain elements of the actor's own personality and place an emphasis on or introduce traits dominant in the personality of the character.

It's a hard task, but it's well worth the effort, for, after all, that tube of greasepaint is a key to that wonderful land of make-believe that is the theater.

Elizabeth Yeatter

A Finished Paper: "What about it?"

It sometimes happens that a writer stays close to his predetermined thesis and develops each succeeding point in enough detail for it to be clear, and yet leaves an unanswered question in his reader's mind. Like the detective novel, which may be engrossing from page 1 to page 217 and still be a failure if page 218 is disappointing, a theme will not be successful if you leave it unfinished or if your ending is not satisfying. The reader must not be allowed to ask, "What about it?" If he does ask that question, one of two things has happened: Either you have not shown him how the idea applies to your life or his, or you have not prepared him for the ending, so that when he reaches it, it seems abrupt; he feels that you had led him to expect more than you have given him.

The following paper, for example, promises more than it provides.

The Federal Government Should Aid Education

A few years ago the president of Amherst College was discussing with one of the school's alumni a prospective fund-raising campaign. It was to be for a million dollars. "Forget about it," the alumnus said. "I'll give a hundred thousand, and nine of my friends will do the same." That was the ideal way of financing education. There was an old-fashioned directness about it that is rare today. Today, in fact, so many people want a higher education and private funds have so dried up that the problem of financing the expansion of our colleges has been brought to the attention of federal legislators. Sufficient funds seem to be available in the collective entity of the federal government.

"We are the government" runs an oratorical phrase. "The government has as a care the education of its citizens" is another. Yet federal aid to education always seems unattractive, both because of the inefficiency of needless bureaucracy and the fear of political control that such aid might bring.

Up to the last sentence, that is a pretty good paper, but at the end it raises questions that it never answers. Why inefficiency, necessarily? Is the bureaucracy needless, demonstrably? What kind of political control? Why should federal aid bring more or different control than state aid, which has long supported public universities? The paper is obviously not finished. "What about it?"

If either your topic or your phrasing raises questions in the reader's mind, he may reasonably expect you to provide him with the answers, or at least to provide the material from which he can construct his own answers. Unless you do one or the other, your paper is insufficiently developed. And an undeveloped paper is not a good paper.

There are three important points to notice as you study these contrasted papers, the undeveloped and the developed. First, the more restricted the idea, the more chance there is to get in the details which alone can make it worthwhile. A cold night in a park cabin is a better subject than a trip from New York to Hawaii to New York. To the writer who can see what details the reader will need in order to understand exactly what the writer feels or thinks, the restricted idea provides plenty of material for a full-length theme.

Second, however, mere length—wordiness—is in itself no virtue. The brief description of "The Mill" is complete; the picture is vivid. You are not being urged to pad your papers, to add detail for the sake of detail itself. Instead, every detail must be carefully chosen to support your main idea, to clarify the thesis or to clarify a lesser supporting idea, to answer legitimate questions your reader might ask. Too much detail smothers an idea; too little leaves the idea nebulous. The successfully developed paper has just enough detail to make the reader see *your* picture, feel *your* feelings, think *your* thoughts, understand *your* ideas.

Third, using enough detail to develop your ideas in a way that answers all the reader's questions is just as important in workaday exposition as it is in description or narration. "The Federal Government Should Aid Education" (page 47), for example, though it poses the problem, never does get to the development of the solution suggested by the title. The passage is unfinished, but as far as it goes, it is concrete and detailed. And it is clearly expository in intention, although not very informative in its development. The student answering an examination question, the engineer recommending the selection of a particular factory site, the county agricultural agent explaining a new farming method, or the freshman explaining a simple process in an English I theme—all of them need concrete, specific detail to make their generalizations understandable.

ORIGINALITY

But a paper may be unified and fully developed and still not be wholly successful. The best themes possess in addition a measure of originality which adds to the interest with which a reader reads. That originality may lie in the topic, in the writer's approach to the topic, in his phrasing, or even in the title he gives to the theme— and the best theme of all will show original touches in all four.[5]

Preeminently, the best themes come from a rigorously honest effort to know exactly what you want to say and to say it as exactly and as effectively as you can. If your papers are developed in the most exact phrasing and with the most appropriate details you can find, they will possess the originality that results from a careful insistence on being yourself. Carelessness and indifference never produce good papers. Trying to write what you think the teacher wants to hear (as distinct from trying to fulfill the assignment) is merely shoddy. Trying to be impressively "literary" will result in being pretentious. Trying too hard to be "different" may result in being grotesque. Above all, be honest with yourself.

It should be obvious at the outset that by the very nature of originality no formula can be offered which will assure you of being original. The most that can be done is to suggest some general characteristics original themes may possess and to offer a few themes illustrating those characteristics. The ability to produce original themes depends in part on the possession of an original mind, but the ability to avoid the commonplace can be developed

---

[5] It is presupposed, of course, that you will be original in the obvious sense that your papers will represent your own work. To submit someone else's work as your own, that is, to use someone else's *phrasing* or *ideas* or *organizational patterns* without giving proper credit, is to find the quickest and most ignominious way of leaving school. If you borrow from other writers, say so. If you don't know how to say so, ask your teacher.

through intelligent practice. And that practice may make the difference between *C* themes and *A* themes, between mediocre writing and writing that will be exciting to read and that you can be proud of having written.

Before we consider ways for securing the kind of originality which makes the difference between the good and the merely average theme, we must first examine the difference between desirable originality and foolish grotesquerie. *Original,* here, means fresh and unhackneyed; it does not mean freakish. Some students lean so far over backward in an attempt to be original that they and their writing fall very flat indeed.

For an obvious example of the merely freakish, imagine how the busy personnel manager of a large corporation felt when he began to read a job-application letter which the applicant, in a misguided attempt to be original, had written backward. The prospective employer read first the signature, then "Yours truly," then the concluding request for an interview. And then he stopped reading and dictated an indignant letter to the head of the Division of Business English at the university from which the applicant had graduated, asking what kind of ridiculous nonsense was being taught there in the Business Letter Writing course. The division head, of course, was as indignant as the businessman. No one in his right mind will read, and no teacher will recommend, a freakish grotesquerie. As Aristotle long ago pointed out, excess of any kind is—excessive. Better the commonplace than the grotesque.

But originality may be secured within the bounds of good taste. A fresh idea or a fresh approach to an old idea is automatically original. Close observation and careful reporting are original, since no two observers see exactly the same things and consequently no two careful reporters report details in exactly the same way. If you are sincere in what you are saying, if you are honestly trying to express your own thoughts, your own feelings, your own responses to a situation or an idea, in your own words—then your paper will be original; and it will be worthwhile and interesting and perhaps fluent into the bargain.

Point of View toward the Topic

It is not easy to think a new thought or to report an experience new in the history of the race, but fortunately it is not necessary. As some of the themes we have already examined illustrate, it is perfectly possible for a college student to look at an old idea or experience in a new way. The following paper, for example, may cast new light on the old relation between the student and the teacher.

Doubt Gets You an Education[6]

When a person is attempting to absorb an education, he should have faith in the things propounded to him by his instructor, but for his own good and the increase of his knowledge he should reserve a particle of doubt. It is all very well to take what is offered, but to really gain insight into a subject there have to be doubts in the mind and independent research to verify or discourage those doubts.

In the universities of today very few instructors have the time to delve as deeply into all the aspects of a certain idea as they would wish to. For a student to really acquire a comprehensive knowledge, he has to take some of the instructor's words with a grain of salt and endeavor to find out for himself just what it is that doesn't ring true.

If, during the entire history of mankind, people had continued to believe fully the teachings and precepts of those who had gone before them, the world would still be at the intellectual level of the Stone Age. All of the world's great thinkers in every field have been led on in their search for new knowledge by doubting some facet of the teachings of earlier scholars.

A complete education of any sort cannot be acquired by unequivocal acceptance of age-old tenets in perfect faith. The same principle applies not only to formal education but to many things in the life of an average individual. "Believe nothing you hear, and only half of what you see," sounds perhaps a little exaggerated, but it really is an excellent idea.

If a person develops the habit of regarding with a bit of skepticism things which are represented to him as verities, that person will acquire a more complete and well-rounded education than the one who blindly accepts everything told to him. To be skeptical and to attempt to verify those skepticisms is to be a better educated man.

James F. Grant

[6] From *The Green Caldron: A Magazine of Freshman Writing,* published at the University of Illinois. Reprinted by permission.

Another fruitful source of theme material lies in the proverbs which enshrine or embalm the vaunted wisdom of the race. Try reexamining the old clichés to see if you really believe them. You have often heard, for example, and probably you have said, "Every man has a right to his own opinion." One student, picking up a chance suggestion from a lecture, has wondered.

The Right to an Opinion[7]

In a speech on this campus several weeks ago the great scientist and thinker, Professor Robert A. Millikan, remarked that no greater fallacy was ever uttered than that every man has a right to his opinion. The words struck me as being most true, a statement long needed. The usual reply to an attempt to correct someone of a prejudice or piece of misinformation is "Every man has a right to his opinion." This has been and continues to be the shield behind which people hide their narrow-mindedness and refusal to accept facts and proofs logically drawn from facts. This fallacy is so convenient to mentally lazy people who follow the way of least resistance, and has been used so much, that it has become an almost universally accepted axiom.

I am maintaining that no person has a right to an opinion that is more than a tentative one. If I were more idealistic, I would say that no person has a right to any opinion that is not the result of much study and thought on the subject, or the result of the study and thought of a reliable authority. I realize, however, that one cannot delve easily into every field, and that he must form some opinions, especially on philosophical subjects, merely on the results of his own observations. Certain convictions must be held and certain assumptions must be made in order for one to build up something to live by, to have a sound philosophy of life, without which man is like a ship without a rudder. One has a right to form an opinion which affects only himself (if such an opinion is possible). One has a right to form an opinion that comes from the heart rather than from the mind. One has a natural tendency to form opinions on every subject on the basis of either knowledge or prejudice, but the point is that these opinions must be subject to change.

When is a person ethically or morally justified in saying that his opinion is such and such on a question that is more than a per-

[7] From *The Green Caldron: A Magazine of Freshman Writing,* published at the University of Illinois. Reprinted by permission.

sonal issue? In the first place, his method of approach must be open-minded; he must cast aside all prejudice and bias. Then he must study the authorities and the facts, and think these over with the dispassionate view of a scientist. But when he has arrived at the conclusion, that is not the end of the study. He must keep in contact with the developments and changes that take place in the subject.

Another means of rationalizing one's mental laziness is merely to say that one man's opinion is as good as another's. Such a view might be excusable if the issue were on a subject on which the authorities greatly differ. For example, the philosophies of Dante, Schopenhauer, Hegel, James, and Bergson are so much in contradiction that they cannot all be accepted as a basis on which to build a philosophy. Since this is true, one's philosophy of life should be built up not on the basis of authority but on the basis of the individual's personal needs. But in more factual subjects which are not merely personal matters affecting the heart more than the mind, one's opinion must be formed from knowledge. Since some people are in a better position to know, some people can and do form more accurate opinions than others. For example, fancy comparing the opinion of the man in the street with the opinion of some eminent biologist on the evolution of man. It is absurd, though very convenient, to say that one man's opinion is as good as another's.

The keeping of one's opinion in a static condition cannot be morally or ethically justified. When the opinions of the people of a nation which is presumably a democracy built on public opinion become static, then progress ceases to take place. Thus every person should form his ideas and convictions on a basis of thought and fact, not only for the sake of society but for the sake of keeping his own personality alive.

R. M. Ewald

That paper, while not strikingly fluent, is original in its fresh approach to an old idea, even though the impulse for that fresh approach came from someone else. It may serve to demonstrate that even a somewhat unimaginative student, if he knows clearly what he wants to say, provides the detail that the reader will need in order to understand what is meant, goes directly to the point, and answers all the reader's questions, can write an interestingly original theme.

Even the very oldest experiences of the race may be treated with a touch of originality by a student who looks at them afresh.

In the following theme the originality lies in the successful effort to present and sustain the child's point of view.

Grandfather[8]

All day the house had been quiet with an air, not of expectancy, but of waiting—just waiting. I hadn't played in the sand as usual. I had been dressed in a new black silk dress, my first silk dress, too. I had walked sedately around or sat primly in a chair and watched the people coming and going, all so silent and serious. Some of them would put their hands on my head for a moment and smile. Once, Uncle Jack took me by the hand, led me into the parlor, and lifted me up so I could see Grandfather, lying in a funny-looking box on wheels. He didn't look very comfortable, either. Maybe it was because men don't like to sleep on white satin; only princesses do that. Grandfather says men like to sleep under the stars, wrapped in a blanket, and sometimes snakes come up and sleep close to them to keep warm. Uncle Dick, my missionary uncle, says that people in China sleep on the floor with only a block of wood for a pillow.

I asked Uncle Jack if he thought Grandfather would take me out to hunt violets when he woke up. He said no, that Grandfather had gone away to be with Grandmother in Heaven and wouldn't ever come back. I guess he meant that Grandfather had gone like I do when Grace goes to school. I go to school with her, only I'm really still at home. I climb up in the Duchess apple tree, where the bottom limb goes straight out before it goes up, and watch Grace till she turns the corner and is behind the hedge. I can't see her then, but I know what she does. She walks down the middle of the road till she gets to the bridge. If it's early, she climbs up and walks the rail. If it's too late, she crosses in the middle, scrambles up the embankment, and walks along the cow-path to the school house. She always goes straight into the school house and puts her books in her desk before she goes out to play. If Mother has sent any message to the teacher, she gives it to her first, so she won't forget it.

All the aunts and uncles and cousins were there for dinner. It made me think of Christmas, only there weren't any presents, and some of them cried. Martha Jean, Uncle Dick's daughter, who is two years older than I am, said that it is proper to cry when someone dies. I didn't know who was dead so I didn't cry. I don't even cry when I cut my foot or get a splinter in it. Grandfather says that only babies cry over things like that.

[8] From *The Green Caldron: A Magazine of Freshman Writing,* published at the University of Illinois. Reprinted by permission.

In the afternoon all the neighbors came and the minister and some more people that I didn't know. They all sat around, or stood around when there weren't chairs enough, and the minister talked a long time about something. He thinks my grandfather is a very good man and has done a lot for the community. I sat in my little rocking-chair, between Mother and Aunt Susan. They both cried. I liked the way Mother did it better than Aunt Susan. She didn't have a nice lacey handkerchief like Mother did, and she was kind of messy about it, anyway.

After a while they all got up and went out. They carried out the box Grandfather had been in and put it in a big truck with curtains on it. Everyone went away but Mrs. Crockett and me. I changed my dress but I didn't feel like playing. I just sat on the steps and held Muffy.

I guess Grandfather really must have gone to Heaven to be with Grandmother, like Uncle Jack said, because it's been a week now and he hasn't been back. I guess he's having a good time, though. He told me once that Grandmother was the most wonderful woman he had ever known and that I looked like her. He left his watch, 'cause he knew I liked to play with it; so I guess he intends to stay quite a while.

Pauline Conard

The writing in that theme is deliberately simple. The originality comes from the sustained point of view and the use of vivid detail to make the reader see and feel what the child saw and felt. That is a good paper, as any instructor would agree, but we might, in passing, consider two possible flaws, just to illustrate the fact that your instructor does not demand impeccability. First, has the student overdone the second paragraph? She intended, of course, to make clear what the child understood from Uncle Jack's queer statement that Grandfather had gone away when he was plainly right there in the box. She interprets it as analogous to her own pretended trips to school with Grace. Yet the paragraph goes into so much detail that the reader might lose sight of the purpose and might feel that much of the paragraph is a digression that obscures the unity of the whole. Too much detail is not as bad as too little, but it can be confusing. Second, is the last paragraph quite equal to the rest? It seems a little strained and a little out of key. The paper might well have ended with the child sitting on the steps, affected by the funereal atmosphere she did not understand and more in a mood to cling to Muffy than to play. But even with those weaknesses, the paper is good freshman work.

With a little thought before you parrot old ideas, with a combination of old ideas into something essentially new, with a slight shift of point of view, but above all with an honest and sincere attempt to look at things through your own eyes and put what you see into your own words, tritely commonplace topics can be avoided. But remember, again, to avoid the merely freakish. The student who devoted seven gory pages to a story of a man pretending to be a dog and battling a Great Dane tooth to tooth to a bloody but pointless triumph had a new topic, all right, but he was wasting his time and the readers'. The unmotivated and impossible situation had no conceivable significance.

Approach to the Topic

"Doubt Gets You an Education," "The Right to an Opinion," and "Grandfather" secure originality by adopting a fresh point of view toward their topics. Originality may also be secured by adopting an unexpected approach to the topic, presenting it, that is, by unexpected methods. A narrative approach to an expository idea, for example, often adds interest to what might otherwise be commonplace and dull. Writers use the method constantly, illustrating a general principle by showing how it applies to particular but typical people and creating characters and situations that exemplify their expository ideas. A magazine article, for example, on the operation of a highway police safety patrol might begin with an account of a particular smashup, the arrival of the safety patrol, and the measures that are taken to determine exactly what happened and to prevent their recurrence. In its extreme form, the narrative method develops into the novel of idea, as *Uncle Tom's Cabin* told the story of one slave to preach the evils of slavery or, more recently, *On the Beach* put into novel form the author's warning of the dangers of nuclear war.

On a somewhat more complex scale, originality of approach may be illustrated by a theme which makes use of a sustained analogy, in other words, by a comparison of two things which are essentially unlike. The student who can see and convey unexpected resemblances, who can use vivid figures of speech or can clarify a whole idea by means of an apt analogy, will have little trouble writing original and interesting themes.

Metamorphosis

Washingtonians who still believe in the tendency of right to prevail and good to overcome evil have watched with amused tolerance the sudden social acceptance of a gay old local girl with a hitherto very sleazy reputation. She long led a boisterous, lusty, bawdy life in an unsavory downtown neighborhood. Never approved by "the better people," she went her painted way, attaining in her prime a notoriety approaching fame.

But with the passing years her charms faded. Badgered by the authorities' almost constant interest in her conduct and decorum, she began to lose her following. Finally she found herself a middle-aged old harpy, lacking in appeal and beset with financial difficulties. Reluctantly, she admitted that she was through and must retire. The old Gayety, the only burlesque theater in Washington, closed her doors.

But there was more vitality in the old girl than Washingtonians realized. She closely watched the struggles of the management of the National, Washington's major legitimate theater, with Actor's Equity over a stiff-necked policy of racial discrimination. And she was rather pleased when the National too closed.

Always an opportunist, the Gayety rattled her bracelets, smoothed her short skirt, and issued a startling announcement to the press. She would comb her hair, take the pledge, renounce her old companions, and go legitimate! After a thorough bath, wearing more subdued makeup and clothing, the "New Gayety" hesitantly opened her house to a new clientele. The remainder of the season was successful.

During the summer closing, the old girl counted her receipts and decided honesty was the best policy after all. She conned her etiquette book, invested in some stylish clothing, and was ready in the fall for her new patrons.

They came, incongruously, in sleek limousines, which drew up to her Ninth Street door to allow their passengers to mingle with the well-groomed crowd before the Gayety. They are still coming. The rest of the area has changed very little. The same garish bars, fifth-rate movie houses for adults only, penny arcades, and pawnbrokers' exchanges surround her as before. The same unsavory crowds pass her lobby. Bums, drunks, seedy civilians, servicemen on leave, callow youths, and predatory females throng the street, and some of them glance at her resentfully as they go by. They do not appreciate her new look; they knew her "when." Impeccable as her social standing is now, they liked her better in the wild days before her metamorphosis.

Martin M. Roudabush

Phrasing

Originality of phrasing, at its most obvious level, may be achieved by any writer who takes the trouble. It consists of consciously avoiding trite phrases and commonplace figures of speech. A good rule is to avoid any phrases or figures you have frequently seen in print. Try to put your own thoughts into your own words. Select exactly the word that says what you mean to say. If you do use figures of speech, look carefully at your subjects and at your figures, to be sure they agree in the pictures they present. (See Chapter 7, on diction, for a detailed discussion.) Vary your sentence patterns, to avoid monotony and more importantly to make them exactly reflect your thought. (See Chapter 6, on effective sentences.) But above all write as honestly as you can. "Fine writing," embroidery, "purple patches," "a 'literary' style"—these are always flaws.

"Originality of phrasing" does not mean excessive elaboration. It takes many forms. For a few examples, we need look no farther than the good papers reprinted earlier in this chapter. "A Summer Experience," pages 41–42, is descriptive and narrative, and is valuable chiefly for the closeness of its observation and the exactness with which it reports details. The verbs and verbals, alone, are worth examining. In the first two sentences we get *straddled, bracing, pitching, shifted, heaved,* and *handed*—all precise. Notable in the rest of it for their precision are *sang out, wheeling, screaming, looping, surfaced, shot up, slamming back, tapped, nudged.* All of them are exact, vivid, and a little unexpected. In "Modern Residential Architecture," pages 43–44, the diction is more formal, in keeping with the tone of the paper, but again it is exact. Further, the thrice-repeated *radical changes* of the first sentence provide an unexpected refrain and tight coherence. The series of *not . . . but . . .* phrases at the beginning of the third paragraph set up a pleasing pattern, and carry it one or two steps beyond the point at which the reader might expect it to end. "The Mill," page 45, uses repetition, sentence length, and sentence rhythm very skillfully.

"The Smell of Greasepaint," pages 45–47, successfully blends an informal tone and a predominant vocabulary of one- or two-syllabled words with enough precisely chosen polysyllables to give the paper body. Originality of phrasing is not beyond the grasp of student writers.

The writer with a sharp ear for the suggestive qualities of words can go beyond the use of exact words and use words with a boldness that is justified by its success. The context makes the words suddenly mean something that they never meant before and probably will never mean again; yet as they are used, they are for the nonce exactly right. The poets constantly use the power of words to suggest many things at once, and the skillful prose writer may use it, too. William Alexander Percy, for example, in his autobiography, speaks of the summer sunlight falling "in splotches and scarves and sudden widths of glitter" on a tree-shaded stream. Describing the smells of his aunt's Virginia farm, he recalls that "the dairy . . . where the crocks of milk and clabber stood in live spring water, smelled cold and slightly sour. The corn-bin had a warm yellow smell like a loaf of bread. . . ." Freshly ground cornmeal tempted him to eat it raw, "so rich and sweet and really fundamental it smelled." *Scarves, cold, warm, yellow,* and *fundamental* were never so used before, but in the context they say what Percy wanted to say.

It will be apparent by now that many matters we have discussed under originality are very closely related to the problems of development. All the papers examined in this section have demonstrated the concreteness and fullness of development which allow the reader to share the experiences or understand the thought of the writer as a unique, individual, perceptive observer. We come back at the end of the section to the point with which we began. With your intended audience in mind to guide your approach, your phrasing, and your choice of details, write with a rigorous honesty to the truth as you see it. Originality will come almost as a matter of course.

Title

Last we come to what in the theme itself stands first of all: the title. In the writing, it is usually best to wait until the theme has been finished to put a title on it, because the title must fit the theme, and even with the best planning a writer cannot be sure of his theme until he has finished it. If you feel a need for a working title as you go—and many writers do—be prepared to reconsider it when the revisions are completed. Write your final title last of all.

A good title stimulates the reader's interest, and in tone, meaning, and implication, it fits the theme. Because no two papers are alike, the title should also be original, although it may well be an old title with a new twist or an old title which, as the reader finally realizes, fits the new work as well as it did the old one. Both Chaucer and Shakespeare, for example, wrote of Troilus and Cressida, and with variation only in spelling, Shakespeare used the names of the chief characters, just as Chaucer did, as his title. *All for Love* is the title of a play by Dryden and a poem by Southey. "A Vision of Judgement" is a poem by Southey, and "The Vision of Judgement" is a satiric poem on the same subject by Byron. Even more appropriately, an apprentice writer may borrow a title from a master for a work of a different sort, and, for example, call a descriptive theme on a garrulous old sailor "The Ancient Mariner." (He should be aware, however, that he thereby invites severe comparison of his apprentice work with the established original.)

More frequent than the directly borrowed title is the modified title, and more frequent still is the title that uses a quotation or an allusion which the reader will recognize as appropriate. Thus, John Steinbeck's *Of Mice and Men* recalls Burns' lines:

> The best laid schemes o' mice and men
> Gang aft a-gley.

The Civil War novel *So Red the Rose* recalls the couplet from the *Rubáiyát*:

> I sometimes think that never blows so red
> The Rose as where some buried Caesar bled.

A teacher's autobiography was entitled *And Gladly Teach,* to recall Chaucer's Clerk of Oxford, of whom Chaucer remarked, "And gladly would he learn and gladly teach." A theme about an optimistic ne'er-do-well might be entitled "Micawber." Or a title may echo a significant phrase in the paper itself, and so be in effect a quotation from the very work it labels. Such a title takes on added significance as the reader reads. Most common of all is the title which merely names the topic or the chief character, thereby briefly describing what is to follow.

But all such titles fit the work by foreshadowing it, not by fully revealing it. A formal expository report, indeed, usually takes a title which as nearly as possible announces the writer's purpose, as in "Pineal Organs: Photoreception, Secretion, and Development." But almost all other kinds of papers are merely foreshadowed by titles which hint at the purpose without openly announcing it. Even the title which explicitly names the topic or the chief character does not reveal what is to be said in the paper itself. Perhaps ideally, the reader should realize just how appropriate a title is only after he has finished the reading. Such foreshadowing titles are often ironic, seeming to say one thing but actually saying something quite different. If the tone of the paper permits, a title may incorporate mild puns, using words which might suggest several meanings. All these characteristics are illustrated by the title "A Fair Look at Life," which a student gave to a paper relating his first adolescent experience with a "girl show" at a county fair.

Good titles, finally, are brief—single words naming the topic or the chief character, or more often two or three or four words in a phrase. On the rare occasions when a full sentence is used, it is likely to be cryptic, as in *America Is West*, a Middle Western anthology. Short titles, foreshadowing the paper, pique the reader's curiosity. If the title fits, that curiosity is satisfied in the reading.

In all these ways—and of course in many others—themes may be given the touch of originality which lifts them above the commonplace, adds interest to the reading, and leads to the instructor's comment: "This theme is one of the best."

EXERCISES

Read the following student theme carefully, and then work out the accompanying exercises.

Why Summer School?

1. As a result of the ever-lurking cloud of Communism, it has become established that every youth will have to serve some time in the armed services of our country. That may seem to some like a very dark and bleak wall across their lives, one before which nothing constructive may be accomplished.

2. To other young men that wall is but an obstacle which has been laid across life's pathway. These men realize that whatever has been started before that barrier is reached may be taken up and completed after the barrier has been surmounted.

3. With that in mind, let us take an overall view of our American educational system.

4. Our grade schools and high schools have nine-month terms, with summer make-up courses in the high schools. Our colleges and universities also have winter terms, but they also have summer sessions. There must be a reason for the college summer sessions, but what is it? Why are there no summer sessions in the high schools?

5. Going to college is usually the first opportunity for young men and women to get away from home strictly on their own. Students graduating from high schools are all approximately sixteen to eighteen years of age. Would you want your son or daughter to leave your home and your care at an age below sixteen? Of course not.

6. But in the colleges and universities the situation becomes different. A student at seventeen does not always compete with other students of seventeen. People of all ages take post-graduate work, beginning work—constantly there are people eager to learn.

7. Going back now and keeping the Communist cloud in mind, let us take a young man of seventeen and a half who has just graduated from high school. This young man has an opportunity to go to a professional school. If he waits one year and is drafted at eighteen and a half, serves his time, and comes home again, what will his outlook be? Will he go on and begin a professional career? Probably not. But by starting immediately after graduation, he can procure a good beginning for his career. Even if he is drafted, he won't have to start from the beginning when he is discharged.

8. With higher education, he will be able to get a better placement in which to serve his country.

9. As you can readily see, summer school is very necessary for life in these times. With the fleeting pace of business and economics, and with the troubled and unsettled world of today, how can anyone say that more education is needless and that summer school should be omitted?

A. Unity

1. Phrase, in a single unified sentence, the thesis that you think the writer intended to develop. Be as specific as possible and try to cover each subordinate point he made.

2. Which details do not fit readily under a unified thesis?

3. Can you explain possible unexpressed connections between the details which seem irrelevant and the thesis he intended to develop?

4. What is the connection between ¶ 5 and ¶ 6? What is the relation of each to the thesis? Is there any possible relation between the last two sentences of ¶ 5 and the overall thesis?

5. With the thesis clearly in mind, rephrase doubtful passages to show the relation more clearly.

6. Has the student ever explained why *summer* school is important? Did he have a clear thesis in mind even before he wrote?

7. Is unity obscured by any shifts in tone or by details out of their logical order? Consider the first sentences of ¶ 2 and ¶ 5. Consider the last sentence of ¶ 6.

B. Development

In considering problems of unity, we have already inescapably touched on problems of development. Here, as is often true, "What are you talking about?" shades into "What do you mean by that?" Questions A3, 4, 5, and 6 may have arisen because the writer forgot his thesis or because he did not use detailed enough phrasing to complete the ideas he was treating.

1. Reconsider questions A3, 4, 5, and 6. Should the problems they are concerned with have been classified under Unity or under Development? Explain your decision.

2. Are the metaphors of ¶ 1 and ¶ 2 specific enough to be vivid? Do the lurking cloud of Communism and the wall laid by the draft across life's pathway create clear pictures? What concrete, specific detail might have been added to sharpen the focus?

3. Paragraph 4 says that we have "summer make-up courses" in our high schools, then asks, "Why are there no summer sessions in high schools?" If you assume that the student was not writing nonsense, what do you suppose the general terms "summer make-up courses" and "summer sessions" meant to him? Has he given enough detail to allow you to be sure that you know exactly what he did mean?

4. Does he ever answer his own question, "Why are there no summer sessions in high schools?" Should he have answered it? Why or why not?

5. In A5, you rephrased ¶ 5 and ¶ 6 to clarify their connections with the overall thesis. If you had been writing them in the first place, would you have added illustrative details to show what you meant by being strictly on your own? What details? How many? Why?

6. Paragraph 6 begins, "But in the colleges and universities, the situation becomes different." What does that mean? What "situation"?

7. What does ¶ 8 mean?

8. What, according to ¶ 9, can you "readily see"? Can you?

C. Originality

1. *If* the writer had kept a clear thesis in mind, and *if* he had provided enough detail to ensure your knowing always exactly what he meant to say, could a paper on this topic have been interesting, whether you agreed with the thesis or not? Why or why not? Is this paper interesting as it stands? Why or why not?

2. Would any other approach to the topic be better? Why or why not?

3. The writer has attempted to be original in his use of metaphors. He has a cloud of Communism lurking in this troubled and unsettled world. He sees the draft as a barrier, a wall, an obstacle laid across life's pathway. Are those metaphors original? Are they vivid?

4. The writer has also attempted to be original by varying his sentence patterns, notably by using both declarative sentences and rhetorical questions he expects the reader to be able to answer. Assuming that he had given the reader enough detail to make clear answers possible, would that variation of sentence pattern have added to the interest of the theme? Has he overused the device?

5. Do you suppose the writer normally thinks and talks in terms of lurking clouds and of obstacles across life's pathway? If he read this theme to a group of his fraternity brothers, would he expect them to understand that he was merely

pampering the queer tastes of English teachers? Is he sincere in his phrasing? Is he trying to be "literary"? Is he saying, as simply and directly and clearly as possible, what he wanted to say?

6. Are unsettled times always troubled? Has the writer gained anything by using both of those paired adjectives? Is he being redundant, that is, is he unnecessarily saying the same thing twice? Is he just embroidering his theme?

7. What is meant by the "fleeting pace of business and economics"? Is *fleeting* a good word here? Does he need both paired nouns? If not, which should he drop? Can you suggest a better noun than either of them?

8. What other phrases might have been improved in revision? Consider, for example, "serve some time," in ¶ 1. What two objections could be made to that phrase? Does it suggest a prison sentence? Should it? Was that suggestion intended? Does it mean, "serve a period of time," or, "serve at an indefinite time"? Is it clear? Select five other phrases you think could be improved.

9. There are no gross errors in grammar or in the mechanics of spelling, punctuation, and sentence structure in the paper. What grade would you give it? Could you rewrite it, retaining the same thesis and most of the details, and improve it greatly? Try it.

Organization

Characteristics of a Good Theme: 6. A logical and effective arrangement of the details.

Good writing develops a single idea, whether phrased as a unified thesis or as a unified statement of purpose. Good writing includes the concrete, specific detail the reader needs before he can understand exactly the idea the writer is trying to present. And good writing is interestingly original. But in addition to all this, it is skillfully organized. All the details which develop the overall thesis, or those which develop the subtheses of lesser sections of the paper, are carefully arranged and presented in the order which will most easily make the intended effect on the audience. It follows that a good paper is thoroughly planned before it is written. Its success is not left to chance. Knowing what he wants to say and the effect he wants to make on the audience he is addressing, the writer must organize his material so that it will have that effect.

For some papers, the problems of organization are easily solved because a natural pattern is inherent in the material, as the natural chronological order of time is inherent in an incident or in a process. But very often no natural pattern inheres in the material. If the details are not to be spilled helter-skelter on the page, some sort of order must be imposed on them, and a logical or psychological order must be sought to substitute for the missing natural order.

Indeed, sometimes—perhaps most often—no single order will solve all the writer's problems. Instead, several different patterns of arrangement must be used at once before the desired effect can be secured.

In this chapter, we shall consider the major patterns that are available to the writer, and shall look at some of the possibilities of superimposing one sort of pattern on another to produce a complex effect not attainable by simple means. Then we shall consider in detail the conventional methods of planning a projected paper— the informal outline for simple papers and the formal outline for more elaborate ones.

THE POSITION OF THE THESIS

You know already that a paper must develop a single idea which should be clearly phrased before you ever begin to plan how to present it. These questions naturally arise: Will that central idea, that thesis sentence, appear in the final paper? If so, where? Why? The best answers to those and all other questions about the writing process will come from your own analysis of others' successful writing. As you read, look for such answers. Here, we can offer only general suggestions.

The thesis, in so many words, sometimes appears in the paper itself. The more formal the paper, the more likely it is that the thesis will be explicitly stated. It may be presented as a single sentence, the most general sentence in the paper, expressing the central idea to which all else is subsidiary. Often, however, it will appear in parts, in several sentences heading various sections of the paper; to reconstruct the author's entire thesis, the reader must recombine these sentences into the unified whole which expresses the paper's central idea. Sometimes part of the thesis is stated in so many words and part of it is merely implied by details which develop an unexpressed generalization. Occasionally, no part of the thesis is explicitly expressed, the entire thesis being implied by the developing details.

Very roughly, we can say that the less clearly the thesis is expressed in the paper, the harder it is for the writer to be sure that his exact idea will be communicated. But if the writer knows precisely what thesis he is developing, keeps it constantly in mind as he writes, and remembers that all of his phrasing and detail must lead to it through implication, clarity can be achieved with an implied thesis. The kind of idea, the audience, and the writer's skill must all be considered in deciding whether or not to present the thesis in the final paper in so many words.

If the thesis does appear, where does it come? Why? It comes at the beginning or at the end—or occasionally somewhere in between. Most often, it comes at the beginning of the paper, either as the first sentence or as the topic sentence of an opening paragraph which as a whole serves as an extended expression of the thesis. If introductory background material is necessary, the thesis may follow the introduction, but we can even then say that it comes at the beginning of the development of the central idea itself.

The principal advantage of placing the expressed thesis at the beginning of the paper is that it provides the reader with a key to what follows. Having been given the central idea, he can more easily see the interrelations of the details that develop it. You might say first, for instance, "Anyone who goes to college may expect to have to work hard while he is there." Then, as you discuss the scope of college courses, the speed of the presentation of course material, the difficulty of securing much individual assistance, the penalties for falling behind in studying, the temptations and the rivalries and the complexities of college life, you can expect your reader to help you in the task of relating each succeeding detail to its fellows, and to understand how they all add up to the necessity for diligent effort on the part of the student during his college career.

The thesis may come, however, at the end of the paper, after all the developing details have been presented. A paper organized in this way is harder to write, because the reader cannot help you relate the details to the thesis until he knows what the thesis is, and as a result, there is a greater danger that the paper will fly apart—will have a scatter-shot rather than a bull's-eye effect. But there are strong advantages to placing the thesis last. The pattern it provides is more interesting than the pattern which puts the thesis first; even an expository paper has an element of suspense when it is skillfully handled. If the reader can be convinced that all of your detail really is leading to a predetermined end which he cannot yet quite see, he will read with interest what you have written. Or suppose you are developing an idea the audience might reject—urging international cooperation on an isolationist audience, for example. It would be well to present your detail convincingly before you state your thesis and show your audience what that evidence implies. And finally, putting the thesis last provides a more emphatic pattern of organization than that which puts the thesis first. In all writing—in the sentence or the paragraph or the whole composition—the end is the most emphatic position. If you can lead your reader up to your thesis and only then present it, he will remember it longer. The pattern is difficult to handle, but it is often very useful.

The thesis may, as a matter of fact, appear at both the beginning and the end, being repeated exactly or, more often, being rephrased to express the same idea in different words. This is the most emphatic pattern of all, and has the double advantage of telling the reader at the outset where you are going and then reminding him at the end where you have been. It is too emphatic, in fact, for a simple paper, because the reader feels he could have understood that simple idea without so much repetition.—We all resent the announcer who tells us two or three times in one commercial to "Go to your corner druggist NOW and *demand So-and-so's* Mange Cure!" But given the right material and the right audience, it is a very effective pattern.

When the thesis is expressed, not in a single sentence, but in several, each of which presents a part of the overall idea, each sub-thesis usually precedes the section of the paper which elaborates that phase of the central thesis. The reader then knows exactly what each section is about, and adds up the parts in his own mind to discover the thesis of the paper as a whole. This pattern is most commonly used with an idea which is too difficult to present all at once, yet is not so complex nor so profound as to be beyond the reader's powers of retention and addition.

To sum up: The thesis sentence may not explicitly appear in the final paper at all, but if it does appear, it may come at or near the beginning, at the end, at both the beginning and the end, or step by step in between.

ARRANGEMENT OF DETAILS

We have been examining the possibilities of arranging the general thesis in relation to the specific developing details. We need now to examine the major patterns of organization which may be used to impose a manageable order on the details themselves. In deciding what order or combination of orders will most effectively present the details, the writer must again consider the kind of idea he is presenting and the kind of reader he hopes to reach. What the intended reader knows or does not know about the topic, his probable attitudes toward it, and the kind of response the writer hopes to secure—all three are important.

There are three kinds of order: *natural order, logical order,* and *psychological order.* The natural orders, like the time sequence of events, are inherent in the material itself; the logical and psychological orders are imposed by the mind of the writer on material which, like weeds in a garden, might occur in any chance pattern or in none at all.

Natural Order

We live in a three- or perhaps a four-dimensional world, a world of up and along and across, of now and of then. Consequently only two natural orders exist: the *order of time* and the *order of space.*

THE ORDER OF TIME

The simplest order is the order of time, the chronological order. If a single chain of events can be isolated, it is natural to present those events chronologically, one after another as they occurred. Simple incidents ("The One That Got Away") and simple processes ("How to Fry an Egg") can hardly be treated any other way.

But the events of time often are important only as a significant chain of incidents, and the very first event in a chain is often not interesting until the chain itself has developed. (What difference does it make if boy meets girl, if they go from the meeting on separate paths?) In narrative, therefore, as in a movie, we often begin at an exciting late point, and then by means of flashbacks explain what went before.

The chronological order is very common, but it demands careful selection of the details, and except in exposition of process or in narrative, it is perhaps most useful in combination with other possible orders.

THE ORDER OF SPACE

The second natural order is the order of space, particularly useful in descriptive writing. It is easy for the reader to follow you if you move from left to right or right to left, from bottom to top, front to back, outside to inside—from point to contiguous point in space. For example, in discussing the complex entity that is America, John Gunther organized his *Inside U.S.A.* by geographical areas and took his reader from one area to another across the familiar map.

Spatial order is frequently the result of mere accident (as it is in group photographs) and so is not very significant. If one of the logical or psychological orders will serve equally well, you might choose it in preference to the natural order of space.

Logical Order

Man likes to call himself a thinking animal, and logic represents the way he believes he thinks. Even though the logical orders have no natural relation to any quality inherent in your material, therefore, they do have a very close relation to the responses of your audience, to say nothing of their relation to your own capacities for understanding the details you are trying to beat into manageable shape. The American government, for example, is a complicated organism, but we can reduce its complexity to understandable order by grouping governmental units as belonging to the executive, legislative, or judicial branches; or considering them as local, state, or federal agencies. We think in logical terms when we think most efficiently, and we must impose some sort of logical order on details before our readers can be expected to understand them.

THE ORDER OF CLIMAX

The order of climax takes advantage of the fact that the final position is the most emphatic position. It arranges details in an order of ascending importance, from least important to most important, saving the loudest bang for the end of the fieworks display. Because no one is much interested in minor attractions if the main event has already occurred, the letdown of an anticlimax results from a failure to build up to the biggest, the best, the loudest, the most exciting, or the most important detail. The order is so common, in fact, that your reader might be seriously distracted by such a faulty climax as, "He is a thief, a murderer, and a road hog." In sentences or paragraphs or whole compositions, climax is important.

THE ORDER OF GENERAL TO SPECIFIC

Another very common order is the order of general to specific, in which large classes or extensive generalizations are introduced before the smaller groups, individuals, or specific details. We have seen that the thesis, the most general idea of a paper, often comes at the beginning; such a paper is following a general to specific pattern. It is common, too, in descriptions to present a general picture before filling in the details (see "S-t-e-a-m-boat A-comin'," pages 76–77). In the chapters of this textbook, and in their subsections, you will usually find overall discussions of the problems to be treated before the details are presented and discussed. Your textbook in zoology or in botany probably discusses phyla before genera, genera before species. In many kinds of writing, the general precedes the specific.

THE ORDER OF SPECIFIC TO GENERAL

Specific to general is the mirror image of general to specific, working from individual instances to general truths, or from individuals to groups. The order is very common in our thinking. The zoologists, for example, had to observe many individual specimens before they could abstract the common characteristics which distinguish a separate species; they had to study the various species before they could identify genera and phyla. You must observe many college students before you can generalize about The College Student. In writing, you might well present types of students, then indicate what characteristics all of them have in common. But the order is less common in writing than the order of general to specific.

THE ORDER OF CAUSE TO EFFECT

The order of cause to effect, as the name implies, begins with a cause and from it traces the probable effects. The order is especially useful in historical writing of all kinds, partly because it is usually supplemented by a chronological order. A book about the influence of the Renaissance on modern thought, for example, would begin with the cause, the Renaissance, and trace its effect on the various elements of our culture, developing each topic chronologically. As an order used in thought, it may be illustrated by the meteorologist who begins with today's weather pattern, considers the probable effects of the interaction of air masses, pressure areas, and wind direction and velocities, and attempts to predict what the cumulative effects will be tomorrow, or five days, or thirty days hence.

THE ORDER OF EFFECT TO CAUSE

The order of effect to cause is the reverse of the preceding. If a fuse blows (the effect), we assume a short circuit (the cause) and begin to look for it. Artemus Ward used to convulse his audiences with a parody of this order by mentioning an effect and then asking earnestly, "Why is this thus? What are the reasons for this thusness?" Any writing which attempts to answer such questions is using this order. In historical thinking of all kinds it is customary to start with Now—since we can scarcely start anywhere else—and work backward in our thinking from the effects with which we are concerned to their probable causes. But notice that few written histories would begin with, say, the modern British Parliament and end up with the Anglo-Saxon council of elders and the Norman *Curia Regis*. The order of cause to effect is the common order in writing.

THE ORDER OF FAMILIARITY

The order of familiarity is eminently a commonsense order, moving from what the reader already knows to whatever is strange to him. It would obviously be foolish to begin unnecessarily with the unknown; the reader would be lost from the beginning and would stop reading as soon as he started. Analogies, for example, take advantage of this order, explaining the complexities of a molecule, say, by comparing its structure to that of the solar system.

THE ORDER OF COMPLEXITY

The order of complexity moves from the simple to the complicated, again in a commonsense procedure. A text in grammar, for instance, would begin by describing the way the main elements of the language work most of the time, before considering the numerous puzzling exceptions.

THE ORDER OF UTILITY

The order of utility presents details in the order in which the reader will need them to understand what is to follow. An elementary text in chemistry, for example, must introduce the complexities of the periodic table and the concept of the atom before it can go on to matters based on atomic structure. An article urging civic reform must first clarify the complex interrelations of the existing corrupt governing bodies before it can present its program for civic betterment.

Psychological Order

Although we think logically whenever we can, we also sometimes respond to ideas and impressions in illogical, but still patterned, ways; and at least three common orders reflect this human tendency.

THE ORDER OF ACCEPTABILITY

The order of acceptability introduces ideas the reader will find pleasant before it introduces ideas he might reject. It concedes the irrefutable points of an opponent's argument before proceeding to the devastating refutation of all the foolish things he has said. It admits the malpractices of some unions, for another example, before defending organized labor in general.

THE ORDER OF THE DOMINANT IMPRESSION

In a way, the order of the dominant impression is a form of the order of general to specific, but it is less logical than psychological. Most commonly used in descriptive writing, it presents first the overall impression, focusing on details which will support, reinforce, and emphasize whatever central concept—such as shabbiness, urbanity, massiveness—the author wishes to stress. Secondary characteristics are likely to be minimized, and if a contradictory detail should be important, it is entered as a striking contradiction of the dominant impression, and hence serves to emphasize that impression by its very unexpectedness.

THE ORDER OF PSYCHOLOGICAL EFFECT

The order of psychological effect arranges material, in a description or narrative, according to the way in which it would catch the eye or the mind of the beholder. It is determined solely by the writer's established point of view. An excited witness to an accident might make much of the fact that "her purse flew right through the windshield" before it occurs to him ever to mention the presence of a woman passenger. A boy might describe the shiny chromium on the family's new automobile, the length of the hood, and the sound of the horn; his father would stress the horsepower and the power steering; his mother is most concerned with the color and the cost. The writer must put himself into the mind of his characters, and as he describes things from their points of view, must select and arrange his details as they would. It is important, however, that the reader sense the presence of the pattern. If the reader feels that no pattern has been imposed at all, the writer has created the wrong effect altogether.

There are, of course, other ways in which details may be arranged, but the orders we have been considering are the most common and the most important.

EXERCISES

A 1. For each of the natural, logical, and psychological orders discussed in the text, suggest a topic and a limiting thesis that might be appropriately developed by that organizational pattern.

EXAMPLE: Order of climax: Topic: The installation of a college president. Thesis: The ceremonies of installing a new college president normally end with his conferring honorary degrees and giving his inaugural address.

2. Explain the fact that a paper developing the thesis in the example under A1 would be organized according to both the order of time and the order of climax.

B 1. List five topics, with a limiting thesis for each, that might well be developed by using either of two different orders.

EXAMPLE: Topic: An ocean voyage. Thesis: The most exciting moments of a typical ocean voyage come during the first hours, in embarking and drawing away from the dock. Appropriate orders: Time, psychological effect.

COMBINING VARIOUS PATTERNS

Papers and parts of papers—sections or paragraphs—might be simple enough to require only one or two of the patterns of organization we have been considering. They might, to illustrate, begin with the thesis and arrange all the subsequent developing details in a general to specific order. But very few papers are as simple as that. Often one pattern governs the overall organization and other patterns govern individual sections or paragraphs, so that you might have thesis first, then some paragraphs developed by an order of complexity and others by an order of climax. Often several orders of different sorts are superimposed in a single passage to produce a more complex effect than any one order can produce alone.

The following paragraph (or "section," since a modern writer would probably break it up into smaller units than Mark Twain employed) is not very complicated in idea. Yet at least five of the patterns we have examined are discoverable in it, besides the thesis-first order of the paragraph as a unit.

"S-t-e-a-m-boat A-comin' "[1]

Once a day, a cheap, gaudy packet arrived upward from St. Louis, and another downward from Keokuk. Before these events, the day was glorious with expectancy; after them, the day was a dead and empty thing. Not only the boys, but the whole village, felt this. After all these years I can picture that old time to myself now, just as it was then: the white town drowsing in the sunshine of a summer's morning; the streets empty, or pretty nearly so; one or two clerks sitting in front of the Water Street stores, with their splint-bottomed chairs tilted back against the walls, chins on breasts, hats slouched over their faces, asleep—with shingle-shavings enough around to show what broke them down; a sow and a litter of pigs loafing along the sidewalks, doing a good business in watermelon rinds and seeds; two or three lonely little freight piles scattered about the levee; a pile of skids on the slope of the stone-paved wharf, and the fragrant town drunkard asleep in the shadow of them; two or three wood flats at the head of the wharf, but nobody to listen to the peaceful lapping of the wavelets against them; the great Mississippi, the majestic, the magnificent Mississippi, rolling

[1] Mark Twain, *Life on the Mississippi*.

its mile-wide tide along, shining in the sun; the dense forest away on the other side; the point above the town, and the point below, bounding the river-glimpse and turning it into a sort of sea, and withal a very still and brilliant and lonely one. Presently a film of dark smoke appears above one of those remote points; instantly a Negro drayman, famous for his quick eye and prodigious voice, lifts up the cry, "S-t-e-a-m-boat a-comin'!" and the scene changes! The town drunkard stirs, the clerks wake up, a furious clatter of drays follows, every house and store pours out a human contribution, and all in a twinkling the dead town is alive and moving. Drays, carts, men, boys, all go hurrying from many quarters to a common center, the wharf. Assembled there, the people fasten their eyes upon the coming boat as upon a wonder they are seeing for the first time. And the boat *is* rather a handsome sight, too. She is long and sharp and trim and pretty; she has two tall, fancy-topped chimneys, with a gilded device of some sort swung between them; a fanciful pilot-house, all glass and gingerbread, perched on top of the texas deck behind them; the paddle-boxes are gorgeous with a picture or with gilded rays above the boat's name; the boiler-deck, the hurricane-deck, and the texas deck are fenced and ornamented with clean white railings; there is a flag gallantly flying from the jackstaff; the furnace doors are open and the fires glaring bravely; the upper decks are black with passengers; the captain stands by the big bell, calm, imposing, the envy of all; great volumes of blackest smoke are rolling and tumbling out of the chimneys—a husbanded grandeur created with a bit of pitch-pine just before arriving at a town; the crew are grouped on the forecastle; the broad stage is run far out over the port bow, and an envied deck-hand stands picturesquely on the end of it with a coil of rope in his hand; the pent steam is screaming through the gaugecocks; the captain lifts his hand, a bell rings, the wheels stop; then they turn back, churning the water to foam, and the steamer is at rest. Then such a scramble as there is to get aboard, and to get ashore, and to take in freight and to discharge freight, all at one and the same time; and such a yelling and cursing as the mates facilitate it all with! Ten minutes later the steamer is under way again, with no flag on the jackstaff and no black smoke issuing from the chimneys. After ten more minutes the town is dead again, and the town drunkard asleep by the skids once more.

Descriptive writing like that looks easy, but the appearances are deceiving. There are many overlapping patterns there, all deliberate, all controlled, and all contributing to the clearly conceived effect Mark Twain wanted to get in the passage.

The topic sentence for the whole section, or at least a generalization that helps to set the mood, the dominant impression, of the whole paragraph, comes in the first two or three sentences. Subsidiary topic sentences appear as the paragraph enters each new phase: "I can picture that old time to myself now, just as it was then. . . ." "And the boat *is* rather a handsome sight, too." "After ten more minutes the town is dead again. . . ." There is chronological order, too, in the whole passage: before the steamboat comes, while it is there, and after it has gone.

Each subsection of the paragraph has its own complex patterns. The first part deals with the setting, the town and the river: "The white town . . . the streets . . . one or two clerks . . . a sow and a litter of pigs . . . the fragrant town drunkard . . . the great Mississippi . . . the dense forest . . . the point above the town, and the point below . . . ." The details move from the general to the specific, and at the same time they move spatially down the street to the river and so out into adventure. There is also a controlling dominant impression, that of expectant lethargy (and the greater of these is *lethargy*). It is not by accident that the pigs "loafing along the sidewalks" offer the most active detail. Quite deliberately, Mark Twain left out of the picture the boys of the town and the dogs; and even the Negro drayman, who on the face of it must have been awake and alert, is not mentioned in the paragraph until alertness is appropriate.

The psychological effect is controlled, too. The point of view is that of the man who affectionately remembers the boy he used to be. Both points of view appear at once, most notably in the description of the steamboat, the details of which are presented in no stodgy, adult order of space, but up and down and back and about, as items catch the eye of the eight-year-old observer. Yet it was the man, not the boy, who noted the "fanciful" pilot-house, "all glass and gingerbread," who was aware of the gaudiness of the grandeur, who realized that the effects were deliberately staged.

No one pattern of arrangement would have given the results the author wanted. Thesis first, a time order superimposed on a general-to-specific order on a spatial order on an order of dominant impression on a controlled psychological effect—all these are present. Such writing looks easy, and it is, in a way. But only when you know clearly what effects you want to make can you learn how to make them. Only by practice can you learn to make them exactly, every time.

Let us try one more passage, a more subtle one this time. Rachel L. Carson, in *The Sea Around Us,* is explaining to to her land-bound audience what life is like in the depths of the sea.

> The last traces of plant life are left behind in the thin upper layer of water, for no plant can live below about 600 feet even in very clear water, and few find enough sunlight for their food-manu-facturing activities below 200 feet. Since no animal can make its own food, the creatures of the deeper waters live a strange, almost parasitic existence of utter dependence on the upper layers. These hungry carnivores prey fiercely and relentlessly upon each other, yet the whole community is ultimately dependent upon the slow rain of descending food particles from above. The components of this never-ending rain are the dead and dying plants and animals from the surface, or from one of the intermediate layers. For each of the horizontal zones or communities of the sea that lie, in tier after tier, between the surface and the sea bottom, the food supply is different and in general poorer than for the layer above. There is a hint of the fierce and uncompromising competition for food in the saber-toothed jaws of some of the small, dragonlike fishes of the deeper waters, in the immense mouths and in the elastic and distensi-ble bodies that make it possible for a fish to swallow another several times its size, enjoying swift repletion after a long fast.[2]

The dominant order in that passage is the order of space: from top to bottom, from the upper layers of the sea to the depths. Next, details are arranged according to the amount of light that penetrates to one layer of life or another. The order of cause to effect is used, as in "Since no animal can make its own food . . . the whole community is ultimately dependent upon the slow rain of descending food particles from above." There is at least a touch of the order of familiarity in the analogy implicit in the word *rain.* The order of general to specific is employed as Miss Carson turns "the slow rain of descending food particles" into, "The components of this never-ending rain are the dead and dying plants and animals from the surface . . . ." The quality of the food supply is con-sidered, again with a dominating spatial order. Finally, with vivid

---

[2] Rachel L. Carson, *The Sea Around Us* (New York: Oxford University Press, 1951), pp. 50–51. Reprinted by permission.

examples, she implies increasing ferocity as greater depths are plumbed. Surely, again, no one pattern of arrangement could have achieved the effect the writer wished to make.

These two passages have been quoted to suggest the sort of careful planning the writer may need to employ if he is to control his readers' responses to his writing. We have, of course, no more than sampled the kinds of complex effects the writer can secure. As you read, examine the methods, the orders, the devices that writers use; and in your own writing, practice them.

As you plan your own papers, consider carefully what organizational pattern or patterns can best produce the effect you wish to make on your reader. There is only one method you cannot follow with any hope of success: You cannot merely spatter details on the page and hope that they will bounce into some sort of order.

PLANNING THE PAPER

The Informal Outline

The intelligent and articulate student, who has read a great deal and written a great deal, can usually depend on his ability to make a paper sound good. But not even that intelligent and practiced student can be sure that he will say exactly what he wants to say and will make the effect he wants to make unless he plans his papers before he tries to write. He may often be able to do most of his planning in his head. On examinations, for example, he will be set clear-cut problems; and he can sometimes read an examination, understand what it calls for, get his central idea in mind, identify the important points, and begin to scribble out his answer —all without any conscious planning and all in the time it takes the slower student next to him to grasp the implications of the question.

But when the writing problem is not laid out in advance, that intelligent student's very glibness may lead him to begin to scribble without any clear idea of where he is going. Because he handles words well, he may get fairly satisfactory grades on his themes in English 1. As long as his paper is fluent, the instructor may assume that what it says is what the student meant to say. Only the student himself can know that the results were entirely accidental. And there will come a day—as assignments grow more complicated, as he needs to organize a research paper in English 2 or to plan a term paper in History 163 or to prepare an Honors Thesis—on which he will need to know how to plan deliberately before he begins to write. On that day, his do-it-in-the-head system, his faith in his own gift of gab, will let him down. When it is no longer a matter merely of saying something that sounds good, but has become instead a matter of saying exactly what he wants to say, he will need to plan his writing deliberately and systematically, and he will not know how to go about it.

The slower student, meanwhile, has been in trouble all along. On the examination, he sees his practiced neighbor begin to write without giving any outward sign of planning the answer. He himself begins to scribble without any clear idea of what he wants to say— and the resulting grade depresses him. Similarly, his freshman English themes never seem to work out as he hopes. Even the early, simple themes of English 1 must develop a central thesis and must present their details in a logically organized pattern. But he has never learned to plan a paper, and he lacks the gift of gab, so his papers from the very beginning are muddled and unsuccessful. Both these students need to learn how to plan consciously before they write. The best way to learn that is to practice using an informal outline.

The informal outline is a stimulant to thought, a guide to purposeful writing, and a useful check during revision. Being informal, it need not be polished. But being an outline, it allows you to think your problem through in advance. Consequently, you can give all your attention during the actual writing to the phrasing of your sentences and the shaping of your paragraphs. It is only a rough preliminary sketch of your paper, but for a simple paper it will provide all the blueprint you need.

We have already met the informal outline, as a matter of fact, in Chapter 1. Making one consists of phrasing your thesis or statement of purpose as precisely as you can, jotting down in brief topics all the details that might help to develop it, and then thinking about those details. Any that seem irrelevant as you reconsider them can be eliminated. Any that occurred to you out of the most logical order can be rearranged. Those that are related to a single phase of the development can be grouped together. Gaps can be filled in and connections can be briefly indicated. All the thinking necessary to plan a simple paper can be done by jotting down rough notes, drawing arrows, crossing out irrelevancies, and numbering items or groups of items to mark their ultimate order. A final quick check will let you sharpen the phrasing of the thesis itself as your own thinking is clarified. In five minutes or so you can be sure that you know exactly what you want to say and how you want to say it. Even the frenzied flight of time during an examination allows for this kind of quick planning, and the controlled writing that results will have a chance of representing you at your best rather than at your chaotic worst.

For example, an Engineering student was faced with an impromptu theme to be written during the fifty minutes of a class period and selected the topic "Advice to the Dean" from the list offered by the instructor. "What can I suggest," he wondered, "that would make the Engineering School curriculum more valuable to the students? What's wrong with it now? For that matter, why am I taking Engineering?" As a trial statement of purpose, he jotted down the very general idea:

PURPOSE: To discuss Engineering and its weaknesses.

Then he set down, as they occurred to him, whatever ideas seemed to be pertinent:

Limited education
All theoretical courses
No practical stuff
Should have broader background
Writing
Lit
History
Need degree for job
Like construction work
Have had experience

Looking over his list, he realized that he seemed to be dealing with two ideas instead of just one. The last three items were chiefly concerned with his reasons for being in the Engineering School; the rest concerned his criticisms of the curriculum. Yet the last three were not entirely irrelevant; as both a student in the school and an experienced construction worker, he was fairly well qualified to discuss the curriculum. If he kept in mind that relation between those items and the rest, they could usefully serve as introductory background material. But most of the details properly concerned the curriculum. The second and the fourth items were the most important, and he rephrased his loose statement of purpose into a precise thesis which emphasized their importance:

THESIS: The Engineering curriculum is too theoretical and too narrow, denying its students both the practical training they will need as engineers and the broad background they will need as human beings.

The first item in his list of topics he crossed out as duplicating the more precise fourth item. The third item rephrased the second, and he crossed it out too. The fifth, sixth, and seventh obviously were subordinate to the fourth, so he circled them and drew an arrow to remind himself of their relation when he reached them in the writing. He now had three groups of details, which he bracketed together and numbered in the order in which he meant to use them.

~~Limited education~~

2   All theoretical courses

~~No practical stuff~~

Should have broader background

3   Writing

Lit

History

Need degree for job

1   Like construction work

Have had experience

The order of the three items in the group he planned to use as introduction was still confusing, and he had not indicated clearly how he could use the group without presenting two ideas instead of one, but he added another arrow and a few scribbled notes, and decided that his outline was complete. He knew now, as he had not known clearly until now, exactly what he wanted to say and how to say it.

THESIS: The Engineering curriculum is too theoretical and too narrow, denying its students both the practical training they will need as engineers and the broad background they will need as human beings.

~~Limited education~~

2 All theoretical courses   (Expand this)

~~No practical stuff~~

Should have broader background

Writing

3 Lit   (Etc.)

History

Need degree for job   Introductory

1 Like construction work   (Why I am· qualifed to

Have had experience   discuss)

The resulting outline was neither neat nor conventional in form, nor even very clear to anyone but the writer. But when it was handed in with the finished paper, the instructor could tell at a glance that the student had thought through his problems and had known where he was going before he started out. More important, the resulting paper developed a clear-cut idea and presented it in an orderly fashion. If the student had begun writing at once, without a plan, he would have had at most only the original vague statement of purpose to guide him, and he would have tried to handle the details in the chaotic and pointless order in which they first occurred to him. A theme so written could hardly have been worth more than a *D* at best. As it was, he thought before he wrote; and even though his final paper was still somewhat too general in its treatment of the theoretical nature of the Engineering courses (because he had left the expansion of that point to the inspiration of the moment of writing instead of clarifying it in the outline), it was still a *B* paper. By devoting ten of the fifty minutes of the class period to planning, he produced a better than average paper instead of one that might at best have barely passed.

Such a quick informal outline, jotted down on a piece of scratch paper or on the back pages of an examination booklet, will give you all the guidance you need for a simple paper which is to be written immediately. It will help you decide what you want to say and will keep you on the track while you are saying it. Until practice in the method has made you certain that you can plan successfully in your head, use pencil and paper and get your informal outlines down where you can see them.

EXERCISES

A 1. For one of the following topics, phrase a specific thesis; then make out an informal outline from which you could write a paper addressed to the generally educated reader.

My intended major subject	Literature to a freshman
Education and the citizen	Tourist accommodations
Definition of a technical term	The real teen-ager
The responsibilities of the student	Types of popular music

2. Identify the orders of arrangement (pages 70–75) by which you have organized the details in A 1.

B 1. Select any paper from Chapter 3, "The Best Themes," and explain specifically and in detail how it is organized. If you see any weaknesses in its organization, explain them and suggest how the organization might have been improved.

The Formal Outline

An informal outline is only a rough working sketch; a formal outline is a detailed blueprint. For a simple paper which is to be planned and written at a single sitting, the informal outline provides sufficient guidance. But many college assignments and very many after-college writing problems call for papers which are not simple at all, but very complicated, and for papers which are far too long to be planned and written all at once. Most English composition students, for example, have to write one or more research papers, at least one of which may extend to five thousand words and be based on weeks of reading in dozens of books and magazines. The unrelated information the student accumulates must be beaten into an orderly pattern which will produce a coherent and unified paper. At every stage of the way, the instructor needs to know what the student is doing and what he intends to do; no mere rough sketch will suffice for either the student or the instructor. More advanced courses may require similar term papers and reports. Many seniors write comprehensive examinations or Honors Theses. Graduate students write term papers, theses, and finally dissertations which may run to five hundred pages or more. The newly hired industrial engineer, after college, may be required to spend several weeks studying the factory and then be told to write a detailed report on what he has learned. The junior executive may be given the task of preparing a complete manual of procedure to which the office force can turn for guidance in any routine situation which may arise. The reporter may spend months digging into the state's treatment of the insane and then write a series of articles exposing the conditions he has found. There is no end to the complex writing problems the student may one day be compelled to solve. The educated man will find many situations in which familiarity with the methods of the formal outline would be extremely useful to him.

If you are already in the habit of making informal outlines for simple papers, learning to use the formal outline will not be very difficult. The formal outline is based on the same kind of thought about your writing problems. It is more complex than the informal outline, because the problems in which you will use it are more complex. It is not easy, because analytical thought is never easy. But it is essentially only the informal outline dressed in company clothes, which are conventionalized, but not greatly different in function from the dungarees, sport shirts, and moccasins you wear most comfortably.

As we studied the informal outline, we saw an Engineering student gradually realizing exactly what he wanted to say, phrasing it in a unified thesis sentence, and deciding that he could best present it to his reader in three steps, which he carefully noted. A formal outline would follow exactly the same process. Its thesis is carefully and precisely phrased and then is broken down into the subordinate parts which must be developed in order to develop the central idea. Like the informal outline, in other words, the formal outline subdivides the central thesis, breaking it down into its major parts and then similarly breaking down each part in turn, as far as the analysis needs to go for complete clarity to the writer and the reader. It is made by an analytical process of dividing and subdividing, treating at each stage smaller and smaller parts of the overall thesis.

This process of subdividing merely follows natural human habits of thought. We cannot think efficiently or even comfortably in units which are too large or too small. The continental United States, for example, is too big and too diverse for us to realize it as a whole. It is easier for us to visualize regions—New England, the Middle Atlantic states, the Middle West, the South, the Southwest, the West, the Northwest. Within each region we think of states— Maine, New Hampshire, Vermont, Massachusetts, Rhode Island, Connecticut. (They are unequal in size, but equal in legal status, equally important.) Within each state, we think of counties or parishes. Within each county we think of townships or hundreds or sections. Finally, we get down to quarter sections, town lots, or the fifty-foot frontage owned by an individual taxpayer. Analyzing by subdivision so that we can clearly see relations is a very familiar process, the basic one in making a formal outline.

The only thing really new about the formal outline is that it has conventional symbols for labeling the items at each stage of the subdividing.

We begin, as we always must, with the thesis, the central idea, the thing we want to say, and we label that "Thesis." The main points by which that thesis is to be presented (or the main points by which it was presented, if we are outlining something someone else has written) are given Roman numerals: **I, II, III.** Each Roman numeral point is in turn broken down into its parts, and the resulting secondary subdivisions are given capital letters: **A, B, C.** Tertiary subdivisions are given Arabic numbers: **1, 2, 3;** quaternary subdivisions are given lower-case letters: **a, b, c.** (You rarely need to go farther than that in your subdividing; if you do, use Arabic numerals in single parentheses first, then use lower-case letters in single parentheses.) The symbols which indicate each rank of subdivision stand out so as to be readily visible, and the outline looks like this:

THESIS: _____

_____.

I. _____

_____.

A. _____.
B. _____
   _____.
C. _____.
   1. _____.
   2. _____
      _____.
      a. _____.
      b. _____.
II. _____.

(And so on, as far as your outline needs to go.)

Because we are subdividing, chopping major ideas into smaller and smaller pieces, we cannot logically have a I without at least a II, nor an A without a B, a 1 without a 2, and so on. But we may have a III, or a V, or even a VII. You should be wary, however, of a IX, or a K, or a 12, because so many items of equal importance at any stage are hard to manage. Both the writer and the reader will get lost if they must keep too many points of similar rank in mind at one time. It is a good, if somewhat rough, rule to reconsider any section containing more than half a dozen items of similar importance; probably some of them could be grouped further.

If a paper demands an extensive introduction, as distinct from a mere opening, the introductory idea should be included in the outline even though it does not directly contribute to the development of the thesis. It is labeled *Introduction*, and if necessary subdivided as if it were a primary point. Most outlines, however, do not include minor introductory material.

There are three additional conventions to be learned. First, no item of whatever rank should deal with more than a single concept; consequently, no item should consist of more than a single sentence or a single topic. Second, each item expresses and summarizes the idea to be developed at that point in the paper; consequently, each item must be phrased as a declarative sentence or topic, not as a question whose answer would be the real idea concerned. And within each section, and wherever else the items are comparable, the sentences should be as nearly parallel as possible, to clarify the similarity of the ideas. Third, one purpose of the outline is to provide a readily clear visual breakdown of the thesis idea; consequently, each item is indented so its identifying symbol will stand out clearly, and items which consist of more than one line are set up in block form, as in the schematic outline on pages 87–88.

Do not assume, finally, that each item, or even each primary subdivision, demands a paragraph in the final paper. Paragraphing, as we shall see in Chapter 5, is both a logical and a psychological problem to be solved with the thesis, the audience, and the length of the paper all in mind. If you were developing the thesis in answer to an examination question, for example, the whole paper might be only one paragraph in length. If you were writing a book, each primary subdivision might call for several chapters. Use your outline to ensure that you understand your ideas; write your paper to present your ideas to your intended audience.

There are only two really useful kinds of formal outlines: the sentence outline and the topic outline.[3]

THE SENTENCE OUTLINE

The sentence outline uses a full declarative sentence for every item of whatever logical value—thesis, primary subdivision, secondary subdivision, and so on down as far as the breakdown goes. It uses only declarative sentences because only declarative sentences directly state ideas, and the outline dispassionately states the ideas in the order of their relative importance. And it uses no more than one sentence for any one item. If you find yourself writing two or more sentences after any one outline symbol, see if those sentences can be combined into a single unified sentence. If they cannot, you must reconsider the item; there must be no more than one idea involved. But remember that a unified sentence need not be a simple sentence; you may use sentences of any necessary degree of complexity.

Sentence outlines have many advantages. Most important, they force you to decide at each step not only what topic you want to talk about, but exactly what you want to say about that topic, stating a complete idea at each point. Second, they fix your ideas in a form

[3] A third type of outline, the paragraph outline, is also common. It consists of the thesis, the topic sentences of each paragraph, and the subordinate details of each paragraph as subpoints. But because there is no necessary connection between the items of an analytical outline and paragraphs of the final paper, it is not very useful to the writer until his plans have been completely formed, and so will not be examined here in detail.

which will be just as clear six days or six weeks or six months later as it was at the moment of writing, so that if your outline is to be used long after you make it out, you will still be able to follow your original plan without stopping to wonder what on earth you had meant to do with some item whose relevance has completely escaped you. Third, a well-made sentence outline is very nearly as clear to someone else as it is to you. As you finish the preliminary work on your English 2 research paper, for example, your instructor can go over a sentence outline with you, see exactly what you are planning to do, and help you strengthen weak spots before the paper is written. The graduate student can submit the plan of his thesis to his adviser; the writer can show the publisher what he means to do with a projected book; the junior executive can get approval on his plans before the typist's time is wasted on an ill-advised manual. Because every idea of whatever rank is fully expressed, the sentence outline provides a clear and easily read blueprint that is understandable at any time, to any reader.

The following outline of an English 2 research paper illustrates not only the methods of formal outlining but also the value of the sentence outline as a blueprint for the final paper. The details still need to be filled in, but the plan to be followed and the approach to be taken is perfectly clear.

The Disappearance of the Greenland Colony

Thesis: After five centuries of varying prosperity, the medieval Norse disappeared from the Greenland colony, probably for a combination of several reasons.

Introduction: Greenland was for several hundred years a successful settlement.

  A. Discovered in A.D. 982, it was settled by Icelanders.
  B. As a republic, the settlement prospered.
  1. It was good-sized.
  2. The church was active.
  3. The Greenlanders could make a living by farming and hunting.
  4. They developed a brisk trade.

I. After Greenland joined Norway in 1261, trade decreased, and Europe gradually forgot Greenland.

  A. After Greenland joined Norway, trade fell off under Norwegian restrictions.

     1. Norway promised to foster Greenland trade, but broke trust by declaring a crippling monopoly.
     2. Under the monopoly legal trade ceased almost completely.
     3. Even illegal trade became unprofitable.
  B. Europe heard little good news from Greenland.
     1. Ivan Bardarsson reported that the West Settlement had been destroyed.
     2. Some of the Greenlanders returned to Europe because of unfavorable conditions in the colony.
  C. Europe gradually forgot the colonists.
     1. Recorded visits to Greenland stopped.
     2. Only isolated mention was made of the colony.
     3. Von Greenlander, about 1540, was the last outsider to see one of the colonists.
     4. Unsuccessful attempts were made to find the settlements again.
II. Greenland was rediscovered, and the extermination theory was proposed to account for the disappearance of the Norse colonists.
  A. Frobisher and others rediscovered Greenland, finding no Norsemen.
  B. The Norsemen were searched for unsuccessfully for many years.
  C. Egede resettled Greenland, looking for Norsemen but finding only Eskimo tales about them.
     1. Egede came to re-Christianize the Norse.
     2. Some time later, the Eskimos told him the Norse had all been killed.
  D. The theory of extermination by the Eskimos was proposed to account for the disappearance.
     1. The Eskimos had migrated into southern Greenland while the colony was still there.
     2. It was assumed that the Eskimos had killed the Norsemen, this being suggested by Egede's news.
     3. Bardarsson's account of the destruction of the West Settlement supported the idea.
III. Later it was suggested that the Norse had been absorbed by the Eskimos, not killed by them.
  A. The Eskimo way of life was well suited to Greenland.
  B. There is much white blood in the Eskimos today.
  C. Early reports support the theory.

D. The evidence of Bardarsson and Egede for extermination is not conclusive.
1. Bardarsson merely assumed a reason for the abandonment of one farm; there could well be other reasons for the abandonment.
2. Egede may himself have given the Eskimos the ideas they reported to him.
IV. Skeletal evidence suggests possible extermination by disease.
A. Skeletons disinterred at Herjolfsnes suggested degeneration under changing climatic conditions.
1. Skeletons, coffins, and clothes were recovered from the Herjolfsnes churchyard.
2. The clothes dated the skeletons and showed that some trade must have continued into the fifteenth century.
3. All the skeletons were degenerate, diseased, and deformed.
4. Several factors indicate a change in climate.
a. This change may at once have cut off trade and made life more difficult.
b. Lacking necessities, the Norsemen died.
5. But Herjolfsnes was an isolated case, and more material was needed to prove the theory.
B. Skeletons excavated in other parts of Greenland show different conditions.
1. Twelfth-century skeletons from Gardar were strong and healthy.
2. Twelfth- to fourteenth-century material from the West Settlement also contradicts the earlier findings.
a. The material was extensive and well preserved.
b. The skeletons were normal: neither degenerate nor diseased.
3. The skeletons do not prove much, but they do suggest that disease and degeneration were not everywhere important.
V. Perhaps the real solution is that the Norse, already diminished in numbers, turned to the Eskimo life, except for those at Herjolfsnes, who degenerated and died.

THE TOPIC OUTLINE

The topic outline, like the sentence outline, begins with a full sentence which expresses the central thesis of the paper. After that, however, all items are phrased as topics only, not as full-sentence predications expressing ideas about the topics. Consequently, the topic outline is far less clear than a sentence outline, even when the topics are carefully polished and made as meaningful as possible within the limits of brevity. Topic outlines are less useful than sentence outlines if any time is to elapse between making the outline and writing the paper, or if the outline is to be submitted to an adviser for scrutiny and suggestion.

The topic outline follows the same conventions of subdivision, subordination symbols, and indention that the sentence outline follows.

For illustration, we can reduce to a topic outline the sentence outline we have just examined.

Thesis: After five centuries of varying prosperity, the medieval Norse disappeared from the Greenland colony, probably for a combination of several reasons.

Introduction: Greenland as a republic.
  A. Settlement.
  B. Prosperity.
    1. Size.
    2. Church activity.
    3. Farming and hunting.
    4. Trade.
  I. Decay as a Norwegian colony.
    A. Trade under Norwegian restrictions.
      1. Crippling monopoly.
      2. Cessation of legal trade.
      3. Unprofitability of illegal trade.
    B. Discouraging reports.
      1. West Settlement destroyed.
      2. Return of some colonists.
    C. Oblivion.
      1. Cessation of visits.
      2. Rare mention.
      3. Last visitor.
      4. Settlements lost.
  II. Rediscovery: Extermination theory.
    A. Rediscovery: absence of Norse.
    B. Unsuccessful search.
    C. Egede: Eskimos.
      1. Missionary resettlement.
      2. Norse reported killed.

        D. Extermination theory.
          1. Early Eskimo migration.
          2. Extermination by Eskimos suggested.
          3. Confirmation in destruction of West Settlement.
    III. Absorption theory.
        A. Eskimo culture suitable.
        B. White blood in Eskimos.
        C. Confirmatory early reports.
        D. Extermination evidence inconclusive.
          1. Only one farm involved.
          2. Idea possibly induced.
    IV. Degeneration theory.
        A. Skeletons from Herjolfsnes.
          1. Recovered from churchyard.
          2. Evidence of late trade.
          3. Evidence of disease.
          4. Evidence of climatic change.
            a. Worsened conditions.
            b. Resultant death.
          5. Isolated case.
        B. Other skeletal evidence.
          1. Gardar: Healthy skeletons.
          2. West Settlement: further contradiction.
            a. Extensive evidence.
            b. Healthy skeletons.
          3. Dubiety of theory.
    V. Probable solution.

Such a topic outline is scarcely more useful than the informal outline, although it does have the advantage of more clearly identifying the relative importance of the subordinate ideas. But too many predicates could be fitted to most of the topics for the topic outline to be wholly clear to anyone other than the original writer, and even he will soon forget exactly what he planned to say about each point. A good paper could certainly be written from that sample topic outline, but perhaps a poor one could be written just as easily. All the topic outline really ensures is that an intelligent writer will treat the topics in a logical order.

For a complex subject, for a paper to be written some time after the outline has been made, for a plan to be submitted to an adviser, a sentence outline is far superior.

EXERCISES

A. The following very rough notes on the topic, "The freshman and his final choice of major subject," are already partially arranged in logical order. No thesis, however, is expressed and the notes are sometimes phrases, sometimes declarative sentences, and sometimes questions or imperatives. Examine them carefully, phrase a thesis, and prepare an analytical sentence outline using all pertinent items. You may rearrange, modify, eliminate, or add items at need.

Some college freshmen genuinely know what they want to specialize in.

An overriding interest in science, or literature, or history, or religion, or engineering, or business (yet which, among all the choices in each field?) may be already established.

The born and confident doctor, lawyer, etc.

Some think they know.

Limited experience may steer them into the wrong fields.

The scientifically minded may go into physics, when he would have gone into astronomy if he had ever met it.

A born Classicist may mistakenly major in Spanish.

Parental occupation may set them wrong.

Good doctors, lawyers, etc., often insist that their children study medicine, etc., regardless of interest or aptitude.

Some know they are in the wrong curriculum, but accede to pressure.

Chiefly that of parents.

"I want my child to have what I missed."

"I suppose I'll have to be a businessman. Most people are."

It's a rare freshman who is strong enough to rebel.

An Engineering freshman who wanted to write musical comedies worked out his own curriculum, over both parental and college objections.

The lawyer's son who wanted to be an engineer.

Many don't know, and know it.

"I'm not interested in anything, really."

"What shall I take?"—sometimes means, "What is required?" Sometimes means, "Help. What will I find of permanent interest?"

Aptitude tests are sometimes useful.

General requirements in first two years are in part designed to force undecided students to sample various kinds of subjects.

(Also designed to introduce all students to the varied approaches to different kinds of truth.)

Indecision not necessarily bad.

Why should an eighteen-year-old completely know his own mind?

Better to sample and find himself than to be forced into the wrong work—which is not always easy to escape.

At least, transfer from one curriculum to another should not be made too difficult.

Let the student who finally does decide have as easy access to his real field as possible.

B. Under your instructor's guidance, select a well-organized expository essay and prepare a thesis and sentence outline showing its structure.

5-

Paragraphs

Characteristics of a Good Theme: 7. Effective paragraphs; clear and smooth transitions.

In both function and size the paragraph stands between the sentence and the whole composition. The sentence is the device by which a writer *expresses* a complete idea. The composition is the means by which he *develops* an idea, a thesis or clear-cut purpose; it is the amplified presentation of the central idea the writer wishes to discuss. In between is the paragraph, the device by which the writer groups sentences to show their interrelations and subdivides the composition into manageable parts, *developing one aspect of the thesis* at a time.

THE FUNCTION OF THE PARAGRAPH

Paragraphs enable the writer and the reader to deal with an idea in stages, somewhat as the chapters of a book do. The indentation at the beginning of each paragraph serves to mark a stopping place or a turning point in the thought, and warns the reader, "Here is a new phase of the development of the thesis." To give that warning is the primary function of the paragraph. How often the warning needs to be provided—that is, how long a paragraph should be and how large an aspect of the thesis it should cover— depends on the topic, on the audience, and even on the medium in which the final paper is to appear. We shall consider those problems presently.

Roughly, meanwhile, the secondary functions of most paragraphs may be considered under four heads, and the slightly different functions of the narrative paragraph under a fifth. Paragraphs are usually used (1) to introduce a paper or a major section of a paper, often sketching the pattern of development that is to be presented later in detail; (2) to amplify and develop an important unit of the thought (most paragraphs fall into this group); (3a) to sum up what has been presented in the several paragraphs of the paper or of a major section of the paper, or (3b) to show the interrelations between one section and other sections preceding it; (4) to provide a transition between major sections of the paper; or (5) to advance narration or to introduce speakers.

Introducing a Paper or a Major Section

As might be expected, these three principal schools of contemporary philosophy—the Idealists, the Realists, and the Pragmatists—reach divergent conclusions as to the possibility of the human mind's discovering the truth underlying given phenomena, because they hold quite different opinions as to the nature of Truth itself. To the fundamental question: What is Truth? and to the respective answers of the Idealist, the Realist, and the Pragmatist, we must now, accordingly, give close attention.

Developing a Major Unit of the Central Idea

It is more beneficial for a person to struggle with a good book that is difficult to read, and to attempt to master it, than for him to read a hundred so-called "light" books. For in struggling with the material of the better book he will be forced to use all of his intellectual powers, to drive deeper into himself. It is argued that this "intellectual struggling" is useless for those who are not intellectually inclined and capable. It is said that this sort of struggling leads on to despair and frustration, that it is an utter waste of time if one can never hope to understand the nature of the material. But this is not so. No person who studies with the end of improving himself is wasting time. Despair he may, become frustrated he may, but he is always moving forward. He is not sliding backward into slothfulness. Perhaps he may never become a scholar. But it is not necessarily the object of the originators of the popular study of the great books to make scholars out of ordinary men and women. The major objective of the study is to make more and more men and women aware of the world they live in and their true place in it as "thinking" beings who will not easily be taken advantage of by scoundrels; who will not easily succumb to the hasty generalization and the mass attitudes which do so much to submerge the individual.

Summarizing a Section

Now, having taken this roundabout road, let's pause to catch our breath and look back over the country we have covered. We have moved from New England's stern and rockbound coast, through its little towns and its industrial cities, to its highland recreation areas in the Green Mountains and the Berkshires. Then, rested, we have plunged into the teeming cities of New York, New Jersey, and Pennsylvania to glance at their heterogeneous populations and their multifarious activities, supported by the rich farming regions inland, each section in its own way busy, and nearly all of them bustling. Now, a little breathless, we are at the Mason-Dixon line. The northeastern quarter of the nation lies behind us.

Interrelating Preceding Sections

If, then, our argument be accepted (and I really do not see how in general outlines it is to be refuted), the conclusion follows inescapably. If free discussion of ideas, free competition of *all* ideas, no matter how wild, how dangerous, how unorthodox they may at first seem, be the one sure way to arrive at truth and to be sure that nothing important is overlooked in the search for truth; if it is the truth which makes a nation free; if it is freedom which in the long run makes a nation and its people strong; and if it is the Western Democracies which freely pursue the truth that makes for freedom and strength, while the Iron Curtain countries suppress truth and seek strength by other, lesser, weaker means— then must the future, given peace, belong to the West. And if we are not given peace, if violent and bloody war from the East should seem to show that strength can be achieved without truth and freedom, why, that is no refutation, but acceptance. For who would resort to war save only those who finally despair of achieving strength by their own chosen, peaceful means?

Providing Transition between Sections

In the second of these lectures I took for examination a single episode in American diplomacy, the Open Door notes of John Hay. Let us now look back at the entire subsequent series of events in our Far Eastern policy.

John F. Kennan

Advancing Narrative Action; Introducing Speakers

In narration, too, the paragraphs fall into one of these four groups, advancing the incidents, characterization, or setting of the story rather than advancing the development of a central idea. But in addition, narration conventionally uses the paragraph in one further way: to mark the entrance of a new speaker in dialogue. Here, unity is a unity of speaker and yet of idea still, since each speaker is advancing the narrative by what he says.

> Ernest kicked at the fire thoughtfully, watching the sparks swirl madly up to the chimney-throat. "What," he said at length, "do you propose to do?"
>
> "Do?" she looked up in surprise.
>
> "Yes, do. You needn't think that you can sit back and leave it to me to get you out of the mess you've made. This is your problem. What, I repeat, do you propose to do?"
>
> "Why, I—don't know."

THE NATURE OF THE PARAGRAPH

Most of what we have so far learned about the whole composition applies also to the paragraph. Like the whole composition, the paragraph must be *unified,* treating no more than one idea which can be expressed by a thesis of its own. (The thesis of a paragraph we shall call a "topic sentence.") It must be *complete,* developing its limited idea fully, concretely, and specifically, leaving no loose ends and no unanswered questions about its central point. And its details must be carefully *organized.* Because we have already considered the function of the thesis in controlling unity and have already discussed the importance of completeness and organization in connection with the whole composition, we can treat those subjects briefly, touching only such problems as are peculiarly paragraph problems. It should be remembered, as we consider paragraph problems, that unity of idea, point of view, and tone are still essential—perhaps, because the whole paragraph is under the reader's eye at once, lack of unity is even more obvious in the paragraph than in the whole composition. It should be remembered that the paragraph-idea, though smaller than the theme-idea, still must be fully developed. And it must be remembered that the patterns of organization we have examined apply to the details within the paragraph just as much as they apply to the arrangement of paragraphs within the theme. In addition, there remain two topics which require special consideration: the *length* of the paragraph; and *coherence* within and between paragraphs, that is, the ways by which the sentences within a paragraph may be bound together and the ways by which the paragraphs of a composition may be bound together.

Unity: The Topic Sentence

Like the composition, the paragraph should be unified, dealing with a single idea which can be summarized in a single sentence. For the paragraph, that summarizing sentence is called the *topic sentence;* and particularly in exposition and argument, it is usually explicitly stated in the paragraph, sometimes more than once. In narration and description, it is less likely to be stated, but even when it is merely implied, the reader should be able to phrase it for himself if he wants to, and the writer must always have it in mind as he writes. When it is stated, the topic sentence is the most general sentence in the paragraph, and everything else in the paragraph is designed to explain it or to make it more vivid.

UNIFIED PARAGRAPH: EXPLICIT TOPIC SENTENCE

Topic sentence stated.

Detailed amplification of topic sentence.

Explanation of reason.

Examples illustrating the explanation and further amplifying the topic sentence.

A good driver "drives ahead of himself." His eyes rove constantly not only from the road surface to the mirror to the car immediately ahead and from side to side, but also as far ahead as he can readily see. On the highway, this may be a quarter of a mile or a mile; in town it may be three car lengths, a half a block, or two blocks. But whatever the driving conditions and whatever the range of his vision, he tries always to be aware of the behavior of traffic on ahead, to be able to interpret that behavior and adjust his own plans safely in advance. Flashing brake lights, for example, on car after car, mean some obstruction of the flow of traffic. Cars edging one after another into a single lane locate the obstruction for him, whether it is caused by repair work or a stalled motor. Swerving by many drivers ahead may mean a bad pothole. Overhead signal lights of contrasting colors warn him that he is approaching a left-turn or a right-turn lane. A one-way flow of cross traffic indicates a one-way street. The absence of

Generalized application of the idea, providing an "ending" for the paragraph.

all such signs cannot promise clear traffic, and he never assumes that it does; but the driver who drives ahead of himself is rarely surprised by the traffic conditions that confront him.

UNIFIED PARAGRAPH: IMPLIED TOPIC SENTENCE

No topic sentence stated, but all details supporting the implied topic sentence: *Washington is beautiful in mid-spring.*

In mid-spring, the Washington air is soft and gentle; the skies are clear or piled high with towering white thunderheads or scattered with little sheep-flocks of cloud. The willows along the Potomac are golden green, the sweep of grass a vibrant emerald, the river coffee-colored with silt after a rain, or jade under the bridges and a deep cerulean as it stretches away to left and right. Over the Arlington hills is flung a patchwork of dark evergreens, soft yellow tulip poplars, wine-red or golden elms, greening oaks and maples—all muted by an overlying cobalt haze. The city itself—gleaming marble, weathered brick, green-tufted streets, and puffs of yellow forsythia or pink magnolia or white dogwood or scarlet azalea or fluffs of cherry blossoms—lies quietly on its hills and in its valleys, beautiful beneath the frosted dome of the Capitol and the sharp, clean sword of the Monument.

Completeness: The Developed Paragraph

Again, like the composition, the paragraph should do all that it promises to do and all that it needs to do to be clear. It must develop its topic sentence and any subsequent general phrasing, leaving no unanswered questions. It must be concrete and specific enough to be clear to the reader.

UNDEVELOPED PARAGRAPH: INCOMPLETE

The *only* trouble? Perhaps.

What prevented it?

Why? "The state of mind" presumably, but we need to know more about it.

The only trouble with any high school is in the state of mind of the student. For my senior year I transferred to a large school in Alexandria. The teachers were good, my schedule was well arranged, and I was eager to learn in each course. Many of the students, too, had fathers in the army, navy, or air force, and they knew how to make a newcomer feel welcome. Nevertheless, I was perfectly miserable for the entire school year.

In five sentences, that paragraph raises at least three questions, but it never answers any of them. Neither the opening topic sentence nor the amplifying details are developed enough to satisfy any reader.

UNDEVELOPED PARAGRAPH: TOO GENERAL

Arriving in New York City, we were lucky enough to spend several days. The crowds and the bright lights were amazing. After our all too short visit we proceeded across the country.

Surely more than that should be said about a visit to New York.

Depending on the subject matter and the purpose of the paragraph and on the audience addressed, there are various ways by which the paragraph-idea may be developed. The writer may amplify the topic sentence by adding explanatory details. He may illustrate his points or exemplify them. Enumeration, analogy, comparison, contrast, tracing of cause and effect—any kind of concrete and specific expansion of the paragraph-idea may be necessary. The topic sentence may be restated at the end in the same or in different words. The details may be summarized or interpreted. Or several of these devices may be employed to answer the reader's questions before the writer moves on to another aspect of the general thesis. The reader must never be allowed to feel that the paragraph is incomplete, nor that it is so general as to be vague and fuzzy.

Organization

The chief difference between the paragraph and the whole composition, so far as organization is concerned, is that the paragraph is much more likely to have its central idea explicitly expressed. As we have seen in Chapter 4, the thesis of the composition may be phrased in so many words, or it may not. The topic sentence of the paragraph, however, probably will be explicitly set down. Some ninety percent of all expository and argumentative paragraphs present their topic sentences directly. (Narrative and descriptive paragraphs, on the other hand, frequently do not.)

TOPIC SENTENCE FIRST

Of those paragraphs which do phrase the topic sentence in so many words, a large majority place it early, in the first or second sentence, so that the reader will know from the beginning what the paragraph is trying to say and can see how each detail contributes to the development of the paragraph idea.

> *Among General McClellan's weaknesses, one of the most important was his constant eagerness to believe himself outnumbered.* Around Washington, during the winter of 1861–62, he had 180,000 men while Confederate General Joseph E. Johnston, at Centreville, had only 60,000. Yet McClellan worked and drilled and wished for reinforcements before he would even think of moving. On the Peninsula, after Pinkerton took over military intelligence, McClellan's tendency grew to an obsession. Before Yorktown, his 90,000 men were bluffed to a standstill by "Prince John" Magruder's 13,000. Before Williamsburg, McClellan halted his 90,000 before Johnston's 50,000, which Pinkerton estimated and McClellan eagerly believed to be 120,000. Before Richmond, 105,000 Union troops were pinned down, defeated, and driven back to Harrison's Landing by Confederate forces that never exceeded 65,000 all told, even with the Richmond garrison and Jackson's troops from the Valley—all because McClellan incorrigibly over-estimated the strength against him. Before Antietam, with Lee's battle orders in his hand and Lee's 40,000 men divided and scattered from Harper's Ferry to Hagerstown, McClellan hesitated to press the attack with his 70,000 troops until after Lee had reassembled his forces. At Antietam itself, Lee stood his ground, then was allowed to withdraw with 32,000 across the Potomac, because McClellan still insisted that his army, battered and battle-weary, but reinforced to full strength, was heavily outnumbered by the battered, battle-weary and unreinforced Confederates.

TOPIC SENTENCE LAST

Sometimes the topic sentence is withheld until the last, to gain emphasis or to allow the writer to present his evidence before he announces a topic his readers might find distasteful.

> More and more students crowd into college. Classes grow larger. Qualified teachers, in proportion to the need, become harder to find. Entrance requirements in the old, established colleges are raised; and new colleges proliferate as the nation tries desperately to provide some sort of advanced education for all who desire it. Yet as the lines outside the admissions offices grow and rising standards within the schools eliminate more students who once would have graduated, there remain many students who are capable

enough, but for one reason or another are content to "just get by." Some of the weakest students, it is true, are doing the best they can; there will always be marginal minds. But most could do much more, could learn much more. That very intelligent, lazy, rebellious boy in the back row: He would like to be an artist, and the sketches that take the place of notes in his notebook suggest that he has the talent; his father, however, is determined to force him into law. That luscious blonde: Her reason for being here is obvious, and he doesn't pay much attention to the lectures either. That pampered mamma's boy at the end of the second row, near the door: If he were not here, he'd be in the army or, worse, working. But why go on? *With potentially good students being turned away, far too many students still are occupying, and wasting, valuable space in college.*

Sometimes the topic sentence is stated early and then restated, usually in different words, at the end, providing a summary of the paragraph and an emphatic reminder of the idea that has been developed.

Occasionally, even in exposition and argument, the topic sentence is merely implied by the fact that all the details support one central idea. Freshman writers, however, might do well to avoid such paragraphs. It is far too easy merely to make random remarks about a topic and call them a paragraph unless the topic sentence is clearly down before you in black and white.

Organization of the details within the paragraph usually follows one or more of the natural or logical orders discussed in Chapter 4. Depending on what pattern will be clearest, arrange the details in the order of climax, or space, or time, or general to specific, or simple to complex, or some other pattern that presents them intelligibly. Again, as is true of the details of the whole composition, the one thing that cannot be done with them is merely to scatter them indiscriminately on the page.

Length

How long should a paragraph be? The answer is complicated by the fact that paragraph length is governed by two somewhat contradictory principles, one logical and one psychological. First, the paragraph must be long enough to develop its topic-sentence idea completely and clearly; but, second, it should not be so long that it strikes the reader as unwieldy nor so short that it seems superficial. The writer must consider the function of the paragraph in the whole composition in applying the first principle; he must consider the subject matter and the audience in applying the second.

Introductory paragraphs, paragraphs summarizing and inter-relating sections, and transitional paragraphs tend to be rather short. Developmental paragraphs, amplifying and clarifying major points in the development of the central thesis of the composition, tend to be longer. Yet a developmental paragraph that presents a very important point may be short, for emphasis.

In avoiding a paragraph that may strike the reader as either unwieldy or superficially brief, the writer must concern himself with the topic, the audience, and even the medium in which the paragraph is to appear. In general, the more serious the topic and the better educated the audience, the longer the paragraphs. Yet a paragraph that covers a full page in longhand may look absurdly brief in type in a printed book, or forbiddingly long in the narrow columns of a newspaper. Not only unity and development and function, but the very appearance of the passage to the intended reader must be considered.

Too long a paragraph frightens a reader. Few of us, no matter how well educated, would willingly read an article, much less a book, which was printed solid, with no indentions to promise sub-divisions of the idea and stopping places for our thought. And most of us feel, as we pick up an article or a book with long, long para-graphs, as if we were faced with heavy going. (*Long*, of course, is a relative term. *Forbidding*, also relative, might be better.)

Too short a paragraph, on the other hand, suggests that the writer has not properly digested or developed the ideas, suggests, in other words, that the job of grouping related thoughts and arranging the material in logical patterns has been shirked or ne-glected, or that the ideas themselves have been treated in too gen-eral terms. When your instructor writes "choppy paragraphing" in the margin of your theme, he often means that the very appearance of the page, with paragraph after paragraph of only one or two short sentences, suggests superficiality.

Somewhere in between the forbiddingly long paragraph and the superficially short one lies the paragraph of just the right length for your purpose and your audience. Sometimes, indeed, writing can be adapted to specific audiences merely by varying paragraph length alone. For example, because modern readers expect shorter paragraphs than readers of the last century did, the paragraph already quoted from *Life on the Mississippi* (pages 76–77) might seem forbidding to a modern reader, and a modern writer would probably have broken that passage up into two or three paragraphs, or possibly even four—the first three general sentences, perhaps, in a paragraph of their own, as introduction; the picture of the river town before the arrival of the steamboat as a second; the arrival of the steamboat, beginning with "Presently a film of dark smoke appears," as a third; and the departure, the last two sentences, as a possible fourth. No change in wording would be required, merely a change in indention. Usually, however, wording and sentence structure (and sometimes even organizational patterns) must be changed as paragraphs are shortened. As a rule we cannot expect to adapt our writing to audiences of various educational levels merely by grouping more or fewer sentences into paragraph units; the whole approach to the subject—the kind of details used to expand the thesis, the arrangement of the details, the tone, the wording, the sentence patterns—must be varied to fit the reader addressed.

Coherence

The problem of coherence is the problem of making clear and smooth transitions between ideas, of making the relations between the sentences of a paragraph clear, and of making the relations between paragraphs and even between multiparagraph sections clear and easy for the reader to follow. The coherent paper is usually the fluent, the flowing, paper.

Basic to coherence in any paragraph or in any paper, it should be understood at the outset, are clear, complete, and logical organization and development of the material. If there is no logical progression of thought from sentence to sentence, paragraph to paragraph, and section to section, coherence cannot be secured by any devices known to writing man. That should be obvious; there is no possible way to clarify nonexistent relationships.

But even well-planned papers may seem bumpy and confusing to the reader unless the writer carefully signals turns in his thought, bridges gaps between ideas, prepares the reader in advance for what is to come. Remember always that even though the writer knows exactly what relations exist between the ideas of his paper, the reader is wholly dependent on the words that are set before him. The writer should as a general rule be twice as clear as he thinks he needs to be; then he may hope to be clear enough for the reader he is trying to reach. There are many kinds of signals and bridges available to the writer, many ways to prepare the reader for what is to come and to announce its arrival when it appears. We shall examine the most common of them under two headings: coherence within the paragraph and coherence between paragraphs.

Coherence within the Paragraph

Given a well-organized paragraph, one in which the sentence ideas logically follow one after another, coherence within the paragraph is usually secured by the use of one or more of five devices: connective words, transitional phrases, repetition of key terms, pronouns looking back to antecedent nouns, and repetition of sentence patterns.

CONNECTIVES

At its simplest level, coherence within the paragraph may be secured by the use of connective words alone. The conjunctions, like *and, but, or, nor, for, because, if, unless, until;* the conjunctive adverbs, like *however, therefore, consequently, moreover, nevertheless, then, so, yet;* transitional adverbs like *similarly, contrarily, likewise, first, second, finally*—all such connective words show relations between sentences or parts of sentences within a paragraph and help tie together the ideas the paragraph presents.

Use connective words with discrimination; they are not interchangeable. Some, like *and, further, furthermore, moreover, additionally,* add similar material to what has gone before. Some, like *but, however, contrarily,* signal a reversal of the thought. *Either, or* and *neither, nor* eliminate one member or the other of paired ideas. The subordinating conjunctions, like *because, if, unless, until,* show such relations as those of cause, condition, or time. Choose carefully the connective word that indicates the true relations of the ideas.

You go your way, *and* I'll go mine. *Then* there will be no occasion for the sort of disagreement we have as long as we are together. *Further,* it is at least possible that after a separation we will more nearly understand each other's point of view *and* can renew our partnership with more successful results. *However,* so long as each is convinced that the other is obstinately wrong, there is nothing to be gained by attempting to work together.

Try reading that without the italicized words. It scarcely makes sense.

TRANSITIONAL PHRASES

Much like the single connective word is the transitional phrase, a group of words working together as a unit to join sentences or parts of sentences and to show their interrelations. In the paragraph just quoted, at least one occurs: *so long as.* Other common ones are *on the other hand, in addition, by the same token, at the same time, a few days later,* and so on. Again, such connectives must be used with discrimination. They are signals to the reader that you are changing direction, and if you signal for a right turn and then turn left, confusion or worse will surely follow.

Among the most amazing changes of the last quarter century are those that have occurred in medicine. One would suppose that any subject to which man has given such close attention for dozens of millennia as he has given to his own aches and pains would have reached reasonable stability long before the one thousand nine hundred and thirtieth year of the Christian Era. *But quite to the contrary.* A doctor who attended the Harvard Medical School in 1930, getting thereby perhaps as good a medical training as any in the world, would have found before 1960 that he was using in daily practice only morphine and one or two other specific drugs of all those that he studied in his Materia Medica courses. *In addition,* he uses quite different splints and casts for broken bones. *By the same token,* he gives quite different advice to his surgical patients, hoicking them out of bed and setting them to all sorts of activity which would have horrified his professors only thirty years ago. He knows new diseases, new treatments for old diseases, new drugs for old treatments of old diseases, new operative *as well as* new post-operative techniques. Even his medical Greek would be Greek to the Harvard faculty of 1930—"psychosomatic," *for a single useful example.* Only two aspects of his life are unchanged: his little black bag and the tendency of illness to strike at the inopportune hour of three o'clock in the morning.

REPETITION OF KEY TERMS

A third very common device for securing coherence within the paragraph is the deliberate repetition or reechoing of key terms. That repetition must be intentional (see also pages 214–215), and the repeated words or phrases must be important enough to the thought of the whole paragraph and exact enough in expressing the ideas of each sentence to bear the piled up emphasis of reiteration.

> From the sea, many millions of years ago, came the first dim forms of life, creeping out upon the barren land from the warm, shallow waters. Sea plants, microscopic sea plants and then well-developed seaweeds, at first attached themselves to the barren rocks and slowly learned to live on land and to grow and to spread; and slowly the land became less barren. Only when sea plants had become land plants could sea animals begin the long metamorphosis into land animals. But when all the conditions were right, simple forms, half-plant and half-animal at first, lived a strange half-life between the surf and the dry shore, then in turn grew and spread and changed, as things will in eons of time, and wandered farther and farther inland from the sea, and learned to run and to fly and finally to stand upright and to speak and to sing. Yet from the sea they all had come and of the sea they all are somehow still, for the salty lifeblood of every living animal is still chemically much the same as the water of the sea itself—sodium, potassium, calcium, mingled still on land as they are in the ageless waters of the oceans.[1]

PRONOUNS

Pronouns substitute for nouns, repeating the noun concept without repetition of the word. Consequently, every pronoun forces the reader to think back to the antecedent noun and by so doing helps to bind together the parts of the paragraph. Care must be taken, of course, to be sure that the pronoun reference (see pages 390–392) will be immediately clear.

> If any one man could be given credit for winning the Second World War, Winston Churchill would have the best claim. In the years between wars, it was *he who* repeatedly warned England of the growing danger, *he who* cajoled and badgered Parliament and the Government into what few preparations were made. To *him*

[1] My indebtedness here to Rachel L. Carson, *The Sea Around Us* (New York: Oxford University Press, 1951), will be obvious.

Britain turned when Chamberlain's belated, desperate efforts to avoid war finally collapsed in futility. After Dunkirk and the fall of France, *he* rallied the British to their grand, solitary defiance of the Axis. *He* worked constantly to bring the strength of America actively into the struggle, and later it was largely *he who* held the disparate Allies together during the months preceding the invasions of the Continent. If *he* had not been on the scene, if *his* work had not been done, the course of the war and probably its ultimate outcome would have been far different.

REPETITION OF SENTENCE PATTERNS

All the paragraphs we have just examined make use of a fifth device which is also commonly used to secure coherence within the paragraph. All of them, in one way or another, repeat whole sentence patterns. In the paragraph illustrating the use of pronouns, for example, *Winston Churchill* or the pronouns *he* and *who* serve as subjects of as many clauses as possible. The result is a tightly coherent paragraph not only because each pronoun looks back to the same noun, but also because the writer has kept the sentence patterns consistent instead of aimlessly shifting the subject from one sentence to the next. For example:

> If any one *man* could be given credit for winning the Second World War, *Winston Churchill* would have the best claim. Between the war, *England* seemed complacent except for his repeated warnings of danger. *Parliament* and the *Government* reduced the strength of the armed forces, and made what few preparations *they* did make only on his urging. When *war* came in spite of Chamberlain's efforts, the *British* turned to Churchill. *France* fell and the *British Expeditionary Force* retreated from Dunkirk, but England's *determination* was strengthened by Churchill's speeches, and *Britain* stood firm against the Axis. *Churchill* then worked to bring the strength of America actively into the struggle, and did much to hold the allied powers together during the months preceding the invasions of the Continent. If *he* had not been on the scene, if his *work* had not been done, the *course* of the war and probably its ultimate *outcome* would have been far different.

In that rewriting of the paragraph, the subject changes in nearly every clause, and the reader must work much harder than necessary to follow the thought.

Even more noticeably, repetition of whole sentence patterns may be used to emphasize the parallel quality of the thoughts and tie them together.

> There is a crime here that goes beyond denunciation. There is a sorrow here that weeping cannot symbolize. There is a failure here that topples all our success.
>
> *John Steinbeck*

CAUTION: OVERUSE OF DEVICES FOR SECURING COHERENCE

Finally, however, a word of caution. Beware of overusing any rhetorical device. It will call attention to itself and away from what you are trying to say. In the following paragraph, for example, the devices for securing coherence—all of them are present, but especially the repetition of key terms and of sentence patterns—assume a significance out of all proportion to their functional value. Use the devices in whatever combination seems best suited to each paragraph, but avoid calling attention to them.

> When the executors began to settle old Mrs. Wintergreen's estate, they were appalled by the magnitude of the task of disposing of all the things which, magpie fashion, she had collected during a long, wealthy, and acquisitive life. They had old glass to dispose of—Sandwich glass and hobnail glass and milk glass and Stiegel glass and dime store glass. They had China to dispose of—bone china and Chelsea china, and even (Wherever did she get them?) thick restaurant mugs. They had brass to dispose of—candlesticks and candelabra, ewers and trivets and doorknockers and bells and belt buckles and harness brasses. They had silver to dispose of—silver trays and silver bowls and silver compotes and silver knives and forks and spoons; sterling silver, coin silver, Sheffield plate, and thinly plated copper. They had rugs to dispose of—rag rugs and Orientals and Wiltons and broadlooms and just plain ruggy rugs. They had chairs to dispose of, all sorts of chairs, from Chippendale to kitchen. They had tables and beds and old-fashioned washstand sets and mirrors and pictures to dispose of. They had three radios and two television sets to dispose of, and house furniture and porch furniture and yard furniture and beach furniture. They had all the clothes she had ever worn in a long, long life to dispose of. They had the house and the land to dispose of. They had, in short, old Mrs. Wintergreen to dispose of—Mrs. Wintergreen, who had never once missed a chance to acquire something and who had never once, in ninety-seven years, herself disposed of a single, solitary thing.

Coherence between Paragraphs

Since very few papers consist of single paragraphs, coherence between paragraphs is as important as coherence within the paragraph. Again, clearly logical organization of the material is basic; confused ideas cannot be integrated by devices of coherence alone. Given logical organization, however, the writer can do a great deal to help his audience follow the development of his thesis.

Four of the devices used to secure coherence within the paragraph are also common between paragraphs: connective words, transitional phrases (which between paragraphs may be expanded at need to full sentences or even to complete transitional paragraphs bridging gaps between major sections of the paper), pronouns looking back to antecedent nouns in preceding paragraphs, and the repetition of key terms. All four occur at once in the following opening sentence of a new paragraph:

> But, besides this, his [Lincoln's] plans long before Appomattox were already moving beyond the mere successful termination of the war and looking toward the re-establishment of the Union, toward binding up the nation's wounds, with malice toward none. . . .

(Notice that the transitions made by these devices are usually made at the beginning of the new paragraph, not at the end of the preceding one. Since the end is the most emphatic spot, it is not often wasted on mere transitions, which, important as they are, are yet less important than the central idea of the paragraph itself. Ignoring this advice can be serious. In "A Dirge" [pages 35–36], the confusion begins merely because the last sentence of the first paragraph should be the first sentence of the second paragraph. From there on, even the writer becomes confused.)

In addition to these four transitional devices, at least three others are commonly used in binding paragraphs into a coherent composition: explicit tie-ins to the thesis of the whole composition, foreshadowings of ideas which are to be developed later, and repetitions of entire paragraph patterns.

TIE-INS TO THE THESIS

Many compositions begin with a clear and explicit statement of the thesis, often indicating from the very first the pattern of development to be followed. When this occurs, the paragraphs which develop each part of the pattern frequently open with topic sentences that look back to the thesis and announce which part is about to be treated. Papers dealing with processes, the operation of mechanisms, and the analysis of causes and effects are especially likely to employ the device. The method may be somewhat obvious, as in the following skeleton paper, or it may be handled more subtly.

Thesis stated; four-part development outlined.	1. I decided to come to the University of Illinois for at least four reasons: it is traditional in my family, it is near my home, it is relatively inexpensive, and it offers excellent training for the profession I hope to follow.
Paragraph looking back to reason 1.	2. First, going to Illinois is traditional in my family. . . .
Transition between ¶2 and ¶3. Tie-in with the thesis, looking back to reason 2.	3. Less important than the family tradition, but still contributing to my decision, is the fact that Urbana and the University of Illinois are only fifty miles from my home, with easy transportation linking the campus with my family and my friends. . . .
Tie-in with reason 3.	4. Further, since I am a resident of the State of Illinois, the tuition at the state university is relatively inexpensive for me. . . .
Transitional phrase. Tie-in with reason 4.	5. Perhaps most important of all, however, is the fact that I hope to become a chemist, and the Illinois Chemistry Department is one of the best in the country. Consequently, I can get excellent training for my future profession right here at my own state university. . . .

FORESHADOWING

"Coming events cast their shadows before," said a poet. And long before the poet phrased it, that idea had been true at least of events and ideas in the world of books. To secure coherence, to prevent a shock of surprise occasioned by the sudden and totally unexpected introduction of an important detail or to prevent the jerk of an abrupt turn of the thought, writers make use of foreshadowing, introducing a detail as casually and as naturally as possible before it becomes important, so that the reader is prepared for the importance it later assumes. The device is particularly prominent in narrative, where traits of character, details of setting, or turns in the action are all carefully foreshadowed. If, as a simple illustration, the hero and heroine are to be rescued from the Indians by the opportune arrival of a troop of the United States cavalry, the reader had better be told early that there is a cavalry post somewhere in the neighborhood. If the denouement is not foreshadowed, the reader will indignantly dismiss it as "contrived," but will accept with pleasure a foreshadowed contrivance as "artistically right." And foreshadowing is just as common, though more subtly handled, in the great novel or the major drama as it is in the Grade B Western. And exposition which uses narrative methods—like most histories or like Rachel Carson's *Under the Sea Wind,* explaining the life of sea creatures, or like George Stewart's *Storm,* a novel explaining the impact of weather on human life—uses foreshadowing in the same way. In *Storm,* for example, under the pressures of the weather, an old fallen tree trunk rolls and tumbles down the mountainside to break the telephone wires of the transcontinental lines; the reader has long known that the tree trunk was ready to roll, though he has not known what the results would be.

In straight exposition, and in argument, ideas are planted or prepared for in advance of immediate need. If you find yourself awkwardly stopping to explain a background concept, reexamine your plan to see whether it might more smoothly have been inserted earlier. In expository and argumentative writing, foreshadowing at its simplest level consists of opening a paper with a statement of thesis which outlines the development to follow; the reader, having been told in advance where the paper is going, recognizes the landmarks when he comes to them. In a different way, it is also present in the repetition of key terms and in the reechoing of sentence patterns, and we shall meet it again in the repetition of paragraph patterns. In all of these, coherence is secured by giving the reader familiar items, items he has been prepared to find. But it is perhaps most successful in complex exposition and argument when it is used skillfully to lead the reader from the topic of one paragraph into the topic of the next by ending one paragraph at a logical point of contact with the topic of the succeeding paragraph. The method is employed, mechanically, in the following excerpts from a paper on types of college students:

> Prominent on every campus is the campus politician. . . . [The paragraph then details the politician's characteristics and activities, and near the close begins to point toward the topic of the next paragraph.] . . . And in his rare moments of leisure, he drops in at the Union (where, to be sure, he continues his work of mending his fences and improving his "contacts") for a cup of coffee and a sociable game of bridge with another B.M.O.C. and a couple of campus queens.
>
> The campus queen herself has such a busy life that it is a wonder she has time for bridge—and she wouldn't have if she weren't "improving contacts" too. . . . [Details of her busy life follow; then the paragraph points toward ¶ 3.] . . . In the fall, she tries to be seen at least once a week on the arm of the captain of the football team, in the winter with the high scorer of the basketball team, and in the spring with the baseball pitcher. She seems to believe that she was especially designed (well designed, she is certain) to adorn the arm of an athlete.
>
> The athlete she goes with endeavors to live up to the Hollywood concept of college almost as much as the campus politician does, or the campus queen. . . .

You see the method, but notice one important point: The topic that is to be major in ¶ 2 is a minor, though logical, detail in ¶ 1, and so on. Otherwise we would risk overemphasizing it in ¶ 1 and losing paragraph unity. (See also page 113.) The second danger in the method is that it easily degenerates into a trick, and if it is used too often or too obviously the reader becomes annoyed by what he regards as a meretricious display of empty technique.

REPETITION OF PARAGRAPH PATTERNS

In the same way that repeated sentence patterns help to tie together the sentences of a paragraph, repeated paragraph patterns help to tie together the paragraphs of a composition. Basically, repeated paragraph patterns reflect a careful paralleling of organization, with similar ideas treated in similar ways at similar points in succeeding paragraphs. The device is perhaps most often used in description and in expositions of comparison and contrast, but it is frequently useful in other kinds of writing.

Probably the easiest way to illustrate its effectiveness is to offer two sample paragraphs in which the reader is led to expect repeated patterns but does not get them. Instead, after following the established pattern for a while, the writer is led away from it by her own detail and finally abandons it altogether.

General tone.
The street.
The houses.

The yards.

Play space.

House furnishings.
Transition, echoing closing and tone of ¶ 1.

The street.

The houses.

The yards.

Play space.

Dress and recreation on Virginia Street.

Dress, recreation on Sixth Street.

Work on Sixth Street.

Work on Virginia Street.

On Virginia Street, in the upper-class section, all is very quiet and peaceful. The street is lined with oak trees and flowers, and the houses have a look of luxury and are well kept. Almost all of them are two-story brick houses with large lawns and plenty of trees and shrubs, and in the back they have large gardens and room for the children to play. The houses have all the modern conveniences for washing, ironing, cleaning, disposing of garbage, and living comfortably and spaciously.

On the other hand, the poor people who live on Sixth Street have almost none of these modern conveniences. Nor is Sixth Street quiet and peaceful. Instead of being lined with oak trees and flowers, the street is littered with paper, tin cans, garbage, bottles, and other rubbish. The houses are usually one-room, tar-paper flats, very dark, dirty, and reeking. The yards, where yards exist, are not large and green and neat, as in the other side of town, but are nothing but small plots of hard dirt, very ugly and with no room for the children to play. Therefore the children must play in the street, where boys and girls form gangs to get, by force if necessary, what the boys and girls of the other section have given to them as a matter of course. The boys and girls of Virginia Street dress well, go to movies and parties, and have a good time, while the slum children dress in rags and have no money to spend for fun. People on Sixth Street work in factories or dig ditches or do anything they can to make a living. People on Virginia Street are businessmen and go to church and clubs and plays. The two sections are completely different.

That student went just far enough with parallel paragraph patterns to make it confusing when she broke away from them. And later paragraphs of that paper, by the way, hopped back and forth between Virginia Street and Sixth Street in a completely chaotic way, compounding the confusion still more with every added sentence. Having established a pattern, the writer should have stayed with it, or left it only for a different pattern that would have worked harmoniously with the first one.

By whatever method or combination of methods seems best suited to the material you are presenting, bind your sentences and your paragraphs and the major sections of your paper into a coherent, fluent whole, signaling all turns of thought and indicating explicitly the interrelations of the ideas. Then, and only then, can your reader give his best attention to the development of the central idea you are striving to present.

EXERCISE

Read the following paper and then answer the questions.

The Need for the Study of the Great Books[2]

1. There is a vital need for the study of the world's great books. The most compelling reason for this study is the decline of popular taste in literature. Writing of the so-called "simple" and "human" varieties is in the ascendant, and there are few indications, if any, to show the existence of a reverse tendency. The great literature of the world, to the creation of which men with fine minds devoted their lives and their energies, has become synonymous on the mass level with stodginess, dullness, and even "highbrowism."

2. The great writers have been replaced by the "new" writers, who are considered clever because "they have discovered sex," and because they borrow liberally from the latest scientific findings in psychology, sociology, etc. Too, they are considered clever because "they know what the people want," and give it to them in copious and unending doses.

3. The cry is raised in many quarters that the study of the great books by the masses is merely another form of the "mass snobbism" set in motion for reasons of profit by the book clubs and other publishers. In answer to this charge it can be said that the study of the great books was instituted by a group of learned men

[2] From *The Green Caldron: A Magazine of Freshman Writing,* published at the University of Illinois. Reprinted by permission.

whose motivation was the sincere desire to help their fellow men to enrich their lives by encouraging them to exercise their own powers of thought. In this they may be compared to certain figures of the Northern Renaissance who sought to bring the writings of the ancients to the widest possible audience. Simply because some alert publishers have exploited the movement for their own profitable ends by bringing out expensive and beautiful editions of great books, thus appealing to the snobbish elements of the nation, does not mean that the originators of the popular study of the great books are trying to spread snobbism.

4. Then, too, it is claimed that the people are not hungry for knowledge so much as they are anxious for diversion. But the mistake here is in the implication that diversion must necessarily be "unprofitable leisure." Why must this be so? Must a hard-working man necessarily flop into his easy chair at the end of his day's work and always switch on the radio, or pick up his funny-book, or go down to the corner tap to guzzle beer and chin pointlessly with his cronies? Can workers divert themselves only by joining bowling teams, by playing cards, by going to the motion pictures, or by attending parties? Certainly, all of these can be considered a part of the class of things that divert one.

5. But they are only a part of the class. There are many other things or pursuits in which diversion may be found, or from which diversion may be gained. Study can divert. "Of course it can," the argument persists, "but it does not entertain." Well, this is but the statement of taste. Those who are against study as such claim that it does not entertain. Those who believe otherwise say that study can entertain. Thus leisure time can be profitably employed, because the person studying for diversion in his leisure time will actually be working toward the betterment of himself. The profitable employment of leisure time is considered to be a mark of the civilized man.

6. Now, an important question arises. Can the study of the great books really bring about a reversal in the downward trend of popular tastes in literature? It can, and for the following reasons. First, most people are interested in developing themselves. They want to be aware of what is going on in the world, and what has gone on in the world. By aiding this desire, the study of the great books helps to set off a trend against inferior tastes. It encourages the individual *himself* to determine the issues in important discussions, to weigh more carefully the sides in disputes or arguments, to look more closely into the nature of things, and to avoid flinging himself into the whirlpool of unworthy mass trends. The study of

the great books will foster a love of fine writing among those who apply themselves to the study. People who study the great books will soon come to recognize the difference between inferior writing and fine writing. Finally, they will devote themselves to the reading of good literature. And if a person reads only cursorily in the great books, he will still come into contact with great ideas and thoughts. Such a meeting cannot fail to have the consequences of making a person take closer stock of himself.

7. It is more beneficial for a person to struggle with a good book that is difficult to read, and to attempt to master it, than for him to read a hundred so-called "light" books. For in struggling with the material of the better book he will be forced to use all of his intellectual powers, to drive deeper into himself. It is argued that this "intellectual struggling" is useless for those who are not intellectually inclined and capable. It is said that this sort of struggling leads on to despair and frustration, that it is an utter waste of time if one can never hope to understand the nature of the material. But this is not so. No person who studies with the end of improving himself is wasting time. Despair he may, become frustrated he may, but he is always moving forward. He is not sliding backward into slothfulness. Perhaps he may never become a scholar. But it is not necessarily the object of the originators of the popular study of the great books to make scholars out of ordinary men and women. The major objective of the study is to make more and more men and women aware of the world they live in and their true place in it as "thinking" beings who will not easily be taken advantage of by scoundrels; who will not easily succumb to the hasty generalization and the mass attitudes which do so much to submerge the individual.

8. No one can deny that the wisdom of the past belongs to all men. It is theirs for the taking. And the wisdom of the past should always be a part of the cultivated man's intellectual equipment. Not merely for ornament, but for use and enjoyment. His knowledge of the past will provide him with an insight into the actions and events of the present time, and even into the future. Some might reply that this knowledge can be gained only over a long period of time and by great effort. No one denies this, least of all those who originated the popular study of the great books. They believe that one should devote not just a few minutes a day to the study of the great books, but rather a lifetime. They believe that men should never cease learning. No man can ever hope to gain even a fraction of all the knowledge of the world. But he can constantly learn.

9. There can be no doubt that the widespread study of the great books would widen the intellectual horizons of men and aid greatly in helping them form cultivated tastes. The individual intellectual effort required for their study is far more valuable than the slickly contrived "How to . . ." articles of the "Digests" and "Women's Magazines," or the flow of books, offering tailor-made philosophies for $3.50 and two evenings of one's time, that constantly clutter up the horizons of knowledge. The study of great books encourages every man to be his own philosopher. Others would deprive him of this privilege and need, and would foist off on him their own ideas and thoughts without regard to his own intellectual powers. No other approach to the problem of bettering popular tastes in literature can be as effective as one which aids the individual to be his own arbiter in matters of judgment and taste. And enough individuals, thus equipped, will be able finally to reverse the decline of popular tastes in literature and in other important things. The study of the great books can bring this about.

Ronald Carver

1. Write out the single topic sentence of each paragraph.
2. In how many of the nine paragraphs is the topic sentence explicitly stated in a single sentence?
3. In how many is it divided between two or more sentences, so that it must be rephrased in order to follow the instructions in question 1?
4. Why are ¶ 2 and ¶ 3 not combined into a single paragraph? Should they have been?
5. Do any of the paragraphs seem to be concerned with more than a single aspect of the central thesis? Consider ¶ 8 in particular.
6. Are any of the paragraphs incompletely developed? too fully developed?
7. Where does the topic sentence appear in each paragraph in which the topic sentence is explicitly stated? What does the writer gain by placing each topic sentence where he does? Should he have used another organization?
8. What pattern of arrangement determines the order of the details in ¶ 4?
9. What is the function of each paragraph?
10. Why is ¶ 2 short? What is the average length of the paragraphs?
11. Point out two examples in the paper of each of the common devices for securing coherence within a paragraph: connective

words, transitional phrases, pronouns looking back to antecedent nouns, repetition of key terms, and repetition of sentence patterns. Point out any sentences which are insufficiently interrelated.

12. How many of the devices mentioned in question 11 are employed in this paper to secure coherence between paragraphs? Which devices? Where are they used?

13. What is the thesis of the whole paper? Are there any tie-ins to link paragraphs to that thesis?

14. Is there any deliberate attempt to bridge the gap between ¶ 6 and ¶ 7? If not, should there have been one? Suggest a device that might have been used.

15. Are there any of the devices for securing coherence between paragraphs which are not used in this paper? If so, select two paragraphs from the paper and rewrite them to illustrate how the devices might have been used.

Effective Sentences

Characteristics of a Good Theme: 8. Mature, concise, and varied sentences that reflect the writer's thought. 9. Compression, or conciseness.

The sentence, the word-group which conveys a complete idea in the larger context of the paper, is the basic unit of thought, the device by which we call attention to a topic, the subject, and then say something about that topic. (Beyond that very loose definition we need not now go. For a fuller discussion, see pages 415–416.) The sentence in English, however, may take many forms, and from all the forms open to him the writer must choose the one which will most nearly say what he wants to say to the reader he is addressing. It must be grammatical, it must be clear, it must introduce its details in the most effective order, it must sound right, it must fit into its proper place in the mosaic of sentences that together make up the paper. The writer, and certainly the student of writing, must consider all of these.

But first, the student of writing should consider a more basic matter: What does it mean to write a sentence, and thereby to invite a reader to read it, to give it his time and attention? It means to express a fully formulated thought, and that obviously means in turn to think first of what is to be said and only then to try to say it. In revision, it means to think again, and if necessary to rewrite until the

123

thought is exactly expressed. Catching a thought to begin with and then conveying it to a reader are both far too hard to be left to the accidental sequence of words aimlessly following one another in merely grammatical patterns. Since the subject of a sentence is "the thing talked about" in that sentence, the grammatical subject ought to be, usually, the logical subject; both the writer and the reader should be concentrating on the concept that is of major importance at that point in the developing central idea. The verb, the heart of the predicate (a *predication* is itself "a fully formulated thought"— and only the subject and predicate together can express it)—should be as exact as possible, not merely any verbish concept that could fit. Modifiers should be carefully chosen; adjectives, adverbs, phrases, or clauses should indicate the relative importance of the qualifying concepts they express and should be so placed as to introduce those concepts when and exactly where they are needed. To write a sentence, then, means to know what you want to say, and to say it as exactly as possible by whatever means best suit the purpose and the audience. It means to have at your command a mature understanding of the English sentence, so that what you write can be effectively expressed.

We shall examine five characteristics of mature and effective sentences. All such sentences are *clear, conventional in form, concise, flexible,* and *euphonious.* Obviously, some of these characteristics of the effective sentence are closely related to other aspects of language, as, for example, both clarity and conciseness are closely related to exactness in our diction, the use we make of our vocabulary. Complete mastery of the sentence, that is, can come only with mastery of other aspects of writing. But in this chapter we shall focus as much as possible on the sentence alone.

CLEAR SENTENCES

First, and most important of all, sentences must be clear. If your reader does not understand what you are saying, all other virtues of your writing are wasted. Some ideas, of course, are more difficult to understand than others; it may be that even the best reader will have to read with close and active attention to follow your thought— as you yourself need to read carefully to understand abstruse ideas. Yet even the most complicated idea must be expressed as clearly as possible. Ideally, insofar as the complexity of the thought will allow, every sentence should be so clear that even the hasty reader will not go astray; it should perfectly reflect and convey every nuance of your thought and should be so exactly right that no change could be made without loss of clarity. That ideal, obviously, is not achieved by any but a careful, skillful writer.

Many confused sentences, of course, are the result of the writer's ignorance of the basic conventions of English usage. Such weaknesses as fuzzy pronouns, lack of agreement between subject and verb, dangling and misplaced modifiers, confusing punctuation, vague or inexact diction—any or all of these virtually guarantee confusion. But many confused sentences are the result of sheer carelessness on the part of the writer, of a failure to keep the reader in mind.

In trying to achieve clarity, the writer should always remember that the living language is the spoken language and that written English is merely an attempt to represent the tones and pace and stresses of spoken English by means of arbitrary symbols strung across a cold page. Readers are first of all speakers and listeners, and reading is essentially an elaborate form of silent listening. Spoken English and written English are of course not identical, because the cold page cannot reproduce the intonation of the human voice, or the expressiveness of the human face, or the lifted eyebrow or shrugged shoulder or pointed finger of human gesture, or the intimacy of face-to-face communication. Written English must of necessity be fuller, more explicit, clearer; yet written English must never divorce itself from the tones and stresses of the spoken language. When it does, clarity is in jeopardy. The writer must always use the rhythms and emphases of normal speech and the attention span of the intelligent listener as his touchstones.

With the listener and speaker constantly in mind, let us examine four elements of sentence clarity—length, complexity, natural stress, and positional emphasis.

Length

Sentences, for modern readers, should not be too long. Perhaps because we read so many newspapers and magazines whose pages are set up in narrow columns, we have become used to much shorter sentences than our grandfathers were accustomed to. Few modern writers would use sentences as long as those, say, of Lord Macaulay or of Cardinal Newman. Whether our modern shorter sentences result from or are tending toward a weakening of our intellectual fiber is beside the point. The point is that modern sentences are relatively short. Length will still vary, of course, according to the complexity of our ideas and the sophistication of our audience; no arbitrary limits can be set. For general writing, we can say only that sentences should not be too short, or allowed to run on too far. If *most* of your sentences have less than ten or fifteen words, they are probably too short. If most of them have more than twenty-five or thirty words, they may well be too long. Consider the desirability of revising some of them.

The skillful writer, balancing and paralleling similar ideas, controlling the reader's responses to each detail, and remembering the rhythms and stresses of natural speech, can go far beyond any limitation of fifteen words, or fifty, or even one hundred and fifty in a single sentence. (For example, consider the fourth sentence in the passage from *Life on the Mississippi*, discussed in Chapter 4, page 76.) But the modern writer does not write extremely long sentences very often.

Frequently the cure for the very long sentence lies in simply rewriting it as two sentences or more. Often the cure involves reducing its complexity, or in consciously striving for a concise yet flexible manner of expression.

Complexity

Just as our sentences are shorter on the average than Lord Macaulay's or Cardinal Newman's, so are they less complicated. We tend now to break up into simpler sentences ideas which the nineteenth-century writer would have combined into involved chains of phrases and clauses, all modifying and qualifying, expanding and limiting a central, major, main-clause idea. This is not to say that the modern writer must or may confine himself to a primer style; it does mean that a modern virtue lies in an avoidance of sentences of undue complexity. Your sentences must be complicated enough to reflect your thought with accuracy, but for the clarity of your own thought, as well as for the clarity of your writing, they should never be any more complicated than they need to be.

Three bits of negative advice may be useful.

1. Avoid unnecessary involutions and convolutions of thought, intellectual mazes into which your reader wanders innocently and trustingly, only to discover finally that he must fight his way out again by main force. The following sentence is reasonably grammatical, and an attentive reader with enough patience could follow it through to the end; yet few modern writers would have left it as a single sentence.

> I have no wish at all to speak otherwise than respectfully of conscientious Dissenters, but I have heard it said by those who were not their enemies, and who had known much of their preaching, that they had often heard narrow-minded and bigoted clergymen, and often Dissenting ministers of a far more intellectual cast; but that Dissenting teaching came to nothing,—that it was dissipated in thoughts which had no point, and inquiries which converged to no centre, that it ended as it began, and sent away its hearers as it found them;—whereas the instruction in the Church, with all its defects and mistakes, comes to some end, for it started from some beginning.
>
> *John Henry Newman*

Once one becomes used to it, Cardinal Newman's prose is admirable; but that sentence is too complicated for a modern reader, whatever his theology, to read with ease and understanding.

The sentence need not be long to be overly complex.

> The caution in the Administration, and among some legislators, is primarily the care that properly is exercised in prescribing drastic drugs before the diagnosis is exact.

As the *New Yorker* would say, "How was that, again?"

2. In breaking up complex ideas, avoid short-circuited thought. Be sure all the connections are perfectly clear to your reader; be sure you have left no thought gaps in passages which are clear enough to you as the writer but which puzzle the reader because he does not readily see connections you left to implication alone.

Suppose, for example, you should think to yourself, "Cats are so sleek, proud, aloof, and graceful that a mere clumsy man should be honored by any attention they deign to pay him"; with that thought in the back of your mind, you try to compliment the Prom Queen who has condescended to go to the movies with you by saying aloud, "You remind me of a cat." She might misunderstand. You have short-circuited the flow of communication, and she may blow a fuse. Indicate the steps in your thinking. Put in your transitional words, phrases, clauses, or sentences; show the connections between your ideas. When you reason from A to B to C, complete the circuit. A reader forced to pass from A to C may never make the connection. In spoken English the context will often clarify nonsense phrasing: "Are your hands clean?" "I'm going in now to do it." But written English should be clear to begin with.

Such thought gaps often occur within a single sentence. General Grant once wrote, in an important order: "Requiring Colonel Oglesby's command with me, however, I have sent a messenger after it to him in this direction." What he meant was something like this: "Because I want Colonel Oglesby's command to join the forces here with me, I have sent a messenger to Colonel Oglesby, ordering him to change his line of march and to march instead in this direction." Or they may occur between sentences. In either event, the writer knows what he means, but forgets that the reader must depend on what he is given. Another military order, far more famous in its result, may illustrate. At Balaklava during the Crimean War, Lord Raglan watched from the heights as the battle was fought in a valley bisected by a ridge. Forgetting that those on the valley floor could not see what he could see, he ordered the Light Brigade to "charge the enemy and capture the guns." But the only guns Lord Cardigan could see were those at the end of a deep defile; so the Charge of the Light Brigade was made up "the Valley of Death," and not against the guns that Lord Raglan had meant, on the other side of the ridge. Never expect your audience to be mind readers.

A great writer may get away with short circuits. A lesser writer must be complete enough to be clear.

3. Avoid chopping up your sentences by throwing in too frequent parenthetical phrases.

> She was, to be sure, quite aware of her own incredible, indeed ineffable, beauty; so aware, it must, sadly, be admitted, that any observer who might, hypothetically, have been able to view her with complete objectivity (if such there could have been) would, perhaps, have come to the conclusion that she was, really, not ineffable at all, but, instead, very nearly unspeakable.

Few readers can squirm with ease through rhetorical barbed-wire like that. A more considerate writer would have eliminated some of those modifiers and rearranged others so that they would fall in a more natural order; and perhaps even then he would have broken up the sentence into shorter ones.

Normal Stress

The writer who keeps the spoken language in mind will try always to phrase his ideas in such a way that the normal stresses of the sentence can fall on important words and key details—in such a way that a reasonably skillful reader could read the sentence aloud without hesitation, breathe naturally during pauses in the thought, scurry over tributary details, and emphasize key points without making any special effort to do so.

Achieving this ideal requires constant attention during revision; and, unhappily, the more clearly a writer knows what he wants to say, the harder it is for him to be sure he has said it naturally. He tends to stress the key points as he rereads his own sentences, whether normal stress really falls on those key points, or falls somewhere else. The more time there is between writing and revising, the more chance there is that the writer can approach his own sentences objectively. And only when he is objective can he read what he has actually put down, as another reader might read it.

The difficulty lies in the fact that the spoken language is more versatile than the written; we can speak sentences we cannot easily write, because when we speak, we can use extra stress to emphasize any part of the sentence and by the tones of our voices and the pauses we use, we can make our sentences say different things. Your instructor, for example, may start to write on your theme, "This paper needs more specific details." He could say that easily enough, whether he meant, "This paper needs more details, preferably specific ones," or "The details in this paper should be more specific"; but in writing he would have to use the longer, more exact sentences to avoid ambiguity.

A speaker can also throw an artificially heavy stress on single syllables.

The distinction between a *ho*tel and a *mo*tel was once easy to make: *ho*tels were central and luxurious; *mo*tels were cheap and inconveniently located. But now, about all one can say is that a *mo*tel is a *ho*tel with a garage or a parking lot.

So long as the contrasting terms are close together, a reader may have no trouble, but if they are so widely separated that he has no warning of the need for extra stress, he may get into trouble.

The hotel you recommended was completely full, but I finally found a room in a motel near a slow bus line.

The normal emphasis falls on *-tel* in both words, and the reader will tend to place it there.

In writing, unless we are to fall back on the cheap and lame device of italicizing the elements on which unexpected stress should fall, we must revise such sentences so that they will be clear when they are read naturally, or substitute other words for the ones requiring abnormal stress. In that last example, for instance, we can use *motor hotel,* instead of *motel,* and avoid all confusion. And by a little practice in shifting the elements of a sentence to throw the normal stress where we want it, we can deal with more subtle problems than that.

Suppose we have written:

One does not expect a restaurant that usually serves appetizing food to include unappetizing dishes in its menu.

The important contrast here, of course, is between *appetizing* and *unappetizing;* yet in both words the normal stress falls on *ap-,* and the stress that falls on *-clude* increases the reader's tendency to overlook the essential negative syllable. Also, placed where it is, *to include* seems to be an adverb modifying *serves* rather than a noun object of *expect,* and the reader may stress it that way, to the utter confusion of the sense. Further, both key words are buried in the middle of the sentence, where their importance is obscured. Many changes could be made in the sentence pattern or in the wording to throw stress on the important elements. We can put the contrasting elements side by side.

If the food of a restaurant is normally appetizing, unappetizing dishes will rarely appear on its menu.

We can place each key term near an end of the sentence where it will be more conspicuous, perhaps at the same time separating the negative idea from the root word to improve the emphasis:

> If appetizing food is characteristic of a restaurant, one scarcely expects that a new dish on the menu will not be appetizing too.

Or we can make the sentence entirely affirmative.

> Unappetizing food is seldom served in a restaurant at which most of the food is delicious.

And so on. The more skillful a writer is in varying his sentence patterns, the better his chances of adjusting the stresses in a sentence so that they will fall where he wants them.

Occasionally a writer will use words in one sense without realizing that his readers may easily understand them in a different sense. In such a sentence, normal stress may fall just where the writer wants it when he reads his own sentence, but fall somewhere else for the intended reader. Confusion is inevitable.

> Only McDowell advanced; and as Lee had replaced Longstreet, who had marched to Orleans the same afternoon, by Anderson, but little was discovered.
>
> *G. F. R. Henderson*

At first reading and at second that sentence seems unintelligible. If Lee had replaced Longstreet, who is Anderson—or where is it? What is the phrase *by Anderson* doing in the sentence at all? And surely there is a thought gap somewhere; the last main clause seems not to follow from the rest. Yet to Colonel Henderson the sentence was perfectly clear. He knew he was saying that Lee, the commander, sent Longstreet to Orleans and put General Anderson in to plug the gap where Longstreet had been. As a result, when McDowell alone of the federal generals advanced to reconnoiter, he was unable to discover much about Longstreet's possible presence in the area. *Lee had replaced Longstreet by Anderson* would have been clear if it had not been split by a modifying clause that shifted the stresses. *Only a little* would have been clearer than *but little*, since *but* the adverb and *but* the conjunction throw different stresses on the rest of the clause. The writer knew what he meant, but failed to see what his reader might make of it.

Even the practiced writer may have trouble deciding exactly where the natural stresses will fall, because, like the diligent apprentice, he knows what his sentences mean, and as he listens to his sentences he apportions his stresses according to his intended meaning. Somerset Maugham, for example, discussing his own development as a writer, reports his final decision.

> I discovered my limitations and it seemed to me that the only sensible thing was to aim at what excellence I could within them.

That is not, certainly, a bad sentence, but to read it as Maugham meant it to be read, one must slightly overstress *could* and must pause unnaturally before going on to *within them*. If Maugham had said (to risk the presumption of revising a sentence by a master of clarity) ". . . aim at what excellence I could attain within them," the natural stress of the sentence would have fallen on a stressable word, rather than on an unexpected little gulp of emptiness.

But difficult as it is for any writer to realize that a possibly inattentive reader may miss the point of a sentence by missing a slightly unnatural stress-pattern, every writer must remember that his readers may be somewhat inattentive, and must try to protect himself by making his sentence stresses as natural as possible. Just as every driver in heavy traffic must assume that other drivers will stay in the marked traffic lanes and obey the lights, but must also assume (if he is to avoid crumpled fenders) that every other driver may be a complete idiot who might do almost anything, so the writer must assume that the reader will know and follow the conventions and pick up his cues deftly, and at the same time must be aware that his readers may not always be fully alert. *He must try to write in such a way that even the inattentive reader cannot possibly go wrong*. The writer must forget what he meant to say and try to reread his sentences with complete objectivity, letting the stresses fall where they may and rearranging his details accordingly.

When you revise your sentences, read them aloud, forgetting so far as possible what you thought you had said. If you find yourself forced to lay an unusual stress on important words, rephrase the sentence so that even the most careless reader would emphasize naturally those details on which you want emphasis to fall.

Positional Emphasis

Slightly different from the emphasis given well-placed details by the natural stresses within a sentence is the general emphasis that can be given a detail by placing it at the beginning, in the middle, or at the end of the sentence unit. Where the first kind of emphasis may fall on single words or even single syllables in a phrase or a clause, the second lends emphasis to the whole syntactical unit, to the whole idea expressed by the first or the last word, or phrase, or clause.

As with larger units of writing, the beginning of the sentence is the second most emphatic position, the middle is the least emphatic, and the end is the most emphatic of all. You can increase the clarity of your sentences if you arrange your blocks of detail accordingly. You can, for example, make a practice of beginning sentences with a key idea instead of with a minor transitional phrase. Let the positional emphasis of the beginning weigh on important items, and tuck your *for example*'s, your *however*'s, your *on the other hand*'s, and your *of course*'s into the sentence somewhere else, early enough to keep the transitions clear, but not so early that opening emphasis is wasted. Similarly, you can avoid letting your sentences trail aimlessly away on minor modifying phrases or other afterthoughts. Save the end for key words and key ideas.

You should never, of course, let your sentences become distractingly artificial. By keeping the spoken language in mind, you can place emphasis where you need it by using slight inversions of the normal order.

The normal order would be

He'll get in at twelve if the train is on time.

But it is entirely natural to say,

If the train is on time, he'll get in at twelve.

By moving the adverbial clause from its normal position at the end of the sentence and placing it at the beginning, we manage to emphasize both the important adverb and the even more important estimated time of arrival.

The normal order would be

She is going to fly to Florida during the Christmas holidays.

But we can change the emphasis by saying,

> During the Christmas holidays, she is going to fly to Florida.

The normal order would be

> The windswept and lonely old haunted house stood at the top of the hill.

But we can change the emphasis by saying,

> At the top of the hill, windswept and lonely, stood the old haunted house.

In almost every sentence, any element, word or word-group, can be shifted from its natural position to some other place in the sentence to secure varying emphasis.

There are some shifts that cannot be made—the ludicrous "misplaced modifier" (see pages 387–390) illustrates that. But usually attention to what you have actually said will prevent *illogical* or *unidiomatic* sentences. Your own common sense should prevent the *illogical* misplaced modifier, like

> Drunk and staggering, the minister's little daughter invited the tramp into the manse.

Your own ear will tell you when an inversion is too *unidiomatic* to use. No native speaker of English would ever say, or write,

> She during the Christmas holidays is to Florida going to fly.

So long as you listen to your own sentences, you can make judicious use of positional emphasis. Used judiciously, it can be a very helpful tool.

EXERCISE

Rewrite the following sentences to increase their clarity. In addition to confusion arising from ambiguous wording, length, complexity, normal stress, and positional emphasis, some of them may lack clarity because of such confusion as that resulting from weak pronoun reference, faulty verb forms, or other grammatical flaws.

> 1. Avoid confusing words that are similar but mean different things.

2. Ambiguity often results from the ease with which, in English, words may function now as one part of speech and now as another—as both noun or verb, for example, or noun or adjective, or participle or gerund, or present tense verb or infinitive —so that the writer fails to see that what he has written could be read quite differently by someone else, as in the headline early in a political campaign: "Jones Forces Open Headquarters"; it can be very confusing.

3. The major element in the story is the relation between Mr. Harding, a quiet, gentle, kindly clergyman, whose income as Warden of Hiram's Hospital, a charitable foundation for old men, is attacked by a young lawyer as contrary to the best interests of the paupers, and his own conscience.

4. What I must do is all that concerns me, not what people think.

5. Across the path of every student, be he never so diligent, so sure of his plans and his topic, so attentive to all details of the process that are suggested by his textbook or in the discussions in the classroom—during which indeed he may ask questions and seek guidance whenever he may need it—there will surely come, as he works on research papers in the library, tantalizing scraps of information that lead him down irrelevant sidetracks and waste hours or whole days of his time although adding greatly to his fund of knowledge and his awareness of the excitement that research can bring.

6. This article presents what seems to be an accurate statement of the facts.

7. A dull but diligent student may learn more from a dull but brilliant professor than a student brilliant but not diligent.

8. It is always perfectly possible that the instructor who seems too dull to be endurable will be suddenly recognized to have been the one remembered best and with most gratitude in later years, though not all the dull instructors who hug that thought to their bosoms would be gratified if they consulted the alumni.

9. If I, personally, had the chance, even briefly, to go to New York, or to some other metropolitan center, to shake the hayseed (I speak, of course, metaphorically) from my hair, I, eagerly, would go, for the change, if for nothing else, wouldn't you?

10. Denver is a mile high, and my husband almost got a divorce before I realized I was trying to cook with an East Coast cookbook.

11. It is often difficult to apply what one knows of theoretical physics to the facts of life as one lives it, as in cooking or

adjusting Venetian blinds to best advantage in different kinds of weather, to offer two examples.

12. Most people seem to believe that what is unnecessary is unwise if unpleasant, but necessarily wise if pleasant.

13. It is an unfortunate American tendency to feel that the "general welfare" should certainly be taken care of in general, but that the minute the government's concern becomes specifically involved in one's own welfare, it is generally wrong.

14. Sweet and sour put up Gretchen the pickles.

15. Male and female created He them.

CONVENTIONAL SENTENCES

To be effective, sentences must be conventional in form. They must above all, of course, observe the accepted conventions of grammar and syntax, so as not to distract the reader by elementary errors that call attention to themselves and by so doing draw attention away from the ideas the sentences are designed to convey. They must be conventionally punctuated. And they must present their ideas in one or another of the standard English sentence patterns.

As we have seen in our rephrasing of an idea to shift normal stresses and emphases at need, a given idea may be expressed in various ways, with some change each time in the exact meaning of the sentence. We have also seen, however, that English, like all languages, follows certain standard idiomatic patterns in arranging words and word-groups like phrases and clauses, and that the placing of such word-groups, consequently, is flexible but not completely free of restrictions. Within these limits, many patterns are available to the writer, all of them established by the conventions of current, national, and reputable usage. With statements, for example, the standard order is Subject, then Verb, then Complement. Each of the basic elements may be modified by various other elements, some with a fixed position (like that of the article before a noun) and some with positions that may be freely changed (like those of many adverbial modifiers). We can invert some of the normal patterns for emphasis: *Dark is the night; Down he fell; The night, dark and gloomy, ...* We can use the expletives *it* and *there* to throw the logical subject after the verb: *It is best to use this pattern sparingly.* We can combine expletive and inversion: *There but for the grace of God go I.* We can expand or contract a concept, using single words, or phrases, or clauses at need. With all this flexibility, our sentences must still be conventional.

The common sentence patterns and the conventions of grammar and punctuation are discussed in the Handbook. Here, we may concentrate on types of sentences, especially on four different ways in which conventional sentences may be classified: by purpose, by syntax, by form, and by completeness.

1. Sentences may be classified according to their **purpose**: as *declarative, interrogative, imperative,* or *exclamatory.*
   a. A *declarative* sentence is one that makes a statement.

   > I see the cat.
   > Although man has had to go out in the rain for many thousands of years, he has still not developed any very successful methods for keeping himself dry and comfortable in wet weather.
   > The upper Mississippi Valley is known as the Middle West.

   Most English sentences are declarative, stating facts or opinions of one sort or another. Any statement of idea is declarative.
   b. An *interrogative* sentence is one that asks a question.

   > What are you doing?
   > Will the *Congressional Limited* from New York get in on time?
   > Where are the snows of yesteryear?

   c. An *imperative* sentence expresses a command or entreaty.

   > Shut the door.
   > Never forget that every American in a foreign land is regarded as representative of his countrymen.
   > Please let me know what you think of my suggestion.

   d. An *exclamatory* sentence expresses more or less strong or sudden feeling. Exclamatory sentences are frequently elliptical, that is, they often omit elements that would normally be necessary for grammatical completeness.

   > How it rains!
   > How are the mighty fallen.
   > A horse! A horse! My kingdom for a horse!
   > What fools these mortals be.

2. Sentences may be classified according to their **syntax:** as *simple, compound, complex,* or *compound-complex.*

   a. A *simple* sentence is one that contains only one clause, one subject-verb combination, one predication. Either subject or verb, or both, may be compounded or extensively modified by single words or phrases. (If these grammatical terms are unfamiliar to you, see Chapter 14.)

> Fido barked.
> The little old man in the baggy brown tweed suit sat happily on the park bench in the sunshine, feeding the pigeons.
> John and Mary danced together all evening.
> Jim sat and glared at them.
> Mary and Jim quarreled the next day and broke off their engagement.

   b. A *compound* sentence contains two or more independent clauses.

> The rain fell and the wind blew.
> The surf thundered on the beach throughout the night; but by noon the storm had abated, and the sea grew more quiet.
> The gulls and the terns, soaring on the wind, were swept far to the south by the storm; however, they beat their way back northward against the dying breeze.

Normally, Standard English does not form compound sentences by combining clauses which differ in purpose.

> AVOID: My problem was not whether to attend college, but rather should I go to a school away from my home town?

If such a shift in purpose is necessary, use two sentences.

   c. A *complex* sentence contains one independent clause and one or more dependent clauses.

> I'll go whenever you are ready.
> Although I haven't studied, I hope to pass the quiz.
> Whoever holds the lucky number will win the prize that the hostess has provided. (*In this sentence, notice, the dependent clauses are directly incorporated in the independent clause, one as subject and one as an adjective modifier. Yet the sentence still has one independent clause and two dependent clauses, and is a complex sentence.*)

d. A *compound-complex* sentence contains two or more independent clauses and at least one dependent clause.

> Fraternity houses must be kept clean, and even though the pledges may feel aggrieved, they will be expected to do most of the cleaning.
> All who wish to go along will be welcome, but everyone who expects to go must be ready by eight o'clock, when the train leaves.

3. Sentences may be classified according to their **form:** as *periodic* or as *loose.*

a. A *periodic* sentence is one (like the present sentence) in which the central idea is not complete until the sentence reaches its final word. (In that sentence, notice, grammatical completeness was reached with *complete,* but the central idea at that point is so unfinished that to stop there would be to phrase a false definition.)

> At the top of the hill, windswept and lonely, stood the old haunted house.
> Elmer, studious and brilliant, actually understands differential calculus.
> There, but for the grace of God, go I.

Because the periodic sentence forces the reader to hold the entire idea in suspension until he reaches the end, and because the end of any sentence is the most emphatic point, periodic sentences are particularly emphatic. You will have noticed, too, that many periodic sentences shift details out of their normal order, and such inversion is another device for securing emphasis. Too many consecutive periodic sentences will therefore produce an over-emphatic style which is annoying—or at least distracting—to the reader, especially when the ideas expressed are relatively unimportant. But to give emphasis to important ideas, periodic sentences are very useful.

b. A *loose* sentence is any sentence which is not periodic. The term *loose* implies no derogation, for periodic sentences are too emphatic and too artificial to be used constantly, and most prose uses both types freely.

4. Sentences may be classified according to their **completeness:** as *full* or as *incomplete.*

a. A *full* sentence is a grammatically complete sentence, containing an expressed (or, as in imperative sentences, an easily supplied) subject and predicate, and not introduced by any subordinating word, unless that subordinating word belongs to a dependent clause. It conveys a complete thought. Probably all your sentences should be full sentences, unless you are writing dialogue.

b. An *incomplete* sentence (also called an "elliptical sentence," an "allowable fragment," or a "minor sentence") is not grammatically complete, but in the context in which it appears it does communicate a clear idea. Incomplete sentences are especially common in colloquial, that is, conversational, English, where meaning is conveyed as much by context, by tones of voice, by facial expressions, and by gestures as it is by words.

We seldom or never hear, for example, a conversation like this:

"Where are you going?"
"I am going to the drugstore."
"Why are you going to the drugstore?"
"I am going to the drugstore to get a package of cigarettes."

Instead we hear, and say,

"Where are you going?"
"To the drugstore."
"Why?"
"To get a pack of cigarettes."

And writing which represents speech, as in narrative dialogue, naturally uses many incomplete sentences.

In two other situations, even in formal writing, incomplete sentences are common. One is in aphorisms:

The more, the merrier.

The other is in making transitions:

To turn to our second reason.

But remember that written English must be clear in itself. It cannot depend on variations of voice or expression to help it convey meaning. Even written dialogue must be more complete than actual conversation in order to be clear, and writing which is not highly colloquial in tone will use incomplete sentences only for very special effects. Your instructor, indeed, may forbid you to use any incomplete sentences at all, feeling that you should first master the full sentence before you try your hand at the sort of writing which requires the special effects provided only by the incomplete sentence.

These four ways of classifying sentences, notice, overlap each other.

America's principal contribution to world-wide culture is Coca-Cola.

That sentence is a declarative sentence, a simple sentence, a periodic sentence, and a full sentence, all at the same time. And any conventional sentence may similarly be fitted into all four of the classification systems.

EXERCISE

Classify each of the following sentences according to their (1) purpose, (2) syntax, (3) form, (4) completeness.

EXAMPLE: James drove to the airport to meet Paula, but because he was late, as usual, he almost missed her after all.
(1) Declarative, (2) compound-complex, (3) loose, (4) full.

1. A boy's will is the wind's will.
2. As with many common quotations, it is hard to say exactly what that sentence means.
3. Ask not what your country can do for you; ask rather what you can do for your country.
4. Please answer by return mail.
5. Fire!
6. Although Bill is a man who is so talented that he could do many things very well indeed, he rarely does anything at all.
7. How many men are content to achieve less than they might?
8. How many men are content to achieve less than they might!
9. The actions of every American abroad may represent his country to every foreigner who is aware of them, but thanks to the newspapers of the world, so may his actions at home.
10. How great a pity it is that it is true.

CONCISE SENTENCES

Concise means "compressed," "brief," "expressing much in few words." Truly effective sentences say as much as possible as briefly as possible. Proverbs, epigrams, aphorisms of all sorts provide good examples of the way complicated ideas may be compressed into brief statements full of suggestion.

> Haste makes waste.
> Look before you leap.
> Strike while the iron is hot.
> Better late than never.
> If youth knew, if age could!
> Knowledge is power.
> Be prepared.

We could go on indefinitely quoting such sentences, any one of which compresses into few words ideas that would provide meat for a full-length theme.

It is not possible, of course, to reduce every idea in our themes to sentences as stark as those. In fact, it is not even desirable, both because the reader would find it difficult to assimilate important ideas so quickly and because the resulting style would be choppy and monotonous. Yet the skillful writer, the master of a flexible sentence style, can say a very great deal in a few specific words without being offensively choppy: Lincoln's Gettysburg Address is a familiar American example.

As a general principle, never use more words than you need; never make a sentence more elaborate than it must be to reflect your thought and to reach your audience. Never write a sentence of twenty words if ten words will do the same work. In revision, ruthlessly eliminate unnecessary modifiers, rambling phrases, vague and fuzzy diction. Make your sentences specific, concrete, concise. Make them go directly, efficiently, and economically to the point. *Make every word work for you.*

Much student writing is wordy, repetitious, vague, inefficient —in short, verbose. One of the major causes, of course, lies in the student's limited vocabulary; a writer cannot use an exact and efficient word that he does not know. (We will return to the problem of exact diction in Chapter 7.) But other causes are almost as important. One is an unawareness on the writer's part of exactly what is to be expressed; instead of doing the hard work of thinking, the writer rambles vaguely around and over the general concept he has in mind and hopes that in the process he has covered the ground. Another cause lies in the misapplication of the teacher's advice to "develop" the topic; instead of learning to use concrete and specific detail to clarify a generalization, the student decides that mere length is a virtue, which it is not. A third cause, closely related to the preceding one, is the feeling that "I could never fill the assigned three or four pages unless I said everything in the longest possible way." And still another cause (sprung from the adolescent's inability to comprehend the adult writing thrown at him by his high school teachers) lies in the mistaken idea that a "literary" style must of necessity be elaborate, tiresome, and incomprehensible; so the student writer embroiders even his most commonplace ideas by using his longest words and his fanciest, most involved phrasing.

The simplest, most direct way of saying something is always the best way.

You can do much to secure conciseness if, in writing and revising, you try consciously to avoid the circumlocutions of euphemisms, deadwood, smothered verbs, jargon and gobbledygook, inflated constructions, and "fine writing." With some overlapping, each can be separately examined.

Euphemisms

Euphemisms are phrases which try to gloss over unpleasant facts or to add dignity to essentially undignified circumstances. They are almost always wordier than they need to be. A euphemistic style says "passed away," or "went away," or, on a fancier level, "entered into his eternal inheritance," instead of frankly saying "died." It says "mortician," or, "funeral director" (and may shortly say "interment engineer"), instead of "undertaker." It says "sanitation engineer," instead of "plumber." It says, expansively and with secret pride, "Due to the unsanitary habituation of his domestic arrangements, his abode was offensively odoriferous," instead of saying, "Because he lived like a pig, his house smelled like a sty." The whole purpose of euphemism is to obscure ideas, not to clarify them. With due regard to the canons of good taste, say what you mean.

Deadwood

Deadwood is useless phrasing of any sort, and as the name suggests, should be pruned out as promptly as possible. If you find unnecessary introductory passages, pointless modifiers, or repetitious and aimless phrasing, blue-pencil them as ruthlessly as you would if you were a magazine editor paying for an article by the word.

> As I think of and ponder on the inner meaning of Thanksgiving, I only wish we were each and all of us truly and properly thankful and grateful for the blessings bestowed upon us in our daily lives.
> At Thanksgiving, I wish we were all thankful for our blessings. (*Eleven words do as much as thirty-eight.*)

In such a sentence, the deadwood can be eliminated by simply omitting it. In other sentences, it can be eliminated by substituting a more exact word.

> He pretended that he acted as he did to save me from embarrassment; but I don't believe that that was his only reason, and I'm not even sure it was his chief reason. (*Thirty-five words.*)
> His ostensible reason for acting as he did was to save me from embarrassment. (*Fourteen words. The term "ostensible" saves twenty-one words.*)

Redundancy, the unnecessary repetition of ideas, also results in deadwood.

> He gets up out of bed at six A.M. in the morning.
> In our modern world of today. . . .
> Why do you repeat that again?
> Spherical in shape, red in color, and heavy in weight. . . .

Smothered Verbs

Another source of wordiness, closely related to deadwood and redundancy, comes from the practice of burying the real verb concept in a noun phrase. In such a style, *compete* becomes *he is in competition with, indicate* becomes *be an indication of, consider* becomes *take into consideration.* A direct statement like *The director recommends . . .* becomes *It is the recommendation of the director. Assigning homework* burgeons into *Assignment of on-the-students'-time work should take into consideration the educative value of activities free of a direct relationship with the immediate objectives of the curriculum.*

Jargon and Gobbledygook

All these forms of wordiness are characteristic of both jargon and gobbledygook. Jargon, as defined by Sir Arthur Quiller-Couch, is the use of "circumlocution rather than short straight speech" and the habitual choice of "vague woolly abstract nouns rather than concrete ones." He lists especially *"case, instance, character, nature, condition, persuasion, degree"*; we might add *proposition, field, line, factor, aspect, situation,* such verbs as *proceed, react,* and going beyond single words, such circumlocutions as *along the lines of, my thought* (or *my idea*) *is, due to* and *due to the fact that, in regard to—* and many other wordy phrases which will occur to you. Whenever, as Quiller-Couch advises, you find yourself using such fuzzy phrasing, stop and take thought. What do you really mean? Each of those words or phrases has a legitimate use, but probably your writing will be the better if you never use any of them.

> In the case of similar propositions along this line, we have always taken a negative position.

That means only

> We have always rejected similar suggestions.

> In my case, the factor I had to consider was the tuition

means

> I had to consider the tuition.

> Here is my thought on this question: Due to the fact that we are as yet insufficiently informed regarding as to whether or not we should proceed to take implementing action or, conversely, should perhaps refrain from taking any positive line at this time, I feel that we perhaps would do better to adopt no definite conclusions and to initiate no line of action until such time as our course is more fully clarified for us

means

> Since we don't know what we're doing, let's wait.

Gobbledygook is a term invented to characterize the jargon of governmentalese, but it also fits commercialese and educationese. The new term really is no improvement over the earlier term *jargon,* but it is becoming the better known, and we can draw at least one distinction: Jargon, by and large, results from mush-mindedness; it thinks it is saying something even though it is not. Gobbledygook, on the other hand, is usually deliberate—and so is far more immoral. Gobbledygook is usually written by men who know what they mean but who do not wish to be too clear, sometimes because their letters or reports must pass through the hands of many superiors with disparate ideas and attitudes, sometimes because they do not want to commit themselves to anything definite, preferring to allow the ultimate reader to interpret their phrasing in any way he likes. We could regard gobbledygook as a purely ethical problem except for one unfortunate fact: Many naïve readers suppose that its pompous obscurity represents good writing, and they try, ill-advisedly, to imitate it.

A government official with one eye on lawyers' prose wrote,

> It is requested that the office of the Secretary be furnished with three authenticated copies of the aforementioned application, said authentication of said copies to provide such official attestation thereof as will render them legally admissible in evidence.

He probably meant,

> Send three notarized copies of the application to the Secretary's office.

There may have been some deliberate intention to "fuzz it up a little" behind this one:

> The effect of the revised regulations is thus reflected indirectly in the totality of the assessment in regard to which the subsequent payments were made.

Sheer bureaucratic timidity explains much "impersonal phrasing":

> It is suggested that the request for compensation be resubmitted with the explanation that corporation business was transacted on the day in question.

Pomposity, inflating and veiling the commonplace or the dubious, says,

> It is desirable that the learning situation be so integrated with the normality of the child's environment that the phenomena of matura-

tion may be utilized to supplement the life-oriented, core course-centered curriculum.

The chief offenders are government officials, businessmen, and pedagogues. Do not imitate them. Anything worth saying should be said in the clearest way. If what you have to say cannot stand clarity, probably it had better not be said at all.

Inflated Constructions

Verbosity also results from using inflated constructions, that is, needlessly blowing up an idea that could be expressed in a single word and saying it instead in a phrase or a clause or even a series of separate sentences, or from using any grammatical construction of greater weight than the detail deserves.

> The house, which was old, was on St. Amelia's Island adjacent to the coast of Florida; it had been there for over two hundred years. This large home had been the residence of many generations of the people who had owned the plantation.

> The large old house on St. Amelia's Island, just off the Florida coast, had been for over two hundred years the home of the owners of the plantation.

Nearly all the sentences illustrating deadwood and jargon and gobbledygook also illustrate the use of inflated constructions. We shall reserve consideration of the cure—reducing predication by properly subordinating lesser ideas to greater—until we consider the flexible sentence later in this chapter (pages 149–158).

"Fine Writing"

Most of the types of verbosity we have so far examined are characteristic of mediocre writers. "Fine writing" (which is emphatically not *good* writing) is a sin of apprentice writers who may someday learn to write very skillfully. "Fine writing" is any writing which is too elaborate for its subject. "Fine writing" is embroidery, preferring big words to little ones, indulging in all sorts of rhetorical flourishes merely to be "literary." It represents what the developing writer thinks of smugly as his "style" and is a source of more or less secret pride. When the instructor objects to it, the student is hurt and bewildered.

But the instructor, if he is to do his critical duty, must still object, because "fine writing" is very distracting to the reader. Save your impassioned prose for moments of high emotional stress. Use your vocabulary with an eye to exactness of meaning and effectiveness of communication, not to its impressiveness. Use every rhetorical device at your command to convey your idea effectively to your reader; if you are skillful, no one can object. But, please, when all you want to do is to say that it's raining, or to ask somebody to pass the potatoes, try not to sound like a third-rate tragedian mouthing *King Lear*.

> As a person nears the threshold of maturity, he must confront the necessity for deciding what field of professional endeavor will most appropriately challenge and absorb his capabilities, and must begin in earnest to prepare himself educationally therefor. So universally is this truth recognized that every institution of higher learning makes the selection of a field of academic concentration compulsory upon all within its walls before they can be admitted to the exalted status of upperclassmen.

That must mean

> All college students must choose a major by the beginning of their junior year.

In every sentence you write, be as concise as you can. The space and time and energy you save can then be used to develop details which really require development.

EXERCISE

Rewrite the following sentences to make them more concise by eliminating euphemisms, deadwood, smothered verbs, jargon, inflated constructions, and "fine writing."

1. It is a simple task to find the class within which the median must lie, but the difficult problem is the exact determination of the proper division point within this median class.
2. The efficacy of hydrochloric acid for eliminating precipitational residues from drainage conduits is indisputable, but the resultant corrosive action is incompatible with metallic permanence.
3. Responsibility cannot be assumed for the production of toxic, noxious, and corrosive residues resulting from the employment of hydrochloric acid as a cleaning agent in plumbing; conse-

quently, it is the urgent recommendation of this agency that an alternative procedure be adopted.

4. Don't use hydrochloric acid in plumbing. It eats hell out of the pipes.

5. I see no reason to cease to consider that I have the right to discontinue my membership by not reenrolling myself in the association.

6. Abide until the domesticated lactating ruminants revert unto their domiciliary shelters.

7. There have been published recently a number of books which attempt to describe the utilization by American manufacturers of professional psychologists to stimulate, by psychological methods, the marketing of goods.

8. Due importance should be credited to the writing of a research paper as an assignment in English in view of the benefit which may be derived from familiarity with its structure and the conventional methods of approach and procedure.

9. Due to the fact that the proposition was definitely controversial, my thought was that further consideration should be given to those factors regarded as insufficiently established by experts in the field.

10. The long ferry ride across the water which separated St. Amelia's Island from the mainland was drawing to a close. I could see the small island in the distance. The palm trees which grew all around its periphery seemed to insulate it from prying eyes.

11. In this modern world of today the sanitary engineer collects domestic waste from the sanitary safes provided by the individual resident, transports it in scientifically designed disposal vehicles to the municipal sanitary landfill, and then proceeds to the quarters of the disbursing officer to collect the remuneration due him for his professional services.

12. The Stock Exchange floor is organized for the purpose of providing for the interchange of information between the representatives of buyers and sellers of stock.

FLEXIBLE SENTENCES

The English sentence is an extremely flexible instrument, one which a skillful writer may mold and shape to his purposes in such a way as to secure almost infinite variety within the conventional patterns, reflecting within each sentence subtle nuances and interrelations of thought, and creating by the interplay of patterns from sentence to sentence a mosaic which itself heightens the effectiveness of the writing. A given detail may be presented in a full sentence, in an independent clause, in a subordinate clause, in one or another kind of phrase, or in a single word. The detail may be shifted about in the sentence to give it greater or less positional emphasis or to take advantage of natural stress. The length of sentences and the type of sentence within the conventional classes we have just been considering (see pages 136–141) may be varied. The very sounds of the sentence may be used to reinforce the sense. There is almost no limit to the variations a skillful writer may exploit.

Because no two men think in exactly the same way, different writers will of course use different sentence patterns. It is, indeed, largely the characteristic sentence patterns a writer employs which form his individual style. No one would confuse, say, the staccato, simple-sentence prose of Ernest Hemingway with the longer, rhythmic complexities of Thomas Wolfe. Yet any writer, as his purpose requires, may employ any sort of sentence; no practiced writer confines himself to set formulas, but chooses skillfully the sentence-tool which will best do the work he wants done.

It is presupposed, of course, that the writer knows what effects he wants to achieve, that his thought is mature and sharply clarified in his own mind before he tries to express it. But it is also presupposed that the writer knows how to use the sentence-tools that lie ready to his hand and can choose a sentence pattern with a fore-knowledge of what it will do.

Simple Concepts

Frequently, of course, a writer has an important but simple idea to express, one for which a single subject-verb predication works most effectively.

Every President must shoulder tremendous burdens.

Whenever a simple sentence with a simple modification works best, it should certainly be used.

But most of the time our concepts are more complex, and the writer bears the responsibility for indicating the relative importance and the interrelationships of the phases of his thought through his arrangement of details and through a judicious use of effective coordination or subordination.

Effective Coordination: Parallelism

Coordinate means "equal." When a writer uses coordinate elements, elements of equal grammatical rank, he says to the reader that he regards the ideas they express as equal in logical importance. Two sentences, two independent clauses, or any two grammatically similar subordinate constructions are coordinate within each pair; and as the writer parallels the kind of element he uses to express related details, he invites the reader to parallel the concepts.

The most emphatic type of coordination is also the simplest: two equal ideas expressed in two simple sentences.

The King is dead. Long live the King.

Obviously, such emphatic simplicity is out of place unless the ideas themselves are so important that the bare, stark sentences will seem justified. Used for unimportant ideas, such coordination is excessive (see Chapter 12), and the result is the primer style of "I see the cat. The cat sees me."

Also highly emphatic, when it is properly used, is the compound sentence. Such a construction, with two ideas expressed by independent clauses within a single sentence, says to the reader by its very form, "Here are two concepts of such prime importance that each deserves a complete predication, and either might have stood alone as a distinct idea. Yet together, even though neither modifies the other, they express a larger idea which itself is a single concept; the whole is something more than the mere sum of its parts."

King Arthur was incomparable; no greater leader ever lived.

Only slightly less emphatic is the compound sentence whose two clauses are connected by a conjunctive adverb.

Vain is the help of man; therefore, trust thyself.

Still less emphatic is the compound sentence whose two clauses are connected by a coordinating conjunction.

The sun shone warmly, and the grass grew greener by the hour.

A fourth type, with more than two independent clauses, can by its punctuation and its choice of connectives suggest varying degrees of separation between its clauses.

She sings with good voice and great sincerity, and she obviously understands the songs; but somehow she falls short of greatness in her performance.

However, the truly unified sentence-idea which can be best expressed by setting logically equal and independent ideas side by side in the same sentence is comparatively rare, and many students grossly overuse compound sentences. It would be a good practice to question the value of every one you write, to be sure the idea cannot be better expressed by subordinating one element to another. Then, when you do permit yourself to use a compound sentence, you can be certain that the form of your sentence, as well as the words, is adding to the effect you want to achieve.

Yet in skillful hands, the paralleling of independent clauses or even of simple sentences can be very effective indeed.

Once, from eastern ocean to western ocean, the land stretched away without names. Nameless headlands split the surf; nameless lakes reflected nameless mountains; and nameless rivers flowed through nameless valleys into nameless bays.

George R. Stewart

The reader expects parallel ideas of any sort to be put into appropriate parallel patterns, and failure to use parallelism can be a distracting flaw. We may keep the effective repetition of key terms in that passage and still seriously weaken the second of those sentences merely by avoiding the parallelism:

Nameless headlands split the surf; and the mountains and lakes were nameless; and nobody had yet given names to any rivers or valleys, to say nothing of naming the bays into which the rivers flowed.

That version of the idea is reasonably grammatical and is perfectly clear, but it has little of the pith and pungency of Stewart's sentence. And notice one other point. Parallelism at any stage is economical. The original sentence contains twenty words; our "revision" contains thirty-five. Even if we shorten the possibly wordy "to say nothing of naming" by substituting "or named," we still save only three words.

Coordination of Minor Elements: Still Parallelism

Even though such effective coordination of independent elements is comparatively rare, coordination of lesser elements, also known as parallelism, is very common. One general principle always governs the innumerable forms parallelism may take: *Similar ideas are expressed by similar sentence elements.*

You have long been familiar with the device. Early in life you learned to use compound subjects, compound verbs, compound complements. Instead of saying,

Craigie is going to the store, and Daddy is going to the store,

you used parallelism and said,

Craigie and Daddy are going to the store.

You said,

Daddy dropped the sack and broke the eggs.

You said,

Daddy broke the eggs and all the bottles.

And as your life grew more complex, you learned to use still more and more complicated parallel compounds, in pairs, in threes (as in the A, B, and C series), or even in larger groups.

Almost any sort of sentence element may be used in parallel construction:

SINGLE WORDS: John and Mary danced, sang, and ate hamburgers. John later crawled wearily but contentedly into his bed.

Mary sat up for hours, gossiping about her exciting evening and listening resignedly to the dull accounts the other girls gave of their tiresome affairs.

Tall, dark men come readily into the lives of petite, blonde girls.

PHRASES: To add to their knowledge of geography and to increase their understanding of their fellowmen, most men are willing to attend a convention in a distant city.

On the land, on the sea, or in the air, it is comforting to have faith in your mechanic.

CLAUSES: If you insist and if I have time, I'll do it for you.

The student who has studied diligently and who has the good fortune to be asked the right questions can face an examination with equanimity.

In your writing—or more likely in your rewriting and revising— watch for every chance to put parallel ideas into parallel sentence elements, whatever function those elements perform in the sentence. Your reader will expect you to use the device, and when you do use it, not only will you write more effective sentences, you will also write concise sentences that will save both you and the reader from wasting time and effort.

Effective Subordination

Instead of being equal and requiring coordination, many of our ideas are unequal and require expression in elements which in one way or another suggest that inequality. If it is essential that we know how to put equal ideas in parallel, coordinate sentence patterns, it is at least as important that we know how to subordinate lesser ideas to greater.

We could say,

> The girl wore blue. The blue went well with her blonde hair. She was charming. She attracted much attention.

But we might better say,

> The charming blonde girl in the becoming blue dress attracted much attention.

Or, if her charm is more important than the attention,

> The attractive blonde girl in blue was charming.

Or

> The charming, attractive blonde wore blue.

Or

> Blue was becoming to the charming, attractive blonde.

And we could say it in still other ways.

Almost any idea can be expressed in many ways, with slight or greater changes in the meaning with each change in phrasing. The writer's problem is to find the best way for his purpose and his audience. Even a simple factual statement may take many forms:

> Abraham Lincoln was six feet, four inches tall.
> Six feet, four inches tall stood Abraham Lincoln.

Abraham Lincoln was tall, measuring six feet, four inches.

Six feet, four inches tall was the stature to which Abraham Lincoln towered.

And so on. Again, the simplest and most direct way of phrasing an idea is always the best way. Unless some special reason, like the maintaining of an established rhythm, makes a more elaborate sentence desirable, the first of those sentences about Lincoln is the best, because it goes straight to the point, with no flourishes.

But not many of our sentences are concerned with the expression of simple and single fact. As our ideas grow more complex, the choice of sentence patterns widens for us; by the exactness of the words we choose and by the constructions through which we present each detail and the position we assign each detail in the sentence, we control the responses our readers make to the ideas we offer for their consideration.

For any given idea, the choices available to us are numerous. The type of sentence we use, its length, its complexity—all may be varied widely. Our basic guide goes back to the simple generalization: *Shape the sentence to reflect the thought.* The purpose of the sentence, the context in which it appears, the audience addressed— on such considerations as these must the final choice depend.

Suppose, for example, you find that in the heat of first-draft composition you have written,

Everybody who lives in a democratic country agrees that the protection of the rights of the citizen is one of the first duties of the state. But every right implies a responsibility, and so there is something just as important as protecting rights and that is fulfilling our responsibilities as citizens, which too many of us do not do.

As you revise the paper, you realize that those two sentences express a major idea of your theme which deserves more emphatic phrasing than your first exploratory circumlocutions gave it. Much can be done to sharpen the idea; many patterns can be tried.

In a democracy, it is essential that the rights of the citizen be protected, but it is no less essential that the responsibilities of the citizen be not forgotten.

This first revision has already gained greatly in conciseness: Twenty-nine words do virtually all the work done by fifty-nine words in the first draft. "Everybody who lives in a democratic country agrees that," for instance, has been reduced to "In a democracy." Three words say as much as nine words said before. Even more important, the detail which at first provided the subject and verb of the first main clause has been reduced to more nearly its proper logical dimensions by being relegated to a prepositional phrase, becoming a brief modifier and leaving the major ideas room to assume a major place in the sentence. Further, the formless rambling of the first version has been disciplined and brought to a balance between the two basic parts of the whole concept. Parallelism has replaced wordy chaos.

But we may not yet be through. The vague "it is" is twice repeated, and the main points appear only as complements to the vapid verb. And the whole second half of the concept is buried in a negative statement, and only the reader who is alert enough to reverse our phrasing will realize the vigorous affirmation we might have made.

We could say it in other ways.

> In a democracy, the rights of the citizen must be protected; but equally the responsibilities of the citizen must be fulfilled.

Or

> The citizen demands protection of his rights; the state may in turn expect fulfillment of the citizen's responsibilities.

Or we may decide that one detail or the other deserves to be given the greater emphasis, and try subordinating one to another:

> Although every citizen expects the state to protect his rights, most men neglect to carry out their political responsibilities.
> Although few men carry out their political responsibilities, every man expects the state to protect his rights.

Or, with as few changes in diction as possible, but with different emphases and consequently a different idea with each rephrasing:

> Two duties are inherent in democracy: the duty of the state to protect the rights of the citizen, and the duty of the citizen to fulfill his obligations to the state.
> No less important, in a democracy, than the state's duty to protect the rights of the citizen, is the duty of the citizen to fulfill his political responsibilities to the state.

A man who slights his political responsibilities risks his political rights.

A man who finds he has lost his political rights may well find that he first neglected his political responsibilities.

The man who is worried about his rights should perhaps be more worried about his responsibilities.

The state must protect the rights of every citizen, even of those who flout all of the responsibilities of citizenship.

To slight one's responsibilities is to jeopardize one's rights.

Who, in a democracy, can shirk his responsibilities without risking the loss of his rights?

How great a risk to our rights is run when we disregard our responsibilities!

Even the man who neglects his responsibilities may demand that the state protect his rights.

—And the idea could be phrased in many other ways, depending on the precise point the writer wishes to make, the audience addressed, the position of the sentence in the mosaic of the whole composition, and the tone of the whole paper.

As our diction is well or ill chosen, the same sentence pattern may be strong or flabby, sharp or fuzzy. But given exact diction, we can vary our sentence patterns and shift the relative positions of details to make our sentences flexible. We must always remember, of course, that the sentence is a tool and not an end in itself. Freakish complexities—like unnecessary or strained inversions, overuse of absolute phrases, too long or too complicated patterns—merely call attention to themselves and consequently take the reader's attention away from what we are saying. But mature thought demands mature sentences. At the very least, our most important sentences should be carefully scrutinized and various patterns should be tried; and no sentence should be allowed to stand unless we are satisfied that it says what we mean.

Variety

Mastery of a flexible sentence style, stemming from practice with various types of sentences and resulting in skill in selecting the sentence pattern which will most accurately reflect your thought, will almost automatically lead to writing in which the sentence patterns are pleasingly varied. Sentence variety is not a virtue in itself, though an absence of sentence variety will be monotonous to your reader, will be distracting, will suggest that your thought is immature, and so will be a positive flaw. Lack of sentence variety in your writing, therefore, is a danger signal; the cure lies less in an attempt to secure variety for its own sake than in a renewed effort to be sure that you know clearly and exactly what you want to say and to be sure that the sentence patterns you choose are those which will most effectively convey that thought to your audience.

EXERCISES

A. The following series of simple sentences presents a concept which might be expressed in many ways. As an exercise in sentence flexibility, write ten sentences, each of which incorporates as many as possible of the ideas in the passage. Vary your emphasis on different parts of the concept, and consequently your sentence patterns, to present variations in meaning. Avoid, however, merely freakish complexity.

We believe in education. The American educational system is varied. Public or private schools are available to all through the high school level. Many go to college. Democracy demands educated citizens. Not all who could profit from college can now attend. This should be changed.

B. Rewrite the following passage to provide coherence and mature flexibility of sentence patterns.

Surprisingly few people ever look up. Many otherwise meticulous housewives never notice cobwebs near the ceiling. They just leave them. Not one housewife in a thousand dusts the tops of doors or the tops of door and window frames. Run a finger along the top of a door. You'll see. Think of the clever child. He discovers that he can nearly always win at hide and seek. He just climbs a tree. In plain sight, he is seldom discovered. He may be discovered, of course. Then he can no longer use trees. But indoors on a rainy day he can still hide from the same opponent. He just climbs to the top shelf of a closet. Much advertising money is spent on signs high above city streets. They are brilliantly lighted. They flash on and off. Few people pay attention.

EUPHONIOUS SENTENCES

Euphonius means "pleasant sounding." It emphatically does not mean "pretty-pretty." The euphonius sentence is pleasant to read; but it is pleasant because its sound reinforces its sense, not merely because it is melodious.

In considering euphony, the craftsman touches the realm of the artist. Many writers whose sentences are clear, conventional, concise, and flexible still lack the sensitivity of ear which alone assures euphony. Some of our greatest poets, even, seem sometimes to have lacked it: Wordsworth, for example, or Browning. But the diligent craftsman blessed with a sensitive ear can approach very close to art, and even the tone-deaf writer can at least avoid the clatter and jangle of harsh cacophony. The student writer is rarely an artist, but even the most unimaginative student can still apply certain general principles which will allow him to produce craftsmanship of a very high order. Cole Porter was no Bach and no Shakespeare, but he lived a long, long way from the dead ends of Tin Pan Alley.

And we should notice, before we consider euphony in detail, that it is not a topic beyond the concern of the engineer, the lawyer, or any other writer of purely workaday prose. The university Admissions Officer should be ashamed of: "By special permission the conditions of admission may be modified." The very sound of his sentence keeps the reader from thinking about the idea. A teacher presenting a discussion of "An Evaluation of Education in the Nation" is standing in his own light. The engineer should avoid recommending that "the bridge should be run from the edge of the ledge below the ridge." Such awkward and useless rhymes are flaws in any writing, because, by distracting the reader, *they interfere with communication.*

Stress

The first characteristic of the euphonious sentence is characteristic also of the clear sentence: When the euphonious sentence is read naturally, the stresses fall on the important words. The euphonious sentence requires no unnatural emphases, no artificial pauses. It flows continuously from one major detail to the next major detail, and its minor details swirl into the thought during the stretches of comparative still water between. It is literally the fluent sentence.

Faulty stress often accompanies other weaknesses, notably lack of satisfactory rhythm. We shall see many examples as we consider other faults. Here, notice two extremes of faulty stress that interfere with ease of reading. The first sentence stresses too many elements; the second give us long clusters of light stresses.

> It is interesting, too, to note not only new scarred areas, but scars still present far beyond time for normal absorption.
>
> It was also the intellectual stimulation of associating with congenial seekers of plain living and high thinking who would at least listen to the young man's half-formulated ideas which helped to free Thoreau from dependence on established, customary assumptions.

Cacophony

The second characteristic of the euphonious sentence is that it avoids its opposite, the unnecessarily harsh, tongue-twisting sounds of cacophony.

> The Eskimo, Googbik, gets great globs of blubber to gulp greedily whenever the surging sea sends stranded whales straight to the beach that stretches before the door of his icy igloo.

Few writers would ever complete a sentence like that. But here is one that was caught only on the seventh revision:

> Food on which the fish might feed is scarce.

It is very nearly as bad as Googbik and his globs of blubber.

In your writing—except when you are trying to achieve special effects—avoid jawbreaking cacophonies of contiguous guttural or spitting dental consonants, the crackling cackle of acrid vowels, and the seriously distracting hiss resulting from accidental series of sibilant *s*'s (as Tennyson put it, "Kick the geese out of the boat"). Excise, at least in revision, the jangles and rattles and clatters, the harshly clashing awkwardnesses you may have permitted yourself to perpetrate in putting down your thronging thoughts—however freely fluent you thought you found your first draft. In revising, read aloud what you have written and *listen* to it. Eliminate all unnecessary dissonances, like the thump and bump of resounding heavy vowels muttering and rumbling pointlessly through your prose;

eliminate accidental alliterations, overly regular rhythms, and the chimes of rhyme you were not aware of at the time you wrote a line, but find as you reread what you have written—a writer who neglects to follow that advice may write clearly and accurately, but he will never write well.

Such writing is both tiring and confusing, even when it is read silently. If you will read the preceding paragraph aloud, your throat and your ear will both tell you how bad it is. And psychologists long ago discovered that when we read silently we make barely perceptible movements with our vocal organs as our minds almost trigger the muscles we use in speaking. (If you wish to test that, open your mouth and relax the muscles; then *think* to yourself, "Got a bottle?" See?) Even if you read very rapidly, long eye spans and all, tongue-twisting prose is physically tiring because it is literally hard to read; it should be avoided for reasons quite aside from esthetic ones.

It is also confusing. As our tongues and lips and vocal cords try to stumble through the verbal gymnastics set for them, our minds are inevitably distracted from the thought we should be absorbing, and communication is broken.

Avoid the harsh sounds of cacophony.

Alliteration and Rhyme

Among the weaknesses illustrated in that tongue-twisting passage are two devices that may, with skillful handling, prove to be virtues. One is alliteration, the repetition of similar initial sounds, at the beginnings of words or of strong syllables. The poet often uses the device; the writer of prose uses it too, but with caution, in pairs or triads of sound. But alliteration, like other rhetorical tricks, ought never to distract the reader from the idea you are trying to convey, as it will if you overdo it. The second weakness that may be a virtue if well handled is rhyme, the repetition of terminal sounds. A more accurate label for the device as it is employed in prose might be *assonance*, which implies only similarity of vowels, not identity of both vowel and consonant sounds. An intentional, well-placed near rhyme is often pleasing to the reader, and echoes of sound help in tying parts of the sentence together. But accidental rhyme, like accidental alliteration, is nearly always bad.

Could anyone seriously pay attention to the thought in such sentences as these?

> Much of the beauty in Thoreau's writing . . . is derived from his ability to take natural facts perceived with the senses by close observation and then use his intuitive writer's instinct for the right word to write what might be described as quite lyrical prose.

(One inevitably wonders what such a writer could know about beauty in anyone's prose.)

> For those who get seasick, I would advise the avoidance of these sea trips. Ships are slow, and air fare is not much greater than sea fare.

Rhythm

In poetry, rhythm may be complicated, but it is regular and stylized enough to enable almost anyone to learn to recognize it and classify it. Rhythm in prose is very nearly as important, but because it cannot be too regular without being distracting, prose rhythm is so extremely complex that no one has ever yet succeeded in developing a system that will codify and explain it. Yet every man who has a sensitive ear and reads widely is aware that some prose halts and stutters and stumbles, not because the writer has been unclear or unconventional, but simply because some writers never seem to realize when they have too many syllables or too few, too many stresses in a bunch or too long a run of words in which no particular stresses appear.

But even though prose rhythm cannot be explained, perhaps its importance may be illustrated by an analogy: The jazz musician, playing without music, may take a chorus on his trumpet and insert all sorts of variations on the basic theme. His improvisation may be brief or it may be extended, but it must in every note be appropriate. If he has no feeling for improvisation, his auditors will be bored or annoyed; if he is successful, they may be wildly enthusiastic. We might say of prose rhythm what Louis Armstrong said of jazz: "If you gotta ask what it is, you'll never get to know."

Yet many people who could not play a note on a trumpet can recognize inept rhythms in a trumpet solo; and many writers who permit themselves to produce nonrhythmic prose could recognize their own ineptitude if they read their sentences aloud and really listened to what they were saying. Most ideas can be expressed in many ways in English—in one-syllabled words or in longer words, in shorter or longer phrases, in clauses of greater or lesser complexity. If a sentence is so regular that it falls into sing-song, if it too noticeably repeats stress patterns, if it halts in the wrong places, if it spills over beyond the point at which it should have paused, try other combinations until the rhythms seem appropriate.

No one, surely, should leave sentences like these in prose which is meant to be taken seriously:

> Even the greatest of geologists are compelled to rely upon theory, logic, and natural laws in reasoning back from effect to cause.
> Yellow grass grew thinly on shale slopes, like hair on scraggy scalps.

Onomatopoeia

Almost from your earliest grade school days you have heard, perhaps with annoyance, of the poets' use of *onomatopoeia*, the conscious use of sounds that reflect the sense. English is full of onomatopoeic words, like *buzz* and *bump* and *hiss* and *crackle*. Even the child who shouts "Bang!" or rattles machine-gun noises over his larynx is illustrating the rhetorical principles involved. The prose writer no less than the poet may command the device. But like the poetical devices of rhyme and alliteration, onomatopoeia must in prose be used discreetly, as an aid to understanding rather than as a mere flourish of ornament. Like all rhetorical devices, onomatopoeia should never obtrude. The reader who admires your writing enough to go back to analyze your methods will be pleased to discover that you have used it; but if he notices it on first reading, you have distracted him and thereby failed in your basic purpose of focusing his attention on your idea.

The sounds of words, the stresses and the pauses of the sentence, and the rhythm of the sentence pattern are all involved in any consideration of onomatopoeia, and the whole problem is too complex for anything like an exhaustive treatment. But the writer who is even aware of its existence can, by listening and by taking pains, make use of the device—at least to the extent of avoiding a harsh and staccato racket in his description of a boy and a girl peacefully together in a canoe under the willows bordering a moonlit lake. He can suggest languor by consciously using long, open sentences full of liquid sounds—*l*'s and *r*'s, *m*'s and *n*'s, *s*'s (in moderation), *o*'s and *ah*'s and *oo*'s. He can, under different circumstances, suggest excitement and tension by using short, choppy sentences full of short vowels and bitten-off consonants. He can make his sentences sputter when he is angry or purr when he is contented; race or glide or amble or stumble or lurch, in harmony with the thought he is expressing. And if he has a touch of the artist in him, in addition to plenty of the conscientious craftsman, he can make his sentences soar and sing, as well.

A few obvious examples of onomatopoeic prose:

> Grandmother stumbled just at the head of the stairs and fell with a bumping, clattering rush into a pitiful crumple at the foot.
> The inhabitants of stagnating Willmore City looked out upon eight miles of curving beach with the blue Pacific rollers lazily tumbling into creamy foam. They decided to announce themselves to the world as a seaside resort, and took the name Long Beach.
> *George R. Stewart*

> Even as I tried desperately to plot the safest route through the boiling rapids, the canoe was seized by sudden whitewater and shot unguided down a sickening swirl, past the boulders, and into the pool of quiet water below.
> I straightened [the airplane] out of the skid, partly by a desperate glance at the bank-and-turn indicator, climbed in a quivering rush of speed up over the glistening smear of lights from the congested area of Camden and Philadelphia, and took up the compass course . . . to Bolling Field, Washington.
> *Beirne Lay, Jr.*

> Smack! Thock! Slump! He's down! Wave the champ to a neutral corner. Pick up the count. ". . . Two, three, four. . . ." The fans are wild. "Nine, *ten!*" "The *win*nah, and *still* champ-i-on, *Joe* PALOOKA!"
> Moving shoreward above the steeply rising floor of the deep sea, from dark blue water to troubled green, [waves] pass the edge of "soundings" and roll up over the continental shelf in confused ripplings and turbulence.
> *Rachel L. Carson*

And a final, detailed look at part of a sentence of Robert Louis Stevenson's about a boy at sea in a small boat:

The whole world now heaved giddily up, and now rushed giddily downward . . . .

That sentence, thanks to its vowels and its consonants, its stresses and its pauses and its pace, has the very sound of the slow, agonizing sweep up the wave, the sickening pause at the crest, and the dizzying slide into the trough below—the very feel of queasiness in a pitching boat. Read it aloud and listen. The first slow vowels, the lighter faster lift of *heaved*, the jiggle of *giddily*, the high halt of *up and now*, the dizziness of *rushed giddily down*—every vowel and consonant is exactly right.

No two readers will respond to a sentence in exactly the same way; but if we listen to the weight, tone, and speed of the vowels and consonants, and the stress and sometimes the pitch of the voice, nearly everyone will read that sentence something like this:

```
                    up,
                        and now
            ly                  rush'
           di-                   d
           gid-                 giddi-
       heaved                        ly
          now
The        world                           downward.
     whole
```

That wave-pattern of sound did not spill itself onto the page by chance. An examination of Stevenson's manuscript clearly reveals the artist's careful polishing to get the effect he wanted.[1]

As Stevenson first wrote it, the first half of the sentence ran—or skittered:

```
            up
                    gid-
            with me      di-
                            ly—
        heaved
            now
      The        world
           whole
```

[1] I am indebted for this information to Margaret Wilsey's article, *"Kidnapped,* in Manuscript," *The American Scholar,* Spring, 1948.

The artist's ear caught that at once as an impossible rhythm, and Stevenson blotted the sentence on the page and substituted the phrasing whose rhythm and pitch would give the effect he needed, ending on the strong high note of *up* instead of on the jiggling which *giddily* suggests when the sentence stresses fall on the word.

He originally began the second half of the sentence as

sick-

en-

now   ing-

ly—

Then he broke off again to rephrase it. After the high note of *up*, he added the delaying syllable *and*, substituted the glissando of *rushed* for the four bumping syllables of *sickeningly*, and echoed the very suggestive *giddily*, which here carries a falling stress. A master craftsman might have ended the wave with *down*, paralleling the sense and contrasting the sound and pitch of *up*. But Stevenson, the artist, went one syllable farther, and instead of *down* he wrote *downward*. That final unstressed syllable is sheer inspiration. It stops the whole thought dead in the trough of the wave and lets the reader feel with the seasick boy the desperate hope that somehow a miracle will prevent another wave from following the one that has just been surmounted and survived.

The reader—any reader—is not, of course, consciously aware of all this as he reads the sentence. (If he were, he would stop reading to admire the artistry, and so would lose track of the idea the artist wanted to convey.) But the effects are there in the sentence; the suggestions of sound and pace and pitch and pause, as well as the basic suggestions of meaning in the words, are all there. And the artistry is there, too, quite deliberately, as Stevenson's manuscript shows, with its first thoughts crossed out and the improvements inserted in revision. That sentence might have read,

> The whole world now heaved up with me giddily, now sickeningly rushed down.

If Stevenson had left it so, it would have been clear, concise, and conventional, and its companion sentences would have proved Stevenson a master of sentence flexibility. But it would have been less than an adequate sentence. He did not leave it so. He wrote, revised, and rewrote until he had said,

> The whole world now heaved giddily up, and now rushed giddily downward.

Perhaps not every sentence we write can normally be given so much attention, even in revision. But every sentence, and every composition, can be improved beyond the accidents of the first draft if we keep the principles of euphony in mind as we give each sentence the best and the most judicious attention we feel we can afford.

EXERCISES

A. What elements of the following sentences prevent them from being euphonious? Rewrite them to express the same ideas but to eliminate unnecessary harshness.

1. In the Brace case, the ace witness for the defense was Pence.
2. The only thing that was keeping me calm was my imagination, which was conjuring up pictures of my saving the situation.
3. He thought of going down to Hatch's candy store to look at the nickel-novel cover pictures in the window.
4. With silent strokes, the Indian drove his canoe over the shadowy water, carefully avoiding any rattle of his paddle against the gunwale to betray his presence.
5. Manuscript evidence [on Anglo-Saxon tools] would seem to imply that the blade of the spade was set at one side of the handle.
6. In the time of the month when the moon is at full, it is pleasant to walk in the fields in the night, or to stroll down a beach by a thundering surf, or to sit at the edge of a mountainous cliff—or to be in the open, wherever you are.
7. When shining shoes, the best policy is to use plenty of polish.
8. Vultures are great, black birds with thin, bare, red, ugly heads.
9. Graceful, aloof, subtle, tactful, analytical—Metternich was all of these, as befitted a diplomat. Doctrinaire, rational, determined, steadfast, he personified conservatism. His unmistakable vanity, pride, self-confidence, and shrewdness did, however, cause controversies among his friends and later among historians.
10. Given time and community support, we can make equality of educational opportunity a reality in the United States.

B. Analyze the following passages to identify elements which make them euphonious.

    1. . . . Every sound is sweet:
      Myriads of rivulets hurrying thro' the lawn,
      The moan of doves in immemorial elms,
      And murmuring of innumerable bees.

                                  Alfred Tennyson

    2. . . . From the long line of spray
      Where the sea meets the moon-blanched land,
      Listen! you hear the grating roar
      Of pebbles which the waves draw back, and fling,
      At their return, up the high strand,
      Begin, and cease, and then again begin,
      With tremulous cadence slow, and bring
      The eternal note of sadness in.

                                  Matthew Arnold

    3. Within the inlet the channel widened and the pale-green water grew murky. . . . The mutter and rumble of the surf grew. With their sensitive flanks the fish perceived the heavy jar and thud of sea vibrations. The changing pulse of the sea was caused by the long inlet bar, where the water foamed to a white froth as the waves spilled over it. Now the mullet passed out through the channel and felt the longer rhythms of the sea—the rise, the sudden lift and fall of waves come from the deep Atlantic.

                                  Rachel Carson

    4. Sometimes of an evening [the priest] would leave the . . . [wigwam], to read his breviary in peace by the light of the moon. In the forest around sounded the sharp crack of frost-riven trees; and from the horizon to the zenith shot up the silent meteors of the northern lights, in whose fitful flashings the awe-struck Indians beheld the dancing of the spirits of the dead. The cold gnawed him to the bone, and, his devotions over, he turned back shivering. The illumined hut, from many a chink and crevice, shot forth into the gloom long streams of light athwart the twisted boughs. He stooped and entered. All within glowed red and fiery around the blazing pine-knots, where, like brutes in their kennel, were gathered the savage crew. He stepped to his place, over recumbent bodies and leggined and moccasined limbs, and seated himself on the carpet of spruce boughs. . . .

                                  Francis Parkman

5. Four times in the known history of the earth have the mountains risen like a tide. Three times have the forces of air and water made head against those mountains, eating away the towering granite peaks into little rounded hills. Two hundred and fifty million years is the period of that cycle—majestic among earthly rhythms.

George R. Stewart

6. Stand for half an hour beside the Fall of Schaffhausen, . . . and watch how the vault of water first bends, unbroken, in pure polished velocity, over the arching rocks at the brow of the cataract, covering them with a dome of crystal twenty feet thick, so swift that its motion is unseen except when a foam globe from above darts over it like a falling star; . . . and how, ever and anon, startling you with its white flash, a jet of spray leaps hissing out of the fall, like a rocket, bursting in the wind and filling the air with light; . . . and how, through the curdling wreaths of the restless crashing abyss below, the blue of the water, paled by the foam in its body, shows purer than the sky through white rain-cloud.

John Ruskin

7. [Glenn Gould] is good, very good. . . . His playing is clean and the piano colors he produces dart and shimmer. Moreover, . . . he is a musician well in advance of his twenty-odd years. His phrases are not simply flat statements of musical fact, but are full of lift and lilt and life.

Jay Harrison

8. . . . By the end of 1863 all illusions had vanished. The South knew they had lost the war, and would be conquered and flattened. It is one of the enduring glories of the American nation that this made no difference to the Confederate resistance. In the North, where success was certain, they could afford to have bitter division. On the beaten side the departure of hope left only the resolve to perish arms in hand. Better the complete destruction of the whole generation and the devastation of their enormous land, better that every farm should be burned, every city bombarded, every fighting man killed, than that history should record that they had yielded. Any man can be trampled down by superior force, and death, in whatever shape it comes, is only death, which comes to all. It might seem incredible when we survey the military consequences of 1863 that the torments of war should have been prolonged through the whole of 1864 and

into 1865. "Kill us if you can; destroy all we have," cried the South. "As you will," replied the steadfast majority of the North.

Sir Winston Churchill

9. In the dark the old man could feel the morning coming and as he rowed he heard the trembling sound as flying fish left the water and the hissing that their stiff set wings made as they soared away in the darkness.

Ernest Hemingway

7 ⸗

Diction

Characteristics of a Good Theme: 9. Compression, or conciseness. 10. Exact and appropriate diction.

The modern student is very fortunate in having excellent dictionaries to which he can turn for guidance during the years when he is developing his vocabulary, and by means of which all his life he can keep a firm grasp on the basic tools of communication. In our study of diction—the words we use—we shall first examine the modern desk dictionary. Later, we shall consider ways by which you can improve your own vocabulary, and the importance of selecting always the exact word and the appropriate word for your purpose and your audience.

THE DICTIONARY AND ITS USE

A good dictionary is basically a selected list of the words in the language and a record of how they are used. As we shall see, it is also much more than that, so that in sum it is the most valuable single reference book you will ever own. Before you buy any other book, buy an up-to-date, well-edited, college-level dictionary. Buy it, and then use it. Your instructor may insist on a particular dictionary. If the choice is left to you, examine the *American College Dictionary*, Funk and Wagnall's *Standard College Dictionary*, the *Webster's New World Dictionary*, college edition, and the Merriam-Webster *Webster's Seventh New Collegiate Dictionary*, and buy whichever seems to you most satisfactory. *Do not try to get by without a dictionary. And do not depend on a "cheap dictionary."*

Your college library owns several general, unabridged dictionaries and many specialized ones. You can and should go there to familiarize yourself with the *Oxford English Dictionary* (also known as the *New English Dictionary* or the *Murray Dictionary*), an invaluable, multivolumed work tracing the historical development of words and providing dated quotations to record the changes which words have undergone. You should also familiarize yourself with the Merriam-Webster *Webster's New International Dictionary of the English Language,* third edition, with the Funk and Wagnall's *New Standard Dictionary,* and with any specialized dictionaries in technical fields in which you are interested. But for daily use, all through college and long after, you should *own* and *use* one of the more limited desk dictionaries already listed.

Remember, as you use it, that it is not infallible. It does not establish standards. Rather, it records the best usage discoverable at the time it went to press. But language will not stand still even for dictionary makers, and consequently every dictionary is more or less out of date when it first appears. New words and new uses for old words come into the language constantly. Other words, especially slang terms, cease to be used. Pronunciations change. Syntactical functions vary. But even though no dictionary can be infallible, unless you are certain that your dictionary is wrong, follow the guidance it offers as the most authoritative guidance available.

Be sure, however, that you understand the guidance that is offered. Far too many students use their dictionaries hurriedly and thoughtlessly, and either fail to get all they could from their dictionaries or misunderstand what they think they have found. Many words, for example, have multiple meanings, only one of which makes sense in any particular context; you cannot merely dip into the word entry and fasten on the first definition you see. Usage labels differ from one dictionary to another; for guidance on usage you must know the policies your dictionary follows. No matter which dictionary you buy, *read the introductory material explaining its methods very carefully.*

Supplementary Sections

What does a good desk dictionary offer? More, probably, than you think. Examine the table of contents to see the wealth of material you will overlook if you use the volume only to check on spellings or definitions of unfamiliar words. Explanatory notes on the methods of the dictionary itself are obviously useful. Useful, too, are the supplementary discussions of pronunciation, of the derivation of words from older English or from other languages, of usage levels, of punctuation and mechanics, of spelling practices, of letter writing, of common abbreviations. Other lists, less useful but handy when you need them, are also available. Any good desk dictionary provides a great deal of reference material besides that contained in the basic vocabulary entries. Study all the supplementary sections in your own dictionary and make use of them.

The Dictionary Proper

The alphabetical vocabulary entries, of course, are the soul and most of the body of the dictionary. Used intelligently, they will yield a vast amount of information. In order to get the most from your dictionary, study the prefatory matter explaining its policies and its methods, and examine the illustrative examples carefully as you do so; then check your understanding by testing yourself on sample pages. If you do not understand what your dictionary tries to tell you by the order of entries, the punctuation, the abbreviations, and even the variations in type, you can go far astray when you think you know what "the dictionary says." The following discussions are concerned with what you can learn about a word by consulting the vocabulary entry; but to learn to read the vocabulary entry, you must read the editor's explanations very carefully.

SPELLING

The word entry itself gives you the standard spelling of the word. If more than one spelling is acceptable, the variants will be given, those noticeably less common being marked specifically as variants of the commoner form. (See *dependence, dependance*.) All spellings listed are in wide use, but in multiple listings, the first is generally preferred in American usage. (See *color, colour*.)

SYLLABICATION

A syllable is a single unit of spoken sound. In writing, if we need to divide a word at the end of a line to maintain a margin, we do so only between syllables, and the dictionary entry is the safest guide to follow. (See *photo-offset*.)

ACCENTUATION

The light and heavy accent marks indicate relative degrees of stress on syllables in the spoken word. (See *accentuation*.)

CAPITALIZATION

The word entry itself, or a subsidiary entry, will show customary capitalization. (See *Pre-Raphaelite*.)

PRONUNCIATION

After the word entry comes a semiphonetic respelling indicating the common pronunciation or pronunciations, if more than one is used by educated speakers. To use the pronunciation entry, consult the brief guide to pronunciation. When in doubt, consult the fuller treatments of pronunciation in the prefaces.

Any pronunciation which is recorded is acceptable. It is generally unwise to try to change an established pronunciation habit to conform to the dictionary preference, so long as your habitual pronunciation is recorded at all.

PART OF SPEECH

After the pronunciation entry come abbreviated indications of the common syntactical functions of the word, preceding the definitions applicable to each function. (See *telephone*.) As a rule, avoid using any word in a syntactical function not recorded in your dictionary.

ETYMOLOGY

The etymological entries are more important than most students realize. By forming the habit of studying them carefully whenever you look up a word, you will become conscious of the interrelations of words built on similar roots or employing similar prefixes and suffixes; you will gain an insight into the ways in which English has freely borrowed from other tongues to build up its prodigious vocabular wealth; and you will gain many clues to the eccentricities of English spelling. (Be sure, as you study the etymological entries, that you understand them, including the abbreviations they employ.)

DEFINITION

The main section of each word entry presents a concise explanation of the basic ideas conveyed by the word, of its denotations (see pages 204–206). For some words, one definition is enough, since the word conveys but one basic idea in any context in which it appears. For many other words, however, several definitions are necessary. To use the dictionary efficiently, you must be careful to select the definition which explains the word *in the context in which you find it*. In order to do that, you must be familiar with the principles according to which your dictionary arranges multiple definitions and with the labels it employs to identify meanings which are restricted to special uses. Detailed explanations of both points are given in the introductory matter at the front of the volume. Here, especially, practice varies from one dictionary to another. Study your own dictionary carefully.

As you look up the meaning of an unfamiliar word, consider the context in which it appears, including its syntactical function, and find the definition appropriate to that context. As a rule, if no restricting label governs that definition, the word may be used in writing addressed to the general, educated audience. Your own intelligence, however, may sometimes suggest that even unlabeled terms will convey little to the particular audience you are trying to reach or are out of harmony with the prevailing tone of your paper.

SYNONYMY

Where several words are roughly synonymous in basic meaning but suggest different ideas and so are used in different contexts, a brief discussion attempts to explain the distinctions between them. Study any synonymies appended to word entries you are consulting, or follow up any cross-references; they may save you from making ludicrous mistakes in diction. (See *ludicrous*.)

FOREIGN WORDS AND PHRASES

Many words which are not yet English are nevertheless frequently encountered in English writing. Such foreign words and common foreign phrases are entered in the general vocabulary but are marked as non-English. If you use foreign words in your own writing, italicize (underline) them. (See *sang-froid* and *weltanschauung*.)

MYTHOLOGICAL OR LITERARY FIGURES

A great many characters from mythology or from literature are identified under regular entries in the general vocabulary. If your reading introduces allusions to such characters, check your dictionary. (See *Sancho Panza*.)

BIOGRAPHICAL OR GEOGRAPHICAL ENTRIES

Names and identifying details about many people and places are included in your dictionary, sometimes in the general vocabulary, sometimes in separate lists. (See *Alfred, Innsbruck*.)

ILLUSTRATIONS AND OTHER MATERIAL

There are numerous inserted illustrations of various kinds. (See *type, zodiac*, and *zone*.)

No more valuable reference book has ever been compiled than the well-edited, up-to-date dictionary; and the college-level desk dictionary that you have been required to buy for your freshman English course is a worthy representative. Examine it, study it, use it —enjoy it. It can be prodigiously helpful so long as you prevent it from gathering dust at the back of your desk.

EXERCISES

A. Write out and hand in to your instructor brief answers to the following questions. Indicate which dictionary you are consulting, including the date or edition.

1. Does your dictionary discuss the varying pronunciation of such words as *ask, bath, laugh?* Where?
2. How does your dictionary use the abbreviations *fr.* and *Fr.* (or *f.* and *F.*) in tracing etymologies?
3. What is generally meant by the abbreviation *Cantab.?*
4. When was Queen Elizabeth I born?
5. Where is Schaffhausen?
6. What is the American and the British spelling practice in regard to the doubling of a final *l* before a suffix beginning with a vowel?
7. Where does your dictionary discuss general practice in the hyphenation of compound words?
8. Where is the University of Delaware located?

B. 1. What are the variant spellings of *eyrie, judgment, dependent, glamour?* Which is preferred in American usage? What is the plural of *bacterium, alumna, basis, echo?*

2. Indicate the syllabication, accentuation, and pronunciation of each of the words in B1, above.

3. Trace the etymology of *circumference, curfew, bonfire, coward, democracy, Icarian, warden, wattage.*

C. 1. How many general definitions does your dictionary list for *wave?* How many specialized definitions? *Wave* may be used as what parts of speech?

2. Define *enervate, colloquial, abstract, general, concrete, specific.*

3. How many synonyms does your dictionary list for *physical?* What are they? Use each in a sentence.

4. Define *in posse, sans souci, ich dien.*

5. Who were *Narcissus, Frigga, Mrs. Malaprop, Japheth, Laertes?*

BUILDING VOCABULARY

A great part of our lives is spent in exchanging ideas with others. And since words represent ideas, are in fact the tools by which we shape and express ideas, it follows that the more words a man commands, the more ideas he can comprehend. (The key word there is *commands.* Words which are only imperfectly understood can obscure more than they clarify.) In a very real sense, until we have the words we do not have the ideas. In college, a very large percentage of the work is word work—reading texts, writing examinations and papers, listening to lectures, exchanging information and opinions with instructors and classmates. The student who misses the import of one word out of ten cannot possibly get as much from his college years as the student whose vocabulary allows him to understand everything he hears or reads.

Increasing one's vocabulary is a vital part of getting an education. The process is slow and difficult, but in the end is very rewarding. But remember that the rewards come in the mastery of clearer thought, not in acquiring an impressive array of polysyllables with which to dazzle and confuse your auditors. You are not being urged to acquire "big words" for their own sake. *The simplest, most direct way of saying something is always the best way.* Only when your word hoard is large can you easily select the exact word which will permit you to express yourself most simply and directly for the audience you are addressing.

Context

We acquire words by listening and reading, by observing how they work in context—the verbal and physical surroundings in which they appear. Our grasp of the words we thus acquire depends very largely on the acuteness with which we observe the context (or the various contexts) in which we meet them. Context may make striking differences. Even familiar combinations of letters may convey quite different meanings in different contextual surroundings.

> You lead, and I'll follow.
> Lead is one of the heaviest metals.
> The more you read, the larger your vocabulary will be.
> Yesterday I read twenty chapters of our history text.
> Man o' War was a fast horse.
> Tie the horse fast to the hitching post.
> That clock always did run fast.
> The train made its run exactly on time.
> She developed a run in her new stockings.
> Walk, don't run, to the nearest exit.
> The two battles of Bull Run were important in the Civil War.
> Do you think the newspaper will run that story?
> The press run of his new book was not big enough to meet the demand.
> After a final run, the fish was brought to the gaff.
> The spring run of shad was unusually large last year.
> This airplane is regularly used in the transcontinental run.

We could go on multiplying examples, but there is no need. Obviously, the context tells us much about the meaning of words.

As we meet new words, we examine them in context. What must they mean, to make sense as they are used? Very often, the context alone gives us (if we are alert and thinking) a clear idea of the meaning of new terms. If we meet the new words again in a similar context, we recognize them and confirm our earlier guesses. And presently we have the new words fixed in our *recognition vocabulary*, that is, the list of words we readily understand when we hear them or read them, even though we rarely or never use them ourselves in speaking or writing.

But context can be misleading—especially if we are not always alert as we read. For many words which we have met again and again, we have only the haziest notion of the meanings. Or, we may fix in our minds very clear notions of meanings which later prove to be completely wrong. An excellent example lies in the word *prodigal*. We have all heard the parable of the Prodigal Son, who prematurely took his share of the family inheritance, spent it, went to work as a swineherd, and finally returned home, to be met with his father's forgiveness and to feast on the fatted calf—much to his brother's annoyance. Whether our sympathies lie with the Prodigal, his father, his brother, or the calf, we all know the word *prodigal*.

Or do we?

How would you define it?

With what word is it synonymous? Repentant? Returned? Replete? Desperate? Forgiven? Traveled? Experienced? Extravagant? Extroverted? Impatient? Impetuous? Impervious? Envied? Pitied?

What is meant by the phrase, "The prodigality of nature"?

Context alone is not an infallible guide.

The Dictionary, the Synonymy, the Thesaurus

Three types of references books are especially designed to help us confirm or correct our own observations of words in context: the dictionary, the synonymy, and the thesaurus.

Of the three, the *dictionary*, which we have already examined in detail in the first section of this chapter, is the most useful. When you meet a new word, or an old word in a new context, the dictionary stands ready on your desk to confirm your impressions of what the word may mean or to correct them if you have come to erroneous conclusions. It offers you a word list, indicates current and obsolete, general and specialized definitions, traces derivations, and suggests interrelations and often connotations. As you presumably already know, the dictionary is invaluable. Whenever you come across a term which is not crystal clear from the context, *go to your dictionary*. Study it intelligently until you are certain you understand the new term in the context in which it appears.

A *synonymy* is useful as a supplement to the dictionary. Its greatest value lies in its attempt to differentiate between the connotations, that is, the suggestions, of words, distinguishing between words which by definition or appearance seem to mean approximately the same thing, but which are by no means interchangeable— for example, *unspeakable, unutterable,* and *ineffable*. It is also useful, although less so than the thesaurus, as a word finder, reminding you of a word you know but cannot at the moment recall. The best of the synonymies is the Merriam-Webster *Dictionary of Synonyms.*

A *thesaurus* is a self-styled treasury of words, arranged usually according to a more or less complicated system of associated ideas, but indexed or alphabetized, so that the user may consult a general conceptual group and from it select the exact term he requires. For the man whose recognition vocabulary is large, it is very useful, but it does not differentiate between the words it lists, and consequently a writer whose vocabulary is not exact and extensive may get into trouble if he tries to select and use words which he does not completely understand. It reminds us of words we already know, but it does little to help us improve our vocabularies. It should be used in conjunction with a good dictionary. The best-known thesaurus is *Roget's International Thesaurus.*

Word Families

The first step in building vocabulary comes in recognizing new words as we hear them or read them. The second comes in observing their use in context and, if necessary, checking our conclusions against the dictionary or some other word list. A third step comes in learning to recognize recurrent parts of words—roots, prefixes, and suffixes—and by so doing learning to recognize family resemblances between a new word and words we already know.

For many of our words are related to other words in the language. This is true of words of native stock—words from the parent Anglo-Saxon—as well as words borrowed from French or directly from Greek and Latin. But because our words from Greek and Latin are by and large more recent borrowings, it is easiest to see family resemblances among words from classical sources. And now that fewer of us learn Greek and Latin, it is all the more important to make a conscious effort to recognize the most common elements taken from those languages and combined in English to form English words. Such words, indeed, will form a high percentage of the new words encountered in college.

As you consult your dictionary, examine the etymologies which trace the derivations of the words. You will soon find familiar elements turning up again and again in various combinations. And presently, when you meet a new word, you may be able to make a better guess as to its probable meaning, for you will now have not only context to help you, but also a growing knowledge of the functions of classical roots, prefixes, and suffixes in Modern English.

Here, we can list the most frequent ones and suggest, by sample words, some of the ways in which they are combined and some of the forms they may take.

Roots

GREEK

anthropos (man) anthropoid, philanthropy, anthropocentric
graphein (to write) graphic, telegraphy, geography
logos (word) logic, geology, dialogue
metron (measure) metric, metronome, micrometer
oide (song) ode, melody, parody
philos (loving) philosophy, philanthropy, bibliophile
phone (sound) telephone, phonograph, audiophone
photos (light) photograph, photosynthesis, photometer
thesis (to hold) synthesis, hypothesis, parenthesis

LATIN

amare (to love) amateur, amorous, amative
aqua (water) aquarium, aquamarine, aqueduct
bene (well) benefit, beneficent, benefactor
dicere (to say) dictate, diction, dictionary
ducere (to lead) education, deduction, reduce
facere (to make, do) manufacture, benefit, perfect
jacere (to throw) reject, inject, objection
lux (light) lucid, elucidate, translucent
mittere (to send) admit, permission, missive
portare (to carry) transport, portable, report
spectare (to look at) inspect, spectacle, prospector
urbs (city) urban, urbane, suburb
volere (to wish) benevolent, malevolent, voluntary

Prefixes

(Notice that the spelling is sometimes affected by the initial sound of the root.)

GREEK

a- (not) amoral, aseptic
anti- (against) antipathy, Antichrist

arch- (chief) archbishop, architect
auto- (self) automatic, automobile
epi- (on top) epidermis, episode
ex- (out of) exodus, eccentricity
hemi- (half) hemisphere, hemicycle
hetero- (different) heterodox, heterogeneous
homo- (same) homogeneous, homologous
hyper- (above) hyperbole, hyperthyroid
hypo- (beneath) hypochondria, hypocrite
micro- (small) microcosm, microscope
mono- (one) monologue, monotony
neo- (new) neophyte, Neoplatonist
pan- (all) panorama, Pan-American
para- (beside) parallel, paratyphoid
peri- (around) periscope, period
poly- (many) polysyllable, polygamy
pro- (before) program, prologue
pseudo- (false) pseudonym, pseudoscience
syn- (together, with) synthetic, sympathy
tele- (far) television, telepathy

LATIN

ab- (from) abduct, avert
ad- (to) adhesion, acclimate, aggression
ante- (before) antedate, antecedent
bi- (two) bisect, biennial
circum- (around) circumference, circumstance
com- (with) coherence, confidence, collaborate, correlate
contra- (against) contradict, contrary
de- (down from) descend, delimit
dis- (away from) dispel, disseminate
ex- (out of) expel, egress
in- (into) inject, illustrate, immigrate
in- (not) innumerable, immeasurable, irreligious
inter- (between) intervene, intercollegiate
intra- (inside) intramural, intravenous
mal- (bad) maladjusted, malevolent
multi- (many) multiply, multilingual
non- (not) noncommittal, nonresident
per- (through) persuade, persevere
pre- (before) preconception, prejudice
pro- (before, for) proclivity, pro-Russian

re- (back) reclaim, reconsider
retro- (back) retroactive, retrograde
semi- (half) semicircle, semimilitary
sub- (under) subversive, submarine
super- (above) superior, superintendent
trans- (across) transition, transportation
tri- (three) triangle, trinity
un- (not) unacceptable, untrustworthy
uni- (one) union, unicellular

Suffixes

(Never modified in spelling.)

GREEK AND LATIN

-able, -ible replaceable, intelligible
-acy illiteracy
-age mileage, cartage
-al natural, formal
-ance, -ence resistance, existence
-ar, -or scholar, doctor
-ate graduate, illustrate
-ic historic, mimic
-ical historical, physical
-ion, -sion, -tion union, dissension, reproduction
-ious glorious, curious
-ism capitalism, opportunism
-ist hypnotist, allergist
-ive recessive, operative
-ment judgment, establishment
-ous onerous, valorous

As you consult your dictionary, be on the lookout for common roots, prefixes, and suffixes. If you learn to recognize family resemblances, you will soon find that you have at least a nodding acquaintance with whole families of words.

The Active Vocabulary

Most of our attention so far has been on building a recognition vocabulary, learning the meanings of new words met in the course of listening or reading. A large majority of the words we "know" remain passively in our recognition vocabulary, helping us understand others, but useless when we wish to make ourselves understood. Yet we are all of necessity speakers and writers as well as listeners and readers, and much of our success in expressing our own thoughts depends on how many words we can promote from our recognition vocabulary to our *active vocabulary,* that is, the words we ourselves use in communicating our ideas to others.

The most important device in improving the active vocabulary is conscious practice. As you meet new words, carefully observe their context and then confirm or correct your guess as to their meaning by judicious reference to the dictionary. Then make a conscious effort to use the new words in a similar context. Be sure, of course, that the occasion is appropriate. A learned word like *acquiesce,* for example, would be entirely fitting in formal writing, but would be out of place in replying to someone who had casually invited you to have a coke at the Union. The inappropriate word is never effective, no matter how exact it may be. Be sure, too, that you are using it exactly. The aim is not to "build a vocabulary" just to have one, but to learn words that will enable you to express your ideas more clearly. Inexact usage will confuse rather than clarify.

You may find it helpful to keep a list in your notebook. As you meet a new word, enter it in your list. Copy down the sentence in which it appears, to be sure you have the word in context, and make up two or three similar sentences using the word. From time to time, run over the list to see how accurately you can define each word and how readily you can use it.

As you write, draw consciously on your recognition vocabulary —preferably during revision—to improve the exactness and the appropriateness of your diction. Question each word, especially each vaguely general word. Do you know or have you ever met a word which will more exactly say what you mean? Could some of your rambling phrases be made more concise if you could recall some half-forgotten word that precisely expresses the concept you are struggling to clarify? If there is such a word somewhere near the tip of your tongue, search for it. We Americans are conditioned to "accept no substitutes." Here the synonymy or the thesaurus is more useful than the dictionary. By looking up the general word with which you are dissatisfied, you can examine the related words until you find the exact word for your purpose. Then, if lingering doubts remain, you can check that recovered word by the dictionary to be sure it really means what you think it does.

Never be satisfied with less than the most exact, the most appropriate word you know; never miss a chance to add a useful new word to your recognition vocabulary and to your active vocabulary. As you speak or write, remember your purpose and your audience. Strive consciously to make your diction as effective as you possibly can.

EXERCISES

A. Select the words which are most nearly synonymous with the italicized words in the identifying phrases. After you have finished, consult your dictionary.

1. an apt *analogy:* (a) science (b) comparison (c) analysis
2. *inert* matter: (a) inactive (b) difficult (c) unerring
3. *latent* power: (a) hidden (b) thwarted (c) exhausted
4. an *inexorable* pursuit: (a) unsuccessful (b) relentless (c) ill-advised
5. a *nebulous* concept: (a) atomic (b) false (c) vague
6. a distinct *entity:* (a) request (b) surprise (c) being
7. a *baleful* look: (a) sinister (b) bound (c) ingratiating
8. *tenacious* of purpose: (a) careless (b) tender (c) persistent
9. an *extant* manuscript: (a) still existing (b) destroyed (c) illegible
10. *tacit* agreement: (a) explicit (b) implied (c) tactful
11. a *plausible* story: (a) credible (b) praiseworthy (c) feasible
12. familiar *aphorisms:* (a) love potions (b) maxims (c) insects
13. a chance *mutation:* (a) silencing (b) discovery (c) alteration
14. a *mendicant* friar: (a) dishonest (b) traveling (c) begging
15. a common *fallacy:* (a) reason for falling (b) invalid argument (c) falsehood

B. Write definitions for *lead, read, fast,* and *run,* as they are used in the sentences on page 178.
C. Select ten of the common Greek and Latin roots, ten of the prefixes and ten suffixes on pages 181–183. For each, list three words containing it. Do not use any of the words listed in the text. Consult your dictionary to be sure the words really are related.

EFFECTIVE DICTION

The writer should question every word he uses to be sure it is doing its full measure of work. As he revises, he should ruthlessly blue-pencil any useless phrasing and sharpen his diction until every word is the most efficient word for his purpose, saying exactly what he means to say, most simply and most directly, to the audience he is addressing.

In learning to reach that ideal, we shall consider first the *exact word*—including the sources of meaning; the difference between concrete and abstract, specific and general words; the ways in which meanings may change from time to time; the confusion of similar words. And then we shall examine the *appropriate word*—the levels of usage, denotation and connotation, literal and figurative language, repetition, and the flaws of redundancy and triteness.

The Exact Word

Using the word that says exactly what you mean presupposes a vocabulary extensive enough to provide freedom of choice. It also presupposes some awareness of how words come to mean what they do, of what kind of word may be exact in itself and what kind needs additional clarifying detail, and of how meanings shift from time to time.

THE MEANINGS OF WORDS

No one can say that a baked combination of flour, water, yeast, and shortening is necessarily *bread*, or *Brot*, or *pain*. One can only say that large groups of people think of a particular kind of food when they hear the sound we represent by *bread*, others when they hear *Brot*, and still others when they hear *pain*. A word, then, is simply a sound or a written symbol for a sound that makes people think of certain things, and the meaning of a word is derived basically from an informal agreement among groups of people to think certain thoughts when they hear certain sounds. It is derived from general agreement on the relationship between a *term*, the word, and its *referent*, the idea to which it points.

Some terms, however, point to more concrete and specific referents than others. There are many kinds of bread—white, rye, whole wheat, Vienna, and many more. The more specific the term, the more nearly both the writer and the reader will think of the same referent when the term is used. The most specific term of all is the proper name, referring to (meaning) only one thing, or the very precise verb, like *boil*, which asserts a sharply definable action. Yet even such terms as these do not mean exactly the same thing at all times to all men, under all conditions. *Allardyce Jarvice III* is a proper name and refers to a single person; yet the term calls up quite different responses from his mother and from the family lawyer who has to spend a great deal of time getting him out of trouble. And the term means different things at different times: When Allardyce Jarvice III was twenty-two, he was constantly in and out of police courts; at fifty-five, he may have become the starchiest of stuffed shirts. *Fido* means one thing to the owner of a particular fox terrier and quite another to the mailman on the route. *Boil* means one thing at sea level and quite another high in the Rockies.

And as we move away from proper nouns and sharply defined verbs, the difficulties multiply. The more general a word is, the less the writer and the reader will think the same thoughts as they hear it. *Fido, fox terrier, dog, animal*—each of those could point to the same referent, but each in turn is more extensive in its coverage and so points less directly to a specific object which both the writer and the reader can visualize clearly. (If the writer says *dog*, thinking of his fox terrier, and the reader reads *dog* and thinks of his own sleepy Saint Bernard, the two minds are going to be some way apart at a moment which might be important.) "He is a *tall* man." Who is speaking, the basketball coach who is used to men of six feet four, or a girl of four feet six? "He is *energetic*." Who says so, the hare or the tortoise? The words themselves can point to all sorts of referents, more or less general, according to the point of view of the speaker.

Abstractions cause as much trouble as generalizations. Many of our words point to referents which exist only as concepts in our minds. *Patriotism, virtue, truth*—each man, according to his own experience and understanding, has his own idea of what such words mean. There exist in nature no tangible referents at all for such terms; we can only say, in illustrative detail, "By such words I mean thus and so, and do not mean such and such." To use the words alone is very nearly futile.

This is not to say that there is no place in good writing for such abstractions as *virtue*, nor for such general terms as *dog*. Such words are essential to the abstracting, generalizing, and categorizing of human experience which make expository writing meaningful. But the writer must never use more abstract or general terms than he needs to use, and when he does use them he must pin them down and relate them to the reader's experience by means of concrete and specific examples. He must try always to give the reader sharply defined referents to show clearly what the abstractions and the generalizations mean to him and what he expects them to mean to the reader. He must *develop* his ideas in enough detail to be clear.

We need not get into such obviously fuzzy terms as *virtue* or *patriotism* to find complexity. What do you really mean by such an apparently innocent term as "a good time"? What is "an easy course"? To one man it is English 1, to another Mathematics 1; yet rarely would both courses seem easy to the same student. Even such terms need concrete, specific development. And the less exactly your words point to particular, individualized referents, the greater the need for illustrative developing detail.

If your instructor, in his comments on your themes, says, "This is too general to be very clear," examine the diction. Have you used too many abstract words, too many general words? Have you left them undeveloped, with insufficient examples and details to make clear exactly what they mean to you? If you have, add whatever is needed.

Yet often our ideas can be expressed more clearly, not by adding details to explain vaguely general or abstract phrasing, but by substituting more exact, concrete, and specific terms.

That thing over there is not very good.

What, precisely, is "that thing"? Where is "there"? And what does "not very good" convey, beyond a general idea of rejection? With the same number of words, we could be much more definite.

That handbag on the table is badly scuffed.

Another illustration·

GENERAL: The man moved along the road.
SPECIFIC: The tramp shuffled down the lane.
SPECIFIC: The policeman stalked across the intersection.
SPECIFIC: The major strode down the company street.
SPECIFIC: Mr. Hyde stumped along the pavement.

Each of those specific sentences says far more than the general sentence that weakly blankets all of them.

The trouble that it takes to find the exact word pays big dividends, both in more exact communication and in more concise and efficient communication. The concrete and specific word not only says much in itself, but it suggests even more. What picture is called up by, "The tramp shuffled down the lane"? The word *tramp* suggests not only a human male, but also something of the man's appearance, energy, and character. How is he dressed? Has he shaved lately? Would you choose him as a partner in cutting through a four-foot log with a two-man saw? Would you ask him to watch your suitcase while you went back for a package you had forgotten? The word *man* could not suggest half so much. Further, consider *shuffled*. Does it add to the idea of the tramp's character? What ambitious, energetic youth ever shuffled, save on the way to school in June? Does the word tell anything about the time of year? Do more people shuffle on a hot, dry day than on a cold, wet one? Is dust involved? What does *lane* suggest? Country, surely. Tree shade, perhaps. Concrete pavement? Certainly not. Much time and space in presenting a picture can be saved by the writer who says, "The tramp shuffled down the lane," instead of, "The man moved along the road." All those suggested details may still need to be filled in and emphasized, according to the writer's need, but a sharp and graphic picture may be filled in much more briefly from that concrete, specific sentence than from a fuzzily general one.

Let us try one more example, this time expository.

> When the thing on the dashboard acts funny, it means you've got trouble with the lights.
> If the dashboard turn-signal indicator flickers, either the flasher or a front or rear bulb has burned out.

The exact word is more efficient than the inexact one.

EUPHEMISMS, JARGON, AND GOBBLEDYGOOK

In studying the effective sentence we have already met euphemisms, and jargon and gobbledygook (pages 143–147). Because the use of such diction almost inevitably leads to wordy sentences, these are all sentence problems. But notice that that wordiness would disappear if more exact diction were chosen. If necessary, review those sections of Chapter 6, concentrating this time on the individual words rather than on the sentence patterns.

COUNTER WORDS, OR UTILITY WORDS

Many of the words we use to blanket thoughts instead of to clarify them were once sharply distinct in meaning. Used by generations of speakers and writers, they have gradually worn down smooth, as coins do when they pass and repass over the retail counters of the world until not only the sharp edges of their designs disappear, but the coins themselves become so thin that not even a discriminating slot machine will accept them at face value. As an intelligent human being, avoid words that have worn so thin they would be rejected by any self-respecting verbal slot machine.

Adjectives and adverbs are the chief offenders. *Awfully, terrible, wonderful, lovely, nice, definitely, lousy.* Who thinks of *awe, terror, wonder, love, discrimination* (to say nothing of *ignorance*), *definition,* or *lice,* when those counter words are used?

It was a lovely evening. I had an awfully nice time.

There are better ways to express that idea, if there really is an idea to express.

Choose always the exact word, the word that has the best chance of meaning to your reader what it means to you.

Sources of Meaning

No one knows how language first began; the ultimate sources of meaning are lost in the mists. But a good deal is known about the development of language and about the family tree of English. Our language is a member of the great Indo-European language family, to which belong nearly all the languages of Europe, including the Slavic, and other languages extending into the Indian Peninsula. All these tongues have developed from a parent language spoken by a people who long ago lived in East Central Europe; and the vocabularies of the Indo-European languages, including most of the English vocabulary, have developed from the relative handful of words that they knew.[1] This development comes largely from changes in meaning, often through imaginatively metaphoric appli-

[1] For a very stimulating discussion, see Charlton Laird, *The Miracle of Language* (New York: Fawcett World Library, 1957).

cation of an established word to a new concept only slightly similar to the previous one. Sometimes, as in naming a new invention, the change is deliberate; more often it is the result of a gradual drift of meaning, or of a playful slanginess that fills a need and so becomes established in the standard vocabulary.

From the single Latin word *caput,* "head," for example, have come into English by various means such words as *capital, capitalize, cap, chief* and *chieftain, cadet, decapitate, capstone, chef, captain,* and many more. To catch a glimpse of the ways in which such proliferation of meanings may come about, let's follow one thread. From *caput* in the sense which has given us *captain* and *chief,* the diminutive *capitellium,* roughly "baby chief," led to a French *capdet,* applied to a younger son accompanying an army at his own expense, as a sort of apprentice officer. From this in turn we get *cadet,* an aspirant for a commission as at West Point, and *cadet,* a younger son or a secondary branch of a family. Probably because the younger generation often behaves in ways that displease the elders, *cadet* as the younger son spawned the British term *cad* for one who, though of gentle birth, does not act like a gentleman. Meanwhile, in a divergent sense, perhaps because shavetails are seldom popular, the French *capdet* or *cadet* also developed the meaning "servant" or "errand boy." The "Auld Alliance" between the French and the Scots introduced *cadet* into Scotland as *caddy,* "a servant." Then it was specialized to "a boy who carries the golf bag," and America has adopted that meaning, too. By such means, through many years and many languages, has the enormous English vocabulary developed.

The Common Patterns of Change

Captain, chief, cadet, cad, and *caddy* all got into English through four common types of changes in meaning, or semantic change. At various times, existing meanings spread out to include other concepts or shrank to more specialized meanings; at the same time, they developed more favorable or less favorable overtones.

Change is always taking place, in these and other ways. We often disapprove of it when we are aware of it at all, but we must admit its existence. In diction as everywhere else in language, the source of correctness is *national, reputable,* and *current* usage. The writer must be sure that he is using words the way his intended audience will interpret them—and the reader must interpret words according to the agreed meanings at the time and place they were written.

Sometimes changes in meaning come quickly. When Prime Minister Chamberlain returned to London from the Munich conference with Adolf Hitler in 1938, he announced that he had agreed to Hitler's demands as part of the British government's policy of appeasement, which would guarantee "peace in our time." Then the bombs began to fall, and *appeasement* changed overnight from "pacification, conciliation" to "sacrificing a moral principle to avert aggression." No Secretary of State now would think of labeling a new proposal as "a policy of appeasement," even though in derivation the word implies "leading to peace." Sometimes changes come very slowly, as with *wan,* which meant "dark, gloomy" when it was applied in the tenth-century *Beowulf* to Grendel, "the wan marsh stalker," but had come to mean "livid, pallid, sickly" six hundred years later, when Sir John Suckling asked, "Why so pale and wan, fond lover?" Quickly or slowly, as men use words the meanings may shift. The writer and the reader must be alert.

The two words *wan* and *appeasement* illustrate the most extreme kind of change, reversal of meaning. Other common changes are less spectacular but just as important. The spreading and shrinking of meaning that brought us *captain, chief, cadet, cad,* and *caddy,* and the favorable or unfavorable overtones of the new words are technically known as **extension, restriction, amelioration, and pejoration.**

By **extension,** words which once pointed to very specific referents expand their meanings to cover general classes. Very often the name of an individual person is used to suggest the type of behavior for which he is best known. Perhaps the most familiar example is *Caesar,* or its form *czar,* for an arbitrary despot. Usually the original specific referent is forgotten: Who thinks of Duns Scotus when he uses the word *dunce* or of generals in the Crimean War when he wears a coat with *raglan* sleeves or buys a *cardigan* sweater? *Canary,* the name of a group of islands, has been extended to a species of bird and from there to a shade of yellow. *Watt* and *diesel* are now common nouns; so are such former trademark names as *thermos, linoleum, cellophane,* and *zipper.* It is by extension, too, that such counter words as *definitely* wilt and lose their firmness.

A great many words are extended metaphorically, as *caput* often was. Its Germanic cognate, *head*, has been metaphorically applied to the governing brains of many a figurative body, as in "the *head* of the house," "the *head* of the English department." It has also moved from its place at the top of the human body to the top of other things, as in "the *head* of the stairs," "the *head* of navigation on the river." Parts of the body are often extended. From a bent *elbow* we get an *elbow joint* in plumbing. From *neck* we get a *neck* of land, like Virginia's Northern Neck or Great Neck, Long Island. We get the *neck* of a bottle, and then a *bottleneck* in traffic. A single point of contact, and not necessarily a close one, often is enough to extend a word from one referent to another one. If enough people adopt it, the new meaning may well be established in the standard vocabulary.

The opposite of extension is **restriction,** by which a term is limited from wide to narrow meanings. *Sterven*, in Middle English, meant only "to die," by whatever means; but the modern Englishman who *starves* has no doubt about what is wrong with him. *Hund*, in Old English as in Modern German, meant only "dog," but its Modern English form, *hound*, means a dog of a certain breed. Similarly, *deor*, "wild beast," has become *deer*. *Corn* is a general word meaning "grain," but it is normally used in different parts of the English-speaking world to refer to the commonest grain of the country: to wheat, or barley, or oats, or maize. Words once general in import often become restricted to more specific referents.

Sometimes words change from worse to better meanings, often rising, as they change, in the social scale—a process called **amelioration.** Many titles of honor had lowly origins. The proud *marshal* was once a groom in the medieval stables, but the man who knew horses grew in importance as the cavalry did, and the marshal now ranks with the five-star generals. The *steward* once fed the pigs and guarded the sty; then he became manager of the estate, and one steward, at least, managed so well that he founded the royal house of Stewart.

Conversely, many words have sunk in the social scale, by **pejoration.** *Hussy* once meant only "housewife," but it would scarcely do now to use it in that sense. *Villain* once meant a man who works around the villa, the country estate. But the country estate seldom makes the profit the town-bred owner expects, and *villain* came progressively to mean a man who must be selling my eggs for his own profit, a man no landlord can trust, a man nobody can trust, and finally a man who prefers evil to good. Words go up and down, are extended and restricted, are subjected to constant change as users understand different things when they hear them.

Those changes we have been considering were largely wrought by time. There are others wrought by differences in environment as their users move from place to place, such, for example, as those affecting *creek*. In England and along parts of the Atlantic Coast where the English first settled in America, *creek* means a "tidal inlet." Washington's Mount Vernon property lay near Hunting Creek, a tidal estuary of the Potomac River. As the early settlers moved westward, they followed the tidal creeks to their feeder streams and carried the word along with them to the foothills. By the time they reached the mountains, *creek* had come to mean a "small freshwater stream," and that meaning has spread across the continent. Especially when words are borrowed from other languages, they are quite likely to take on new meanings in their new environment.

Still other changes result from change in culture. *Manufacture*, by derivation, should mean "made by hand." Yet the Industrial Revolution largely displaced the handcraftsman, and *manufacture* now implies "made by machinery." To replace it, we go to Anglo-Saxon roots and say *handmade*. Many people who have not bought ice for years still say *ice box* instead of *refrigerator*.

Many words have been borrowed by English from other languages, including nearly all the words we have been considering, often with some change in meaning. Most borrowings have come from other Indo-European languages, but nearly every tongue that Englishmen have dealt with is represented in our vocabulary in one way and another. As a single example, *moccasin* is an Algonquian word that is now occasionally used even in British English.

Finally, many changes come through misunderstanding of an established word in context, as *aggravate*, from "to make more severe," has developed the meaning "to irritate" or "to annoy," and as *infer* is absorbing the meaning of *imply*. Changes even come,

paradoxically, because speakers and writers have such limited vocabularies that they coin new words to fill gaps that do not really
exist: *finalize* says no more than the verbs *end* or *finish*, and the
nouns *end* or *finish* say as much as *finalization*, and more quickly.
Such changes are actively occurring now, and many readers object
to them very strongly.

All these changes in meaning, however, have introduced new
words into the language, and in the long run have enriched the
vocabulary and allowed English to express more ideas more efficiently. Yet probably every one of them encountered objections
when it was new. The writer needs to be wary of words that are in
the process of changing, for such words distract many readers;
and he must always be sure that the words he is using have not
taken on new meanings for his audience. The Secretary of State
may no longer use *appeasement* in its old sense; the Tidewater
writer may not use *creek* to mean a milewide tidal estuary unless
he is writing for a restricted Tidewater audience, any more than
a modern writer would use *deer* to mean any sort of wild beast, or
hound to mean *collie* (unless, since *hound* has in some circles pejo-
rated, he wished to express a very derogatory opinion of that collie).
The general usage indicated by an up-to-date, well-edited dictionary
will serve as the best guide to national, current, and reputable
usage—always provided that some overnight change, like that
suffered by *appeasement*, has not shifted the meaning of a word
since the dictionary came off the press.

CONFUSION OF SIMILAR WORDS

Next to the use of unnecessarily vague, general words instead
of exact, specific words, probably the apprentice writer's greatest
trouble with diction comes from the confusion of words that sound
or look more or less alike, but mean quite different things. The
results can be very amusing, whether the mistakes are made by
Mrs. Malaprop, Sam Goldwyn, or a college freshman.

Sometimes trouble of this kind seems to result from sheer
heedlessness—the use of *to* for *too*, *it's* for *its*, *there* for *their*, *then*
for *than*, even though everyone surely must know the words apart.
There can be no possible excuse for such errors in diction in college
writing—or any other writing. Sometimes the mistakes lie close to

carelessness in spelling–*though* for *thought, latter* for *later.* There is little excuse for those errors, either. And since no two words mean exactly the same thing, and since the purpose of writing is to say what you mean, there is not much excuse for the educated man's confusing any common words which happen to sound or look alike.

Examine the following list of words which freshmen frequently confuse. If you cannot distinguish between the paired words, begin now to learn to use them properly.

accept, except

adapt, adopt

adaptation, adoption

advice, advise

affect, effect

allot, a lot

all ready, already

all together, altogether

allusion, illusion, delusion

almost, most

attributed, contributed

beside, besides

born, borne, bourn

canvas, canvass

capital, capitol

censor, censure,

cite, sight, site

coarse, course

complement, compliment

compose, comprise

conscience, conscious

continual, continuous

dairy, diary

decent, descent

desert, dessert

dining, dinning

economic, economical

expect, suspect, suppose

formally, formerly

forth, fourth

hear, here

in, into

incredible, incredulous

instance, instants

irrelevant, irreverent

its, it's

knew, new

know, no

later, latter

lead, led

liable, likely

lie, lay

loose, lose, loss

moral, morale

passed, past

personal, personnel

populace, populous

practicable, practical

precede, proceed

principal, principle

quiet, quite

raise, rise

respectably, respectfully, respectively

right, rite, wright, write

set, sit

shone, shown

statue, stature, statute

stationary, stationery	threw, through
suspect, suspicion	to, too, two
than, then	who's, whose

Avoid the misuse of words which happen to be similar.

A third source of trouble comes with words that lie near the fringes of student vocabularies, as do some of the words just listed, or that are so common they are used without thinking. These are the words that are *almost* familiar. *Prodigal* (see page 179) is such a word. So are *enervate, esoteric, imminent, incipient,* and *livid.* Many students, oddly, use *plausible* when they mean *feasible,* and so on. At the other extreme, some of the commonest words in the language cause trouble, the simple conjunctions and prepositions. *And* appears where the context calls for *but. For* as a conjunction rarely appears at all in student writing. *In, into, on, of, about,* and *to* are flung about in wild confusion—not in phrases which idiomatically require an unexpected combination, but in their simplest uses. English teachers, though appalled, are at least used to it. Other literate readers are just appalled.

As you make your last revisions on a paper, look carefully at the words you have actually written on the page. Many "errors in diction" are really heedless slips of the pen, wrong words that the writer would readily recognize as wrong if he ever really looked at them. But we tend to "see" what we think we wrote, not what is actually on the page, and many such mistakes are overlooked in proofreading. But it does no good to say, "Oh, you know what I mean!" The reader must depend on what you allowed to stand in your final copy, and will argue, not unreasonably, that if you did not mean what you said, you should not have said it.

EXERCISES

A. In the following paper, the major faults, including the wordiness, result from weaknesses in diction. Even the occasional tendency of the writer to back into a sentence seems to stem from his inability to command the exact word. Rewrite the paper, eliminating vagueness, wordiness, and inaccuracy of diction. If necessary, draw on your imagination for appropriate detail, but depend as far as possible on finding the exact words that eluded the writer.

The morgue is the place where people found passed away are taken to have a name put to them. I have been to it, and it is a grotesque location.

Upon entering in the building, I was soon impressed by its sanitariness. Every speck of its white tiled walls to its slippery linoleum floor was immaculately clean on every conspicuous place. As I entered the front office, I was greeted by a motherly old gentleman garbled in what appeared to be a policeman's uniform. He seemed to be very distressed. He stuttered in speaking and winked his left eye, which seemed to be teary, every once in awhile.

After inquiry to him of the morgue and its action, I was questioned if I'd like to view the balance. I pondered on the thought some, and when I aroused my courage I said, "Okay. Thanks."

The first compartment that we went in was called the inquest room. It was small and had the look of a little court room, with a witness stand and a judge's pulpit, and a table and ten beaten-up chairs. In the back of the room in back of the table there were many benches spreading the width of the room. A light on a cord with no shade tried to light the room.

We then proceeded to walk down a long, narrow hallway which smelled from formaldehyde. It ended at two large swinging doors which entered a fairly large room. A wall almost all window adjoined this room with the next-door room. As the man opened the door into the adjoining room, I sensed the formaldehyde once again and noticed the definite fall in the temperature. This was undoubtably the refrigerator room for the storing of the corpses. I noticed the small compartments which divided one wall of the room into eighteen divisions. As he opened one of the compartments I was startled to see the pale image of a man's head with a sheet covering the remainder.

We then exited this room and proceeded to a room which I was astonished to see was a neatly equipped operating room. Of course it wasn't an operating room, but an autopsy room. There were metal tables with holes in the bottom. Scalpels, clamps, and sheers decorated the wall. On each side of the room was a layer of shelves on which were chemicals and different jars occupied by different parts of bodies for the coroner to examine.

The cold of the storage room had now disapated, but I shuddered anyhow when we were proceeding down a hallway and there I saw it lying at the side of the hallway. It was a coffin, and inside it was a skeleton covered with mold and mildew.

I told the nervous old gentleman that I had to go. As he walked down the last corridor and showed me the door, he said, "Thank you for the visit. I hope we see you here again."

B. Rewrite the following sentence to make the diction as exact and specific as possible.

1. What is that funny noise?
2. She is all right.
3. Kenney is a man of very high principals.
4. The degree of success in arriving at a solution was in every case dependent upon the nature of the case.
5. Circumstances, sir, prevented me from studying the lesson; however, I cannot answer your question.
6. All during the weekend, the weather was awful.
7. If you do something wrong, you will loose my respect.
8. When using someone else's stuff in a paper, site the source.
9. Ever since Alexis got a C instead of a B, he has past me without speaking.
10. A friend and I expended a pleasant day.

The Appropriate Word

In addition to exactness of meaning, effective diction must possess another quality: it must be *appropriate*. Not only must the words you use say what you mean to the reader you are addressing; they must say it in a way that will be in harmony with your subject and your purpose, the tone of your writing, the level of your language. And they must not only mean, by definition, what you think they do; they must suggest what you want them to suggest.

LEVELS OF USAGE

Let us begin our study of appropriate diction with a discussion of the various levels of language. The differences between them are chiefly matters of vocabulary, even though they are also characterized by differences in grammar, sentence patterns, paragraph length and complexity, and certain other aspects of language. Some scholars object to the term *levels*, on the ground that it suggests that some levels are higher and therefore superior. They prefer the term *areas* instead. Yet neither term is exact, and *levels* is well established. We need only be aware that different subjects, different purposes, and different audiences may require different levels.

We do not express our thoughts in the same way on all occasions or in all surroundings, as every student knows who first discusses his academic shortcomings with his fraternity brothers in the Union and then walks over to keep an appointment with the dean. Further, some topics themselves call for a more formal treatment than others: the relation of God to man, the meaning of life and death, the position of the individual in the state—these and many other topics virtually demand a more dignified treatment than would be appropriate, say, in a postmortem on a football game. Our subject, our purpose, and our auditors all affect the level of language we use.

Five language levels may be distinguished: formal, informal, colloquial, vulgar, and (with some overlapping) slang and cant. Of these, all but the vulgar are on occasion used by educated men.

Formal language is language in full dress. It is the language used on formal occasions by those who might be expected to use the "best" English. The presidential address, the state paper, the sermon from the pulpit, the leading editorial, the major speech, the serious article or essay on a serious subject—all these would be couched in formal terms. Students are inclined to believe that the formal must be pompous and stuffy; it is not, except when it is used by pompous and stuffy people, who can make any level pompous. But it is serious and dignified. It is impersonal. It is conservative in grammar and sometimes complex in syntax. It makes full use of all the available resources of vocabulary, with discrimination and without embarrassment in the face of terms which in informal circumstances might seem a little pretentious.

It might, for example, say,

> Fourscore and seven years ago our fathers brought forth on this continent a new nation, conceived in liberty, and dedicated to the proposition that all men are created equal.

Clearly, no one would now use "fourscore and seven" for any but a formal occasion, and in informal intercourse, written or spoken, we would probably say something like this:

> Eighty-seven years ago our ancestors established the United States in an attempt to secure freedom and equality.

But notice that the two ideas are not quite the same, and that no amount of circumlocution could make the informal phrasing both say and suggest exactly what the formal version does. The meta-phoric suggestion of human birth and dedication to a formal creed adds religious overtones that the informal version completely lacks. Nor is formal writing old-fashioned. The speeches and writings of Sir Winston Churchill, Adlai Stevenson, John F. Kennedy, and many others offer eloquent twentieth-century examples.

Much of our writing, nowadays, is done on a carefully *in-formal* level. Less conservative than the formal, less dignified, in some ways less discriminating and so less exact, it is still very useful and thoroughly respectable. It is language in business clothes—well dressed, conventionally dressed, carefully dressed, but dressed for daily action rather than for formal occasions. Most books, including most textbooks; most articles in the carefully edited magazines; most lectures, as distinct from formal addresses; most editorials and most feature articles and most "columns"—are all couched in in-formal English. In short, informal English is today the normal writ-ten English of the educated man.

According to the subject, the purpose, and the audience, in-formal English exhibits a wide range, from a high informal that lies very close to the formal to a free informal that employs many elements of the colloquial.

Colloquial language is language in sport clothes. It is still fully dressed—for the occasion—and it is still dressed according to established conventions; but those conventions are looser than the conventions of either formal or informal usage. There are many constructions which the educated man will employ in ordinary conversation but which he never writes even in a freely informal paper (for example, the once controversial "It is me," or "Who did you sell your old car to?"). Colloquial English is *conversational* English, the language used by educated men in casual talk together, but only rarely in writing. (The word *colloquial* has no connection with *local*. Colloquial English is not the English peculiar to a locality or a region. *Colloquial* means literally "pertaining to talking together"; the term is related to *locution*, "speech," to *eloquent, elocution, loquacious*.) Brief sentences, fragmentary sentences, pro-nouns with implied antecedents, slang phrases, extreme informality of many kinds—all these are characteristic of conversational English. There are, of course, many constructions common to uneducated speech (*ain't got none*) which the educated man never uses, however informal the situation; and even in the easy informality of casual talk, the man whose ideas are clear cut expresses them in exact terms.

Colloquial English is written chiefly when the purpose of the writer is to represent conversation, as in plays or narrative dialogue, or when his purpose is to represent the free flow of easy thought.

Vulgar English, also called *nonstandard* or *illiterate,* is language in well-worn overalls. It is the language of the uneducated—clear, and in its own way conventional, but not used by those who have learned the standard forms. (*Vulgar,* here, has no suggestion of crudely indecent; it means only "pertaining to the common people, the *vulgus.*") It uses *ain't got none* (which, notice, is perfectly clear), instead of the colloquial-informal *don't have any* or the high informal *do not have any* or the formal *have none.* It may say *have went* instead of *have gone, not hardly* instead of *hardly,* and so on. It tends to use common words, not because they are the most exact words for the purpose but because they are the only words the user knows. Often, when it does use "big words" it misspells or mispronounces them, or mistakes their meaning. Clear and often effective as it is, it has no place in college writing or in college speech, with the single exception of writing designed to represent the language habits of the uneducated.

Slang and *cant,* in slightly different ways, are language in uniform, that is, language addressed to special, limited groups. For that reason, neither is effective in writing addressed to a general audience. Slang is ephemeral, meaning one thing today and nothing at all tomorrow. No language is so bad as out-of-date slang. *Twenty-three skiddoo, the snake's hips, horsefeathers, sad, corny, square*—each seems ludicrous as soon as a new phrase replaces it. Further, slang is often peculiar to a locality as well as to a moment in time. The students of one college are often nearly unintelligible to their friends from other campuses. Slang may be and often is adopted into the colloquial and sometimes even into the formal vocabulary; the up-to-date dictionary will record that acceptance if it occurs. In general, slang should not be used in college writing unless it will be fully intelligible to the audience addressed and is appropriate to the tone of the paper. And remember that someone has remarked that slang is invented by brilliant minds and used by lazy ones. Never employ slang merely to avoid the trouble of finding more exact phrasing.

Cant, linguistically, is shoptalk—language peculiar to a trade or a profession. Two doctors discussing an interesting case will be unintelligible to the patient. College students speak glibly of *sections, credit-hours, mid-terms, quality-point indexes.* Carpenters talk of *shims* and *jigs,* printers of *ems* and *quads* and *cuts.* Most trades and professions, most technical subjects have their own private language which would be entirely inappropriate in general writing. The dictionary will mark with a technical label terms confined to cant vocabularies. They may be used for a nontechnical audience only if they are defined or otherwise explained.

It should, finally, be noticed that most words, like the prepositions and conjunctions and the commonest nouns and verbs and modifiers, and most elements of grammar and syntax—in fact, the bulk of the language—are shared by speakers and writers of all levels.

The level of language to be used will depend on the subject and the purpose of the paper and on the audience addressed. Select the level that will be appropriate to the occasion, and be consistent in language level throughout any paper.

EXERCISE

Identify each of the following passages as formal, informal, colloquial, or vulgar. Under what circumstances might each be appropriate?

1. Ira David Sankey was known as the "singing evangelist." He was tall, stout, imposing, rather unctuous, and wore English mutton-chop whiskers. His was not a great voice in the musical sense, but he knew how to put fervor into it.

   Earnest Elmo Calkins

2. One day it turned out that we were rich. Papa had won a big case. He bought a new buggy and a new harness for Tom and there were five hundred dollars left over. With outlaws getting scarcer, that was a lot of money for a lawyer to have all at once.

   Marquis James

3. Men become attached to certain particular sciences and speculations, either because they fancy themselves the authors and inventors thereof, or because they have bestowed the greatest pains upon them and become most habituated to them.

   Francis Bacon

4. It's no good asking for a simple religion. After all, real things aren't simple. They look simple, but they're not.

C. S. Lewis

5. What did she care if she got six dollars a week? Or two! It was worth while working for nothing, to be allowed to stay here. And think how it would be in the evening, all lighted up—and not with no lamps, but with electrics!

Sinclair Lewis

6. Happiness lies not in the mere possession of money; it lies in the joy of achievement, in the thrill of creative effort.

Franklin D. Roosevelt

DENOTATION AND CONNOTATION

Denotation refers to the literal definition of a word, to the sense most people have agreed to give it, to what Porter G. Perrin has called its "core of meaning." *Connotation* refers to all a word suggests, its emotional flavor, its favorable or unfavorable or neutral tone, the verbal company it keeps.

On the simplest level, for example, are *domicile, residence, abode, home, house*. All of them may be defined as denoting the building in which we live, but they are by no means interchangeable, because their connotations are different. *Domicile* and *residence* are quite different for tax purposes, and a man may pay taxes in two states as a result, even though he has no *house* in either state, and even though *home,* to him, may be somewhere else altogether.

We have seen that *appeasement* changed its meaning almost overnight. What changed was its connotations. Prime Minister Chamberlain expected and got cheers for his "policy of appeasement," that is, of "compromise leading to peace." But war followed, and the cheers were succeeded by hisses. Now *appeasement* carries unfavorable connotations. *Man of vision* is favorable; *visionary* is unfavorable. The connotations of words, the attitudes they suggest to a hearer or reader, are very important.

Connotations develop for various reasons, but two are particularly important. First, words that point to unpleasant referents tend to develop unfavorable connotations. *Snail* (and particularly *slug*), *spider, snake, rat, stink* all carry unpleasant suggestions for most readers. We make use of them when we call someone a rat or a snake in the grass. Similarly, *home* and *mother* are favorable for most of us. Second, even when we are not wholly aware of the etymologies of words, the connotations they had for our remote ancestors sometimes cling to them, and a careful writer adds strength to his diction by making use of such derivational overtones. To say "History is a shambles" is to compare it to a slaughterhouse. *Adore* still carries overtones of reverence, as for a divinity. *Coward* no longer says directly "with the tail between the legs," but the idea lingers. The more one knows about the history of words, the better his chances of using connotations wisely.

Further, because of connotations, some words simply will not go with other words. We cannot say, without creating confusion,

The notorious general was widely praised for his heroics.

Notorious denotes "widely known," but it connotes "unfavorably known." *Heroics* connotes useless grandstanding; it is not synonymous with *heroism*. These unfavorable terms sound wrong when they are used with *widely praised*, unless, indeed, that phrase is itself so badly chosen as to be completely misleading.

The villain twirled his mustachios and gaped at the helpless heroine.
Little Mr. Stutterfutz sidled up to the counter and glared at the cashier.
A farmer who plans successful contour plowing must gloat over the shape of his fields.

In each of those sentences, one verb is preposterously wrong, because of its connotations.

Often, a good dictionary will help you discriminate among words whose denotations lie close together but whose connotations are quite different. Consider the following, for example:

¹gaze \'gāz\ *vi* [ME *gazen*] **:** to fix the eyes in a steady and intent look and often with eagerness or studious attention — **gaz·er** *n*
syn GAZE, GAPE, STARE, GLARE, PEER, GLOAT mean to look (at) long and attentively. GAZE implies fixed and prolonged attention (as in wonder, admiration, or abstractedness); GAPE suggests an openmouthed often stupid wonder; STARE implies a direct open-eyed gazing denoting curiosity, disbelief, insolence; GLARE is a fierce or angry staring; PEER suggests a looking narrowly and curiously as if through a small opening; GLOAT implies a prolonged gazing expressing undue or malignant satisfaction

Thoughtful examination of such synonymies may allow you to avoid ludicrous mistakes.

But a dictionary cannot always prevent the apprentice writer from using a word which is inappropriate because its connotations are wrong. Practice, a sensitive ear, and much reading are the best guides.

LOADED TERMS, SLANTING

The reader must be as alert to connotations as the writer is, first to catch the full intended flavor of what he is reading, and second to guard against "loaded terms" designed to influence his judgment. (See also Chapter 8.) By using words with favorable or unfavorable connotations, a writer may slant his report strongly.

THE FACTS: A government economist proposes a change in the administration's policy of credit control and offers as his reason a new theory about the relation between supply and demand.

EDITORIAL COMMENT FAVORING: Now at last economic scientists understand how to avoid those wild fluctuations of credit and prices which have jeopardized our national standard of living ever since Adam Smith and the other eighteenth century "political economists" first began to be aware of what they called "the law" of supply and demand. Dr. Rutabagger's cogently reasoned proposal deserves the most respectful consideration.

EDITORIAL COMMENT OPPOSING: Another wide-eyed visionary is urging us to tinker with the natural laws of economics, claiming anew, as so many self-styled "economists" have claimed before, that the best-known economic law of all, the law of supply and demand, can be repealed by wishful thinking on the part of bureaucrats. Fortunately, Congress can be depended upon to see through Rutabagger's crackpot notions.

LITERAL AND FIGURATIVE LANGUAGE

"Stay away from that girl. She's pure poison ivy!"

Literally, that would be a very confusing remark. How could any girl (female, young, human) be poison ivy (herbaceous, vine-like, toxic, of the genus *Toxicodendrons*)? It is hard to make any sense out of that obviously well-intentioned advice. Yet what native speaker of English would be even momentarily bewildered? We are all familiar with the fact that we may literally say one thing and mean something else altogether.

Literal language, meant to be taken at face value, causes no trouble, so long as our diction is exact. And so long as we are dealing with matters of fact we are likely to be using language literally, to mean no more and no less than it says.

One meter equals one hundred centimeters.

No more, no less. Face value. Nothing up the sleeve. But notice that in this very paragraph at least two nonliteral concepts appear. "Face value" and "nothing up the sleeve" are metaphoric; taken literally, they would be nonsense.

We have seen the function that metaphors and other poetic fancies have played in developing the vast vocabulary of English, both in providing new denotations (from *caput* to *captain* and *caddy* and *cad*) and in allowing sharp connotative distinctions to arise (the *priceless* is far from the *worthless*). We should notice, now, two other points.

First, we cannot avoid figurative language, even when we wish to be most literal. (*Avoid* implies "to make empty," here, of imagination; *figurative* implies "dealing with symbols"; *language* implies "sounds produced by the tongue"; *wish* implies "to desire strongly" and is directly related to *Venus*, that highly desirable goddess; *literal* implies "taken letter by letter.") No one can even speak of figurative language without using figurative language as he does so.

Second, the limitations of language on thought are such that no one can ever say *exactly* and only what he means: Try answering, *exactly*, the commonplace question, "How do you feel?" Try defining, *exactly*, any word you choose, in as many words as you like. Not even the scientist, for all his careful selection of terms, ever says exactly what he means to mean: Our colleges offer courses and graduate courses in "solid state physics"; yet even a student of high school physics knows that no such thing as solidity can exist in matter; we merely agree to talk as if the seemingly solid were real. At best, we say *approximately* what we mean, and we hope that our examples, our connotative suggestions, our readers' imaginations will somehow bridge the gap between what we would like to say and what actually can be said.

> . . . Ah, bitter chill it was.
> The owl for all his feathers was a-cold.
> The hare limped trembling through the frozen grass.
>> *John Keats*

The examples suggest the chill as statistics never could.

> . . . Winter had set in, and already *dead* Nature was *sheeted* in *funereal white*. Lakes and ponds were frozen, rivulets *sealed up*, torrents *encased* with stalactites of ice; the *black* rocks and the *black* trunks of the pine-trees were beplastered with snow, and its *heavy* masses *crushed* the *dull* green boughs into the drifts beneath. The forest was *silent* as the *grave*.
>> *Francis Parkman*

The death motif of the diction suggests the lonely desolation Parkman could not directly convey.

Figurative language, in other words, is not mere decoration daubed onto something that could be said more plainly without it. It is an inescapable and vital tool for conveying thought, for suggesting what cannot be directly stated, for crossing somehow the appalling gulf between what our words generally mean to millions of speakers of English and what they specifically and uniquely mean to us, now, as we write or read.

The varieties and complexities of figurative language are almost endless. Over two hundred figures of speech have been classified and named, and we use all of them, more or less consciously. But a limited few are particularly important.

> He's a gay dog if ever I met one.
> Oh, what a tangled web we weave
>> When first we practice to deceive.
> Aunt Ellie is as fussy as a bluejay.
> You're a fine one, to talk about your aunt like that!
> I'm so mad I could burst!
> Your suggestion is Utopian, but impractical.
> The wind sighed through the shutters.
> The waves pounded furiously against the jetties.
> The little countries are twisting the lion's tail.

None of those ten sentences make very good sense, interpreted literally; yet we constantly use such expressions, and we expect to be understood when we do it. They illustrate eight of the most common types of figurative language: metaphor, simile, irony, over-statement (hyperbole), understatement (litotes), personification, allusion, and symbol.

Metaphor is an implied comparison, boldly speaking of one thing in terms that normally belong to something else, as in *The ship plowed the waves.* The metaphor may be implied by the verb, by specific adjectives or adverbs, or even less directly by modifying phrases or clauses. Many common words—like *enthrall, enchant, enslave, panic, bottleneck, educate*—are themselves more or less obvious metaphors.

> The captain barked his orders.
> Have you heard Charlie crow over his latest triumph?
> The office is bogged down in detail.
> You're throwing good money after bad.
> I'm in the doghouse this week.
> He's lost in a fog of confusion.

Simile is explicit comparison, saying that something is *like* something else.

> Aunt Ellie is as fussy as a bluejay.
> He's got a backbone like a piece of spaghetti.
> She always looks as if her wrinkles hurt.
> Dr. Johnson said being on board a ship is like being in jail with the chance of drowning.

Irony says one thing but means something else. It often runs through an entire passage, so that the literal-minded reader may come out with an impression diametrically opposed to the one the writer intended and more alert readers receive. One must read the implications between the lines or in the tone of voice, rather than the explicit statement; and as a writer, one must walk carefully along the narrow line dividing the oversubtle from the blatantly obvious.

> You're a fine one, to talk about your aunt like that!
> A student as brilliant and diligent as Dick is bound to flunk something.
> Brutus is an honorable man.

Overstatement (hyperbole) is deliberate exaggeration.

> I'm so mad I could burst!

He doesn't have enough sense to pull in his head when he shuts a window.

If you're so much as one minute late, I'll never speak to you again.

I'm going to slice him up in half-inch cubes and fry him in deep fat.

Understatement (litotes) is deliberate minimizing.

That was no mean achievement.

I would not be unhappy if I inherited a million dollars.

Oh, yes. This little diamond tiara *is* rather an amusing piece.

I'll admit that when I collided head on with the bus it slowed me up a little.

Personification, as it is most commonly used in contemporary writing, is the attribution of human characteristics to nonhuman objects.

The wind sighed through the shutters.

The old oak crooked a friendly elbow to make an inviting seat for the children.

The waves pounded furiously against the jetties.

We rarely now use the obvious personification of giving proper names to abstractions, speaking familiarly of Fate, Ambition, gentle Spring, or, on a much lower scale, Mother Nature, Old Sol, Old Man Winter; and personification of any kind may weaken the writing unless it is sharp, vivid, and appropriate.

Allusion is reference, either directly or by borrowing familiar phrasing, to literature, history, or contemporary life, to enrich our own writing by inviting the reader to associate with it familiar suggestions drawn from outside. Three precautions must be observed: First, be sure the allusion really is familiar to your audience, or the associative value is lost. Second, unless the passage would be clear even without recognition of the allusion, you may merely confuse where you meant to clarify. Third, when the allusion takes the form of borrowed phrasing, be careful not to borrow so much that your reader suspects you of plagiarism.

Dinwiddie is the Shakespeare of the advertising world.

Like Mr. Micawber, Jack always expects something to turn up.

Caesar had his Brutus, Charles I his Cromwell, and George III—.

All right, Rip van Winkle. Wake up, or you'll be late for your eleven o'clock class.

> Between the lunch and the quitting,
>   Along about three or four,
> Comes a pause in the day's occupations
>   That is known as the coffee hour.

Symbols are concepts that represent some cultural abstraction—through common usage, as the lion represents Great Britain and the eagle represents the United States; through the frequent usage of writers, as white symbolizes innocence or spring symbolizes youth and hope; or through the repeated use by a single writer, as blood and sleep become symbolic in *Macbeth*. A limited sort of symbol is known as a *sign,* in which one thing directly suggests another, as a clock suggests the passage of time. Symbols and signs lie close to simile, metaphor, and allusion, but they are critically fashionable these days, and you should be aware of them.

Caution: Certain dangers, besides those suggested as we considered each type, are involved in the use of all figures of speech. We fall easily into triteness, into forced figures, and into mixed figures.

Be wary of using tired, overfamiliar figures. As with all trite phrasing, figurative language which has been used by many other writers comes in time to mean little, and instead of adding vivid suggestion to your writing, it merely suggests that you are too lazy even to think for yourself. *As limp as a wilted collar, pretty as a picture, the only pebble on the beach, scared to death, big as a house, nutty as a fruitcake, Mother Nature, Old Man Winter—*presumably all such figures were vivid and exciting when they were first used. But that was long ago. Never use stock figures. (See also pages 215–216.)

Be wary, too, of figurative language that is so complex, so farfetched, produced by so painful a strain that it could not in any conceivable circumstances express a genuine resemblance. Never let your reader find himself thinking, "Oh, come now!"

> As timid little Mr. Stutterfutz resolutely faced the one-armed bandit, I was inescapably reminded of a fire-breathing dragon planning the delightful devastation of a defenseless countryside.
> Climbing that flight of stairs to the dorm seemed every night like spending a dozen eternities toiling up the frozen and forbidding wastes of the Himalayas.

> This new historical romance by the incomparable Bessie Scriver is unquestionably the greatest, the most stupendous, the most colossal literary achievement since the Phoenicians invented the alphabet.

Be wary, too, of incongruous confusion in your imagery, of superimposed pictures that do not go well together—like a double exposure that seems to show the minister coming out of the neighborhood saloon. Mixed figures usually result from a lazy imagination that uses trite figures without ever really thinking about the images they suggest.

> The Ship of State is bogged down in a fog of red tape.
> She entered the room like a frigate under full sail, slithered into a chair, and cooed at the ambassador.
> Chaucer stood with one foot in the Middle Ages and with the other pointed to the rising star of the Renaissance.

(That last example is an old favorite and suggests that there is more than one way to write deathless prose. But few of us wish to be remembered for our obvious mistakes.) Mixed figures may result, also, from an inexact vocabulary. A student who speaks of "delving knee deep" presumably does not know that *delve* means "dig," not "wade." No one who looks carefully at what he has said should have any trouble.

To avoid faulty figures of speech, apply two contradictory bits of advice: First, hesitate to use any figure which occurs to you so readily that you might suspect it to be trite. Second, hesitate to use any figure which does not come with some degree of spontaneity; any strain involved in producing a figure will probably be felt by the reader.

Yet if you do avoid these dangers, the skillful use of figurative language will often let you suggest far more than you say, and will add richness and an interest to your writing that may raise it far above the merely adequate commonplace.

IDIOM

Idiom refers both to the structural patterns peculiar to a language and to a phrasing whose meaning cannot be explained logically or grammatically by examining the meanings of the individual words which compose it. If your instructor says of a passage you have written, "This is unidiomatic," he means simply, "We wouldn't express this idea this way in English."

My cow has over the fence jumped.
She for Christmas is to Florida going to fly.
To town going I am.
I do my own work, and you will do same likewise.

None of those sentences are English. The words are all English words, but they are not sung to an English tune. The structural patterns are not the patterns peculiar to the language.

Idiomatic phrases whose meanings are somehow different from the sum of the meanings of the parts may be illustrated by the obstinacy with which certain words "take" certain prepositions. We may, for example, *differ from* someone when we are not alike or *differ with* someone when we disagree. But we never under any circumstances *differ at* anyone at all. And many words are similarly particular about the prepositional company they keep. Further, we make many tense and mood combinations by adding together verbs and auxiliary verbals and prepositional adverbs in a complicated but perfectly regular way: *I am going, I am going to go, I am going to go on reading, I have been doing,* and so on. Similarly we add prepositional adverbs to verbs to make new verbs: *to put, to put up, to put up with;* and depending on context, one such combination may mean several things. For example, we can *put up* a tent, *put up* a shelf, *put up* a card table (whether we are getting ready to use it or have finished using it), *put up* preserves, or even *put up* a bluff. Those phrases vary in informality, but all are idiomatically established. How could anyone explain them by adding together the meanings of *put* and *up?*

As in any language, there are many idiomatic quirks in English, and they trip up the foreign student constantly. (Why do we say, "I am in town" but "I am in the city"? Why do we say, "Allow me to go" but "Let me go"?) But difficult as such idioms may be for the foreign student, they rarely trouble the native speaker. It is the exact preposition, the verb-adverb, and, very rarely, the idiomatic word order that bother the native speaker; for the first two, at least, the dictionary can often be of help (see *differ* in your dictionary). If your instructor scribbles *idiom* in the margin of your theme, check your dictionary and read carefully what you wrote on the page.

REPETITION

Repeating words may be either a virtue or a vice. As we have seen (Chapter 5), the repetition of key words or key sentence patterns may bind the sentences of a paragraph or the paragraphs of a composition into a tightly coherent unit. Intentional repetition may also give us the pleasure of recognizing a recurrent refrain which in itself is satisfying, quite aside from its value in securing coherence.

> . . . The place felt exciting, and we were visited by a fresh sense of the surrounding city: . . . the air drill poised ready to open the pavement, the dentist's drill poised ready to open the tooth; the conductor's baton poised ready, the critic's pencil poised ready. . . .
> *E. B. White*

Only a very insensitive ear could miss the effectiveness of those lines, and the principal device they employ is repetition.

But in fumbling hands, repetition can be very bad. If the repetition serves no function, if the repeated words or syllables are not key words deliberately reiterated to secure coherence or emphasis, but instead are minor words lazily allowed to recur because it is too much trouble to select more exact terms or to phrase the sentence in such a way as to avoid repetition, the effect will be at first irritating and finally monotonous and repelling. And remember that you are not avoiding repetition if you merely shift words from one form or one construction to another; it is the jangle of needlessly recurring sounds that is bad.

> The road ended in a mass of spruce trees entangled in very heavy vines. It was very late at night when we reached the cottage, which gave a very eerie first impression as it sat there at the end of the road, so very empty and lonesome.
>
> In this particular situation, nothing in particular could be done.
>
> The student's study can also be stimulated if he can find a job directly connected with his studies. Doing work which ties in closely with his studies gives the student an opportunity to see how his classroom study helps in practice.
>
> In high school, I was more interested in movies, sports, and other outside interests than I was in schoolwork.
>
> Much of the farmer's food is prepared from fresh products produced on the farm.

None of those useless repetitions should have been allowed to stand beyond the first revision.

REDUNDANCY

Redundancy (or more strictly, tautology) is wordiness resulting from unnecessary repetition of idea, saying the same thing twice. Redundancy is never good.

> John got home at two A.M. in the morning.
> The globe is spherical in shape.
> The scenic sight that spread before them was visible to the eye as a panorama that extended all around them.
> The actors were superb and also pretty good.

A writer who knows the meanings of the words he uses and pays attention to what he is saying can easily avoid such asininities.

TRITENESS (See also page 211.)

"You took the words right out of my mouth!" That astonished cliché is usually no compliment to either side. It probably means only that both participants in a conversation are thinking in and expressing themselves by trite expressions so commonplace that each knows in advance exactly what phrases the other is about to use. Trite, hackneyed, worn-out, overused clichés come easily to the tongue or pen because they have often come there before—so often that they no longer say exactly what anyone means; they only settle down limply over the approximate thought, covering it but not expressing it.

Trite means literally "worn out"; *hackneyed* means "available for anybody and everybody"; *cliché* means "that which is stereotyped." Avoid all "stock expressions," commonplace, secondhand phrases. Say always exactly what *you* mean, in the words that precisely express *your* thought.

Here are a few examples:

a blushing bride	a groaning board
a reluctant bridegroom	to do justice to a repast
mother love	to partake of refreshments
worldly goods	tired but happy
a proud father	last but not least
a dull thud	a tragic end
a blunt instrument	a ripe old age

to no avail	I thought I'd die
in the arms of Morpheus	a bolt from the blue
the time of your life	rears its ugly head
in no uncertain terms	a cold sweat
stew in your own juice	beautiful but dumb
none the worse for wear	raining cats and dogs

If you find yourself using phrases that you have seen or heard again and again, stop and ask yourself, "What do I really mean?"

As you write, and even more as you revise what you have written, question every word. If any word is doing less than its share of the work, throw it out and put a more exact or a more appropriate word in its place.

EXERCISES

A. Rewrite the following passages to eliminate phrases which are inappropriate because they are inconsistent with the dominant level of usage, unidiomatic, repetitious, redundant, or trite.

1. The question of the type of diet and its relation to health and fertility is a source of much controversy. Some sources say protein consumption and fertility are in direct, others in inverse, proportion.
2. The bullet emanated from the pistol with a loud report.
3. It is difficult to see that Buchanan would have done better to have done differently from what he did.
4. Modern man continues to be enthralled by the beauty of Greek legends, but finds it hard to understand how anyone could revere gods with the morals of a passel of cats.
5. In my candid opinion, if we put our shoulders to the wheel, we can bring our affairs to a satisfactory conclusion.
6. His nomination can be taken for granite, but his election is very doubtful.
7. What are the essential qualities necessary to a satisfactory definition?
8. That guy couldn't hardly act the part of Casper Milquetoast without rodomontade.
9. I have no interest nor sympathy with those who bound out of bed whistling every morning at 6 A.M.
10. We have witnessed a rapid descent in business activity, but we should bottom this month and have a fourth quarter turn-up that will set the market bullish-wise.

11. Tired but happy, and none the worse for wear, we returned our trusty steeds to the stable.
12. Because his bank balance was lower than he liked, he paid only one third of his tuition when he registered, deferring the balance until later in the term.
13. In any examination, devote careful attention on the instructions, particularly for instructions concerning a choice of questions.
14. It is now believed that the earth is not a globular sphere, nor even ovoid in shape; instead it is said to be like a squat pear.
15. His insouciance is intolerable. He needs to be gigged.

B. Rewrite the following passage to eliminate words whose connotations make them inappropriate.

> The show was terminated. After four weeks of rehearsal and ten performances, the drama was finally over. The curtain was depressed; the house, void. Below the stage, the actors were eliminating their cosmetics. They sat in small congregations, but no one vocalized. Even the atmosphere seemed weary and a little crestfallen. I sat in a corner alone, scantily apprised of the people encircling me. Every emotion had vacated me long ago, and now I was simply tired. Eight weeks of excessive endeavor and imperfection of sleep were at last demanding liquidation. In the far corner of the chamber someone was lachrymose. A forced, shrill laugh arose from the assemblage around the little, dirty, broken mirror. It was hot. The grease paint was scented with an aroma like burning rubber. The room was unbearable. I arose and tardily climbed the long wooden staircase that conducted me to the stage.

C. Identify the types of figurative language illustrated by the following sentences. Revise any forced or mixed figures.

1. George Eliot always looked as if her clothes had been cut out with a knife and fork.
2. This schism has deep roots which may serve as the foundation of a tempest in the Kremlin.
3. The wind roared furiously through the trees.
4. Launched on the course charted by Calhoun, the southern leaders soon ran the ship of state on the rocks.
5. The Union gravy would make fine wallpaper paste.
6. If she is eighteen, I'm a mummy's grandmother!
7. I'm so tired I couldn't claw my way up to the basement.
8. Now is the winter of our discontent/Made glorious summer by this sun of York.

9. A diller, a dollar, Mr. Robinson. You might as well cut class altogether as come at this hour.
10. The hilarity of the audience was somewhat less than discernible.
11. She always speaks to her husband as if they were to be married in an hour.
12. I wish somebody would buy him a fifth of rodenticide.
13. The standard gearshift is like the letter H.
14. The captain stormed into the mess hall.
15. The reaction is triggered by the addition of the catalyst.

Reasoning and Persuasion

In considering reasoning and persuasion, we shall be concerned with thought processes that are basic not only to many kinds of writing, but to most of our conscious activity; but we shall be focusing largely on a kind of writing we have not heretofore considered: effective argument, in which especially evidence and reasoning are presented persuasively in order to convince a possibly hostile reader that certain opinions are preferable to others. As we concentrate on argument, however, we should remember that logical thought is important too in description, narration, and exposition as well—in arranging and presenting details, evaluating evidence, and drawing sound conclusions. To write effectively, to read intelligently, to live a fully humane life, we must know something of the patterns by which we think.

Truth is difficult to identify, and the workings of our minds as we grope our way toward truth are very complex. Logicians and psychologists are far from a complete explanation of the processes of reasoning, and certainly we cannot reach one in a single chapter. It must be understood at the outset that we are dealing only with broad and oversimplified outlines and with obvious thought patterns. We can do little more than sketch the major methods by which man attempts to discover truth and to base his opinions on reasonable inferences drawn from dependable evidence, and by which he attempts to persuade others to adopt his beliefs. We can use *truth* only as most men use it, to mean that which in practice seems most probable, all the evidence considered. It is on this pragmatic sort of truth that all of us, always, must act. It will be much, however, if we can learn to distinguish between fact and opinion, to discriminate between valid evidence and false evidence, to catch a glimpse of the kind of inference which may be reasonably drawn from a given piece of evidence, and to recognize the basic methods by which we think at the rational level. In addition, we can learn to be wary of some of the common fallacies and emotional appeals by which, irrationally, our trains of thought are often shunted onto sidetracks and we are led to "make up our minds" without ever using our minds at all. Finally, we shall examine specifically some of the problems common to argument, that is, writing designed to persuade others to adopt our reasoned beliefs. Our attention in this chapter will be focused sometimes on the writer and speaker, sometimes on the reader and listener, but always on man as a rational, though human, being.

FACT AND OPINION

Basic to any understanding of reasoning and argument is an understanding of the difference between fact and opinion. Facts are things which exist, deeds which are done, events which occur. Facts are actual and true, regardless of what we think about them. A rock on which we can stub our toes, a contract and the signatures on it, the smell of alcohol on a driver's breath, a battle which has occurred and the debris it left, a promise given or withheld—all these are facts. Opinions, on the other hand, represent our inferences about facts, our evaluations, our judgments, our beliefs. A statement which is factual in form, a statement, that is, which is phrased *as if* it presented fact, can be proved or disproved as true or false; everyone who considers the evidence impartially must come to the same conclusion. Opinion, on the other hand, can never be proved or disproved; it can only be accepted as probable or rejected as improbable, and impartial observers of the evidence may reach differing conclusions. Yet, in spite of the uncertain nature of opinion, we must form opinions and act on them at least as often as we may act on facts. We need, however, to be aware of the difference. To test factual statements, we have only to examine the evidence, but to test statements of opinion, we must examine both the evidence of fact and the inferences drawn from it. Similarly, in presenting a factual argument, we need only offer the evidence for the facts; but before we can expect an audience to adopt an opinion, we must first offer the underlying facts and then explain the reasoning upon which the opinion is based.

If I say, "Many college classrooms contain chairs equipped with writing-arms," I am making a factual statement, and by examining representative classrooms, you can easily test its truth or falsity. Whether or not these chairs are comfortable, esthetically pleasing, or convenient for writing themes, however, are matters of opinion, and so are the precise meanings of *comfortable, pleasing,* and *convenient.*

> That cube measures six inches on each side.
> Lake Superior is the largest of the Great Lakes.
> California is bounded on the west by the Pacific Ocean.
> The Smoot-Hawley Act set the highest tariff rate of any tariff measure in United States history.

All of these statements are factual, and their truth may be ascertained by anyone who wishes to test them.

So far, we have considered clear-cut examples. But statements may be factual in form whether or not they express truth. "The sun rises in the west every morning" is a factual statement, but when the evidence is examined, the idea the sentence expresses is clearly false. A witness may swear that Scarface MacKonochie could not have been robbing the cigar store at seven o'clock because he was in Ozzie's Bar and Grill at seven o'clock, no matter what a dozen other witnesses may say; but one story or the other must be false.

Even the most convincingly detailed statement may not be true.

> My opponent in this congressional election accepted a bribe of $17,339.47, from Edward H. Sinster, at 728 East 43rd Street, at 8:37 Eastern Standard Time, on January 27, 1964.

Well, maybe he did, but we shall want to examine the evidence before we make up our minds. The statement is convincing merely because it is factual in form and because it is highly detailed. The danger to our thinking lies in the fact that, although we all know that there is little to prevent a writer or speaker from announcing confidently that black is white, we too often tend to forget it; we are all too ready to accept without question any statement presented in factual form, unless our own knowledge of the facts arouses our suspicions. All propagandists are quite aware of our gullibility; the Hitlerian technique of "the big lie"—used by many besides Hitler—depends on our readiness to accept as true whatever we are offered as the truth. We must remember that factual statements can be tested, and that anyone who offers a factual statement which really expresses truth will be quite willing to have us apply the pertinent tests which will prove it.

Often, the distinction between fact and opinion rests on precise definitions of common but vague terms. How soon after shaving does the average man "need a shave"? At what point does the man who needs a shave become a man with a beard? How tall is tall? How dark is a dark complexion? Policemen trying to make sense out of the descriptions furnished by eager witnesses could tell you that no two quite agree on "the facts," and that identification is usually based on the lowest common denominator. It is not easy, in other words, to be sure when a "fact" is a fact.

Just as important to us as the statements of fact are the statements that go beyond fact into opinion by expressing value judgments or otherwise interpreting facts. "That six-inch cube would make an attractive base for a lamp." Would it, really? The opinion is based on esthetic judgment, and some observers might differ.

> Lake Superior is more beautiful than Lake Ontario.
> California is the best state in which to live.
> High tariffs are better for the economic welfare of the United States than low tariffs.

On all these statements, many would disagree. Yet in deciding what we must do on numberless occasions, we must act as our judgment tells us to act, even though incontestable proof for our opinions cannot be found.

Very often, fact and opinion appear together in the same statement.

> Congress plunged with eagerness into the question of tariff revision.

The facts are that hearings were begun, a measure was introduced into the House early in the session, and new and somewhat higher tariff rates were adopted. But *plunged* and *eagerness* have introduced the writer's attitude, his opinion of the way Congress went about its work; they are loaded terms of a sort we should recognize and be wary of when we read or when we write such a sentence. (See also page 206.)

Or, when we discuss a topic, we may slip from fact into opinion as we pass beyond the range of the demonstrable. S. I. Hayakawa has pointed out that no one can argue the question of whether or not angels watch over your bed at night. Similarly, we deal with fact when we say that the Stone of Scone was taken from the Scots by Edward I and carried to England, where it was placed in the Coronation Chair—so much is historical. Whether or not the stone is identical with the one that served as Jacob's pillow, whether or not it was conveyed from Palestine to Ireland and thence to Scotland are matters of legend and are beyond proof. Acceptance or rejection of the legend can be no more than opinion.

What to do about it? As a writer, be able to stand behind any statement you make. Have the evidence to support statements of fact, and explain the reasoning behind opinions. Especially, avoid statements that are broader than they need to be. One student, for example, wrote, "The prosperity of America is due to the policies of the present administration," when all he meant was "Many voters believe that the prosperity of America is due to the policies of the present administration." Why raise hackles unnecessarily? If something seems merely possible, it should not be announced as probable or stated as if it were certain. In outlining an opinion held by the opposition but rejected by the writer, you must be careful not to phrase it in such a way that you seem to believe it yourself. The distinctions between fact and opinion, and between opinions of varying degrees of probability, should always be kept clear.

As you read, keep these distinctions in mind. For matters of fact, consider the evidence; for opinion, consider the evidence and the reasonableness of the inferences based on the facts. And as you write, give your reader the evidence and make clear to him the reasoning by which you have reached any opinions you are asking him to adopt.

EXERCISE

In the following sentences, identify the elements of fact and the elements of opinion. For elements of opinion, comment on the probabilities.

1. London is one of the largest cities in the world.
2. London is one of the most exciting cities in the world.
3. It is difficult to write clearly.
4. Essay examinations reveal what students know about a course and betray weaknesses in their understanding of it.
5. Charles II "never said a foolish thing, and never did a wise one."
6. An opinion cannot be true unless it ceases to be an opinion and becomes a fact—so, an opinion cannot be true.
7. A Leica is a better camera than a Brownie.
8. The nature of one's language determines the "facts" one can recognize.
9. Facing the jury confidently, the prosecuting attorney deliberately distorted the facts of the case in his summing up.
10. The legendary King Arthur was probably, in historical fact, a Romanized, Celtic military leader who defended Britain with some success against the early Anglo-Saxon invaders.
11. There are sixteen ounces in a pint.
12. "A pint's a pound, the world around."
13. We boast of our material progress, but archaeologists of the future may know our times as the Age of the City Dump.
14. Twentieth-century structures are superior to those of any preceding century.
15. Time has no existence outside the human mind.

THE NATURE OF EVIDENCE

Before we examine the nature of evidence, one important preliminary remark must be made: *Assertion is NOT evidence.* It proves nothing merely to say that such and such is true, no matter how loudly or how repeatedly we say it. Probably the greatest single weakness in student arguments lies in dependence on the unsupported assertion of debatable opinions or dubious "facts." It results either from a failure to distinguish real fact from opinion, or from an inability to realize that an intelligent reader might conceivably hold differing opinions on key issues in the argument. One may depend on assertion only when the audience can be counted on to accept the truth of factual statements and to understand the inferences drawn from them, or when the writer's integrity, knowledge, and judgment have been so firmly established that the audience will accept his word as authoritative.

Now, if assertion is *not* evidence, what is?

Valid evidence, the signs which point to truth or strong probability, may be considered somewhat loosely under four heads: facts, observation, the testimony of witnesses, and the reasoned opinions of authorities.

Facts

The defendant in a criminal trial may protest his innocence, and witnesses from Ozzie's Bar and Grill may give him an alibi, but his lawyer will have difficulty explaining how his gun with his fingerprints turned up at the scene of the crime. That gun and those fingerprints and their presence at the scene are facts, and those facts are evidence. True, they may be misinterpreted. The defendant may be able to prove that someone else borrowed the gun and used it on the night in question. Courts are more reluctant than laymen to jump to conclusions on circumstantial evidence alone. But often, as in the Lindbergh kidnaping case, the evidence of facts may pile up so convincingly that only one interpretation is reasonably possible, and the opinion based on them may be accepted as sufficiently probable to justify action. Whenever interpretation is not too difficult, the evidence of facts alone provides a case that is hard to refute. Did Neolithic man know how to make pottery? Here is a piece of pottery buried with his undisturbed bones. The most plausible way to account for the facts is to assume that pottery was familiar to him. Did you have some unauthorized help with your last theme? Why are these corrections on your rough draft in someone else's handwriting? The best evidence is the evidence of facts.

Observation

One very short step beyond the facts themselves is the evidence of our own senses, our observation of the facts.

> I know there is a curb there because I just stubbed my toe on it.
> There is jam on Johnny's face. I can see it.
> This steak weighs fourteen ounces. I can read the scales.

In each of these examples, we are reaching conclusions through our own observation of the facts. But it is important to notice that already an opportunity for error has crept in as we have moved beyond fact into opinion by interpreting the facts before our eyes. The lawyer and the psychologist are very much aware of how easily an honest witness may draw false conclusions by interpreting facts incorrectly, by failing to consider all the facts, or by unconsciously imagining the presence of "facts" which were not really present at all but which his preconceptions have led him to think should have been there. The conflicting testimony about an exciting accident offers a ready example. Or, for another example, are you sure that steak really weighs fourteen ounces? The scales may be wrong, or the butcher may be weighing his thumb. The sleight-of-hand magician makes constant use of our tendency to imagine that we have observed whatever we assume should be present. We must try consciously to "stick to the facts," even though it is often difficult to be sure just where the facts end and our own inferences begin. (What, for example, do you really see when you "see" a mirror?) Observation must be handled carefully.

We are, perhaps, least likely to be wrong when we deal with the evidence of our own senses; but we must test our conclusions, because seeing should not necessarily be believing. We must be as sure as possible that we are considering all the facts and only the facts, and are making allowances for our own preconceived notions.

Witnesses

Very often we cannot ourselves observe the facts but must depend instead on the testimony of witnesses, of others who have observed the facts. The judge and jury in a court of law, indeed, are not allowed to know the facts from their own observations; they are required to listen to the testimony—usually conflicting—of those who were present on the occasion in question, and to resolve the disagreements as best they can. And all of us are constantly making use of such outside testimony to form beliefs about things we do not know from our own observation. I believe, for example, that there was an accident on the Highway Bridge this morning, although I was not present myself. But Bill was there, saw it, and told me all about it. I know him to be truthful and to have no reason for misleading me; so I accept his account as evidence of something I did not see myself. Did Professor Snodgrass really assign the next forty pages for tomorrow? I was not in class, but Betty says he did, and I believe her and prepare the lesson accordingly. In many ways, we depend on the testimony of witnesses.

Our witnesses, need not, of course, speak to us in person. Their evidence may be documentary. Aunt Emma writes that Johnny has been sick but has now gone back to school. We believe her. The witness who cannot appear in court swears to a written deposition setting forth what he knows. We learn a great deal about fourteenth-century England by reading Chaucer. The historian studies letters, wills, deeds, court records, and contemporary writing of all kinds, and is often most interested in indirect testimony which touches a point incidentally when the witness's attention is directed toward something else. Directly or indirectly, witnesses may come to us hot from the scene, or they may speak to us across the centuries.

In dealing with the testimony of witnesses, as in dealing with the evidence of our own senses, we must, of course, be aware of the possibility of honest mistake. And we must be aware of a new factor: a deliberate intent to deceive. Betty told me that Professor Snodgrass had assigned the next forty pages for tomorrow. But ten pages is his usual assignment. Could she be trying to get even with me for laughing at her new dress last Saturday night? Could the politician "viewing with alarm" the mistakes of his opponent be distorting the facts to catch my vote? Before we accept any testimony, we must "consider the source." The testimony must be evaluated to eliminate possible honest misinterpretation of the facts, or self-interest, or prejudicial bias, or insufficient background for adequate reporting. Any of these factors might result in false testimony and must be taken into consideration as we form our conclusions.

And beyond this evaluation of the competence of the witnesses we must remember that now *two* sets of interpretations of the facts are involved: the one made by the witnesses themselves and the one we ourselves make of what we are told. The Indians who tried to describe the Mississippi River to the early French explorers of the Great Lakes region were telling the exact truth when they said that a little farther on there was a great river which flowed into the sea. They were in a position to know the facts, and they had no intent to deceive. The Frenchmen who listened were guiltless of any desire for self-deception when they assumed that "the sea" must be the Pacific Ocean. Yet the Frenchmen were influenced by preconceived notions of American geography, and many a fruitless attempt to find a river route across the continent resulted from that second-hand interpretation of the facts. Not only must we evaluate the testimony and the veracity of the witness; we must also attempt to evaluate our own evaluation.

Authorities

The fourth source of evidence lies in the opinions of authorities, that is, of the experts, those who have studied the facts, examined the testimony of the witnesses, considered all the evidence, and reached more or less trustworthy conclusions. Whose opinion do you accept when you want to know what to do when you are ill, Aunt Agatha's or the doctor's? The professor who has spent an honest and intelligent lifetime studying the reign of Queen Anne is probably better able to comment on the background of Alexander Pope's *Rape of the Lock* than your sophomore roommate who has attended most of the lectures in History 13. How is a given word used? What do the modern, well-edited dictionaries say? How many people live in Kalamazoo? The latest census report provides the best guess. We must often consult authorities and follow their lead.

The authorities, however, may be wrong, and equally well-qualified authorities may disagree, just as the alienists disagree over the mental competence of the defendant in a murder case— or as reputable dictionaries disagree over the proper hyphenation of a word. Authorities often must rely on other authorities or on witnesses, and someone's interpretation always creeps in, at least slightly; there may be prejudice somewhere along the line or even flat mistake. The doctor interpreting symptoms in the light of his expert knowledge may still treat you for the wrong disease. The scientist's opinions are often overset by the discoveries of later scientists. Historians disagree, not only over why things happened, but even over what did happen. Critics argue, and economists, and many other kinds of authorities. But for all that, the authorities offer the best guide available, especially if we check one against others. The doctor is still more likely to be right than Aunt Agatha.

What we must do is compare the authorities and test them as we test witnesses. Are they in a position to know the facts? Is their knowledge up to date? (The most recent are not always the best, but at least they have had a chance to profit by the work of all the preceding authorities.) Are they as nearly unprejudiced as human minds can be? What are their preconceptions and biases, and how should such bias be allowed for? Finally, what is their evidence, and how sound is their reasoning?

EXERCISE

In 1868, Thomas Henry Huxley published, under the title "On a Piece of Chalk," a lecture given in Norwich, England, as a part of his campaign to explain the scientific bases of Darwinism to the English public. Selecting chalk, the bedrock on which Norwich is built, as his topic, he sought to prove its origin in deep-sea sedimentation, to demonstrate the vastness of geologic time. The following statements summarize the first part of his argument, in which he shows that the chalk consists of "the dried mud of an ancient deep sea."

Identify the kinds of evidence—as fact, observation, testimony of witnesses, or authority—*that the statements present.* Notice in particular that, even though he was a noted biologist, he did not assert any debatable opinions without other evidence until *after* he had established his own right to speak as an authority, although he did allow himself to testify as a witness to facts he had personally observed.

1. Well diggers in Norwich dig into chalk.
2. Chalk underlies all of the county of Norfolk, and forms the coastal cliffs from Yorkshire to Dorset; it underlies all of southeastern England except the Weald of Kent and Sussex, to a depth in some places of more than 1,000 feet; it extends from Ireland to Central Asia in an irregular oval 3,000 miles long.
3. If together we examine the nature and origin of chalk, we can see the solid foundation of some startling scientific conclusions.
4. As we all know, to burn chalk is to make quicklime. Chalk is a compound of carbonic acid gas and lime, and heat drives out the gas, so that we see the lime but not the gas. If chalk is dropped in vinegar, we can see the gas bubbling out; the lime dissolves. Chemically, then, chalk is carbonate of lime.
5. Carbonate of lime is widespread as limestone; it also is the familiar deposit in your teakettles.
6. If you slice chalk thin, you can see its structure with a microscope. A slice of teakettle deposit would show only layers of a mineral substance, but a slice of chalk shows minute granules and well-defined globular bodies averaging a hundredth of an inch in diameter.
7. By separating these bodies from the matrix, one can see them as chambered structures, the commonest being called *Globigerinae.* They provide the clue we shall follow.

8. Someone might suggest that these bodies result from crystallization, as water crystallizes into fernlike shapes in winter. Some learned men, in former times, supposed that all fossils were formed this way. But no such explanation is now acceptable, because experience has shown that mineral matter never does assume the forms found in fossils.

9. Better evidence of the organic nature of *Globigerinae* lies in the fact that similar skeletons are now being formed by living creatures in the ocean.

10. These living *Globigerinae* were discovered when the needs of marine surveying led to the invention of a device to bring up samples of the sea-bottom from great depths. In 1853, mud from 10,000 feet down was sent for examination to two able microscopists, Ehrenberg of Berlin and Bailey of West Point. Both found that the mud was composed of the skeletons of living organisms just like the *Globigerinae* already known to occur in chalk.

11. When the trans-Atlantic cable was proposed, knowledge of the sea-bottom became essential, and in June and July, 1857, Captain Dayman was sent by the Admiralty to ascertain the depth and collect samples of the bottom over the whole route of the cable. The specimens of Atlantic mud he procured were sent to me to examine.

12. From the specimens taken, we know that the sea floor from Ireland to Newfoundland is covered with mud which chemically is carbonate of lime, and which physically consists of *Globigerinae* imbedded in a granular matrix, substantially the same as the *Globigerinae* of the chalk.

13. *Globigerinae* of all sizes, from the smallest to the largest, occur in the Atlantic mud; and in many of the shell-chambers is soft animal matter, the remains of the living animal which built the shell from the carbonate of lime dissolved in the sea-water, according to a pattern which can be imitated by no other known agency.

14. It is hard to believe that animals can live at the depths from which living *Globigerinae* have been brought up, and it is at least possible that they do not. About 5% of the mud specimens consists of the silicon remains of *Diatoms* and the silicious skeletons of *Radiolaria*, which certainly do not live at the bottom of the ocean, but on the surface. These remains have fallen from the surface, sometimes through 15,000 feet of water. If they lived at the surface and fell to the sea-floor after death, *Globigerinae* might too. But both positive and negative evidence

all points the other way. The *Globigerinae* are too heavy to float, and they are not found at the surface with the *Diatoms* and *Radiolaria*. It has also been noticed that the deeper the sea, the greater the proportion of *Globigerinae,* and that deep-water *Globigerinae* are larger than those living in shallower waters, so that they can hardly have been swept by currents from the shallows to the depths.

15. (Living starfish, clinging to the lowest part of the sounding line, have been brought up from a depth of 1,260 fathoms. Dr. Wallich ascertained that the sea-bottom at that point consisted of *Globigerina* ooze, and that the stomachs of the starfish were full of *Globigerinae*.)

16. "The living *Globigerinae* are exclusively marine animals, the skeletons of which abound at the bottom of deep seas; . . . there is not a shadow of reason for believing that the habits of the *Globigerinae* of the chalk differed from those of the existing species. But if this be true, there is no escaping the conclusion that the chalk itself is the dried mud of an ancient deep sea."

THE PROCESS OF REASONING

Reasoning is the subtle and complex process by which we arrive at opinions based on the pertinent evidence. Fallacious reasoning leads to mistaken opinion. Emotional appeals lead us "to make up our minds" without using our minds at all. We need, therefore, to examine not only logical reasoning but also the fallacies and emotional appeals which lead us astray. Because reasoning is both subtle and complex, customarily consisting of chains of inference drawn from the implications of the evidence, logicians and psychologists are still uncertain about many elements of the process. But in spite of their disputes, we can add greatly to our own understanding of ourselves by at least glancing at the way in which chains of inference may lead us to valid conclusions, even though the logical steps involved may be obscured; by examining the classical descriptions of logical method; and by considering the major logical fallacies and some of the obvious emotional appeals.

Implication and Inference

Facts, the bedrock of evidence, mean nothing by themselves. As we studied the nature of evidence, we were constantly aware of the danger that the observer or the witness, and even the authority, might introduce error by his selection or interpretation of

the facts. The facts provide *implications*—hints, suggestions, starting points for thought. The human mind must discover those implications and from them draw the proper *inferences*—the logical
conclusions that give useful meaning to the facts. All of the possible
implications are present in a given fact; we select those that have
meaning for us. To a geologist, for example, a diamond implies past
conditions of heat and pressure in the earth; to a stonecutter, it
implies the hardness he needs for saw teeth; to a jeweler, it implies
a gem to be set; to a debutante, it implies a society wedding; by
each, the secondary implications may be ignored as irrelevant.
Usually, of course, there are many implications that are relevant
for our purposes, and from them many inferences may be drawn.
Our reasoned opinions are normally the end result of incredibly
complicated chains of implications and inferences as we move from
evidence to what we hope will be valid conclusions.

An example will be instructive, and no less useful for being
both famous and fictional. At the beginning of "The Adventure of
the Blue Carbuncle" Sherlock Holmes shows Dr. Watson an old hat,
abandoned, along with a Christmas goose, after a street brawl. On
a card tied to the bird's leg was "For Mrs. Henry Baker," and the
initials "H.B." were legible on the lining of the hat. Holmes challenges Watson:

> "Here is my lens. You know my methods. What can you gather
> yourself as to the individuality of the man who has worn this
> article?"
> I took the tattered object in my hands and turned it over rather
> ruefully. It was a very ordinary black hat of the usual round shape,
> but was a good deal discoloured. There was no maker's name; but, as
> Holmes had remarked, the initials "H.B." were scrawled upon one
> side. It was pierced in the brim by a hat-securer, but the elastic was
> missing. For the rest, it was cracked, exceedingly dusty, and spotted
> in several places, although there seemed to have been some attempt
> to hide the discoloured patches by smearing them with ink.
> "I can see nothing," said I, handing it back to my friend.
> "On the contrary, Watson, you can see everything. You fail,
> however, to reason from what you see. You are too timid in drawing
> your inferences."
> "Then, pray tell me what it is that you can infer from this hat."
> He picked it up and gazed at it in the peculiar introspective
> fashion which was characteristic of him. "It is perhaps less sug-

gestive than it might have been," he remarked, "and yet there are a few inferences which are very distinct, and a few others which represent at least a strong balance of probability. That the man was highly intellectual is of course obvious upon the face of it, and also that he was fairly well-to-do within the last three years, although he has now fallen upon evil days. He had foresight, but has less now than formerly, pointing to a moral retrogression, which, when taken with the decline of his fortunes, seems to indicate some evil influence, probably drink, at work upon him. This may account also for the obvious fact that his wife has ceased to love him."

"My dear Holmes!"

"He has, however, retained some degree of self-respect," he continued, disregarding my remonstrance. "He is a man who leads a sedentary life, goes out little, is out of training entirely, is middle-aged, has grizzled hair which he has cut within the last few days, and which he anoints with lime-cream. These are the more patent facts which are to be deduced from his hat. Also, by the way, that it is extremely improbable that he has gas laid on in his house."

"You are certainly joking, Holmes."

"Not in the least. Is it possible that even now, when I give you these results, you are unable to see how they are attained?"

"I have no doubt that I am very stupid, but I must confess that I am unable to follow you. For example, how did you deduce that this man was intellectual?"

For answer Holmes clapped the hat upon his head. It came right over the forehead and settled upon the bridge of his nose. "It is a question of cubic capacity," said he; "a man with so large a brain must have something in it."

"The decline of his fortunes, then?"

"This hat is three years old. These flat brims curled at the edge came in then. It is a hat of the very best quality. Look at the band of ribbed silk and the excellent lining. If this man could afford to buy so expensive a hat three years ago, and has had no hat since, then he has assuredly gone down in the world."

"Well, that is clear enough, certainly. But how about the foresight and the moral retrogression?"

Sherlock Holmes laughed. "Here is the foresight," said he, putting his finger upon the little disc and loop of the hat securer. "They are never sold upon hats. If this man ordered one, it is a sign of a certain amount of foresight, since he went out of his way to take this precaution against the wind. But since we see that he has broken the elastic and has not troubled to replace it, it is obvious that he has less foresight now than formerly, which is a distinct proof of a weakening nature. On the other hand, he has endeavoured to conceal some of these stains upon the felt by daubing them with ink, which is a sign that he has not entirely lost his self-respect."

"Your reasoning is certainly plausible."

"The further points, that he is middle-aged, that his hair is grizzled, that is has been recently cut, and that he uses lime-cream are all to be gathered from a close examination of the lower part of the lining. The lens discloses a large number of hair-ends, clean cut by the scissors of the barber. They all appear to be adhesive, and there is a distinct odor of lime-cream. This dust, you will observe, is not the gritty, gray dust of the street but the fluffy brown dust of the house, showing that it has been hung up indoors most of the time; while the marks of moisture upon the inside are proof positive that the wearer perspired very freely, and could, therefore, hardly be in the best of training."

"But his wife—you said that she had ceased to love him."

"This hat has not been brushed for weeks. When I see you, my dear Watson, with a week's accumulation of dust upon your hat, and when your wife allows you to go out in such a state, I shall fear that you also have been unfortunate enough to lose your wife's affection."

"But he might be a bachelor."

"Nay, he was bringing home the goose as a peace-offering to his wife. Remember the card upon the bird's leg."

"You have an answer for everything. But how on earth do you deduce that the gas is not laid on in his house?"

"One tallow stain, or even two, might come by chance; but when I see no less than five, I think that there can be little doubt that the individual must be brought into frequent contact with burning tallow—walks upstairs at night probably with his hat in one hand and a guttering candle in the other. Anyhow, he never got tallow-stains from a gas-jet. Are you satisfied?"[1]

We can seldom be so certain as Holmes was with the writer behind him. (Even he, notice, is careful with his *probably*'s and *perhap*'s, and he overlooks entirely the possibility that the hat came to Henry Baker at second hand.) But we can and do work constantly with implications and the inferences to which they point.

For a simple example, if you hear water dripping in the kitchen sink, you may infer one of two conclusions: either the faucet

---

[1] From *The Adventures of Sherlock Holmes* (1892). Reprinted by permission of the Trustees of the Estate of Sir Arthur Conan Doyle, and of John Murray (Publishers) Ltd.

was not turned off tightly, or the washer is so worn that the faucet leaks. To decide which is more probable, you need to consider two other factors: the habits of those who use the sink, and the age of the washer. If A habitually leaves a dripping faucet, you infer: "A failed again to turn off the water." If the faucet is normally turned off and it has been some time since the washer was replaced, you infer: "That washer is worn and needs to be changed."

Such an example itself implies the prior existence of certain assumptions. A drip, for instance, implies a leak. We assume that a leak may be the result of human carelessness or of mechanical failure. The human being who has been careless before may well be careless again. Mechanical failures result from discoverable causes. Washers deteriorate with age and need replacing. And so on. Our inferences are governed by our prior assumptions—so much so that we may completely misread the implications of the evidence. The skillful detective story writer knows this well, and plants his clues confidently with a hint at one basic assumption to mislead the reader; then on page 203 he produces another assumption which turns the inferences inside out, and triumphantly demonstrates the real solution. To Dr. Watson and the police, the disappearance of Neville St. Clair means that he is dead. To Sherlock Holmes, it suggests that he may instead be in hiding, himself a villain. And evidence is often similarly misinterpreted outside the covers of books.

Throughout the Judeo-Christian world, for instance, it was long assumed as a matter of course that the Biblical account of the creation was to be read as a divinely inspired, literal report. The geological and paleological facts of uplifting, erosion, sedimentation, glaciation, and fossilization were variously interpreted in the light of that assumption; but not until the middle decades of the nineteenth century was the assumption itself modified and modern inferences made possible. Yet the inferences were not hard to come by. The early Greeks, like Heraclitus or Empedocles, had long ago pointed in the direction that geologists and biologists are now going. Politically, for a second example, men assume that the leaders of their own party are somehow inherently better than those of the other party, and interpret the facts uncovered by a Senate investigation as evidence of corruption or of mere partisan harassment, depending on whose ox is being gored. All of us have basic assumptions of which we are scarcely aware, and those assumptions may determine the inferences we can draw unless we can identify the influence they may have on the validity of our thinking.

With awareness of our assumptions and a care for reasonable probabilities, however, we can usually distinguish between valid and invalid assumptions. Suppose a given student flunks out of school at the end of his first semester. There may be many explanations, but some will be more reasonable than others. We may reasonably infer that he neglected to study, or that he allowed too many "outside activities" to absorb his energies, or that he was poorly prepared, or even that he lacked the intelligence to do college work. It is less likely that "the teachers had it in for him," or that the standards of the college are unfairly high, or that each teacher was told to fail a certain percentage of the students and coincidence caught him in the unfortunate group in each class. For another example, a passerby with no connections with either party to an accident testifies to what he saw. We may want to make allowances for his excitement, but we can probably assume that he is not biased in favor of either party. A college professor of economics expresses an opinion about high school curricula. We can assume that he knows something about college students, about college-level teaching, and about economics, but we cannot assume without more evidence that he knows much about high school curricula.

Usually, many implications and inferences follow from a given set of facts and provide a chain which more or less justifies our ultimate conclusion. A builder digging the basement for a house in a subdivision on an old estate in Kentucky comes across several forgotten human skeletons, scraps of cloth, bits of shoe leather, and a few silver coffin handles. Numerous guesses are offered to explain the facts: "An Indian graveyard," says the operator of the bulldozer; "Murder," says someone else. "An old burying ground for slaves," says a third. But the shoe leather and the coffin handles rule out the Indians; the multiplicity of skeletons and the formal burial rule out the probability of murder; and the silver coffin handles virtually rule out the slaves. The find must indicate a forgotten burying ground for fairly sophisticated white settlers, but whether or not they belonged to the family that long owned the estate, no one now can say. Many implications, many assumptions, and many inferences are involved in the chain; but the conclusion seems reasonably valid, in spite of the complexity of the process by which it was reached.

Even though thought is incredibly complex, a beginning at understanding the process can be made, with some oversimplification, by examining the classical descriptions of two basic methods of reasoning: We observe individual phenomena and reach general conclusions about them; then we use these general conclusions to make predictions about similar phenomena. For example, you drop a watch—or better yet, see someone else drop one—and observe the shattering results. After only one such experience—or perhaps at the most, three or four—you reach the general conclusion that it is not good for a watch to be dropped. When, subsequently, your year-old nephew grabs your watch, you hastily apply your general conclusion to the new situation and take your watch away from him for fear he will drop and break it. You have been using the two basic patterns of thought: *induction* and *deduction*.

EXERCISE

Select a convenient physical object—say a notebook, an old shoe, a woman's purse, or a piece of furniture. What facts about it are observable? What inferences may logically be drawn from the implications which your observed complex of facts presents?

Inductive Thought

Inductive means "leading into." Inductive thought begins with the observation of representative individual phenomena—as many of them as are necessary to reach valid conclusions—and arrives at a general law concerning them, thus:

The scientist (or any careful thinker) makes his observations consciously and controls them so far as he can, but for most of us, our inductive generalizations, the assumptions on which we order our lives, our personal stock of "general laws," are the half-conscious accretions of our total experience. The result is that we are scarcely aware of the process of inductive thought which lies behind them. Consider the numerous general assumptions that make up your stock of "laws."

> It is unwise to touch a hot stove.
> December is colder than July.
> A motorist should carry extra water when he crosses Death Valley.
> Eight o'clock classes come too early in the morning.
> The Irish are pugnacious.

All these (and of course many more like them) are inductive generalizations based on repeated observations of phenomena—sometimes your own, sometimes those of others. Your wariness of hot stoves was established early; of eight o'clock classes, late. Your expectation of cold in December and heat in July developed gradually, from your own observations and the comments of your family and friends. Your conviction that an Irishman likes to fight perhaps comes from the comic strips.

Those "general laws" are not equally valid. Below the equator, cold weather comes during our summer. Some Irishmen—for example, Oliver Goldsmith—are conspicuously gentle. It follows that our casual generalizations are not automatically expressive of truth. We must test our generalizations as the scientist does; and, like him, we must be aware of the process by which we reach them. We must be sure, first, that we are taking all the facts into consideration. A shockproof watch could be dropped on a down pillow without damage. Second, we must be sure our instances are fair and representative. Every member of Beta Theta Pi may assert that fraternities are valuable additions to the campus, but general student opinion may not agree. Third, we must be sure that our instances are numerous enough. To discover what the student body thinks of the football coach, we really should ask every student, but if we ask enough representative students to provide a fair sample, we can form a reasonably good generalization. Finally, we must be sure that our evidence actually supports our conclusion.

HASTY GENERALIZATION

The danger in inductive reasoning is that we will "jump to conclusions" and decide too quickly that we have found a general law when really all we have is a *hasty generalization*. We have already seen a number of them. One swallow does not make a summer, nor do the opinions of half a dozen coeds make a fair sampling of student opinion in general. But notice that only one example may justify drawing a generalized inference. Biologists were sure that the fish known only from fossils as *Coelacanthidae* had long been extinct until an unmistakable coelacanth was drawn up in a net off the African coast. That single specimen disproved their theory, and the subsequent recovery of others has merely confirmed the evidence provided by the first. More important than the number of instances is the representative character of the instances. A political worker ringing doorbells in a prosperous suburb may form an opinion of his party's chances that differs greatly from that formed by a precinct worker in the slums; neither one can accurately predict the results of the election. Finally, we must try to consider all the implications of our facts. The skull and jawbone of Piltdown Man were certainly facts, but it required the discovery of secondary facts to lead paleontologists to the truth.

To avoid hasty generalization in inductive reasoning, we should apply four tests to all inductive generalizations:

1. Have we taken all the facts into account?
2. Are the instances fair and representative?
3. Are the instances numerous enough?
4. Does the announced generalization necessarily follow?

CAUSAL REASONING

A special form of inductive reasoning deals with causes and effects. If a given phenomenon is regularly followed by a particular result, and if there appears to be a necessary relation between the two, we say that the phenomenon causes the result.

Identifying causes is difficult. Often we are concerned only with *proximate* causes, that is, those which act immediately to produce the effects. Or we are concerned with *necessary* causes and *sufficient* causes, that is, those which must be present before the effect can occur and those which seem in themselves important enough to lead to the effect. Usually we need to look for *concomitant* causes: several present at once and all necessary.

There are two chief dangers to guard against in causal reasoning. The first is oversimplification: selecting one in a necessary complex of causes and assigning it undue primacy—not all slum children are delinquents. The other is confusing cause with effect or both with sheer coincidence. Which comes first, the chicken or the egg? A man spills a drink on the boss at an office party. When he is later passed over for promotion, he is sure the boss holds a grudge against him. Whose policies caused the Great Depression? President Hoover was in office when it began, and he was chosen as the scapegoat.

CAUSAL REASONING: POST HOC, ERGO PROPTER HOC

This particular form of faulty reasoning, in fact, is so common that it has a special name, being known as "the *post hoc* fallacy." Just because one phenomenon preceded another in time, we must not assume that it caused the other. Walking under a ladder at 8:50 probably will not cause you to fail a quiz in your ten o'clock— unless, indeed, you are so superstitious that the incident is still haunting you more than an hour later; and even then the superstitious cast of your mind might be considered the real cause. Beware of arguing "after this, therefore because of this": *post hoc, ergo propter hoc*. Between two events, look for a real connection, a plausible, probable, cause-and-effect relation.

We must always test causal reasoning by asking these questions:

1. Is the assumed cause sufficient to produce the effect?
2. Does the result regularly and necessarily follow?
3. Might there be other causes? Is the assumed cause an oversimplification?
4. Is the assumed cause merely coincidental?

ANALOGY

Still another type of inductive reasoning is reasoning by analogy, that is, reasoning which assumes that things similar in some respects will be similar in others. But sometimes the assumed similarities do not exist; thus reasoning by analogy is often misleading. You learned inductively long ago, for example, that most English verbs form their past tenses and past participles by adding -*ed* to the infinitive form. In your reading you come across a new verb, say *saccharify*, which you decide to use yourself. By analogy with other verbs (and with due regard to spelling analogies) you quite properly employ *saccharified* as a past tense. Analogous reasoning has been helpful to you. But the three-year-old child who reasons the same way and says, "We buyed it at the store," unwittingly illustrates the basic danger in the method. Things similar in some ways may very well be quite different in other very important ways. Analogy breaks down unless the things being compared are really similar at the point of comparison.

Analogy is also used in argument merely as vivid illustration. Lincoln urged the voters not to change Presidents in the middle of the Civil War by warning them against swapping horses in the middle of a stream. He remonstrated with the critics of administration policies by comparing them to people who would let a man get halfway across Niagara Falls on a tightrope and then start shaking the rope. Both analogies made effective illustrations, but they proved nothing at all. Changing Presidents in wartime may be bad, but it is not really very much like swapping horses in midstream; steering the Ship of State (to suggest a third, metaphoric analogy) is not much like walking a jostled tightrope.

ANALOGY: FALSE ANALOGY

Such illustrative analogies are never proof, but they are often very persuasive. Often dangerously persuasive, too, are "false analogies," which do not illustrate the point at issue but instead obscure it by offering a comparison in which the resemblance is too remote to be relevant, or one which is flatly untrue.

> Parents should not attempt to judge the school system or criticize the methods of its teachers. To do so is like trying to tell the doctor how to remove Johnny's appendix.
> I have served for years on the City Council, whereas all my opponent has ever done is stand up before the Council and object to its decisions. Would you elect an untried boy to do a man's work?
> Where there's smoke, there's fire.
> Anybody who objects to federal old-age health insurance would probably like to abolish the fire department and go back to the days of the bucket brigades.

We must always test an argument by analogy by asking, "Are the point at issue and the analogous example sufficiently alike to justify the conclusion?"

The *method of reasoning,* notice, has nothing to do with the manner of *presenting the results* in an argument. In analyzing an argument, ask yourself always how the thinker reached his decisive opinion and what kind of decision he reached. In inductive thought, we examine details and reach general principles. The public opinion pollsters, for example, question representative voters, then decide what the general opinion is. Yet typically the polls are presented in the paper with the logical conclusion as the headline and the details of questioning later. As a logical process, the thinking is still inductive.

EXERCISES

Identify each of the following as inductive reasoning, causal reasoning, or reasoning by analogy. Determine the validity of each conclusion by applying the appropriate tests. Identify any hasty generalizations, *post hoc* fallacies, or false analogies.

1. Indiscriminate use of pesticides is harmful to birds.
2. When many automobiles in the line of traffic ahead of you try to move out of the lane they are in, you may expect some kind of obstruction in the lane.
3. Over three-fourths of the students who did well on the test as a whole missed question 4. It must have been confusingly phrased.
4. Charlie told Professor Snodgrass that he didn't finish his research paper because he had mononucleosis. I'm going to try that on Coberly. If it works once, it ought to work again.
5. The dean was angry when I went in to see him, so he refused to approve my petition for a change of grade.
6. I don't like pizza. I tried some once and it was as soggy as a wet pot holder.
7. Most business executives have large vocabularies. The way to be a business executive is to learn a lot of words.
8. My English teacher is unfair. I always got A's in English in high school, not C's.
9. Carlyle said that democracy is unworkable, and that one might as well expect the captain of a ship to take a vote of the crew every time he wanted to tack his ship.
10. I wouldn't put soda in a drink if I were you. I did, just last night, and this morning I had a dreadful headache.
11. Dictionary editors attempt to determine what words mean by carefully examining the contexts in which they appear. The principle is explicit in the prefaces of most dictionaries.
12. My teacher said *plausible* doesn't mean the same thing as *feasi-*

ble, but that's what it means in the theme I wrote, and context determines meaning.

13. A straight line is the shortest distance between two points. Try measurements.
14. Making a formal outline for a short theme is like using an electric garbage disposal unit to get rid of an eggshell.
15. This is the kind of rain that floods Roosevelt Street.

Deductive Thought

The second basic form of thinking is concerned with the application of inductive generalizations to particular instances—with predicting that what we have observed to be true of phenomena in the past will be true of a similar phenomenon in the future.

Deductive means "leading away from." Deductive thought begins with a general law and proceeds from it to the particular, thus:

Having decided that it is not good for a watch to be dropped, you take yours away from your year-old nephew, having reasoned,

No watch should be dropped.
This is a watch.
Therefore, this should not be dropped.

—although you probably did not phrase your thoughts so formally.

THE SYLLOGISM

The formal pattern of deductive thinking is called the *syllogism.* It consists of three parts: the *major premise,* the *minor premise,* and the *conclusion.* A valid major premise makes a statement which is presumed to be true of all members of a given class, the minor premise identifies a particular instance as a member of that class, and the conclusion says that what is true of all members must be true of the individual member.

MAJOR PREMISE: All men are mortal.
MINOR PREMISE: Socrates is a man.
CONCLUSION: Therefore, Socrates is mortal.

The most common pattern may be reduced to a formula:

	Affirmative	Negative
MAJOR PREMISE:	All A's are B.	No A's are B.
MINOR PREMISE:	C is A.	C is A.
CONCLUSION:	C is B.	C is not B.

You may remember it by arranging the terms alphabetically around a figure 3:

All   A's   are   B.

C ⎯⎯ is ⟩ A.

C ⎯ is ⟩ B.

In mathematics, things equal to the same thing are equal to each other, but in logic the elements of this formula may not be rearranged with impunity. We cannot argue,

All A's are B.   All A's are B.
All men are mortal.   Socialists are liberal.
C is B.   C is B.
Fido is mortal.   He is liberal.
C is A.   C is A.
Fido is a man.   He is a Socialist.

We have rearranged the formula, and the resulting argument is clearly invalid.

There are two important variants to this common (or *categorical*) form.

One, called the *disjunctive* syllogism, deals with alternatives and strictly requires two in an *either-or* relationship, like the questions in the game of Twenty Questions or the binary items fed into a computer.

MAJOR PREMISE: All matter is either organic or inorganic.
MINOR PREMISE: This object is not organic.
CONCLUSION: This object is inorganic.

The second, called the *hypothetical* syllogism, sets up a condition and its necessary result, shows that a particular set of circumstances satisfies the conditions, and concludes that the result will follow as a matter of course.

MAJOR PREMISE: If a satisfactory student misses the final examination because of a genuine emergency, he is eligible for a grade of *Incomplete*.

MINOR PREMISE: Mr. Birch's case satisfies these conditions.

CONCLUSION: Mr. Birch is eligible for a grade of *Incomplete*.

In all deductive reasoning, we must be certain that our premises really state truths—that *all* A's are B, and not merely *some* A's; and that C really belongs in Class A—or we must qualify our conclusions to fit the probabilities. If only *some* A's are B, and C really is A, all we can say is that C *may be* B, or *is probably* B, or *could be* B. We must be certain that the terms which seem similar all mean the same thing. And we must respect the basic formula. Otherwise any conclusion will be a *non sequitur:* "It does not follow."

NON SEQUITUR

A *non sequitur* is any conclusion which cannot logically be inferred from the premises, whether (1) the minor premise does not really fit under the major premise because the terms of the premises are mixed, (2) the formula is rearranged, or (3) the conclusion is simply irrelevant.

Fraternities are frivolous organizations.
Phi Beta Kappa is a fraternity—

(Wait a minute. The terms are mixed, and any conclusion will be a *non sequitur.*)

Some college students are lazy.
He is a college student—

(Again the terms are mixed. He may not be a member of the limited class named in the major premise.)

Hard work is honorable.
Stealing refrigerators is hard work—

(Isn't *hard work* in the major premise somehow different from *hard work* in the minor one?)

All city governments need more income.
Licensed gambling will produce more income—

(The formula has been rearranged. Any conclusion will be a *non sequitur*.)

> Examinations are considered important even when a student is too nervous to do good work.
> This is an examination, whether I am nervous or not.
> Therefore, examinations are unfair.

(There may be a valid chain of inferences here, but, as the syllogism stands, the conclusion is a *non sequitur* because it is irrelevant to the premises.)

Finally, if your reader or hearer declines to accept as true the statement made by either the major or the minor premise, the whole argument is unconvincing, although the syllogism itself follows the formula exactly. Logic, we should remember, can be used for false purposes as well as for true.

> All Irishmen are pugnacious—

(But Goldsmith was not. I do not believe the major premise and will follow the argument no further.)

> Murderers should be hanged.
> He is a murderer—

(I don't know whether he is or not, because he hasn't been tried yet. I want no part in a lynching.)

There are numerous other ways in which the syllogistic formula may be distorted to produce fallacious results, but virtually all of them may be avoided by applying four tests to the argument:

1. Does the major premise really present a general truth?
2. Does the particular instance identified by the minor premise really belong to the class named by the major premise?
3. Do the terms which appear to be identical really point to identical referents?
4. Does the announced conclusion necessarily follow?

In considering the nature of evidence, we have seen that assertion is not evidence. One of the greatest weaknesses of student arguments lies in the mere assertion of the truth of a premise without offering supporting detail. The opposition may not believe that it is true, and will regard any conclusion as a *non sequitur* and the rest of the argument as invalid.

Everyone knows that required courses are a waste of the student's time—

The Democratic party attracts the best men—

Once the nation has adopted a policy, it must stick to it—

If such "truths" were self-evident, there would be no need to argue. Unless your premises are accepted, the whole argument based on them will collapse.

THE ENTHYMEME

As you are already aware, in practice we seldom think in terms of the formal syllogism (though sometimes, in an elaborated argument, all the elements are present, in one form or another). Instead, we more often use a clipped form known as the *enthymeme*, that is, a syllogism for which any one of the three elements has been implied rather than explicitly stated. We say,

> If you don't study, you'll flunk. (*Omitted: Those who don't study, flunk—the major premise.*)

Or we say,

> You'll pass. He passes all Betas. (*Omitted: You're a Beta—the minor premise.*)

Or we say,

> All freshmen are required to take English, and you're a freshman. (*Omitted: Therefore you must take English—the conclusion.*)

The tests we used to check the validity of the syllogism also apply, of course, to the enthymeme. We need merely to be a little more alert to consider whether or not we accept as valid whatever element has been omitted from the argument.

CHAINS OF DEDUCTION

Very often, perhaps most often, deductive reasoning becomes even more informal than it is in the enthymeme. We not only leave out one of the elements of a syllogism; we compress a whole chain of syllogistic reasoning into what seems on the surface to be a single thought. Having tried the Union coffee time and again, you have established a generalization: All Union coffee is bitter. As a friend offers you a cup of coffee at the Union, you hastily reason,

> All Union coffee is bitter.
> This is Union coffee.
> Therefore, this is bitter.
> I dislike bitter coffee (another inductive generalization).
> This is bitter coffee.
> Therefore, I shall dislike this.
> I do not wish to drink what I dislike (another inductive generaliza-
> tion).
> I shall dislike this.
> Therefore, I do not wish to drink this.

And you decline the proffered cup, saying instead, "I'd rather have a coke," as the result of a scramble down a second chain.

The more complex the chain, the harder it is to apply our tests to the individual syllogisms; but if we run into disagreement, we shall have to reconstruct the argument in order to find the point of dispute. We shall usually find that somewhere we have assumed the truth of a premise that has not met general acceptance. Whenever this happens, the whole argument breaks down until we can establish the disputed premise as valid. It is precisely these rejected premises which appear most often in student themes as unsupported assertions. They will certainly be questioned unless they are bolstered by the evidence.

Again, the *method of reasoning* has nothing to do with the manner of *presenting the results* in an argument. Ask yourself always how the thinker reached his decisive opinion and what kind of decision he reached. In deductive thought, we apply general principles to particular circumstances, and the logical conclusion— wherever it comes in the paper—is more specific than the premises which support it.

In practice, as we shall see, few arguments are entirely deductive (or entirely inductive), and in a largely deductive argument, we virtually never find a syllogism laid out explicitly, and carefully shaped to the formulas. Instead we may find introductory material, an announced major premise or general principle, and the evidence and reasoning to support it, which may include subsidiary syllogisms and the support they need. Then we may find the minor premise and its evidence, and finally the logical conclusion. Or the logical conclusion may *begin* the paper, with the evidence and reasoning presented afterward. Or the basic argument or its parts may be enthymemes. We need to reduce the argument to its bones to see its nature. Reread the passage from "The Adventure of the Blue Carbuncle" to see how deductive reasoning may be presented. Sherlock Holmes is there presenting a long series of syllogisms to Dr. Watson. One of them, for example, might be reconstructed to show the bones:

MAJOR PREMISE: A purchaser who has a hat-securer attached to a new hat has foresight.

MINOR PREMISE: The purchaser of this hat had a hat-securer attached.

CONCLUSION: The purchaser of this hat had foresight.

The major premise of that syllogism is virtually self-evident, so Holmes offers no support. He assumes, safely, that Dr. Watson will accept it as the result of inductive observations of his own. In that sense, the basically deductive argument is a matter of compounded thought, with inductive and deductive elements intermixed.

EXERCISE

Identify each of the following as syllogism or enthymeme. For each syllogism, reconstruct the formal argument and identify the major premise, the minor premise, and the conclusion. If any syllogisms are invalid, explain why. For each enthymeme, supply the missing element. If any of the resulting syllogisms are invalid, explain why. If a deductive chain is involved, reconstruct the chain.

1. As hard as it is raining now, Roosevelt Street must be flooded.
2. Judging from all the elementary mistakes in this paper, you're either very careless or very ignorant.
3. The way that dog chases cars, he's going to be killed. You ought to break him of that habit.
4. The repetition in this paragraph is distracting because it serves no discernible purpose.
5. There must be a cat in the yard, the way that mockingbird is squawking.
6. If the grass is not mowed soon, the whole yard will have to be raked.
7. Be sure to read Professor Snodgrass's new book before you write your research paper. His work is invariably significant.
8. There was no mistake in your grade of F. No one can pass this

course without having written a research paper, revised all themes, and taken the final examination.

9. If you leave that camera in the car in plain sight, it may be stolen even though you lock the car.

10. The senator's proposal is unacceptable. It would place in the hands of one small segment of the population the power to control the production, and therefore the price, of a commodity essential to many elements of our economy.

Compounded Thought

In practice, the methods of inductive thought and those of deductive thought usually interact and intermingle, as we run almost instantaneously through the complex process of evaluating the evidence presented by a given situation, of considering pertinent inductive generalizations from our stock of general laws, and of applying them deductively to the particular situation confronting us. In other words, we examine the implications of whatever facts are presented to us, draw the inferences to which they lead, and reach the most nearly valid conclusions we can. Usually many sets of inductions and deductions lie behind even our simplest thought. A driver on a busy street, for example, suddenly realizes that a car in the next traffic lane is inadvertently edging toward his front fender. He honks to alert the inattentive driver and swerves as much as he safely can, avoiding an accident. It is all over in an instant and seems almost instinctive. Yet even in that simple response there is a chain of compounded inductive and deductive thinking that is almost too complicated to follow.

Inductively, our driver has previously established several general laws: Automobiles, left to themselves, tend to continue in the direction in which they are already moving. Two automobiles traveling on converging courses at the same rate of speed over the same distance will collide. Collisions are to be avoided. Attentive drivers usually do not deliberately ram other cars. Inattentive drivers may be recalled to alertness if they hear a warning horn. A driver may safely swerve away from one line of traffic if he is careful not to interfere with traffic on the other side. We could identify still others, but these will suffice.

Deductively, these generalizations are applied to the particular circumstances. For example, one of the numerous syllogisms hidden behind the driver's instantaneous response is

Inattentive drivers may be recalled to alertness if they hear a warning horn.
This driver is an inattentive driver.
Therefore, this driver may be recalled to alertness if he hears a
warning horn.

And our driver honks accordingly. The entire chain of reasoning—
"Our automobiles are on converging courses and will collide unless
we do something about it. I don't want a collision; so I'll honk to
wake up the other driver, meanwhile swerving as far as I can"—
could be analyzed in detail to show how inductive generalizations
are used as premises for deductive syllogisms, or how the conclusion
of one syllogism may become the major premise or the minor premise of another. But perhaps it is already clear that the two basic
patterns of thought can be identified in compounded chains of
inference if it becomes necessary.

Usually it is not necessary. What is necessary is that we understand the basic patterns, so that if our arguments are challenged—or
if we are dubious of someone else's arguments—we can examine
and test the arguments in order to identify and correct the fallacious reasoning, whether the trouble results from faulty inductions,
from invalid premises, or from untenable conclusions.

EXERCISES

1. With two men on and the score at 5 to 4 in the last of the ninth
   inning, the manager of the losing team sends in a pinch hitter.
   The catcher signals for a high, fast pitch; the batter does not
   swing; and the umpire calls "Ball one," as the batter expected.
   Reconstruct the reasoning of the catcher and the batter.
2. With temperature at 34° F, the weather forecast is changed at
   2:30 on Friday afternoon to warn of a chance of snow beginning
   about 5 P.M. The director of the Department of Public Works
   considers calling up emergency crews to spread salt on the main
   traffic arteries and alerting standby crews for snow removal. Instead, he notifies the police that crews will be alerted for possible
   night work. Reconstruct his reasoning.
3. Under the circumstances outlined in 3, above, the chief of the
   Traffic Division of the Metropolitan Police cancels all leave and
   notifies the precinct captains that patrolmen should be held on
   duty until 6 P.M., or until further notice. Reconstruct his reasoning.

Three Common Fallacies

Fallacies are errors in reasoning. As we examined inductive thinking and deductive thinking, we considered four very important types: *hasty generalizations, post hoc fallacies, false analogies,* and *non sequiturs.* There remain three others that are equally common and equally dangerous: *the faulty dilemma, begging the question,* and *ignoring the question.*

FAULTY DILEMMA

A dilemma is a "two-horned" proposition, an argument that places an opponent squarely between two equally unpalatable choices. International politics, especially, produces many awkward dilemmas. Between World Wars I and II, Britain was caught between her commitments to the Arab nations and her sympathy for Zionist ambitions. The establishment of Israel by the United Nations did little to solve her problems. Similarly, Russia found herself caught between her chance in Castro's Cuba to confront the United States with armed missile bases in the Caribbean and her unwillingness to precipitate war; under pressure by President Kennedy, Premier Khrushchev accepted public defeat and withdrew the missiles. We ourselves have had to choose between our sympathies with newly independent nations and our loyalty to such old friends as Britain, France, and the Netherlands; or between our commitments to Nationalist China and the international facts of life. In domestic politics, an officeholder must often choose between his own strong convictions and the vociferously expressed opinions of his constituents or his party. A student on an examination must frequently decide whether to admit that he doesn't know the answer or try to bluff—and perhaps fail either way. A dilemma can be very real.

A **faulty dilemma,** however, is one that offers a choice between two courses of action—or two answers—but ignores and thereby attempts to conceal alternative possibilities. The classic example is the "Have you stopped beating your wife?" question. The soda fountain clerk mixing a malted milk offers you a faulty dilemma with the sudden question, "Do you want one egg in it or two?" (at ten cents an egg). The politician offers one when he screams, "Elect Joe Doakes or doom the nation to disaster!" The disjunctive syllogism (see page 244) is especially susceptible to the faulty dilemma.

All college students are either underclassmen or upperclassmen—

(That sounds all right, until you think of graduate students.) When faced with a dilemma, examine it for concealed alternatives.

BEGGING THE QUESTION

To **beg the question** is to present a proposition in terms that assume as proved a point still under dispute. A partisan newspaper editorial begs the question when it announces,

> No thinking American could approve so unacceptable a policy as the one the Administration is suggesting.

If the policy under debate were really unacceptable to every thinking American, it would never have been presented for consideration. The prosecuting attorney in a murder trial would beg the question more than once if he thundered at the jury,

> Are you willing to take upon your souls the responsibility for releasing this dangerous murderer to prey again and again on innocent, law-abiding citizens?

The very purpose of the trial is to determine whether or not the defendant is a murderer.

A debater begs the question when he "argues in a circle," when, that is, he assumes a point (often "for the sake of the argument"), proceeds to a conclusion on the strength of it, and then, having "established" his conclusion, announces triumphantly that this conclusion proves the original assumption. Much of the fun of the Gilbert and Sullivan operas comes from Gilbert's skill in playing with such circular reasoning. In *H.M.S. Pinafore*, for example, the central argument is clear:

> Assume that naval officers must come from well-born families. Suppose two babies are confused by a nurse, so that the well-born one is believed to be "the other." Then, when both enter the Royal Navy, the wrong one, naturally, rises to become a captain and quite unreasonably holds command over his former foster brother. But let the truth of their birth come out, and the false Captain automatically becomes an Able Seaman, and Ralph, the former seaman, logically becomes "the Captain of the *Pinafore*."

But circular reasoning can be very serious indeed. Before World War II, both Mussolini and Hitler encouraged large families, to provide more potential soldiers for strong armies. The growing population then obviously needed more land and more resources—*lebensraum*. To get it, the dictators went to war, and countries at war obviously need more soldiers for strong armies. Will Durant called it "a veritable pinwheel of logic"; yet millions of lives around the world were drawn into the vortex of the tornado it created.

In student argument, however, the commonest form of begging the question is the one we have already met in considering the *non sequiturs* that always result: the assertion as true of unacceptable and unsupported premises. Those premises may well be valid; perhaps they usually are. But to depend on assertion alone, without evidence and without proof (unless your hostile audience will accept it at face value), is to beg the question and lose the argument.

IGNORING THE QUESTION

To **ignore the question** is to talk about something else, to evade the point at issue. The student in an examination who does not know the answer to the question asked, and who, pretending that he misunderstood, optimistically answers some vaguely similar question instead, is ignoring the question. The lawyer with a weak case who stays away from the evidence and strives instead to impress his own personality on the members of the jury is ignoring the question, whether he browbeats them or tries to get them to laugh at his jokes. One of the most common and at the same time most obvious ways of ignoring the question is to resort to the *argumentum ad hominem*, the "argument against the man," which, instead of discussing the issues, attempts to discredit the man who supports the opposing side. Mudslinging political campaigns provide frequent examples. A candidate who years ago was exempted from the draft as a conscientious objector may find it brought up as implied cowardice. Side issues and "red herrings" of all sorts, name-calling and glittering generality, in fact, all the emotional appeals we shall next consider, are concerned with ignoring the question. That is their very reason for being.

All seven of these fallacies are common and dangerous. Watch out for them.

EXERCISES

Identify the common fallacies exemplified by the following.

1. The *Literary Digest* in 1936 mailed ballot cards to people whose names had been culled from telephone directories all over the country. The "straw votes" returned were cast overwhelmingly for Landon. Yet Roosevelt won the election despite the *Literary Digest* prediction.

2. Albertus Magnus, "the head of scholasticism, . . . decided in [the Virgin's] favor the question: 'Whether the Blessed Virgin possessed perfectly the seven liberal arts.' . . . 'I hold that she did, for it is written, "Wisdom has built herself a house, and has sculptured seven columns." That house is the blessed Virgin; the seven columns are the seven liberal arts. Mary, therefore, had perfect mastery of science.' "

Henry Adams

3. "Let us assume, for the sake of the argument, that whatever is good for America is good for the world, since America is one of the leading nations of the world. High tariff rates make it possible for American manufacturers to compete in the American market with foreign manufacturers who can produce more cheaply because they pay lower wages than the American standard of living permits American workers to live on. Because under a high tariff American manufacturers can profitably compete in the American market, American prosperity is supported and American generosity to the less efficient nations of the world is made possible. And American generosity is necessary because foreign manufacturers simply cannot meet American competition for the American market, the world's richest market. We must remain prosperous because we must continue aiding other nations to stay solvent. So it is obvious that high American tariff rates are not only good for America and for the free world, but are indeed essential to the free world's very economic survival."

4. Park it or drive it!

5. Old Withers is well known in this state, all right. He's been running for some office or other ever since anybody can remember. Now when he talks about graft in the statehouse, he expects people to take him seriously. "Often a bridesmaid, but never a bride!" Who'd listen to him?

6. Since President McClanahan assumed office in 1963, the enrollment of students in the college has increased by nearly 20 per-

cent. Clearly the president's policies have greatly strengthened our academic standing.

7. Senator Blooper, touring Europe as a member of the Senate Committee on What and Why Not, deplored the importation of plastic eidolons into the United States without duty. An editorial in the *Ruritanische Morgenblatt* in turn denounced the United States for reversing its policy of encouraging trade with members of the Common Market.

8. Admittedly the police department is corrupt, but better that than no police at all.

9. Go by railroad, and arrive in the middle of town, where you want to be, and not in the middle of nowhere, miles from the city.

10. I'm glad you asked that question about my conviction for so-called nonpayment of taxes. I am reminded of a story. It seems there were two Irishmen, Pat and Mike. Pat said to Mike, "I hear yez hev been in jail fer not payin' yer income tax." And Mike answered, "Begorrah, an' how could anybody be payin' fer an income that he can't see fer the whizzin' by of the outgo?" Are you fully aware, my friends, how the cost of living has been allowed to climb—nay, forced to climb—since . . . ?

EMOTIONAL APPEALS[1]

Two sides of our natures, the rational and the emotional, get badly mixed up, and because thought is painful and arduous, we often allow ourselves to be unduly influenced by our emotions. We have been talking about reasoning; it is time we concerned ourselves rather with the ways in which anyone who has a slightly dubious ax to grind—whether he is an unscrupulous political demagogue, or an advertiser, or an editor or writer, or only the classmate who wants us to cut class and go to a movie—seeks to overpower our reasoning by appealing to our emotions instead of our intelligence. Insofar as they can be treated in logical terms at all, they invariably lead to *non sequiturs*, as could be seen very readily if they were expanded into the syllogisms they imply.

[1] Much of the following section is based on the work of Clyde Miller and the Institute for Propaganda Analysis, supplemented by material suggested by Vance Packard, *The Hidden Persuaders* (New York: David McKay Company, 1957).

All those who use Brand X soap become rich executives.
I wish to become a rich executive.
I should use Brand X soap.

Not only are premises invalid, but the syllogistic formula is badly scrambled; yet we are bombarded with such arguments so constantly that some have even suggested we are losing the power of logical thought and are in danger of acting entirely on emotional impulses.

There are, to begin with, innumerable insidious ways of pricking our emotions and getting us "to make up our minds" without using our minds at all. Appeals to fear, to love, to pride, to hope, to greed, to hatred, to our sense of humor—we cannot begin to examine them all. All we can do is consider some of the most common emotional appeals and let our awareness of their characteristics make us wary of others like them.

But as we consider them, we should also realize that a touch of emotional appeal is not necessarily bad in itself. Even sound intellectual proof will customarily be presented in terms to which the audience will respond favorably; only an idiot would present a good case in terms calculated to make his audience reject it. Only an excessive or a dishonest use of appeal to emotion is bad. If we learn to recognize emotional appeals when we see them, we can discount them adequately with a simple rule of thumb: *The more emotional the appeal, probably the weaker the case.* No one lays down a real smoke screen unless he has something to hide.

NAME-CALLING

Name-calling (also called mudslinging) is the use of bad labels designed to make us reject an idea because we are prejudiced against the terms in which it is presented. The phrase "this creeping socialism" may disguise a proposal to provide milk for grade school lunches. The proposal may be a bad proposal, but it is hardly "creeping socialism." Be wary of such labels as *Red, reactionary, left-winger, old fogey, un-American, extravagant, imperialist, isolationist.* Such terms are loaded terms and are not designed to help you think clearly about the ideas they conceal. Again, ask yourself, "What is the idea worth without the bad labels?"

GLITTERING GENERALITY

A glittering generality is a good label, a general term designed to make us respond favorably to an idea because we are prejudiced in favor of the terms in which it is presented. "This gallant leader of men—." Could that mean a modern Jesse James? "Social security," "the system of free enterprise," "the pioneer spirit," "justice" (especially "simple justice"), "this man of vision" (the opposition may be using the bad label "visionary")—all such good labels are likely to be concealing something. What is the idea itself worth?

For both Name-Calling and Glittering Generality, it is valuable to try to reduce the idea to neutral terms which will avoid slanting the presentation either way. It may not always be possible to eliminate all opinion and leave only fact, but the closer you can get to fact, the better.

TESTIMONIAL

Testimonial pretends to be authoritative opinion. It quotes some prominent person who is willing to say publicly that a given idea, outside his special field, is good or bad, and attempts to transfer his prestige to the idea concerned. The baseball player who testifies to the quality of a make of baseball bat is an authority testifying in his own special field, but when he starts talking about cigarettes, he is off-base; and so is the great mathematician talking politics, or the singer discussing economic theory, or the wealthy debutante who flashes a multicarat diamond and murmurs the name of a brand of soap. Increasingly, no specific testimony is offered, the device having perhaps become too obvious. But the direct association of name or face accomplishes the same result, even if the personage has to be explicitly identified as a "famous fashion designer," or whatever, for the uninitiated. Apply the tests used for the testimony of authorities: Is this person an expert on this subject? Is he reliable? up to date? prejudiced?

PLAIN FOLKS

Testimonial is often based on snobbery. Plain folks is the other side of the coin. It attempts to convince us that an idea or product or a man is "of the people," that other very ordinary people just like us have accepted it. Every political candidate pretends to like fishing and babies and farming, to be a "plain ordinary guy." The "cracker barrel philosopher" makes even quite commonplace ideas seem profound when he utters them in a back-country accent. What is the idea worth in itself?

BAND WAGON

Band wagon appeals to our faith in the majority, to our desire to be one of a crowd. If many others have accepted an idea or a product, why shouldn't we?

> This book is the current best seller. Everybody is reading it.
> Twenty million housewives buy this brand of soap.

Jump on the band wagon! Go with the crowd! But what is the idea worth?

TRANSFER

Transfer, the broadest of the emotional appeals, attempts to carry the responses we have toward one thing over to something else. Even though it is by no means new (we have long had pretty girls in advertisements for all sorts of things), research in the last decade or so has given the publicist greater skill in handling the device. We see fewer efforts these days to tie together such diverse items as puppies and cigarettes, and are given instead more and more figures with which, in psychosociological cant, we can "identify" ourselves. "To identify" is to put oneself in the picture, to transfer to oneself the characteristics of another or to imagine some direct relationship with another. The term indicates a new insight into an old phenomenon and helps to explain, for example, our personal sense of involvement in a tragic play or a romantic novel. Those who seek to manipulate our minds for their own purposes use our tendency to identify ourselves with others to appeal directly to our emotions, especially to fear, to pride, or to concupiscence.

Direct appeals to fear, for ourselves or others, can most easily be seen in insurance advertisements: We identify ourselves with the man driven into the night with his family by fire, or we identify our own families with those bereaved, and bereft of support, by the death of an uninsured breadwinner. On a larger scale, we are led to identify ourselves with those who will be affected by proposed social programs, like the abolition of poverty or the broadening of civil rights, by appeals to our hopes for or our fears of the consequences.

Appeals to pride in many forms—snobbishness, desire for status, desire to conform or to be a nonconformist—are common weapons in the salesman's arsenal, whether he is selling automobiles or electric back scratchers or ideas. Sleek automobiles of the latest model are shown drawn up before luxurious homes, and we are invited to identify ourselves with the owner or his mink-clad companion. The "planned obsolescence" of styling appeals to our pride in being up-to-date. It encourages us in all things to avoid return to the "horse-and-buggy days," materially or ideologically, but instead to be proud of our shiny status symbols.

Also very common are more or less subtle sexual appeals, like the ubiquitous pretty girls and the virile men with whom we can identify ourselves in one way or another. They turn up in many places; recently no political campaign has been complete until a covey of movie stars has rallied to the support of each candidate. There are, too, the tattooed cigarette smoker, with his hint of recklessness and adventure; the suavely piratical beard or eye-patch; the throaty female "Sure" of the beer commercial; the sly double meanings of slogans. (One of the last backfired: A leading cigarette was widely advertised as "a *man's* smoke," but the women in the market declined to be attracted and decided instead to let the men smoke it. The appeal was shifted to stress loyalty to the brand.)

Finally, there are still examples of transfer which appeal to our emotions without asking us to identify ourselves directly with some attractive figure. Appeals to patriotism, for example, may picture the Founding Fathers, mention some cheap blended whiskey, and leave it to us to make the connection if we can. "Old Ironsides" illustrates an insurance company's appeal. The flag appears in full color on a newspaper masthead. Babies, kittens (but rarely cats), mountain scenery, honored names (who could doubt the integrity of a company named for Lincoln?), the stern and rockbound coast or the little white churches of New England, and many more things for which we feel respect or affection may be used with wild irrelevance.

IMAGES

The deliberate development of "images" for our public figures or institutions in order to manipulate our responses is a growing device. We are increasingly being given jerry-built façades which show us only what the public relations consultants have decided we will respond to favorably. The idea itself is not new. William Henry Harrison's supporters turned the mansion on Berkeley Plantation into a more appropriate log cabin and Harrison into a poor man's son. The senior Rockefeller was converted from a ruthless monopolist into a philanthropist dispensing millions to public charities and dimes to caddies on the golf course. What is new is the building of whole political campaigns around a controlled and selected image: the "father image" of President Eisenhower's second campaign, for example, which was so well established that the Democrats hesitated to attack it; instead they learned the technique and built an "older brother—successful son image" for President Kennedy's campaign. A number of major corporations have recently shifted their images, a great public utility becoming the little man's friend or the great manufacturing complex becoming the unselfish patron of research and education. When such jobs are skillfully done, they are hard to detect; but we can at least be aware that the manipulators are at work.

HUMOR AND THE BIZARRE

An appeal which is difficult to classify and which may touch at one point or another on many of the other appeals is the intentional appeal to humor ("intentional," because if the others are too obvious, they may seem funny when they are not supposed to). The lawyer staying away from the evidence and making the jury laugh is indulging in the fallacy of ignoring the question, but the compact car that refuses to take itself seriously in its advertisements is parodying the emotional appeals of its competitors. The shapely movie comedienne and a double meaning in the copy provide both the sexual transfer and a welcome laugh at it. Cartoons, shaving-cream jingles, adverse images like that of the Bulbsnatcher, satiric prose—these and many more illustrate the humorous appeal.

The use of the bizarre is not quite the same thing. There may be a nervous laugh involved, but the chief reliance is on shock or bewilderment. The fate in store for the man who uses the wrong bitters in his drinks, the nonchalant man-about-town seated sideways on a white horse to plug a brand of whiskey, the grammatical solecisms of Madison Avenue prose—even the deliberate misspellings in the counter-signs of a department store—are all depending on our response to the strangely incongruous. Whether we like it or not, we may well remember it. Like the appeal of humor, the use of the bizarre has long been a writer's device, too. The deliberately tortured prose of Thomas Carlyle offers a good example; its shock value underlined his idea.

CARD STACKING

Card stacking is dealing from a crooked deck. It is presenting a favorable case, regardless of the truth, by distorting or ignoring inconvenient evidence that supports the other side. It is shifting the grounds of the argument, deliberately lying, misquoting the opposition or distorting by quoting out of context, making an excessive use of emotional appeals, using half-truths as if they were all of the truth, consciously begging the question, making the worse appear the better case by any underhanded means. It is prostituting the human powers of thought. It is the unforgivable intellectual sin. It is very common.

In considering these emotional appeals, we have often dealt with advertising because the impact of an advertisement must be quickly made, and as a result the appeal can often be easily identified. Many of our examples may seem trivial in consequence, since no one is greatly harmed if he is tricked into buying one bar of soap instead of another one. Yet the skillful and unscrupulous use of such appeals can be deadly serious. It was largely by these means that the Nazis led the highly educated German nation into the madness of the Third Reich. We seem to be in no danger now of such dreadful results, but we should be aware of the deliberate efforts of the manipulators to predetermine our personal, professional, and national decisions. In the face of such efforts, it is harder than ever for us to get at the truth.

EXERCISE

Identify the emotional appeals exemplified by each of the following.

1. "Because our great candidate dares to expose their plots, liberal extremists are screaming in fits of fanatical frustrations. Without any real issues to present except more taxes, more giveaways, more socialism, they hurl childish epithets from the moral sewers at this stalwart of freedom for fear that the voters will finally junk the free-wheeling rocketeers of the federal debt and return the nation to fiscal sanity."

2. "The Man-Size Deodorant!"

3. "We want to make people think of this soap as fresh and cool and ladylike. How about running a series of ads with old-fashioned bouquets—nosegays, you call 'em—all lace and lilies of the valley and forget-me-nots and things, and a bar of soap in the middle of them?"

4. "Smokey says, 'Real campers don't build fires at all.'"

5. "No novel has stayed longer on the booksellers' shelves! No writer has touched the nation's heart as Bessie Scriver has done!"

6. "For the man who has everything—We suggest a mink-lined, electrified barbecue apron."

7. REVIEW: "There are very brief moments of first-rate comedy. Miss De Jour and Mr. Poe, for example, become, incredibly, almost believable in the last scene of the first act, and while it was doubtless not intended, their annoyance at the ineptness of the lighting was thoroughly amusing in an otherwise tremendous bore of a play."

8. "You can depend on Senator Reesing to represent *you* in his fourth term in Washington. He is one of us and knows our problems. Although his duties have kept him in Washington most of the time, he has maintained his home and his interests here. He raises his own cattle on his farm in the Valley, pays the same taxes we all do, and is always glad to hear from us whenever we have problems."

9. "Eat Pop-up. Mickey Mantle does."

10. "Smoke travels farther, stays cooler, tastes milder in a king-sized cigarette."

PERSUASIVE WRITING

We have been considering the complexities of thought and the effects our emotions may have on our thinking, and especially in the latter discussion we have been largely concerned with the problems of the reader rather than with those of the writer, because you need to be able to recognize shoddy logic in order to avoid being taken in by it. Now, we shall consider the problems of the writer of argument, in which especially evidence and reasoning must be handled with understanding as we search for truth and then seek to persuade an audience that we have found it.

To persuade means "to present an opinion in a convincing way, so that the reader accepts the conclusions of your argument as more probable than the conclusions of the opposition." The term sometimes implies an appeal to the emotions rather than to the intellect, but it aways points to conviction as the result. Those who appeal chiefly to the unthinking may rely chiefly on emotional appeals, but we are not and should not be concerned with writing designed to move the viscera instead of the brains of our readers. Our concern is not with benumbing minds, but with arousing them; and those whom we seek to persuade should ideally be more amenable to logic than to emotional appeal, just as we ourselves in listening and reading should learn to recognize and to scorn appeals merely to the emotions and should instead weigh the rational appeal of logic.

In description and narration, the important logic is the logic of space and of time and the logic of believable responses in believable situations. In writing which deals with ideas—in most exposition and in all argument—the important logic is both that of rational arrangement of material, so that each idea proceeds clearly and coherently from the one before it, and that of evidence and reasoning, of fact and sound opinion based on fact. In exposition of opinion, particularly, and in argument—which presents an opinion not only clearly but convincingly, so that the reader will be led to adopt it as his own—the facts must be clearly presented, and the chains of inference supporting the opinions must be clear and capable of withstanding close examination by readers who may disagree. Both sorts of writing should provide the details which ought to lead a fair-minded reader to adopt the opinion being expressed.

The problems of organization, of clarity, of full development of ideas which we have repeatedly faced in other kinds of writing appear also in persuasive writing and are solved by the same means. There are in addition, however, a few special problems involved in persuasive writing which we need now to consider.

The writer should assume, throughout his writing, that his audience is or may be hostile. One does not persuade a reader who already agrees; one merely reinforces his belief. Persuasion involves changing a fixed and opposed opinion, or forming an opinion where there was before only a neutral and amorphous void. To reach either kind of audience, the writer must state his case fully, state it convincingly, and show why it is superior to the opposing case.

Before you can even begin to write, you must yourself have thought through the problem. First you must define the topic very clearly in your own mind. Until you know what disputed question you are trying to answer—now for yourself and later for your reader—you cannot know what is relevant and what is not. This is elementary, but a great deal of fuzzy argument results from failure to take this first step. Next, you must identify the major issues, the crucial points of disagreement.

There are few topics on which those who disagree hold no opinions in common; the points of agreement must be found to serve as basic premises on which the argument can be built. There are few, too, on which all points of disagreement are equally important; the degrees of importance must be recognized because they determine the degrees of emphasis to be given to each issue. For example, if the argument is concerned with the desirability of a change in established practice, three questions will identify the primary issues: (1) Is the present practice unsatisfactory? (2) What different practice do you propose? (3) In what ways and to what degree will the proposed practice be more satisfactory than the present one? It is on these primary issues in particular that you must focus your search for truth. Then you must identify the subsidiary issues, and their relationships to each other and to the problem as a whole.

With the issues in mind, you must then examine the evidence—all of it, including subtle appeals to your own emotions and prejudices—and evaluate the divergent interpretations that may be drawn from it. What are the implications of this evidence? What varying inferences may be drawn? Which inferences seem most nearly valid? Why? What basic assumptions underlie your choices, and what differing assumptions may be held by your potential readers? Examine your own reasoning for hidden fallacies. *Think* about the problem. No one who has failed to do all this has any right to maintain his "opinion" at all.

When you have decided clearly what you yourself believe, you need to think as carefully about why others disagree. A written argument is a one-man debate in which the writer must work out both sides—or all sides—of the question, with no prompting from a present and alert opposition; there is no chance for rebuttal, none for countering arguments you had overlooked in your own thinking. Instead, you must turn yourself inside out and examine carefully the case against you. Why have your opponents adopted the other side, particularly on the major issues? You must always know your opponent's case, because you must always answer that case. If you cannot answer it, you had better change your own mind. Certainly you have no business trying to persuade someone else to reject a case that you cannot logically refute. Some of the opposing case will be irrefutable; not all of the truth will lie where you first supposed it would. Such truth as you find in the opposing case may then be incorporated in your final thinking, and the thesis that your argument presents will thereby lie that much closer to the ultimate truth on the question.

Then, writing the argument consists in leading the presumably hostile reader through the same processes of thought that you have yourself gone through. How the material is organized and what detail you need to develop the thesis will vary, of course, according to how much your reader knows about the topic, but there are certain problems peculiar to argument that must be solved in one way and another as you write.

Most importantly, you must be aware of when your reader can be counted on to agree with you and when his opinion may differ from yours. Whenever he differs, you must support your opinions with evidence and with a demonstration of your reasoning. Even when he agrees, generalizations may need supporting detail. When he disagrees, lack of support results in his rejection of your statement; and if the statement is a premise, rejection means the collapse of whatever part of the argument is based on it. Further, since the reader does disagree, the detail you use must not only make clear what your general statement means, as it does in exposition, but also provide the proof that your statement is true. You need, therefore, more detail than you need in exposition, and perhaps detail of a different kind. In making your selection, decide what details have convinced you that, despite opinions to the contrary, the truth lies where you think it does.

A second problem peculiar to argument is that the writer cannot expect his reader to work with and for him. We should always say as exactly as possible what we mean, but in exposition we can count on the reader's trying to understand us sympathetically. In argument, however, the reader distrusts us and may magnify any flaws that he finds. It is never good to have to fall back on, "Oh, you know what I mean"; in argument it may be fatal.

Third, the writer must present the opposing case in order to refute it. If he does not consider the evidence from all points of view and make clear, fairly, what the opposition believes, he will be suspected at worst of card stacking and at best of ignorance. Many an argument based on sound evidence and valid reasoning is ineffective because it seems one-sided. The reader must never ask vainly, "But what about —?" In presenting the opposing case, however, the writer must never let the reader wonder which side is which. In outlining what "they" believe, for example, the writer must make it clear that he does not accept the opinion as sound. If the writer keeps clearly in mind his own point of view, he will avoid bewildering his reader.

Finally, the writer must present his case exactly and fully, not only to be clear but to avoid fallacies in the written argument. If the preliminary thinking has been carefully done, presumably no fallacious reasoning has led the writer to invalid conclusions, but the reader must depend on what is before him on the page. Unless the writer makes clear all the stages of the reasoning, for example, his conclusions may be logically valid in his own mind but may seem to be *non sequiturs* or hasty generalizations as they are presented. Unless he examines illustrative analogies carefully, they may be inappropriate and may seem to be false. If he asserts a premise without supporting it, or allows himself to overstate it, he may seem to be begging the question. If in his fervor he chooses terms for their favorable connotations, and overstates the case that way, he will certainly seem to be resorting to emotional appeals, which to an intelligent reader are always suspect. To use words whose denotations and connotations are both appropriate is entirely justified; to appear to be using a "glittering generality" to obscure the truth is not. But if he directs his case to his audience and says exactly what he means, these problems can be solved.

In summary, know your case and your opponent's case, and show your reader what you believe and why you believe it. Remember that assertion alone is not evidence. Stick as closely as possible to facts; present the evidence fairly, clearly, and completely. Test your own reasoning and your opponents', and demonstrate the reasoning on which your opinions are based. Leave distortion and evasion to the charlatan; you are concerned with finding truth. Do not be afraid of presenting your case in favorable terms, but remember that the best case is convincing even in the baldest and most neutral terms, and that even the best case is suspect if it is accompanied by an excessive appeal to emotions.

Decide what you think.
Focus on the major issues.
Present the evidence fairly.
Demonstrate the soundness of your conclusions.

EXERCISES

A. Write a persuasive paper to present your considered opinion on one of the following topics.

1. The present grading system is (or is not) fair.
2. Examinations do (or do not) adequately measure a student's knowledge.
3. Fraternities are beneficial (or are harmful) to their members.
4. Fraternities are beneficial (or are harmful) to the college.
5. College students (or engineers, or scientists, or education majors, or business administration majors, or classics majors, and so on) should (or should not) be permanently exempted from military service.
6. The city (or the country, or a small town, or the suburbs) is a good (or a poor) place for a child.
7. A liberal (or a practical) education is most valuable.
8. Students desiring a college degree should be forced to satisfy strict curricular requirements (or should be allowed to choose their own courses so long as they meet minimum requirements for hours and credit points) (or should be required only to pass set subject-matter examinations, without reference to course attendance).

B. On a separate sheet, list specifically the major issues you have tried to meet in your paper. List briefly the points you regard as strongest in your own case. List in clear detail the points you regard as strongest in the opposing case.

C. Indicate, by specific paragraph and line references, the processes of reasoning you have used in your paper.

9—

The Research Paper

A very important part of your English composition course is that dealing with the research paper, or the "library paper," or the "source paper," or the "term paper"—all names for the same project.

Until now, you have focused your attention on expressing your own ideas, re-creating your own experience, passing your painfully acquired knowledge on to others who might be saved some of your pain as a result. But the human race has been acquiring knowledge, often at the price of intolerable pain, for many thousands of years. One of the major purposes of the research paper project is to teach you how to get at the experience and knowledge of the men who have gone before you, who have observed and thought and recorded what they have learned just so you could make use of it. The libraries of the world are full of knowledge that you can put to good use if you know how to find it. The research paper project is primarily an introduction to the best ways to find out what the race has already learned.

Another purpose is to give you a chance to learn how to manage really complicated problems of organization and expression, in a long paper whose material has come from many sources representing many points of view, about which you have a chance to exercise your own intelligence in weighing, selecting, rejecting, and shaping the material into a final form of your own—perhaps as a new and significant judgment, certainly as a new and original organization, phrasing, and evaluation of what is known about your topic.

Still another purpose is to give you practice in critical reading. (See also Chapters 8 and 10.) You will find printed sources which sound equally authoritative. Yet some will be sadly ignorant, or out of date, or fanatically "riding a thesis" so that any evidence of whatever sort is interpreted with prejudice and warped into position in the imposing edifice the writers have decided in advance to build. Or you will find sources whose authors are honestly and sincerely and intelligently trying to find the truth; yet they will disagree violently. It is enlightening and valuable to learn to judge for yourself and to evaluate what you read.

And most immediately practical of all, a final purpose is to teach you what to do when a professor in one of your advanced courses announces casually, "There will be a term paper due before Christmas. It will count as one third the grade in the course."

If at this point you are thinking, "Here we go again. I've already learned all this in high school," forget it. This is not an exercise in finding two or three popular books and a *Reader's Digest* article to tack together into a "reading report." Some of what you have already learned, of course, will be useful to you, but it would be a great mistake to coast until the project is half-completed and then realize that there is more to learn than you expected.

THE USE OF THE LIBRARY

For thousands of years, the human race has been storing up its collective wisdom in libraries. No two libraries are exactly alike. The region in which a library is located, the interests of its donors or its directors, the accumulated results of losses and acquisitions— all these factors make the collection of any one library different from that of any other. Your library's share of "the best that has been thought and said in the world," however, will give you quite enough raw material for your freshman research paper. It is obvious that you do not have the time or the energy to read through all the books, magazines, newspapers, pamphlets, and manuscripts it contains in the hope of stumbling on facts or opinions which have a bearing on a particular subject you are interested in; but, fortunately, you do not have to. Even though the collection of each library is unique, the machinery by which you can search that collection for material you can use is standardized. The same research tools and methods can be used in any library in the country. Standard reference books, catalogues, and indexes save you from having to guess where to look for material, or from having to wonder what your library owns and what it lacks.

The Card Catalogue

The card catalogue—rows of filing cabinets filled with three-by-five-inch cards listing every book in the library's collection, usually in three different ways—is an invaluable aid to research. From it can be found what *books* the library contains, alphabetically listed by the author's name, the first important word of the title, and the subjects treated. Whether the library contains twenty thousand books or eight or nine million, a knowledge of the nature of the card catalogue is essential to the student.

The basic card is the author card, printed by the Library of Congress and distributed to libraries all over the country.

```
   E
 175.9
 .S34  Schlesinger, Arthur Meier, 1888–
 1934        New viewpoints in American history, by Arthur Meier
         Schlesinger ...  New York, The Macmillan company, 1934.
             x p., 2 l., 299 p.  20½ cm.
             Originally published 1922.
             "Bibliographical note" at end of each chapter.
             CONTENTS.—The influence of immigration on American history.—
         Geographic factors in American development.—Economic influences in
         American history.—The decline of aristocracy in America.—Radical-
         ism and conservatism in American history.—The rôle of women in
         American history.—The American revolution.—Economic aspects of
         the movement for the Constitution.—The significance of Jacksonian de-
         mocracy.—The state rights fetish.—The foundations of the modern
         era.—The riddle of the parties.
             1. U. S.—Hist.—Philosophy.  2. U. S.—Hist.  3. U. S. Pol. govt.
         I. Title.
                                                             34–25367
             Library of Congress        E175.9.S34  1934
                                           [3]                973.04
```

The typed number in the upper left-hand corner is the "call number," the number by which the librarian knows where in the stacks of books the particular volume is shelved. It is not important that you understand how the librarian arrives at that number, but it is extremely important that you copy it down exactly and completely as you fill out a "call slip" for a book. If you do not, you will have to go back to the card catalogue and get it.[1]

The first line of the printed card gives you the author's name, surname first, and the dates of his birth and, unless he was living when the card was printed, his death.

Second is the title of the book (capitalizing only the first word and proper names), the author's name as it appears on the title page, the edition (if other than the first), and the facts of publication, that is, the place of publication, the publisher, and the date.

In your final paper, you will need that information; consequently you should note carefully everything offered in the first two elements of the catalogue card.

The rest of the information provided by the card does not appear in your final paper. But do not, on that account, ignore it. From the third item you can get an idea of the size of the book—how many pages and how large a volume. You can tell whether or not it contains illustrations, maps, charts, or a bibliography that might be useful to you, and even sometimes how many times it has been reprinted, which suggests something of its value.

Even more important is the fourth item (which, unfortunately, does not often appear), the analysis of the contents. If that analysis is given, it will tell you at once whether or not the book will touch your particular phase of the general subject the book deals with.

Next—and again very important to you—are the subject headings under which the book has been classified. This element of the card will often suggest related subjects that should be consulted, and will give you key terms to keep in mind as you consult not only the card catalogue but also the other kinds of indexes to library material.

Finally, there are a series of numerical entries that are useful chiefly to librarians—the Library of Congress call number (which will also be listed in the upper left-hand corner if your library uses the Library of Congress system), the Dewey Decimal classification number (which will be listed as the call number if your library

---

[1] If you wish to know more about the classification systems, study any one of several good handbooks on library practice which your librarian can recommend.

follows that system), the Library of Congress card number, the copyright number, and so on.

Most books are listed not only by author but also by title and subject. From whichever angle you approach the card catalogue, you will get clues that will lead you to book sources. You should, however, follow up the other avenues of approach besides the avenue you first took. Usually, for example, you will begin with subject cards. But you should remember to look also at the author cards of an authority who turns up frequently; there may be other books of his bearing on the subject which the library has neglected to list under that particular subject heading. The subject headings are rather specific—history, for example, touches and overlaps many other concepts. They must be used intelligently and imaginatively, because your material may be scattered widely. Check related subject headings; they may lead you to useful sources. And use the cross-reference cards suggesting other ways of cataloguing related material, or use the *Library of Congress Subject Headings,* a ready-made cross-reference volume. A "see" card or a "see also" card should never be ignored. The first indicates that you are consulting the catalogue through a key term the library does not use and tells you what term to look for; the second suggests a closely related subject heading that may provide important additional material.

One important source of material is often overlooked. Biography may not be filed under any other subject matter heading, so that such a major source, say, as Freeman's four-volume *R. E. Lee* may not appear at all under U.S.—History—Civil War. Yet Volumes II and III are at least as important as Freeman's *Lee's Lieutenants.* Be sure to check biographical material for people who are importantly involved with your topic.

A few remarks might be made about the ways in which librarians file the catalogue cards. A little browsing in the catalogue will do more to teach you than any amount of direct advice, but some helpful hints may be offered.

Books *by* a writer are filed before books *about* him.

Abbreviations are filed as if they were written out in full—*U.S.* comes where *United States* would come. *Mac, Mc,* and *M'* are all filed as if they were *Mac.* Numerals are filed as if they were spelled out. *Von* and *de* are ignored, and the last name is used instead, as in *Rochambeau, Comte de.*

Single key words in phrases come before compounds, or, as the librarian phrases it, "short comes before long."

Slave labor	Slavery
Slave songs	Slavery and abolition
Slave-trade	Slavery and the church

Historical subdivisions are arranged chronologically; otherwise subdivisions of a topic are arranged alphabetically.

U.S.—History—Colonial Period
U.S.—History—King William's War, 1689–1697
U.S.—History—King George's War, 1744–1748
U.S.—History—French and Indian War, 1755–1763
U.S.—History—Revolution

But

Slave-trade
Slave-trade, Africa, West
Slave-trade, Brazil
Slave-trade, History
Slave-trade, U.S.
Slave-trade, West Indies

Follow through the listings under all possible subject headings before you decide the library contains no books dealing with your topic (including general books overlapping the topic).

Periodical Indexes

Magazine articles provide much of our current reading, but magazine articles are not listed in the card catalogues, though the magazines themselves will be. To find articles which have appeared in magazines or in other publications issued periodically, there are many very useful periodical indexes. Every student should be aware of the major indexes: *Poole's Index to Periodical Literature* (indexing many periodicals published during the nineteenth century), the *Reader's Guide to Periodical Literature* (a more useful index covering popular magazines of the period from 1900 to the present), the *International Index to Periodical Literature* (which lists articles in many scholarly magazines in the humanities and some of the sciences), the *Industrial Arts Index* (engineering and business), and the specialized indexes, of which there are many, covering the student's particular interest. The last two, and the specialized indexes which can include more periodicals as they try to cover less ground, are especially important. *Never* stop with the *Reader's Guide*. It indexes the popular magazines on the newsstands, and the authors of the feature articles listed in it are very likely to have acquired what they know by the same process of library research that you are learning. They are professional writers, but amateurs in the subject matter. Like them, you need to consult the experts, whose contributions are in the professional journals and the scholarly books.

As you use any of the periodical indexes, be sure that you understand the system they follow. Consult the explanatory material at the front of the volumes for full discussion of their abbreviations, the order of details, and so on. We shall later see that you need to record all bibliographical material according to a specialized system conventionally followed in research papers. Before you can translate an index entry into the system you must use, it will be essential that you understand both systems thoroughly.

Newspaper and Pamphlet Indexes

Most newspapers are not indexed, but since most papers print the same news on the same day, two particular newspaper indexes can be used to locate news stories in nearly any paper. One is the *New York Times Index*, and the other is the (London) *Times Index*.

Pamphlets are less completely indexed, but two indexes are very useful, as far as they go. The *Vertical File Service Catalog* indexes much pamphlet material and should be consulted. The *Document Catalogue* and the subsequent *Monthly Catalogue* list many government publications.

Specialized Indexes

There are many specialized indexes of various kinds and of varying value; among them are the following:

> *Agricultural Index*
> *Art Index*
> *Book Review Digest*
> *Chemical Abstracts*
> *Dramatic Index*

Education Index
Engineering Index
Index to Legal Periodicals
Index Medicus
Modern Humanities Research
  Association Bibliographies
Psychological Abstracts
Public Affairs Information Service

Make use of any specialized indexes available; you can locate them by consulting Winchell, *Guide to Reference Books*, Robert W. Murphy, *How and Where to Look It Up*, the *Bibliographic Index*, or—after you have really looked for yourself—the librarians.

Reference Books

Reference books, like the telephone directory, are designed to be consulted for specific and classified information about limited subjects. The periodical indexes we have just been considering are reference books, and there are many others, some of which, like the general dictionaries, are already familiar to you. Among the most important are the encyclopedias, the dictionaries, the biographical dictionaries, the yearbooks, and the atlases.

GENERAL ENCYCLOPEDIAS

General encyclopedias attempt to present objective and authoritative articles on as many topics of general interest as possible. Because they differ, of necessity, one from another and edition from edition, it is well to consult several rather than only one. Among the best edited and most dependable are the following:

Encyclopedia Americana and its annual supplement *The Americana Annual*
Encyclopædia Britannica and its annual supplement *The Britannica Book of the Year*
Collier's Encyclopedia (This is designed primarily for high school use and will often provide a good introductory article from which you can—and should—go on to the adult encyclopedias listed above.)

It is usually best to use the latest available editions, which will present the results of the most recent scholarship. Only if you wish to know what was thought about a given topic at an earlier period (or if your topic has been dropped from late editions) should you consult an edition other than the most recent one.

DICTIONARIES

In addition to the standard unabridged dictionaries,

The New Century Dictionary of the English Language
Funk & Wagnall's New Standard Dictionary of the English Language
Webster's Third New International Dictionary of the English Language,

every student should be aware of two or three comprehensive historical dictionaries.

Dictionary of American English on Historical Principles
Mitford M. Mathews, *Dictionary of Americanisms*
Oxford English Dictionary on Historical Principles (also called the *New English Dictionary* or the *Murray Dictionary*)

These multivolumed dictionaries are invaluable in tracing the development and change of meanings and in determining what a word may have meant to an author writing in an earlier time—the Anglican *Book of Common Prayer,* for example, in praying, "Prevent us, O Lord, in all our doings," is confusing until you understand the sixteenth century use of *prevent.*

BIOGRAPHICAL DICTIONARIES

At least four biographical dictionaries should be familiar to every student, and there are many others in specialized fields.

Dictionary of American Biography, and supplement
Dictionary of National Biography (British), and supplements
Who's Who in America
Who's Who (British)

The first two are concerned with prominent persons no longer living, the second two with prominent living persons.

YEARBOOKS

Yearbooks contain valuable factual information about events

of each year. There are many, but among the most important are the following:

The Americana Annual
The Britannica Book of the Year
American Year Book
Facts on File
New International Year Book
World Almanac and Book of Facts

ATLASES

The three best-known atlases are the following:

Encyclopædia Britannica World Atlas
Columbia Lippincott Gazetteer of the World
Rand McNally Commercial Atlas and Marketing Guide

Early in your work on the research paper you should familiarize yourself with the very important general reference works that have been listed. In addition, you should examine carefully the specialized periodical indexes, biographical dictionaries, technical dictionaries, and encyclopedias offering information about your special field of study. Consult Winchell, *Guide to Reference Books* or some similar guide (there are many), browse through the library Reference Room, and consult the reference librarian. Remember that she should not be expected to do your work for you, but part of her job is to know the best reference sources for specialized investigations. Make use of her expert knowledge.

EXERCISES

A. What would be the best source to consult if you wished to find the following information?

1. A list of the principal books by Sir Winston Churchill.
2. The tonnage of steel produced last year in the United States.
3. The career of Francis Scott Key.
4. A sketch of the early history of Jamaica.
5. The approximate date at which *prevent* appeared in print with its modern meaning.
6. The philosophical publications of Herbert Spencer, who lived in England from 1820 to 1903.
7. The location and height of Mount Everest.

8. Articles in historical periodicals, between 1950 and 1960, on King Richard III of England.
9. Newspaper accounts of the death of Ernest Hemingway in 1961.
10. Specialized encyclopedias in religion and ethics.

(If you go to the library to look up the information, handle the reference books carefully. When many students look up the same items, books wear out rapidly.)

B. Prepare and submit to your instructor a list of the specialized encyclopedias, specialized periodical indexes, and specialized biographical dictionaries necessary to anyone doing research in the field in which you expect to major.

C. After careful examination of the books, write out and submit to your instructor a brief statement of the content and scope of the following: *Oxford English Dictionary, Cambridge History of English Literature,* Bartlett's *Familiar Quotations, Book Review Digest, Webster's Biographical Dictionary,* Winchell, *Guide to Reference Books.*

D. Consult your library's card catalogue to discover how many books your library contains from which you could secure detailed information about Lady Jane Grey. Include in your list biographies, specialized histories of the period, and the pertinent volumes of general histories. Follow up all "see" and "see also" cross-references.

RESEARCH PAPER PROCEDURE

Selecting a Subject

When your instructor announces that the time has come to begin the research paper project, you need first to find an answer to the question of what to write about.

If you are given a choice—and many instructors, for a number of good reasons, prefer to assign topics—you should select a topic you are interested in. For one thing, you will find the task more pleasant if you are interested in the topic from the first. Almost any subject will become interesting as you learn more and more about it, but initial interest will help carry you through the chores of preparing the preliminary bibliography and doing the preliminary reading. You might select a topic you already know a little about, or you might take this opportunity to investigate a subject you have always wanted to study but never have had time for.

First, of course, your subject should be one which cannot be settled from a single source. The process of making steel in a Bessemer converter is not a research topic. All explanations will be essentially the same. Choose a topic that can teach you what the library project is designed to teach.

Second, your topic, obviously, should not be too big. An assignment to write a two- to five-thousand-word paper may be appalling at the outset, but you will soon find, as you begin to learn more and more about the topic, that a surprisingly little bit goes a long way. All that has been said in earlier chapters about restricting subjects can be repeated to good purpose now. Limit, subdivide, pare, and prune your subject till you have a chance to learn it thoroughly and really say something useful about it. Stone Age man? Too big, too vague, and too widespread. Aurignacian man in France? Better, but still too big. The religious beliefs of Aurignacian man? Still too big, by the time the ramifications are covered. The cave paintings? Possible, but it would slip over into the religious beliefs and get out of hand. The cave paintings of Lascaux? That might be about right. If it proved to be still too big, the paper could be restricted still further—to the discovery, say, or to the precautions taken to preserve the paintings from tourists and fresh air. One good way to find a limited topic is to notice points which a general article on the subject treats with only incidental comment. An article on the Tower of London, for example, touching on many events in its nine hundred years of history, mentions "the notorious theft of the English crown by Thomas Blood." The Tower of London is too big a topic, but many subtopics that catch your interest will turn up even in a brief account. Your final choice will depend partly on the material you find available in your library. But remember to select a topic small enough to be worth working on. As you do your early reading, focus on smaller and smaller aspects of your general subject until you settle on a topic you can handle in the time and space at your disposal.

Also, for various reasons, the topic you decide to investigate should not be too new, or too technical, or too regional, or too controversial. Let us consider each of these limitations in turn.

Your topic should not be too new. A major purpose of the project is to teach you to use the facilities of the library, and libraries are chiefly collections of books and magazines. Your subject, then, must be old enough to have had time to get into book and magazine form. The exciting news story on the front page of today's newspaper would make a poor subject; the sources would be largely newspaper stories and columnists' speculations. Not only would it be hard to locate pertinent material, but many libraries are reluctant to have too many people handle their flimsy newspaper files until they have been microfilmed, and you would be limited then to a very few papers. Again, too new a subject would be one, of whatever age, that has not been studied by experts in primary research. (Primary sources are letters, deeds, wills, bills of lading, and so on and so on.) It is not always chronological age that counts here. Douglas Southall Freeman, for example, found as he began to work on his biography of Washington that nobody ever had bothered to study plantation life along the Potomac in the days of Washington's youth. He had to begin with the primary sources before he could write a chapter on the world Washington grew up in. Only by searching the card catalogue and the various indexes can you tell whether a given subject is too new in this sense. And finally, a subject which for one reason or another is being kept secret would be "too new" for your purposes. New processes, commercial secrets, new weapons, new policies—none of them would be open to you. Select a topic old enough to have been treated fully in books and articles.

For quite different reasons, your topic should not be too technical. A report on a technical subject for a nontechnical audience is hard to write, but that is no real objection; the practice would be good for you, and as the *New York Times* or *Time* or many other exemplars demonstrate, success is perfectly possible. But if the subject is too technical for you to understand yourself, the problem becomes important. Medical subjects, for example, are often discussed only in the professional medical journals and only in medical jargon. Unless you already know the terminology doctors use in talking to each other, you may be wholly unable to make sense of your sources, and you have too little time to preface your research with a course in medical terminology. The material is there, but as far as you are concerned, it might as well not be there at all.

The same difficulty arises with a topic on which much of the material is in a foreign language you cannot read.

A regional subject might be excellent if you are yourself in the right region. A history of Jefferson County, Kentucky, for example, might be written in Louisville. But it might be very difficult to find much material if the same topic were tried in Kansas, in a library which might have almost no material at all on Jefferson County, Kentucky. Library collections, remember, differ greatly. Check the card catalogue and the periodical indexes before rejecting a regional topic, but do not be surprised if you discover that little material is available. It would be better to choose another topic than to go to the expense in money and time to arrange for interlibrary loans or to travel to the distant libraries where your material is stored. The research scholar often must do that, but you can learn library research and term-paper methods just as well with a topic that can be handled right at home.

Finally, the subject should not be too controversial. Avoid topics on which you yourself have violent prejudices. You need to learn to get rid of such prejudices, or at least to base them on valid evidence and clear thought; but the freshman research paper is perhaps not the best place in which to do that. Again, be sure the topic is one in which truth, or a high degree of probability, can be found. Do not, for example, set out to discover by means of library research which of the two and seventy jarring sects represent true Christianity, nor, for that matter, which philosophical definition of Truth itself is the true one.

Your instructor may suggest further limitations. Here we need to consider only one more: To get the greatest good from the assignment, it is well to select a subject which will allow you to produce a *judgment* rather than a mere *report*. A judgment is a paper in which you can reach conclusions of your own after thoughtfully evaluating all the evidence. One of the fascinating problems of American history, for example, concerns the final career of Aaron Burr, who had been Thomas Jefferson's Vice-President and, but for Alexander Hamilton, would probably have been President in Jefferson's stead. What was his scheme to detach the Lower Mississippi country from the United States? He was acquitted in his trial for treason. From the evidence, available then or since uncovered, should he have been acquitted? Did he himself really know what he intended to do? What is the evidence and how do you think it should be interpreted? Such a subject gives you a chance not only to write a good paper, but even to write a brilliant one.

A report, on the other hand, is well worth doing, but it can never be brilliant. It deals with a purely factual topic and consists of a clear presentation of all the facts, offering no opinion because facts do not admit opinion; they are either true or false. A report could be written, for example, on Aaron Burr's conspiracy, indicating merely what occurred, who was involved, and how the trial went; but the topic almost demands an evaluation of the evidence and an attempt to explain Burr's actions. If you agree that the second would be a more valuable paper, you will see why your instructor may well feel that a judgment is superior to a report.

In summary, ask yourself, first, what subjects you are most interested in and would most like to study. Limit your choice to a topic small enough to handle. Avoid the too new, the too technical, the too regional, the too controversial. And if you wish to show what you really can do, and if you wish, incidentally, to learn as much from the assignment as possible, select a topic which will allow you to form your own opinions of the meaning of your material.

With your topic selected, you are ready to go to the library.

EXERCISE

Submit to your instructor for his comments a list of six carefully restricted topics on which you would like to do research. Explain briefly why you are interested in each topic and why you believe it would be a good subject for a research paper.

Preparing a Preliminary Bibliography

The next job is to find out what material on your subject is available in your library. For that, you need to make up a preliminary bibliography, listing, in a form that will later be very convenient, the books and the articles which from their titles look promising.

The tools for this, of course, are the card catalogue, the general and specialized periodical indexes, and any specialized bibliographies you may be able to find. But before you begin to record authors and titles, go to the reference room and read a good encyclopedia article on your subject. One of the well-edited, up-to-date general encyclopedias will be best for most topics, such as the latest edition of the *Britannica* or of the *Americana*. Or if the topic is highly specialized, a more limited encyclopedia may be better, such as the *Encyclopedia of Religion and Ethics* or the *Encyclopedia of the Social Sciences*. There are two good reasons for going first to the encyclopedia: You will get from it an authoritative and objective introduction to the subject, and can from the beginning work with some knowledge of what is important and what is generally known about it; second, the encyclopedia will probably give you, at the end of the article, a selected bibliography of the most important sources, and will consequently tell you from the first what books and articles you cannot afford to miss, however much you may be able to add to them. Record all such bibliographical information from the encyclopedia before you turn to the card catalogue and the periodical indexes.

Then comb the card catalogue, following up all cross-references to related subjects. Begin with the subject cards, where all the *books* on your topic should be recorded. Do not forget to note especially books which contain bibliographies and books which are themselves special bibliographies on the subject, all of which will be listed by subject cards. Do not overlook general books on larger topics including your subject. If your topic, for example, is the attempt to place Lady Jane Grey on the English throne instead of Mary Tudor, you may find only one or two books on that topic by itself. (Even the Library of Congress lists only thirty-nine.) But the history of England would have been quite different if the plot had succeeded; any general history of England will at least mention it. More limited histories of the Tudor era will give it in more detail. Studies of Mary Tudor or of the Tudor monarchy or of the powerful Dudley family of Northumberland will all provide material. Use the card catalogue intelligently.

Do the same thing with the periodical indexes, both the general indexes, like the *Reader's Guide,* and the specialized indexes which alone will lead you to the very important detailed articles written by scholars or other experts on your topic. Suppose, for example, you are interested in a literary problem, say the disputed authorship of *Piers Plowman.* There are literally scores of professional publications devoted to literary scholarship, none of which are indexed in the *Reader's Guide* because the *Reader's Guide* is concerned only with magazines aimed at the general reader, and the general reader is not very much interested in the esoteric controversies of literary scholarship. If you wish to find out what scholars think of *Piers Plowman,* you must turn to the *International Index to Periodicals* or the *Modern Humanities Research Association Bibliographies,* which do index professional journals in the humanities. Similarly, a student interested in a medical subject must examine the *Index Medicus,* a chemist must comb *Chemical Abstracts,* and so on. Do not report to your instructor that there is no material available (and do not be satisfied yourself with your preliminary bibliography) until you can honestly say that you have examined all pertinent volumes of the specialized indexes, in addition to the general indexes and the card catalogue. The specialized articles listed may be too technical for you, but at least look at them to make sure.

You should also use, of course, any other bibliographical aids you can find. Be alert to pick up hints from the footnotes of the books and articles you work with. Follow up a reference in the text to any authority who is unfamiliar to you. Check the bibliographies. You are trying to discover what has been written about your topic; be sure nothing important gets by you. You may well find, when you look at a newly discovered book or article, that it is not very useful after all, but you can never know that until you do look at it.

BIBLIOGRAPHY CARDS

As you find each new possible source, make a careful record of it on a three-by-five-inch card, using a separate card for each item that looks promising. Then you can add to your alphabetical list of sources or withdraw items from it without any of the confusion that would result from trying to keep a helter-skelter list in a notebook.

The purpose of the preliminary bibliography is to give you a convenient list of the sources that might be helpful. After your paper is finished, you will be expected to append a final bibliography which will give your readers a list of the sources you have actually used. It will save time and trouble and will help prevent mistakes if you take down the items for your preliminary bibliography in the form and with the detail you will ultimately need. Your instructor, indeed, will probably examine your bibliography cards to be sure you understand the method, so that care from the beginning not only will save you trouble with the paper itself, but may even save your having to do much of the work over again to satisfy some of the course requirements.

The form of the bibliographical entry differs slightly for each type of source—for books, encyclopedia articles, magazine articles, pamphlets, and unpublished manuscripts, like theses.

But for all types of sources, three bits of information are expected: *author, title, facts of publication.* (The facts of publication are also called the "imprint.") As we shall see, the three-by-five-inch bibliography card recording each source may and often should contain additional information, but those three items are standard. For each source, *take these three items down in full* when you first come across the source and save yourself possible trouble later. And take them down in the recommended form, avoiding abbreviations or other shortcuts.[2]

BOOKS

Author: Last name first, to facilitate alphabetizing. If two or three authors are listed on the title page (not the cover or the spine), the book will be alphabetized in your bibliography under the surname of the first author listed. That author's name is given surname first. The names of the other authors, however, are recorded in normal order.

If more than three authors are given on the title page, the first alone is used, and the rest are indicated by *et al.*, meaning "and others."

If the work of many authors has been collected in one volume, as in an anthology, the book is listed under the name of the editor, with his function indicated by the abbreviation *ed.*

An edition of a classic work, or a translation of a foreign work, is listed under the name of the author (unless that name has become

[2] The bibliographical forms discussed and illustrated are those of the revised *Style Sheet* of the Modern Language Association with one major modification, the inclusion of the publisher, borrowed from Kate L. Turabian, *A Manual for Writers of Term Papers, Theses, and Dissertations* (Chicago: University of Chicago Press, 1955).

almost part of the identifying title, as in Homer's *Iliad*), and the name of the editor or translator follows, identified as *ed.,* or *trans.*

If no author is listed, the book should be listed alphabetically by title, disregarding initial *A* or *The.*

Title: The title of the book, as it appears on the title page, is entered on the second line of the card. If the title is extremely long, it may be shortened, but be sure to include all significant, identifying terms.

The titles of complete works, like books, are put in italic type by the printer; in longhand or in typing, they are underlined.

Facts of publication: For books, the standard entries are place of publication, publisher, and date. (The date may be given on the title page, or as a copyright date on the back of the title page, or merely as a date appended to a preface or introduction. Use the title page date if one is given.)

All three of the standard entries need to be entered in your bibliography so that a reader who wishes to follow up your references may easily find the same edition (with the same pagination, misprints, revisions, and other details) that you used.

If for any reason one of the three entries cannot be found, indicate that fact by the abbreviations *n.p.* (no place given), *n. pub.* (no publisher), or *n.d.* (no date).

The normal bibliography card for a book by one author looks like this:

Yarwood, Doreen

The Architecture of England

London: B. J. Batsford, 1963

Examples of the various complexities you are likely to run across follow *in the form the entries should take in your final bibliography.* (On the preliminary cards, author, title, and facts of publication should each be listed on a separate line, as in the sample card above.)

One author:

> Yarwood, Doreen. *The Architecture of England.* London: B. T. Batsford, 1963.

A second work by the same author:

> ———. *English Costume.* London: B. T. Batsford, 1953. [The use of a long dash instead of repeating the author's name emphasizes the repetition. In this book, the title page uses the abbreviation *Co.* You may either follow the title page usage, or put all entries in one consistent form, or omit the word altogether.]

Two authors:

> Batho, Edith, and Bonamy Dobrée. *The Victorians and After.* New York: Robert M. McBride Company, 1938.

More than three authors:

> Dock, Lavinia, *et al. History of American Nursing.* New York: The Macmillan Company, 1922. [Omitted: Sara Elizabeth Pickett, Clara D. Noyes, Fannie F. Clement, Elizabeth G. Fox, Anna R. van Meter.]

A collection of the work of many authors:

> Kreymbourg, Alfred, ed. *An Anthology and a History of American Poetry,* 2 vols. New York: Tudor Publishing Co., 1930.

An edition other than the first:

> Nedham, Carter. *Individuality and Conformity,* 2nd ed. New York: Arkwrite Company, 1966.

An edition of a classic:

> Carlyle, Thomas. *Sartor Resartus,* ed. by Charles Frederick Harrold. New York: The Odyssey Press, 1937.

A translation of a foreign work:

> Zweig, Stefan. *Mary Queen of Scotland and the Isles,* trans. by Eden and Cedar Paul. New York: The Viking Press, 1935.

Lang, Andrew, Walter Leaf, and Ernest Myers, trans. *The Iliad of Homer*. New York: The Modern Library, n.d. [The author's name has become so merged with the title that the translators are more important in identifying the edition used.]

A book of more than one volume:

Trevelyan, G. M. *History of England,* 3 vols. Garden City, N.Y.: Doubleday & Company, 1953.

One volume of a set of volumes:

Trevelyan, G. M. *History of England,* Vol. I. Garden City, N.Y.: Doubleday & Company, 1953.

A book in a series:

Faulkner, Harold Underwood. *American Political and Social History,* 4th ed. Crofts American History Series, Dixon Ryan Fox, general ed. New York: F. S. Crofts & Co., 1946. [Notice that this entry also identifies a late edition and an editor distinct from the author.]

A book with a "corporate author":

Workers of the Writers' Program of the Works Project Administration. *Washington, D.C.: A Guide to the Nation's Capital,* revised ed. American Guide Series. New York: Hastings House, 1942.

REFERENCE BOOKS

The following form is suitable for articles from many kinds of reference books, like the *Dictionary of National Biography,* as well as from the general encyclopedias.

Author: As with book entries, last name first on the first line of the bibliography card.

Many, though not all, encyclopedia articles are signed by the authors' initials at the end of the article. The authors' full names are listed at the front or back of the volume, or sometimes of the first or last volume of a set. If you are certain that the article is not signed, the first entry on your card cannot be an author entry and is the title entry instead. But find the author if possible.

Title: The title of the *article,* not of the encyclopedia, is the title of your source. Titles of works which appear as parts of larger wholes, as one article is part of the larger encyclopedia, are put in quotation marks.

Facts of publication: The facts your reader needs before he can understand where your article appeared are the title of the encyclopedia (underlined), the date or edition of the encyclopedia (normally the most recent, unless an earlier edition is somehow superior), the volume number, and the inclusive pages of the article in that volume.

The normal bibliography card for an encyclopedia article looks like this:

> Fraser, Alexander Campbell, and
> Richard Ithamar Aaron
>
> "John Locke"
> _Encyclopaedia Britannica_ (1964),
> XIV, 273-274

The entry would appear in the final bibliography as

Fraser, Alexander Campbell, and Richard Ithamar Aaron. "John Locke," *Encyclopaedia Britannica* (1964), XIV, 273–274. [An alternative form, equally acceptable, would enter the date, volume, and pages as: (1964), 14:273–274. Whichever form you adopt, use it consistently.]

MAGAZINE ARTICLES

Author: Last name first, if the article is signed. If the article is anonymous, alphabetize it under the first key word of the title.

Title: The title of the article, in quotation marks.

Facts of publication: The underlined title of the magazine (in full, not abbreviated as it is to save space in the periodical indexes), the volume, the date, and the pages. Two forms are common, as with encyclopedia entries. Whichever form you use, be consistent throughout your bibliography.

If, in addition to numerals representing volume and pages, you need to use numerals representing series, numbers, or sections. identify the numerals by the abbreviations **ser., no., sec., vol.** (or **vols.**), and **p.** (or **pp.**).

The normal bibliography card for a magazine article looks like this:

The entry would appear in the final bibliography as

Viertel, John. "Generative Grammars," *College Composition and Communication*, XV (May, 1964), 65–81.

Or

15:65–81 (May, 1964).

Many magazine articles, as well as chapters or excerpts from books, are reprinted in anthologies or in casebooks for composition courses. When such reprints are used in research papers, the author and title are, of course, those of the original article or excerpt. If the original facts of publication are indicated, they should also be given in the bibliography. In addition, however, full credit must be given to the immediate source. The result is in effect a double entry.

An excerpt in an anthology:

Becker, Carl L. "The Ideal Democracy," from *Modern Democracy*. New Haven, Conn.: Yale University Press, 1941. Reprinted in Kenneth L. Knickerbocker, ed. *Ideas for Writing*, 3rd ed. New York: Holt, Rinehart and Winston, Inc., 1962, pp. 318–332.

An article in a casebook:

Reed, Glenn A. "Another Turn on James's *The Turn of the Screw*," *American Literature*, 20:413–423 (January, 1949). Reprinted in Gerald Willen, ed. *A Casebook on Henry James's "The Turn of the Screw."* New York: T. Y. Crowell Company, 1960, pp. 189–199.

GOVERNMENT PUBLICATIONS

Author: Often, no author is named in government, industrial, and similar publications. If the author is named, of course his name should be entered, but if the work is anonymous and the government agency or the corporation assumes responsibility for it, enter the name of the agency or corporation as a "corporate author." Use the smallest division of government that will be recognizable to your reader; the author card in the card catalogue may or may not help you reach your decision. Arrange the name to alphabetize the work under the key term; that is, use Agriculture, United States Department of, rather than United States Department of Agriculture or list the work under the title.

Title: As the title of a complete work, underline it.

Facts of publication: This is often the hardest part of the entry to determine. Remember that the purpose of the entry is to enable a reader to secure a copy of the work, and to provide whatever information will be most useful to him. For example, most federal government publications are printed by the Government Printing Office, and publications designed for general distribution are usually available through a branch of the same agency. For such publications, the Government Printing Office should be listed as publisher. But if the work is for use within a government agency, the agency using it should be listed as publisher. If the publication is one of a series, the titles and numbers of the series should be given if they will be useful. Dates, when available, should always be given.

The following examples illustrate a few typical entries:

Commerce, United States Department of. *Employee Handbook.* Washington, D.C.: United States Department of Commerce, 1949. [No author is listed; the work is designed to be used within the department.]

Goheen, Howard W., and Samuel Kavruck. *Selected References on Test Construction, Mental Test Theory, and Statistics, 1929–1949.* Washington, D.C.: United States Government Printing Office,

1950. [The work is designed for general circulation and may be obtained through the Government Printing Office.]

Hall, Milton. *Getting Your Ideas Across through Writing.* Training Manual No. 7. Washington, D.C.: Federal Security Agency, 1950.

Electronic Determination of Tolerances. Washington, D.C.: Industrial Researches Company, 1964.

NEWSPAPER ARTICLES OR NEWS STORIES

Author: If the article or news story is signed, the author's name should of course be recorded. Usually, however, no author is identified, and the title of the article or story must serve as the first entry.

Title: The title (often no more than a headline or a single topic, like a name heading an obituary) should be enclosed in quotation marks, as part of a larger whole.

Facts of publication: The underlined title of the newspaper (the name of the city is underlined only if it is part of the title of the paper), the date, the page and section number if the paper has section numbers, and sometimes the column—all these help the reader find the article you are citing. It is often difficult to determine which of several editions is involved. That information would be useful, because the makeup of newspapers changes from hour to hour; but the clues to the edition are usually hidden, and in general the same edition will be distributed to libraries beyond the immediate place of publication. As a result, editions are rarely identified in bibliographical citations.

A typical signed newspaper entry would appear in the final bibliography like this:

Raskin, A. H. "Steel Talks Wait as Owners Want Light on Prices," *New York Times,* April 1, 1952, sec. 1, p. 1.

UNPUBLISHED MANUSCRIPTS

University students often have access to specialized treatments of their topics in the form of typed and bound manuscripts prepared as theses for the master's or doctor's degree. These should be consulted if they are available, and of course should be included in the bibliography if they prove useful.

Author and title are always given and should be listed. The title, somewhat oddly, is enclosed in quotation marks even though the work is complete in itself. Since the work is unpublished, there are no "facts of publication," but to let the reader know where the source may be found, it is identified as an unpublished thesis (or dissertation), and the university and the date are indicated.

A typical thesis entry would appear in the final bibliography like this:

> Rorabacher, Louise E. "Victorian Women in Life and in Fiction." Unpublished thesis, Ph.D. (Illinois, 1942).

Make out a bibliography card for each promising source as you come across it. Take down all the information you will later need in the form you will later need to use. Keep your cards in alphabetical order as you go. The method may seem like a good deal of extra trouble at first, but in the long run it will save time and effort.

ANNOTATING YOUR BIBLIOGRAPHY

At least two additional entries should be made on each card, not for the final bibliography, but for your own working convenience. The first is the library call number by which you may get the book or bound volume of the periodical from the library stacks. When you first locate the item in the card catalogue, enter the call number in a corner of your bibliography card; thus you will save later unnecessary trips back to the card catalogue when you want to withdraw the volume. The second additional entry on the bibliography card is a brief note indicating the value of the source to your paper. When you examine a book or article, make a note of its value on the bibliography card. If you discover, for example, that a source with a promising title is really of no use to you, a note to that effect will save your having to look at it again after you have forgotten what you thought of it. Similarly, a source may give you valuable information without actually providing a single specific detail for your paper; yet a reader following up the subject should know about it. A note on the bibliography card will remind you to include that item in your final bibliography even though you make no direct reference to it in your paper.

The preliminary bibliography, carefully kept, is an invaluable tool. Use it in any way that you can.

EXERCISE

Submit to your instructor the cards on which you have listed your preliminary bibliography. Be sure that you have consulted both general and specialized periodical indexes as well as the card catalogue. Do not overlook pertinent chapters or sections in books covering wider topics.

Making a Tentative Outline

As soon as the preliminary bibliography is well under way —as soon, that is, as you have reaped the ready harvest from the card catalogue and the periodical indexes—it is time to map out the general lines you think the investigation may follow. So far, of course, you know very little about your subject, but you have already read a general encyclopedia article, and as a result you do know something of the main topics your intensive reading will cover; you may even already have glimpsed some of the gaps in your knowledge that you can hope to fill.

Before you go any farther, make out a list of the questions you hope finally to be able to answer. They will still be fairly general, but be as specific in phrasing them as you can. Those questions will sketch for you the sections into which your paper will probably fall, and they will help you recognize important items as you read. Suppose, for example, you want to write a paper on Edgar Allan Poe as a literary critic. What questions will your paper eventually have to answer?

1. How much criticism did he write?
2. When?
3. Where did it appear?
4. What critical principles did he follow?
5. How influential was his criticism, that is, what did his contemporaries think of it?
6. What do modern scholars and critics think of his critical work?

There may well be other questions that will occur to you as you work on the problem, or you may find that you have included questions that later prove to be unimportant. But at least you have from the very beginning some sort of framework to build on, and you can always add or subtract questions and expand or contract the questions already asked, as your reading goes on.

The next step is an easy one. The questions should be translated into topics which will make up a tentative outline of what you hope to learn as you work. There should also be a clearly phrased statement of what you intend to do, as specifically limited as possible. (Later, a thesis may form in your mind, but that cannot be phrased until you have done much of the reading and know where your paper is going.) Just now a clear statement of purpose is enough.

PURPOSE: To find out what critical writing Poe did, and how good it was in the opinion of his contemporaries and of modern scholars.

1. What he wrote
2. When
3. Where
4. His critical principles
5. Contemporary opinion (or influence)
6. Modern opinion

Be prepared at any time to reconsider your tentative outline as your knowledge grows. Here, for example, the first three topics are obviously related, and the three together are less important than any one of the other three. Perhaps the first three topics can be covered in the final paper in a single section—or perhaps other similar items will need to be added. The fourth point in the tentative outline will obviously need to be expanded as you learn more about Poe the critic. You might guess to begin with that he would be highly personal in his criticism, that he would favor romantic writers, and that he would stress esthetics. But that expansion can come as you begin to see what lines he actually followed. Point 5 might grow in the direction of his influence on other writers or in the direction of his contemporary reputation among laymen; it might even prove to be two points before the work is done. The final point may prove less important than you expect.

But with the tentative outline as a guide, you can direct your reading from the first. As a book or article on Poe touches Poe the critic, you will not only know that here is something you need to make notes on, but even know what use you may be able to make of the information. Your note-taking, in other words, will be purposeful from the first; and the tentative outline will save you from missing some fact or opinion you should record, will save you from making notes on masses of information you later have no use for, and will enable you to keep your growing collection of information in some sort of manageable order as you work. Any one of those results would justify the initial difficulty of thinking about your problem in advance. All together, they offer overwhelming reasons for making out a tentative outline as early as you possibly can and expanding or contracting it as your work shows the need.

EXERCISE

Submit to your instructor the tentative outline you have prepared to guide your reading and note-taking.

Reading and Evaluating Sources

Your purpose in reading is to find the answers to the questions you have asked yourself about the subject, to discover new questions, and to fill in the detail which will develop the topics in your tentative outline. It is usually well to begin with a book or an article written for the general reader rather than for the specialist, particularly if the subject is one that you know little about. The popular book or article probably will yield little that you can use in your final paper, but it will from the first give you a picture of the main outlines of the subject you are beginning to study. As a popularized book, it may well present a superficial and perhaps a distorted view, but your later reading will correct that, and just now it will tell you early in your reading what is generally known about the subject, so that as later reading fleshes out your understanding you will recognize the importance of new details as you meet them. *Take no notes on the first book.* Later you may want to skim through it again and pick up anything of importance in it, but it is a waste of time to make careful notes before you know what is important and what is not.

Your preliminary bibliography contains many books and articles that may or may not be useful to you. If you are working on Poe as a critic, for example, any book on Poe might provide information, but as you work you will find that most of them, perhaps, offer you little help. It is not necessary, however, to read every word of every book and article in your preliminary bibliography to find the helpful sources. Instead, by using the prefaces, tables of contents, and indexes of the books, and by skimming the promising sections of books and the promising articles, you can quickly eliminate useless sources and concentrate your attention on the useful remainder. Prefaces are often ignored, but usually the preface can be an invaluable aid to the reader. In the preface the author is very likely to sketch his approach to the subject and indicate his methods. He may present his reasons for employing a particular arrangement in preference to some other, and he is very likely to explain what he is trying to do in the book. Also, the reader can often see evidence of the author's particular point of view, and can pick up warnings of whatever bias he should be aware of as he reads. Make use of prefaces. They are not as dull and unrewarding as many people suppose. Make use, too, of tables of contents and indexes. The table of contents may help you quickly to discover the sections of the book that contain the kind of information you need, or you may find that your phase of the topic is not touched by the book at all. If the book is indexed, your work is still further simplified. Remember that the author may have used slightly different key terms from the ones you think he should have used; check all the possibilities that occur to you. With that precaution, you can usually go from an index directly to the parts of the book that concern you.

Articles, unfortunately, do not have prefaces, tables of contents, and indexes. They must be examined directly. But even here it is not necessary or wise to plod doggedly through every word in hopes that something will turn up. Skimming is an art that you should develop as quickly as you can. Remember all that you have learned about writing, and make use of it in your reading. Look for statements of thesis, usually toward the beginning of books or chapters or articles. Look for summaries toward the end. Be alert to pick up topic sentences of paragraphs and larger sections. As you run your eye over a page, the key terms of your subject will jump out at you. Skimming an article on Poe to see if it mentions his criticism, you will be especially aware of such words as *critic, criticism, critical,* and they will stand out on the page to warn you to stop and read carefully. Even if you find that the sentence says only, "This was a critical winter in the poet's life," you will not have wasted much time. Look for dates that cover the period you are interested in, or look for proper names that you know might appear in a discussion of your phase of the larger subject. Only when you hit real pay dirt should you begin to read with careful attention to detail.

When you do hit pay dirt, read with your full mind, bringing to bear everything you have learned about the subject. In the book or article that treats your subject, what is the thesis? What are the main parts? What is the writer's particular approach to the subject? What are the implications of what he is saying, or perhaps of what he is leaving out? Is he objectively looking for truth or is he riding a prejudice? Question him, argue with him. Get everything from the source that you can. Read actively and intelligently, not passively and limply. (See also pages 224–228.)

As you read, you will begin to see why a research paper cannot be a mere rehash of one or two books. The writer of the first general book that you read seemed confidently to know all there is to know about the subject; yet the more you learn, the more you realize how much he left out, and how many other ways there are of interpreting the facts he presented. The authorities will usually agree on the major facts, even though particular facts may come to you from one source and another. It is the interpretation of the facts and the approach to the subject that differ from one source to the next. It can be said, for example, that there is no history, there are only interpretations by historians. One man is concerned with political, another with economic, another with social interpretations. As a writer approaches facts from his own point of view, he will see something in them that another man sees from a different angle— the presumed motives behind an action, for example, may change the whole meaning of the action. The movements of Richard of Gloucester, for instance, after the death of Edward IV may be read as those of a villainous usurper or of a loyal Protector of the Realm in the minority of his brother's son. Even the attempt to present the facts themselves is often colored by the viewpoint of the beholder. Read, for a very interesting illustration, the eyewitness accounts of a battle from opposite sides. The Union colonel who seized Little Round Top at Gettysburg and the Confederate colonel who attempted to seize it were both convinced that the other side heavily outnumbered them. The two reports seem to be talking about completely different engagements. No wonder that the historians who have to try to find truth from such evidence come up with conclusions that differ. Your task is to weigh the evidence, consider the sources, and reach your own conclusions in the best light of your own intelligence.

(There will come a time in your reading when you feel an impulse to say, "Everything I'm reading says the same thing all the rest say." Resist the impulse. It means only that you are still reading popular or general sources. Go back to the indexes and dig deeper.)

You will not, of course, settle the questions for all time, but you have one advantage over the writers who preceded you: You are the latest in the field and can profit by their mistakes. One man has corrected another, and the third and fourth and fifteenth have corrected all of their predecessors. Each has introduced new facts or new ways of looking at the facts. You have a chance to use all the available evidence, and may well come a little nearer the truth than anyone else has done.

There are certain tests that should be applied to each source as you read. First, who is the authority you are consulting? Find out all you can about him, in the biographical dictionaries or the membership rolls of learned societies or the lists of the faculties of his college, or the card catalogue listing his other books, or wherever information may turn up. The Research Professor at the greatest university may not be the best man in the field, but he probably is not the worst. The writer of many books on a subject may be more dependable than a tyro—or he may not. Second, what do other authorities think of his work? The *Book Review Digest* will often tell you, or the specialized periodical indexes will lead you to reviews of his work. Third, *when* was the book or article written? The latest source is certainly not always the best, but an early one may well be out of date. Other things being equal, work with the most recent sources. Fourth, how much does the writer you are consulting know about the subject? The more you yourself learn about your subject, the easier it becomes to recognize superficial work. Fifth, how clear and how detailed are the evidence and the argument he offers to support his contentions? Do his theories cover all the facts, or has he ignored some inconvenient fact that might upset them? Are his explanations as simple as the circumstances permit, or has he built an unnecessarily complicated case? Finally, is he in general agreement with other authorities, or in violent opposition to them? Remember that the rebel might be right. The first man to say that the earth travels around the sun was closer to the truth than all the authorities who agreed that the sun travels around the earth. But the burden of proof is on the man with the new idea, and his evidence and argument must be scrutinized with a skeptical, although open, mind. Apply these tests to all your sources, weighing and evaluating as you read, using all your intelligence to come as near as possible to probable truth in your final conclusions.

Taking Notes

As you read, you will find yourself constantly coming across new facts, and, particularly, new ways of looking at the old facts. Take careful notes on everything new to you and important to the subject, so that when you write your final paper you will know whom to credit for the ideas you are borrowing.

Notes, like the preliminary bibliography entries, should be taken on cards so that they can be rearranged, added to, and otherwise shuffled at will. Facts and important opinions and pertinent questions will come to you in the accidental order determined by the purpose of whatever authority you happen to be consulting. They would soon be hopelessly jumbled if you tried to keep them on the pages of a notebook. Instead, use four-by-six-inch cards (large enough to give you room but not too large to handle easily) and *take one note to a card*. If an item happens to be related to two or three of the topics in your tentative outline, fill out a card to be filed under each topic. This extra effort will seem like unnecessary trouble at the time, but it is far worse to know at the last moment that somewhere you have a note you need, if you could only find it. Here, as everywhere else in the research paper project, the more pains you take at each stage of the work, the easier the final task becomes.

As you take each note, record its source carefully, so that you may know later exactly where you got it. It is not necessary, however, to write down author, title, and the facts of publication on every card. If you are using only one book, for example, by Joseph Wood Krutch, all you need to identify the note is "Krutch," and the page or pages on which you found the item. Later, your bibliography card will provide you with all the additional information you need. If you have two sources by the same author, use a short title to identify each one. If you have two authors with the same last name, use initials. And so on.

At the top of the card, write the topic from your tentative outline under which the item belongs. That way, no matter in what accidental order you pick up useful details, you can always keep related details together, and from the beginning will have your material at least loosely arranged in manageable form.

Most of your notes should be summaries of what your authorities are saying. Be sure your summaries are *your own words*, not thinly veiled quotations of the source. Take down in direct quotation only phrasings that are particularly striking, or statements for which you may later want the prestige of the exact words of a recognized authority. Such quotations as you do take must be copied exactly as they are in the text (spelled and punctuated, for example, as the original writer left them). They must fairly represent the author's intended meaning, not distort it when they are taken out of context. You may omit parts of the original, indicating the omission by the three dots of the ellipsis mark; you may insert explanatory material in square brackets; and you may use capitals and lower-case letters according to the final sentence pattern of your own paper. But you must be sure no distortion of the writer's original meaning results. Mark all quotations in your notes with quotation marks, to be sure you will later know exactly where paraphrase stops and quotation begins.

A typical note card looks like this:

Daniel, p. 62   Chamber Tombs:
                                 Distribution

"Single chambers occur in two areas" of south-west Iberia: Almeria (circular, dry wall or orthostat wall); central and northern Portugal ("polygonal megalithic chambers"). Rectangular tombs rare in south-west, and when covered are round barrows. "... the long barrow... is non-existent in Iberia."

Except as aids to your own memory, you will not need source notes on details that are presented by virtually all the authorities, such as the birth dates of prominent people (on which all your sources will agree). But in your final paper, you will be expected to acknowledge your indebtedness for any details that have come, or that look as if they probably came, from particular sources, for individual interpretations of facts, for statistics or charts or tables you have borrowed from one of your authorities, and for passages you are quoting verbatim. For your own protection and convenience, record carefully the sources of all such material. You will need the information as you write the final paper.

Plagiarism through Ignorance

It is important here to consider briefly the nature of summary and paraphrase and the problem of plagiarism. When a teacher, or a textbook, says, "Most of your notes should be summaries," or, "Mark all quotations in your notes with quotation marks to be sure you will know exactly where paraphrase stops and quotation begins," the matter seems so elementary and the injunction so clear that often no more is said about it. But when the final paper comes in, the instructor recognizes phrases and sentence patterns that are completely unlike the student's usual writing; no quotation marks indicate that the student is borrowing directly, although a footnote may acknowledge indebtedness for the ideas. When the instructor checks the source, he finds that the striking phrases and the uncharacteristic sentences come from the source, though perhaps with slight modifications. He calls the student in to examine the honesty of the paper, and often the student is genuinely bewildered. He has been taught to write précis in high school; he has not copied his source word for word; he has given credit for the information in a footnote. What has gone wrong? Sometimes he is expelled from college without ever finding out. (Sometimes, unhappily, he knows perfectly well.)

Just what does it mean to "use your own words"? We can best explain by using examples. William Gaunt, in a book entitled *London* (New York: Viking Press, 1961), p. 25, wrote:

> Would you know how a merchant prince of the fifteenth century lived? In what stately surroundings, Crosby Hall, moved stone by stone and timber by timber from Bishopsgate to Cheyne Walk in 1908, can tell. . . . It is just as it was, . . . with its oriel window and oak roof, as when it belonged to a prosperous wool-stapler of the late Middle Ages; when after his death in 1475 it was occupied by Richard, Duke of Gloucester; and after 30 years again by Sir Thomas More.

Those are his exact words, and if they are used, they will of course be given a footnote to acknowledge the source. As a long quotation—say, over six lines—they will be indented and single-spaced, as in the sample page on page 316. The format means "this is quoted," so no quotation marks are needed. (A shorter quotation, with quotation marks, would be double-spaced and folded into the text, with the sentence patterns of the text adapted to the grammar of the quotation so that they fit smoothly together.)

There are several ways the passage may be used, *all calling for a footnote reference;* there is one way it may *not* be used.

1. It may be paraphrased. Using the names and the date and such key terms as *wool-stapler,* and in this case using the unavoidable chronological organization, you may say essentially the same thing in your own words and in your own way. It would not be indented in the paper:

> Crosby Hall, although it has been moved from Bishopsgate to Cheyne Walk, is unchanged from the days of its occupancy by a London wool-stapler who died in 1475, its occupancy after that by Richard, Duke of Gloucester, and thirty years later by Sir Thomas More. With its oriel window and its oaken roof it is a fine example of the home of a wealthy merchant at the end of the Middle Ages.

Because the idea and the information came from Gaunt, the paraphrase calls for the same kind of footnote as the direct quotation.

2. It may be summarized:

> Crosby Hall, successively occupied by a wool-stapler who died in 1475, by Richard, Duke of Gloucester, and by Sir Thomas More, exemplifies the houses of wealthy fifteenth century merchants.

A footnote is still necessary.

3. Part of the information may be borrowed as fact:

> Sir Thomas More lived in Crosby Hall, in Bishopsgate, about 1505.

A footnote is still necessary, unless your topic is such that the same information can be found in most of your sources.

4. Part of the phrasing may be borrowed directly:

> Crosby Hall shows the "stately surroundings" in which "a merchant prince of the fifteenth century" lived.

A footnote is still necessary.

The only way in which it may *not* be used, the way which

raises strong suspicion of an intention to gain for oneself the credit for organization and phrasing that rightfully belongs to William Gaunt, is to adopt his wording with only slight modifications:

> Would you like to know how a merchant prince of the fifteenth century lived? In what stately surroundings, Crosby Hall can tell. It is just as it was, including its oriel window and oak roof, as when it belonged to a prosperous wool-stapler; when it was occupied after 1475 by Richard, Duke of Gloucester; and after thirty years more by Sir Thomas More.

No footnote can prevent the reader from thinking that you must have known that the sparkle in that passage, as well as the facts, belonged to Gaunt.

Unless you are careful as you take notes to mark all direct quotations clearly, you may not know, later, what phrasing is your own and what belongs to your sources. The college Disciplinary Committee may well regard the matter as very serious.

The Final Outline

When the investigation is finished—the sources combed, the facts and opinions collected, your questions about the subject answered—it is time to sit down and think about what you have learned. You are now, in some measure, an authority on the subject yourself; at the very least, you know a great deal more about it than the other members of the class. Your task now is to present what you have learned in such a way that a generally educated reader can understand it and learn from it too. Before you can do that, you must be sure that you have not merely swallowed, but have also thoroughly digested, the material. A successful research paper cannot be merely a hodgepodge of undigested facts, nor an aimless stringing together of impressive quotations, nor a rambling presentation of interesting but unrelated remarks about the topic. It must be a clear, unified, and coherent paper about the subject you have been studying.

The tentative outline has enabled you, as you worked, to keep the material in some sort of order, and with luck you may have hit from the first on the best order possible. But re-examine that order now with the needs of the final paper in mind. The tentative outline represented what you at first thought you might discover. Additions and changes have had to be made as you worked, and now you know a great deal about the subject. What have you learned? What thesis would best summarize your new knowledge? What main points will you have to present and develop in order to clarify that thesis? Try various combinations as you attempt to beat the material into shape. It is time to expand your tentative topic outline into a formal sentence outline which will show you and your instructor that you have really passed the collected information through your brains and understand it thoroughly.

The outline for the final paper should be a full and formal sentence outline for at least two reasons. (See Chapter 4.) First, if you can get down on paper a clear and specific statement of thesis and can subdivide that thesis into main points which not merely indicate the topics you mean to discuss but say something definite about those topics, and if the progression of the resulting ideas is logical and clear, then you can know that you have mastered the subject and that your thinking has been well done. Writing the paper itself will be easy, as by now it should be. Second, a full sentence outline enables your instructor to check your plans before you write. He can see exactly what you expect to say, and he has a chance to help you avoid any last-minute trouble. The research paper is probably the biggest single project of the year, and the grade counts heavily in your final standing in the course. If you and your instructor together can work over an intelligible sentence outline, he can usually suggest the chief difficulties you will need to watch out for as you write. But he can do this only if he can understand exactly what you are planning to do. And only a sentence outline, made out in detail, will let both of you scrutinize your plans.

EXERCISE

Submit to your instructor your final outline, the cards on which you have listed your final bibliography, and the cards on which you have taken your notes.

The Final Paper

The final paper will consist of four sections: the title page, the outline, the text complete with footnotes indicating the sources of your detailed evidence, and the final bibliography. The third of these, the text, is obviously the most important of the four.

The title page should contain at least the title of your paper, your name, and the course and section number.

The outline that accompanies the final paper may well be the sentence outline that served as a guide to the writing of the paper, or your instructor may require that that sentence outline be reduced to a carefully phrased topic outline. In either case, it is often useful to treat the final outline as a combined table of contents and index, indicating the pages in the text at which each idea is presented.

The text, the paper itself, is the heart of the project. The material in it has come to you from reading rather than from experience, but the unity, the organization, the development, and the phrasing are your own. It is you who give meaning to the information you have accumulated. Except for indicating where you learned what you know, writing the paper is no different from writing any other paper. You need not try to work in all the evidence you have collected if honest and judicious selection can make your point just as well. You must not distort what seems to be the truth by ignoring inconvenient evidence, of course, but you may and should select the clearest and most pertinent. Since it is the most important single piece of writing done in the course, the paper on which you have spent the most time and the one dealing with the most complex material, bring to bear in writing it all you have learned about writing during the year. You should find, as a matter of fact, that it is also the easiest paper of the year to write. You know more about the subject matter than usual, you have given more thought to the development of the idea, and you have, besides, steeped yourself in the writing others have done on the same subject. Perhaps for the first time during the course, you can put your full attention on the actual writing job and can concentrate on phrasing your ideas in the most effective way, on making the clearest and most graceful transitions, on saying well the things you want to say. If you have done the work you should have done in preparation, you may well be surprised and proud over the results.

FOOTNOTING

There is only one thing new about the text of the research paper: the necessity for using clear and conventional footnotes to acknowledge your indebtedness to the writers from whom you are borrowing details. It is not necessary or expected, remember, that you use footnotes to document details that might be found in most treatments of the subject. But it *is* necessary to use a footnote at any point at which you know that a particular source provided the fact, the opinion, the pattern, or the exact phrasing you are presenting. As you read, especially in the scholarly journals, notice how your authorities footnote their articles.[3]

Footnotes are conventionalized shorthand devices for saying to the reader, "I got the information I have just given you from so-and-so. He said it in his book or article with such-and-such a title. If you care to look into the matter further, you will find it on such-and-such a page."[4]

That thirty-nine word remark to the reader can immediately be shortened to the name of the author, the work cited, and the page, as in

Arthur Guilfoyle, *The Ebb of the Confederate Tide at Gettysburg* (Chicago, 1963), p. 327.

And there are a number of conventional abbreviations that make subsequent notes even briefer. See pages 314–315 for a full list. Here, we may consider the most common. If the next note should refer again to the same work and the same page, the useful abbreviation *ibid.* (for the Latin word *ibidem*, "the same") will shorten your remark to the reader to those four letters alone. Or if another author's name and work intervenes, you may after the first reference to Guilfoyle's book use his last name only and the page, as in

Guilfoyle, p. 390.

A numeral after and slightly above the end of the detail you are documenting will announce to the reader that a note is ap-

---

[3] There are in fact, many different systems, but the differences are matters of minor detail, such as punctuation. Most of them are based on the University of Chicago *Manual of Style,* and the pertinent forms may be examined in Turabian, *A Manual for Writers of Term Papers* (see note, page 287.) The form here recommended is that of the revised Modern Language Association *Style Sheet,* which is somewhat simpler and is now widely followed.

[4] That description applies to the most common type of footnote, the source note. There are also explanatory notes, like this one, which add useful information that could not gracefully be blended with the text. A third type of note combines the other two by citing a source and then adding explanatory comment.

pended; the same numeral at the foot of the page (before and slightly above the note) tells him which note to consult.

A sample passage would look like this:

some illegal trade, most of which probably came from Lynn and Bristol in England. [16] During the last years of the fourteenth century, however, Greenland trade became unprofitable to Europeans. African ivory, Russian fur, and Dutch and English cloth had replaced Greenland commodities in the European market, and the voyage to Greenland had become increasingly risky. [17] The trade dwindled and ceased.

About 1345, Ivar Bardarsson, steward of the bishop's farms in the East Settlement, accompanied an expedition sent to find out why there had been no news from the West Settlement for several years. He found no human beings at the one farm he stopped to investigate, but there were cattle there, and sheep roamed about

---

[16] Stefansson, <u>Greenland</u>, p. 160.

[17] Norlund, p. 143.

untended. From this limited evidence he con-
cluded that the Skraelings (Eskimos) had
recently slaughtered the entire settlement.[18]
In 1355, another expedition was sent to find
the missing Greenlanders, but it was unsuccessful.[19]

After 1367, we hear little about the colonies.
In such isolation, life must have become more
unattractive and difficult. Some of the settlers
took passage on visiting vessels and returned
to Europe.[20] The last recorded visit of Ice-

---

[18] The story is told in Vilhjalmur Stefansson,
Unsolved Mysteries of the Arctic (London,
1939), pp. 28-29; Nansen, p. 127; Norlund,
p. 134.

[19] Nansen, p. 128.

[20] Stefansson, *Greenland,* p. 86; Nansen,
pp. 96, 100.

Typical footnote problems are illustrated in the following
sample notes.

A first reference to a book:

[1] William Carter, *Charles Dickens* (New York, 1964), p. 28.

An immediately succeeding second reference to the same book and
page:

[2] *Ibid.*

An immediately succeeding reference to the same book but a different page:

> ³ *Ibid.*, p. 328.

A first reference to a magazine article:

> ⁴ Edward Wagenknecht, "Dickens and the Scandalmongers," *College English,* 11:374 (April, 1950).

Or (an alternative form):

> ⁴ Edward Wagenknecht, "Dickens and the Scandalmongers," *College English,* XI (April, 1950), 374.

An immediately succeeding reference to the same article and page:

> ⁵ *Ibid.*

A reference to Carter's book, last cited in footnote 3:

> ⁶ Carter, pp. 42–44.

A reference to Wagenknecht's article, last cited in footnote 4:

> ⁷ Wagenknecht, p. 376.

A reference, at secondhand, to something available to you only as a quotation by another source:

> ⁸ Pieter de Haugen, *Hoera de Koningin,* as quoted by Edgar Gilbert, *Modern Holland,* II, 269. [If it is possible to examine the original source, of course you should do so; if one useful detail is there, others might be also. Footnote 8 also illustrates, incidentally, a reference to a work of more than one volume.]

An immediately succeeding reference to Gilbert's book cited in footnote 8:

> ⁹ Gilbert, II, 297. [*Ibid.* could not be used here, since that would refer not to Gilbert, but to de Haugen.]

A reference to editorial material in an anthology:

> ¹⁰ Stephen F. Fogle, "What Poetry Does," in *A Brief Anthology of Poetry,* ed. by Stephen F. Fogle, p. xi.

A reference to an unsigned newspaper editorial:

> ¹¹ "Interstate Tax Chaos," *Washington Post,* June 18, 1964, p. A22.

A reference to an encyclopedia article:

> ¹² Morris William Travers and H. Grayson Smith, "Liquefaction of Gases," *Encyclopædia Britannica* (1951), 14:176. [The only difference between this first footnote reference and the bibliography entry is that the note cites the specific page to which reference is made, but the bibliography entry cites the inclusive pages covered by the article.]

A later reference, not immediately succeeding, to the same article:

14 Travers and Smith, p. 180.

A reference to an authority personally consulted:

15 Wood Gray, Professor of American History, The George Washington University, in a personal interview, February 27, 1964. [Such a note is rare, because a reader would find it difficult to consult the same source to check your accuracy or to obtain additional information. But an important point should not be omitted from your paper merely because it is not based on a published source, and if you consult an authority in person, you must credit him with the material he provides.]

A second reference to an author with more than one entry in the bibliography:

16 Harrison, *Over the Hill,* p. 77. [The title must be repeated, since a reader referring to the bibliography could not easily tell which work had already been cited. If the note immediately preceding had referred to the same work, however, *Ibid.* would be perfectly clear.]

Other footnote problems will occur as you work, but if you remember that the purpose of the footnote is to inform your reader of the source of borrowed material, and if you understand the details of the method illustrated, you should be able to adapt your notes to the system.[5]

Abbreviations and symbols: The following abbreviations and symbols are conventional in footnoting. You will often see them in your sources, and you may have occasional need for them yourself. For any others that you find, consult your dictionary. (Those in italics are from Latin and are put in italics because they are foreign words. They are underlined in longhand or typing.)

above: appearing earlier in the same article. See *supra.*
art(s).: article(s).
below: later in the same article. See *infra.*
bk(s).: book(s).
c. or *ca.:* about, approximately; used with dates.

5 The system presented is that commonly used by scholars in the humanities. The sciences frequently follow a different pattern, numbering their alphabetized bibliography items and making source references to those items by inserting in the text, in parentheses, the bibliography number and the page to which reference is made, as (17:39). Even science majors, however, will have occasion to write papers for advanced courses in the humanities, and the system illustrated in detail in the text should consequently be learned. Unless your instructor otherwise directs, follow the models in the text in your composition course research paper.

cf.: compare.

chap(s).: chapter(s).

col(s).: column(s).

ed(s).: editor(s), edition(s).

et al.: and others.

etc.: and so on. Not italicized, because it is now common English. But use it sparingly.

et seq.: and following; used of the pages following a cited page.

ff.: and following; used of the pages following a cited page. Now more common than *et seq*.

fig(s).: figure(s); used to refer to charts, diagrams, and so on.

ibid.: the same, used as a ditto sign to refer to an immediately preceding reference. May be used with a page change. When it is the first word in the footnote, as it usually is, it is capitalized.

infra: later in the same article. Not an abbreviation, it is not followed by a period. "Below" is now more common.

loc. cit.: in the place cited; used instead of *op. cit.* for magazine and encyclopedia articles, or for any source which is part of a larger, integral whole. Usage of *loc. cit.* varies, but this is its essential function. The author's name (or the title of an unsigned work) must accompany it. Often used with a page change.

MS(S).: manuscript(s).

n.d.: no date given.

n.p.: no place given.

n. pub.: no publisher given.

no(s).: number(s).

op. cit.: the work (opus) cited; used to refer to a previously cited book. The author's name and the page reference must always accompany it.

p(pp.): page(s).

passim: here and there throughout. Used, rarely, to indicate that pertinent material is scattered all through an indicated work. Use specific pages wherever possible. No period because it is not an abbreviation, but a complete word.

sec.: section.

ser.: series.

[*sic*]: thus in the original; used to indicate that an obvious error occurs in the source and that the quotation is exact. Used in square brackets, because it is a remark inserted in the quoted text. No period, because it is not an abbreviation.

supra: earlier in the same article. Not an abbreviation, it is not followed by a period. "Above" is now more common.

trans.: translator(s), translation.

vol(s).: volume(s).

Make use of these common abbreviations to save yourself the trouble of writing unnecessarily long footnotes. Since you will be expected to recognize and use these abbreviations in papers written for advanced courses, your instructor will not look with favor on long footnotes which appear to be attempting to evade the task of learning the use of the shorter forms.

THE FINAL BIBLIOGRAPHY

The final bibliography, the last section of your research paper, presents an alphabetized list of the sources you have found helpful in preparing the paper. All sources to which you have made footnote reference must be included, and it is often helpful to your reader to include any particularly good sources that you have not referred to directly. The bibliography thereby gives your reader a selected reading list on the topic you have studied. Practice differs here. Consult your instructor.

The forms of the final bibliography entries have already been illustrated in the discussion of the preliminary bibliography (pages 289–295). Consult those examples, and study the models offered in the attached student research paper. Follow the models exactly, in the order of details, in the information given, and in punctuation.

A FINAL WORD

You have a long, hard job ahead of you; there is no way in which digging information out of the library can be made painless. But if you follow the advice and the methods we have been discussing, and if you work intelligently and steadily throughout the time allotted to the project, you will find that it is not as hard as it may seem at first, and you will even discover, about the time you get into the intensive reading, that it really can be fun.

Examine the following typical student research paper for its methods of unifying material gathered from varied sources, its development of its topic, and its use of documentation.

The Problems of Slums and Urban Blight

JAMES A. INCE

The problems arising from slums and urban blight are not new; they have probably been with civilization for as long as there have been cities. At least, references to slums and related problems have been found in the earliest written histories.[1] The major factors responsible for slums are varied and intermingled, a combination of social and economic problems.

> The slum is a residential area (comprising one or more lots, city blocks, or rural plots) in which the housing is so deteriorated (through poor upkeep ordinarily combined with obsolescence, age, depreciation, or change in consumer demand), so substandard (owing to builders' or owners' ignorance of principles of construction, planning, equipment, and hygiene, or to the deliberate ignoring of such principles), or so unwholesome (owing to narrowness of streets, crowding of buildings upon the land, or proximity of nuisances such as noxious factories, elevated railways, overshadowing warehouses, railroads, dumps, swamps, foul rivers, or canals) as to be a menace to the health, safety, morality, or welfare of the occupants.[2]

This definition by no means encompasses all the factors that produce slums, but it is comprehensive enough to indicate the scope of the problem.

Although slums have been with us since the beginning of history, only in comparatively recent times has the general public become fully aware of the deplorable conditions existing in these areas.[3] This condition is due in part to the concept of democracy as it has developed over the past two centuries. We know now that to say that a child raised in a slum area has equality of opportunity with a child raised in more favorable surroundings is absurd.[4] The foul atmosphere in which a slum child is raised saps his vitality, corrupts his morals, and usually leaves him with a hostile attitude toward society. It thus materially reduces his chances of becoming

---

[1] Harold M. Lewis, *Planning the Modern City* (New York, 1949), II, 17.
[2] James Ford, *Slums and Housing* (Cambridge, Mass., 1936), I, 13.
[3] Lewis, p. 19.
[4] *Ibid.*

a well-adjusted and useful member of society. Another reason for public awareness is our rising standard of living, which has widened the gap between slum dwellings and the average home. This consciousness of the wide difference between the living conditions of different segments of our population is being manifested in legislation by federal and local governments for the redevelopment of blighted areas. Examples of such legislation are the Housing Act of 1949 and the subsequent amendment in 1954, with major emphasis on the prevention of slums and blighted areas.[5] In order to eliminate slums completely, we must first eliminate the factors responsible for our blighted areas. It will be necessary to make detailed studies of the causes and effects of slums. The redevelopment problems will have to be studied and solutions recommended. Most of all, there will have to be cooperation between the federal government, local governments, and the general public.

The factors responsible for slum conditions can be divided into the broad categories of primary and secondary causes. Obsolescent housing is an important primary cause of slum conditions. With the advance of design and technology in building houses, the old structures are no longer attractive to most tenants. As it becomes increasingly difficult to keep tenants in these obsolete buildings, the rents are usually lowered and the buildings allowed to deteriorate because it is no longer profitable to keep them in good repair.[6] Other important factors are overcrowding, development of heavy traffic, noxious industrial odors, and uneconomic use of land.[7]

Finally the important factor of land speculation is a cause of blight, in that properties are held for prices at which there is no possibility of appropriate and economic development in the location. The speculator anticipates sale for a higher-value use than exists, and so reduces his expenditures for maintenance to a minimum. He is not interested in the property as presently used in the existing community, hoping only to make a profit on his invested capital by sale. The tragedy of this practice is that there is little or no possibility of such sales except in isolated and fortuitous cases; yet each such high-priced sale is used by scores of owners in the neighborhood as an indication that they also may expect a windfall.[8]

[5] *Ibid.*
[6] *Ibid.*, p. 36.
[7] Ford, I, 446.
[8] Lewis, p. 36.

The secondary factors responsible for slum conditions are not very important individually, but collectively they constitute a major problem. Some of these factors are physical, such as unsuitable building sites, inadequate street systems, or the shift of a city's business district to a new location.[9] Other secondary factors are mainly economic. Incomes that are too low to provide money for adequate housing chain many people to slum areas.[10] On the other hand, high costs, including taxes and mortgages, which are not in keeping with the earning ability of an area may cause its abandonment and subsequent deterioration.[11] The two causes interact disastrously. The effects of these various factors which tend to bring about slum conditions are felt not only by the individuals directly concerned but also by the entire community as the blight spreads.

There are, of course, other bad effects within the slum itself. Slums in general have a higher juvenile delinquency rate than surrounding areas. The lack of playgrounds and supervision of children's activities in these areas aggravates this condition.[12] Adult crime seems to flourish more in blighted areas than in other sections of the city. High disease and mortality rates are commonplace in slum areas. Communicable diseases are easily spread by the overcrowded conditions, filth, and lack of adequate sanitation.[13] One of the many studies made of the social effects of slums should illustrate the magnitude of the problems.

> The San Francisco Planning and Housing Association made a study of two contrasting residential areas with results that students of the subject know to be common in all cities. The "clean bright" Marina area of 53 blocks and 12,188 people was checked against the blighted area known as Geary-Fillmore with 41 blocks and 13,750 people. Marina had, in the period studied, 133 fires, Geary-Fillmore had 251; Marina had 17 juvenile court cases, Geary-Fillmore had 100; Marina had 39 "police" cases, Geary-Fillmore had 4,771; Geary-Fillmore had 36 times as many tuberculosis cases, 66 times as many hospital cases, and three times as many infant deaths as Marina.[14]

[9] *Ibid.*, p. 35.
[10] Robert E. Alexander and Drayton S. Bryant, *Rebuilding a City* (Los Angeles, 1951), p. 6.
[11] Ford, I, 447.
[12] *Ibid.*, p. 448.
[13] *Ibid.*, p. 376.
[14] James Dahir, *Communities for Better Living* (New York, 1950), p. 78.

This is not an isolated example. Similar studies in other large cities have found the same results—crime, juvenile delinquency, and disease are widespread in slum areas.

The social effects of slums on a community are only part of the problem. The cost of fire and police protection for blighted areas is exceedingly high, and these areas drain heavily on the city treasury for such services as relief and medical attention.[15] Without a doubt, if the cost of social services for the entire city were as high as the services for slum areas, the city would go bankrupt.[16] Since the people living in these deteriorated sections of a city have low incomes, the revenue to pay for the social services must come from taxpayers residing in other sections.[17] This inequality causes many people to move to the suburbs, thereby lowering the city's already faltering tax base.[18] If concrete proposals are not made for the redevelopment of blighted areas, this flight to the suburbs will continue to grow in the years to come.[19]

The redevelopment of a blighted area is a complex undertaking and requires a well-organized and aggressive city plan. Often redevelopment plans pay too much attention to slum clearance and too little to slum prevention.[20] Sufficient consideration is not given such problems as size of city lots, architecture, and recreation areas. Little is accomplished by erecting developments that will be tomorrow's slums. Effective zoning is essential to any redevelopment project. Industries should be near, but not in residential areas.[21] Considerable attention must be given to housing standards. Each room of a house should have adequate light and ventilation. Minimum standards should be established for sanitation and general cleanliness of buildings. These housing standards should be applied to suburban communities as well as redeveloped urban areas, for suburban developments that lack adequate design and planning can easily become the slums of the future.[22] —— Park, Virginia, located about thirty miles from Washington, D.C., is a good example of a poorly designed community that is very likely to become a

[15] Ford, I, 431.
[16] *Ibid.*
[17] Alexander and Bryant, p. 1.
[18] Lewis, p. 35.
[19] *Ibid.*
[20] Ford, I, 495.
[21] *Ibid.*, p. 615.
[22] Ford, I, 477.

blighted area within the next twenty years. The entire community consists of houses having the same architectural layout. The houses are small and poorly constructed, and have the general appearance of summer cottages. Many of the residents work in Washington, D.C., thereby creating a transportation problem. Elimination of housing developments similar to —— Park is one of the major problems in preventing future slums.

One of the most difficult problems in redeveloping blighted sections of a city is relocating the displaced population. In almost every location where slums are torn down and replaced by new housing developments, there are more families in the slum than can be adequately housed in the rebuilt area.[23] Care must be taken that these displaced families do not move to areas already overcrowded. Because of the low incomes of these families, the only practical solution seems to be an expanded program of low-cost government housing.

Another major obstacle in the way of urban redevelopment is financing. Slum rehabilitation through private effort is usually economically unfeasible. If private capital were used to finance redevelopment projects, the rents of the new buildings would have to be quite high.[24] Using private capital would therefore defeat the purpose of slum rehabilitation: to replace slum areas with housing developments for low-income groups.[25] As mentioned earlier, land speculation is one of the main causes of high costs. Some method must be found to obtain at a fair price the land that needs redeveloping.[26] Other high costs stem directly from our postwar inflation, and little can be done about them. The only way these financial problems can be overcome and an adequate slum clearance program can be carried out for the country as a whole is through government assistance.

In fact, the federal government already gives considerable assistance to local slum clearance projects.

In the Housing Act of 1949, the Congress declared, in part, that the general welfare and security of the nation and the health and

[23] Coleman Woodbury, ed., *The Future of Cities and Urban Redevelopment* (Chicago, 1953), p. 517.
[24] Ford, II, 572.
[25] *Ibid.*
[26] Lewis, p. 38.

living standards of its people require the elimination of substandard and other inadequate housing through the clearance of slums and blighted areas, and the realization as soon as feasible of the goal of a decent home and a suitable living environment for every American family, thus contributing to the development and redevelopment of communities and to the advancement of the growth, wealth and security of the nation.[27]

Federal financial assistance is available to local governments to assist them in the clearance of slum areas and for future redevelopment of these areas. These programs are carried out by private enterprise in accordance with local plans. The federal government does make decisions on the acceptability of the plans, but local governments can proceed on most general matters without further approval.[28] The federal government provides up to two-thirds of the net project cost, and the local government must furnish the rest in the form of cash, land, public utilities, or site improvements.[29]

Another way in which the federal government aids local communities in the fight against urban blight is through low-rent public housing. Since the main economic factor compelling most families to live in substandard housing is low incomes, these housing projects are essential to the elimination of slums. The housing projects are constructed, owned, and maintained by local housing authorities operating under state enabling acts.[30] If the United States Public Housing Administration determines that a community has a need for low-cost public housing, it usually grants a loan, which must be approved by local authorities, for preliminary work. After the housing is complete, the federal government pledges a subsidy which will cover the difference between operating expenses of the project and the amount obtained in rent.[31]

It appears that federal assistance will have to be continued for an indefinite period. Local governments are unable to raise sums of money large enough to finance adequate slum clearance programs because the federal and state governments have tapped available

[27] Meyer Kestnbaum, "Twenty-five Federal Grant-in-Aid Programs," *Final Report of the Commission on Intergovernmental Relations* (Washington, D.C., 1955), p. 147.

[28] *Ibid.*, p. 148.

[29] *Ibid.*

[30] Kestnbaum, *Final Report of the Commission on Intergovernmental Relations* (1955), p. 223. Hereafter cited as *Final Report*.

[31] *Ibid.*

sources of revenue to such an extent that little more can be added to the tax burden.[32] While cities are unable financially to undertake a large-scale renewal program, however, most cities could accept more responsibility for the prevention of slums than they are presently willing to do.

> The shocking neglect of many municipal governments in failing to enforce and modernize existing housing and building codes has done much to bring about widespread conditions of urban blight and has resulted in governmental subsidies on an increasing scale. Local governments should accept responsibility for the broad goals of raising housing standards, eliminating and preventing slums and blight, establishing and preserving sound neighborhoods, and laying a foundation for healthy community development. Local governments should recognize the interrelationship of these activities and should work continuously to improve administrative and fiscal coordination among all local agencies and programs involved in planning, development and enforcement of codes and ordinances, slum clearance, public housing, and other related elements.[33]

State governments have also shirked their responsibilities in the field of slum clearance.[34] This is one of the primary reasons why the federal government has been forced to enter the field of public housing on such a large scale, despite the fact that slum clearance is an exercise of police power and ideally belongs at the municipal and state levels.[35]

Together with government assistance, furthermore, slum clearance needs the support of the general public. In order that our governmental units may plan expansion and renewal of our cities effectively, it is necessary for the private citizen to give his support.[36] The people of a community must let their elected officials know how they feel about having a well-planned community.[37] Groups of public-spirited citizens can do much to prevent the occurrence of slum conditions. They can encourage the improvement and

[32] Guy Greer, *Your City Tomorrow* (New York, 1950), p. 113.

[33] Kestnbaum, *Final Report*, p. 224.

[34] *Ibid.*

[35] *Ibid.*

[36] John Popham, "National Citizens Planning Conference," *New York Times*, June 11, 1957, sec. 1, p. 26.

[37] Luther Gulick, "Five Challenges in Today's New Urban World," *American City*, 71:149 (December, 1956).

upkeep of tenements and call on homeowners with suggestions on how their property can be improved. If they cannot secure voluntary cooperation, they should report all violations of the housing code and make sure that city officials require property owners to clear up all discrepancies. If enough private citizens actively support slum clearance projects, the job of ridding our cities of slums will progress at a faster pace.

The success or failure of slum clearance and urban renewal will ultimately depend on the success of modern city planning techniques.[38] City planning, like any large undertaking, requires a great deal of teamwork. This is why it is important that government and private persons cooperate to rid our cities of slums and blighted areas. It should be the goal of everyone concerned to see that adequate housing is brought to the level of our public school system— available to the entire population.[39]

[38] Henry S. Churchill, "City Planning in the United States," *Encyclopedia Americana* (1957), 6:718.
[39] Lewis, p. 21.

BIBLIOGRAPHY

Alexander, Robert E., and Drayton S. Bryant. *Rebuilding a City*. Los Angeles: The Haynes Foundation, 1951.

Churchill, Henry S. "City Planning in the United States," *Encyclopedia Americana* (1957), 6:718–726.

Dahir, James. *Communities for Better Living*. New York: Harper and Brothers, 1950.

Ford, James. *Slums and Housing*. 2 vols. Cambridge, Mass.: Harvard University Press, 1936.

Greer, Guy. *Your City Tomorrow*. New York: The Macmillan Company, 1950.

Gulick, Luther. "Five Challenges in Today's New Urban World," *American City*, 71:149–150 (December, 1956).

Kestnbaum, Meyer, chairman. *Final Report of the Commission on Intergovernmental Relations*. Washington, D.C.: United States Government Printing Office, 1955.

――――. "Twenty-five Federal Grant-in-Aid Programs," in *Final Report of the Commission on Intergovernmental Relations*. Washington, D.C.: United States Government Printing Office, 1955.

Lewis, Harold M. *Planning the Modern City*, Vol. II. New York: John Wiley & Sons, Inc., 1949.

Popham, John. "National Citizens Planning Conference," *New York Times*, June 11, 1957, sec. 1, p. 26.

Woodbury, Coleman, ed. *The Future of Cities and Urban Redevelopment*. Chicago: University of Chicago Press, 1953.

10~

The Critical Paper

Criticism, as we shall use the term, is judicious evaluation of the quality, significance, technique, truth, or beauty of a work produced by man; or it is an appreciation or an interpretation of such a work. The "work" may be a bridge or a symphony, a history or the performance of a pianist, an epic or a detective story or the whole nature of tragedy. We shall be concerned with the criticism of writing—utilitarian or artistic or both—and with both the judging of the relative value of a particular book and the analysis and interpretation of established works. To get practice in the presentation of critical evaluations of books, you will probably be expected to write book reviews in your English composition course. Your instructor will demand more than the synoptic "book report" you may have done in high school to prove that you really had read an assigned book. He will expect to see a developing capacity for critical thought. In your composition class or in later literature classes, you will be expected to write analyses and interpretations of numerous kinds.

In considering critical writing, we shall concentrate on the book review, since that is the kind of critical writing you will have most occasion to do during your college years. In considering the book review, we shall examine first the task of the reviewer and the elements of nonfiction and of fiction which the reviewer usually must take into account in forming his judgment. Then we shall examine the way he presents his judgment in the final review. Much of what is said can be applied with only slight adaptation to the problems of evaluating movies or plays or art, or to the writing of critical reviews of any sort.

Finally, we shall at least glance at the work of the critic in analyzing and clarifying the nature of literature itself—of explaining and interpreting the artist and his art to the rest of mankind.

THE CRITICAL REVIEW

Forming the Judgment

Any work which is to be criticized should be read carefully. It is not fair either to the author of the book or to the reader of the review to presume to pass critical judgment on a work which has been only sampled or hastily skimmed. The college student, reading for an assigned review, should read with care and with full attention to what the author is trying to say and to how he says it.

The purpose of the author and his success in achieving that purpose form the basis for the reviewer's favorable or unfavorable judgment of the book, which must be criticized primarily on how well it does what it set out to do. Obviously, for example, an elementary textbook or an article summarizing generally accepted knowledge about its topic should not be condemned because it does not introduce discussions of the latest esoteric controversies. A philosophical treatise should scarcely be expected to contain vivid description. A discussion of the best ways of preventing pulsating vibrations in a suspension bridge need not be keyed to the understanding of the readers of the *Ladies Home Journal*. Nor is the writer's purpose important to the critic only when he is reviewing nonfiction. A novel of adventure may be excellent even though it does not concern itself with the psychological analysis of its characters; the novel of character need not possess an involved and exciting plot.

On the other hand, if the writer has failed to achieve his purpose, or even to be sure himself what his purpose was, the critic is obliged to point out the inadequacies if he is to do his critical duty. If the textbook omits essential elementary material or is confusingly written, it does not fulfill its purpose. If the philosophical treatise is not logically constructed, if the engineering report is not clear to those for whom it was written, if the adventure story has an improbably contrived plot or a dull one, the reviewer must say so. To be able to recognize such deficiencies, the critic must be careful to determine exactly what the author's purpose was, and for what kind of audience he was writing.

Very often, in books of nonfiction, the author explicitly announces his purpose and discusses his methods in a preface. No reader, and especially no critic, should ignore prefaces, and no critic should condemn a writer for not doing something he has explicitly said in his preface he was not trying to do. The critic should, however, be aware of any failure on the part of the writer to do what he proposed. The critic may even decide for good reason that what the writer was trying to do was not worth doing, or that the methods adopted were ill chosen. Still another book, for example, presenting the old evidence and the old arguments for the exploded legend of the lost continent of Atlantis would scarcely be worth doing. A book presenting possible new evidence but burying that new evidence under an inconsequential drift of old stuff might be worth doing, but might better have been done another way.

Such examples presuppose some knowledge of the subject of the book; but how can one criticize a book on a subject about which he knows nothing? Even the apprentice critic may reasonably be expected to familiarize himself at least with what is generally known about the subject of any book he is reviewing. The general and specialized encyclopedias, the biographical dictionaries, the periodical indexes, and the card catalogue are available to him in the library. (See Chapter 9.) He should consult them as he needs to in order to make an intelligent and informed decision on the author's purpose and methods and on the value of the book.

Having read carefully, and with the author's purpose, audience, and methods clearly in mind, the reviewer must measure the book by the criteria that apply. The greater his own experience with similar books and the more sensitive and sophisticated his own responses, the more valuable his final judgment will be. But even the apprentice reviewer can apply certain commonsense criteria and produce a more valuable judgment than one based only on the fact that he enjoyed the book or found it dull. He may, particularly, ask and answer three questions: (1) What kind of book is it?

(2) What are the characteristics of a successful book of that kind?
(3) How many of those characteristics does this book possess?

The varieties of nonfiction are not easily classified; but before the reviewer can begin to judge a book he must decide at least roughly what type of book it is. Is it expository or fictionalized biography, history, exposition of fact or opinion in science or philosophy or political theory or some other field, personal memoir, travel book, text?——These categories overlap, and they do not begin to exhaust the possibilities. But in each, certain qualities will be important and must be measured, in addition to the characteristics of nonfiction of any type. Until the reviewer has decided what kind of book he is reviewing, he does not know what to look for. And if he is mistaken in his classification, he may form the wrong judgment altogether, as the student reviewer did in "Hell on Earth" (page 339), in which a rental library exposé is treated as a significant treatise on criminology.

Characteristics of Nonfiction

Certain salient characteristics are expected of any work of nonfiction. We can consider them, roughly, in the order of their importance.

First of all is significance. With the author's purpose and audience in mind, how important is the book? What contribution does it make to the knowledge of its specialized audience or to that of a wider audience? Dr. Kinsey's study of the gall wasp would certainly be of little interest to an astronomer or a debutante, but to entomologists it is very important and it was written for entomologists. Einstein's reports of his theory of relativity were written for physicists and mathematicians, but their significance for the rest of the world is incalculable. A popular treatment of a scientific topic would have little value for scientists—but may have much value for the nonscientific audience to which it is addressed. The reviewer must consider first the book's significance.

Second in importance is the newness of the material, or of the approach to or grouping of the material, or of the conclusions. A book presenting new facts, like Darwin's report of his biological observations during the voyage of the *Beagle*, makes a contribution of greater or less importance to the knowledge of its audience. Professor Toynbee's regrouping of the known facts of history makes a contribution. Darwin's *Origin of Species* offered new and important conclusions based on a study of old facts. H. G. Wells' *Outline of History* brought old facts to a new audience. Each in its way is new and important.

Third is the accuracy of the facts and the reasonableness of the inferences based on them. Other things being equal, the most accurate and most reasonable book is the most valuable—although a book which is inaccurate in some of its facts may be stimulatingly influential in its conclusions, just as one which is wrong in most of its conclusions may contribute important new facts. How carefully does it present its evidence? How logically does it draw inferences from the evidence to support its conclusions? (See Chapter 8 if these terms are strange to you.)

Fourth is the scope of the book. How completely does it cover its topic, considering the author's purpose and his audience? Does it present all the material it should, and is the presentation balanced?

Fifth is clarity. How easily understandable is the book for its predetermined audience, in organization and in phrasing? The more significant the book, the less important is clarity. It was said that only half a dozen men could understand Einstein's first exposition of his theory of relativity; yet it was not on that account unimportant. But in general, the clearer the book—to its audience—the better.

Last is readability, closely related to clarity but not identical with it. The first four characteristics are concerned with the content of the book; these last two are concerned with style. The critic must evaluate both what the author is trying to say and how he says it. In nonfiction, as in fiction, there may be vast differences in readability. Bishop Berkeley and Herbert Spencer, for example, are perhaps equally important as philosophers and their writings equally significant; yet Berkeley is easy to read and Spencer is very difficult. The qualities of good writing with which we have been concerned throughout the text are no more important to the creative writer than they are to the writer of workaday exposition or argument.

In addition to these general characteristics of good nonfiction, of course, each type of writing and each book possesses special characteristics of its own. History and biography, for example, may well be vivid, vitalizing their topic as well as presenting it clearly and accurately. Memoirs and travel books lie close to imaginative narration and description. An account of American place names may be fascinating reading. A popularization of the facts and theories of oceanography may be beautifully written. The critic must go beyond the list of general characteristics as he asks himself, "What are the characteristics of a book of this type, and how many of those characteristics does this book possess?"

Judging Fiction

College students read more fiction, perhaps, than nonfiction, except for their textbooks; but most of them have very little idea of what to look for in evaluating it, aside from the crude test implied by, "I liked the book" or "I didn't like it." Your college composition course may require you to review one or more novels, or it may confine your critical writing to nonfiction. If you are required to review a novel, you will find it immediately practical to consider in detail the major types of novels and the important elements of the novel. If you are not so required, you will at least find increased enjoyment in your own reading if you know what critics look for in judging fiction—in somewhat the same way the initiated spectator enjoys a cattle show far more than his city cousin does, or in the way the artist sees more in an exhibit of painting than is apparent to the man who merely knows what he likes.

Again, as with nonfiction, the reviewer of fiction must determine the writer's purpose and must then ask and answer three questions: (1) What kind of book is it? (2) What are the characteristics of a successful book of that kind? (3) How many of these characteristics does this book possess?

Types of Novels

Even though there is a great deal of overlapping, at least three types of novels may be recognized: the novel of plot, the novel of character, and the novel of idea, each distinguished by the element on which the author's purpose has led him to lay the greatest emphasis.

THE NOVEL OF PLOT

The novel of plot is the novel in which the action, the interrelation of the incidents, is the most important feature. The adventure story, like *Treasure Island;* the detective story, *Murder's Little Helper;* the rental library "love" story, *Forever Amber;* novels of suspense, *Escape;* much historical fiction, *Ivanhoe*—in all these and many others the most important thing is what happens. So long as it happens naturally and interestingly, and so long as the story seems reasonably plausible in the telling, the author achieves his basic purpose.

THE NOVEL OF CHARACTER

The novel of character is more complex than the novel of plot. Its purpose is primarily to trace the developing character of human beings, sometimes in the face of exciting action, but more often in fairly quiet circumstances. Somerset Maugham's *Of Human Bondage* is almost purely a novel of character; the principal concern is to show what made Philip Carey the man he was. *Madame Bovary* is a novel of character, as is *David Copperfield,* or *Silas Marner,* or Thomas Wolfe's *Of Time and the River.* All these novels and many more, perhaps most serious novels, are novels of character, examining in detail how various kinds of human beings grow or wither or at least change under the circumstances of human life.

THE NOVEL OF IDEA

The novel of idea is preeminently the novel written to present a thesis or a theme (though theme is often important, too, in the novel of character). The novel of idea is exposition or argument in narrative form, and more than in plot or in character, the novelist is interested in presenting a thesis effectively. Many of Dickens' novels—*Oliver Twist, Bleak House, Hard Times,* for specific examples—seem chiefly concerned with securing social reform or with changing social attitudes. The novels of Lloyd C. Douglas are designed to disseminate religious ideas. Satirists like Sinclair Lewis or John P. Marquand or George Orwell used their novels to call attention to social phenomena of which they disapproved.

None of these classifications are exclusive. The novel of plot makes some attempt to people its scenes with believable characters, and may develop a theme; the novel of character may develop a theme or present exciting incident; the novel of idea pays greater or less attention to plot and to characters. And some novels decline to fit neatly into any of the three groups: W. H. Hudson's *Green Mansions* and George R. Stewart's *Storm* come to mind as examples.

But, somewhat roughly, most novels may be classified as novels of plot, or of character, or of idea, depending on which element is predominant.

Elements of the Novel

The reviewer needs next to consider at least five elements of the novel as he forms his judgment of how well a particular novelist has achieved his purpose. *Setting, plot, characterization, theme,* and *style* are the basic elements with which the novelist works, with greater or less emphasis on each according to the type of novel concerned. (See also pages 346–348.)

SETTING

The action of every novel takes place on some kind of stage. That stage is the setting. It may be vividly portrayed or lightly sketched; it may be relatively minor, or it may—as in *Green Mansions*—be the most important element in the book. In any event, it will be treated differently by different novelists. In many novels, the setting is a major element—Egdon Heath dominates Hardy's *Return of the Native,* and the fair and smiling or bleak and barren landscapes echo the turns of fortune in *Tess of the D'Urbervilles.* Many historical novels, like *Gone with the Wind,* are chiefly distinguished by the care with which they reproduce the times in which they are laid.

In reviewing a novel in which setting plays an active role, the critic must ask himself, first, whether the emphasis on the setting is justified, and, second, whether the setting is graphically presented. Even if the setting is minor, the critic must still try to determine whether it is as vivid as it should be, or whether it is unnecessarily, even disturbingly, blurred.

PLOT

The plot is the main story, the pattern of action which raises a conflict and eventually resolves it, and which not only determines what will happen, but when and how and with what results. (Nothing happens by chance in a novel of any consequence at all—at least since the early picaresque novels. Every incident either prepares for later events or grows out of those that went before, according to the predetermined plan of the author.) The novel which depends chiefly on plot is generally considered to be the least significant sort of novel—adventure stories, detective stories, suspense novels, all books in which the most important question is "What happens?" However, plot is probably the most generally interesting element of all, and a good plot well presented is not to be sneered at. The apprentice reviewer, writing a book review for a college composition course, needs only to remember that plot is not everything. If he keeps in mind the importance of determining the writer's purpose and judging the book by the writer's success in achieving that purpose, he will avoid the common student mistake of condemning a book like *Middlemarch* or *The Way of All Flesh* merely because it lacks an exciting plot.

In any novel in which plot is important—and few novels are completely plotless—the critic's problem is to decide how successfully the plot is presented. Do the incidents follow each other logically and naturally, given the conditions set up within the novel itself? Is each turn of the action adequately foreshadowed, or do things happen fortuitously, depending on unlikely coincidence? In a novel of plot is the action interesting enough to be worth the reader's time and trouble?

CHARACTERIZATION

The characters are the people of a novel, and characterization is the way the novelist portrays his people. In a novel of character, of course, characterization is the dominant element, but in virtually every novel, characterization, at least on an elementary level, is important. Do the people of the novel act and talk like real people? Are they individuals or merely stereotypes? Is their motivation credible? Do they respond to the circumstances of the story in a natural way, or do they act or talk "out of character" to suit the convenience of the novelist, or because the novelist does not know people or cannot write natural dialogue? Do they change, for better or worse, as they are subjected to the circumstances of the story? Should they change?

How does the novelist present his characters? Does he merely tell about them, or does he let them reveal themselves by what they do and say? Does he, perhaps, show them through the eyes of other characters, as Stevenson does Mr. Hyde or as Galsworthy does

Irene Forsyte? Are even the minor characters vivid, as they are in Dickens? Is the author better at depicting some types or classes of people than others? Are male and female characters equally credible? Adults and children? Are the characters easily distinguishable, or does the reader have trouble telling which is which, even after he has had time to get acquainted?

THEME

The theme of a novel is its basic text, what the author is trying to say about life itself, the philosophic concept underlying the work. Sometimes the theme is distinct and can be succinctly phrased; sometimes it represents little more than a fundamental attitude on the part of the novelist. Good critics often disagree on theme, or emphasize different aspects of a theme they do agree on. Novels of plot usually have no theme worth worrying about. (Would anyone maintain that *Treasure Island* was written to show that a boy who helps his widowed mother and is kind to blind beggars may be led to buried gold?) Often the novelist wants only to present exciting action. Novels of character, however, are often saying more than appears on the surface, and certainly novels of idea are concerned with presenting a theme. *Madame Bovary*, for instance, is a novel of character, tracing the progressive degeneration of a bored woman searching for romance. But one might say that its basic theme is that a romantic education is necessarily foolish preparation for life in a realistic world, filling giddy minds with illusions which lead inevitably to dissatisfaction; or, even more generally, that our illusions cause our major disappointments. Thomas Hardy's novels all develop the general theme that Fate is against mankind, that there can be no enduring human happiness in this hostile universe. (At such a point theme strongly overlaps tone—the general attitude of defiant pessimism in Hardy's writing.) *Of Mice and Men* underlines the futility of planning for the future. Some of these are novels of idea, others are novels of character; all of them develop clearly defined themes.

Where a basic theme is present, the critic must take it into account, or he may miss the whole point of the book; at the very least he will fail to understand why the characters behave as they do or why certain incidents are included. His review, based on misconception of the author's purpose, must necessarily suffer. He may, if he likes, take thoughtful exception to the theme, but he must not miss it altogether.

STYLE

Style, in its broadest sense, means the way the book is written: its diction (see Chapter 7), its sentence patterns (see Chapter 6), the kind of detail the author selects to expand and develop his story, the technique by which he moves from incident to incident or from chapter to chapter, the way he presents his characters, the kind of dialogue he writes, the amount and kind of description he uses, the point of view, the imagery, the tone—everything, in short, which concerns his technique as a novelist. Because each novelist presents his material in the way that seems most natural to him, and because no two novelists see things in exactly the same way or think in exactly the same way, it is largely the style which sets the work of one novelist apart from the work of all others. Ernest Hemingway and Thomas Wolfe and William Faulkner and John Steinbeck— each is distinctive; each has his own style.

It is important to observe that style is not mere rhetorical embroidery laid on to something that could better be said in a simpler, plainer way. It may, indeed, in itself be simple, as the style of Hemingway is simple. Where it is elaborate, as the style of Thomas Wolfe is elaborate, it should represent still the best efforts of the author to say what he wants to say, making the effect he wants to make. Student writers and student critics are too obsessed with the idea that style is something necessarily fancy and something quite apart from the writer's natural habits of thought.

They are too obsessed, also, with the belief that style is merely a matter of diction and sentence structure, though they may have some awareness of prose rhythms and of something vaguely known as "symbolism." Those all help make a "style," certainly. But so does a writer's tendency to be specific or to generalize; to compress much into epigrammatic statements, like Bacon, or to expand and qualify and add and subtract ideas, like Henry James; to look at events from the outside, like Arnold Bennett, or from deep inside the minds of the participants, like Virginia Woolf. Attitude, tone, conventionality or originality—all of these, too, are matters of style in the broadest sense.

The reviewer needs to be conscious of style for two reasons. First, as we shall see when we turn to the presentation of the critic's judgment in the review, the reviewer needs to indicate the general flavor of the book, and it is largely style which gives a book its flavor. Second, whenever style is not appropriate to the matter being presented—for example, Thackeray's cynical comments on his "puppets," or the orotundity of Dr. Johnson's style, which led a friend to remark that he always sounded "like a whale talking to little fishes"—the book is flawed because the reader is distracted from the idea the writer is presenting and thinks instead of the irrelevant manner of presentation. Whenever the style is harmoniously suited to the material, it actively aids in the presentation but does it in a way that will escape notice if the critic is not alert. He must consider the style as an essential part of the book.

In forming his judgment of a novel, then, the critic must first determine the type of novel and then examine the author's treatment of setting, plot, characterization, theme, and style. In judging nonfiction, he must consider the special characteristics of each type of book, and evaluate the book's significance, newness, accuracy and reasonableness, scope, clarity, and readability. Only when he has thus formed a careful judgment should he turn to the writing of his review.

Presenting the Judgment

As the reviewer forms his judgment of the book he is criticizing, he must be constantly aware of the purpose of the original writer. As he presents his judgment to his own audience in his review, he must be equally aware of his own purpose.

The professional reviewer, writing for the book review section of a newspaper or a magazine, is trying to help his reader decide whether or not to read a given book, just as the dramatic critic or the music critic tries to help him decide whether or not to see a given play or movie or hear a given orchestra or singer or opera company. He must remember his readers and what they will look for in a book. Few detective stories, for example, are really first-rate novels, but neither the author nor the reader expects that much; so long as the book is plausible and plays fair within the formulas of the detective story type, the purpose is achieved. The reviewer must always measure a book by the yardsticks that apply to it and must try to present his judgment in a way that will be of genuine help to his readers in deciding whether or not to read the book.

The student reviewer in an English composition course is writing for a reasonably well-educated audience. Consequently, the standards by which he measures a book are high. The book must not be judged out of its class—the elementary history text must not be condemned because it does not offer startlingly new theories. But the book he is reviewing may be measured against the best of its class and judged accordingly. Most composition-course book reviews are written in emulation of the professional reviewers on the staffs of the better newspapers and magazines. The *New York Times*, the *New Yorker*, or the *Saturday Review* offer good models.

There is no infallible formula for producing a good book review, but for the average book the reviewer usually considers three questions: (1) What kind of book is it? (2) What is the flavor of the book? (3) What is its value? If we remember the purpose of the review, it is easy to see why each question should be clearly answered.

1. WHAT KIND OF BOOK IS IT?

Readers have different tastes. One man enjoys historical fiction about the American Revolution; another abhors fiction but reads avidly any nonfictional account of that period. A third man prefers biography. A fourth wants novels of character. A young reader insists on fiction with an exciting plot. An older one prefers to savor the ripe philosophical comment of a sage observer of mankind. A professional man wants new facts or theories in his professional field. Each wants to know, as he picks up a review of a new book, "What kind of book is it?" The reviewer who neglects to answer that question, either directly or by implication, has failed in his duty to his audience.

2. WHAT IS THE FLAVOR OF THE BOOK?

Equally important is the flavor of the book, for books of the same general type may differ widely in the way they are written. The Frenchman André Maurois' appreciative *Miracle of England,* for example, differs from Arthur Lyon Cross's *A Shorter History of England and Greater Britain* in a way perhaps suggested by the flavor of their titles. In all sorts of nonfiction, books vary widely, and that variation affects both their flavor and their value. One writer is accurate in handling detail; another is careless with detail but brilliant in the suggestiveness of his conclusions. One presents his evidence carefully and draws reasonable inferences from it; another is obviously biased and ignores all inconvenient facts; a third may be inept in nearly every way. Some books are highly significant in content but written in an almost unreadable style. Some are facile but foolish. And novels, even within the same general type, may differ greatly in the way they are written. Historical novels, for example, may range from *Forever Amber* to *Henry Esmond*. They may be peopled with stereotyped characters sprinkling their speech with "Gadzooks" and "forsooth" and behaving like no human beings that ever lived on earth; or their characters may be vital, credible people struggling with the vividly realized problems of their times. The tone of any book may range from saccharine to bitter. The novelist's approach may be romantic or realistic. His plot may be gripping or contrived or boring. There may be great differences in theme or characterization or setting or style. No two books, fiction or nonfiction, are alike in style. By direct comment, by selected quotation, by implication, the reviewer must indicate the flavor of the book.

3. WHAT IS ITS VALUE?

Certainly, the critic must indicate his judgment of the value of the book. Criticizing means judging, evaluating—indicating, remember, the good qualities of a book as well as the bad ones. The fundamental business of the reviewer is to suggest to the reader whether or not the critic believes the book worth reading, and his reasons for thinking that it is or is not. To fulfill his obligations as a critic, he suggests the criteria by which he has judged the book and indicates how well it measures up to the standards it should have met.

This formula for a standard review, notice, cannot be applied mechanically. Frequently, one element or another will demand special emphasis. Certain features of the book may be outstandingly good or bad, or may have been given special attention in the book according to the original author's particular purpose. They should receive corresponding attention in the review. The reviewer may vary the order in which he answers the three major questions, or the answer to one of them may be implied by the way he answers one of the others. A new book by a well-known writer may be measured against his earlier books. A book may be set against similar books by other writers or of other periods. There are many variations to this standard pattern. As the reviewer, remember always your own purpose: to present your considered judgment of the work you are reviewing, clearly, specifically, and effectively.

Three reviews follow to illustrate some of the ways in which the reviewer meets his obligation to his audience. The first is a student review of a work of nonfiction. Perhaps mistaken in its judgment, it is nonetheless clear, and it expresses an independent opinion. The second is a brief professional review of a second work of nonfiction. The third is a student review of a novel.

A student review of a work of nonfiction:

Hell on Earth[1]

Teddy Roosevelt once said, "There are two things about the French I could never understand or tolerate; they are French Guiana and the French Foreign Legion." Not only Roosevelt, but the whole world has wondered about the great French penal colony. Periodically, since Guiana's birth in 1852, humanity has been shocked by tales of terrorism and brutality emanating from there. But so completely has French Guiana guarded its dark and dismal secrets, only vague and garbled rumors of conditions in Guiana have reached the general public's ear.

The man in the street doesn't associate the name Guiana with the more famous name Devil's Island, and, if he did, the chances are he would have to consider several moments before settling on their location. The reason for this amazing lack of knowledge is quite simple. The French government and the administration of Guiana could never hope to keep the partial truth of Guiana from the world, but they have done the next best thing. They have endeavored, since the famous Dreyfus case, to obscure and destroy all documents and witnesses that could supply to the public the evidence needed to corroborate the stories and rumors that have come out of the place. The French government and the Guiana administration have, in effect, reduced the colony to one of those evils which, from constant repetition and insufficient evidence, become boresome to the public.

[1] From *The Green Caldron: A Magazine of Freshman Writing,* published at the University of Illinois. Reprinted by permission.

Such was the case until *Dry Guillotine* appeared. The world became "Guiana-conscious" again, for here was an account written by René Belbenoit, an escaped prisoner from Guiana. But not an ordinary prisoner! Not a semi-intelligent, illiterate, bestial hulk of a man! Here was a burning intellect, kept alive in a frail ninety-pound body. After spending fifteen years in this hell, in a climate and under treatment that had killed thousands of men—big, strong men, far better equipped by nature than he—René Belbenoit, literary, versed in several languages, living but for the day he would tell the world of his experience, escaped from Guiana. This emaciated mite of a man, all his teeth gone, his body racked with fever, with but a few years to live after the privations he had suffered, arrived in America as a stowaway on a tramp steamer. He had not traded his health for nothing—he carried with him a precious oilskin-wrapped bundle containing thirty pounds of closely written manuscript. From that thirty-pound bundle *Dry Guillotine* was made, a work which treats the subject so clearly and objectively (and objectivity must have been especially difficult for one who had suffered as long and as deeply as had Belbenoit) that no reasonable person could doubt it is the absolute truth. The work is fully substantiated by documented evidence: Belbenoit worked for some months as custodian of the official archives of French Guiana, cataloging them, by the special request of the Civil Governor.

Dry Guillotine is the odyssey of a man's will, of the fighting, unquenchable spark, the mysterious, intangible force that drives men on after their bodies have quit. At the age of twenty-one, Belbenoit was sentenced to eight years at hard labor in Guiana. Upon arriving there, he was faced with the choice all newly arrived prisoners faced—the choice of staying there, trying to endure the burning sun, the omnipresent mosquitoes and insects, the bad housing and poor nutrition, the brutal treatment of the guards, and the back-breaking jungle labor camps, where prisoners labor naked in the sun and die like flies; or trying to escape. The very air seemed to whisper the answer—"escape or die."

And Belbenoit tried. For four unsuccessful attempts he tried, for fifteen years of the most terrible hardships he tried, until, finally, on his fifth try, after twenty-two months of unbelievable sufferings, he escaped through the jungles of Central and South America. On this series of escape attempts René weaves a fascinating pattern of prison life. The dreaded islands—*Isles du Salut* (Isles of Salvation), including Royal Island, home of *La Case Rouge* (the Crimson, i.e., The Bloodstained, Barracks); Saint Joseph, where the terrible solitary cells are; and Devil's Island, the tiny island on which political prisoners are kept—are painted with an unforgettable brilliance. The terrible labor camps of *Chavein, Kourou,* and *Godebert,* the blockhouse at *Saint Laurent,* the sordid capital city of Cayenne, the *libères* (freed convicts, still required to remain in Guiana), the *fort-a-bras* (roughnecks), the *momes* (sexual perverts), and the *incos* (incorrigible prisoners) leap into life before your startled eyes. They hold you half thrilled, half sickened, in your chair.

I believe that *Dry Guillotine* will stand the test of time; its theme, penology, will be of interest to all generations, and it is perhaps the greatest expression of man's inhumanity to man ever written. The book has great sociological significance. . . .

Sociologists, human welfare workers, child educators, criminologists, parents, and all others having the interests of the species at heart, and even those that don't—the anarchist, the nihilist, the malcontent, and the criminal—will find in *Dry Guillotine* a vital interest; for it is something that affects every one of us. No one can say when he, or someone dear to him, will be faced by the law's long arm; and when that happens you would like to feel that the law you face is a fair and just one, that it will give you all due and just consideration, that if you are convicted, you will not have to suffer such a man-destroying, soul-destroying hell as Guiana, that you will have a chance to serve your term and to rehabilitate yourself afterwards. For these reasons, and because it is a profound study of the meaner side of human nature, I recommend *Dry Guillotine.*

Robert Wright

QUESTIONS

1. It seems probable that the student reviewer has misjudged the kind of book he has read, presumably because of lack of experience. Yet as he sees the book, he has presented a well-written review. This review presents a good deal of the material in the book. Is it merely a synopsis, or does the reviewer offer a clear judgment?
2. Does he tell so much about the book that he spoils it for you? Does he tell it in a way that helps you decide whether you want to read the book?
3. Does he indicate clearly his opinion of the significance of the book? of its newness? of its accuracy? of its scope? of its clarity? of its readability? Considering the audience to which the book

is addressed, what is the relative importance of each of these elements?
4. Where and how does the reviewer indicate the type of book and the flavor of the book?
5. Do the reasons he offers for recommending the book seem adequate? Has he overlooked other and possibly better reasons? Has he overestimated the value of the book?

A brief professional review of a book of nonfiction (*The Stream of American History* by Leland D. Baldwin):

The Stream of American History[2]

Dr. Baldwin's magnum opus is written from the viewpoint of the conservative with a conscience. He approaches his task as one who sees history as a continuous process, and sees it whole. In these two thoughtful, fact-crammed volumes, he tells the American story not as an isolated phenomenon in the Western Hemisphere but as a prodigious offshoot of the European civilization which transformed the Western world. Dr. Baldwin is primarily concerned with what he calls the "American mission," which at various times has been called expansionist, isolationist and exemplary. His judgments are reasonable, judicious, and qualified where necessary; the prose is lively and crisp. The author is especially persuasive in his treatment of the contemporary scene, which does not fill him with the despair it has engendered in others. As a historian, he is aware that at least since 1775 we have lived constantly in a state of transition, and have always been plagued by more or less confusion. Yet democracy continues to flourish here amid our million voices. This work is not only history—it is also entertaining and instructive reading which will make you think better of your country.

Richard R. Smith

QUESTIONS

1. The reviewer seldom answers his questions on kind, flavor, and value mechanically, in that order. This review illustrates one way in which the answers may be efficiently interwoven. Where and how is each question answered?
2. Is the review too brief to do justice to its subject? What sort of expansion would you suggest?

[2] From the *Washington Post*, April 12, 1953. Reprinted by permission.

A student review of a novel:

To Kill a Mockingbird: A Review

Harper Lee's novel, *To Kill a Mockingbird*, is the kind of story that is mistakenly called "heartwarming." I think instead that I would choose the word "heartbreaking." It is the story of two children, Jeremy Atticus Finch (Jem) and Jean Louise Finch (Scout), of their childhood in a sleepy Alabama town during the 1930's, and of their introduction to a bewildering adult world full of contradictory values and conflicting standards of morality. Raised by their lawyer-father Atticus Finch and their colored housekeeper Calpurnia, Jem and Scout find it difficult to understand the vague concept which their prim Aunt Alexandra calls "background," or the hypocrisy which allows the citizens of Macomb to condemn Hitler for hating Jews, but to refuse to conquer their own prejudices in order to give a colored man a fair trial, or the hatred of cruelty which motivates Atticus to hide from his children his ability as a marksman. Their childhood is the awakening to disillusionment which every childhood must be, but their father's appointment to defend a Negro in court rips away the childish fantasy-barriers which should melt slowly before approaching adulthood, and forces Jem and Scout to see all the kindness and cruelty of humanity in one short summer. And here is the eternal heartbreak of mankind, more pitiful here because these children are not prepared for it. "Naw, Jem," says Scout, "I think there's just one kind of folks. Folks." But Jem replies, "That's what I thought, too, when I was your age. If there's just one kind of folks, why can't they get along with each other? If they're all alike, why do they go out of their way to despise each other?" Yet where is the evil? The conclusion to which the children finally come is the one which Atticus tried to teach them when he said, "Remember, it's a sin to kill a mockingbird"; the conclusion which their neighbor, Miss Maudie, explained to them by saying, "Your father's right. Mockingbirds don't do one thing but make music for us to enjoy. They don't eat up people's gardens, don't nest in corncribs, they don't do one thing but sing their hearts out for us. That's why it's a sin to kill a mockingbird." So obvious, so clear even to a child. And yet heartbreakingly unclear, it would seem, to some adults.

Miss Lee tells her story in the first person, through the eyes of Scout, an irrepressible tomboy who worships her older brother and hates the thought of growing up to be a lady. The book becomes

Scout's story, told simply and convincingly, a story so engrossing that the beauty of Miss Lee's language, the art of her similes—she describes a shadow as being "crisp as toast"—her eye for detail, and her apparently effortless creation of living human beings slips past the reader as part of the whole, only to be noticed when one goes back and reads the book again. The characters are completely real, with the habits and eccentricities of all real people. Scout herself is a refreshingly realistic child. She is not cute, or artlessly naïve; she is just a little human being. And this child describes the people she knows: Miss Stefanie Crawford, the neighborhood gossip; Miss Maudie, with her acid tongue and her boundless capacity for understanding; Dill, Scout's playmate, whose fantastic imagination leads the three children into countless scrapes; Calpurnia, the literate and cultured Negro who raises Jem to be a gentleman and Scout to be a lady, but who reverts into dialect when she is with her own people; and Atticus, whose strict sense of justice and morality forces him always to be completely honest with his children, lest they lose respect for him. Through Scout, Miss Lee presents them all, telling us enough in a few brief sentences and a few scraps of conversation so that we know them as well as she does. This book is beautifully written; the grasp of conversation is perfect; Miss Lee never uses an incongruous or an inappropriate word.

The plot of the novel is complicated and involves dozens of people; yet to the reader it seems simple and clear. The emotions which the characters feel are complex and hard to describe; yet the reader understands them perfectly. Perhaps the chief charm of this book, apart from its humor and its general perfection, is its lack of pretension. Miss Lee is dealing with a theme "of universal significance," but she doesn't try to relate her story to the whole human race. She lets the reader do that job. She covers the field of human emotion from good-natured laughter to complete frustration and heartbreaking despair, but she never says, "This is a portrait of humanity." She never even implies it. The reader is drawn completely into the situation, and is led subtly to the desired conclusion, but at the end he is left with the impression that this conclusion is a product of his own powers of deduction and sensitivity. And in this quality lies the book's value. This book will be remembered by those who read it, not because it baldly states eternal truths, but because it leads the readers to their own formulations of these truths. Miss Lee has done a commendable job, and she has written a compassionate, forthright, and thoroughly enjoyable book.

Candace Carroll

QUESTIONS

1. What central thesis gives unity to this student review?
2. What aspect of the novel gives unity to each of the paragraphs? How does the purpose of each paragraph determine the selection of details for the paragraph?
3. To what extent has the writer combined her discussion of type, flavor, and value with discussions of significant elements of the novel?

THE CRITICAL ESSAYS

The book review is probably the most common type of critical writing required of students in all curricula; but criticism goes far beyond reviewing, and many composition courses, centering your attention on writing of the highest quality, will expect critical essays of interpretation and analysis as you learn more and more about the subtleties of the expression of human thought and emotion through language.

The varieties of critical writing are almost endless. As critics seek to understand what an author has done, how he did it, and why the work produces the effect that it does, the different interests of different critics result in different approaches and different evaluations. Obviously we cannot examine all the possibilities in detail. That would require a book in itself.[3] What we shall do is consider some of the critical problems which lend themselves to student treatment in papers of manageable length. In so doing, we shall consider varied types of literary works—essays, novels, short stories, plays, poems—but without intending to apply all problems to all types or to limit a particular approach to the type we use as illustration. We shall consider, first, critical papers dealing with a single work in itself, and then at least suggest papers that deal with works in their setting.

[3] No wholly satisfactory book of this sort for beginning college students is yet available, though two or three having appeared close together suggests that the void may soon be filled. B. Bernard Cohen, *Writing about Literature* (Chicago: Scott, Foresman and Company, 1963), Edgar V. Roberts, *Writing Themes about Literature* (Englewood Cliffs, N.J.: Prentice-Hall, Inc., 1964), and Richard D. Altick, *The Art of Literary Research* (New York: W. W. Norton & Company, 1963) are all useful in different ways, and I am indebted to all of them throughout this section. Many critical case books present collected essays that will provide helpful illustrations of varied critical approaches to a single work.

The simplest kind of paper on a single work is the *summary*, which may be assigned early in the term, or on a test, to check on your ability to understand what you read and on your ability to identify the relative importance of sections and details. Simple as it seems, the summary of a work is not expected to be merely a concise account of the ideas or events as they appear, but an identifying of the main idea or purpose of the work and the most important subsidiary points. The length of a summary and the depth of its detail depend on the time and space available. It may be adapted to any type of writing.

Distinct from the summary is an *explication* of a work, or more commonly of a typical brief passage. It calls for an explanation of the meaning of the passage: a close analysis of the denotations and connotations of words and phrases and of the cumulative and sometimes paradoxical suggestions of its imagery or symbols; a recognition of allusions and a clarifying of their contribution to the total effect; and usually, at significant points throughout, a paraphrasing of what the author has said. Because explication is called for only when a passage is highly compressed, as in poetry or a Baconian essay, or obscure because of unfamiliar vocabulary, syntax, or details, the essay of explication is usually longer than the passage itself. If this strikes you as absurd, remember how long it sometimes takes your instructor to explain to the class just what a poem or a difficult passage in prose says to a careful and experienced reader.

A third type of critical paper deals with *analysis of structure*. Structure concerns both the organization of the work and the effect of that organization on the reader's understanding or emotions. Again close reading is essential; you must know what the writer was trying to do (or what, after intelligent scrutiny, it seems to you that he has done). Then you must discover the parts into which the work falls, not chapters or stanzas or books or volumes (though the last two often indicate broad elements of structure) but the main sections of the developing work. Finally you must decide what each contributes to the unity of the whole and how each has affected the reader.

For brief example, the first nineteen chapters of *The Way of All Flesh* introduce the great-grandfather, grandfather, and father of Ernest Pontifex, the central figure of the novel, and trace the drifting of each generation away from the true genius of the family to the smugly hypocritical way of life and thought into which Ernest was born. Because the purpose of the novel is to present Ernest's struggle to adapt himself to this way of life which is wrong for the Pontifex line, and to emphasize the inevitability of the true Pontifex nature's ultimately reasserting itself, Butler treats each generation in greater detail as it drifts farther from its proper life. The great-grandfather is rather briefly shown, but is made enviably admirable. The grandfather's life and character are given in greater detail, and the reader's sympathy with him is progressively alienated. The father too begins with the reader's sympathy; yet as he settles into his false life, he becomes more and more odious. The reader is fully prepared to struggle with Ernest to escape. The structure is wholly appropriate. The next section presents Ernest's childhood, youth, and young manhood, in all of which he tries unhappily to conform to his father's life, with disastrous results; the reader remains sympathetic, but becomes increasingly exasperated with Ernest's obtuseness. And so on through the novel.

Another type of paper may deal with *analysis of a character,* usually with a secondary character. What kind of person is this? What effect does he have on the action or on other characters? What is his function in the story—or poem, or play? The housekeeper in *The Turn of the Screw,* for example: Depending on how you interpret Henry James' purpose in the novelette and the meaning of the tale, what is Mrs. Grose like? What is her relationship to the children and the governess? What do her nature and her presence in the story enable the author to do? And always, why do you think so?

Similarly, *analysis of incident or of detail* can add greatly to literary insights. Nothing comes into good writing without purpose. Since the best work leads to unity of effect, everything the writer includes should contribute something more than padding to fill the distance between the covers. Examine an incident in a story or a novel or a play, particularly one that seems at first to be irrelevant to the design. Why does Shakespeare, for example, break the mounting tension of the tragedy in *Hamlet* with a low-comedy scene between the gravediggers? Why does Spenser call up and catalogue the nymphs in stanzas 3 and 4 of his "Epithalamion"? Why does Mark Twain include the fatal quarrel between Dr. Robinson and Injun Joe in *Tom Sawyer?* You may find, indeed, that the incident or detail is truly irrelevant and that the structure is at least at that point faulty. But present your reasons carefully.

We have already considered the nature of style as we considered the critical review (pages 335–336). Even though that was a sketchy treatment, we need not go into it again, for much of this book is concerned with style, Chapters 6 and 7 especially. Nor can we examine the complexities of prosody, that is, of poetic meters and rhythms, of rhyme schemes and the poet's special use of assonance and alliteration and onomatopoeia. Those you will certainly be given by your literature text or by your instructor. Here, we need only list as an important critical topic the *analysis of style or of prosody*.

As a final item in our discussion of critical papers dealing with a single work in itself, we shall consider, instead, the problem of *point of view*. The term has long been common in the critical vocabulary, but interest in the functions and the complexities of point of view is very high at the moment. In its basic sense, point of view means the position from which the action of a narrative is seen. If the story is told by a participant from his own observation, the point of view is first person, with the problems attendant upon getting the "I" into all of the action or at least letting him hear about it plausibly. If the action is presented without an explicitly participating narrator, the point of view is third person; sometimes it is "omniscient" so that the writer-narrator sees equally well into all the thoughts and motives of all the actors, but more often it is "limited" to a thorough presentation of one character, with other characters and the action presented as they would appear to him; or it may be "shifting" from one character to another at different stages of the narration. Obvious technical problems accompany each of these approaches, and the critical reader has long been alert to the restraints imposed by point of view in this simplest sense.

Yet even in that sense it is not as simple as it appears. Who *is* this "I" who is telling the story? What facets of his character does the writer present? What façade, what *persona* is this Speaker? Even in narrative, that can become very complex. In *Treasure Island*, the "I" is only young Jim Hawkins, soon after the adventure (except that Stevenson wrote himself into a box, so that for a time the "I" had to be Dr. Livesey). But who is the "I", the Speaker, in *Great Expectations?* Not Pip. Not Mr. Pip. Not even Philip Pirrip, though the Speaker says at the beginning that his name is Philip Pirrip. Instead, it is Mr. Pirrip, somewhere in his late middle age, when all the events of the novel and most of its unnarrated sequelae are behind him, and he can look at Pip and Mr. Pip and Philip Pirrip and all they knew and did through eyes that none of them could have commanded. Who is the Speaker in Shakespeare's sonnets? Possibly Shakespeare, though the critic-scholars have knotted themselves into pretty tangles when they have assumed that. Who is the Speaker in Dean Swift's "A Modest Proposal"? Certainly not the dean; they have almost nothing in common. Who is the Speaker in Browning's dramatic monologues, all of which are first person? Various people, even Browning, sometimes.

In *Wuthering Heights*, a little of what Mr. Lockwood writes about happened directly to him, but most of what he tells us is told him by Mrs. Dean, so that the "I" is now one person and now the other, with complicated results in determining what the ultimate reader can be told about events and motives that Mrs. Dean knows only from hearsay. In *A Connecticut Yankee* the speaker is first, ostensibly, Mark Twain, then Hank Morgan. But sometimes Hank Morgan speaks in Samuel Clemens' highly indignant voice—to the frequent ruination of the unity of the work. In any of these, what is the relationship between the Speaker in the work and the writer himself? Finally, who is the Speaker, say, in the Declaration of Independence, or in one or another of the Federalist Papers? in an editorial in your favorite newspaper? in one of your textbooks?

A paper carefully examining point of view and its effect on what is said and how it is said and even why it is said can lead to fascinating critical insights.

In addition to all these critical approaches to a single work in itself are critical essays dealing with a work in its setting. These we need only touch on, because all but the first two or three types probably need more knowledge than the student in an elementary course can command without background reading which will in itself give him illustrative models to follow.

First, bridging the gap between a single work and a work in its setting, are essays of *comparison or contrast* examining the similarities and differences between one work and another, one character and another, one treatment of an idea or a technical problem and another, and so on. They may be on comparable items by the same author, by different authors, of different literary movements or periods, or whatever other pairings seem significant.

Second, the scholar critic may deal with *biographical relationships* between the author's life and his works. To what extent, for example, are Thomas Wolfe's novels alike because they are largely concerned with Wolfe himself as the central figure? How did the limited range of Emily Brontë's experience affect *Wuthering Heights*? What is the relationship of Samuel Butler to Mr. Overton on one hand and to Ernest Pontifex on the other, and to what extent is *The Way of All Flesh* autobiographical? Is Wordsworth himself the Speaker in his poems? How does the fact that Gerard Manly Hopkins was a Catholic priest help in understanding "The Windhover"?

A third critical problem concerns works or writers and their *historical relationships.* They may reflect the life of their times—*Beowulf*, Chaucer's "Prologue," most of Dickens. They may deal with the ideas and movements of their times—Milton's *Areopagitica;* Byron, Wordsworth, Shelley, and the democratic movements of the early nineteenth century; Dryden's varied allegiance. They may shape their times—Sir Walter Scott's impact on not only the image but the reality of Scotland. The writer and history are a rich field.

Very close to the writer and history is the writer (or a work) and the *literary conventions* of his time. A writer is always influenced by what has been done before him, and some writers determine what will be done afterward: Chaucer was followed by many imitators; Wordsworth and Byron set new patterns; Keats influenced Tennyson; T. S. Eliot and James Joyce have changed tomorrow. The shifting of conventions can be traced in the Arthurian cycle—Gildas, Geoffrey of Monmouth, Chrétien de Troyes, Malory, Tennyson, and now *The Once and Future King* and the musical *Camelot.* The complexities of literary convention are endless, and of course any critical writing on these and similar topics will require not only work in the course but a good deal of additional reading in the library to provide the necessary background.

Finally (not to exhaust the possibilities of the critical essay, but to make an end somehow), are the most difficult critical writings of all: those which not only identify and classify but also shape literary *genres, trends,* and genuine *movements.* The giants of criticism are rare, but there is plenty of room for practice. As

W. H. Auden put it, "Our intellectual marines/ Landing in little magazines/ Capture a trend." Presumably even giants start small.

Four essays follow to illustrate some of the many ways in which a student's reading may lead to critical papers. The first is an explication of a short story, with emphasis on the theme. The second compares two treatments of a single idea and reaches a personal judgment concerning the validity of the opposed opinions. The third is an analysis of a character and his effect on a play. The fourth is an analysis of one use of imagery, testing a suggestion made by another critic.

The Meaning of Maturity[4]

Joseph Conrad's avowed task of authorship is to

> hold up unquestioningly, without choice and without fear, the rescued fragment before all eyes in the light of a sincere mood. It is to show its vibration, its colour, its form; and through its movement, its form, and its colour, reveal the substance of its truth.[5]

True to this task, "The Secret Sharer" is a study in depth of the attainment of maturity by one individual. The events presented in it are selected, arranged, and interwoven to form one fine fabric which is the central effect of the story, but one distinction must be clear: they are presented, not interpreted. Because of this non-interpretive mode of presentation, "The Secret Sharer" has a most provocative characteristic. Inspecting a fine tapestry under varying light conditions causes one to perceive different highlights; in a similar manner, reading Conrad's story with special attention to different elements of its construction causes the reader to perceive more than one theme.

The most obvious theme of "The Secret Sharer" is the captain's alienation. In the captain's own words: "All these people had been together for eighteen months or so, and my position was that of the only stranger on board" (p. 100). How this feeling of alienation

---

[4] From *Chandelles: A Magazine of Freshman Writing*, published by the United States Air Force Academy. Reprinted by permission.
[5] Robert G. Davis, *Ten Modern Masters* (New York: Harcourt, Brace & World, 1959), p. 538. All subsequent references are to the same text.

affected him inwardly is also revealed as he says, "But what I felt most was my being a stranger to the ship; and if all the truth must be told, I was somewhat of a stranger to myself" (p. 100). The captain also feels uneasy because he is "untried as yet by a position of the fullest responsibility" and wonders "how far [he] should turn out faithful to that ideal conception of one's own personality every man sets up for himself secretly" (p. 100). By his own statements we learn that the captain does not measure up to these standards as the story begins; however, he does change as the story progresses to become a fully mature individual. Thus, the main theme of "The Secret Sharer" is an explanation of his coming of age and the forces which cause it.

Less obvious but equally important are the themes concerning Leggatt, the secret sharer, for the forces introduced by this ethereal being are the cause of the captain's maturing. Leggatt's confession of murder has great impact on the captain's moral outlook. The very similarity of their situations precludes the "normal" response of censure from the captain and forces him to look beyond a simple black and white judgment of Leggatt's crime to see the justification for Leggatt's seemingly unforgivable act. That the captain can see this justification is the first sign of his inward change. To describe the emotion which makes this understanding possible, Conrad uses the phrase, "the expression of my sudden pity for his mere flesh." In other words the captain felt compassion for his double. Davis simply states that the "risky and perhaps unwarranted help given the stranger seems mysteriously to protect his protector" (p. 71). Perhaps it would be more accurate to say that the change brought about in the captain by this feeling of compassion is the only protection he needs, for this change is his maturing. In short, the sharer is the ingredient necessary to the captain's change, but an understanding of how Leggatt precipitates this change must await the resolution of one more issue.

This last issue is the true nature of Leggatt. Is he a ghost? His unusual mode of arrival would certainly seem to indicate this, for the captain relates his first impression of the sharer as such:

> With a gasp I saw revealed to my stare a pair of feet, the long legs, a broad livid back immersed right up to the neck in a greenish cadaverous glow. One hand, awash, clutched the bottom rung of the ladder. He was complete but for a head. A headless corpse! (p. 103)

Because of the nature of the story, this explanation is possible, but such a device seems too macabre for Conrad to use simply for effect without making it an integral part of the story, and the character, Leggatt, definitely loses stature by being regarded as merely a ghost. A more reasonable explanation is that Leggatt does actually exist. But if he does, why does Conrad continually reiterate the idea that Leggatt is the captain's double when it is obvious from the scant description given that they differ greatly? To me a more satisfactory explanation is that Leggatt exists only in the captain's mind, created there as the product of his intense isolation. In other words, during the captain's protracted period of estrangement, his mind has given life to the fictitious sharer. This hypothesis is consistent with the statements that they are both *Conway* boys of similar backgrounds, experience, and attitudes, and it is strongly supported by the captain's statement: "and all the time the dual working of my mind distracted me almost to the point of insanity. I was constantly watching myself, my secret self" (p. 115).

If we accept this explanation of Leggatt's origin, we can proceed to evaluate the impact of this assumption on the story. First, Leggatt is presented as the younger counterpart to the captain, a person having insufficient maturity for command. Added to this he lacks mature responsibility, a tragic flaw which has made him a killer. In other words, Leggatt represents those qualities of which the captain must rid himself if he is to become his own master. The expulsion of these qualities would remove the source of his feelings of unworthiness, ending the struggle within him between a youth's emotions and a man's responsibilities. Secondly, if Leggatt exists only in the mind of the captain, the conversation between them actually took place there, too. In other words, the captain's maturity was brought about by the power of his own mind, not by some external force. This is a strong indication that Conrad feels that maturity is attained by knowing oneself.

That the captain himself recognizes the true meaning of their parting is shown by the statement:

I felt suddenly ashamed of myself. I may say truly that I understood— and my hesitation in letting that man swim away from my ship's side had been a mere sham sentiment, a sort of cowardice. (p. 128)

The effect of this painful parting is also presented by the captain as he says:

> I was alone with her. Nothing! no one in the world should stand now between us, throwing a shadow on the way of silent knowledge and mute affection, the perfect communication of a seaman with his first command. (p. 136)

With this parting he became a worthwhile commander. The captain's was a difficult decision. He had to abandon forever the emotions and traits of his younger life or remain forever unfit for command as was the captain of the *Sephora*. His decision that it is best to forget the past is a passable theme in itself, but the part played in this decision by the captain's self-examination and isolation make "The Secret Sharer" much more than a mere repetition of the old theme of progress or death. It is an excellent study of the meaning and attainment of maturity.

Gregory H. Canavan

Moral Law versus Man's Law

In an ideal situation, the moral law as standing for divine law would always prevail. Men would do good simply for the sake of obeying a spark of divinity within themselves. However, the world is not ideal, and men are often ignoble. Men can only live together in a society if order is imposed upon them; man's law must reinforce the moral law. For its own survival, society must demand adherence to its laws and can accept no plea that a higher law requires that man's law be flouted. As it is expedient that men live together, it is essential that they obey a rigid, uniform code.

I have reached the foregoing conclusion from reading two works of quite dissimilar origin but of similar theme—the conflict between moral and man-made law. The first work, *Antigone,* by Sophocles, upholds moral law above life itself. Antigone, the heroine, has defied the state in order to give her brother burial, and for her crime she must die. However, she goes to her grave in inner triumph. She has defied an unjust ruling of the state. In her insistence upon a personal upholding of moral law, she has elevated herself. She has become a symbol of devotion to a force higher than man. She has fulfilled her duty to the gods.

Antigone is noble in solitary defiance. Yet should all men follow her selfless path? In *Billy Budd,* Melville confronts this question. His main character, Billy, is innocent of all evil, but he is provoked by a force of evil to commit an act of murder. In the realm of moral law, Billy should not be punished, for he is guiltless. ("As a man thinketh in his heart, so is he.") However, the murder occurs on a ship, and to Melville a ship symbolized society. The question becomes one of whether or not Billy can go free without disrupting the discipline of the ship. Can man disrupt society and not be punished? Captain Vere decides that Billy must receive punishment, for otherwise the crew might mutiny. By analogy, the innocent must sometimes suffer to keep order in society.

Melville's doctrine of expediency for the sake of order is harsh and possibly even immoral. However, I must agree with it. Although a man must obey a moral law in order to live in peace with himself, he must obey man's law in order to live in society, even at the price of inner discord. Man's law is the expedient which maintains a workable civilization. Without man's law, and man's conformity to it, all is chaos.

Rita Forman

"And Some Have Greatness Thrust upon Them"

Shakespeare's play, *The Tragedy of Richard II*, is not a true tragedy, even though the action turns—and turns and turns—on a fatal flaw which from the beginning paves Richard's way to Pomfret Castle. Yet here is no mighty soul, no discovery of a flaw which leads to efforts to correct it (he never knows it is there), no change at all. The only tragic thing is that Richard has been thrust into a position calling for a greatness he does not have. We are drawn towards him by the beautiful poetry and by the fact that, even in the most unkingly situations, "he yet looks like a king." But while we may feel sorry for him, we are constantly repelled by his inconstant capriciousness, and our real sympathies finally lie with the strong, purposeful deliberation of Bolingbroke.

Richard is the very epitome of a capricious man. He is highstrung, moody, and incalculable. He has sudden flights of fancy, and acts out his life with the full-blooded temperament of an actor who knows all the tricks but does not understand his role. He is a child of whim, and his caprices are the paving stones in the pathway that leads to his downfall.

From his opening words, we know his character. In the first scene of the play, he addresses John of Gaunt, "time-honoured Lancaster," to ask if the participants in "the boisterous late appeal/ Which then our leisure would not let us hear" have come to wait again upon his judgment. In a scene full of poetry and fury, Richard fails to "make leopards tame" and decides to let Mowbray and Bolingbroke settle their quarrel by duel. In the third scene, when the duel is on the very point of starting, Richard gives the order to lay down arms, for he has suddenly decided to banish both of them. When he has pronounced their sentence, he is at once seized by Bolingbroke's thought of "how long a time lies in one little word," as, yielding to Gaunt's plea, he shortens Bolingbroke's banishment by four years.

This early, the way to Pomfret is clear, and all that is left is for him to pave the rest of it. This he soon begins to do, when, angered by Gaunt's dying words, he rashly orders the seizure of Gaunt's estates to finance a desire to go and fight in Ireland. On his return he "weeps for joy," and salutes "my gentle earth." Then in the same breath he launches a farfetched flight of fancy in which he implores the earth to yield toads, spiders, and nettles to make his enemy falter. Next he plunges into a speech full of confidence with a change of mood in keeping with his character. News of his fleeing troops makes him pale, but in the same moment he remembers that he is king, and once more his thoughts are raised on high. He takes Scroop's bad tidings calmly at first, but on hearing of his betrayal by his friends, he flies into a fit of anger which quickly gives way to depression and despair. So in one scene the king passes through the moods of ecstasy, trepidation, confidence, fear, fury, and despair.

The rest of the play follows the same pattern of whimsical cavorting on his road to Pomfret. In the climax, when he hands over the crown, he epitomizes his character with the opening words of his speech: "Ay, no; no, ay . . ." Finally he is killed in the dungeon of Pomfret Castle, after passing through many inconstant moods and weaving fantastic images on the theme of time.

No tragedy, this, except as irresponsible responsibility is tragic. The play moves, but Richard never moves: he merely darts; the others move. Whim and not reason was his foremost guide as he faced the need of greatness thrust upon him.

Richard T. Moll

The *Einfuhlung* of John Keats[6]

Probably no other author of the English language has been placed so much in a class by himself as John Keats. Literary critics

[6] From *Wingover: Cadet Writings in the Humanities,* published by the United States Air Force Academy. Reprinted by permission.

continue to debate whether to group Keats along with the many so-called Romantic poets who preceded him, with the didactic Neo-Classicals who were his contemporaries, or with the early "modern" poets. It is not the purpose of this paper to enter into this controversy, and it is only mentioned here to establish the *uniqueness* of Keats' work. One of the reasons for this prominent position which Keats holds is his use and extraordinary handling of certain poetic qualities and techniques. Two of these outstanding qualities, praised by Richard Fogle in his introduction to *John Keats: Selected Poetry and Letters*,[7] are "synaesthesia" and "empathy."

According to one dictionary definition, synaesthesia is a "sensation produced in one modality when a stimulus is applied to another modality, as when the hearing of a certain sound induces the visualization of a certain color." Although this definition is accurate, it leaves something to be desired when relating it to Keats' poetry. Fogle uses both synaesthesia and empathy as examples to emphasize Keats' extraordinary ability to concentrate, intensify, and unify. He feels that in Keats' work, "Synaesthesia is either a transference or a fusion that relates different modes of sense experience . . ." (p. xi). He further states that "in Keats it acts chiefly to fuse and unify" (p. xii).

Fogle has already analyzed, from the viewpoint of its synaesthetic qualities, what is probably the most highly "synaesthetic" stanza that Keats ever wrote; namely, the second stanza from "Ode to a Nightingale." However, most of the synaesthesia which Keats employed occurs in one- and two-line groupings rather than in, and throughout, an entire stanza as in the case just mentioned. For example, in "Lamia" Keats refers to "jealous curls" in his description of Hermes (p. 252). Later in the same work, Keats speaks of "words she spake . . ., as through bubbling honey," where both sound and taste are fused into one mode of perception (p. 253). Among the most quoted lines from Keats, and ones which best exemplify his use of synaesthesia are those from the twenty-sixth stanza of "The Eve of St. Agnes":

> Anon his heart revives: her vespers done,
> Of all its wreathed pearls her hair she frees;
> Unclasps her warmed jewels one by one;
> Loosens her fragrant bodice; by degrees . . . (p. 223).

In a lecture at the Air Force Academy, John Ciardi gave an example of the intensity with which Keats wrote by quoting these

[7] New York: Holt, Rinehart and Winston, 1960. All subsequent references are to the same text.

lines. He stated that in the original manuscript, Keats scratched through *fifteen* different words before he finally became satisfied with "warmed" as an adjective for jewels. No explanation is necessary for the reader to see how Keats has transferred and fused the sensations of sight, sound, touch, and smell into the lines by the use of "wreathed pearls," "warmed jewels," and "fragrant bodice." Once having read these lines, it is difficult, if not impossible, to imagine any other words appropriate in their place.

In psychology, the word "empathy" usually refers to the mental "entering into the feeling or spirit of a person," whereby one person can more fully understand the inner emotions and outward actions of another. Fogle defines poetic empathy as "a way of thinking in which the poet seems to project himself into and identify himself with his subject." He says that in Keats "empathy is a sensuous imagination that gives life and meaning to bodies and forms" (p. xiii). Keats' own idea that the poet had no real identity of his own, but was a part of his poetic images, gives substance to this definition.

Though Fogle quotes lines from a poem to illustrate Keats' use of poetic empathy, it appears that the mood or empathetic feeling which Keats generates stems not from a few words, but rather from a group of phrases or, in some cases, the entire poem. For instance, in "Endymion" the reader not only understands, but can actually *experience* the melting resistance of the speaker as he describes his newfound love:

> Who could resist? Who in this universe?
> She did so breathe ambrosia; so immerse
> My fine existence in a golden clime.
> She took me like a child of suckling time,
> And cradled me in roses (p. 103).

And who can help but place himself in the position of Porphyro and feel his self-same emotions as he gazes upon his fair Madeline disrobing in the moonlight? If one were to read Keats' ode "To Sleep" with the proper concentration and rhythm, he might very well find himself soon nodding his head with heavy lids. It is through this quality in Keats' writing that the reader can enter not only into the experiences of the poet's creations, but also into the character of the poet himself. For if the poet is not more than what he writes, then it is only logical to assume that the experiences which his poetry extends to its readers must contain some small portion of its writer.

It seems rather anticlimactic to state here that Keats was a master of the use of such poetic qualities as synaesthesia and empathy. The precise definitions of these terms, even by qualified literary critics, do not include everything that they should. Instead, we might combine them into a slightly more vague, but nevertheless more inclusive, term used by many German philosophers—*Einfühlung*. Literally translated, this word means "in-feeling." However, it includes not only the psychological implications of empathy, but also a type of fusion or unity between the spirits of two or more separate entities. Certainly Keats has been able to do this with his poetic subject, whether they be living or inanimate.

No better statement of the significance of *Einfühlung* in Keats can be found than that given by Richard Fogle.

> The significance of synaesthesia and empathy in Keats is primarily that they are poetic ways of thinking and feeling, not logical yet intelligible and effective. They are methods of unifying, of demonstrating valuable relationships. In their concentrative power and swiftness of action they correspond with and reinforce the general tendencies of his poetry toward intensity and complexity of experience (pp. xiv–xv).

R. L. Howell

11

Writing Good Examinations

In many of your college courses, the instructor will know little more about you than he can learn from the answers you write in mid-term and final examinations. Your entire grade in the course and your standing in college will depend on your ability to say quickly and clearly exactly what you want to say. Everything that you have learned in your composition course about unified, clear, and effective writing should be put to use. For if your instructor cannot determine, as he reads your paper along with dozens of others, just what it is that you are trying to say, he will probably assume that you yourself do not really know, and he will mark down your paper accordingly. Some poor examinations, of course, are poor simply because the student does not know much about the course material, but a great many more are poor because the student fails to realize that carelessly written papers cannot do him justice— or, perhaps, that they do him exact justice by suggesting that he has a sloppy mind. Nothing can be done to help the student who does not know the course material. But the student who knows the course and still gets mediocre grades can be helped a great deal.[1]

College examinations, as a matter of fact, are not as difficult as your sophomore friends insist. But many of them call for integration

---

[1] In addition to studying this chapter, such a student would do well to read carefully J. N. Hook, *How to Take Examinations in College.* College Outline Series (New York: Barnes & Noble, 1958). It is available at any college bookstore.

and discussion of facts and principles in a way that seems hard to students who are used to objective tests but are not used to the essay type of examination. It is the purpose of this chapter to consider the kind of examination you will frequently encounter in your college career and to suggest procedures that will help your answers reflect your true knowledge and ability. We shall consider first the purpose of the essay type of examination, and second the best procedures to follow in writing the answers.

THE PURPOSE OF THE ESSAY TYPE OF EXAMINATION

The purpose of any examination is to reveal what you have learned about the course. An objective test is easy to give and easy to grade and shows readily how many of the facts of the course you can recognize at examination time. But an objective test does not so readily show how many facts you can bring up out of your memory without prompting, and it usually does not show at all how thoroughly you understand the facts and the general principles of the course. Well-phrased essay questions can easily reveal your knowledge of the facts; they can also require you to distinguish between items of major and minor importance or to recognize that items major in some circumstances can be minor in other contexts. They can let you show your awareness of general principles and your ability to apply them to new facts, or to correlate them in new ways within the course or between the course and the rest of your experience. They can allow you, as an objective test never can, to write a brilliant examination. They also quickly betray superficiality. A student who can answer an objective test perfectly might still have little idea of what the course means. He might easily select the right answer to such a question as "Simon de Montfort's Parliament met in 1261, 1265, 1295 (choose one)," yet have no clear idea of the importance of de Montfort's Parliament nor of its relation to the Model Parliament of Edward I. The instructor might well prefer to ask a broader question: "Discuss the importance of Simon de Montfort's famous Parliament, (a) to the British, (b) to the United States." In such a question, the student is put to a real test, and under a grim instructor one such question might constitute the entire examination. (No student, by the way, could provide an exhaustive answer to that question in the time allowed by even the longest examination. The instructor does not expect it. What he wants to find out is what you regard as important enough to include in the time you can give to the answer, how you arrange the details you elect to present, and what interrelationships you indicate between them.)

Usually, essay questions are not so sweeping as that. In a two- or three-hour examination, you can expect to be asked six to ten questions that will touch on the major divisions of the course and show how well you understand them. To answer such questions successfully, you must be sure not only that you understand the course material, but that you understand the questions and write understandable answers.

The better the student, paradoxically, the more he needs to keep in mind the purpose of the examination: to find out what he knows about the course. Unless he does so, he may be either too humble or too self-assured, and in either event he will write a less successful examination than he might. If he neglects to remember the purpose of the examination (and that often the examinations provide the sole evidence on which grades are based), he may hesitate to include full and clear statements of elementary points, feeling that it is presumptuous of him to lecture to the instructor, who knows far more about the material than any student does. But if, in humility, he omits the elementary points, the instructor may wonder if he knows them. Such a student will do well to write as if he himself were lecturing to the class; his very humility will prevent him from being brash. If, on the other hand, a student is too self-assured, he may omit the elementary points on the ground that the instructor will of course assume that he knows such things, that such knowledge can be taken for granted. But if the instructor could take knowledge for granted, he would not need to ask the question. Again, he may wonder if the student really does know them.

Keep in mind always the fact that the purpose of the examination is to give you a chance to show what you know about the course. Give the instructor the evidence he needs in order to decide.

PROCEDURES TO FOLLOW

The process of taking an examination consists of five almost equally important steps: preparing, reading the examination, planning the answer, writing, and checking what you have written.

Preparing

REVIEW

Preparing for an examination begins on the first day of the semester. Then, and on all subsequent days, review the day's work, looking for the major divisions and for their interrelations as you put your notes and your thinking in order after class. Tie each fact carefully to the major principle it illustrates. Before the examination—as long before as possible—review in the same way the section of the course to be covered.

It is an excellent practice to give yourself occasional quizzes and trial-run examinations. If you were the instructor, what questions would you ask? Make up a test, as searching a test as possible, and then write out careful answers. If you do that, few exams will trouble you.

RELAX

Go to the examination itself in as relaxed a state as possible. If you have reviewed properly throughout the semester, you do not need to cram. If you have not reviewed properly, cramming will do little more than confuse you. In either event, you will do better on the examination if you get a good night's sleep the night before.

GO EQUIPPED

Take to the examination a dependable pen and at least one pencil, and enough paper. Avoid disturbing yourself and your neighbors by running out of some essential piece of equipment at a moment when neither you nor they can afford to be interrupted. And by all means take a watch, bought, begged, or borrowed. You should always be aware of the time as you work—the time that has passed, the time to be given each question, and the time that remains in the examination period. The instructor may announce the time occasionally, but his announcements should never take you by surprise.

ARRIVE ON TIME

Try to avoid arriving so early that you have time to stew, but try even harder to avoid arriving so late that you disturb your neighbors and deprive yourself of time that should be spent working on the examination.

Reading

READ THE ENTIRE EXAMINATION FIRST

Since the examination will probably touch on the high points of the course, reading through the examination gives you a last-minute opportunity to see the course pattern through the instructor's eyes and consequently to orient yourself and your knowledge to the thinking of your audience, the instructor who will read and grade your paper. Second, knowing what all the questions are before you write any of the answers will prevent your answers from overlapping. You will not be led into wasting on question 1 details which are far more pertinent to the nearly related question 4; instead, you can use what you know in the places at which it will do the most good. Third, you will have a chance to see and understand any specific instructions that should be followed, such as those giving you a choice of six out of eight questions. (It does no good to write on all eight. Your instructor will merely read the first six and stop, meanwhile thinking that you are not very bright to have missed the obvious indication of how much he thought you should do in the time allowed.) If you are given a choice, by the way, it is best to answer the questions in order, since many instructors prefer to read all the answers to a single question before going on to the next one; if you have answered question 1 at the end of your paper, the instructor cannot give it quite the reading he would have given if he had found it in its proper place. Pay particular attention to instructions indicating the relative importance of the questions, such as parenthetical indications of their point value. Obviously, a question worth 50 percent should get five times the thought and time given to one worth only 10 percent. Finally, reading the entire examination before you try to answer any of it will stir up your knowledge of the course; and if you know in advance what all the questions cover, you can make hurried notes on pertinent items as they float to the surface of your mind and then will have them available for use when you turn to the later questions.

It is a serious mistake, although a common one, to isolate each question in turn from the rest of the examination and attempt to answer it in a vacuum. A choppy, repetitious, impoverished paper is very likely to result.

Too many students skim a question hastily, pick up one or two key terms, and think they know what the question calls for. They may overlook an inconspicuous but vital negative and go haring off in exactly the opposite direction from the one they were invited to take. More commonly, they fail to give due consideration to qualifying modifiers, so that their answers roughly parallel the right ones, but diverge too much to be worth full credit. Most commonly of all, they deprive themselves of the help to be gained from clues built into the carefully written question by the very terms in which it is phrased. Students constantly wail, "What does he *want?*" A careful reading of the question itself would often point them toward the answer.

Certain stock terms, in particular, should indicate at least the scope of the answer that is expected.

Discuss means "treat fully," sketching backgrounds, clarifying at least major and perhaps secondary points with specific illustration or detail, showing pertinent interrelations, and indicating your understanding of the implications of the question. *Never* dash off a brief and superficial answer when you have been told to discuss.

Explain means "make plain," as fully as is necessary for clarity. The extent of the answer expected depends on the extent of the concept concerned.

Sketch, or **trace,** means "survey the high spots."

Analyze means "break down into its component parts."

Classify means "group and arrange to emphasize relationships."

Summarize means "present briefly, but don't leave out anything important."

Define, or **identify,** or **characterize,** means "distinguish this term, or this person, from all others that are similar." All three are clear injunctions to be as specific as possible.

Enumerate, or **list,** means "set down briefly, one after another, without undue elaboration."

Illustrate, or **exemplify,** means "give examples," showing thereby, rather than by definition, that you understand the concept.

Compare, strictly, means "show how these things are similar." Many instructors, however, use it to mean "show both similarities and differences."

Contrast means "show how these things differ."

Evaluate means "weigh and judge." If it is used with a series of items, it means "indicate relative importance." If it is used with a single item, it means "show the importance of the item."

Make use of the clues provided by such terms, or of any clues provided by a carefully phrased question, always being as concise and as specific as possible. As a rule, it is a waste of time to do more than you are told to do. And certainly you should be careful to do no less.

Planning

The biggest single cause of unsuccessful examinations is failure to plan an answer before writing it. Too many students, panicky at the flight of time, dive headlong into the writing without ever stopping to think what they want to say; the more they know about the course, the more confused their answers are likely to be. Ideas are spilled helter-skelter on the page, without purpose and so without result. Some points are developed at too great length, so that no time is left to develop others equally important. And some points, perhaps more important still, are omitted altogether. It is usually clear from such answers that the students have attended the lectures and read the text, because they have used terms they could have learned in no other way; but it is not at all clear that they have understood what they have heard and read. These are the students who explode bitterly, "I knew that stuff cold! I really hit that exam! And he had the nerve to give me a *C!*" But the instructor probably thought that the *C* was generous.

These same students, in their English composition classes, learned to make hasty informal outlines (see pages 80–83) before they tried to write impromptu themes. It is certainly no less important in a crucial examination to get a central thesis clearly in mind, jot down the points that must be covered, and arrange them in the most effective pattern. The margins or the back pages of a blue-book are ideal for the purpose, and the instructor might even be favorably impressed by evidence of an attempt to think about the questions he has asked.

Students wail, "But we don't have *time* to outline!" The answer is that you cannot afford to spend time on a jumbled paragraph. If you have five equally important questions to answer in a fifty-minute test, you have exactly ten minutes for each question. You may spend the ten minutes hopefully spilling words on the page, or you may take two or three minutes to think about what you are doing and so give yourself a chance to do something worthwhile. A brief answer that says something is far better than an answer perhaps one-third longer that seems to have been written with an eggbeater.

To write a successful examination, you must know what the question calls for, focus your answer on a central thesis that gives the answer point and direction, include at least the most important details, and finish your writing in the time available. If you can do the necessary planning quickly, in your head, so much the better; Phi Beta Kappa keys are to be worn with pride. But if you want to stay in school, you had better plan your examination answers in one way or another.

Writing

Questions, of course, will differ widely and will call for differing treatment. Almost every type of writing you have practiced will be useful at one time or another. But a few bits of advice will apply to almost any essay type of examination.

First, write legibly and completely, finishing your adverbs, for example, with a readable *-ly*, not a hastily scrawled wriggle; carelessness is at best irritating, and at worst may be confused with ignorance. Write on only one side of a sheet of paper, unless you are using a bound bluebook. This is more important than it sounds; since readers do not expect to find material on the back of a sheet, you may well lose credit for answers that the instructor did not know were there. And identify the question you are answering, by number and by paraphrasing the question in your answer, so that answers to similar questions will not be confused with each other.

All of these simplify the reader's task, and your instructor will be grateful.

Second, every answer, like every other piece of writing, should clearly develop a central thesis. Unity is no less important in final examinations than it is in themes, or term papers, or a report to be read by the president of the corporation. Most answers, as a matter of fortunate fact, call for the simplest sort of overall organization, that which begins with the thesis and then develops it by means of examples or details. In one respect, the thesis of a good examination answer takes a special form: It combines in the opening sentence the gist of the question and the most essential points of the answer, thereby identifying the question and simultaneously indicating the direction the answer is to take.

For example, we saw earlier a sweeping question about the importance of Simon de Montfort's Parliament, (a) to the British, and (b) to the United States. The thesis of the extensive answer that question demands might be this:

> Simon de Montfort's famous revolutionary Parliament of 1265 was important because it first included as regular members representative burgesses from the established boroughs, and by so doing set the pattern for Edward I's so-called Model Parliament of 1295, which was accepted as a precedent in determining the composition of subsequent British Parliaments, whose development in turn was paramount in determining the form eventually to be taken by the Congress of the United States.

Much detail will be required to develop that thesis fully, but from that first sentence of the answer, the instructor knows two important things: the student's understanding of the question involved, and the direction the answer proposes to take. Like any good thesis, it is a one-sentence summary of the central idea, covering by implication everything that is to be said later. The battle for the grade on that question is already two-thirds won by the student. He needs now only to provide an intelligent development of the thesis in the time allotted to the question.

Third, having ensured unity by a clearly stated opening thesis, the good answer must include all the important subordinate details and must indicate their interrelations. Here, the informal outline is the best guarantee. If you have stopped to think through your answer, to jot down the points you want to cover, and to arrange them in an effective pattern, you can be reasonably confident that you will develop your thesis intelligently.

You must, however, be specific in your development. Next to the jumbled, unplanned answer, the vaguely general answer is the worst offender in student examination papers. The instructor will be exasperated, not pleased, if everything you say *might* be right. By the very nature of generalizations, they could mean several things. Pin yours down with specific diction and with enough specific detail to make clear exactly what you mean.

> *Realism* is a literary term meaning that the writer writes about things as they really are, as he sees them when he looks at life, and not just as they are written about in books. Whether the details are good or bad, the realist is not afraid to write about real life.

What does that mean? Generously interpreted, it is probably true; but assuming that any good writer "writes about things . . . as he sees them when he looks at life," the definition could apply equally well to naturalism, or impressionism, or romanticism, or cynicism, or almost any other ism in the course. How are things, "really"? What is "real life," as distinct from some other kind of life? When are details "good or bad"? When they are well or poorly presented? When the hero reveals a fatal flaw? When the ashcan is dumped in the dining room? When Harriet Beecher Stowe writes about Little Eva, or Dickens writes about Bill Sykes, or Hardy writes about Tess at the dairy farm? That answer proves little more than that the student was taking an examination in literature and not in philosophy. Such vaguely general, wordy answers are worthless. Never use more general terms than you must. Never leave any generalization unsupported by specific details and examples.

As you develop your thesis to show specifically what your generalizations mean, be careful to indicate your awareness of the difference between fact and opinion. For matters of opinion give the evidence behind them or cite the authorities you are following. Here, again, the brilliant student needs to remember the purpose of the examination: to find out what he knows about the course. If you wish to go beyond the superficial, elementary points that your classmates are presenting, be sure to indicate briefly that you are familiar with those details before you launch into a discussion of more esoteric theories. And if you disagree with the commonly accepted opinions, be sure you make it clear that you know what those opinions are and give your reasons for disagreeing. Few instructors will insist that you parrot their lectures or swallow their personal conclusions uncritically, but all instructors want to be sure that you understand what they have devoted a semester to presenting.

The same advice applies to definitions, especially to those the instructor may have dictated and carefully discussed. Such definitions normally represent effort to clarify key terms that must be understood within a particular context. To substitute a spur-of-the-moment phrasing of your own for the meticulous phrasing you are presumed to understand may raise grave doubts about your understanding of the course itself. If you have good reason to think that the accepted definition should be modified, be sure that your knowledge of the accepted definition is unmistakable.

Finally, as you write an examination, make use of all you have learned about writing effectively. Be exact and appropriate in your diction, using the technical terms of the course wherever they fit and using always the most efficient wording for your purpose, so that your answers will be concise and to the point. Make your sentences as clear and mature and flexible as possible. Let your paragraphing indicate the relative importance of your ideas (though for most questions a single, developed paragraph will probably suffice). And insofar as time will allow, be as accurate as possible in spelling, punctuation, grammar, and other mechanics. Your instructor does not expect polished prose (though he will welcome it), but he may well be annoyed if he has to beat his way through semiliterate gibberish. And if he cannot understand easily what you are trying to say, he may well suppose that you do not yourself understand the course. Even the occasional misguided instructor who says, "Don't worry about your English. I want the facts," usually means only, "Don't waste time on the spelling of technical terms." He may not realize that students usually take his comment too literally and abandon all attempt to be clear. Many of the low grades he gives on examinations, which he assumes reflect ignorance of the course material, really could have been much higher if the writers had been more careful of the organization and phrasing of their answers. One wiser instructor always prefaced examinations with the injunction: "English is my native tongue. Please write in that language." Any instructor will think more highly of you if you write your examination in English.

Checking

The final stage in producing a good examination is checking what you have written to be sure you said what you meant to say. Reread the question and read your answer, looking at what you put on paper, not merely at what you intended to say. Do not be afraid to make corrections. Your paper should be as neat as possible and should be clearly legible, but no instructor will object to occasional crossed out items or interlinear insertions. You can often improve an answer a great deal by reading it over and revising it hastily.

We suggested earlier a five-question, fifty-minute test, in which all questions are equally important. Ten minutes at the most can be allotted to each question. It would be a good plan to take five minutes to read and ponder the entire examination; then devote two minutes to planning each answer, five minutes to writing it, and two minutes to checking it. The resulting paper will be shorter than if you had written frantically for the full fifty minutes, but it may well be a better paper than you knew you could write.

EXERCISES

A. As you review a day's assignment or study for a mid-term or for a final examination, write out five questions that in your opinion would make a good test over the material. Write answers to the questions. Examine your answers critically, comparing them with the treatment given the material in the text, in the lectures, and in a book on the same subject, other than the textbook in the course. If you were judging your own knowledge and understanding of the course solely on the answers you wrote, what grade would you give your paper? Why?

B. Study critically the answers you actually wrote in a course examination. If possible, compare your paper with one graded A. Assuming that your paper has been fairly graded, why were your answers evaluated as they were?

C. Rewrite the answers to the examination studied in Exercise B. What changes have you made, and why?

The Handbook

12-

The Most Common Errors

Characteristics of a Good Theme: 11. Conventionally
acceptable mechanics.

* There are exercises for items marked with an asterisk.

The purpose of this chapter is to bring together in one place the most common errors in grammar, syntax, and punctuation. (The most common error of all, misspelling, is treated in a chapter of its own, Chapter 15.) We shall consider these common errors briefly and illustrate their nature and the methods of correcting them. Working with this chapter as you revise your themes should result in your learning to avoid the errors altogether. Some, though not all, of the errors discussed here are considered in more detail in other chapters, often from a slightly different point of view. You should consequently follow up all cross-references to other parts of the book, to be sure you thoroughly understand the errors you are making in your themes before you attempt to correct them. If you find terms that are unfamiliar to you, consult the index or your dictionary. If the explanations in the text are still not clear, consult your instructor.

The first three errors we need to consider—fragments, comma splices, and run-ons—result primarily from carelessness in punctuation or from inability to recognize grammatically complete ideas. If they persist in your themes despite your efforts to eliminate them, it will suggest that you are unable to identify the fundamental constituents of the sentence. You may need to study the chapters on effective sentences and on grammar carefully.

1. FRAGMENTARY SENTENCES—Frag

A sentence, in the context in which it appears, conveys a complete idea. Sometimes, especially in dialogue representing conversational speech or in informal writing representing the free flow of easy thought, complete ideas are readily conveyed by grammatically incomplete sentences (see Full and Incomplete Sentences, pages 138–141). But normally, especially in serious exposition and argument, your reader will expect a subject and a finite verb in a grammatically independent predication.

Faulty fragmentary sentences (and we are concerned here exclusively with faulty ones) are usually of two kinds: They may be long strings of modifying phrases and clauses, but with no complete independent clause to carry the burden—imposing, but actually saying very little; or they may be afterthought modifiers that really belong to, and should have been connected with, a preceding main clause. Fragments of the first type need a main clause. Fragments of the second type need to be repunctuated to tie them onto the main clause they are modifying. (See also P12e.) A few students write faulty fragments of a third type: fragments that contain only a verbal instead of a finite verb.

Often, if you read aloud what you have written, the tones and pauses of your own voice will warn you that your punctuation is misleading or that you have forgotten to complete your thought. But to use this test on your own writing, you must read the signals your punctuation and phrasing actually give. If you read what you _meant_ to say, instead, the test will not help you.

a. No Complete Predication

I think the idea expressed by Jacques Barzun of offering lectures or general courses for nonscience majors, which would give a general understanding of scientific principles and methods and yet not force a student who will never be a chemist to wade through a lab manual and still come out with no clear idea of science.

Do not, as this student has done, allow mere length to confuse you. Such a fragment often accompanies the use of too long and too complicated sentences.

b. Afterthought Modifiers or Appositives

He was here Wednesday afternoon. Immediately after he arrived from New York. (*A comma instead of a period, or no punctuation at all, would make such a passage more effective.*)

I do not believe the argument that Professor Barzun presented. Because a laboratory course at least introduces a student to scientific techniques, without which no real understanding of methods or even principles can exist. (*Comma. The second word-group is merely a modifier.*)

A student cannot merely be told, for example, that measurements must be precise, but must have experience. For instance, the dismay of missing an "unknown" because of a few too many drops of a reagent. (*Perhaps a dash.* Dismay *is in apposition to* experience.)

c. No Finite Verb in a Main Clause

The doctor whom I consulted recommending no strenuous exercise. (*Such a fragment may result from the careless omission of a linking verb, or perhaps from inability to distinguish between finite verbs and verbals.*)

Our language governs the way we think, but at the same time the way we think, governing as it does the kind of language we can use. (*The first clause is complete, but not the rest of the sentence.*)

d. Fragments in Dialogue (see also P5e)

In normal speech, of course, incomplete sentences are common, and dialogue often uses them. But in punctuating dialogue and accompanying orientation phrases, be careful not to create unintentional fragments which would not convey complete ideas in normal speech.

FAULTY: "I am quite sure," he insisted. "That you are wrong."

CORRECTED: "I am quite sure," he insisted, "that you are wrong."

2. COMMA SPLICES (OR COMMA FAULTS, OR COMMA BLUNDERS)—Cs

A comma splice results when two independent clauses are run together with insufficient punctuation. (See also P1.) Your instructor will regard repeated comma splices as serious errors because repeated comma splices, like repeated faulty fragments, suggest that you are unable to recognize complete ideas. The "rules" are simple. Learn first to follow them implicitly, and later you may learn how to modify them to suggest subtle sentence relations.

a. Rule: Independent clauses not connected by *and, but, or, nor,* or *for* are separated by a semicolon or made into two sentences.

(But see also Excessive Coordination, pages 382–383, and P1.)

A comma splice results when a comma is used instead of the semicolon.

> Certain bacteria, such as *Escherichia coli* and many soil bacteria, bring about the reduction of nitrates to nitrites, nitrogen as nitrates is essential to plant growth. (*A semicolon after* nitrites, *or a period, would prevent confusion. The comma splice results because the comma is insufficiently heavy to identify the main break in the sentence.*)
>
> Soil bacteria of all types are useful, however, they do not all function to the same end. (*Conjunctive adverbs, like* however, *are not simple conjunctions.*)

Many writers use commas, however, when the clauses are short and the connection is so close that no confusion will result.

b. Comma Splices in Dialogue (see also P5e)

In punctuating dialogue and accompanying orientation phrases, be careful not to create unjustifiable comma splices.

> COMMA SPLICE: "I will not go," he said, "you may be sure of that."
> CORRECTED: "I will not go," he said. "You may be sure of that."

3. RUN-ON, RUN-TOGETHER, OR FUSED SENTENCES—Run-on

Even worse than the comma splice, which confuses the reader by tying together two independent clauses with a comma when a semicolon is needed, is the run-on sentence, which jams together two independent clauses with no punctuation at all.

a. Independent clauses connected by *and, but, or, nor,* or *for* are generally separated by a comma, unless the clauses are short and the connection is very close. Failure to use such a comma may result in a confusing run-on sentence.

> I intend to go with your brother and you may do as you please.

b. Most confusing of all are two independent ideas without any sort of connective and without any punctuation.

> Students should be careful of punctuation trouble will result if they are careless. (See Cs2a.)

NEVER "correct" a comma splice by removing the comma, leaving no punctuation at all. The resulting run-on sentence will be worse than the original error.

EXERCISE

In the following passage, identify and correct all fragmentary sentences, comma splices, and run-on sentences.

A common college phenomenon which worries students and their parents more than it should, the mood of cynical disillusionment which overtakes almost all intelligent students sooner or later. It comes most often to sophomores. Which is one reason sophomores are so hard to tolerate. Sometimes it does not come until the junior year rarely does it come as early as the freshman year or as late as the senior year. But come it nearly always does and for very good reasons. For one thing, the hitherto unquestioned certainties which the student brings to college with him in his mental baggage without really knowing why he believes them are not only laid open to question, but are sometimes dismissed as not being even worthy of consideration. Then, the study of the way we think and of the logical fallacies which trip the unwary, the study of the nature of evidence and of the dangers of gullibility, the confusing difference between fact and opinion—all of these suggest that a case could be made for almost any idea or any side of any argument. And instructors who are equally intelligent and equally admirable maintain sharply opposed opinions, class discussions develop convincing arguments for adopting contradictory conclusions. Truth seems undiscoverable and even reasonable probability seems all but unattainable. Disillusionment, skepticism, and cynicism—doubting everything but doubt itself—offer an uncomfortable but fairly dependable protective armor and the more sensitive the student, the more eagerly he dons it. To wear it defiantly until increasing knowledge and growing wisdom enable him once again—this time through his own thinking—to say with some confidence, "This I believe."

4. EXCESSIVE COORDINATION (See also pages 149–154.)—**Co-ord**

Frequent comma splices or run-on sentences (see above) are usually a sign that the writer uses too many compound sentences, consisting of equal (coordinate) independent clauses. A compound sentence, remember, says to the reader, "Here are two independent ideas, neither modifying the other—equally important, yet together expressing a single, unified idea." Such a logical relation is fairly rare in mature thought. Far more often one of the ideas is in some degree and in some manner really subordinate to the other, and the sentence pattern expressing them should reflect the true relation of the ideas.

a. "Stringy Sentences"

Avoid the excessive coordination of "stringy sentences," long chains of primer sentences tied together with *and*'s or *but*'s or *so*'s.

> I came early on registration day, and I knew exactly what I wanted to take, but I had to wait in long lines everywhere I went, and my adviser insisted that I take chemistry, and several of the classes I wanted were full, and the cashier said my papers were filled out wrong, and nothing worked right for me, so I spent all day, and even then I ended up with a terrible schedule.

These clauses are roughly parallel, but because the ideas are not logically equal, the parallelism is faulty. To reflect the thought accurately, the sentence should be broken up, and some of the independent clauses should be reduced to subordinate clauses or modifying phrases.

> Although I came early on registration day and knew exactly what I wanted to take, I ran into long lines, closed classes, an adviser who insisted on adding chemistry to my program, and a cashier who sent me back to correct my papers. It took me all day to register, and even then I ended up with a terrible schedule.

b. "Choppy Sentences"

Avoid "choppy sentences," incoherent passages lacking the transitional words or phrases that would indicate the relation between the ideas.

Flying is an excellent way to travel. There are long stretches of boredom. The passengers sitting by the windows can see very little. Passengers in the aisle seats can see nothing at all. One can pass the time by reading and eating. The air lines provide up-to-date magazines and excellent food. The fares are high, but roughly equivalent to those of Pullman travel. Accidents are usually fatal, but are very rare, considering the passenger-miles traveled. Flying is comfortable and is the fastest form of transportation. To get from one place to another, flying is best.

That paragraph is bumpy and confusing, but all it lacks is adequate transitions.

Flying is an excellent way to travel. In spite of the long stretches of boredom resulting from the inability of the passengers by the window to see very much and of those in the aisle seats to see anything at all, one can pass the time by reading the up-to-date magazines and eating the excellent food provided by the air lines. The fares, it is true, are high, but they are roughly equivalent to those of Pullman travel. It is also true that accidents are usually fatal, but they are very rare, considering the passenger-miles traveled. Most important of all, flying is comfortable and is the fastest form of transportation. For those who wish primarily to get from one place to another, flying is best.

In developing the ability to write flexible sentences (see pages 149–159), and incidentally developing your own ability to think clearly, take great care in subordinating lesser ideas to greater. According to the relative importance of the ideas, use single-word modifiers, phrases rather than clauses, compound subjects and compound verbs, subordinate clauses rather than main clauses. Save your main clauses for your most important details. Shift the position of the main clauses in your sentences, and shift the position of the lesser modifiers, so that emphasis will fall where you want it. Attempt consciously to use all the elements of the English sentence that you know, varying your sentence patterns to reflect your thought as exactly as possible. Avoid, of course, confusingly involved sentences, and avoid sentences chopped up by too many parenthetical elements. Keep your reader and the effect you want to make always in mind. If you do all of that, sentence variety will automatically follow.

EXERCISE

Rewrite the following passages so that they will clearly reflect the writers' thought, without choppiness and without confusing complexity. Reorganize if necessary.

1. There are only two times a day in which a man can get himself into trouble. One is daytime. The other is nighttime.

2. Big-city intellectuals dislike Suburbia. They say suburbanites must conform. The suburbs are dull. No intellectual challenge is provided. None is tolerated. The houses are all alike. Status symbols are all-important. The size of one's car or power mower determines position. Whether one lives in the middle of the "project" or on the edge is important. The PTA is the center of life. Children take up all their parents' time. Men commute. It is a woman's world.

3. Shopping centers are replacing the downtown stores as the source of the family's needs and the result is that the middle of most cities is blighted and so more people move away or stay away and so more deterioration follows and city businessmen and city planners are worried, but no very satisfactory solutions have yet been found.

4. A modern drugstore is likely to be a member of a chain. They are all alike. The doors are marked "In" and "Out." Near the doors are cash registers. They are inside a fence with turnstiles. Only the tobacco counter is outside the fence. The fountain lunch counter may be too. It will be along one side. Behind the fence are aisles of shelves full of goods. Above the shelves are signs saying "Cosmetics," "School Supplies," "Cameras." It is hard to know where to look for what you want. At the back are the drugs. The store is clean, but it is all impersonal and I miss the old drugstore.

5. I turned restlessly in my bed this last morning of camp, aware only of the sound of my own thrashing movement and of the whimper of a nearby screech owl, trying to forget the litter we had made in packing up to leave, trying to forget the work which had yet to be done before we could get away. But incautiously glancing at the filthy floor, with duffel bags and suitcases standing open amid the still unpacked spoils of camping, eagerly awaiting the yet-to-be-stored miscellany of toothbrushes, wash

384

cloths, soap, towels, forgotten whistles, trophies, leather work, the shorts and socks and shoes and blouses which could not be put away until just before our departure made me suddenly conscious of the many tasks remaining to be done before our departure and exhausted me in the very prospect; so, pulling the rather soiled top sheet up over my head, I made a final effort to go back to sleep.

5. FAULTY SUBORDINATION (See also pages 154–159.)—Sub

a. Illogical Subordination ("Upside down subordination")

Avoid illogically subordinating major ideas to minor ones.

When the attempt was made to hold up the First National Bank, I was just walking down Main Street, paying no particular attention to anything. (*Surely, the attempted holdup is more important even to an egocentric writer than the fact that he was walking inattentively down the street. Putting that idea in the main clause would give it more emphasis.*)

As I was walking down Main Street, paying no particular attention to anything, the attempt was made to hold up the First National Bank.

Usually, the context makes clear what should be important and what is minor.

b. Overlapping Subordination

Avoid overlapping subordination, the awkward repetition of identical forms of pronouns, of subordinating conjunctions, or of prepositions.

This is a job which I will do with a zest which cannot be exceeded.
She said that she would take that one and that I should take this one.
He failed because he couldn't answer the exam questions because he hadn't slept the night before.
I will go with you with pleasure.

If modifiers or other elements are parallel in importance, however, the repetition of connectives clarifies the relationship. Do not vary connectives merely for the sake of change.

EXERCISE

Rewrite the following passage to correct any faulty subordination.

The pattern of your sentences should reflect your thought, be-cause you should choose and arrange sentence elements carefully. Main clauses imply important ideas. Subordinate clauses should express ideas that are secondary but which are still of major impor-tance. Though lesser ideas may go into phrases or single words (a strong single word may be more emphatic than a flabby phrase). The beginning and the end of a sentence are usually more emphatic than the middle. An inverted sentence pattern is more emphatic than a normal one, and a modifier out of its normal position—if the rela-tionships are clear—is more emphatic than one standing where it would be expected to stand. By varying these elements by changes in structure and position, and by carefully introducing concepts in the order in which you want them considered, you may control your reader's responses to your thought by suggesting the impor-tance of each point by the weight you give it.

6. DANGLING MODIFIERS (See also pages 462–471.)—**Dng**

As you practice using different kinds of sentences, develop-ing your ability to write mature and flexible sentences that will reflect the turns of your thinking, you may find yourself sometimes writing dangling modifiers. Do not allow the recurrence of the symbol **Dng** to discourage you from further experiments; you can-not learn to handle new tools skillfully without practice. Instead of being discouraged, learn how to avoid dangling modifiers and how to recognize and correct such dangling modifiers as may have slipped in during the heat of composition. When you have done that, you will have mastered a new sentence pattern that will be very valuable to you.

Dangling modifiers are verbal clusters or elliptical adverbial clauses with nothing to modify.

a. Dangling Participles

DANGLING: *Seated one day at the organ,* a new chord shaped itself under my fingers. (*Who was seated?*)

CORRECTED: *Seated one day at the organ,* I played a strange new chord. (*Main clause revised to contain a modifiable word.*)

CORRECTED: *As I was seated one day at the organ,* a strange new chord shaped itself under my fingers. (*Participial phrase changed to adverbial clause. Notice that this sentence, though structurally satisfactory, is stylistically weak because of the shift in voice.*)

b. Dangling Infinitives

DANGLING: *To learn to handle new tools,* repeated practice is necessary. (*Who is to learn?*)

STILL DANGLING: Repeated practice is necessary *to learn to handle new tools.*

CORRECTED: *To learn to handle new tools,* you must practice repeatedly. (*Main clause revised to contain a modifiable word.*)

CORRECTED: *Before you can learn to handle new tools,* repeated practice is necessary. (*Infinitive phrase changed to adverbial clause.*)

c. Dangling Elliptical Clauses

DANGLING: *When planning to move,* damage to some of your furniture should be accepted as inevitable. (*Who is planning?*)

CORRECTED: *When planning to move,* you should accept damage to some of your furniture as inevitable. (*Main clause revised to contain a modifiable word.*)

CORRECTED: *When you are planning to move,* damage to some of your furniture should be accepted as inevitable. (*Elliptical clause expanded to full clause. This revision may be stylistically awkward. A "correction" may still produce a weak sentence.*)

d. Confused Thought

The hardest kind of dangling modifier to discover and correct in revision results from a basic confusion of thought. It can take many forms.

On my first day in high school, too unnerved to eat breakfast, I left the house twenty minutes early—much to my mother's dissatisfaction. (*The dissatisfaction must refer to the failure to eat, not to the early departure. The sentence will have to be completely rewritten to make it clear.*)

Many modifiers which are technically dangling do not cause any confusion at all; you can find examples in all but the most formal writing. You need to be aware of the problem, nevertheless, for a dangling modifier of which you are unaware may raise a laugh over a point you meant very seriously.

7. MISPLACED MODIFIERS—Mm

Misplaced modifiers are modifiers which are all right in themselves, and do have something in the sentence to modify, but which are put in the wrong place, so that they seem to modify an element you did not mean to qualify. The essential difference between dangling modifiers and misplaced modifiers is that the former cannot fit logically anywhere in the sentence; the latter merely do not belong where you put them.

Remember that *modifiers go as near as possible to the elements they modify.* An adjective (word, phrase, or clause) will consequently try to attach itself to the nearest noun; an adverb will try to attach itself to the nearest verb, adjective, other adverb, or the whole clause in which it appears. Whether modifiers precede or follow the element they modify, and whether their position is fixed or is relatively free is a complicated matter of structure and idiom. If you are uncertain about that, see Chapter 13. If a modifier is placed near an eligible element which it was not intended to affect, the modifier has been misplaced and confusion will certainly follow, sometimes with unintentionally amusing results.

Correcting a misplaced modifier is easy: Move it from the confusing position and put it where it will be clear. Sometimes, as in the first example below, you may need to rephrase the whole sentence.

a. Carelessness

MISPLACED: Look at that odd boy with the checked trousers about a block behind.

MISPLACED: Friday I started for the ocean in a jeep which was about two hundred miles away.

MISPLACED: I have been looking forward to taking English for a long time.

MISPLACED: Professor Snodgrass objects to students who sleep while he is lecturing shamelessly.

b. *Only*, etc.

One special problem causes particular trouble: *Only* and *almost* and *nearly* and *completely* are words that in informal English may move around in a sentence rather freely. There is no real confusion when we say,

This bus driver only drives as far as Clarksburg.
The fullback only smokes after the football season.

But many readers have been taught to object to such floating adverbs, and sometimes there might possibly be a question as to what we really mean. And sometimes the misplacing of such adverbs can be a serious functional error, making it impossible for the reader to be sure what you mean.

> He almost solved the problem in his head. (What does that mean? Was the problem ever solved?)

To be sure that your writing is clear and to avoid distracting your reader unnecessarily, it is best to put such adverbs as near as possible to the elements in the sentence they are intended to modify.

> This bus driver drives only as far as Clarksburg.
> The fullback smokes only after the football season.
> He solved the problem, but he finally had to use pencil and paper.

c. "Squinting Modifiers"

Another special problem arises with a modifier which stands between two elements it might modify, so that the reader cannot tell which it was intended to affect. (It is called a "squinting modifier" because it looks both ways. Perhaps "cockeyed modifier" would be a more accurate name.)

> CONFUSING: The man who is honest usually is happy.
> IMPROVED: The man who is honest is usually happy.

Such modifiers are perfectly clear when they are spoken, because the pitch and juncture given them makes confusion unlikely. But no such aid to understanding is present in the written sentences.

The problem often accompanies comma splices or run-on sentences.

> CONFUSING: I will not go, until you have apologized, I will not even stir from this chair.
> IMPROVED: I will not go. Until you have apologized, I will not even stir from this chair.

EXERCISE

In the following sentences, distinguish between dangling modifiers and misplaced modifiers. Rephrase all faulty sentences to correct the errors.

> 1. Having always enjoyed reading, standard grammar and idiom have never been any trouble to me.

2. To absorb English idioms from reading, your reading rate must not be extremely fast.

3. Seven miles below me I could see the pattern of the river system very clearly.

4. To find an unoccupied parking place, a fireplug should be found.

5. When parked by a fireplug, a ticket is not unexpected.

6. Thoroughly boiled, she served the cabbage and announced dinner.

7. Studying calculus, the neighbor's children are distracting.

8. Do not cross yellow line when on your side.

9. She talked to the professor with knowledge and understanding.

10. To avoid parking problems, the bus is best.

11. Our dog is as old as my sister, who is fourteen but still in good health.

12. Although very well constructed, Mary lives in an old and odd-looking house.

13. His lectures are confusing, and I fear sometimes intentionally confusing.

14. After spending two weeks fishing in the mountains, the office seemed very confining.

15. Howling through the treetops, I could hear the wind.

8. REFERENCE OF PRONOUNS—Ref

Third person pronouns substitute for nouns already explicitly expressed in the sentence or passage. Rarely, demonstrative or relative pronouns refer to and summarize a concept clearly implied by a whole preceding predication. (See pages 430, 416.) Until you are sure of the clarity of your writing, be certain that there is an expressed substantive near enough to the pronoun for the reference to be unmistakable, and be certain that there is only one eligible antecedent to which the pronoun might refer.

a. Implied Antecedents

Avoid using a pronoun to refer to an antecedent which has been merely implied by the preceding phrasing.

I have always envied the teacher's life, and I have decided to become *one.* (Teacher's *is an adjective in function, not a noun. The noun* teacher, *to which the pronoun is intended to refer, does not appear in the sentence at all.*)

I accept the Universe! *which,* on the whole, is just as well. (*Such a pronoun really refers to the idea of* acceptance, *implied by the verb. The construction is well established, and if no confusion results, no one will notice it. It is not used, however, in strictly formal writing, and you might well avoid it in college work.*)

b. Ambiguous Antecedents

Do not use a pronoun to refer ambiguously to one of two or more eligible antecedents.

John handed Elmer *his* book.

Ambiguity also occurs when forms of the same pronoun are used to refer to different antecedents.

When a driver is waiting for a parking space and another driver edges in ahead of *him, he* may try to cut *him* off. (*The reader may be able to solve the puzzle, but the writer's job is to set no puzzles in the first place. It is never adequate to say, "Oh, you know what I mean." The reader is concerned with what you have said.*)

If the skin receives too much sugar, *it* stores *it* up, and *it* interferes with the normal functioning of the oil glands.

Be particularly careful of using *it* as a pronoun and *it* as an expletive in the same sentence. If there is any possibility of ambiguity or awkwardness, avoid the construction.

It is a stubborn condition, and *it* is hard to correct *it.*

Ambiguity can also occur through the position of eligible antecedents in the sentence.

The Buick skidded on the wet pavement and crashed into a shed. *It* was totally demolished. (*Pronouns tend to refer both to the nearest eligible antecedent and to an eligible antecedent functioning in the same way as the pronoun. Here,* it *could refer either to* Buick *or* shed, *since both are third-person singular,* Buick *and* it *are both subjects, and* shed *and* it *stand side by side.*)

Avoid the awkwardness of parenthetical explanation of ambiguous pronouns. It is better to be clear in the first place.

WEAK: John said that *he* (John) would do *his* (Jim's) work for a slight fee.

BETTER: John promised to do Jim's work for a slight fee.

c. Antecedents in Subordinate Constructions

Avoid using a pronoun to refer to an antecedent functioning in a subordinate construction.

I envy the life of a teacher, and I plan to become *one*. (Teacher, *the intended antecedent, is merely the complement in a modifying phrase, and consequently the reference is obscured.* One *tends to refer instead to* life, *the nearest major eligible noun.*)

d. Demonstratives with Implied Antecedents

If you use the demonstratives to refer to an implied antecedent (see page 390), be sure the reader would have no trouble supplying the omitted substantive.

ACCEPTABLE: Many teachers will object to demonstratives lacking a clear antecedent. *This* [objection] should be considered before you employ the construction.

CONFUSING: The first step in planting a lawn is preparation of the soil. *This* must be turned over to a depth of six inches. In former days, *this* was accomplished by using a spade and a strong back. Now one can rent a small tractor and do the work faster and more efficiently. *This* also breaks up the soil into a fine texture in the same operation.

EXERCISE

Clarify all confusing pronoun reference in the following sentences.

1. As the fan oscillated on the rickety table, it squeaked.
2. Because I thought they were very good, I gave the books to my nephews.
3. An emotion does not explain its meaning. It has none; it must be provided for it.
4. Before heads of state are driven through the streets of Washington, they are decorated with flags and hosed down if they need it.
5. Jane looked despairingly at the battered copy of the outside reading list. It was barely legible, and it was so long it would take forever to read every book in it.

6. I had always supposed that college courses would be easy for me, but it assumes a preparation I have not had.
7. It said in the paper that it will snow, and if it does, it will tie up the holiday traffic.
8. With her figure, she should never have bought that dress. It bulges in all the wrong places.
9. John told Jim that he would do his English lesson.
10. The archaeologists are contradictory in this report on the evidence concerning Cretan writing, which is confusing.

9. AGREEMENT OF PRONOUNS—PAgr

Pronouns agree with their antecedents in person, gender, and number. "To agree" means to correspond in form. If the antecedent is third person, masculine, and singular, for example, the pronoun will be third person, masculine, and singular. The antecedent of first and second person pronouns is determined by context. All nouns, including clauses and phrases, are treated as third person.

a. Person

Pronouns agree with their antecedents in person. There is only one point that needs to be mentioned. The indefinite pronouns (*one, each, everyone, everybody,* and so on) are third person in origin, but *you,* used informally as an indefinite pronoun, is second person. *You* may be used only when all readers might reasonably accept it as personal in reference.

Avoid, for example, sentences beginning: "Have you ever looked at yourself in your new dress and thought . . . ?" Half of the human race would have to say, bristling, "No, of course not!"

b. Gender

Pronouns agree with their antecedents in gender.

In English, gender is determined by sex and consequently causes little grammatical trouble. If the antecedent names a female, the pronoun is feminine; if the antecedent names a male, the pronoun is masculine; otherwise the pronoun is neuter. The few exceptions (ships, for example, are feminine) cause no trouble.

In sentences containing both masculine and feminine antecedents, a masculine pronoun alone is sufficient.

RIGHT: Every man and woman votes according to his own best judgment.

393

UNNECESSARILY ELABORATE: Every man and woman votes according to his or her own best judgment.

c. Number

Pronouns agree with their antecedents in number.

The men went their way.
The man went his way.

The following complications need to be examined.

1) ANTECEDENTS WITH *and*

Two or more antecedents connected by *and* take a plural pronoun, regardless of the number or position of the individual nouns.

Bill and Elizabeth went to New England for their vacation.
The foreman and the men did their work efficiently.
The men and the foreman did their work efficiently.
BUT: Every bolt and cog in the machine does its share of the work.

2) ANTECEDENTS WITH *or* OR *nor*

Two or more singular antecedents connected by *or* or *nor* take a singular pronoun.

John or Joe will get his way.
Neither John nor Joe will get his way.

If the antecedents differ in number, the pronoun agrees according to the logic of the idea.

Neither the captain nor the men knew what initiated their action.
Neither the captain nor the men knew what initiated his action.

3) AFFIRMATIVE AND NEGATIVE ANTECEDENTS

If one of two antecedents is affirmative and the other negative, the pronoun agrees with the affirmative antecedent.

The men, but not the superintendent, will be paid extra for their overtime work.
Not the superintendent, but the men, will be paid extra for their overtime work.

4) *Either,* AND SO ON

Either, neither, everyone, nobody, and so on, are treated as singular in formal writing and take singular pronouns. Informally, they often take plural pronouns. Be sure that the form you use is consistent with the tone of your paper.

> FORMAL (usually preferred in college writing): Everybody in the class conscientiously did his own work.
> INFORMAL AND COLLOQUIAL: Everybody did the best they could.

The reason for the difference is that formal English tends to follow the form of the words; informal and colloquial English tend to follow the meaning. If in a formal context you find you have written a sentence which demands that the second pronoun be plural, recast the sentence to avoid the indefinite pronoun.

> After the completion of the ceremony, everyone entered their automobiles and formed a procession.
> After the completion of the ceremony, the participants and the spectators entered their automobiles and formed a procession.

5) *Each,* AND SO ON, PLUS A PLURAL MODIFIER

Each, either, neither, everyone, and so on, followed by a modifying phrase containing a plural noun, are still singular (but see point 4, above) and take a singular pronoun.

> Each of the students did his best.
> Neither of them was present when his name was called.
> Every one of them misunderstood the problem and consequently got his answer wrong.

6) *None*

None may be either singular or plural.

> None of them deserves credit for his work.
> None of them were there when they were called.

7) COLLECTIVE ANTECEDENTS

Collective nouns (naming groups of things) are either singular or plural, depending on whether the writer means to refer to the group as a unit or to the individual members of the group. A pronoun agrees with the intended number of the collective ante-cedent.

> RIGHT: The board of directors announced its decision.
> RIGHT: The board of directors voted to pay themselves extra fees.

10. AGREEMENT OF VERBS—VAgr

A verb agrees with its subject in person and number, what-ever the subject is and wherever in the sentence it is located.

The following complications need to be examined.

a. Person of Nouns

All nouns are third person. The point is more important than it may sound. No one in college ever writes "He don't," but many college students write sentences with singular nouns as subjects and a *don't* somewhere along the line as a verb.

b. Singular Subjects plus Plural Modifiers

A *singular* subject followed by a phrase containing a plural noun is still singular and takes a singular verb.

The silhouette of the mountains looms against the evening sky.

c. Singular Subjects with *as well as,* and so on

A *singular* subject followed by a parenthetical phrase intro-duced by *as well as, in addition to,* and so on, takes a singular verb.

> Monday, as well as the remaining days of the week, begins very early in the morning.
> The happy laughter of the children, in addition to the banging of the garbage cans they are playing with, distracts me badly.

d. Subjects with *and*

Two or more subjects connected by *and* require a plural verb.

> Marjorie and Lois were glad to see each other again.
> Men and women are accorded equal voting rights.

e. Subjects with *or* or *nor*

If two or more subjects of differing number are connected by *or* or *nor,* the verb agrees with the nearest subject.

The teacher or the students are wrong.
The students or the teacher is due for a surprise. (*If such sentences seem awkward or illogical, they may always be rephrased.*)
The students are due for a surprise, or the teacher is.

f. Affirmative and Negative Subjects

If one of two subjects is affirmative and the other negative, the verb agrees with the affirmative subject, regardless of which is nearer the verb.

Not the general, but the privates, were unhappy at the thought of a night march.
The privates, but not the general, were unhappy at the thought of a night march.

g. Subjects and Subjective Complements

The verb agrees with the subject, not the subjective complement.

The only drawback to the apartment is the neighbors' noisy children.

h. Subjects after the Verb

The verb agrees with the subject even when the subject follows the verb, as it does in questions and after the expletive *there*.

Is Lois sitting in that uncomfortable chair from choice?
Are there any reasons for your decision?
There are three reasons for my decision.

(The expletive *it* also throws the logical subject after the verb, but with *it* the verb is always singular, even though the logical subject may be plural.)

It has been seven weeks since we have seen her.

i. Indefinite Pronouns

The indefinite pronouns (*each, everyone, everybody,* and so on) are singular and require a singular verb.

Everybody has done his work promptly.
Each of the students has done his own work.
Every man and woman has contributed greatly.

j. None

None may be either singular or plural.

None of them deserves credit.
None but the brave deserve the fair.

k. Collective Nouns

Collective nouns may be either singular or plural, depending on whether the writer is thinking of the group as a unit or of the individual members of the group. The verb agrees with the intended number of the collective subject.

SINGULAR: The board of directors decides all policies.
PLURAL: The board of directors vote themselves extra fees for every bit of extra work they do.

l. Relative Pronouns

If the subject is a relative pronoun, the verb agrees, for all practical purposes, with the antecedent of the pronoun.

There are many men who are always too tired to work.
He is one of those men who are always too tired to work. (*The logical relation of the ideas can be seen more readily if the sentence is rearranged: Of those men who are always too tired to work, he is one.*)

There are old and honorable literary precedents for *one of those men who is* (Addison, Swift, Johnson, Jefferson, Macaulay, *et al.*), but many readers still strongly object to it.

He is the only one of those men who is not always tired. (*In this sentence, the adjective clause modifies the singular* one: *Of those men, he is the only one who is not always tired.*)

m. Quantities, and so on

Quantities considered as units, fractions modified by a phrase containing a singular noun, and some nouns plural in form but singular in meaning—all express singular ideas and take singular verbs.

Two weeks is the normal vacation period in business.
Two-thirds of the crop is ruined.
Mathematics is a confusing subject.

Two-thirds of the apples are spoiled.
The news is good tonight.

EXERCISE

Choose the correct form from the pairs in parentheses in the following sentences.

1. On the library steps there (has, have) gathered the usual group of students, men and women, to smoke and relax.

2. Relaxing on the library steps is one of the numerous ways which students (has, have) to avoid studying.

3. Every one of the few students who (is, are) too far behind in (his, their, his or her) work to relax (wishes, wish) (he, they, he or she) had studied earlier.

4. Either you or she (is, are) going to give tomorrow's speech.

5. Glenn is the only one of all of the students on this campus who (was, were) voted Most Likely to Succeed in high school who (shows, show) that (his, their) success may be academic.

6. Either of the candidates (is, are) well qualified because of (his, their) past experience.

7. The student body anxiously (awaits, await) the Registrar's reports of (its, their) grades.

8. Intelligence and application—(this, these) (constitutes, constitute) the secret of success in college.

9. (Is, are) any of the proposed solutions to the problem of poverty likely to work in all circumstances?

10. Either the instructor in the classroom or the deans of the various colleges and divisions (handles, handle) disciplinary problems.

11. The recognition of negative characteristics, as well as awareness of similarity, (is, are) essential to making satisfactory classifications.

12. Nine-tenths of what one learns in class (is, are) probably going to be forgotten before long.

13. The one-tenth that (remains, remain) (is, are) your general education.

399

14. Even in your professional specialty, three-fifths of your knowledge (is, are) all that you are likely to retain for instant use, of the five-fifths you originally learned.

15. Everybody (has, have) to hope that (he, they) will not need part of the dormant two-fifths of (his, their) information in an emergency.

11. SENTENCE CONSTRUCTION (SHIFTS)—Cst

a. Point of View

In a number of places in the text, "point of view" has been used in a rhetorical sense to refer to the position or attitude from which events are seen or ideas are considered—the "Speaker" behind a piece of writing. Here, we use it in a grammatical sense, related but more tightly restricted, to refer to consistency in grammatical forms—to tenses and sequence of tenses, to mood, to voice, to person, and to number; or it may refer to a structural or a logical consistency from one end of a sentence to the other.

The fundamental principle is clear: The writer must keep in mind his relationship—in time, mood, number, and so on—to what he is saying. Changes within a single theme or even a single sentence are not only possible, but are sometimes mandatory. What is important is that *shifts in point of view should not be illogical.*

1) SHIFT IN TENSE (THE TIME RELATION OF VERBS AND VERBALS)

The bull still had lots of life in him when the picadors entered the ring. These men teased the bull until he charges them. They then gouge the bull's back with their long lances. The ground was becoming stained with blood wherever the bull stands. (*Shift from past to present to past to present.*)

Taxiing up to the hangar, the pilot went in to make his report. (*The action named by the participle occurred before that of the main verb; a perfect participle,* having taxied, *would express that time relation.*)

2) SHIFT IN MOOD, VOICE, AND PERSON

The process of carving figures from soap begins with the collection of materials. The would-be sculptor needs an idea, a bar of soap, and a small-bladed knife. First, carve out the rough outlines . . . . (*Shift from indicative mood, third person to imperative mood, second person.*)

He browns the meat and the onions. Then the sauce is poured over the meat . . . . (*Shift from active voice to passive voice.*)

If one is to get from college all that college can give, you must put into college all that you can give to it. (*Shift from third person* one *to second person* you.)

b. Sentence Patterns

In addition to the shifts in point of view just illustrated, another kind of shift is very common. In the heat of composition, students often begin a sentence according to one pattern and then forget where they were going and shift in mid-sentence to a different pattern altogether. Or revision of one part may throw another part off.

In its simplest form, this kind of shift may merely repeat an element already included.

I knew that, if I left the job to her, that she would do it in the least efficient way.

Or some vital element may be omitted from the sentence, such as parts of a verb phrase or prepositions demanded by an idiom.

This problem has and will be carefully studied. (*Omitted:* been, *to complete the verb phrase* has been.)

I am as good or better than you. (*Omitted:* as, *leaving the idiomatic comparison* as good as *unfinished. Perhaps the best phrasing for that idea:* "I am as good as you, if not better.")

Or if the writer jumps across a gap in the thought in mid-sentence, the two ends of the sentence may seem to have little or no structural or even logical connection with each other.

Watching us intently, nevertheless the sun went down immediately behind the deer, which made them a difficult target for all our care to prevent discovery.

To have been able to judge exactly what the scope of registration would be this year would have been hard to predict.

c. Faulty Predication

A predication is a statement of an idea, but a faulty predication is literal nonsense. Usually, it burbles out in the haste of composing and is not caught in revision because the writer reads what he meant to say instead of what he put down on the page.

1) ILLOGICAL USE OF *to be* (FALSE EQUATION)

The most comfortable method of traveling is an automobile.

The copper wheel process is one of the best types of ornamentation.

Many automobile accidents are youth and the desire to show off. (*Perhaps that nonsense results from the omission of* caused by, *but as it stands, the predication is faulty.*)

To her grandchildren, a grandmother is a doctor, teacher, part-time parent, playmate, and many other occupations.

I intend to illustrate my thesis by examples which are the chief reasons for the development that took place. (*In this sentence, the choice of a more exact verb than* are *would have solved the problem. Presumably the student avoided* illustrate *and* exemplify *to prevent repetition. It would have been better to change the infinitive.*)

A few constructions which logically result in false *to be* equations are increasingly common, but many readers object to them and are distracted.

Doing well in college is when you make the Dean's List.

A construction to watch out for is where . . . . (*A thing is never a* when *or a* where. *Suspect any* is when *or* is where *sentences.*)

The reason I won't go is because . . . . (*This phrasing is becoming increasingly common, but it is still wordy, if not ungrammatical. Avoid* reason is because. *Say "I won't go because . . ." or "The reason . . . is that . . . ."*)

2) FAULTY APPOSITIVES

The play irritated my father, an unmitigated piece of trash. (*The appositive belongs to* play, *not to* father. *Yet it stands by* father.)

Mary flirted openly with Kenny, a sure sign that she was quarreling with Bill. (*What substantive does* sign *repeat?*)

Skill with any musical instrument requires diligent practice, a category into which I certainly do not fit. (*Nothing in the main clause names a category.*)

3) INCOMPLETE OR ILLOGICAL COMPARISONS

My study habits are better than John. (*Omitted: than John's are. This is both incomplete and illogical.*)

I am so tired tonight. (*We can stress* so *in speaking, but in writing it suggests* so tired that . . . *and seems incomplete.*)

402

Swimming is one of the most relaxing and beneficial exercises of any other sport. (*The* other *makes nonsense of the sentence.*)

Alert students are sometimes troubled by the distinction between figures of speech (such as metaphor, metonymy, and synecdoche) and faulty predications. The difference is that the good figure of speech is appropriate and intentional; the faulty predication results in inappropriate nonsense. Furthermore, the faulty predication is not the same as a faulty figure of speech. The first results from lazy carelessness in the choice of diction (usually *to be* instead of a more exact verb) or from failure to recognize other pairings of unlike ideas. The second results from a misguided effort to gain clarity by an inappropriate figure. The writer of a faulty predication plods indifferently into a logical quagmire; the writer of a poor figure of speech leaps without looking and lands with an intellectual pratfall.

Sometimes—in the heat of composition—two or three ideas overlap and get scrambled. This sort of shift (and any of the others) can happen to the best of us. But it is a sad freshman who does not recognize and correct such shifts when he revises his themes, as the writer of the following sentence, faced with an extra semester of instruction and practice, should have realized.

When I consider the above-mentioned mistakes plus some others, it will all boil down to the fact that it is the cause of disinterest or just trying to get by, because yet today there remains the fact that the taking of this course is still a means toward an end and still not caring whether I make a *D* or *A* but only whether I pass or flunk is the only interest I have for this course because my true interest is numbers and their association to each other and not with the association of words and ideas of words which would make my other courses easier, if I had a control over my English or rather rhetoric.[1]

12. FAULTY PARALLELISM—//Cst

Putting similar ideas into similar constructions is an important device for securing effective sentences. (See pages 151–154.) The human mind likes to run in grooves, and a reader is pleased by skillfully repeated patterns. Parallelism, the deliberate use of similar

---

[1] From "Rhet as Writ," *The Green Caldron: A Magazine of Freshman Writing,* published at the University of Illinois. Reprinted by permission.

constructions for similar ideas, is very common as a result. It is so common, in fact, that your reader will be irritated and confused if you fail to use parallel patterns where he expects them or do use them with dissimilar ideas where he does not expect them.

a. Similar Ideas

Use similar constructions to express similar ideas.

FAULTY: I enjoy swimming, hiking, and to fish.
PARALLEL: I enjoy swimming, hiking, and fishing. (*Three gerunds are parallel; two gerunds and an infinitive are not.*)
FAULTY: He was an old man of ninety-seven and tired.
PARALLEL: He was an old man of ninety-seven, and he was tired. (*Two clauses are parallel; a clause and an adjective are not.*)
PARALLEL: He was an old, tired man of ninety-seven. (*Two adjectives are parallel.*)
FAULTY: This is an important job and which must be done carefully.
PARALLEL: This is a job which is important and which must be done carefully.
PARALLEL: This is an important job, and one which must be done carefully. (*Two nouns,* job *and* one, *are parallel; a noun and an adjective clause are not.*)
NOT PARALLEL, BUT CORRECT: This is an important job which must be done carefully.

Notice that all the examples of faulty parallelism so far considered result from misuse of the coordinating conjunction *and*. *And* connects only equal elements.

A similar error results from misuse of the correlative conjunctions, such as *either–or, neither–nor, not (only)–but (also),* which always work in pairs to connect equal elements.

FAULTY: Either John will do this job or let it slide.
PARALLEL: John will either do this job or let it slide.
FAULTY: Not only will John do this job, but ask Frances to help him.
PARALLEL: John not only will do this job, but will ask Frances to help him.

When you use correlative conjunctions, be sure each member of the pair is followed by grammatically similar elements.

Other kinds of faulty parallelism are more complex, sometimes involving a lack of logical comparability even though grammatical

404

parallelism is maintained, or otherwise failing to balance ideas which ought to be treated alike.

> Here is the typical regular Navy officer of today: an average of seven years in the service, high school graduate, has a good technical education through a service school, is usually quite competent, and well satisfied with his career.
>
> No one really cares what you do, but only can you keep it secret.
>
> By using the French idioms in each lesson, the student is able to enlarge his vocabulary, also making him able to express himself more accurately. (*This one is the kind that poses problems for the instructor. It might be marked* //Cst, *or* Cst, *or even* K.)

b. Dissimilar Ideas

Do not use similar constructions to express dissimilar ideas.

The principal trouble here arises with constructions that look like A, B, and C series, but do not deal with logically similar elements.

> FAULTY: I put on a surgical gown, a skull-type cap, and tied a mask around my face.
>
> CORRECTED: I put on a surgical gown and a skull-type cap, and tied a mask around my face. (*The first* and *now connects two nouns,* gown *and* cap; *the second connects two verbs,* put on *and* tied. *The comma separates the dissimilar elements.*)

In revising your themes, be alert for all such shifts in construction. Remember that although you may know what you mean, your reader must depend on what you actually say.

13. AWKWARDNESS—K

A final problem which remains to be mentioned is that of awkwardness. It is a complex problem which may take many forms and may be related at one and the same time to weakness in grammar, to shifts in construction, to the uncertainty in diction and idiom which plagues those who have never done much reading, and to haste in writing and slackness in revising. It is very hard for an instructor to put a finger on, because it results in writing which is not exactly ungrammatical but is certainly not fluent.

The following passages, for example, offer nothing which a student should be proud of having written. They could be analyzed in detail, and their weaknesses could be specifically indicated. Yet few instructors have the time for such detailed analysis as would be required, and the margins of themes leave too little room. Most instructors, consequently, would mark them as awkward and hope that the student, when he revised his theme, would ask himself, "Now, what did I really mean to say here? What would be the easiest way to say it?"

> Had not the people of the ages been able to record their history and do so well, we would be lost in knowing about the past.
> There was no grammar as such, because everybody would not have been in that class if he or she did not know it.
> I could get little satisfaction from having helped to any extent mentally subnormal children if I were one in a grade-series of teachers. With a limit to the time or level of development, the teacher cannot fully practice a good program with a follow-up and check to keep the children from backsliding or becoming fixed at one level when there is more capacity than has been developed.

And finally:

> In speaking to friends and fellow students and also from my own personal experience, I have found it rather difficult to advance in position in the business world without a college education. I have always worked with one idea in mind, that is, the hope of advancement. In this hope I am at this time deeply disappointed. I have failed to reach the step of the ladder that I feel I am capable of standing on. Why? Well, my superiors have told me that I have not sufficient education. I pointed out to them that I did have the experience and intelligence to handle the job. In this they agreed, but they wanted the piece of paper to show that I had had the education. At this stage, I could not produce the evidence. So the only outlook I had was to enter college.

How would you mark a passage like that to show the student his weaknesses? Every line has something wrong with it, and yet very few of the errors are so clear cut that reference to the handbook would do very much good. In despair, the instructor contented himself with the general comment: "A good deal of awkward phrasing, in which you don't say quite what you mean. See me in conference."

There is no quick cure for a bad case of awkwardness, but practice in writing, reading aloud what you have written, attentiveness to the rhythms and idioms of Standard English as you read what others have written, care in knowing before you write what you want to say, and critical revision of what you have written—all these will help.

EXERCISE

Rewrite the following passages to make them clear and effective. Identify the kind of error involved.

1. As the plane droned on, some talked, watched movies, read, and others were asleep.

2. As soon as they are corrected, these inadequacies in the curriculum will improve the college greatly.

3. To appoint Ira to a committee is to be sure that, though it may take time, that the job will be well done.

4. The grill work is well-designed, unobtrusive, and stainless steel.

5. One should work carefully and do the best that you can do, within the limits of the importance of the task.

6. We were playing football in the side yard and having a lot of fun until Uncle Will comes out and starts coaching.

7. I have a great deal of interest and respect for your opinion.

8. Among the numerous skills developed by a good course in English composition are a knowledge of the basic structure of the language and confidence in your ability to express yourself fluently.

9. My grandmother is acquisitive and retentive—anything and everything from old dresses and letters and knickknacks to long since abandoned old rocking chairs in the attic.

10. My ability to play basketball was not great, but it was at least better than the average boy.

11. Sawmills, mining wastes, atomic energy plants, and chemical refuse are responsible for the pollution of salmon streams.

12. The biggest change from high school to college was the differences in teaching.

13. The average American traveling in Europe does not know the languages of the country he is in nor anything about the customs. They are Ugly Americans.

14. Wherever one goes in this country, you find people having different ideas on that which it is necessary to be done, but all of them Americans and wanting what is best for everybody, which makes education important and a free press.

15. Abolishing poverty, not only in Appalachia but in the blighted hearts of city slums, is a vital problem for all of us, and which will take time to solve.

16. Roses are perhaps the most popular flower, but they are hard to care for, being more susceptible to insects and disease.

17. The town's present real-estate assessment is $25,643,159.00, which under the statutory law of 18 percent pertaining to debt limit of real estate, is $4,615,768.62.

18. Love may be based on common interests, or on loneliness and propinquity, or for many other reasons.

19. The easiest way to write faulty predications is out of your head.

20. Professor Snodgrass was maneuvered into resigning, the best thing President McClanahan has done since taking office.

13-

Grammar

Characteristics of a Good Theme: 11. Conventionally acceptable grammar.

Gr   Grammar

* There are exercises for items marked with an asterisk.

THE IMPORTANCE OF GRAMMAR—Gr

For those who cannot trust their own language habits, some knowledge of "grammar" offers the easiest way of correcting habits that are not in accord with general educated usage, of learning to recognize and avoid "mistakes"—whether those mistakes are functional, actually getting in the way of the reader's comprehension, or merely conventional, violating an established usage although not preventing understanding.

You already know most of the grammar of spoken English, though you probably do not know how to explain it in words and very likely have never thought of most of it as grammar at all. But you do speak English. You know the basic forms of English words (*morphology*), the basic ways to arrange them (*word order*), and the use of words that mean little in themselves (*function words*) but indicate the relationships of more meaningful words. Most remarkable of all, you know how to pitch your voice, high or low or gliding from one pitch to another, to give variations of meaning to an utterance. You know how to give greater or less vocal emphasis to parts of an utterance. You know how to vary the pauses between parts of an utterance to join or separate what would otherwise be a meaningless series of sounds. In other words, you know how to use the very important devices of *pitch, stress,* and *juncture.* In spoken English all of these are fundamental parts of the grammar. And the spoken language is the vital, living language.

412

Written English is a complicated set of symbols that represents spoken English, but in some ways does it awkwardly. The difficulties you may have with written English are our primary concern. Many of them arise because written English lacks the pitch, stress, and juncture signals of spoken English, except as typography and punctuation can suggest them. Others arise because morphological changes in the forms of words (showing tense, case, number, and so on), which once were of major importance, are now incomplete remnants of a dead system and consequently are sometimes hard to remember. Still others arise because written English must be fuller, clearer, and more precise than spoken English; you cannot merely write down what you might say. And still others arise because you have never seen much sense in learning a subject that did not seem to have much use outside an English class; consequently, though you have met "grammar" often, you may never have learned how to make use of what you know.

But now, having entered college, you are preparing yourself for admission to the educated minority, and you need to know the minority dialect used by educated people. Again, you already do know most of it, but wherever your habits differ, you need to learn the constructions that educated speakers and writers use—particularly educated writers.

For it is the usage of those who are presumed to know the language best that makes the "rules" of the educated dialect, not logic nor lawgivers nor the practice in other dialects, though all of those to some extent influence educated usage. And to learn to adjust your habits to educated usage, you must know something of the basic structure of the language, Grammar, of whatever kind (and there are several kinds), is an attempt to classify the elements of a language in order to describe how it works. Just as algebra is generalized arithmetic, English grammar is, or should be, generalized English, by which one can make or understand meaningful statements about the language instead of having to treat every new sentence as a new and unique phenomenon. Language is less exact than numbers, and grammar is less fixed and less complete than algebra. Scholars still strongly disagree about what approaches, what systems of classification, and what terminology provide the best description of Modern American English. (It has been wisely said that all grammars leak.) But for all the disagreements, it is possible to generalize about what usually occurs. We shall use familiar terminology wherever possible, borrow from varied approaches to grammar when it is convenient to do so, and try to describe the national, current, and reputable usage that makes up the language of the educated man.

But it is not enough to say of a disputed locution that it is nationally and currently used by most reputable writers. There is a time lag in grammatical understanding, as there is in many things. The primary purpose of all worthwhile writing is to convey the writer's idea as effectively as possible to the reader he wants to reach. Those readers may not be as sophisticated linguistically as the writer is; they may respond unfavorably to a construction that he knows is quite well established, and the possibility of such an unfavorable response must be considered. Suppose, for example, that the writer ends a sentence with what looks like a preposition. He may know it is not a preposition, but is an adverb, and that English has long made use of verb-adverb combinations to produce new verb-ideas. (For example, in the phrase *to put on shoes, put* and *on* combine to express the idea of the formal *don,* itself an old and now forgotten verb-adverb phrase, *to do on. Shoes* is the object of the verb-adverb combination, not of *on* alone. Because this adverb *on* looks like the prepositional *on,* however, the student would perhaps do well to avoid it at the end of a sentence. It will seldom be noticed anywhere else.) If the reader is startled by any construction and loses track of what the writer is trying to say because he thinks instead of the way the idea is phrased, there is a flaw in the writing which reduces the effectiveness of the paper. So we shall sometimes say, "This is not wrong. Don't worry about it when others use it. But avoid it yourself, because many readers will be distressed and distracted by it." Alexander Pope is now somewhat out of fashion, but his advice is still good.

> Be not the first by whom the new is tried,
> Nor yet the last to lay the old aside.

We shall try to find a middle ground and to recommend constructions which are clear, modern, and effective.

THE FUNCTIONS OF SENTENCE ELEMENTS

1. THE SENTENCE ITSELF—Gr 1

Grammar is chiefly concerned with the sentence. Although consistency in grammatical point of view does relate one sentence to another in such matters as tense and person and number, most grammar consists of analyzing the elements of one individual sentence at a time. We shall be working with sentences throughout most of this chapter.

But what is a sentence? Basic though the concept is, and familiar as the word is, "a sentence" is so hard to define that we can best fall back on combining many definitions, each clarifying some one aspect of the sentence and all together suggesting the meaning. The word *sentence* is related to the word *sense,* and in very general terms, a sentence is an utterance that makes sense in itself, in the context in which it appears. The old grade school definition is inadequate: "A sentence is a group of words having a subject and a verb and expressing a complete thought." But not all sentences have a subject and a verb, though most of them do. And what is a complete thought? It is a structure that makes sense in itself, in its context. Someone asks a question, and you answer, "Yes." In its context, *yes* makes sense, and in speech or writing dialogue it is certainly a sentence. "Where—?" "The drugstore." "Ouch!" "George?" These could all be sentences—minor sentences, though not full sentences. (See pages 139–140.)

But in written English, especially outside of dialogue or stream-of-consciousness prose, sentences usually are also grammatically complete with subject and verb and a complete idea. For grammatical completeness alone, another definition has been phrased: A sentence is "a structure not included by any formal device in any larger structure"—by such elements, that is, as subordinating conjunctions, like *until* or *if.* "George is here" is a sentence, but "If George is here" is not; it is made dependent on some kind of larger structure by that *if.*

Still another definition looks to the spoken language for its clues, but written sentences can be read aloud and tested by the clues offered by the voice; so this definition can be useful too:

"A sentence is an utterance between two full stops of the breath, usually ending with a change of pitch." With practice, you can hear the signals of pitch, stress, and juncture (pauses). We will need them often.

Many other definitions have been phrased, but we can get along with a combination of these three: "A full sentence is a grammatically complete and independent utterance, spoken between full stops of breath and ending usually with a change of pitch; it makes sense in itself and in its context." It is a *predication*, an expression of a fully formulated thought. Much of the rest of this chapter will be concerned with examining details behind that definition.

2. THE ELEMENTS OF THE SENTENCE—Gr 2

English, as a spoken language, is made up of sounds and sound combinations, and anyone who pretends to anything like a thorough understanding of the language must know what they are and how to identify them. We do not need to be so thorough. It is interesting to know that there are different grammars and different approaches. Depending on our approach, we could learn to say that the elements of the sentence are phones, segmental phonemes, suprasegmental phonemes, or morphemes, or constituents, or clusters, or vowels and consonants, or words and phrases, or headwords, or kernels and strings, or transforms, or various other things. Those terms and many others are important to one or another of the currently active attempts to describe Modern English.

Unfortunately, none of these new grammars is complete or foolproof, and there is none with which all college students are already familiar. For our purposes, even though the traditional terminology of Latin-based grammar causes some trouble when it is applied to English, we can perhaps get along best with the terms most students already know, and merely modify, at need, the way we look at them. In those terms, the elements of the written sentence are letters and words representing sounds. The words are roots (or stems), and one or two to a word, and part-words like prefixes and suffixes (see pages 180–183). Some words are only roots, some are prefixes and roots, some are roots and suffixes, and some are all three. Sometimes each word functions as a unit (as in

Frank snores. Charlie catches fish. Some students are lazy), but they sometimes go together in word-groups with the whole word-group functioning as a unit (as in [*The old man*] [*in the corner*] [*has been sitting*] [*in my favorite chair*] [*since the day before yesterday*], [*when he first came in*]). Some of the word-groups are phrases, some are clauses, and some are just clusters of words attached to a major word, the "headword" in the group. Whether the functioning unit is a single word or a word-group makes very little difference in the way the unit functions.

3. THE FUNCTIONS[1]—Gr 3

Whether as single words or as word-groups, all elements of the sentence (with the single exception of the expletives *it* and *there,* in *It is* and *There is/are* sentences) function in one of six ways, as *subjects, verbs, complements, modifiers, connectives,* or *absolutes.* These functions must be understood, because we shall be using these terms constantly throughout the chapter.

a. *Subject:* **A word or word-group indicating the topic of the sentence, telling what the predication is about.** (*Test: Who* or *what* did or is or has done to it whatever the sentence asserts?)

   S
John teaches.

      S
The squirrel in the tree jabbered incessantly.

      S
Whoever left the door open should have shut it.

     S
To leave doors open in winter is foolish.

     S
Does *the draft* disturb you?

  S
It does.

[1] For this simplification of Otto Jesperson's analysis of functions, I am especially indebted to George A. Gullette and James M. McCrimmon, *Writing Effectively* (New York: Holt, Rinehart and Winston, 1941).

417

The subject normally precedes the verb in statements and exclamations, and normally follows the verb or splits a verb phrase in questions.

b. *Verb:* A word or word-group that tells what the subject does or is, or what is done to it. (*Test:* What does the subject *do? Is* it something? *Is* something *done to* it?)

    S   V

John *teaches.*

    V   S   V

Does John *teach?*

        S   V

The squirrel in the tree *jabbered.*

        S V

The noise *is* incessant.

    S   V

It *becomes* worse by the minute.

            S   V

Much fruitless thought *has been expended* on the nature of the verb.

    V

Sit down.

The verb normally follows the subject in statements, and precedes the subject or straddles it in questions. In requests or commands (imperatives) the subject normally does not appear at all.

c. *Complement:* A word or word-group that completes an otherwise incomplete idea initiated by a verb, a verbal, or a preposition.

Complements are restatements of the subject, or modifiers of the subject, or objects. (*Test:* The subject acts on *whom* or *what?* The subject is *what?* Something is IN, ON, UNDER *what?*)

        S   V   C

Dr. Reesing teaches *"The Age of Milton."*

       S   V   C

"The Age of Milton" is *a senior course*.

       S   V   C   C

The course is *a requirement* FOR *English majors*.

              C   V   C

In studying *Milton,* read *the text* carefully.

    (*Studying,* as a verbal, may itself require a complement.)

    S V   C

Muriel is IN *the library*.

    S   C V   C

Relaxing IN the *library* is *popular*.

        V   C   C   C

Please give *me your name and address*.

      S   V   C   C

Dr. Reesing is *chairman* OF *the department*.

The complement normally follows the verb, verbal, or preposition.

1) COMPLEMENTS MAY RESTATE THE SUBJECT

Subjective complements follow forms of the verb *to be* and a few other "linking verbs," like *to become,* which assert conditions or states of being; subjective complements tell what the subject is.

      S   LV   C

Dr. Reesing is *chairman* of the department.

    S LV   C

Honesty is the best *policy*.

       S LV   C

The best policy is *honesty*.

2) COMPLEMENTS MAY MODIFY THE SUBJECT

Predicate adjectives also follow *to be* or other linking verbs.

    S LV C(M)
Grass is *green.*

    S   LV   C(M)
Relaxing becomes *habitual.*

    S LV C(M)
Relaxing is *pleasant.*

3) MOST COMPLEMENTS ARE OBJECTS

They follow verbs of action in the common actor-action-goal pattern of the sentence. There are three types of these.

           V   C
DIRECT OBJECT: The storm destroyed the *village.*

        V   C
Dr. Reesing teaches *"The Age of Milton."*

        V C   C
INDIRECT OBJECT: Give *me* the *book. (Book* is the Direct Object. Such a sentence always has two objects; the Indirect Object precedes the Direct Object; the two complements name different things.)

      C   C
Tell the *dean* the *truth.*

               S   C   C
OBJECTIVE COMPLEMENT: The fraternity elected *Richard president.* (*Richard* is the Direct Object. Such a sentence always has two objects; the Direct Object precedes the Objective Complement, and the two complements name the same thing.)

4) OBJECTS OF PREPOSITIONS OR OF VERBALS

Complements may be the headwords in prepositional phrases (see pages 461–462), or they may complete verbals instead of verbs (see pages 449–453). Both are *objects.*

        C
IN the *room . . .*

C

TO the *barricades!*

C

FLYING an *airplane* . . .

C

TO TELL the *truth* . . .

        C   **C**

I want you TO TELL *me* the *truth.* (The phrase *you to tell me the truth* is direct object of *want.*)

Subjects, verbs, and **complements** are the most important elements of the sentence. Everything else is related to them in one way or another.

EXERCISE

In the spaces to the left, indicate the function of each italicized element. Use the symbols S for subject, V for verb, and C for complement.

_____ 1. Some women *should be struck* regularly, like gongs.

_____ 2. I never struck a *woman,* dear, for sport.

_____ 3. Sentences 1 and 2 are *quotations* which do not necessarily disagree.

_____ 4. Great minds often *flock* together.

_____ 5. *Flying an airplane* is more exciting than driving a slow car.

_____ 6. *Whoever attempts to fly an airplane,* however, should have had some experience.

_____ 7. In an emergency, inexperienced people *have* sometimes *managed to fly.*

_____ 8. As Icarus found, though, the novice is seldom *successful.*

_____ 9. Give *Icarus* credit for trying.

_____10. The credit given *him* might take the form of a commemorative wreath.

d. *Modifier:* A word or word-group that describes or limits, or qualifies, or identifies some other element, making it more specific.

Modifiers may affect subjects, verbs, complements, other modifiers, or even whole predications. (*Test:* Does an element serve to make some other element more specific?)

M(C)

Andrea was *absent.* (Describes Andrea, and also completes the incomplete verb-idea.)

M   **M**

The *absent* Andrea slept *late.* (*Absent* describes Andrea; *late* tells how she slept.)

M M   **M**

The old man *in the corner* . . . . (Tell which man, describes and identifies.)

M   **M**   **M**

Jack's car was damaged *very badly.* (*Jack's* identifies the car; *badly* qualifies *was damaged,* and *very* qualifies *badly.*)

M

If it does not rain soon, the crops will be ruined. (Qualifies the whole main predication.)

The positions of modifiers are sometimes fixed and sometimes flexible. We shall examine that problem as we consider types of modifiers later. Notice, at the moment, that they tend to stand as near as possible to the elements they modify.

e. *Connective:* A word or word-group whose chief function is to tie parts of the sentence together, indicating subordination or coordination between the parts, reducing a main element to a modifier, or doing something similar.

In addition to this grammatical information, they convey various ideas of relationship: *in* is not *under; and* is not *but; instead of* is not *in addition to.* They are very important in enabling us to express complicated ideas. (*Test:* Does the word or word-group work chiefly to show connections between major elements in the sentence?)

Con

The old man *in* the corner . . . (Makes *corner* a modifier of *man.*)

Con

In spite of his laziness, he accomplished a good deal. (Ties *laziness* to the main idea and sets up the conditions under which he worked.)

     Con   **Con**   **Con**

Writing *and* speaking have much *in* common, *but* are not identical.

  Con   **Con**

Because they are similar, one cannot always test the clarity *of* written

   Con   **Con**   **Con**

English *by* ear alone, *since* what is clear *when* it is spoken may not

   Con

be clear *when* it is read.

Connectives usually begin the word-groups to which they belong, and most of the time they stand between their word-groups and the sentence elements to which their word-groups are connected.

f. *Absolute:* **A word or word-group included in the sentence but having no grammatical effect on it.**

Terms of address, grunts and groans, digressive comments, and so on are all absolutes. (*Test:* Does the element in any way change the grammatical structure of the rest of the sentence?)

   A

Dean Linton, what should be done with a student who is absent all the time? (The absolute aims the sentence at its target, but has no grammatical effect.)

       A

The answer, *of course,* is that such a student should fail. (*Of course* comments on the obviousness of the idea, but it does nothing else.)

     A

An alert student—*but I do mean "alert"*—can learn enough grammar to correct his bad habits. (The digression comments on the main idea and emphasizes part of it, but does nothing else.)

A

There is, *alas*, not much hope for an inert student. (Just a groan.)

Absolutes may appear anywhere in the sentence. Notice that they are always set off from the rest of the sentence by commas.

In summary, except for the expletives *it* and *there*, all elements in an English sentence function in one (occasionally two) of these six ways: as Subjects, Verbs, Complements, Modifiers, Connectives, or Absolutes. So do the *separable* elements within word-groups. Once we realize that fact and learn to identify these six functions, the patterns of English become relatively easy to understand.

EXERCISES

A. In the following sentences, underline all single-word modifiers, connectives, and absolutes. Above each, identify the function by the symbols M, Con, or A.

1. These ashtrays do not always prevent cigarettes from rolling off and burning the table.

2. Regardless of how one feels in winter, in summer no one objects to an invasion of a polar-Canadian air mass.

3. Bright, clear, invigorating days, with low humidity and low temperatures, are Canada's gift to the United States.

4. When they come, muggy air from the Gulf of Mexico is pushed back toward the Gulf.

5. I hope, of course, that Canadians do not begrudge us the temporary use of their air.

6. Oh, let us rejoice in the existence of that long, undefended border between the two nations.

7. The liberal arts and the sciences have been called two separate cultures, because the specialists in one often know too little about the other.

8. In the twentieth century—the age of space and plastics—can anyone be considered liberally educated if he knows nothing about science?

9. Can any scientist be considered educated at all if he knows nothing of those liberal arts by which man has always developed his most human, or humane, potentialities?

10. If ever there really are two separate cultures, Lord Snow and Mr. Leavis, they both will be destroyed.

B. By means of the symbols S, V, C, M, Con, A, analyze the function performed by each word in the following sentences.

        S   V M C Con M   C   Con V Con M   C
EXAMPLE: John hit the ball over the fence and ran to first base.

1. Swimming in the ocean is fun.

2. I dislike grammar.

3. The clock struck twelve.

4. Snodgrass is the treasurer of the club.

5. Oh, how I hate arising in the morning!

6. Shannon and I worked on the magazine.

THE BASIC SENTENCE PATTERNS

We have sketched the nature of sentence elements and the ways in which those elements can function. Now we need to look briefly at the basic patterns of English sentences. Subjects, verbs, and complements are relatively limited in the positions they may assume, because *word order* is one of the most important grammatical devices in modern written English. In Anglo-Saxon days, when form changes were elaborate, word order was less important, and English, rather like Latin, could indicate function by the forms of the major words. But now we have few form changes (just enough, in fact, to cause us trouble occasionally). We depend chiefly instead on word order and function words to mark grammatical function. Consequently, although variety of pattern is still possible, there are basic patterns we normally use. If you know them, they can often help you to identify subjects, verbs, and complements that are otherwise obscure.

All sentences do one of four things: make statements, ask questions, issue commands or requests, or utter exclamations. For the first two, there are eight common structural patterns, for the third there are six, and for the fourth there are three. Any of them may admit additional elements, such as modifiers, but the elements listed are essential to the pattern.

Statements—active

1. S   V—Mortals die.
2. S   LV   M—Washington is beautiful.
3. S   LV   C$^{(SC)}$—Deans are administrators.
4. S   V   C$^{(DO)}$—Deans counsel students.
5. S   V   C$^{(ID)}$ C$^{(DO)}$—Addison gave Ann a kitten.
6. S   V   C$^{(DO)}$ C$^{(OC)}$—We made Eisenhower President.
7. It is   M   S(word-group)—It is unlikely *that he will appear.*
8. There   LV   S   M—There are difficulties here.

Questions—active

Patterns 1 through 6:   S   V+?   V   S+?   V   S   V+?

1. Mortals die?
2. Is Washington beautiful?
3. Are deans administrators?
4. Do deans counsel students?
5. Did Addison give Ann a kitten?
6. Did we make Eisenhower President?

Pattern 7: Is it   M   S?—Is it unlikely that he will appear?
Pattern 8: LV   there   S   M?—Are there difficulties here?

Commands and requests

Patterns 1 through 6: The S disappears from the statement pattern. Only *second-person* statements with some form of future verbs can be transformed into requests.

Statement: S   V + ___ You will report for induction.
Command: V + ___ Report for induction.
Statement: S   V + ___ You will send me the free booklet.
Request: V + ___ Send me the free booklet.

Patterns 7 and 8 do not occur.

Exclamations

1. *How* or *what*   S   V ___ How it rains.
2. *How* or *what*   C   S   V ___ What a joke it was.
3. *How*   M   S   V ___ How green the grass is.
   (Stress and pitch signals may lend other patterns exclamatory
   force in spoken English. An exclamation point may do the same
   in writing.)

PARTS OF SPEECH AND FUNCTIONS

The most familiar, but in some ways the least satisfactory
method of classifying sentence elements is as "parts of speech."
Because the established terms are familiar and convenient, everyone
who discusses English grammar uses them in some degree; consequently it is essential to know them. But it is also important to realize that the system is not foolproof. First, it is not a system of logical
classification in which one and only one set of criteria is applied
throughout. (Of the customary eight parts of speech, some are
classified by meaning, some by function, and some by position in
the sentence.) Second, it is a system designed to describe Classical
Latin and not Modern English, and although the two languages are
related, the system does not fit English perfectly. Third, the same
word in English may function in several different ways, so that a
word may be a subject in one sentence, a verb in another, and a
modifier in a third, or even belong to one class by form but another
by function, like possessive pronouns. We shall try to solve these
problems by classifying words according to their function in a given
sentence. We shall try to define the parts of speech by their most
common meanings, their forms, and their characteristic functions.

We usually identify eight parts of speech: *nouns, pronouns,
verbs, adjectives, adverbs, prepositions, conjunctions,* and *interjections.* In addition to these, there are the verbals, which it is convenient to consider separately.

427

4. NOUNS

a. Definition

Nouns are names, and often names are nouns. They name people, places, things, qualities, and concepts: *Jack, Kankakee, desk, warmth, honesty*. Here we classify by meaning.

Nouns have characteristic forms. They usually may be either singular or plural: *boy-boys, ox-oxen, witch-witches* (but *mush, news* have only one form). They may have a possessive form: *boy's, ox's, witch's-witches'*. They may be preceded by *a, an,* or *the*.

Nouns function as Subjects, as Complements, and sometimes as Modifiers.

>   **S**   **C**
> The *snow* drifted across the *roads*.

>   **M**   **S**
> The *mountain passes* were choked.

>   **C**   **S**
> In *time,* all *traffic* stopped.

>   **M**   **S**
> The *weatherman's prediction* was fulfilled.

Or nouns may be appositives to Subjects or Complements, renaming the idea more specifically and functioning the same way.

>   **S**   **S**
> His *sister, Mary,* was here. (*Mary* is an appositive, in apposition to *sister*.)

As Subjects or Complements, the position of nouns is determined by the basic sentence patterns. As Modifiers, they precede the words they modify, usually other nouns.

b. Classes

From different points of view, nouns may be classified in several ways. There are *common nouns* and *proper nouns:* the first name groups of things; the second name individuals. There are *abstract nouns* and *concrete nouns;* the first name intangible concepts; the second name tangible things. There are *general nouns* and *specific nouns:* the first name classes; the second, units within those classes—and a noun may be general in respect to some other noun and specific in respect to a third noun. Notice that these three classifications overlap. Every noun may be classified in all three ways. *Harry,* for example, is at once a proper noun, a concrete noun, and a specific noun. *Virtue* is common, abstract, and general.

COMMON NOUNS: desk, virtue, boy, copper
PROPER NOUNS: Tom, Dick, Harry, the White House
ABSTRACT NOUNS: virtue, truth, beauty
CONCRETE NOUNS: desk, boy, Harry, the White House
GENERAL NOUNS: vegetable, plant, organism (*Each of those is more general, dealing with a larger class, than the one before it.*)
SPECIFIC NOUNS: tree, oak tree, the Treaty Oak (*Each of those is more specific, dealing more nearly with a unit, than the one before it.* Tree *is specific in relation to the general noun* plant, *above.*)

Nouns offer very little trouble, except for the difficulty of realizing that an intangible abstraction, like *truth,* is a thing, and that its name consequently is a noun. When a word functions as a noun, that is, as Subject or Complement, you may call it a noun (or a substantive). Even words which normally function in other ways may be called nouns (or substantives) when they function as Subjects or Complements; or they may be classified by form according to their normal use. Either way, you may get into an argument.

Many are called; *few* are chosen.

You may say that *many* and *few* are Subjects and so are nouns; or you may say that what is meant is *many men, few men,* that the true subjects are "understood," and that *many* and *few* are adjectives and Modifiers. In either event, you should be prepared to defend your decision against disagreement.

EXERCISE

Underline the nouns in the following sentences and identify the function of each as Subject or Complement.

1. Many freshmen are confused by terms they hear during the first semester in college.

2. A few definitions of common words might be useful.

3. A school that is called Somewhere or Other College is one providing courses and awarding degrees in the liberal arts, and usually the sciences, at the bachelor's level.

4. Within a university, a "college" is one of a group of associated academic faculties; the "university" itself is the resulting association, the unity of diverse parts.

5. A "school" is a professional college, usually awarding advanced degrees.

6. A "division" may be a part of a college, or it may be a separate administrative unit; concerned with academic work, it nevertheless does not usually award degrees.

7. Schools and colleges have self-governing faculties under the direction of a dean, and an independent college also has a president, as does a university.

8. Departments are concerned with particular academic disciplines—like English, history, foreign languages, philosophy, chemistry—and the courses and major curricula in those disciplines, and are administered by heads, or chairmen.

9. Academic ranks commonly are instructor, assistant professor, associate professor, and professor.

10. Outside the academic group are numerous administrative officers, like the Director of Admissions, the Registrar, the Comptroller, the Bursar, the Business Manager, and all the others needed to keep house.

5. PRONOUNS

a. Definition

Pronouns are words that substitute for nouns, allowing us to avoid awkward repetition. Whatever meaning they have they take from the context. (See Chapter 12, **Ref.**)

b. Classes

There are eight classes of pronouns.

PERSONAL: I, you, he, they, and so on
RELATIVE: who, which, that, what (= that which)
DEMONSTRATIVE: this, that, these, those
INTERROGATIVE: who, which, what, and so on

REFLEXIVE: myself, himself, themselves, and so on
INDEFINITE: one, you, they, it, everyone, and so on
INTENSIVE: myself, yourself, and so on
RECIPROCAL: each other, one another

The personal pronouns have different forms for case, person, number, and gender, and so do the reflexives, the indefinites, and the intensives, all of which resemble the personals. The relative *who, whose, whom* show changes for case.

Like nouns, personal, relative, and indefinite pronouns may function as Subjects, as Complements, or (in the possessive case only) as Modifiers. Interrogative pronouns function as Subjects. Reciprocal pronouns function as Complements. The rest function as Modifiers. Except for the relatives, which begin their word-groups, and the intensives (*I* MYSELF), pronouns take the same functional positions as nouns in the basic sentence pattern.

c. Troublesome Relatives

Fortunately, only the relative pronouns cause very much trouble. They are very common, appearing in most noun and adjective clauses, but students often do not recognize the relatives as pronouns in the way they readily recognize the personals as pronouns. Much of the difficulty some students have with clauses would disappear if they remembered that *who, which,* and *that* (and such compounds as *whoever*) are pronouns and may be Subjects or Complements in subordinate clauses.

d. *Who, Which, That*

Minor trouble with relative pronouns also occurs in choosing between *who, which,* and *that. Who* is used only to refer to persons, *which* to refer to nonpersons, and *that* to refer to either. Use: The person *who,* the thing *which,* the persons or things *that. That* is never used now with nonrestrictive adjective clauses. (See pages 490–492.)

EXERCISE

Underline the pronouns in the following passage and identify the function of each as Subject, Complement, or Modifier.

The wolf trotted into his den and flopped down in his favorite chair. (It was not a very comfortable chair, but it was one he liked, which is all that matters.) "I met the silliest girl today," he remarked to his wife as she brought him his pipe and slippers. "She was on foot, but was wearing a riding hood, for one thing. It was red, and not very appropriate for such a green child—." (His wife sneered at this pun, but he ignored her.) "She stopped me in the woods and carried on a long, pointless conversation about the contents of a basket which she was carrying. And then later I ran onto her again, and—." He paused to be sure he was getting his wife's full attention. "Here's the payoff, my dear. She decided I was her grandmother!" He smiled reminiscently and gently smacked his lips. "However," he added, "silly as she was, I rather liked her. She was a good girl."

e. Case

Case is the property of nouns and pronouns which shows by changes in the form of the words whether they are functioning as Subjects (subjective, or nominative, case), as Complements (objective, or accusative, case), or as Modifiers (possessive, or genitive, case).

For Modern English nouns, word order (position in the sentence) has largely replaced changes in form to indicate function. We place Subjects first, before the verb, and place Complements after the verb or the preposition they are completing; the same form of the noun is used for both functions. Possessives are formed by adding an apostrophe and usually an *s* to the common case forms. The only real difficulty with case in nouns, consequently, comes in the formation of the possessive case. For a discussion of that problem, see pages 522–523.

The case of pronouns causes more trouble. We use pronouns oftener than we do nouns, and consequently have retained a fuller declension for case, especially with the personal pronouns, which still have three case forms.

> SUBJECTIVE CASE (pronoun functioning as Subject or subjective Complement):
>> I—we
>> you—you
>> he, she, it—they
> POSSESSIVE CASE (pronoun functioning as Modifier):
>> my, mine—our, ours

your, yours—your, yours
his, her, hers, its—their, theirs

(Where possessive forms occur in pairs, as in *my, mine,* the first member is used when the pronominal adjective precedes the noun it modifies: *my, our, your, her,* or *their* book. The second member of each pair is used as a predicate adjective or as the object of the preposition in a phrasal possessive: This book is *mine, ours, yours, hers,* or *theirs.* He is a friend of *mine, ours, yours, hers,* or *theirs.*)

OBJECTIVE CASE (pronoun functioning as Complement):
me—us
you—you
him, her, it—them

In spite of the relatively full declension of the personal pronouns, they ordinarily cause little difficulty. But there are at least six fairly common situations which students do find confusing.

1) SUBJECTIVE COMPLEMENTS

Use the *subjective* case for a subjective Complement.

It is *I*. This is *he*.

This usage has all but vanished from conversational English. Even well-educated speakers commonly *say* "It is me" in ordinary conversation. But in written English, except that which is imitating speech, as in dialogue, you are expected to use the subjective case for a complement following the verbs of being, the "linking verbs." (See pages 439–440.)

2) WORDS IN PAIRS

When words are used in pairs, use the case demanded by the function of the pronoun.

This is between *you* and *me*. Give it to John and *me*.
The class nominated *her* and *me* to represent it.
She and *I* will be there.
(*If such sentences seem awkward, they may always be rephrased to avoid the construction, as, She and I were nominated to represent the class. She will be there, and so will I.*)
We Americans are proud of our country.

Europe sometimes distrusts *us* Americans.
Let *us, you* and *me,* go. Let's *you* and *me* go.

In all such sentences, the function can be seen more readily if the pronoun is used alone. No one would say, "This is between I," "Me will be there," "Give it to he," or "Give it to I," "The class nominated I," "Us are proud," "Europe distrusts we," or "Let I go." (The mere existence of another word functioning in the same way should not be allowed to obscure the function of either member of a pair.)

3) AFTER *than* OR *as*

Normally, use the *subjective* case after *than* or *as.*

He is as tall as *I.* She is smaller than *I.*

Such constructions are considered to be parts of clauses the rest of which is merely "understood," as if you had said, for example, "He is as tall as *I* (am tall)." If the full clause, however, would demand the objective case, it should be employed.

I like her better than (I like) *him.*

4) MODIFYING GERUNDS

If the pronoun modifies a gerund, use the *possessive* case.

Imagine *his* singing being so pleasant. (*Gerunds are verbal nouns. See page 449. It is the singing that is to be imagined; the pronoun merely modifies it. With nouns before gerunds the objective case is often used.*)

5) SUBJECT OF INFINITIVE

Use the *objective* case for the subject of an infinitive. (See pages 449, 451, 464.)

They thought *him* to be the greatest general in the war.
I want *them* to go.

6) WITH THE INFINITIVE *to be*

The infinitive *to be* is followed by the same case as the case that precedes it.

They thought *him* to be *me.*
I was thought to be *he.*

f. *Who* and *Whom*

The relative or interrogative pronoun *who* probably causes more trouble with case than all the other pronouns put together. With nouns, position in the sentence has become relatively fixed, and we can tell the function of a noun by its position: If a noun comes before the verb, it is usually subject; after, it is usually object. But *who,* like all relatives, begins its clause; it may appear first in a sentence or a clause and still be an object of a verb or of a preposition. Or it may actually be the subject in its own clause and yet seem to be an object of a preceding verb or preposition that really has nothing to do with it. We are never quite sure when we should use *who,* and when we should use *whom.* In conversation, the problem does not worry us; most *speakers* say *who* when the pronoun comes at the beginning of the sentence, regardless of its function, as in, "Who did you invite?" "Who did you give it to?" But the educated *writer* still carefully distinguishes between the subjective case and the objective case, according to the *function of the pronoun in its own clause.* In written English, we need to be precise.

If you can identify the verb, the problem is not hard to solve. Ask Who? or What? before the verb; the answer will be the subject. If there is no other substantive as subject, use *who.* If there is some other subject, the relative must be a complement; use *whom.*

Fortunately, the difficulty occurs in relatively few constructions.

1) SUBJECT IN A CLAUSE

Use *who* when the pronoun is *subject* in its own clause.

He spoke to the man *who* was here yesterday.
Who told you that?

Do not allow a parenthetical clause coming between *who* and its verb to obscure the function of *who* as subject.

Who do you think will win? (*If the sentence were merely Who will win? there would be no confusion. The presence of a parenthetical clause does not affect the main clause.*)
He spoke to the man *who* (I thought) was here yesterday.

When the relative pronoun (usually *whoever, whichever,* and so on) is *subject* of a noun clause, the *subjective* case is used, regardless of the function of the clause as a whole.

435

The prize will be given to *whoever* calls the station first. (*Whoever is the subject of* calls. *It is the whole clause which is the object of the preposition* to.)

2) OBJECT OF A VERB OR VERBAL

Use *whom* when the pronoun is *object* of a verb or of a verbal.

Whom did you invite? (*Did invite is the verb, and* you *is its subject. The pronoun is object of the verb and in the* objective *case.*)
Tell me *whom* you really came to see. (*Cf.* You came to see *him.*)

3) OBJECT OF A PREPOSITION

Use *whom* when the pronoun is *object* of a preposition.

Whom did you give it to? (*A more formal sentence would be, "To whom did you give it?" Such a sentence is sometimes too formal for the prevailing tone of a paper, and seems stiff and pedantic. But the* objective *case would be used for the relative pronoun in either sentence.*)

g. Whose

When the pronoun *who* is used as a possessive Modifier, the form is *whose.*

Whose books are these?

Do not confuse *whose,* the possessive pronoun, with *who's,* the contraction for *who is.* In informal writing, *whose* is sometimes used as a possessive form for *which,* in place of the formal *of which.* In college writing, it is perhaps best to follow the formal usage.

Remember: The case of a pronoun is always determined by *its function in its own clause.* If the relative pronoun is Subject in its own clause, use the subjective *who;* if it is a Complement in its own clause, use the objective *whom.*

h. Person, Number, Gender

These three aspects of nouns and pronouns cause little trouble except as problems in pronoun agreement. See Chapter 12, **PAgr,** for a discussion.

EXERCISE

In each of the following sentences, select the form which would be used in formal writing. Identify the function of each pronoun.

1. (We, us) students of grammar lead difficult lives.

2. I think (we, us) should study harder.

3. No matter how popular Professor Snodgrass is with the rest of the class, I like Professor Highfill better than (he, him).

4. (Who, whom) do you suppose I saw today?

5. (Who, whom) do you suppose was at the airport when I landed?

6. Although he is big, he is very graceful, and I admire (his, him) dancing.

7. (His, him) dancing is a pleasure to watch.

8. He is a man (whose, who's) integrity is unquestioned.

9. Kenney sent his best regards to Marjorie and (I, me).

10. You ask for the best candidate, and that is (I, me).

11. This is no time for (he, him) to be loafing.

12. I am sorry, but I cannot tell you (who, whom) the winner is.

13. It was (they, them) who called on us yesterday.

14. As delegates, the girls elected Mary, Martha, and (I, me).

15. Mary and Martha are not as wise as (I, me).

6. VERBS

a. Definition

The verb is the heart of the sentence. There is always a verb expressed in a full sentence, and implied in any minor sentence in which it is not explicit. Once you have found the verb, the rest of the sentence can be worked out easily.

Verbs are not easy to define. In meaning, they name actions, like *run, walk, sleep;* or "states of being," like *is, become.* They tell what the subject does or is, or what is done to it.

In form they are clearer. Verbs are words or (more often) word-groups with such forms as *to be, ran, walked, walking, to write, written, sings, to shout.* (A few auxiliary verbs—*can, must, shall,* and the like—lack some of these forms.)

In function, true verbs function only as Verbs. We shall presently need to distinguish verbs from verbals, but at the moment it is enough to know that true verbs may be inflected to show differences in person and number; verbals may not.

The position of verbs is determined by the basic sentence patterns.

V

The snow *drifted* across the roads.

V

The mountain passes *were choked.*

V

Traffic *is going to be* delayed a long time.

V

That *is* too bad.

Verbs have many forms, to indicate *number* (one or more than one), *tense* (time in relation to the writer's point of view), *mood* (*indicative,* stating fact; *subjunctive,* expressing doubt; or *imperative,* giving a command), and *voice* (*active,* with the subject doing the acting; *passive,* with the subject being acted upon). And there are related forms which are not true "finite" verbs at all, but *verbals,* functioning not as Verbs, but as nouns, adjectives, or adverbs, as Subjects, Complements, or Modifiers.

Each of these aspects of verbs causes trouble, and we must accordingly consider each in turn. For the verb is in a very true sense the heart of the sentence. Once you understand verbs, finding the Subjects, the Complements, and the Modifiers, and identifying clauses, will be relatively easy.

First, we will consider the finite verbs, the forms which function as Verbs in asserting action, condition, or state of being of the subject in a clause or a sentence. Then we will consider the infinite, unlimited forms, the troublesome verbals, which function as nouns, adjectives, or adverbs, that is, as Subjects, Complements, or Modifiers.

b. Kinds

There are three kinds of finite verbs: *transitive* verbs; *intransitive* verbs; and *linking,* or *copulative,* verbs.

1) TRANSITIVE

Transitive verbs name and assert the presence of an action and require an object which receives the action. The action of the verb is "carried across" to the object. We cannot, for example, say merely, "He installed." We must tell what or whom he installed, as in "He installed the furnace," or "He installed the new chairman in his office." When any verb has an object as a Complement, we call it a *transitive* verb.

2) INTRANSITIVE

Intransitive verbs are *not* transitive. They do not, that is to say, require an object as a Complement. They express ideas which are complete in themselves, so that we may have a sentence with no more to it than Subject and Verb alone: "Jesus wept." Intransitive verbs may be modified by adverbs, and they often are; but they do not take Complements. Some verbs, *rise* for example, are always intransitive. We do not say, "I rise the flag," or that anybody "rises" anything.

It should be noted that many verbs may be either transitive or intransitive, depending on the idea being expressed. Every sentence must be analyzed according to the way the words function in that sentence. We can, for example, say, "Jesus wept tears of compassion." In that sentence, *wept* is transitive precisely because it has an object, *tears.*

According to the use of the verb in the given sentence, a verb which requires an object as Complement is *transitive;* one which does not require an object is *intransitive.*

3) LINKING

Linking verbs (also called copulative verbs, "coupling" verbs, or copulas) might be considered a form of intransitive verbs. They express no action, and so cannot pass action on to a receiving object.

But they do require a Complement. They are the verbs of condition or states of being, such as, principally, *be* in all its forms, and sometimes *appear, become, feel, look, seem, smell, sound, taste,* and some others, when these verbs express no idea of action. The Complement that linking verbs require is either a substantive which renames the subject (a predicate noun or predicate pronoun, word or word-group, that is, a subjective Complement), or an adjective which modifies the subject, a predicate adjective. (*To be,* especially, is occasionally completed by a predicate adverb.)

> It is I. (It *and* I *are the same person.*)
> George VI was King of England. (George VI *and* King *are the same person.*)
> She is charming. (Charming *modifies* she.)
> The roast smells good. (Good *modifies* roast.)
> I feel fine. (Fine *modifies* I.)
> John is here. (Here *completes the otherwise incomplete verb-idea and modifies* is.)

In the examples, these linking verbs express no action; they are, except in the last example, essentially equals-marks. (It = I. The roast = good.) If you remember that linking verbs are usually little more than equals-marks, you will not be distressed by the fact that the same verbs used in another way may express more active ideas. When we say, "The velvet feels soft," we are using *feels* as a linking verb. When we say, "My fingers feel the velvet," we have a transitive verb taking an object.

Linking verbs, then, take no objects because they express no action. They are rarely modified by adverbs, because adverbs customarily qualify or describe or limit actions. But linking verbs do require subjective Complements or predicate adjectives. The subjective Complement renames the subject; the predicate adjective modifies the subject.

Verbs, true verbs, whether transitive, intransitive, or linking, function in only one way, as Verbs. They assert that the subject is acting or is existing in a certain way. They are "finite." That is, they are limited to specific person and number. (If that term "finite verb" has puzzled you, remember that it means any verb functioning as a Verb.)

EXERCISE

Underline the finite verbs in the following sentences. Identify each as transitive, intransitive, or linking. Identify the objects of the transitive verbs and the subjective complements or predicate adjectives completing the copulas.

1. Old MacDonald had a farm and assorted livestock, and on top of that had to plow, plant, and harvest crops.

2. MacDonald must have expended a tremendous amount of energy.

3. Not everything is said in a song that could be said.

4. Every English sentence has a verb, whether the verb-idea is important or not.

5. We use the expletives (*it is,* or *there is* or *are*) when the verb-idea is of very minor importance, because the expletive pattern throws strong emphasis on the subject.

6. Avoid the expletive pattern, therefore, whenever a stronger verb would be useful.

7. A sudden burst of rain drenched the Saturday shoppers.

8. I have sat patiently for an hour, but I would like to know whether or not the doctor is really in the office.

9. Doctors know that time cures many illnesses, so they give patients time to be sure they are really sick.

10. One patient waited so long that he found an item for rent included in the doctor's bill.

c. Number

English recognizes two numbers: *singular,* when only one is involved; *plural,* when two or more are involved.

The chief trouble that occurs in the number of verbs arises from the fact that an *s* must be added to the stem of the verb to form the third person *singular,* present indicative.

I think	I run	I say
You think	You run	You say
He (or John) thinks	He (or John) runs	He (or John) says

Since in nouns an *s* indicates plural, some students have unnecessary trouble with verb agreement (see pages 396–398) because they fail to remember that an *s* ending in a verb is a singular ending. And since all nouns including noun phrases and clauses are third person, as well as the third person pronouns, that confusion can be serious.

d. Tense

Tense, with either verbs or verbals, means *time,* the time of the action or state asserted by the verb in relation to the time point of view of the speaker or writer.

1) THE SIX BASIC TENSES

It is usually said that English verbs have six tenses, formed by combining the "principal parts"—the infinitive, the past tense, and the participles: *begin, began, begun, beginning; wait, waited, waited, waiting*—according to systematic patterns. These key tenses are the *present,* now; *past,* a single time before now; *present perfect,* a recently completed action or sustained action begun in the past and carried up to the present; *past perfect,* sustained action begun and ended in the past: *future,* single action later than the present; and *future perfect,* sustained action later than the present. (*Perfect* means "completed," "perfected.")

On that simplified basis, our verb conjugations may be illustrated by following an irregular verb, first person singular, through its tense forms in the indicative mood.

> PRESENT: I begin. (*Time, now.*)
> PRESENT PERFECT: I have begun. (*Time, before but leading up to now.*)
> PAST: I began. (*Time, before now.*)
> PAST PERFECT: I had begun. (*Time, before some past time.*)
> FUTURE: I shall (will) begin. (*Time, after now.*)
> FUTURE PERFECT: I shall (will) have begun. (*Time, before some future time. The terminal future point is normally indicated by an adverbial modifier.*)

442

The same tense relation may be seen graphically.

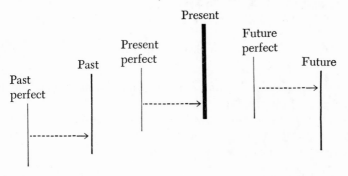

2) OTHER TENSE FORMS

Actually, English verbs are far more flexible than that conventional classification suggests. We can and do express all sorts of time and mood relations beyond that simple six-tense system by varying our verb forms. This convenient flexibility arises from the way our verbs are constructed: We name the action we have in mind by the last member of the verb phrase and modify our tense and mood concept by combining "auxiliary" verbs or prepositional adverbs or adverbial phrases in varying patterns with that naming form.

In analyzing sentences, therefore, we must almost of necessity consider as a unit the whole verb-group. Unless you are trying specifically to identify the elements of such a verb phrase, call the entire unit a verb, without worrying about the number of words that may be involved. To appreciate the complex tense and mood concepts that English can express and to understand the use of verb phrases as units, consider the following:

> PRESENT: I *run*. (*But we seldom use this simple present to express present action. The two following are more common.*)
> I *am running*. (*Called the "progressive present."*)
> I *do run*. (*Called the "emphatic present."*)
> FUTURE (with modal overtones): I *shall run* in the 440 in next week's meet.
> I *am going to run* in the 440.
> I *run* in the 440 in every track meet.

443

I *should run* in the 440, but I *would* rather *run* in the 220.
I *may run* in both the 440 and the 220.
I *plan to run* in the 440.
I *am to run* in the 440.
The coach wants me to change, but I *am going to go on running* in the 440.

And we use *can, could, did, have, had, might, must,* and *ought* as auxiliaries, too.

These complexities naturally are very confusing to foreign students of the language, but fortunately only a few forms cause the native speaker and writer any trouble.

e. Tense Problems

1) PAST FOR PAST PARTICIPLE

The educated dialect makes distinctions between the past tense and the past participle that some nonstandard dialects do not. Variations in the pattern grate on the educated ear. The trouble comes with the use of past tense forms with auxiliaries for other than simple past tenses, or the past participle as past tense. The problem occurs only with irregular, "strong" verbs, since regular verbs have identical past tense forms and combining forms.

I *went;* but I *have* or *had* or *am* or *was* or *shall be gone*
I *saw;* I *have,* etc., *seen*
I *did;* I *have,* etc., *done*

NEVER: *I have did,* or *I done; I have saw,* or *I seen.* Of the "principal parts" of a verb, the past tense form is used *only* for the past tense. Misuse of the past tense form with auxiliaries is the most obvious indication of uneducated speech or writing. Except in dialogue representing uneducated speakers, it has no place in college writing, and few instructors can bring themselves to pass a theme in which the slip occurs.

2) *Of* FOR *have*

A second glaring error is the use of *of* as if it were an auxiliary verb. In speaking, we often slur *have* in an unstressed position so that it sounds like *of.* But in writing we must use the verb. In dialogue, to reproduce the sound, use the contraction *'ve.*

WRONG: I would *of* come if I had known.
CORRECT: I would *have* come if I had known.
INFORMAL DIALOGUE: I would've come if I'd known.

3) *Shall* AND *will*

A great deal of time is wasted worrying about *shall* and *will* in future and future perfect tenses. British and American usages differ, and neither has ever consistently followed the patterns you may have struggled with—*shall* in the first person, *will* in the rest. Although it is scarcely worth much thought, some readers will worry about it, especially in formal writing. The same rules are said to apply to *should* and *would*. Actually, *should* and *would* often still carry their Old English meanings of obligation and willingness, respectively, with the result that the minute you begin to apply "rules" to them, you are liable to write something you do not mean at all. Use whichever form seems natural. It is probably also "correct."

I should go = I ought to go, and suggests *I do not really expect to go.*
I would go = I am willing to go, but often more than suggests *I am not going.*

With *should* and *would*, relax and be natural; it is safest.

4) OVERUSE OF *would*

Compound tenses with *would* now sometimes suggest, not willingness, but past habitual action, as in, "Each summer, we would spend two months at the seashore." But avoid a *would* phrase in sentences in which the simple past or the past perfect expresses your true point of view.

This would be easy if you *examined* (not *would examine*) your point of view as writer.

5) SPECIAL USES OF THE PRESENT

Three special uses of the present tense need to be mentioned: the present tense expressing *habitual* or *characteristic action,* the present tense expressing *universal truth,* and the *historical present* in narrative.

HABITUAL ACTION

Habitual or characteristic action is often expressed by the present tense, regardless of the tenses of other verbs in the sentence.

He told the police that whenever he *comes* to town, I *call* on him.

UNIVERSAL TRUTH

Universal truth is expressed by the present tense.

He knew that five fives *are* twenty-five.
Galileo discovered that the earth *travels* around the sun.
In *David Copperfield,* Dickens *presents* a picture of his own boyhood.
Chaucer *says* that murder will out.

HISTORICAL PRESENT

The historical present uses the present tense in particularly exciting moments to make the reader feel that the action described is taking place before his eyes. Douglas Southall Freeman, for example, describing Pickett's Charge on the last day of the Battle of Gettysburg in *Lee's Lieutenants,* tells in the past tense of General Longstreet's reluctance to order the attack, of the beginning of the charge, and of the growing carnage. At the height of the advance, Freeman slips into the historical present:

> . . . On the left, where Mayo had no support, the ground was littered. Discouraged soldiers were turning back or were lying down among the dead.
> Garnett has halted to deliver his first volley. Kemper is doing the same thing. Faintly audible through the wrathful roar of a hundred Federal guns is the high quaver of the rebel yell. This time, where the smoke is swept away for a moment, the colors are higher on the hill but they are less numerous. . . .

Then as the tide rolls back, he returns to the past.

Because narrative recounts events that have already occurred, the past tense is the normal narrative tense. Unless the action is crucial, the use of the present tense in narrative suggests an uneducated speaker of the "So I says . . . , an' he says . . ." type. See Damon Runyan's short stories for a skillful use of the present tense to convey social comment about the speaker.

446

6) SEQUENCE OF TENSES

"Sequence of tenses" concerns the interrelations between the tenses of the verbs and the verbals in a sentence or a longer passage.

The tense of the verb in the first main clause governs the tenses of the other verbs and those of the verbals in a sentence. Assuming that your first main clause says exactly what you mean, it is taken as the starting point, and all other verb and verbal tenses are determined by the temporal relationships between them and the tense of the verb in the first main clause.

From one sentence to the next, keep the tenses of the verbs in the main clauses consistent. Do not illogically and unnecessarily shift from one tense to another. On the other hand, if the time relations among the things you are writing about change, you must change the tenses in main clauses accordingly.

Within a sentence, use the tenses in subordinate clauses that logically indicate the time relations to the action of the verb in the main clause. (See the tense chart, page 443.) Remember that there will often quite properly be differences between the tenses of the main clauses and those of subordinate clauses, or even between the tenses of two subordinate clauses.

> He *says* (present) that he *was* (past) there while she *was being questioned* (past passive progressive).

f. Mood

Mood (or mode) is a property of verbs which indicates the speaker's attitude toward the verbal idea, as fact or as contrary to fact, as command, as possibility, and so on. English uses the *indicative* mood of fact most of the time, but also uses the *imperative* mood for commands, expresses various modal overtones by verb phrases with *can* and *may*, *should* and *would*, and so on, and occasionally still uses the *subjunctive* mood of doubt. Only the *subjunctive* mood causes trouble, because it is rare and fading fast. We retain it in a few situations, chiefly involving the verb *to be*.

In conditions contrary to fact:

> If I *were* you . . . (which I am not).
> If it *were* true . . . (but it is not).

(Sometimes, as in the two examples following, the subjunctive seems archaic or very formal.)

> If this *be* treason . . . (but I do not think it is).
> *Were* I able . . . (but I am not able).

In parliamentary action:

> I move this *be* accepted.
> *Be* it enacted . . . .

In wishes, and after *demand, insist,* and so on:

> I wish I *were* going. I demand (or insist) that he *come*.

After *as if* or *as though:*

> He looks as if he *were* ill.
> I feel as though I *were* causing you too much trouble.

There are other moods—the potential, for example—that we express through regular forms of auxiliaries to indicate the possible, the permissible, or the obligatory. They cause us no trouble.

g. Voice

In the *active* voice, the subject does the acting or is in the condition asserted by the verb.

> He runs. He seems bored. I am giving the orders.
> We endorse these products.

In the *passive* voice, we follow a regular system in transforming the Complement of the transitive verb into the Subject, and use a verb phrase with some form of *to be* plus the past participle.

> These products are endorsed by us.
> The orders are being given by me.

The passive is used chiefly when the doer of the action is unknown or unimportant.

> A caricature of the teacher was scrawled on the blackboard.
> Cows are milked twice a day.
> The boy down the street was struck in the head by a baseball.

Use the active voice whenever possible. It is stronger and more emphatic than the passive voice, and consequently leads to more effective writing. Avoid the "weak passive."

PREFER: We use and endorse these products.

AVOID: These products are used and endorsed by us.

EXERCISE

Correct all errors in number, mood, and tense sequence in the following sentences.

1. Had I a-knowed I could've rode, I would've went; but even if I had've went, I couldn't've et nothing.
2. Aldiborontiphoscophornio, how left you Chrononhotontologos?
3. When I go to the beach, I would sit at the edge of the tide and let the water purl around me.
4. I move that Senator Snort makes the nominating speech.
5. Mabel was kissed squarely on the end of her nose by Jim, by Jove.
6. Joan liked me ever since she was a child.
7. I should be grateful if you would fill my order promptly.
8. Whoever buys the tickets numbered in the even hundreds are to receive a door prize.
9. I did not know before I read it in the paper that until last week the President had been planning to go to England when Parliament next meets.
10. Casey was struck out.

7. VERBALS

Verbals are verb forms which do not function as Verbs—or, if you prefer, verbals come from verbs, look something like verbs, and have certain verb characteristics, but are not true finite verbs; instead, they are nouns, adjectives, or adverbs which name actions, but function as Subjects, Complements, or Modifiers. Because of their verbal ancestry, however, they may have Subjects or Complements of their own, as we shall see when we consider verbal phrases.

There are three kinds of verbals: *gerunds, participles,* and *infinitives.*

a. Gerunds

Gerunds function as Subjects or Complements. They (or the first member of a word-group verbal) always end in *-ing,* and they always function as substantives, that is, as Subjects or Complements.

449

S

Swimming is good exercise.

C   C

I prefer *sitting* to *standing*.

C

He devotes his attention to *loafing*.

C

One should be thankful for *having survived* the perils of adolescence.

The only trouble with gerunds comes in distinguishing them from present participles. Remember that gerunds are verbal *nouns*. (To associate the two, remember the *n* in *gerund* and the two *n*'s in *noun*.)

b. Participles

Participles function as Modifiers, and when they stand near substantives they readily attach themselves. Most of the time, in fact, they do modify substantives, but they sometimes modify whole clauses, adverbially. When they stand first in the sentence, however, they always seem to be modifying the Subject, and dangling participles may result. (See **Dng.**)

There are two basic participial forms, *present* and *past*. In more complex tenses, the basic participial tense form may be found in the first member of the verbal group.

1) PRESENT

Present participles always end in *-ing*. They look like gerunds, and are distinguished from gerunds only by the fact that they function as adjectives, whereas gerunds function as nouns. (To associate the terms, remember the *n*'s in *gerund* and *noun*, the *a*'s in *participle* and *adjective*.)

S

GERUND: *Swimming* is good exercise.

M

PARTICIPLE: The *swimming* horse seemed nearly exhausted.

M

PARTICIPLE: *Having been swimming,* the boy had wet hair.

M

PARTICIPLE (PREDICATE ADJECTIVE): The fish are *swimming.*

(If you wish to call the phrase *are swimming* the verb, many would agree.)

2) PAST

Past participles end in various ways. Usually, they end in *-ed,* like simple past tenses, with which they are easily confused. (In "She burned the steak," *burned* is verb in the past tense. In "The burned steak had to be thrown away," *burned* is past participle, modifying *steak.*) Or they end in *-t,* as in "The burnt child shuns the fire"; or in *-en,* as in "A broken reed makes a poor staff." Or sometimes they are formed by an internal vowel change, as in, "Sprung rhythm is characteristic of Hopkins' poetry."

Participles are verbal *adjectives.* (Again, remember the *a* in *participle,* and the *a* in *adjective.*)

c. Infinitives

Infinitives function as Subjects, Complements, or Modifiers. They normally consist of *to* plus the "name form" of the verb, that is, the form you would look for if you were trying to find the verb in the dictionary (the name form is the first member in a phrase). The *to,* however, is not always present. We say,

Allow me *to go.*

but

Let me *go.*

In both sentences, *go* is an infinitive.

Notice that the infinitive without *to* looks just like a present tense verb, and may be distinguished from the verb only by the fact that it functions, not as a Verb, but as a noun, an adjective, or an adverb, that is, as Subject, Complement, or Modifier.

S   C

NOUN: *To know* her is *to love* her.

M

ADJECTIVE: The man *to elect* is the man who can best fill the office.

M

ADVERB: I went *to buy* a loaf of bread.

V

VERB: I *buy* bread frequently.

d. Split Infinitives

Aside from the problem of distinguishing infinitives from verbs, the chief trouble with infinitives occurs with "split infinitives." It would obviously be awkward to say.

I went *to* as cheaply as possible *buy* a loaf of bread.

Split infinitives are weak precisely because they are awkward, but it sometimes happens that it is still more awkward to avoid them. How else could one say, "We hope to more than double our enrollment"? Remember, however, that many readers have long been convinced that no infinitive should ever be split. Avoid the construction whenever you can.

Because of their derivation from verbs, verbals may show changes for tense and voice, they may have subjects or take objects or subjective complements, they may be modified by adverbs, and they always *name* actions, conditions, or states of being. But they do not function as Verbs, asserting that the action is going on. Instead, they function as nouns, adjectives, or adverbs, as Subjects, Complements, or Modifiers. They cannot be used without an accompanying finite verb.

e. Verbals in Fragments

It is failure to distinguish between verbs and verbals which leads to the writing of many *fragmentary sentences* containing one or more verbals, but without a true verb in a main clause to assert action or condition actually occurring. Do not allow mere length to fool you; a sentence must have a finite verb in a main clause.

FRAGMENT: John, being eager to work and always ready to do whatever he could find that needed doing.

Remember: Verbals look like verbs, but do not function as Verbs.
Gerund—ends in *-ing;* used as a noun.

Participle—ends in -*ing,* or -*ed,* or -*t,* or -*en,* or shows an internal vowel change; used as an adjective.

Infinitive—"name form" of the verb, usually preceded by *to;* used as a noun, an adjective, or an adverb.

f. Tense Sequence with Verbals

The tense of a verbal is governed by its time relation to the main verb in its own sentence.

A *present participle* is used for action occurring at the same time as the action of the verb.

Sailing into the harbor, the captain sighed in relief.

A *perfect participle* indicates time prior to that of the verb.

Having weathered the storm, the sloop sailed into the harbor.

A *present infinitive* indicates the same time as the time of the verb, or a time later than that of the verb.

John wanted *to take* Mary to the dance.
I hope *to see* you next winter.

A *perfect infinitive* indicates time prior to that of the verb.

He was thought *to have been seen* near the accident.

EXERCISE

In the following sentences, underline the verbals. Identify each as a gerund, present or past participle, or infinitive. Identify each as noun, adjective, or adverb. Indicate the function (S or C) of the verbal nouns. Indicate the elements modified by the verbal adjectives and adverbs.

1. I am glad to be the one chosen to commend you for your fine work.

2. Students and professors alike seem to feel that there is somehow more virtue in having forgotten something than there is in never having learned it, though neither is eager to give the other much credit for virtue of that kind.

3. Both students and professors, being human beings, have a full share of human failings.

4. Building a building is more profitable than having one built.

5. Gerunds, being verb forms rather than true nouns, do not have plural endings.

6. Eating, quarreling, twittering, and roosting are among the starling's principal activities.

7. To dream, as Hamlet knew, is not always pleasant.

8. The nightmare is the dream to be feared by living dreamers.

9. In that sleep of death, what dreams may come to ramp across the soul-nerves of our souls.

10. I am sorry. I had not intended to think of that.

8. MODIFIERS

a. Adjectives

Adjectives function only as Modifiers of substantives, either immediately before the substantive or after a linking verb, as predicate Complementary Modifiers. They describe the substantive, or identify, designate, point out. They tell what the substantive is like, or which one it is.

They take many forms—*blue, successful, intense, happy, warm, tall*—and they show regular changes for comparison—*blue, bluer, bluest; successful, more successful, most successful.*

Single-word adjectives normally precede the substantive or follow a linking verb. The first is called an *attributive* adjective; the second a *predicate* adjective. Word-group adjectives (phrases and clauses) normally follow the substantive.

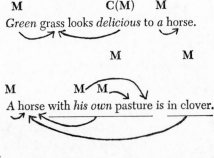

M   M

M   M
There was *a* man in *our* town who was wondrous wise.

Notice that the articles, *a, an,* and *the* designate which one and are adjectives.

If you can recognize substantives, that is, nouns and other naming words that function as Subject or Complement, and can recognize the limiting or describing function of Modifiers, adjectives should cause no trouble.

b. Adverbs

Adverbs indicate such diverse ideas as the time or duration of an action, the manner in which it is done, the degree of intensity of adjectives or adverbs, and many other things: *rapidly, slow, slowly, very, not very* (both are adverbs), *intensely, actively.*

Many adverbs are formed by adding the suffix *-ly* to adjectives: *rapidly, intensely, successfully,* though when *-ly* is added to nouns it produces adjectives, as in *manly.* (The *-ly* comes from *like: intense-like.*) They are usually inflected to show comparison: *rapidly—more rapidly—most rapidly.*

Adverbs function as Modifiers, and serve to qualify verbs, adjectives, other adverbs, and whole predications. Perhaps the easiest way to identify them is to recognize that they are Modifiers but are not modifying substantives.

Single-word adverbs normally precede adjectives or other adverbs. When they modify verbs, they often follow them or split word-group verbs. But many adverbs, especially the word-group adverbs, move around freely.

> Phrase ideas *carefully;* a *well*-chosen word; thinking *deeply; no,*
> I will *not* do it; *usually* truthful.

M
MODIFYING VERBS: He ran *awkwardly*

M M
MODIFYING ADJECTIVES: It is *very* warm.

455

M M M

MODIFYING ADVERBS: It is *not* very warm.

TELL HOW: It rained *hard* (*Adverb of manner.*)

TELL WHERE: He is *here*. (*Adverb of place.*)

TELL WHEN: Registration begins *tomorrow*. (*Adverb of time.*)

TELL WHY: He dieted *to reduce*. (*Adverb of purpose.*)

TELL WHY: He won *because the judge is his brother*. (*Adverb of cause. Such adverbs are normally clauses.*)

TELL WITH WHAT RESULT: He won, *so he was given the prize*. (*Adverb of result. Normally clauses.*)

TELL UNDER WHAT CONDITIONS: We will come *if it doesn't rain*. (*Adverb of condition. Normally clauses.*)

TELL WITH WHAT CONCESSIONS: *Even though you forbid it*, I will do it. (*Adverb of concession. Normally clauses.*)

TELL TO WHAT DEGREE: He is *very* lazy. (*Adverb of degree.*)

COMPARE: I am not as tall *as you*. (*Adverb of comparison. Normally clauses.*)

REVERSE A VERB OR A MODIFIER: He is *not* lazy. (*Adverb of negation.*)

AFFIRM OR DENY: *Yes, no. Yes,* I did it. (*Adverb of affirmation or negation.*)

CONNECT EQUAL CLAUSES: I go; *however*, I shall return. (*Conjunctive adverb. Other common conjunctive adverbs are* consequently, nevertheless, moreover, therefore, accordingly, so, yet, then.)

INTRODUCE QUESTIONS: *Where* are you going? (*Interrogative adverb.*)

EXERCISE

Identify the adjectives and the adverbs in the following passage. Include all possessive nouns or pronouns. Indicate what each modifies.

The little old lady laid her old-fashioned string bag carefully on the counter and nervously plucked off her lace mittens. Tentatively, she peered into the dim recesses at the back of the cigar store, quickly counted the all-male sales force, and cleared her throat timidly. "I am," she announced to the burly, straw-hatted clerk who had brusquely asked if he could help her, "a professional baby-sitter. In my time I have watched many television shows, and I have carefully observed the sly, or audacious, or misguided, or successful techniques employed by many a slippery customer. I believe I am," she smirked proudly, "one of the nation's foremost experts on skull-duggery, shrewdness, and sheer violence." The store clerk gaped uncomprehendingly. "I see," she continued hastily, "that you do not quite realize the inner purport of my comments." A glint of light along the nickeled barrel of a .32 momentarily distracted the clerk's attention. The little old lady purred, not very gently, "This is a stick-up, Bub."

c. Verb-Adverb Phrases

One very common use of adverbs is to form entirely new verb-ideas. This would cause no trouble if the adverbs concerned did not look so much like prepositions. These prepositional adverbs are essentially parts of the verb and might best be so regarded. *To put,* for example, means one thing; *to put up* means something else; *to put up with* means something else still. These verb-adverb phrases may take objects, but those objects are not the objects of preposi-tions, at all, and such phrases may not require objects. Yet many readers are deeply disturbed if what looks like a preposition comes at the end of the sentence, and if you end a sentence with a verb-adverb phrase, they will be distracted from what you are saying to worry about the way that you say it. Do not worry unduly if you must use the construction, but try to avoid using it at the end of the sentence. Few will ever notice it if it comes anywhere else.

These verb-adverb phrases are most common in informal and colloquial usage. *To put up with* means essentially the same thing as *to tolerate.* If the overall tone of your paper is formal, harmony of tone and exactness of diction both may suggest that you avoid a verb-adverb phrase and use a more formal verb instead.

d. Confusion of Adjectives and Adverbs

Be careful, too, not to confuse adverbs and adjectives. If you are in doubt as to whether a given word is properly adverbial, con-sult the grammatical classification given it in your dictionary. Sometimes the problem arises because of different usages in conversational English and most written English. Thus, many *say,* "It *sure* was hot," or "That was a *real* nice party"; but we are more likely to use *surely* and *really* when we write. Written English nearly always needs to be more precise than spoken English.

9. CONNECTIVES

a. Prepositions

Prepositions function only as Connectives. They connect substantives to some other part of the sentence and show the relationship involved. The resulting prepositional phrase functions as a Modifier, but we will postpone consideration of such phrases until we can consider the functioning of groups of words.

Prepositions are usually little words, and they indicate such abstract relations as direction, position, duration, and so on. They are most easily identified by the fact that they are invariably accompanied (usually followed) by substantive Complements, as in *in* town, *under* the rug, *during* the storm, *to* Tom, *between* the dark and the daylight, *at* the party, *concerning* your objection.

Prepositions normally stand first in the phrase, and consequently precede the substantive headword. But it has never been true in English that they may not follow the substantive on occasion, as in "Tell me what you are thinking *about.*" The latter usage, however, is rare in formal writing; and as with the verb-adverb construction, you might avoid it at the end of a sentence whenever you can gracefully do so.

Notice that the substantives which are objects of the prepositions may be and often are modified by adjectives, but that fact need not obscure the essential relation between the preposition and the object. Ask the question Whom? or What? after the preposition; the substantive that answers the question is the object, and the whole word-group is a modifying phrase.

b. Conjunctions

Conjunctions function only as Connectives. They connect words or groups of words (phrases or clauses), and they work chiefly to provide grammatical information about the relations of other words in the sentences. They are not, however, interchangeable in meaning. *And* is not *but; unless* is not *until.*

There are two kinds of conjunctions that we need to consider: *coordinating* and *correlative conjunctions,* connecting only grammatically equal elements; and *subordinating conjunctions,* which usually introduce adverb clauses and indicate their relation to the main clause.

1) COORDINATING AND CORRELATIVE CONJUNCTIONS

For all practical purposes, we can say that there are five coordinating conjunctions: *and, but, or, nor, for.* A few other connectives are sometimes loosely used as coordinating conjunctions, such as *while* when it means *and* or *but,* as in "I am going to town, while you may do as you please," but they cause little trouble. Remember that *and, or* and *nor* always connect equal elements. *But* always does unless it is a preposition meaning *except,* as in "Anyone but John would know that," or an adverb meaning *only,* as in "But little good can come of such action." *For,* the conjunction, is not quite a coordinating conjunction, but it is punctuated as if it were (see page 481), so that we may treat it as a coordinating conjunction in considering the one aspect in which it might give trouble. Use *and, but, or, nor,* and *for* to connect only grammatically equivalent elements, and remember that they are the coordinating conjunctions. They stand between the elements they connect.

Coordinating conjunctions connect equal words.

John *and* Mary danced *and* sang.
John, *but* not Mary, sang.
John *or* Mary will call you.

They connect equal phrases.

He went around the house *and* down the cellar stairs.
He went into the house, *but* not up the stairs.

They connect equal clauses.

If it rains *and* if we can't get the car, we won't go.
This little pig went to market, *but* this little pig stayed home.
You may go, *or* you may stay here.

A subtype works in pairs, called *correlative* conjunctions, with compound subjects, complements, or modifiers: *either . . . or . . . , neither . . . nor . . . , not only . . . but (also) . . . .* Each member of the pair stands before one member of the compounded element. (See also //**Cst.**)

> You will *either* do the work of the course, *or* fail.
> It is *not only* dark, *but also* late.

2) SUBORDINATING CONJUNCTIONS

Subordinating conjunctions connect subordinate clauses to main clauses and show the relation between them.

Most subordinating conjunctions introduce adverbial clauses and connect them to the main clause. The most common are *if, because, unless, until, though, although, even though, when, while, where,* and so on.

> *If* it rains, I won't go. I won't go *even though* you ask me. Come *when* you please.

When *that* introduces a noun or adjective clause having some other subject, *that* may be a subordinating conjunction, or it may be a relative pronoun and object of the verb.

> I know *that* he will do it. (*Subordinating conjunction.*)
> There is a view *that* you will never forget. (*Object and therefore a relative.*)

c. Conjunctive Adverbs

Finally, a number of transitional words are at least partly adverbial, though they connect first and modify second. They are the *conjunctive adverbs: however, moreover, nevertheless,* and so on. Unlike the other connectives, they may stand at many points in any given sentence.

10. INTERJECTIONS

Interjections function only as Absolutes, that is, they do not function in a sentence at all; they are merely there. They are always thrown into a sentence parenthetically. The emotion they express may be violent, or may be very mild indeed.

> *Oh,* that I were a glove upon that hand.
> She said, *alas,* that she could never love me.
> *Well,* perhaps it is better so.
> *Why,* how can you say such a thing?

FORMAL GROUPS

11. PHRASES

A phrase is a group of words without an essential subject and verb, functioning as a unit.

As we are well aware, there are many kinds of phrases, but we need to consider only three or four kinds. From the point of view of form, we will examine *verb phrases, prepositional phrases,* and *verbal phrases.* From the point of view of function, the same phrases may be called *verb phrases, noun phrases, adjective phrases,* and *adverbial phrases.*

a. Verb Phrases

Verb phrases are very common, because Modern English normally indicates changes in tense, mood, and voice by combining verbs and verbals (by combining a basic form naming the action with various auxiliary, or "helping" verbs). And Modern English creates many new verb-ideas by combining verbs with prepositional adverbs. In most sentences, consequently, the verbs consist of more than one word; they are word-groups built of verbs and adverbs, or of verbs and participles and infinitives. Consider, for example, such verb phrases as *had been going, had gone, have gone, was going, am going, do go, shall go, can go, am going to go, shall have been going, should have been going, am willing to go, am going to go on going, would have gone*—and so on, almost *ad infinitum.*

Treat these verb-groups as single verbs. If you wish to break down such a phrase as *should have been going* into verb, infinitive, past participle, and present participle, you may do so, of course, but since that particular verb-idea can be expressed in no other way, the exercise will have little effect on your understanding of the sentence. Call such phrases *verbs* and be done with them.

b. Prepositional Phrases

Every preposition has an object; as a result, every preposition introduces a prepositional phrase. Prepositional phrases consist of the preposition, plus its object, plus any modifiers of that object. The object itself may be a phrase or even a clause, and the modifiers may be phrases or clauses. No matter. The word or the group of words that answers the question Whom? or What? after the preposition comprises, with the preposition itself, a prepositional phrase.

> He went *down town.*
> He went *into the city.*
> He walked *from school to the center of town.*
> She went *to the dance which promised to have the longest stag line.*
> Give it *to whoever comes to that door which opens directly on the street.*

Prepositional phrases function as Modifiers—as adjectives or as adverbs.

M

ADJECTIVE: They bought the house *on the hill.* (*Tells which house.*)

M

ADVERB: He went *down town.* (*Tells where; adverb of place.*)

M   M

ADVERB: *In 1800,* the federal government moved *to Washington.* (*In 1800 tells when;* adverb *of time.* To Washington *tells where; adverb of place.*)

c. Verbal Phrases

Since there are three kinds of verbals—gerunds, participles, and infinitives—there are three kinds of verbal phrases: *gerund phrases, participial phrases,* and *infinitive phrases.* Each kind of verbal phrase functions in exactly the same way as the verbal headword. Gerund phrases function as nouns; participial phrases function as adjectives; infinitive phrases function as nouns, as adjectives, or as adverbs.

The verbal phrase, of whatever kind, consists of a verbal plus a subject or an object, plus (perhaps) modifiers. The modifiers or subjects or objects may be single words or phrases or clauses, but the resulting word-group functions as a unit. The key headword of the phrase is the verbal, and the phrase functions in whatever way that headword functions.

1) GERUND PHRASES

Gerunds are verbal nouns ending in *-ing*. Gerund phrases, then, function as nouns, that is, as Subjects or Complements.

> **S**
> *Doing swan dives* is fun.

> **S**
> *Hitting the ball over the fence* is unfair to the fielders.

> **C**
> I enjoy *eating too much dinner.*

> **C**
> My chief pleasure is *eating good food.*

> **C**
> Professor Snodgrass persists in *grading papers for English as well as for history.*

2) PARTICIPIAL PHRASES

Participles are adjectives, and participial phrases function as adjectives, that is, as Modifiers of substantives. (From a slightly different point of view, participial phrases sometimes seem to modify the whole predication and consequently to be adverbial. See, for example, the second sentence below—and also see **Dng**.)

> **M**
> Douglas, *swimming the turbulent stream,* was nearly exhausted.

> **M**
> *Swimming the turbulent stream,* Douglas was nearly exhausted.

> **M**
> The ball went over the fence *surrounding the ballpark.*

3) ABSOLUTE PHRASES

One special form of participial phrase, consisting of a noun plus a participle, modifies the following main clause and so functions as a rather loose adverb—so loose that it is called an *absolute phrase.*

> *The rain having stopped,* the game was continued.
> *The game being over,* we left the stadium.

463

The construction is well established in English, but many readers find it stilted. Consequently, it should be used chiefly in formal writing, and then sparingly.

4) INFINITIVE PHRASES

Infinitives may be nouns, adjectives, or adverbs, and so infinitive phrases function as nouns (S or C), adjectives (M), or adverbs (M).

S   C

To keep one's nose to the grindstone is to limit one's view of life.

C

I want *him to come to the party.* (*Him is subject of the infinitive. The whole phrase is object of the verb.*)

M

The best place *to catch the biggest fish* is under the noses of scoffing witnesses. (*Adjective: modifies* place.)

M

He came *to see what he could see.* (*Adverb of purpose: tells why he came.*)

Infinitives, in fact, do many things, not all of them as easy to classify as these. Like adverbs, they cover a great deal of ground for us.

EXERCISE

In the following sentences, underline all phrases. Identify each as verb phrase, prepositional phrase, gerund phrase, participial phrase, or infinitive phrase. Indicate the function of each as noun, verb, adjective, or adverb. Indicate the function of each as Subject, Verb, Complement, or Modifier.

1. To Washingtonians, as to all Americans, the majesty of the government of the United States is awe-inspiring despite occasional grumbling.

2. But that awe is somewhat dented by the realization that the

FBI, or the Department of State, or the Treasury is a man across the street or the fellow next door.

3. To be a lieutenant colonel or a commander in the Navy is great in the outposts of the service, but in the Pentagon it is merely to be one more worker in the swarm.

4. In directing traffic consisting of swarms of lieutenant colonels, a policeman who served in the army as a private sometimes succeeds in getting his revenge.

5. In the opinion of some Washingtonians, it is not at all difficult to explain the frustrations of rush-hour traffic.

6. Substantives answering the question Whom? or What? after participles are objects of the participles in participial phrases.

7. Having identified a participle, you need only to determine whether or not it has an object to decide whether or not it is part of a participial phrase.

8. Identifying participles and distinguishing them from gerunds depends on recognizing the functions of the verbals.

9. Include all word or word-group modifiers of the headword to identify a complete phrase, not forgetting modifiers of modifiers.

10. After having identified the complete phrase, it is often useful to work backward from the end of it to determine the separate elements of which it is composed.

12. CLAUSES

A clause is a group of words containing both a subject and a verb and functioning as a unit. In one sense, any subject-verb combination is a clause, but as a rule we use the term *sentence* (simple sentence) if a predication has only one such combination.

There are two kinds of clauses: *independent clauses* (also called *main clauses,* or *principal clauses*) and *dependent clauses* (also called *subordinate clauses*).

a. Independent Clauses (Main Clauses, Principal Clauses)

Independent clauses are little trouble to anyone who can recognize complete sentences. They contain a subject and a verb and are not introduced by any subordinating word. They express a grammatically complete thought and could stand alone as complete sentences. All that distinguishes an independent clause from a sentence, indeed, is the fact that the writer did not choose to let it stand alone.

Three sources of difficulty arise. First, a given utterance may express a complete thought in context and still scarcely be called a clause: "I am going to do it." "Why?" (*Why*, with neither subject nor verb, is not a clause.) Second, an independent clause may well contain noun clauses as Subjects or Complements, or adjective or adverb clauses as Modifiers, as in, "Whoever demands guidance may follow a guide who knows as little as he does himself; and both may go astray." There are four subject-verb combinations in the first main clause; yet there is only one independent predication: "A may follow B." The other three clauses within the main clause are subordinate. Third, grammatical completeness may not be logical completeness. In "He was here" we have a grammatically complete statement, even though clarity of meaning depends on knowing who *he* is. The test is always, Could this group of words stand alone, in this context?

b. Dependent Clauses (Subordinate Clauses)

Dependent clauses contain subjects and verbs and are introduced by a subordinating word (which is not always explicitly expressed). They function as nouns (S or C), as adjectives (M), or as adverbs (M). We shall consider each kind in turn.

1) NOUN CLAUSES

Noun clauses are substantives and function as Subjects or as Complements. They are usually introduced by relative pronouns (*who, which, that, whoever, whichever, whatever,* and so on).

S
Whoever calls the station first will get the prize.

C

I will take *whichever you reject.*

C

Give it to *whatever charity you select.*

When *that* is used to introduce a clause having some other subject, *that* may be a subordinating conjunction.

He always knew *that* something would turn up.

After a few verbs, notably *tell* and *know*, noun clauses functioning as objects may be introduced by *when, where, why,* and so on. These noun clauses look like adverbs, but they answer the question What? after the verb, not When? or Where? or Why? They are objects, not Modifiers.

C

Tell Mother *where you have been.*

C

I know *when he came in last night.*

Compare

C

I know *whom you mean.*

M

I heard him *when he came in last night.*

To determine whether a subordinate clause is a noun clause, there are several tests you can apply. First and best, does it function as a noun, as Subject or Complement? If so, it is a noun clause. Second, if you find it hard otherwise to identify Subjects and Complements, does the clause answer the questions Who? or What? before the verb, or the questions Whom? or What? after a verb or preposition? If it does either, it is a noun clause, Subject or Complement. Third, can it be moved to any other position in the sentence? Subjects normally come before the verb, and objects normally follow the verb. If the clause cannot be moved easily, without rephrasing the sentence altogether, it will be either a noun clause or an adjective clause; the other tests will settle the question.

EXERCISE

Underline the noun clauses in the following sentences. Identify the subject, the verb, and the introductory word of each noun clause. Identify the function (as S or C) of each noun clause.

1. "Who steals my purse steals trash."
2. Do you suppose Iago really carried trash in his purse?
3. Perhaps that apparent admission demonstrates that Iago was deceitful in all things, small as well as large.
4. Eight o'clock in the morning is an hour when no man should be abroad, let alone in class.
5. Registration clerks seem to believe that every student should have at least one eight o'clock class every term.
6. The administration argues that classrooms must be used at all suitable hours.
7. To say that eight o'clock in the morning is "suitable" is ridiculous.
8. It would be just as sensible to say that eleven o'clock at night is suitable, or that three in the morning is.
9. Don't say anything like that where anyone can hear you. The administrators might forget when they had decided to begin the school day and schedule a class for three in the morning.
10. If any such proposal is made, address your protests to the chaplain or to whoever else may have influence with the powers that be.

2) ADJECTIVE CLAUSES

Adjective clauses do nothing but modify substantives. They are usually introduced by relative pronouns. They usually follow the substantive they modify.

He is the man *who spoke so persuasively.*

He is the man *that you told me to meet.*

Occasionally, the pronoun is omitted, especially in informal writing. But it can be readily supplied.

He bought the house (*that* or *which*) he had long wanted.

Rarely, some introductory element other than a relative pronoun will be used with adjective clauses. The clauses still modify substantives.

There comes a time *when all must work.*

This is a period *in which cooperation is essential.*

Unlike single adjectives, which usually precede the nouns they modify, adjective clauses follow their nouns, coming immediately after the noun unless another modifier intervenes.

He is a man *who should go far.*

There was a man in our class *who knew all the answers.*

If you have a sentence containing a substantive immediately followed by *who, whom, which,* or *that,* plus a verb, you can be sure you are dealing with an adjective clause.

As a further test, notice that adjective clauses, like noun clauses, cannot be moved around in the sentence. They must follow the substantive they modify, and the position of that substantive is determined by its function.

EXERCISE

Underline the adjective clauses in the following sentences. Identify the subject, the verb, and the introductory word of each clause. Identify the substantive each adjective clause modifies. Identify the independent clauses in each sentence.

1. Adjective clauses are subject-verb combinations which modify substantives.

2. Substantives are nouns or other words or word-groups which function the way nouns function.

3. The words which introduce adjective clauses (relative pronouns or subordinating conjunctions) stand at the beginning of the clause.

4. A student who cannot recognize adjective clauses needs to

learn to recognize subjects and verbs, relative pronouns, and subordinating conjunctions.

5. The most common relative pronouns in adjective clauses are *who, which, that, whichever, whoever,* and *whomever.*

6. Whenever a sentence contains a noun which is followed by a relative pronoun and a verb, you can be sure that it contains an adjective clause.

7. In an adjective clause which is introduced by a subordinating conjunction (most often *that* or such combinations as *in which*), a substantive following the conjunction functions as the subject.

8. Do not overlook such adjective clauses, in which the subordinating conjunction looks like a relative but is not the subject.

9. Any sentence containing a noun that is followed by either a relative pronoun and a verb or a subordinating conjunction, a substantive, and a verb probably contains an adjective clause.

10. As you are no doubt aware, the sentences in this exercise indicate some of the means by which you can identify adjective clauses.

3) ADVERB CLAUSES

Adverbial clauses, like adverbs, are Modifiers. They tell How? Why? When? Where? Under what conditions? With what result? and so on, about another clause, or they complete a comparison of an adjective or adverb.

They are introduced by subordinating conjunctions, among the most common of which are *if, because, unless, until, though, although, as, than, where, wherever,* and so on.

If it is too hot, the picnic will be canceled.
Unless you tell me, I'll never know.
If you study *whether or not you are in the mood,* you should be ready for surprise quizzes. (*Whether or not you are in the mood* modifies *if you study.* Together they modify the main clause.)

I was doing fairly well *until she began to help.*
Whenever you are ready, we can begin.
He is stronger *than I am.*
Hercules worked harder *than most people do.*

Adverbial clauses are often placed at the beginning of the sentence, because the end is a more emphatic spot and should not be wasted on a mere Modifier. But notice that the adverbial clause, alone among subordinate clauses, often *may be moved around in the sentence.* It may come first, before the main clause, or it may follow the main clause. We can say either

Because you are here, I am happy.

or

I am happy *because you are here.*

You may, consequently, recognize adverbial clauses by their function as Modifiers of a clause or of an adjective or adverb; by the presence of an introductory subordinating conjunction like *if, as, because, until,* and so on; or by the fact that they may usually be moved around in the sentence without necessitating major rephrasing of the sentence-idea.

EXERCISES

A. Underline the adverbial clauses. In each adverbial clause, identify the subject, the verb, and the introductory word. Identify the element each adverbial clause modifies. Identify the independent clause in each sentence.

1. Students should be especially careful early in a term to keep up their work, because the end of any term is always busier than anyone expects it to be.

2. Have you seen Mabel since she was operated on for appendicitis late last term?

3. Because Mabel was in the hospital at the end of the term, she had to take an Incomplete in all her courses.

4. Not all students who fall behind in their course work are as lucky as Mabel was last term.

5. Roger, when he failed Chemistry 2, took Chemistry 1 over again as an auditor.

6. Professor Fetterwate announced that he was resigning as head of the Physics Department because of his health.

7. Wherever there is a college, there is at least one popular coffee and coke joint.

8. Whatever *do* you suppose became of Judge Crater?

9. If you can recognize subordinating conjunctions, you can tell adverbial clauses from noun clauses; if you can identify the word or word-group that a clause is modifying, you can tell adverbial clauses from adjective clauses—always assuming that you can recognize a clause.

10. Unless you can find subjects and verbs readily, understanding clauses will be very difficult.

B. Identify the phrases and subordinate clauses in the following sentences. Explain the form and the function of each.

1. Many students who are quite willing to learn the special terminology of a science course rebel at learning grammatical and rhetorical terms.

2. "So long as I can correct a sentence," they complain, "there is no sense to my learning to label mistakes, to memorizing what different kinds of mistakes are called in the textbook."

3. One answer to that is that knowing the labels leads to understanding the mistakes, because the labels serve to classify common errors and thereby group many errors under a single, manageable category.

4. Another reason is that every sentence is unique, so that only the ability to classify and label mistakes will allow the student to consult a handbook for guidance when he knows that a sentence is faulty but does not know how to correct it.

5. If he can look at a sentence and say, "There is a dangling participial phrase," he can consult any handbook and discover what to do to correct it.

6. If he can recognize nonrestrictive adjectives or adverbs, he can quickly learn how to punctuate the sentence in which they appear.

7. Without a knowledge of terminology, however, he and his teacher are nearly helpless in the task of trying to correct habitual errors.

8. All the teacher can say is, "That sentence is wrong, and so is that one, and so is that one."

9. If, in addition to this traditional terminology, he knows something of the terms and the methods of the structural linguist or the transformational grammarian, he can greatly increase his understanding of English and can further refine his control of the writer's medium.

10. But one who understands the terms we have been using, as we have used them, can work readily with almost any grammatical reference book he may later consult.

14-

Punctuation

Characteristics of a Good Theme: 11. Conventionally
acceptable punctuation.

P   Punctuation

* There are exercises for items marked with an asterisk.

THE IMPORTANCE OF PUNCTUATION

The living language is the spoken language, which the written language reflects. When we speak, we have much besides words to help us communicate our ideas. We have facial expressions—our own and our listeners'. We have gestures, ranging from the lifting of an eyebrow or the tilting of the head through a shrug of the shoulders and a flick of the fingers to violent pounding on a desk or the stamping of a foot. The one word *yes* can be said in a way that will mean vigorous affirmation, coy and hesitating consent, dubious willingness to suspend disbelief, or scornful rejection. A *lighthouse keeper* and a *light housekeeper* are quite different. *John will do it* is a comforting statement; *John will do it?* may be hopeful or despairing. In addition to facial expressions and gestures, which are themselves systematic, we can give many shades of meaning to a spoken phrase by systematic variations of the tone or the emphasis of our voices or by pauses of varying length—and usually by combinations of all three. These oral devices for conveying grammatical information, and consequently meaning, are known as *pitch, stress,* and *juncture.* We have found these concepts useful in considering basic grammar. They are at least as useful in learning conventional punctuation. We need not worry about the details of the four meaningful degrees of stress, of pitch, and of juncture, since they are difficult to distinguish. But we do need to know that they exist and are important to us.

When we write, we are trying, somewhat clumsily, to put into black marks on white paper all the kaleidoscopic richness of the human voice and oral delivery. The experienced and skillful writer varies his sentence patterns to achieve shifting emphasis. He chooses words that reflect his meaning, words that will produce soft sounds, strong sounds, melodious sounds, or jarring cacophony—and he still has black squiggles on white paper. But even the least experienced writer has at his command the major device which helps convey the tone, pace, vehemence, interrogation, and pauses of oral delivery. For these effects, all writers must depend heavily on twelve marks of punctuation. One little mark alone, in shifting combinations, manages to do very nearly 85 percent of the work. Next to words, the comma says most to your readers—if you use it skillfully. But if you use commas in a way your readers do not expect, commas can do almost as much as misused words to make your writing confusing. The other eleven marks of punctuation, too, give your readers clearly defined signals as to how you would have spoken the lines if you had been speaking instead of writing. If you use any of the marks of punctuation in a way your readers do not expect, you are depriving yourself of the standard device which helps the writer represent the flexibility of the human voice.

In other words, it is extremely important to you to learn the commonly accepted conventions of punctuation.

Fortunately, English sentences fall into one or another of certain limited sentence patterns. The skilled and practiced writer can vary the basic combinations widely. But even the beginning writer can learn to give his reader the most important elementary clues to his meaning. As a matter of comforting fact, an understanding of the conventional punctuation of four troublesome sentence patterns will solve many of your punctuation problems. Those four sentence patterns comprise the following:

1. The sentence with two independent clauses
2. The sentence with an introductory modifier
3. The sentence interrupted by parenthetical elements
4. The sentence containing elements in series

In the discussion that follows, we shall be concerned first with those four troublesome sentence patterns. Their punctuation is largely a matter of comma usage, though one or two other marks are also involved. Then we shall examine the miscellaneous uses of the comma and the overuse of the comma. Finally, we shall consider the other marks of punctuation, which cause relatively little trouble.

TWO FUNDAMENTAL PRINCIPLES

Modern English punctuation chiefly indicates the pitch and juncture patterns of spoken English, and they in turn usually indicate the grammatical structure of the sentence. Once in a while the structures and the pitch-juncture signals are at odds (as they are when we say "Yessir" but write "Yes, sir"), so that we need to be aware of them both. Whenever our standard punctuation practices seem illogical, we can only accept them as established conventions which give our readers the signals they are used to.

Two common practices reflect the relationship between punctuation and structural patterns:

1. WE DO *NOT* NORMALLY USE PUNCTUATION TO SEPARATE SENTENCE ELEMENTS THAT BELONG TOGETHER STRUCTURALLY

Subjects and verbs and complements, for example, belong together structurally. Essential modifiers standing in normal positions belong structurally to the elements they modify. Even though slight pauses may occur between such elements, they are normally not separated.

2. WE *DO* NORMALLY USE PUNCTUATION TO SEPARATE ELEMENTS THAT DO NOT BELONG TOGETHER STRUCTURALLY

Most introductory elements, like introductory adverbs, belong logically and structurally to the predicate or to the whole main clause, but they stand before the subject, and we separate the two. Nearly all elements out of their normal positions are set off. Nonessential (nonrestrictive) modifiers are set off. Absolutes are set off. And so on. Accompanying changes in the pitch of voice, and decided pauses, usually mark the spots at which punctuation belongs.

These two principles underlie not only the conventional punctuation of the four troublesome sentence patterns, but many of the other "rules" of punctuation as well.

Those "rules" are at best codifications of what most reputable writers do in certain conventional situations to suggest how they would speak their sentences if they could talk to you. To begin with, learn these basic punctuation conventions and follow them. Your reader expects you to give him conventional clues. Do not worry if you observe variations in the punctuation of experienced writers. After you have become thoroughly familiar with the conventions and know what your reader expects and what your punctuation says to him, you too may make skillful variations from the standard forms to suggest subtle nuances of meaning. But while you are learning, follow the rules.

THE COMMA: THE FOUR TROUBLESOME SENTENCE PATTERNS

1. SENTENCES WITH TWO INDEPENDENT CLAUSES

a. With coordinating conjunctions: Two independent clauses which are connected by *and, but, or, nor,* or *for* are usually separated by a comma.

> Every writer should revise his work carefully, for even Homer nods.
> He entered the grounds by the garden gate, and the full glory of the garden in spring burst upon him.
> He proposed to Jane, and Mary has not spoken to him since.

Read those sentences aloud and listen to what you do with your voice at the comma. At *carefully, gate,* and *Jane* your voice rises, then drops to a level tone or a little below, and there is a perceptible pause before you go on to the conjunctions that follow. You have warned the listener that more is to follow in the sentence, but that the first major part is finished. The reader interprets the comma at that point as the same kind of signal.

The failure to use a comma in such a sentence often misleads your reader. The function of coordinating conjunctions is to connect grammatically equal words, phrases, or clauses. If you do not use the comma between clauses, your reader may be momentarily confused, since he may assume that the conjunction is connecting two nouns in a compound object and may have to back up and reread the sentence when he finds himself deep in a new, unannounced predication. See, for instance, the last example above. It could be very confusing without the comma.

The inclusion of the conjunction *for* perhaps should be explained. It is not, strictly, a coordinating conjunction. But to avoid confusion with the preposition *for,* conventional writers customarily set off *for* clauses.

481

Compare the following examples:

I did it for you. (For _is a preposition._)
I did it, for you told me to. (For _is a conjunction._)

We can depict graphically the rule for the punctuation of such sentences with a coordinating conjunction.

| (Independent clause) | (Con- junction) | (Independent clause) |

———————————— **,** & ————————————

1) SEMICOLON WITH INTERNAL COMMAS: IF THE INDEPENDENT CLAUSES CONTAIN POTENTIALLY CONFUSING INTERNAL COMMAS, USE A SEMI- COLON INSTEAD OF A COMMA BETWEEN THE CLAUSES TO INDICATE THE GREATER IMPORTANCE OF THE MAJOR BREAK IN THE SENTENCE EVEN THOUGH THE CLAUSES ARE CONNECTED BY A COORDINATING CONJUNC- TION.

He rode madly up hill and down dale, through forest, field, and stream; and still the fox eluded him.

2) THE DASH RARELY USED

Only rarely should independent clauses be separated by a dash. Study the primary functions of the dash (P12) and be sure you are using the dash properly before you use one in a compound sentence.

b. Without coordinating conjunctions: Two independent clauses _not_ connected by coordinating conjunctions (_and, but, or, nor, for_) are separated by a semicolon.

No one spoke to him as he walked through the village; no one seemed to recognize him. (_Two independent clauses, no con- junction._)

The surroundings seemed thoroughly familiar; however, he did notice some changes. (_Two independent clauses connected by a conjunctive adverb, not by a coordinating conjunction._)

Washington weather is much maligned; even though other regions have a similar climate, Washingtonians are fond of insisting that their weather is worse. (_Two independent clauses, the second preceded by an adverbial clause. There is no coordinating con- junction._)

If you read these sentences aloud, you will hear a more distinct change in pitch between the clauses, and a maximum juncture at the main break in the idea, as if the clauses were separate sentences—which, indeed, they could be, so far as structure goes.

In such sentences, a comma would be adequate only if the clauses were short and no confusion could result. Often, a subordinate clause intervenes between the independent clauses. Use the semicolon, still, to indicate the main break in the sentence, as in the third example just above.

c. Comma Splices (See also **Cs.**)

The use of a comma instead of the heavier semicolon between the independent clauses of such sentences results in the *comma splice* (also called the *comma fault* or the *comma blunder*), which can be very confusing to the reader. As we shall see, the comma is used to set off many lesser elements from the central main clause. If you use one between two independent clauses, the reader may be confused until he stops to analyze your sentence.

> CONFUSING: After the storm, cracks appeared in the bridge pavement, the piers and the cables, however, were undamaged. (If the main break in the sentence, after *pavement,* had been indicated by a semicolon, no confusion would have resulted.)

Listen to your voice, first as it stumbles through the confusion caused by the comma, then as it marks the main break in the sentence that a semicolon after *pavement* would indicate. Notice that the term "comma splice" refers only to this misleading use of a comma between independent clauses.

1) CONJUNCTIVE ADVERBS

The same rule enables you to handle the punctuation of sentences connected by conjunctive adverbs like *however, moreover, nevertheless, consequently, then,* and sometimes *yet* and *so.* They are not coordinating conjunctions and may in fact be used along with coordinating conjunctions. Unless *and, but, or, nor,* or *for* is present, use semicolons between independent clauses.

2) *So*

So is a special problem. In the first place, students grossly overuse it. Avoid it on general principles. If you must use it as a connective between clauses, ask yourself just what it means. If it is synonymous with *consequently,* it is a conjunctive adverb and connects clauses that probably should be separated by a semicolon. If it means *so that,* the succeeding clause is not an independent clause at all, but an adverbial clause of purpose or result, and the punctuation falls under P3b.

3) TEST

Could the clauses stand alone? If so, they are independent and equally important. The reader expects to be warned that one clause does not modify the other. Commas are not enough warning, and a comma between independent clauses not connected by *and, but, or, nor,* or *for* splices the clauses together with insufficiently heavy punctuation.

Read the sentences aloud, comparing the pitch and juncture signals for commas and for semicolons.

d. Run-on sentences

If you are so little conscious of your own meaning that you run together two independent clauses without any punctuation at all and consequently without giving your reader even the slightest warning, you commit the cardinal sin of writing a **run-on** or a **run-together sentence,** which is worse than a comma splice because it confuses your reader still more thoroughly.

> WRONG: His sunburn was painful for a week he was in agony.
> WRONG: He is a stimulating teacher everybody says there is none better.
> WRONG: He wrote steadily for an hour the results were terrible.

Correct such sentences by applying the principles discussed in both **a** and **b** above. Wherever you think the main break in the sentence should come, indicate it to the reader by using the proper punctuation.

We can depict graphically the rule for punctuating compound sentences without a coordinating conjunction.

| (Independent | (Independent |
| clause) | clause) |

———————————————   ;   ———————————————

e. Possible subordination of one clause

Before we leave the punctuation of compound sentences, we might consider one final point. Should those sentences be compound sentences at all? Remember that the form of the compound sentence says to the reader, "Here are two distinct and independent ideas, neither modifying the other, yet both belonging in one sentence because together they express a single, unified idea." That is not a very common rhetorical or logical necessity. If your themes frequently contain comma splices or run-on sentences, stop and consider. Are your sentences really reflecting your thought? Should the compound sentences have been broken up into two simple sentences, or should one independent clause have been reduced to a subordinate clause or a modifying phrase or even a single modifying word? (See also pages 149–158.)

Graphic Summary

The punctuation of sentences with two independent clauses is normally handled in one of these ways:

With *and, but, or, nor, for:*

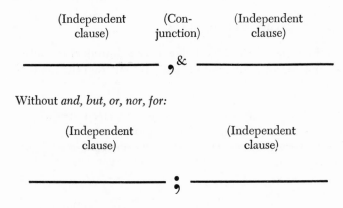

| (Independent clause) | (Con- junction) | (Independent clause) |

Without *and, but, or, nor, for:*

| (Independent clause) | | (Independent clause) |

EXERCISE

Punctuate the following.

1. There is a great deal of good expository writing in English but most of it is topical and goes out of date quickly.

2. We are all firmly convinced that men possess certain inalienable rights however it requires uncommon tolerance to recognize that our own rights are also the rights of other men.

3. The first of our troublesome sentence patterns concerns compound and some compound-complex sentences comma splices and run-ons do not occur in other kinds of sentences.

4. The usual practice of educated writers serves to establish a convention which readers expect you to follow failure to follow it, therefore, may confuse your readers badly.

5. My lawn is composed of bluegrass chickweed and sorrel also thrive in it.

6. Two of Rachel Carson's books attracted wide attention: _The Sea Around Us_ made us sit up and think of Rachel Carson, _Silent Spring_ made us sit up and think.

7. Law is the ethical minimum to be merely legal is to be morally sleazy.

8. The FDA reported, as the main deleterious side effect, heart damage, kidney, liver, and other visceral damage and damage to the nervous system sometimes resulted also.

9. Ruth flirted outrageously with Kenney and Caleb and Dick flirted with her.

10. The careers of most men are decided by chance, choice in comparatively few cases is the determining factor.

2. INTRODUCTORY ELEMENTS

a. Adverbial clauses and verbal clusters: Introductory adverbial clauses and verbal clusters are usually set off from the main clause by a comma.

> As soon as the sun came out, the sidewalks began to steam.
> If you wish to see a doctor's excuse, I can get one.
> To find your way around in the city, get a good map.
> Having dragged himself out of bed, he decided he might as well go to class.

Your voice, again, will warn you by signals of pitch and pause that there is a break in the construction of the sentence. A comma signals that break to the reader.

We can depict graphically the rule for the punctuation of sentences introduced by an adverbial clause or a verbal cluster.

486

(Clause or verbal)   (Independent clause)

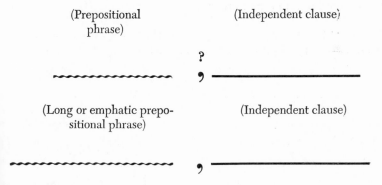

b. Prepositional phrases: An introductory prepositional phrase is often *not* separated from the main clause. If the phrase is long, requires special emphasis, or might be misread, it may be set off by a comma.

> NO COMMA NECESSARY: To the right of the door is the drinking fountain.
> In a troubled world personal peace of mind is hard to secure.
> COMMAS PROBABLE: In every examination throughout the entire semester, Professor Snodgrass flunked Gertrude.
> In short, she failed the course.

Usage here is divided. The best test is provided by your own voice. If you read your sentence with a decided pitch-pause signal after the prepositional phrase, use a comma; if not, leave it out. The same test can be applied to single introductory adverbs, though they seldom cause trouble either way.

We can depict graphically the rule for the punctuation of sentences containing introductory prepositional phrases.

(Prepositional   (Independent clause)
phrase)

?

(Long or emphatic prepo-   (Independent clause)
sitional phrase)

EXERCISE

Punctuate the following sentences containing introductory modifying elements. Be prepared to explain why you use or do not use a comma in each sentence.

487

1. For the latest weather forecast dial 936-1212.
2. Until we get a heavy rain the forest will be tinder dry.
3. To prevent disastrous fires the governor has closed the state parks by executive order.
4. As you no doubt already have discovered when you are asked to write a theme during a class hour it is useful to have a list of interesting topics filed in your notebook.
5. Many places, like banks, still provide convenient counters at which to write checks, but since the triumph of the ball-point pen few places now provide blotters.
6. Occasionally one can substitute Kleenex for a blotter, but the result is seldom a happy one.
7. To the student who is concerned only with his grade a satisfactory grade will probably come; to the student who is concerned only with how much he can learn will probably come not only a satisfactory grade, but also satisfaction.
8. Pausing after the delivery of a ringing phrase the mayor awaited applause.
9. To a surprising number of otherwise well-taught students dashes and hyphens are virtually identical.
10. After all there is but one race—humanity.

3. PARENTHETICAL ELEMENTS

Any element which does not vitally modify the sentence or which is out of its normal order in the sentence may be considered parenthetical or interpolated (that is, "stuck in"), whether it comes in the middle of the sentence, at the end, or even at the beginning, like the special cases discussed in P2 above. Any such element, since it is not essential to the elements it stands by, is separated from the rest of the sentence, "set off," by commas.

The voice signals of pitch and pause are normally clear with all such parenthetical elements. The pitch rises before the interpolation and again at the end of it, and there is a decided pause, after which the pitch is markedly lowered. With essential modifiers, on the other hand, neither pitch change nor pause occurs. With a parenthetical element at either end of the sentence, of course, only one set of signals occurs, but in any position the signals are unmistakable in the spoken sentence. Commas signal the break in writing.

Notice the signals in the following sentences.

Dr. Bradley, who tries to keep abreast of new discoveries, spends a great deal of time reading medical journals.

> Any doctor who tries to keep abreast of new discoveries must spend a great deal of time reading medical journals.
> Come out, wherever you are.
> John, is this clear?

The problem in punctuating, when the elements come in the middle of the sentence, usually lies in forgetting to set off the element at *both ends.* One comma merely separates the subject from the verb or the verb from the complement. Two commas give the reader the structural signals he needs.

The most common types of parenthetical interrupters may be considered separately.

a. Absolutes: Absolutes are set off by commas.

Absolutes are words or phrases, rarely clauses, that do not grammatically affect the sentences in which they appear. Interjections, transitional words or phrases, nouns of address, nominative absolutes (absolute phrases), adverbs of affirmation or negation (*yes,* and *no* when it is not directly modifying a word in the sentence) —all these are absolutes and are set off by commas. All can be removed from the sentence without affecting the sense of the sentence, and all are set off by commas.

> Oh, why do you say that?
> I say it, of course, because I believe it to be true.
> I say it, as you might have known, because I believe it to be true.
> Tell me, John, when you expect to go.
> Yes, I'll go with you.

b. Nonrestrictive modifiers and appositives: Nonrestrictive modifiers and nonrestrictive appositives are set off by commas.

Since *nonrestrictive* is a negative term, here and in each subsequent discussion under this general rule it will be necessary to consider the restrictive elements first, in order to understand the nonrestrictive elements.

A *restrictive* element is one that is so vital to the understanding of the sentence that it could not be omitted without seriously disturbing the clarity of the sentence. It restricts (limits) the meaning so sharply that it cannot be removed. It belongs to the sentence, and we do not separate elements that belong together. We read them together without a change in pitch and without pause, and we do *not* set them off in writing.

A *nonrestrictive* element, on the other hand, may add useful information, but it does not so sharply restrict the meaning that it cannot be removed without materially changing the meaning of the sentence. In reading or speaking, our voices separate it from the rest of the sentence. It is, consequently, parenthetical and is set off from the rest of the sentence by commas.

1) NONRESTRICTIVE ADJECTIVE MODIFIERS: NONRESTRICTIVE ADJECTIVE MODIFIERS ARE SET OFF BY COMMAS.

To understand the nonrestrictive adjective modifier, we need first to consider the restrictive adjective modifier.

A *restrictive* adjective modifier is a phrase or a clause that particularizes, limits, points out, designates, *identifies* the noun it modifies. *It tells which one of several possible things the sentence is about, and it is not separated from its noun either by the voice or by punctuation.*

> RESTRICTIVE: The man in the tweed suit is not listening. (*There are several men present, but only one is in tweeds, and only he is not listening.*)
>
> RESTRICTIVE: The book I borrowed from Budd was very interesting. (*There are many books. I am talking now about the one Budd lent me.*)
>
> RESTRICTIVE: The click of the light switch woke me up. (*Clicks occur often. It was that one click that disturbed me.*)

We can depict graphically the function of the *restrictive* adjective modifier.

(Several pos-　　　　　　(Restrictive
sible nouns)　　　　　　　modifier)

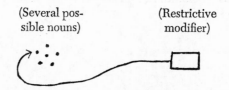

A *non*restrictive adjective modifier, as the name suggests, is *not* restricting, not identifying. It does add useful or interesting information, or it would not be there at all, but *it could be left out without destroying the sense of the sentence,* and both our voices and our punctuation separate it accordingly.

NONRESTRICTIVE: Mr. O'Neill, who is wearing a tweed suit, is not listening. (*There is only one Mr. O'Neill in the group, and he is already identified by name. The tweed suit is incidental. The sentence would be clear without that modifier.*)

NONRESTRICTIVE: *Europe since 1914*, which I borrowed from Budd, was interesting. (*The title identifies the book. Where I got it is merely additional information, not necessary to the sense of the sentence.*)

We can depict graphically the function of the *nonrestrictive* adjective modifier.

(Identified noun)		(Nonrestrictive modifier)
●	**+**	⬜

Compare these examples:

	Several men	The one in the tweeds
RESTRICTIVE: The man in the tweed suit is asleep.		

	O'Neill	A tweed suit
NONRESTRICTIVE: Mr. O'Neill, who is wearing a tweed suit, is asleep.	● **+**	⬜

	Several eggs	The egg I broke
RESTRICTIVE: The egg I broke was no good anyway.		

	Eggs	Protein
NONRESTRICTIVE: Eggs, providing protein, are welcome at breakfast time.	● **+**	⬜

491

Nonrestrictive adjective modifiers could be omitted without destroying the sense of the sentence, and consequently are parenthetical and are set off by commas—*two* commas if the element comes in the middle of the sentence.

Very often, however, the modifier, as an adjective phrase or clause modifying an object, comes at the end of the sentence. Your voice will give the same pitch-pause signal at the beginning of the element; one comma clarifies the pattern for the reader.

Please awaken Mr. O'Neill, who is wearing a tweed suit.

We can depict graphically the punctuation of sentences containing *nonrestrictive* modifiers,

(Part of main idea)	(Nonrestric- tive modifier)	(Rest of main idea)

———————— **,** ∼∼∼∼∼∼∼∼ **,** ————————

(main idea)	(nonrestrictive modifier)

———————— **,** ∼∼∼∼∼∼∼∼∼∼∼

2) NONRESTRICTIVE ADVERBIAL MODIFIERS: NONRESTRICTIVE ADVERBIAL MODIFIERS ARE SET OFF BY COMMAS.

The distinction between restrictive and nonrestrictive adverbial modifiers is less clear-cut than that between restrictive and nonrestrictive adjectives and appositives. Sometimes only the writer can be sure of the exact degree of separation he wishes to indicate, and the reader must hope that the punctuation is dependable and that the modifiers which have been set off were really meant to be nonrestrictive. If the writer is careless here, confusion will inevitably result. Your voice provides the best guide. Read the sentence aloud as you would speak it, and use a comma where pitch and pause signal a break.

Sometimes the adverbial modifier is clearly necessary to the sense of the sentence and therefore could not be omitted. Such modifiers are not set off.

RESTRICTIVE: I have not seen her since yesterday morning.
RESTRICTIVE: I will not do it unless there is no one else for the job.

Sometimes the adverbial modifier merely adds a useful but nonessential idea and could be omitted without vitally changing the central thought. Such modifiers are set off by commas.

NONRESTRICTIVE: I will do it, unless you can find someone else who wants the job.

The two may be represented graphically.

(Main clause) (Restrictive adverbial modifier)

(Main clause) (Nonrestrictive adverbial modifier)

3) NONRESTRICTIVE APPOSITIVES: NONRESTRICTIVE APPOSITIVES ARE SET OFF BY COMMAS.

An appositive is a noun repeating another noun and making it more specific. A restrictive appositive identifies. A nonrestrictive appositive, like the nonrestrictive adjective modifier, merely adds interesting information; it does not identify which one of several possibilities the sentence is about. Since the appositive follows another noun, it never begins the sentence, though it may end the sentence. The same signals of pitch and juncture (pause) that mark the nonrestrictive modifier will warn you to set off nonrestrictive appositives.

Examples should make the distinction between restrictive and nonrestrictive appositives clear.

RESTRICTIVE: The poet Keats died young.

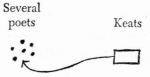

Several poets Keats

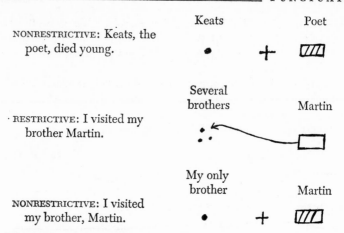

NONRESTRICTIVE: Keats, the poet, died young.

RESTRICTIVE: I visited my brother Martin.

NONRESTRICTIVE: I visited my brother, Martin.

c. Elements out of order: Elements out of normal order in the sentence are set off by commas.

> Happily, he sang all through his bath.
> The horse, old and infirm, was retired to pasture.

Many elements in English can be shifted into a slightly unusual order for changes in emphasis. Adverbs, for example, may precede the main clause; adjectives may follow nouns instead of precede them; conjunctive adverbs, like *however,* may go into the middle of a clause instead of between clauses. All such elements may change the normal flow of thought; when they do, they are parenthetical and are set off by commas.

d. Tests

1) REMOVE PARENTHETICAL ELEMENTS FROM THE SENTENCE.

To determine whether an element of any sort is parenthetical and should be set off, try removing it from the sentence. If the remainder of the sentence is grammatically and logically complete and essentially the same without it, the element is parenthetical and should be set off by commas.

2) READ THE SENTENCE ALOUD.

An even better test, for *most* parenthetical elements, we have already learned. *Read the sentence aloud and listen to your voice.*

494

If you pause, before and after the element, if the tone of your voice rises and falls, if you "read around" the element, the element is parenthetical and should be set off by commas. This "pause test" is not valid for all questions of punctuation, and of course is of no help at all to anyone who reads in a stumbling monotone; but with a few exceptions, such as *sir* in "Yes, sir," it will work in determining whether or not a given element is parenthetical. Listen for the commas. If your voice inserts them, insert them in the written sentence.

e. Reminder: Set off parenthetical elements at both ends.

If the parenthetical element comes in the middle of the sentence, *be sure to set it off at both ends of the element.* Only rarely do students fail completely to recognize that an element is parenthetical. What they often do fail to do is indicate clearly to the reader where the parenthetical element both begins and ends. *One* comma with a parenthetical element merely chops the sentence confusingly in two, separating subject from predicate or verb from complement. *Two* commas are essential if the parenthetical element comes anywhere except at the beginning or the end of the sentence. (See also P6a, b.)

f. Rule

The rule for the punctuation of sentences containing parenthetical elements may be represented graphically.

(Part of main idea)   (Parenthetical element)   (Rest of main idea)

(Parenthetical element)   (Main idea)

(Main idea)   (Parenthetical element)

g. Modifications

Four modifications of the rule should be mentioned.

1) SLIGHT PARENTHESIS: ELEMENTS THAT ARE ONLY SLIGHTLY PAREN-
THETICAL ARE USUALLY NOT SET OFF.

I am indeed pleased to be here.

2) ELEMENTS TO BE MINIMIZED: PARENTHETICAL ELEMENTS THAT ARE
TO BE MINIMIZED ARE ENCLOSED IN PARENTHESES, NOT COMMAS.

She is sure (I talked to her yesterday) that he will do it.
Chaucer (1340?–1400) held court positions under three kings.

3) ELEMENTS TO BE EMPHASIZED: PARENTHETICAL ELEMENTS THAT ARE
TO BE STRONGLY EMPHASIZED ARE SET OFF BY DASHES, NOT COMMAS.

Conventional punctuation—and this you must believe—helps your
reader understand your sentence.

4) WITH INTERNAL COMMAS: PARENTHETICAL ELEMENTS THAT WOULD
NORMALLY BE SET OFF BY COMMAS ARE OFTEN SET OFF BY DASHES IF
THEY CONTAIN INTERNAL COMMAS.

The three youngest boys—John, Elmer, and Stanley—ran home
crying.

The pitch and juncture signals given by the voice when such
sentences are spoken differ, subtly but distinctly, from each other
and from the signals that call for commas in the patterns we have
been considering under P3. They are difficult to describe without
special training, but all of us use them constantly in speaking and
listening; they can just as successfully be used in punctuating.

EXERCISE

Punctuate the following sentences to set off parenthetical elements conventionally. Be prepared to justify your punctuation.

1. A comma most of the time represents a change in the pitch of
   the voice and a distinct pause in the breath both of which can
   easily be heard in a spoken sentence.

2. It is precisely these pauses and changes in pitch the comma signals that make it unwise to break up a sentence by using too many parenthetical elements.

3. Spoken a style with too many interrupters is called "roller coaster prose"; read silently it seems more like briar patch prose because the reader's mind is snagged by the commas.

4. Omitting the commas however merely ignoring the problem is to force your reader unwillingly to determine if possible the structures underlying your sentences and to guess at the degrees of separation between them.

5. It is better instead to learn to give the conventional signals which can be done by paying attention to both structure and sound.

6. Throughout the country the growth of populations and of industries in addition to increasing use of air conditioning in towns and irrigation on our farms is producing a potential inadequacy of water supplies.

7. Increasingly men look to the ocean for future resources whether of food, of water, or of minerals.

8. Man races for the moon and the stars lest he outgrow the earth.

9. Already the moon long a symbol of romance and happy-ever-afters has become a symbol of man's greed instead.

10. What fools as Puck remarked these mortals be.

4. COORDINATE ELEMENTS IN SERIES

There are two common patterns involved in this item: the A, B, and C series, and coordinate adjectives modifying the same noun but not affecting each other.

a. A, B, and C series: Coordinate words, phrases, or clauses in an A, B, and C series are best separated by commas.

Here, admittedly, usage varies. Many reputable writers do not use a comma before the *and* when the elements of the series consist of words or short phrases. But because the function of *and* is to connect, it is safest in college writing to indicate clearly to the reader that B and C are no more closely related than A and B. Almost all writers use the comma before the *and* in a series of long phrases or of clauses. When *or* is used, most conventional writers use the comma in all cases.

Both the structure of the sentence and the pitch and juncture signals of the voice suggest the use of commas between all the members of the series, as you can confirm by listening to your reading of the following examples.

> Toast, coffee, and eggs are common foods for breakfast.
> Toast and coffee, bacon and eggs, and ice cream and cake are three combinations often found together.

It is perhaps the double pull of both these criteria that leads many readers to object to the omission of the comma before the *and* at the end of the series. Justification for the omission lies in the modern tendency to reduce the amount of punctuation. The clarity of the series is the ultimate guide.

Until you are certain that your writing is skillful enough to guarantee perfect clarity, use

$$A, \quad B, \quad and \ C.$$

> John, Elmer, and Stanley were the three youngest boys.
> He looked in the closets, behind the bureau, and under the bed.
> If my work is done, if Mary will go, and if the weather is cool, I'll go to the Bay with you on Saturday.
> We chose an excellent day for the picnic, the girls provided excellent food, and we all enjoyed ourselves thoroughly. (*This example, containing a series of independent clauses, represents a special problem. If the clauses had been so long that the reader might have become confused, the use of commas would have resulted in an apparent comma splice. To prevent confusion, semicolons might be used in a series of long independent clauses: A; B; and C.*)

b. Adjectives in series: Coordinate adjectives modifying the same noun but not affecting each other are separated by commas.

> The exhausted, miserable child sobbed herself to sleep.
> The excited, happy rooters cheered the team.
> The old, infirm horse was retired to pasture.

It is not always easy to decide just when such adjectives cease to be coordinate (that is, performing equal functions in the sentence) and begin to have more or less subtle effects on each other, so that one functions adverbially. Often, too, the final adjective and the noun form a virtual compound, so that the earlier adjective modifies both words together and not the noun alone.

The dress was too youthful for the little old woman who bought it.
She should never have purchased a yellow silk evening gown.

1) TESTS FOR COORDINATE ADJECTIVES

Insert an *and* between the adjectives. Since *and* will connect only equal elements, if the *and* will fit, it follows that the adjectives are coordinate. If the *and* will not fit comfortably, it must
follow that the adjectives, instead of being coordinate, are actually
affecting each other in some way. Therefore they belong too closely
together to be separated.

> He cut a switch from the sour apple tree. (*No one would say, "The
> sour and apple tree." The adjectives are not coordinate and should
> not be separated.*)
> The exhausted and miserable child sobbed herself to sleep.

Try the adjectives in some other order. If they are truly coordinate, any order should be possible, though one may be logically
preferable.

> The miserable, exhausted child . . . .
> (*But no one would say:* The apple, sour tree . . . .)

Read the sentence aloud and listen to your voice. The pitch
and juncture signals of *the old, infirm horse* are quite different
from those of *the little old lady* or *the sour apple tree*.

2) NOTE: NO COMMA BEFORE THE NOUN

The final adjective is *not* separated from the noun.
This is the pattern:

$$\text{Adjective}\ \text{,}\quad \text{adjective noun}$$

Coordinate adverbs are less common than coordinate adjectives.
When they occur, they are punctuated as adjectives are punctuated.

> The crowd cheered excitedly, happily.

EXERCISE

Punctuate elements in series in the following sentences according to the practice of strictly conventional writers.

1. The wind blew the windows rattled the thunder rolled and the rain beat upon the huddled houses.
2. John and Mary danced sang and ate hamburgers.
3. The old gray mare does not look much like Man o' War.
4. Think on this doctrine: that reasoning beings were created for one another's sake that to be patient is a branch of justice and that men sin without intending it.
5. How can I marry such a pretty little girl when I have a wife and three children at home?
6. Through the valleys down the mine shafts and beneath the cabins the wind raged.
7. The captain on the bridge the engineer in the depths of the ship and the steward chasing cups across the galley floor knew that the ship was pitching heavily.
8. The battered leaking vessel lurched head-on into the waves.
9. Presently almost abruptly, the ship passed out of the storm, and the sea was amazingly calm.
10. Before a storm, a calm oily sea is a frightening portent.

GRAPHIC SUMMARY

The conventional punctuation of the four common troublesome sentence patterns has been depicted graphically as each was discussed. It is helpful to see those graphic representations all together.

1. TWO INDEPENDENT CLAUSES

(Independent clause)   (Coordinating conjunction)   (Independent clause)

——————————— ,& ———————————

(Independent clause)   (Independent clause)

——————————— ; ———————————

2. INTRODUCTORY ELEMENTS

(Adverbial clause)   (Independent clause)

～～～～～～～～ , ———————————

(Verbal cluster)   (Independent clause)

〰〰〰〰〰〰〰 **,** _____

(Prepositional   (Independent clause)
phrase)

〰〰〰〰〰〰〰 **?** _____

,

3. PARENTHETICAL INTERRUPTERS

(Part of   (Parenthetical   (Rest of
main idea)   element)   main idea)

_____ **,** 〰〰〰〰〰〰 **,** _____

(Parenthetical
element)   (Main idea)

〰〰〰〰〰〰 **,** _____

(Main idea)   (Parenthetical
                                    element)

_____ **,** 〰〰〰〰〰〰

4. ELEMENTS IN SERIES

A **,** B **,** and C

Adjective **,** adjective noun

EXERCISE

Punctuate the following sentences, illustrating the four most troublesome sentence patterns, according to the practice of strictly conventional writers.

1. When I am punctuating sentences that someone else wrote I can do very well.
2. The trouble comes with sentences of my own I know exactly how the sentences should be read and can't see when my punctuation has been misleading.
3. You must learn of course to punctuate your own sentences correctly.
4. Other people's sentences other people's punctuation and other

people's meaning are problems the other people must solve for themselves.

5. America broke away from England in the eighteenth century and as a result many American idioms reflect eighteenth century British practice.

6. The British often object to "Americanisms" but as a matter of fact many of the expressions they object to merely represent older to them outmoded British usage.

7. Not every Tom Dick and Harry can manage to occupy the White House.

8. Considering the difficulty of securing the nomination by a major political party for the presidency we have succeeded in electing an astonishing number of good Presidents and an incredibly small number of poor ones.

9. To a reasonable being that alone is insupportable which is unreasonable.

10. Neither death nor exile nor pain nor anything of this sort is the true cause of our doing or not doing any action, but our inward opinions and principles.

11. As a man thinketh in his heart so is he.

12. The human voice is an elaborate flexible instrument capable of lending many shades of meaning to a spoken English sentence written English a far less flexible instrument must depend on precise diction careful control of the form and position of sentence elements and a sensitive handling of the conventions of punctuation.

13. It is little wonder therefore that writing well is difficult and reading well is demanding.

14. Unfortunately the more exactly one knows what he wants to say, the more dissatisfied he is likely to be with his best efforts to say it.

15. Writing revising rewriting—these must be stopped at some point as time and deadlines pass.

16. A dialect is a system of speech peculiar to a region a class and a time in sounds words and constructions.

17. The written English of the educated American is a dialect a minority dialect indeed from one region to another dialect differences occur even within educated written English.

18. Without intensive study no one can say though many do say even many who should know better that a particular locution is the only standard pattern.

19. There are of course many locutions that are not used in educated

writing unless that writing represents nonstandard usage as in dialogue.

20. There are many locutions too that many readers object to even though they are well established the writer uses them at his own risk.

21. No student of language maintains that "anything goes" the rhetorical effect of one's language must always be considered.

22. Ideally your thought should flow without distraction into the reader's mind your sentences should be so carefully controlled that they are read exactly as you wish them to be read.

23. Punctuation is a matter of major importance it helps determine how easily the reader can read your sentence as you wished it to be read.

24. There are many ways in which a practiced writer can suggest subtle variations of thought by varying the basic punctuation patterns but even the inexperienced writer who studies the basic patterns can be fairly sure that he will not lead his reader badly astray.

25. If you believe it is easy to say exactly what you mean think of all the successful lawyers you know who make a practice of breaking each other's carefully drawn wills and contracts.

5. MISCELLANEOUS USES OF THE COMMA

a. Prevent misreading: Elements that might be mistakenly read together are separated by commas.

Occasionally, to say what we want to say, we are forced to put side by side elements that might be confusingly read together. To warn the reader of the separation, we use a comma between such elements.

Whatever is, is right.

b. Contrasted elements: Contrasted elements are separated by commas.

Not John, but Peter, was given the most responsible duty.
Peter, not John, was the older.

c. Dates: Commas are used to separate the month and the year, and the day of the month from the year when the day is given.

October, 1492
October 12, 1492

Commas are customarily omitted, however, if the form *12 October 1492* is used.

When the date occurs in the middle of a sentence, most writers use a comma also after the year.

> Columbus arrived in America on October 12, 1492, and opened the New World to European exploration.

d. Addresses and geographical items: Commas are used to separate the parts of an address or other geographical item.

> His address is 110 Kenner Avenue, Indianapolis, Indiana.

When the address occurs in the middle of a sentence, most writers use a comma also after the name of the state.

> If 110 Kenner Avenue, Indianapolis, Indiana, is no longer the right address, write in care of his parents.
> He once lived in Washington, D.C.

When the geographical item occurs in the middle of a sentence, most writers also use a comma after the last element.

> Paris, France, is a beautiful city.

e. Quotations (including comma splices and fragments in dialogue): Commas are used to separate such orientation phrases as *he said* from the *direct* quotations they introduce.

> He said, "I am ready for the exam."

When the orientation phrase occurs in the middle of the quotation, punctuate the entire passage according to the sentence pattern of the whole.

> "I will do as you ask," he said. "It would be foolish to disobey." *(The first clause and the orientation phrase make a full sentence; the following clause makes a full sentence. They are punctuated accordingly.)*
> "She denies it," he pointed out; "however, the evidence is clear." *(The quoted sentence, exclusive of the orientation phrase, is a compound sentence without a coordinating conjunction and requires a semicolon. The orientation phrase does not change the pattern.)*
> "Give me liberty," he cried, "or give me death." *(The first part of the quotation, with or without the orientation phrase, could*

*stand alone as a sentence, but the second part could not. It must
be included in the basic sentence.)*

Avoid **comma splices** (see **P1c** and **Cs**) in sentences like the first and
second examples above. Avoid **fragmentary sentences** (see P7a and
Frag) in sentences like the third example above.

With these miscellaneous conventions, pitch and juncture signals are subtle and may be missed. It is perhaps best merely to
learn the half-dozen constructions involved.

EXERCISE

Punctuate the following sentences illustrating the most common
miscellaneous uses of the comma. If necessary, adjust the capitalization.

1. What a piece of work is a man how noble in reason how in-
    finite in faculty in form and moving how express and ad-
    mirable in action how like an angel in apprehension how like
    a god.
2. Two miles above the sky was laced with clouds.
3. Huntsville Alabama should not be confused with Huntsville
    Texas.
4. Dorothy is a Texan not only by birth but also by choice.
5. One's choices not one's innate characteristics are one's own
    responsibility.
6. Beyond the railing on which he leaned fifteen feet below the
    water foamed and tumbled.
7. "Tell me" she said "why you look at me so curiously."
8. "I was wondering what kinds of people invent new styles of
    make-up" he answered "what a fiendish sense of humor they
    all must have."
9. His address is 2029 G Street Northwest Washington D.C.
    20006.
10. On October 11 1492 Columbus sailed the ocean blue.
11. By 13 October 1492 he had discovered not the continent the
    Vikings had long known nor the continent the Polynesians
    traded with but a rather small island.
12. As a result of the voyages of Columbus and the subsequent
    reports both continents are named not Columbia but America.
13. What a wonderful thing is publicity writers make history.

505

14. "What is so rare as a day in June?" the poet asked and was answered by the calendar "any day in February is rarer."
15. For the right answer the right question is important.

6. OVERUSE OF THE COMMA

Since we do not separate elements that belong together, the overuse of commas can be as confusing as the omission of commas where your reader expects to find them. Remember, too, that commas signal pitch and juncture patterns and that consequently excessive commas produce a distractingly bumpy prose.

It is not quite true that the foregoing rules cover all the possible sentence situations in which commas may be useful, but in your college writing it might be well to avoid using a comma which cannot be justified by one of those rules.

Avoid unnecessary commas, particularly in the following five situations.

a. Do not use a comma to separate subject and verb.

No idea is expressed unless both subject and predicate are present. The two "belong together" as much as any two grammatical elements can. Even when the subject is a long noun clause, or a noun modified by a long restrictive phrase or clause, avoid a comma after the subject and before the verb unless confusion will result without it.

Whoever comes to the office to claim this package may have it.
The little old man who came every day to feed the pigeons was a friend of mine.

Note: Parenthetical elements coming between subject and verb are set off by *two* commas; they do not affect the syntax of the main clause. (See also P3e.)

Old Mr. Saunders, who came every day to feed the pigeons, spent a great deal of money on cracked corn.
Horatio Hornblower, the incomparable naval officer, won every war he entered.

b. Do not use a comma to separate verb and complement.

An incomplete subject-verb idea demands a complement; consequently that complement belongs to the verb and should not be separated from it.

> The answers are clear and comprehensive.
> He told us that he would surely be there.

Note: Parenthetical elements coming between verb and complement are set off by *two* commas; they do not affect the syntax of the main clause. (See also P3e.)

> I shall explain, as clearly as I can, all I know about the problem.

c. Do not use a comma to separate restrictive modifiers from the words they modify, nor to separate restrictive appositives from the words with which they are in apposition. (See P3b.)

This rule may be applied not only to restrictive adjective and adverb phrases and clauses, but also to the last member of coordinate adjectives in series before a noun and to the first in a series of coordinate adverbs after a verb.

> The man who answered first was wrong.
> The girl's shrill, petulant voice echoed through the house.
> She spoke harshly, stridently.
> Shakespeare the poet only rarely took suggestions from Shakespeare the businessman.

Note: Since the relative pronoun *that* is now used only with restrictive adjective clauses, or with noun clauses functioning as subject or complement, the punctuation of *that* clauses is simple. *Do not set off* that *clauses,* except in A, B, and C series.

> This is the book that I told you to read.
> The charity that begins at home arouses our greatest interest.
> That you can do it if you try is unquestionable.
> He said that he would think about it, that he would call me, but that I should not call him.

d. Do not normally use a comma before *and* or *or* connecting words or phrases, except in A, B, and C series. (Such a comma may be used if the degree of separation is distinct or if confusion might result from its omission.)

> He was uncomfortable and cross.
> He will do all that he can for you and will let you know what happens.
> You will pay that bill by tomorrow or be sued.
> John, Tom, and Mary went to the movies.

e. Do not separate coordinating conjunctions (*and, but, or, for, nor*) **from the clause, phrase, or word they introduce.**

> The clouds gathered, and the rains came. (*A comma after* and *lends entirely too much emphasis to the connective.*)

Conjunctive adverbs, like *however* and *nevertheless,* may or may not be set off, depending on how formal the rest of the punctuation is in the passage.

EXERCISE

Correct the punctuation of the following sentences by removing unnecessary commas. Insert any commas that are required.

1. Driving inland from the East Coast, one passes, the Tidewater, the Piedmont (or foothill region), and a relatively low range of mountains before one comes to the Appalachians.
2. To the true Easterner, the area between the Atlantic, and the Appalachians is the only one, which is of any consequence, for, beyond the Appalachians the West begins.
3. It is amazing, how many people, in this country, would be surprised, to think of Ohio—or Nebraska—as, "the West."
4. Lord Dunsany, an English scholar and critic, once invented a sentence to illustrate excessive punctuation: "Moreover, Jones, who is, also, of course, Welsh, is, perhaps, coming, too, but, unfortunately, alone."
5. The pitches and junctures in Lord Dunsany's sentence, are enough, to make a reader seasick.
6. Despite the length of time it has taken scholars to classify the uses of pitch, stress, and juncture in English, children have long been aware of it, and just for fun read the wrong signals into passages of prose, roaring with laughter at the results.
7. Experts in double-talk, too speaking rapidly give, the right signals but, for, the wrong structures and listeners, puzzled, wonder why they do not quite understand.
8. A foreigner speaking English may get the words and the forms of words and the order of words perfectly and still be difficult to understand because he misses the signals of pitch, stress, and juncture and consequently misses the English tune.
9. From time to time and place to place the system of signals

changes, but it is always systematic, and understood by all, who speak the dialect.

10. The signals, that are understood by a group of speakers, constitute the system for that group.

OTHER MARKS OF PUNCTUATION

In the foregoing discussion of the four troublesome sentence patterns, the miscellaneous uses of the comma, and the dangers of the excessive use of the comma, we have considered about eighty-five percent of all punctuation. There remain to be considered eleven other marks of punctuation (some few uses of which have been treated as we worked with the troublesome sentence patterns). Fortunately, these other marks of punctuation are chiefly employed in clearly defined and stereotyped situations. Once their functions are understood, they give very little trouble.

7. PERIOD (.)

a. Marking the end of a sentence: The period is used to mark the end of a declarative sentence, an imperative sentence (unless it is very emphatic), and many exclamatory sentences which express only mild emotion.

> Many coeds regard classes as annoying interludes separating weekends.
> Shut the outside door.
> How tired we all were after the party.

Note: The period should not be used to create **fragmentary sentences.** Except in very unusual circumstances, be sure that everything you write as a sentence expresses a complete thought. (For full discussion, see **Frag** [Chapter 12], and pages 415–416. See also P12e.)

> WRONG: My brother, who everybody knows is far more energetic than I and who has developed a native resourcefulness by a strenuous career as a newspaperman.
> WRONG: I will gladly do it for you. After you have paid me for the three previous jobs.

b. With abbreviations: The period is used after abbreviations and after initial letters representing words.

Etc., Mrs., *ibid.*, A.D., J. L. Smith.

Exceptions: Periods are not used with initials representing government agencies, with an increasing number of other organizations, or with abbreviations (clipped forms) which have become recognized words in their own right. (Such clipped forms are usually very informal.)

TVA, AEC, CIA, MLA, AAUP, exam, ad, taxi

8. QUESTION MARK (?)

a. Direct questions: The question mark is used after an interrogative sentence, one which asks a direct question. It is not used after a declarative sentence reporting an *indirect* question.

Where did you get that notebook?
He asked where I got this notebook.

The use of question marks is especially important in two situations, chiefly because many students fail to use them and thereby mislead a reader. The first is at the end of a long sentence which has been made interrogative by the inversion of the subject-verb order of declarative sentences.

Did you read the story in the paper which told of the discovery by archaeologists of one of the earliest cities in the Fertile Crescent, the presumed area of the birth of civilization?

The other is at the end of a sentence which does not invert the declarative subject-verb order, but depends instead on the interrogative pitch and juncture signals.

John will do it?

The question mark is used after a sentence rendered interrogative by a parenthetical question coming at the end of the sentence. It is usually not used if the parenthetical question comes elsewhere in the sentence.

I wish I knew how he can afford to date her, don't you?
You think, don't you, that I never study.

b. Indicating doubt: The question mark, usually in parentheses, is used to indicate doubt about the accuracy of some statement.

Chaucer was born in 1340(?) and died in 1400.

c. Not used to label irony

Do *not* use the question mark to call attention to ironic remarks. If your jokes are so feeble that they need to be labeled, you are perhaps better off if your reader overlooks them.

WEAK: He is a scholar (?) and a football player.

9. EXCLAMATION POINT (!)

a. Marking the end of a sentence: The exclamation point is used after an emphatic exclamatory sentence, after a strong interjection, or after an exclamatory question.

Your house is on fire!
Whew!
How can you stand it!

b. Not to be overused

Do *not* overuse exclamation points. They are known as "screamers." Save them for occasions when you want to scream.

c. Not to be doubled up

Do *not* attempt to show that this time you really need an exclamation point by using two or three at once. Use them sparingly, and one will be enough.

WEAK: Honestly! I was so mad! ! He was late! ! !

EXERCISE

Punctuate the following sentences conventionally.

1. Who, me
2. Has it really occurred to you that I might have meant someone else
3. Be reasonable enough, won't you, to admit your guilt
4. Brutus is an honorable man
5. He asked Father William why he continually stood on his head

6. The President is unquestionably the greatest living American, don't you think
7. Look out We're going to hit him
8. She glared at him angrily "You're crazy"
9. He replied, inquisitively, "You think so   Why"
10. He asked why she thought so

10. SEMICOLON (;)

The semicolon (not to be confused with the colon) functions as a heavy comma, but is used principally between elements which are grammatically equal. Overuse of the semicolon between unequal elements confuses the reader. The pitch and juncture signals for semicolons, particularly between independent clauses where they most often appear, are essentially the same as those for a period: a sharp dropping of the voice, followed by a full stop of the breath, that is, the maximum juncture. Only the logical unity of the resulting sentences distinguishes between periods and semicolons, and valid differences of opinion are usually possible.

a. Compound sentences without coordinating conjunctions: The semicolon is used to separate independent clauses not connected by a coordinating conjunction. (See also P1b and Cs.)

Professors tend to stress theory rather than practice in their courses; they realize how much more stable theories are than the variable methods by which theories are applied.

We wish that we could accept your invitation; however, we have a previous engagement.

As the second example above indicates, conjunctive adverbs (like *however, nevertheless, accordingly, therefore*) may connect independent clauses. But they are not coordinating conjunctions; they are primarily adverbs. When they occur between clauses without an attendant coordinating conjunction, separate the clauses with semicolons. (See also P1b, c.)

Note: Do *not* assume that semicolons always precede conjunctive adverbs. If the conjunctive adverb is inserted parenthetically within a clause, it is set off by commas as a parenthetical interrupter. (See also P3.)

He has studied hard all semester; therefore he has little need to cram for exams. (*A comma after* therefore *would be more formal.*)
He has studied hard all semester; he has little need, therefore, to cram for exams.

EXERCISE

Punctuate the following sentences conventionally.

1. The Dean was present however he slept all through the meeting.
2. That was not the first important meeting moreover in which he had been caught napping.
3. He was a man of action at the same time he was a man of dreams.
4. There is no history there are only the interpretations of events by historians.
5. The farther into the past an event recedes, the more likely historians are to reach agreement while we might as well accept their opinions we should realize that probability is involved rather than certain truth.

b. Compound sentences with coordinating conjunctions and internal commas: The semicolon is used instead of the comma between independent clauses connected by a coordinating conjunction whenever internal commas might obscure the importance of the main break in the sentence.

After swimming, riding, dining, and dancing, they retired to their rooms; and being somewhat wearied by their exertions, they slept soundly till the following noon.

c. Between members of an A, B, and C series with internal commas: Semicolons are used instead of commas to separate the members of an A, B, and C series whenever commas within the members might confuse the reader.

Abel, Martha; Ambrose, Murray; Berger, Henry—these names led the class roll.

11. COLON (:)

The colon (not to be confused with the semicolon) is used between a formal introductory passage and that which follows. Unlike the semicolon, which is used between grammatically equal elements, the colon separates elements which are logically equal but are often grammatically quite different.

a. The colon is used between independent clauses when the second clause repeats or develops the idea of the first.

> The Duke of Wellington was a perfect example of the strictly honorable English gentleman: after a long separation and without any intervening indication of interest on either side, he married his youthful sweetheart because he believed he had once led her to expect him to do so.

b. The colon is used between a generalizing statement and the formal series of details which particularizes it.

> Three types of governmental functions are carefully distinguished in the Constitution: administrative functions, legislative functions, and judicial functions.

c. The colon is used between a formal orientation phrase and a formal quotation.

> Jean Jacques Rousseau long ago observed: "If children are not to be made to do things merely for the sake of their obedience, it follows that they will learn nothing until they recognize in it a real and immediate profit or pleasure."

d. The colon is used between the salutation and the body of the letter in formal correspondence.

> Dear Sir:
> Your very interesting suggestion has been referred to . . . .

e. The colon is used between titles and subtitles.

> *Middlemarch: A Study of Provincial Life*

f. In Biblical references the colon is used between chapter and verse.

> Ecclesiastes 12:12

g. The colon is used between hours and minutes numerically represented.

> 10:45 P.M.

12. DASH (—)

The dash (not to be confused with the hyphen) is a useful and quite legitimate mark of punctuation, but with two exceptions it does not substitute for any other mark of punctuation. (See P12g, h.) Indiscriminate use of the dash, therefore, is not only an indication of the writer's unwillingness to learn conventional punctuation, but is an imposition on the reader, since it forces him to decide what kind of punctuation was intended. A dash in the wrong place is always annoying and often confusing.

Remember that the dash is an emphatic mark. It suggests sharp and often sudden breaks in thought, and it is marked by very distinct pitch, stress, and juncture signals, characterized chiefly by abrupt and emphatic shifts. It is sometimes considered more appropriate in informal than in formal writing, because formal writing tends to be more measured and more calm than a dash will permit.

In print, a dash is at least twice the length of a hyphen. To indicate a dash in typing, use two hyphens with no space between them and the preceding and succeeding words, or space-hyphen-space.

a. With a sentence broken off: The dash is used to suggest that a sentence has been sharply broken off.

> I tell you—. But, no, I will not tell you after all.

b. With an emphatic appositive: The dash is used to emphasize an appositive.

> There is one room the sovereign of England may never enter—the chamber of the House of Commons.
>
> Only one man—the President—can appoint justices to the Supreme Court.
>
> [Notice that commas would be normal in both sentences if emphasis were not required; see P3b(3).]

c. With digressions: The dash is used to set off an emphatic digression.

> You must not—and I mean this—use dashes indiscriminately.
>
> It was last Thursday—no, it was the Tuesday before—that I wrote to Henry about it.

d. With an emphatic parenthetical element: The dash is used to emphasize a parenthetical element which might normally be set off by commas. (See P3.)

> Unlike the public figure, if an ordinary man should undergo a nervous breakdown—which, under certain circumstances, could happen to anybody—he could at least secure a reasonable privacy.

e. Indicating decided and emphatic hesitation: The dash is used in informal writing to suggest a decided and emphatic hesitation before adding an afterthought.

> I will gladly do it for you—after you have paid me for the three previous jobs.

Note: This punctuation will provide, legitimately, the effect student writers often attempt to secure by putting the afterthought into a fragmentary sentence. (See P7a and **Frag.**) Use it, however, sparingly; overuse is distracting.

f. Between a series and a summarizing passage: The dash is used between a series and a summarizing passage.

> Beauty, family background, wealth, an excellent education, a prosperous and happy marriage—all these explain her arrogant self-assurance.

g. Setting off parenthetical elements with internal commas: Dashes are used as substitutes for commas to set off parenthetical elements containing internal commas.

> Considering the manifold blessings of civilization, everyone—man, woman, and child—should know as much as possible about first aid.

h. In place of colons in informal writing: Dashes sometimes substitute for colons in informal writing.

> FORMAL: Bacteria fall into two groups: aerobic and anaerobic.
> INFORMAL: Bacteria fall into two groups—aerobic and anaerobic.

i. The dash splice in compound sentences

Avoid the dash in place of the semicolon between independent clauses not connected by coordinating conjunctions. (See P1c and P10.)

On rare occasions the clauses of a compound sentence may be held tightly enough together by logic to provide a unified sentence in spite of the abrupt separation of the dash, but normally such a dash destroys unity. If you need the emphasis of the dash, it may legitimately be used between two sentences.

13. PARENTHESES ( )

a. To minimize a parenthentical element: Parentheses are used to **enclose elements interrupting a sentence when that material is to be minimized,** providing the reader with necessary information but offering the least possible distraction from the main idea. The pitch patterns of parentheses and dashes do not differ greatly, but the stress is light with parentheses and the junctures are less abrupt. The effect is much less emphatic.

> John Keats (who died at the age of twenty-six) was perhaps the most promising young poet that England has ever produced.
>
> Parenthetical (interpolated) material may be set off by commas, parentheses, or dashes, depending on the degree of emphasis desired.

b. With other punctuation: When parentheses occur at a point in **the sentence which requires other punctuation, place the other mark of punctuation** *inside* **the final parenthesis if the other mark belongs to the parenthetical material,** *outside* **if it does not.**

> Enrollment in English courses will take place in Monroe Hall (Room 103).
>
> The 1920's were a period of roaring prosperity. (But the farmer even then was in trouble.)
>
> If tomorrow is a windy day (and the weather report suggests that it may be), there will be little passing in the football game.

c. Misuse with material to be deleted: Do *not* use parentheses to **enclose material you wish to delete from a manuscript. Instead, draw a line completely through the material to be omitted.**

> WRONG BECAUSE CONFUSING: He accepted the offer (although) in spite of the fact that it was disappointing.
>
> RIGHT: He accepted the offer ~~although~~ in spite of the fact that it was disappointing.

517

d. Parentheses always occur in pairs. Do not forget to close the parenthesis by inserting the) at the end.

> CARELESS: Solomon was given to thoughtful meditation (he had many, many wives.
>
> RIGHT: To avoid comma splices, you must first memorize the five coordinating conjunctions (*and, but, or, nor,* and *for*).

14. BRACKETS [ ]

a. To enclose material inserted in a quotation: Brackets are used primarily to insert explanatory or connective material of your own in passages quoted from another writer.

> "For this story [*A Study in Scarlet*] which first introduced Sherlock Holmes, the most famous and the most profitable detective of all time, Dr. Conan Doyle received exactly £ 25 [then worth $125]."

b. With other punctuation: When brackets occur at a point in the sentence requiring other punctuation, place the other mark of punctuation *inside* the final bracket if the other mark belongs to the bracketed material, *outside* if it does not.

15. QUOTATION MARKS (" ")

a. Double quotation marks except with internal quotation: Quotation marks in American practice are double (" ") except when a quotation occurs within another quotation. Do not attempt to distinguish between quotations of varying importance by using single quotation marks (' ') in anything other than an internal quotation. (Because British practice reverses American practice, you have sometimes seen single quotation marks where you expected double ones.) Follow American practice when writing for American readers.

b. With direct quotations: Double quotation marks enclose all material directly quoting the exact words of a speaker or writer. They are *not* used with indirect quotations.

> "I can't do the impossible," he said. "What do you take me for, a marine?"
> Lincoln began quietly: "Fourscore and seven years ago. . . ."
> "I will be there," he promised.
> He promised that he would be there.

518

"On November 6, 1817, died the Princess Charlotte, only child of
the Prince Regent, and heir to the crown of England."

Lytton Strachey

**c. With a quotation of more than one consecutive sentence: When
a quoted speech or passage consists of more than one consecutive
sentence, use quotation marks to enclose the entire quotation, *not*
to enclose separate sentences.**

WRONG: "I will gladly go with you." "I was going that way anyway."
RIGHT: "I will gladly go with you. I was going that way anyway."

**d. With a quotation of more than one paragraph: When a quoted
passage consists of more than one paragraph, *begin* each paragraph
with double quotation marks, but do not use closing quotation
marks until the end of the quotation.**

**e. With nicknames: Double quotation marks are used to enclose
nicknames, unless the nicknames are already familiar to your
reader.**

"Butch" Cabot, "Spike" Lowell, and "Ladyfingers" O'Toole shared
the leadership of the segment of Boston society I knew as a child.
Stonewall Jackson was one of America's greatest generals.

**f. With words as labels or in an unusual sense: Double quotation
marks are used to enclose a word used as a label or a word used
in an unusual way. In both usages, the quotation marks have the
same effect as the phrase "so-called."**

A word or phrase in which the sounds reflect and reinforce the
meaning is called "onomatopoetic."
Elmer's "industry" is closely akin to other people's idea of laziness.

**g. With words as words (now rare): Rarely, double quotation
marks are used to enclose a word used as a word, that is, as a combination of letters without reference to the meaning. More commonly now such a word is put in italics (underlined).**

OLD-FASHIONED: You have too many "and's" here.
BETTER: You have too many *and*'s here.

Note: Avoid "apologetic quotation marks" to enclose slang or colloquial phrases inappropriately employed in formal writing. The

519

use of quotation marks in such situations is now old-fashioned. Modern writers will use a slang or colloquial term without apology *if it is appropriate* (that is, if the intended reader will understand it and if it is in harmony with the tone of the whole). If it is not appropriate, do not use it.

> OLD-FASHIONED AND INEPT: We did the best we could with the job, and even if the result wasn't "top notch," at least it would "come pretty high up" on anybody's scale.
>
> VERY INFORMAL: We did the best we could with the job, and even if the result wasn't top notch, at least it would come pretty high up on anybody's scale.
>
> FORMAL: We gave our best efforts to the task, and even though the result fell short of perfection, it was not a result of which we needed to be ashamed.

h. With titles: Double quotation marks are used to enclose the titles of works which are parts of larger wholes, such as stories from a collection, articles from a magazine, chapters from a book, poems from a collection, and so on. Titles of complete works are now commonly put in italics (underlined). (See also **Ital.**)

> "The Adventure of the Empty House" (a story from the volume entitled *The Return of Sherlock Holmes*), "Cheap Clothes for Fat Old Women" (an article from the magazine entitled The *Atlantic Monthly*), "Matter Prefatory in Praise of Biography" (a chapter from the novel entitled *Tom Jones*), "My Last Duchess" (a poem from the volume entitled *Dramatic Romances*)

i. With other marks of punctuation: American practice, followed by all but a few American writers and publishers, is easy to learn. British practice is more complex, but since you are writing for American readers, learn and follow the American practice.

1) WITH PERIODS AND COMMAS: PERIODS AND COMMAS GO INSIDE QUO-TATION MARKS, REGARDLESS OF THE LENGTH OR THE NATURE OF THE QUOTATION.

> "Butch," "Spike," and "Ladyfingers" led the gang.
> "Speak to me of my beauty," she purred.
> "Aw, go on," he responded brusquely.
> The reaction is technically known as "reduction."

2) WITH COLONS AND SEMICOLONS: COLONS AND SEMICOLONS GO OUT-
SIDE QUOTATION MARKS, REGARDLESS OF THE LENGTH OR NATURE OF
THE QUOTATION.

> "Some books are to be chewed and digested": Bacon's essays them-
> selves are not to be read hastily.
> "Give me liberty or give me death"; that spirit is not dead in
> twentieth-century America.

3) WITH QUESTION MARKS AND EXCLAMATION POINTS: QUESTION
MARKS AND EXCLAMATION POINTS GO INSIDE QUOTATION MARKS IF
THEY BELONG TO THE QUOTED MATERIAL; OTHERWISE THEY GO OUT-
SIDE QUOTATION MARKS.

> He asked, "Are you going?"
> Did he say, "I am going"?
> Did he ask, "Are you going?"
> "Help!" he cried. (*Notice that we usually do not double up punctua-
> tion. The exclamation point replaces the normal comma before
> the orientation phrase.*)
> He said, of all things, "No comment"!

EXERCISE

Punctuate the following sentences illustrating the uses of quotation marks.

1. He spoke with quiet exasperation. You have neglected to hand
   in five themes. You have missed nearly half of the meetings
   of the class. You made a score of fifty-three on the final examination. And you complain because you failed the course!
2. But I've got to get a B, or I can't be initiated, the boy insisted.
3. I would suggest, the professor replied, that you consider that
   point somewhat earlier in the next term, if you are still in
   school.
4. Professor Snodgrass is just an old meany.
5. That chapter called Oxidation and Reduction is the hardest one
   in the book.
6. The American Way is harder to define than many people realize.
7. Stonewall Jackson was one of Lee's principal generals; Old
   Pete Longstreet was another.
8. Where were you on the night of June the third? the prosecutor
   thundered.

9. I was at home, she answered, reading a story entitled Injured Innocence, from a book called Perilous Pitfalls.

10. Her own definition of innocence was what interested the jury.

16. APOSTROPHE (')

a. To indicate the possessive case: The apostrophe is used to indicate the possessive case of nouns and of indefinite pronouns. It is *not* **used in the possessive case of personal pronouns nor with the relative pronoun** *who-whose.*

boy—boy's	boss—boss's
man—man's	bosses—bosses'
men—men's	Moses—Moses'
everybody—	one—one's
everybody's	one's self *or* oneself

NOT: hi's, her's, it's, who's
USE: his, hers, its, whose
It's is a contraction of *it is.*
Who's is a contraction of *who is.*

1) NOTE: WHEN TO USE THE APOSTROPHE ALONE, WHEN TO USE APOSTROPHE AND "S."

To decide when both an apostrophe and an extra *s* are needed to form the possessive case of nouns and indefinite pronouns, remember that the apostrophe is *always* needed. If, when you pronounce the possessive case, you add an extra *s*- (or *z*-) *sound* to the form of the common case, use an extra *s* in addition to the apostrophe.

man + *s-sound* = man's
boss + *s-sound* = boss's
bosses + no *s-sound* = bosses'
Moses + no *s-sound* = Moses'

The man is here. The man's coat is torn.
He is the boss. John married the boss's daughter.
They are the bosses. To marry the bosses' daughters would be bigamous.
Moses led the Children of Israel out of Egypt. Moses' writings are well known.

You can trust your own pronunciation. Proper names about which you are in doubt probably have alternate forms.

> I went down to St. James' Infirmary.
> He is our ambassador to the Court of St. James's.

2) IN COMPOUNDS: IN COMPOUNDS, THE POSSESSIVE FORM USUALLY APPEARS IN THE LAST WORD.

> The King of England's horse
> Everybody else's opinion
> The man in the street's opinion

b. In contractions: The apostrophe is used in place of an omitted letter in a contraction.

> cannot—can't
> do not—don't
> it is—it's
> could have—could've (not *could of*)

c. To indicate the plural of symbols: The apostrophe is used to form the plurals of letters, words used as words, numerals, or other symbols. It is *not* used to indicate plurality in ordinary nouns.

> You have too many *and*'s in that sentence.
> Add two 2's and the result is 4.
> He sprinkles &'s throughout his writing as if it would exhaust him completely to write *and*.
> WRONG: They are leader's of the movement.
> RIGHT: They are leaders of the movement.

17. SUSPENSION POINTS (ELLIPSIS MARKS) (. . .)

a. To indicate an omission from a quotation: Suspension points (*three* dots) are used to indicate that something has been omitted from a quoted sentence.

> You cannot make a philosophic individualist into a good citizen. As the world is constituted at present, . . . probably it would be better to have hundred-percenters and A-1 patriots than to have reasonable individuals living reasonable lives.
>
> *Lin Yutang*

You are under a moral obligation, when using suspension points this way, to omit nothing which would change the sense of what you are quoting. In the example above, an expansive detail, "with fierce national conflicts," was omitted. The omission did not distort the original. When the omission comes at a point in the original which requires other punctuation, add the other punctuation to the three dots, before them or after them according to the position of the omitted material in the original.

> Germany's payments, moreover, were fixed . . ., and the *de facto* relationship between war debts and reparation was clearly recognized.
>
> *F. Lee Benns*

> Then with a spilling, tumbling rush of water falling down into its trough, it [a wave] dissolves . . . .
>
> *Rachel L. Carson*

b. In dialogue: Suspension points are used, most commonly in dialogue, to indicate a decided but not emphatic hesitation, or to indicate that an uncompleted sentence trailed away into silence. (See also P12a, e.) These uses are rare, and suspension points should be used sparingly.

> "Mary. . . ." He spoke with soft embarrassment. "I . . . I missed you, . . . Mary."
> "The treasure is hidden in. . . ." But the feeble old voice had faded away. My father was dead.

EXERCISES

A. Punctuate the following sentences according to strictly conventional usage. Capitalize where necessary. Be prepared to defend your decisions.

1. This is an exercise reviewing all that we have studied about punctuation consequently you must be alert for any sort of problem may occur

2. There will be no trick sentences or at least not many

3. Any sentence which lacks the normal aid that conventional punctuation provides is to some extent tricky

4. How sweet the moonlight sleeps upon that bank Sandra quoted meaningfully Harold clutched his fraternity pin firmly and ran

5. Many people who have lived for years in Washington D C maintain residences in another state where taxes are lower

6. Death taxes and clichés these no man can escape

7. Three may keep secrets if two be away

8. If sweet are the uses of adversity civilization is getting sweeter by the minute or should I say by every tick of the scientists' clocks

9. Our food is denatured pasteurized and reinvigorated and all of it tastes like old wallpaper paste

10. Wallpaper half of the time is plastic and paste as likely as not is a glutinous fraud

11. In the 1930s we laughed at the Germans *ersatz* materials how proud we are of our own synthetics many of which were developed from German patents incidentally

12. We fire rockets at the moon and flash madly around the inner reaches of space all the time dodging the left over junk from dead but still orbiting bric-a-brac

13. Many cities like Baltimore Maryland can boast mile after mile of rusting junk piles so perhaps space is as good a place to throw new junk as any other

14. Meanwhile although man has been going in and out through the rain for many millennia no one yet has invented a convenient comfortable way to go out in the rain without getting wet

15. Why doesnt some scientist think about some of the important problems of life

16. Names on the Land by George R Stewart is an excellent history of American place naming

17. The History of New York is one of its most interesting chapters

18. I will contribute upon one condition that my name not be made public

19. The time has come gentlemen to what time is it anyway

20. America needs you and I do mean you to preserve her institutions whenever they are threatened and to improve them wherever they are faulty

21. How long ago it was that Wordsworth said The world is too much with us

22. Life comes before literature as the material always comes before the work

23. He rushed into the room crying the house is on fire

24. Do not I said to him icily say the house is on fire tell us specifically what part of the house and inform us clearly of the seriousness of the conflagration before you stampede us into making utter fools of ourselves by calling the fire department quite unnecessarily

25. He said that he was sorry and that he would do better when we got another house

B. Punctuate the following passage.

One of the things that cannot be too often emphasized as you perhaps have heard before is the importance of writing about subjects you are interested in. If you will stop for a moment before you start work on a theme to think of the topics offered to twist those topics to fit subjects that you know something about to consider whether or not the theme can be made more to you than a mere exercise if you will do this until you have hit on an idea you really know about and are interested in your theme assignments will be easier to fulfill and your themes will be more interesting to read. Also you are quite likely to discover that somehow you have written better and more accurate English than you knew you could. Not even Shakespeare could have written his best when he was bored. Why should you try You may complain But the topics themselves seem dull. The only answer is that they shouldnt. Many students have written well on similar topics many times before. The topics are designed to fit your knowledge and your interests they were selected for those reasons. Remember three things you cannot learn to express yourself clearly unless you sincerely constantly try; unless you see your effort as useful to all the rest of your work in college and after unless you are interested in what you are saying and eager to say it well.

15-

Spelling

Characteristics of a Good Theme: 11. Conventionally acceptable spelling.

Sp   Spelling

HISTORICAL BACKGROUND

Correctness in spelling, as in any aspect of the language, is established by *current, national,* and *reputable* usage. Fortunately for twentieth century users of English, the standard of correctness in English spelling is clear cut: Most English words are properly spelled in only one way, and that way can be learned and used confidently. Neither the audience you address, the tone of your writing, nor the level of language you adopt has to be considered in spelling.

Even so, English spelling offers many complicated problems. It is not as illogical as it seems, but the logic behind it is the logic of history, and the history of our language has been very complex indeed. Many of our words, for example, came from the language our Anglo-Saxon forefathers spoke. Many other words came to us from Latin through the French of the Normans who conquered England in 1066 and formed the ruling class for some three hundred years thereafter. Other words came directly from classical Latin as still later borrowings. Others came from Parisian French, or were taken from classical Greek, or were borrowed from one or another of the many languages the far-ranging English have been in contact with over the years. And the spelling of all these words has been affected by the way the English-speaking peoples have pronounced them.

The effect of the changes in the sounds English speakers have given to their words can be seen in such a word as *priest*. Christianity touched the Angles and Saxons soon after they left their homeland in the north of Germany, fifteen hundred years ago, and the Greek word *presbyteros* was adopted to signify the spiritual elders of the tribes who taught the new doctrines. Over the centuries, that word wore down to *preost*, and that to *priest*. Then when the sixteenth century reformers of the faith wanted a new word to signify the leaders of the new sects, they went back to Greek and borrowed the same word all over again, and we have the priest on one side and the presbyter on the other. Similar changes have taken place in far shorter periods. In such words as *brought*, or *thought*, the *gh* was pronounced (somewhat like the Scottish *ch* in *loch*, or the German *ch* in *achtung*) in Chaucer's day, less than six hundred years ago. Two hundred years ago, all reputable speakers pronounced *deaf* to rime with *leaf*, and some grandmothers still pronounce it that way. Yet as the sounds have changed, the spelling has often remained the same.

There have been, also, other complicating factors. The scholars do not like the illogicalities of spelling any more than students do, and they have made many attempts (often misguided ones) to introduce order and simplification to the confusion. Sometimes they have attempted to go back to the "original word." Latin scholars, for example, decided that since Chaucer's word *dette* had made its way into English from the Latin *debitus*, it would be simpler and more "proper" to spell it *debt*. Other scholars decided that the perfectly good Anglo-Saxon word *iland* must have been derived from the same root as the word *isle*, which came into the language later from Norman French; so they spelled *iland* as *island*. In another sort of change, after the settlement of America, Noah Webster decided that American writers should drop the *u* from such English spellings as *colour* or *labour,* and spell the words *color* and *labor.* Although it is usage alone that establishes correctness, these particular prescriptions took hold; the best writers began to use the prescribed forms; and because those forms are now used by the best writers, they are now correct.

Not all attempts to simplify spelling have been so successful. As recently as the turn of the present century, Theodore Roosevelt threw all the weight of his tremendous energy and all the prestige of the presidential office behind a new effort to "simplify" English spelling. The federal government, many colleges, and some publishers adopted such spellings as *tho, thru, altho,* and *thoro.* But the reputable writers, the court of final appeal in such matters, simply refused to use them, and now they are rarely or never seen in books or carefully edited periodicals.

Nor are current schemes to simplify English spelling likely to be any more successful. The problem is more complex than it seems at first glance. Ideally, words should be spelled phonetically, that is, as they are pronounced. Yet even so apparently simple a solution is complicated. We have already seen that sounds change, sometimes quite rapidly. (We all know people who still meticulously retain the French pronunciation of the word we all spell as *garage,* carefully saying GA·RÁHZH where most of us say GA·RÁHDG and where the lower-class Englishman says frankly GÁRE·IDG.) Our spelling was almost phonetic when Chaucer was writing, just before the introduction of printing tended to fix spellings; and then the sounds changed, and have kept on changing. If we are to spell words as they are pronounced, the first question is: As they are pronounced when? Shall we be constantly changing spelling as our sounds change? It is hard enough now to learn a fixed spelling, much less to try to keep up with constant changes. Another question arises: As words are pronounced by whom? The Englishman, the Australian, the Bostonian, the Mississippian, the Chicagoan—all pronounce words differently. Whose pronunciation shall be taken as the standard? And who shall decide when an accepted spelling is to be changed? With all these considerations in mind, it should be clear that there is not much chance that spelling will be made easier. It will be necessary for you, rather, to improve your spelling to conform to standard practice.

THE IMPORTANCE OF SPELLING

Nothing is more obvious to the educated reader, nothing brings quicker scorn, than poor spelling, at least partly because everyone has some trouble with spelling and consequently few have patience with what seems to be lazy unwillingness to improve. The educated writer is expected to spell as others do, and no excuses are accepted.

And improvement can certainly be made, even though improvement is harder for some people than for others. (If you are a really bad speller, if you genuinely try but still have trouble with common, little words, if you literally cannot see the difference between such words as *trial* and *trail*, you have a special problem that needs expert help. But you can still improve. Your college Reading Clinic may be qualified to help you, or in large cities special remedial centers—some better than others—are available. You cannot go to them too soon.) Most poor spellers have merely never taken the trouble to learn to spell the comparatively few words they miss. As long as they were given *A*'s and *B*'s for their work, there really seemed to be no need to learn.

But your college instructors may prove less lenient. Since most students can spell conventionally, and since most poor spelling is merely a sign of laziness and indifference, college instructors, in English or any other subject, have little patience with it. Unless the instructors are unusually charitable, the day of *A*'s and *B*'s is over for the careless speller. And after college, the handicap imposed by poor spelling grows. At all stages of your career, poor spelling will brand you as ignorant, and will amuse as well as confuse your reader.

IMPROVING SPELLING DEFICIENCIES

Learning to spell, as late as your college years, is hard. It will require constant, individual effort for a long period, because your habits—bad habits here—are firmly fixed, and it will take determination and persistence to correct them. Fortunately, however, hard as the job is, it is not as hard as you think. You already spell most words and most types of words correctly. Even a word you habitually miss is usually correct except for one or two letters. Further, your misspellings fall into discoverable groups and can be corrected by groups. To improve your spelling, you need first to learn what words you misspell and how you misspell them, second to learn the patterns of English spelling which will help you determine the proper forms, and third to discover ways to fix especially difficult words in your memory.

1. PERSONAL SPELLING LIST

Before you can begin to improve your spelling you must know where the trouble lies. What words and what types of words do you misspell and how do you misspell them? To discover where your trouble lies, keep a personal spelling list in your notebook. From every theme, from every other piece of writing you do, record the words you miss. Write out, this one more time, the misspelled form of the word as well as the correct spelling. (If you are a really bad speller, keep the list on three-by-five-inch cards, so that you can easily look to see if a given word has already been entered. If it has, make a check mark for each recurrence.) Any words you find yourself missing three or four times should be given particular attention. This list of your own problem words has a number of advantages. One of them is that it warns you to *doubt* your handling of particular words as you write, for obviously until you doubt your present practice, you can scarcely begin to form new habits. Not less important is the fact that it teaches you which words or types of words to doubt, so that you need not any longer regard the whole problem with numb despair.

2. DIAGNOSING THE TROUBLE

After a few themes have provided you with a representative sample of your mistakes, examine your misspellings, if necessary in consultation with your instructor. What kind of mistake are you making? You may find—and you should be embarrassed if you do—that practically all your errors result from sheer carelessness. If you can spell all the words that you use when you are thinking about spelling, your problem is easily solved: *Think about spelling* as you revise your themes, or even as you write them. There is no conceivable excuse for carelessness in a matter that can have such immediate bad effects.

The chances are, however, that the difficulty will not be so easily removed. An intelligent student who spells badly is more likely to have something besides carelessness to cope with. You may find that you do not know when to double consonants before suffixes, or when to use *ei* instead of *ie*, or when to drop or retain a final *e*. If some such confusion troubles you, most of your misspellings can be corrected by using the "spelling rules" you have repeatedly met but never mastered. They will frequently give you a clear path to follow, particularly if you remember that they are not "rules" at all, but very useful generalizations about what happens in large classes of words.

You will probably discover, though, that the trouble lies deeper than that. You may confuse the vowels in unaccented syllables, which we do not normally pronounce clearly, so that your ear is no guide even if you pronounce words properly. Or you may find that you misspell because you do *not* pronounce words properly, that you omit or add syllables unconventionally; that is, you spell what you say, but do not say what your readers assume you are trying to write. *Canidate* for *candidate* is a ready example; others are *strickly* for *strictly,* or the dropping of -*ed* from past participles. Or you may confuse similar words, even such common words as *to* and *too*.

Currently, the most frequent difficulty of all arises from the way you were first taught to read. (It is not always your fault if you are a poor speller, but it will be if you remain one.) If you were taught to read from the first by recognizing whole words at once, instead of by syllables—if in the first grade you saw and recognized *cat* instead of *c-a-t*, and later *separate* instead of *sep-a-rate*—you may never really have seen the words you misspell. Thousands of students, even when they are writing common words, begin and end with confidence and glory, but slither through the middle as best they can. All they know of a given word is that it begins and ends with certain letters, that it takes up approximately an inch on the page, and that there are no conspicuous letters, like *k*'s or *x*'s, anywhere in it. So they write *convience,* call it *convenience,* and think, "I just can't spell."

Examine your misspellings carefully and try to identify your personal difficulty. The examples just given do not exhaust the possible kinds of trouble, but they do include the most common ones, and they should suggest the diagnostic method that will make it possible for you to work intelligently at the task of improving. Once you learn where your trouble lies, work on that trouble, in recurring words or in new words that bother you. Remember that *you never miss a whole word;* without making careless mistakes anywhere, concentrate on the parts of the word you do miss.

3. USING THE DICTIONARY

Whenever you enter a word in your spelling list, go to your dictionary for the correct spelling. Do not guess; *know* that you are entering it correctly. And do not just glance at the word, then write it down and forget it. You know already that that method will do no good, since you now have to turn to the dictionary again and again for certain words, without ever learning them. Instead, make intelligent use of the dictionary; it is one of your strongest allies.

a. Syllabic division

Look at the word carefully, syllable by syllable, with particular attention to the syllables you misspell. (If you are uncertain about the system your dictionary uses to indicate syllabic division, consult the explanations at the front of the book.)

b. Pronunciation

Pronounce the word carefully, syllable by syllable, stressing the troublesome part.[1] (If you are uncertain about the system your dictionary uses to indicate pronunciation, study the detailed discussion.) Our spelling is far from phonetic, but in a sense most of our words are spelled as they are pronounced. If a word contains a "long *a*" sound, for example, the vowel may be spelled any one of several ways (as in *gate, hail, day, steak, rein, obey, fiancée,* or even *gauge*), but you can be sure it is not spelled *ow* or *ck*. The letter *a*

---

[1] This careful, syllabic pronunciation, stressing the syllables which may cause trouble, is a device to use in studying spelling, not in normal speech. Overprecise pronunciation in speaking is no solution to anything. In fact, since many troublesome syllables are troublesome because they are not stressed in normal speech, misapplication of this advice might merely lead to confusion.

in a word may not represent the long *a* sound of *gate*. It may represent the *a* of *arm*, or *can*, or *bath* (however you pronounce that), or *raw*, or any one of four or five other sounds. But it will not represent the sound in *foot*. Some of our consonants are "hard," like the *g* of *rag*, or "soft," like the *g* of *rage*. Some are "voiced," like the *s* of *lose*, or "voiceless," like the *s* of *loose*. A few consonantal sounds may be spelled several ways, like the *f* sound of *fish* and the *f* sound of *enough* or of *philosophy*. But most of our consonants represent fairly definite and identifiable sounds, and those sounds call for definite and dependable letters. Within these limits, and in this sense, most of our words are spelled as they are pronounced.

Pronounce the word carefully, *by syllables*, when you look up the spelling, and much of your difficulty may vanish. If you adopt such careful pronunciation as a regular practice when you are checking spelling, you should in time begin to recognize familiar letter combinations as they recur, and you will begin to be able to predict what combinations may be possible. Our later discussion will suggest the ways by which you can learn to choose the right combinations for any particular word.

There is at least one further way in which careful pronunciation by syllables as you check the spelling of a word will help. If you habitually leave out certain syllables, if you write *convience* for *convenience* or *rember* for *remember*, you can spot the difficulty readily by pronouncing the troublesome word as you revise your paper. In each of the examples just given, you would find yourself a syllable short. It should be no great trouble then to insert the missing syllable.

c. Derivation

It is often helpful to know something about the ancestry of a word. For one thing, it helps you to understand the presence of letters no longer pronounced, like the *gh* in *thought* or even like the *b* in *debt*, which has never been pronounced in English. It helps you to see relations between words you might not otherwise recognize as members of a word family. *Anthropology* and *philanthropy*, for example, share the Greek root word for man, *anthropos*. Recognizing such roots will help fix a shaky spelling. Also there are many classical or Anglo-Saxon prefixes and suffixes which constantly reappear. (See pages 181–183.) Recognizing them in a new word,

535

and knowing something of how they affect spellings, will often help. Whenever you can, use the derivation of a word to help you remember its present form.

d. Entry in personal spelling list

After you have taken these three steps, enter the word in your personal spelling list.

4. VISUAL SPELLING

a. The image in longhand

As you enter the word in your spelling list, correctly spelled and in your own handwriting, _look at it._ Look at the whole word, but focus your attention particularly on the syllables you misspell. If it is a word you habitually misspell, this will be the first time you ever saw the word as it should look in your own handwriting. You have seen it frequently in print, but the visual patterns made by a word in print and in your own longhand are quite different things. Fascinate and _fascinate_ do not look very much alike, and seeing the word in print a thousand times will do little to make you realize you have done something wrong if you read over your own themes and see _facinate_ on the page.

b. Fixing the image

Look at the word you have just written (correctly, remember) for a full minute. Now close your eyes and see if you can visualize it. You will not be able to see it as clearly as you can see your own signature, the specimen of your handwriting you have seen most often, but you should be able literally to see the word. If the image is vague, look at the word again and again until you can see it clearly. (Inability to form such visual images may be a sign of a special problem. Bad spellers who cannot form visual images should seek expert help, beginning with the college Reading Clinic or special classes in spelling.)

Fixing such a visual image of the correct form will at least help to warn you, as you revise a paper, that a given word is wrong, and it may well help you to get it right. You already use the method, in an unmethodical sort of way. How many times have you turned to a sheet of scratch paper and tried out various combinations "to see

536

which looks right"? If you have given yourself clear visual images of the correct form of these troublesome words, you can very easily pick out the correct combination.

5. FINGER SPELLING

We usually do not realize how much of our spelling is done by our fingers, without much prompting from our brains. When you want to write the conjunction *and,* for example, you never think *a-n-d.* You just write *and.* Again, how often do your thoughts get ahead of your hand? You are writing, say, "I plan to explain my opinion," and the *pl* of *plan* gets mixed up with the *pl* of *explain;* when you revise you wonder how on earth you came to write, "I plain my opinion," as if you were your own two-year-old nephew just learning to talk. In the same way, *rember* for *remember* is probably a finger mistake, the first *em* carrying over into the second. If your misspellings often contain such slips as *thought* for *though, throught* for *throughout, posses* for *possesses,* much of your trouble may lie in bad finger habits—that, and carelessness in proofreading. Some students, too, have trouble with different words when they type than when they write in longhand. Fingers again.

In order to teach the muscles and nerves of your fingers to write a word correctly, *make them write it correctly.* After you have fixed the visual image of the word, practice writing it. Write it out ten or a dozen times. The next day, do it again. *Do not* try to increase the dosage. If you set out to write the word twenty times or a hundred times instead of ten or a dozen, you will soon cease to concentrate, and your fingers will fool you by reverting to their old habits until you are actually practicing your mistakes. It is better by far to write a word correctly ten times a day for ten days than a hundred times at a single sitting.

6. MEMORY AIDS

In spite of all your efforts to follow these directions diligently, a few words will get by you. Or perhaps you are fortunate enough to be bothered by only a few words to begin with. There are ways to learn even these words. If you find that certain words are causing trouble again and again, throw your dignity away and invent memory crutches to help you. It doesn't matter how ridiculous they are.

In fact, the more ridiculous they are, the easier it will be to remember them. The pun involved in "The cemetery is full of ease" may be painful, but that pain will keep you from writing *cemetery* with an *a*. "The end of *friend* is *end*" may make little sense, but it will help you spell *friend*. "There is *a rat* in *separate*" may be sheer nonsense. What of it? It is useful. The word *lice* may help you remember the *li* of *relieve* and *believe* and the *ce* of *receive, deceive, conceive, perceive*.

The more you know about languages, of course, the easier the problem becomes. If *license* bothers you, and you know Latin, remember *licentia;* the second consonant could only be a *c*. If *discipline* bothers you, a medieval collection of rules to be followed by monks was called *Disciplina Clericalis*. The student who knows Latin can be sure of the spellings of *license* and *discipline* if he remembers the pronunciation of *licentia* and *disciplina*. Many other words can be similarly fixed in mind. You must, however, work at this consciously, or you will find yourself using English spellings in French class and French spellings in English themes, and being wrong both times.

But even if you know only English, there are many devices you can use. Try capitalizing trouble spots; write *con-VEN-i-ence*. Try mispronouncing for spelling alone. Does *separate* cause trouble? When you have to write it, say SEP-*AY*-RATE to yourself. Or shift a word from one part of speech to another. If you are uncertain of the third vowel of *definite* and habitually write the syllable with an *a*, remember that we clearly pronounce accented vowels and slur unaccented ones. (Really we pronounce most unaccented vowels about alike, as *uh*, like the last sound in *China*.) Shift the doubtful word into another part of speech, one in which suffixes shift the accent. You can never identify the third vowel in *definite*, but in *definition* the accent falls on the doubtful syllable; the letter could only be an *i*. Even the difficult *-able, -ible, -ance,* and *-ence* words can be managed, particularly since you will probably find that very few of them bother you. The shifted stresses of *dispensable—dispensation, existence—existential,* and such words can often help. Verbs ending in *-hend* go to adjectives in *-sive* or *-sible: comprehend—comprehensive —comprehensible*. One you can remember because it seems odd: *resistance* BUT *resistible*. Visual images, finger spelling, memory aids, and regular patterns all help.

7. REGULAR PATTERNS

It was suggested earlier that most words are spelled according to their sounds, as those sounds are represented by limited letter-combinations which follow regular patterns. Some of those patterns you know already, and many others cause you little trouble even though you are not consciously aware of them. Wherever such patterns will help you in learning to spell troublesome words, make use of them. Think of other words of similar sound and spelling, words you spell correctly already. They may help you see the pattern they are following.

A few patterns may be pointed out, to suggest the method or to indicate combinations you might not easily discover for yourself.

a. Length of vowel

In such words as *rate, secede, stripe, rope, brute,* the long vowel is followed by a single consonant and a silent *e*. When the *e* is dropped before certain suffixes (see also Spelling Rules 8c, d, and e, page 543) the vowel sound remains long and the consonant remains single, as in *rating, seceded, striping, ropy, brutish.*

Short-vowel sounds often occur before single consonants without a final, silent *e,* as in *brag, bed, drip, drop, rut.* Followed by vowels, as in many suffixes, the consonants are usually doubled: *bragging, bedding, dripping, dropped, rutted.*

Become is one of the few words that trip you here. It has a shortened vowel, but a single consonant and a silent *e;* with the suffix, it does not, as many students suppose, double the *m.* It is *becoming,* not *becomming.* (Notice that you will tend to pronounce those two with slightly different vowel sounds, if you really stop to think.)

b. *un-, dis-, mis-*

Such common prefixes as *un-, dis-, mis-* do not affect the spelling of the root word to which they are added. There is one *s* in *dis-,* one initial *s* in *satisfy,* and the two, joined, provide a double *s: dissatisfy.* But *appear* has no *s,* and so when *dis-* is added, only one *s* can be needed: *disappear.* The same principle applies to *unnatural, unappetizing, misspell, mistake.*

The list of common prefixes that begins on page 181 provides convenient samples of typical words in which they occur. By no means all the possibilities are illustrated, but if you have prefix trouble, examine that list.

c. *in-, com-*

A difficult variation of that pattern occurs with *in-*, *com-*, and a few other prefixes that are less common. As before, the prefixes do not affect the spelling of the roots, but the roots often affect the spelling of these prefixes. Before Latin roots beginning with *l, m,* or *r,* the *n* of *in-* is changed to the same letter as the initial of the root. Thus there are two *l*'s in *illuminate* (*in* + *luminare*), two *m*'s in *immediate,* two *r*'s in *irresistible.* (Before Anglo-Saxon roots the change does not occur: *inlet, inmate, inroad.*)

Com- becomes *con-* before most consonants: *concave, confess, conjugate,* and so on. Before *l* and *r,* the *m* becomes *l* or *r,* like the *col-* and *cor-* in *collaborate* and *corroborate.*

Among the others we might mention *ad-,* which accounts for the doubled letters early in such words as *account* itself, *affiliate,* and *aggression.*

d. *-ly, -ness*

Such suffixes as *-ly,* or *-ness* are simply added to the root. The chief troublemaker is *-ly.* Does the root word end in *l?* If so, when you add *-ly,* you will have two *l*'s as in *real* + *ly* = *really, cool* + *ly* = *coolly,* and so on. Similarly, *barren* + *ness* = *barrenness.*

e. Shifts in parts of speech

A *b* in a verb often becomes a *p* in a noun, as in *describe—description.* A *d, r,* or *t* in a verb often becomes *s* in a noun, as in *decide—decision, inquire—inquisition, convert—conversion.* The *c* in *-ence* nouns often becomes *t* in adjectives: *influence—influential, difference—different—differential, confluence—confluent.*

f. Plurals

Do plurals bother you? We usually add an *s* to the singular: *boy—boys.* If the singular ends in an *s* (or *z*) sound, or in a *ch, sh,* or *dg* sound, we add a syllable when we pronounce the plural, and we spell it *-es: classes, matches, brushes, judges.*

When a noun ends in *y* preceded by a consonant, we change the *y* to *i* and add *-es: lady—ladies, baby—babies.* When a noun ends in *o*, we usually add *-es: Negro—Negroes, hero—heroes, potato —potatoes, tomato—tomatoes.* (Be careful to remember why the *e* appears. Do not pull it back into the singular and write *heroe,* or *potatoe.*) There are many nouns ending in *o,* however, which add only *-s.* They are likely to be musical terms from Italian sources, like *sopranos, pianos, solos;* but there are some others, like *silos.* If your visual image of the word or a memory crutch does not help, doubtful words ending in *o* had better be checked in the dictionary.

g. Troublesome prefixes and suffixes

Some troublesome prefixes and suffixes remain. It is easy to confuse *ante-* and *anti-, de-* and *di-, dis-* and *dys-, hyper-* and *hypo-, inter-* and *intra-, per-* and *pre-.* The only cures lie in studying the derivations of the words and the meanings of the prefixes, and in pronouncing the words carefully. Fortunately, only a few words may bother you. Your own spelling list will tell you which words recur, and your clear visual images of those words will serve to keep them straight.

8. SPELLING RULES

Last in the devices which will help you improve your spelling are the spelling "rules." They are like the regular patterns in spelling we have just been considering in that they indicate what usually happens in certain common spelling situations. They are unlike them in that they are extremely, even excessively, familiar to you, and so far they may not have helped very much. But if you really try to use them, they will help a great deal. (The "rules" are not rules, of course, but merely codifications of what is done most of the time, hence the "exceptions" that have long plagued you.)

Actually only about half a dozen of the rules are really helpful. You have seen them often before, but this time, perhaps, you mean business.

The following six rules are the most useful.

a. *Ie* and *ei*

When a word with an *ie* or an *ei* is pronounced with a long *e,* the most frequent form is *ie.* The *ei* usually follows a soft *c.* You know the rhyme,

I before *e*
Except after *c*.

Use it.

Many people find the code word *lice* more useful (*i* follows *l*, as in *relieve, believe,* and *e* follows *c*, as in *receive, conceive.* In *lice* itself, *i* comes before *e*, as it most often does). If that method seems more memorable, use the code word *lice*. If you remember that *the rule applies only to the long e sound,* there are nine fairly common exceptions—or perhaps only six: *either, financier, inveigle, leisure, neither, seize, sheik, species, weird.* (They can be put into a sentence of sorts: *Neither financier could inveigle the sheik to seize either species of weird leisure.*) But some people pronounce *either* and *neither* with a long *i*, not a long *e*, and the British pronounce *leisure* to rime with *pleasure*, so none of these three can be called a universal exception: If the word is pronounced any other way than with a long *e*, the spelling is usually *ei*. Some examples of words pronounced other ways: *weigh, neighbor, counterfeit, foreign, reign.* Some exceptions: *fiery, friend, mischief, view.*

After all that discussion—and all the times you have read similar discussions—it scarcely seems reasonable to remark that only four words ever bother you, and only two bother you often. It might be simplest just to learn them:

receive, deceive, perceive, conceive

b. Doubling final consonant

When a word ends in a single consonant preceded by a single vowel, with the accent on the final syllable (or on the only syllable, if there is only one), the final consonant is doubled before a suffix beginning with a vowel.

strip + *ing* = *stripping*
whip + *ed* = *whipped*

The rule is important. Every sentence has at least one verb, and by far the greater number of our verbs form their past tenses and past participles by adding *-ed*. All of them form their present participles and their gerunds by adding *-ing*. So those two endings alone, on verbs alone, bring this rule into play over and over. And other forms occur, as in

begin—beginner   *occur—occurrence*
bid—bidder   *quiz—quizzes*

Remember that the rule applies only to words of one syllable or to words accented on the last syllable. If the accent falls earlier, or if the accent shifts to an earlier syllable when the prefix is added, the final consonant is *not* doubled. Thus:

bénefit, bénefited
prefér, preférred, but *préference*

c. Final silent *e* before consonants

When a word ends in silent *e,* retain the *e* when adding a suffix beginning with a consonant, as in *achievement, arrangement, completely, desperately.*

Some common exceptions: *argument, awful, probably, truly, wholly.*

In such words as *development, developement, judgment, judgement,* the first form is more common in American usage, the second in British. For an American audience, prefer the American spelling.

d. Final silent *e* before vowels

When a word ends in silent *e,* drop the *e* when adding a suffix beginning with a vowel, as in *achieving, arranging, completing.*

Some exceptions:

After soft *c* or *g* before *a* or *o,* as in *advantageous, courageous, noticeable.*

To prevent mispronunciation or confusion with other words, as in *hoeing, shoeing, dyeing, singeing.*

e. Consonant plus *y* before suffixes

Words ending in a consonant plus *y* change the *y* to *i* before any suffix not beginning with *i.* The suffixes *-es* and *-ed* are especially common. The suffix *-ing* provides the chief exceptions.

baby, babies; city, cities; dry, dries; try, tries
happy, happily, happiness; duty, dutiful, dutiable
BUT: *study, studying; cry, crying; try, trying* (Both the *y* and the *i* are pronounced.)

f. SEED words

Words that end in the sound SEED usually spell the final syllable *-cede,* as in *concede, precede, recede, secede.*

Three words use -*ceed*: *exceed, proceed, succeed.*
One word uses -*sede*: *supersede.*

9. SPELLING LISTS

The following lists are made up of words that students often use and often misspell. Examine all of the lists carefully and learn the spelling of any words in these lists that you are unsure about. Since these are common words, your instructor will be very unfavorably impressed by inability to spell them correctly.

a. Words often misspelled because of careless pronunciation

SYLLABLES AND LETTERS OMITTED

accidentally	laboratory	really
Arctic	length	recognize
boundary	liable	representative
candidate	library	sophomore
curiosity	literature	strictly
everybody	mathematics	superintendent
February	miniature	surprise
generally	occasionally	temperament
geography	probably	usually
government	quantity	valuable
history		

SYLLABLES AND LETTERS ADDED

athletics	height	privilege
disastrous	hindrance	remembrance
drowned	lightning	similar
elm	mischievous	suffrage
entrance	momentous	translate
grievous	prejudice	umbrella

SOUNDS CHANGED OR LETTERS TRANSPOSED

accurate	formerly	perform
description	introduce	preparation
despair	irrelevant	restaurant
divide	optimistic	sacrilegious
existence	particular	separate

b. Similar words often confused

accent, ascent, assent
accept, except
advice, advise
affect, effect
aisle, isle
all ready, already
all together, altogether
allowed, aloud
allusive, elusive, illusive
altar, alter
angel, angle
aught, ought
baring, barring, bearing
berth, birth
born, borne
breath, breathe
Britain, Briton
buy, by
canvas, canvass
capital, capitol
choose, chose
cite, sight, site
close, clothes, cloths
coarse, course
complement, compliment
conscience, conscious
core, corps, corpse
council, counsel, consul
dairy, diary
desert, dessert
device, devise
dual, duel
dyeing, dying
fair, fare
finally, finely
formally, formerly
forth, forty, fourth
hear, here
heard, herd
hole, whole
holy, wholly

huge, Hugh
human, humane
instance, instants
irrelevant, irreverent
it's, its
knew, new
know, no
later, latter
lead, led
lessen, lesson
loath, loathe
loose, lose
luxuriant, luxurious
material, matériel
medium, media (*pl.*)
mind, mine
moral, morale
of, off
passed, past
peace, piece
personal, personnel
plain, plane
planed, planned
precede, proceed
precedence, precedents,
  presidents
presence, presents
principal, principle
prophecy, prophesy
quiet, quite
respectably, respectfully,
  respectively
reverend, reverent
right, rite, wright, write
sense, since
shone, shown
staid, stayed
stationary, stationery
statue, statute, stature
steal, steel
straight, strait

545

than, then
their, there, they're
therefor, therefore
threw, through
till, until
to, too, two
track, tract

troop, troupe
waist, waste
weak, week
weather, whether
which, witch
who's, whose
you're, your

c. General Spelling List

(This list does not necessarily include all the words or all the forms of words in the specialized lists. Study all three lists carefully.)

absence
absurd
accept
accidentally
accommodate
accompanied
accumulate
accustomed
achieved
acquainted
across
address
advantageous
advice
advise
aerial
affect
aggravate
aggression
agreeable
aisle
alley
allotted
all right
already
altar
alter
altogether
alumna(ae)
alumnus(i)
always

amateur
among
amount
analysis
analyze
angel
angle
annual
answer
anxiety
apartment
apology
apparatus
apparent
appearance
appreciate
appropriate
Arctic
argument
arithmetic
around
arouse
arrangement
arrival
article
ascend
assassin
association
athlete
athletics
attacked

attendance
attractive
audience
auxiliary
awkward
bachelor
balance
banana
barbarous
baring
barring
battalion
bearing
becoming
before
beggar
beginning
believe
believing
beneficial
benefited
berth
birth
biscuit
born
borne
boundaries
breath
breathe
bridle
brilliant

Britain
Britannica
Briton
bulletin
buoyant
bureau
business
busyness
cafeteria
calendar
candidate
cannot
can't
canvas
canvass
capital
capitol
captain
carburetor
career
carriage
carrying
cavalry
ceiling
cemetery
certain
changeable
changing
characteristic
chauffeur
choose
chose
chosen
cite
climbed
close
clothes
cloths
coarse
colonel
column
coming
commission

commit
committed
committee
comparative
comparison
compel
compelled
competent
competition
complement
completely
compliment
comrade
concede
conceivable
conceive
conferred
confident
connoisseur
conqueror
conscience
conscientious
conscious
considered
consistent
contemptible
continuous
control
controlled
convenient
coolly
copies
corner
corps
corpse
council
counsel
country
courageous
course
courteous
courtesy
criticism

criticize
cruelty
curiosity
curious
curriculum
cylinder
dealt
deceit
deceive
decent
decide
decision
deferred
definite
definition
descend
descendant
describe
description
desert
desirable
despair
desperate
dessert
device
devise
dictionary
difference
digging
dilapidated
dining
dinning
diphtheria
disappear
disappoint
disastrous
discipline
discussion
disease
dissatisfied
distribute
divide
divine

547

doctor	experience	guidance
doesn't	explanation	handkerchief
don't	extension	handsome
dormitories	extraordinary	harass
drudgery	extremely	having
dual	familiar	height
duel	fascinate	hero
dyeing	February	heroes
dying	fiery	hesitancy
ecstasy	Filipino	hindrance
effect	finally	hoping
efficiency	financial	hopping
efficient	financier	huge
eighth	forehead	Hugh
eligible	foreigner	hurriedly
eliminate	foremost	hygiene
embarrass	forfeit	hypocrisy
eminent	forgo, forego	imaginary
emphasize	formally	imitation
employed	formerly	immediately
employees	forth	impromptu
encouragement	forty	incidental
encouraging	fourth	incidentally
enemy	frantically	incredible
entirely	fraternities	independence
environment	friend	indigestible
equipment	fundamental	indispensable
equipped	furniture	inevitable
equivalent	further	infinite
erroneous	gage	influential
especially	gallant	ingenious
etc.	gauge	ingenuous
exaggerate	generally	initiation
exceed	genius	innocence
excel	ghost	innocents
excellent	government	instance
except	governor	instants
exercise	grammar	intellectual
exhaust	grandeur	intelligence
exhilaration	grief	intelligent
existence	grievous	intentionally
exorbitant	guarantee	intercede
expense	guard	interested

invitation
irrelevant
irresistible
it's (it is)
its
itself
knowledge
laboratory
laid
later
latter
lead
led
legitimate
leisure
liable
library
lightning
likely
literature
livelihood
loneliness
loose
lose
lying
magazine
maintain
maintenance
maneuver
(manoeuver,
manoeuvre)
manual
manufacture
marriage
material
matériel
mathematics
meant
medicine
medium(s),
    media (pl.)
merely
messenger

metal
mettle
miniature
minute
miscellaneous
mischievous
misspell
momentous
moral
morale
mortgage
mosquitoes
murmur
muscle
mussel
mysterious
naïve
naphtha
naturally
necessarily
Negroes
neither
nevertheless
nickel
niece
nineteen
ninetieth
ninety
ninth
noticeable
notoriety
nowadays
nucleus
obedience
oblige
obstacle
occasion
occasionally
occur
occurred
occurrence
o'clock
of

off
officer
omission
omitted
oneself, one's self
operate
opinion
opportunity
optimism
optimistic
organization
origin
original
outrageous
overrun
pageant
paid
pamphlet
parliament
parliamentary
particularly
partner
passed
past
pastime
peace
perceive
perform
perhaps
permanent
permissible
perseverance
persistent
personal
personnel
perspiration
persuade
phenomenon(a)
physically
Philippines
physician
picnic
picnicking

piece	propaganda	respectfully
plain	propeller	respectively
plane	prophecy	restaurant
planed	prophesied	rhetoric
planned	prophesy	rheumatism
pleasant	prove	rhythm
politician	psychology	ridiculous
politics	publicly	sacrifice
possess	pulling	sacrilegious
possession	purchase	safety
possible	pursuit	salary
potato	quantity	sandwich
potatoes	quarter	scarcely
practicable	quiet	scene
practically	quite	schedule
practice	quiz	science
prairie	quizzes	scientific
precede	rarefied	secretary
precedence	ready	seize
precedents	realize	sense
preceding	really	sentence
prefer	recede	sentinel
preference	receive	separate
preferred	recognize	sergeant
prejudice	recommend	several
preparation	refer	severely
presence	reference	shepherd
presents	referred	shining
presidents	regard	shinning
prevalent	region	shone
primitive	reign	shown
principal	rein	shriek
principle	relieve	siege
prisoner	religion	significance
privilege	religious	significant
probably	remembrance	similar
procedure	renown	sincerely
proceed	repetition	site
profession	replies	smooth
professor	representative	soliloquy
prominent	reservoir	sophomore
pronounce	resistance	source
pronunciation	respectably	speak

specimen
speech
statement
stationary
stationery
statue
stature
statute
stopped
stopping
strength
strenuous
stretch
strictly
studying
succeed
successful
suffrage
superintendent
supersede
supplement
suppress
surely
surprise
syllable
symmetry
temperament
temperature
tendency
than
their

then
there
therefor
therefore
they're
thorough
thousandths
threw
through
tired
to
together
too
tournament
track
tract
tragedy
transferred
treacherous
tries
truly
Tuesday
twelfth
two
typical
tyrannically
tyranny
unanimous
undoubtedly
universally

unnecessary
unprecedented
until
unusually
usage
using
valuable
vegetable
vengeance
view
vigilance
village
villain
warring
weather
Wednesday
weird
welfare
whether
which
wholly
who's
whose
witch
women
won't
writer
writing
written
yacht

16–

Manuscript Conventions

Characteristics of a Good Theme: 11. Conventionally acceptable mechanics.

There are a number of conventional practices in handling manuscript with which you should be familiar. Most of them apply not only to themes, but to writing of any kind. Consult this chapter for advice if you find that you do not know how to handle one of the conventional, mechanical problems in writing.

1. LEGIBILITY—Leg

Your instructor will be pleased if you can type your papers; but even if you type, there will be many papers, like impromptu themes and examinations, which must be written in longhand. Remember that every paper must be legible. No one will ever discover the virtues of a paper that cannot be read. It is a sign of careless disregard of the reader, not of superior eccentricity, to form your letters so individually that they cannot be deciphered. Distinguish clearly between capital letters and lower-case letters. Distinguish between *a*'s and *o*'s, *e*'s and *i*'s and *l*'s, *m*'s and *n*'s and *w*'s and *u*'s and *v*'s. Avoid flourishes that encroach on letters in the lines above and below. Write at least as plainly as a fifth-grader does, or type your papers. The symbol **Leg** always calls attention to an illegible or a messy manuscript, and the general symbol **Ms** often does.

2. THE PAGE

a. Paper

Many colleges specify particular kinds of theme paper or bluebooks for college work. If no such specification is made, handwritten papers—in blue or black ink—should be submitted on 8½″ × 11″ white bond paper, ruled for ⅜″ lines. Do not use colored paper or flimsy paper, either unglazed paper or the thin, ripply paper that is designed for carbon copies. Do not use legal-size paper or small notebook paper. Do not use narrow-lined notebook paper, which crowds your writing and makes it very difficult for the instructor to read it.

If you type your papers, use white, 8½″ × 11″ paper, unruled. Use one side of the sheet only, with either typing or longhand.

b. Margins

Never crowd your pages. Leave your instructor room for helpful comments. Standard margins are, top, 1½″; left side, 1½″; right side, 1″; bottom, 1″. If papers are submitted in a folder, allow extra margin at the left.

All lines, including the last line on the page, should be carried over as nearly as possible to the right-hand margin, except for the line that ends a paragraph.

c. Spacing—#

Typed papers are always double-spaced, except for business letters and inserted quotations of over six lines, both of which are single-spaced with double spacing between paragraphs or between quotations and text.

In longhand on lined paper, write on each line. Do not skip lines between paragraphs.

Leave a space between your title and the text.

If you are not familiar with standard spacing in typing, such as the single space after commas but double after periods, consult any typing manual.

d. Indention—] or ¶

Paragraphs should be indented ¾″. If the paper is typed, five or six spaces is standard for paragraph indention.

3. PAGING

Number all pages, after the first, with Arabic numerals, at the top center or in the upper right-hand corner. The first page is left unnumbered, or numbered with an Arabic 1 at the bottom.

Roman numerals are often used for sections or chapters or volumes, and preface pages are usually numbered (at the bottom of the page) by lower-case Roman numerals. Roman numerals are never used for text pages. Arabic numerals are rapidly superseding Roman numerals for all uses. To translate Roman numerals into Arabic, or vice versa, consult your dictionary, under *numbers* or *Roman numerals*.

Having numbered your pages, keep them in order.

4. ENDORSEMENT

Your instructor will probably prescribe the form you are to use in endorsing your themes. If no form is prescribed, be sure at least to put your name on the outside of all papers.

It is usually not necessary to endorse any but the last page of the paper.

5. FINAL REVISION

The final copy submitted to your instructor should be as neat as possible, and revisions should be kept to the minimum. But no instructor will object to a few neat corrections on the paper he reads. In deciding whether to correct on the page or recopy, apply common-sense tests: Does the paper look as if you thought it worth taking pains? Can it be read easily?

a. Insertions—ᴧ

Insertions should be written above the line and centered over the point at which they are to be read into the text. A caret (ᴧ) is used *below* the point of insertion, thus:

> not
> Children should be impertinent to their elders.
> ᴧ

In typing, a virgule (/) is often used instead of a caret.

> not
> Children should/be impertinent to their elders.

b. Cross-outs, material to be deleted—δ, ϑ

If you wish the reader to omit words or phrases, strike through them (cross them out) with a heavy straight line. Do not enclose them in parentheses. Parentheses have a quite different function (see page 517), so that your reader, instead of omitting your unwanted phrases, will try to read them in and will usually be confused as he tries to make sense of what you have said.

Commonly, the grading symbol δ means, "You have included something here which should have been omitted."

c. Designating paragraphs—¶, No ¶

If you decide, belatedly, that a passage should have been paragraphed separately, mark it at the beginning of the passage with the symbol ¶. If you have inadvertently set up as a paragraph a passage that really belongs with the preceding paragraph, mark it at the beginning **No** ¶. But use these two symbols rarely. Your paragraphing should mark turns of your thought (see Chapter 5), and excessive use of ¶ and **No** ¶ suggests that you have been careless in your thinking. It is usually better to recopy the page.

The principal use of these instructions for last-minute revisions should come in impromptu themes. These, too, should be legible and as neat as possible, but probably your instructor will not expect you to waste the limited time of a single class period by making an impeccable final copy. Put your time, instead, on planning, writing, and revising.

6. TITLES

Titles are centered at the top of the first page, with a space between the title and the text.

a. Capitalization in titles

Major words of a title (all but the articles, and prepositions and conjunctions of less than six letters) are capitalized. The first word and the last word are capitalized. If you type your themes, full capitals may be used, throughout the title.

Do not use quotation marks or italics (underlining) unless they are called for. (See Italics, page 561, and Quotation Marks, page 520, for their special uses.)

b. Titles as antecedents

Your title and your theme are separate items. The title fore-shadows the theme (see page 61), but it should not be treated as if it were the opening sentence. In particular, avoid using a first-sentence pronoun referring to the title as antecedent. For example, do not begin a theme entitled SHOES with, "They are an utter abomination." If necessary, repeat the title.

A common exception is the book review which uses the title of the book as the title of the review, and then begins, "This book . . ." or "Miss Scriver's new romance. . . ."

7. CAPITALIZATION AND LOWER CASE—Cap, Lc

a. Capitals—Cap

1) PROPER NOUNS AND ADJECTIVES

Capitalize the names of particular persons, places, things, events, periods, and so on, and adjectives derived from such proper nouns.

John Doe	General Motors
Louisville	the Civil War
the Treaty Oak	the Colonial Period
Wednesday	English
June	Spanish

the Coronation of Elizabeth II

Except in journalistic practice, *street, county, river,* and so on, in geographical names are usually capitalized as part of the proper name.

First Street, Fairfax County, the Ohio River

2) THE FIRST WORD OF A SENTENCE

Capitalize the first word of a sentence.

3) THE FIRST WORD OF A QUOTATION

Capitalize the first word of a direct quotation except when the quotation is incorporated in your own sentence.

He asked, "Where are you going, my pretty maid?"
The chairman's speech was "full of sound and fury."

4) THE MAJOR WORDS OF A TITLE

Capitalize the first word, the last word, and other major words of a title (all but articles, and prepositions and conjunctions of less than six letters).

A Guide to the Nation's Capital
All Is Lost
Thoughts Concerning Glory

5) TITLES OF HONOR

Capitalize titles of honor preceding proper names.

Dr. Cole, Professor Tupper, Mr. Green
BUT: He asked the professor to go over the paper with him.

6) THE FIRST WORD OF A LINE OF POETRY

Capitalize the first word of a line of poetry.

7) SALUTATION AND COMPLIMENTARY CLOSE

Capitalize the first and last words of the salutation of a letter, and the first word of the complimentary close.

8) *I* AND *O*

Capitalize the pronoun *I* and the vocative interjection *O*.

b. No capitals—Lc

Lc means "lower case," no capital.
Do not capitalize unnecessarily.

1) POINTS OF THE COMPASS

Do not capitalize words naming points of the compass when you are indicating a direction. Such words, however, are capitalized when they refer to specific areas of the country.

Indianapolis is east of Denver.
He was born in the East.

2) SEASONS

Do not capitalize seasons.

I like spring best of all the year.

3) NOUNS OF FAMILY RELATIONSHIP

Do not capitalize nouns of family relationship unless they are used as substitutes for names or as titles preceding the name.

She is the mother of three children.
Tell me, Mother, where you put it.
He is my uncle.
Give it to Uncle George.

4) ACADEMIC CLASSES

Do not capitalize academic classes.

Most sophomores are more arrogant than most freshmen.

5) ACADEMIC COURSES

Do not capitalize academic subjects unless they name particular courses or are proper adjectives.

I like history better than German.
My best course is History 171.

6) WORDS LIKE *high school* AND *college*

Do not capitalize words like *high school* and *college* unless they are parts of proper names.

> I never studied in high school, but I have to study in college.
> He is a member of the Columbian College of The George Washington University.

8. ITALICS—Ital

In longhand or typing, indicate italics by a single straight underline.

a. Emphasis

Italics are used for emphasizing words or phrases. The device should be used sparingly; it is better to secure emphasis by means of the sentence structure. (See Chapter 6.)

> Italics for emphasis should *not* be overused.

b. Titles of complete works

Italics are used for titles of books, magazines, newspapers, and other complete works, including works of art.

> *Lee's Lieutenants*   *Paradise Lost*
> *The Eroica Symphony*   The *Saturday Review*

The in newspaper or magazine titles is not italicized, and is not capitalized unless it begins the sentence. If an identifying city name is an integral part of the name of a newspaper, it is italicized as part of the title, otherwise it is not.

> He always reads the *New York Times*.
> The picture appeared in the Louisville *Courier-Journal*.

Titles of short poems, even though they are complete works, are usually put in quotation marks instead of italics.

> Carl Sandburg's "Fog" is well known.

c. Names of ships, planes, and so on

Italics are used for names of ships, planes, trains, Pullman cars, and so on.

The U.S.S. *Missouri*	the *Denver Zephyr*
the *Spirit of St. Louis*	the *Altamont*

d. Foreign words and phrases

Italics are used for foreign words and phrases and their abbreviations. If a foreign word has been established in English, it is not italicized. When in doubt, consult your dictionary.

> Private Jones addressed the general with complete *sang-froid*.
> He astonished the general, and vice versa.

e. Words, letters, and the like, as symbols

Italics are used for words, letters, figures, and the like, used as symbols without reference to their meaning. The older practice of enclosing such words in double quotation marks is less common, but is still sometimes seen.

> There are too many *and*'s in that sentence.
> Is that letter an *a* or an *o*?
> Avoid the symbol & in general writing.

9. HYPHENS AND SYLLABICATION— = / or Syl

Hyphens function in two ways: They join words or word-parts to form compounds, and they divide words at the end of a line to preserve margins. The hyphen should not be confused with the dash; the two serve quite different functions. (See P12.)

a. Hyphens— = /

1) COMPOUND NOUNS

English often runs words together to form new noun, adjective, or adverb concepts. Usage varies widely, but in general it may be said of compound nouns that first there are two words, then a hyphenated compound, and finally, as the compound becomes familiar, a single word, written solid. Thus, *base ball* became *base-ball* and finally *baseball*.

2) COMPOUND MODIFIERS

Compound adjectives and compound adverbs sometimes reach the stage of single words when both elements are monosyllables or when the compound is very common, as in *upstate, inshore, overnight, nearby;* but usually with adjectives and adverbs the choice is between two words or a hyphenated compound. Adverbs ending in *-ly* are never hyphenated. With adjectives, hyphens are often used when the adjective precedes the noun; but predicate adjective compounds are usually written as two words.

A clear-cut example. The example is clear cut.

3) GUIDES TO COMPOUNDING: THE DICTIONARY

Whenever you are in doubt about whether to hyphenate a compound, consult your dictionary. If you do not find the compound you are seeking in the general vocabulary, study the discussion of the use of compounding hyphens in the special article in the dictionary. There are numerous subtleties in the use of compounding hyphens. The dictionary is the best guide.

4) GUIDES TO COMPOUNDING: ACCENT

One indication that a compound noun may have become a single word lies in the stress, pitch, and juncture patterns of the spoken sentence. If you strongly accent the first element of the compound and slight the rest—as in *baseball, basketball, playwright, scorekeeper*—the compound is probably one word. If you read two or more words together in a breath with a rising pitch, but divide the accent fairly evenly—as in *mother-in-law, hanger-on, light-year, city-state, soul-stirring, sky-high*—the compound is probably hyphenated. If the signals fall somewhere in between, the dictionary is the only guide.

5) SOME CATEGORIES

a) A PREFIX PLUS A PROPER NOUN

Compounds composed of a prefix plus a proper noun are commonly hyphenated: *pro-British, un-Christian.*

b) COMPOUND NUMERALS AND FRACTIONS

Compound numerals (numbers consisting of two words, from twenty-one to ninety-nine) and fractions are commonly hyphenated; but fractions containing a compound numeral as one member are not hyphenated between members: *twenty-three, two-thirds;* but, *three twenty-sevenths.*

c) COMPOUNDS WITH *self*

Compounds with *self-* are usually hyphenated: *self-styled, self-appointed.*

d) HYPHENS TO AVOID CONFUSION

Compounds resulting in confusing vowel combinations or possible confusion with other words are regularly hyphenated: *anti-imperialist, co-owner, re-creation* (distinguished from *recreation*).

e) COINED COMPOUND ADJECTIVES

Any coined compound adjective read together in a breath with evenly divided accent and preceding the noun is hyphenated: *a not-to-be-sneezed-at opportunity.*

b. Syllabication—Syl

Hyphens are used to separate syllables of a word that must be divided at the end of a line to maintain a margin. The hyphen always comes at the end of the line on which the word begins; it never precedes the succeeding line. The hyphen comes always between syllables, that is, between elements of the word that are pronounced as distinct units of sound. Never divide a one-syllable word, no matter how long: *stretched* is one unit of sound and cannot be divided. Never divide in the middle of a syllable.

The dictionary is the best guide to the proper syllabication of a word, but certain conventional practices may be indicated.

1) DIVISION BY SYLLABLES, ACCORDING TO PRONUNCIATION

Words are divided by syllables, according to pronunciation, and they should preferably be divided so that the part of the word left at the end of the line will suggest the pronunciation of the whole word. Avoid such breaks as *serv-iceman, prefer-ence.* Never separate a word which is pronounced as a single syllable, even though its written form contains a suffix which in some other word is pronounced as a separate syllable. *Stretched,* as noted above, has only one syllable, though *wretched* has two. (Even when the *-ed* forms an extra syllable, separating it saves only one space.)

2) A SINGLE-VOWEL SYLLABLE

With words containing a single vowel as a separate syllable, divide after the vowel: *sepa-rate*.

3) A ONE-LETTER PREFIX AND A TWO-LETTER SUFFIX

Avoid leaving a one-letter prefix on the first line and avoid carrying over a two-letter suffix to the second line. Avoid such breaks as *a-bove, wretch-ed*.

4) DOUBLED CONSONANTS

When the addition of a suffix has caused the doubling of a final consonant, or when a word normally contains a doubled consonant, break between the consonants, as *sit-ting, neces-sary*.

But a word normally ending in a doubled consonant retains the two consonants in the one syllable when a suffix is added, as *fill-ing*.

5) HYPHENATED COMPOUNDS

Hyphenated compounds are preferably divided only at the hyphen, as *soul-stirring*.

6) SINGLE-WORD COMPOUNDS

Single-word compounds are preferably divided between the elements of the compound, as *scorekeeper* becomes *score-keeper*.

c. Other uses of the dividing hyphen

1) IN SPELLING OUT

Hyphens are also used to divide the letters of a word to indicate that the word is being spelled out.

The answer is *n-o*, no.

2) IN REPRESENTING STUTTERING

Hyphens are also used to divide repeated letters representing stuttering.

I'm n-n-not f-frightened.

3) IN PAIRING COMPOUNDS

Hyphens are sometimes used to indicate that the last part of a compound has been suppressed but will be supplied by the last part of a paired compound to follow.

We live in a three- or perhaps a four-dimensional world.

10. ABBREVIATIONS—Abr

In general writing, *avoid abbreviations,* including the ampersand (&).

The following abbreviations, however, are established and may be used in any but the most formal writing. (And since *Mrs.* has no other form, it may be used whenever you need it.)

TITLES PRECEDING NAMES: Mr., Messrs., Mrs., Dr., St. (saint)
TITLES FOLLOWING NAMES: Esq., Jr., Sr., M.D., Ph.D., etc.
COMMON LATIN PHRASES: i.e., e.g., etc., ad lib., viz., A.D. and B.C., A.M., P.M., VS.

In informal writing, government agencies, and the like, are now often abbreviated to their initials. Be sure, however, that the abbreviation will be clear to your reader.

For specialized writing, common abbreviations are listed in your dictionary.

11. REPRESENTATION OF NUMBERS—N

a. General principles

Usage in the representation of numbers is divided, but some general principles may be suggested.

1) NUMBERS OF ONE OR TWO WORDS

In general writing, write out numbers that can be expressed in one or two words, as *one, twenty-three, two hundred, seven million.*

2) NUMBERS OF MORE THAN TWO WORDS

Use figures for numbers requiring more than two words, as *276, 1337, 9,277,438.*

3) CONSISTENCY

Be consistent in the representation of numbers within a single paper. If most of them can be expressed in one or two words, write out all of them. If most (or even many) would require more than two words, use figures for all.

b. Special conventions

A few special conventions are generally observed. (See also Paging, page 556.)

1) NUMBER BEGINNING A SENTENCE

Never begin a sentence with figures. Write out the number or rephrase the sentence.

> AVOID: $2,300 was the price of that car.
> BETTER: That car cost $2,300.

2) FIGURES FOR STATISTICS

In all but very formal writing, use figures for statistics. If some numbers in a paper are statistical and some are not, consistency may be ignored to indicate the difference.

> ACCEPTABLE: Each of the two investigators reported that 43,000 bushels had been wrongfully sold, that 37,000 bushels had been allowed to spoil, and that 750,000 bushels remained in storage.

3) FIGURES FOR DATES

Use figures for dates, except in very formal social correspondence.

> Kenny was born June 14, 1914.

But ordinal numbers representing days of the month, when the year is not given, are more commonly written out.

> PREFERRED: He was born June fourteenth.
> POSSIBLE: He was born June 14th (or June 14).

4) FIGURES FOR STREET NUMBERS

Use figures for street numbers.

> 2802 Massachusetts Avenue

5) FIGURES FOR DECIMALS

Use figures for decimals.

The tolerance allowed was .001 of an inch.

6) FORMS FOR PERCENTAGES

Figures are usually used for percentages.

He gets a 10 percent (or 10%, or ten percent) commission.

7) FIGURES WITH A.M. AND P.M.

Use figures for the time of the day when given with A.M. and P.M.

It is now 4:19 P.M.

8) FORMS FOR NUMBERED STREETS

Numbered streets are written out unless local usage prefers figures. Thus, in New York, numbered avenues are written out; numbered streets are given in figures: *Fifth Avenue, 42nd Street.*

9) NUMBERS STANDING SIDE BY SIDE

When two numbers must stand side by side, the first number is often written out and the second given in figures, to prevent confusion.

He owned six 10-ton trucks.

17 —

Glossary of Troublesome Phrases

Characteristics of a Good Theme: 10. Exact and appropriate diction.

This section is designed to provide brief advice on the use of words and phrases that often trouble college students. The trouble stems from a variety of sources. Sometimes it arises because a locution that is common in the student's dialect is not used in the dialect of educated writing. Sometimes it arises because of changing linguistic custom, so that older readers (and all college teachers are at least slightly older) are conscious of shibboleths that may no longer be observed by contemporary writers of the first rank. (Some shibboleths have never been observed, even by those who are most disturbed when someone else violates them. The disturbance, however, is itself an important fact to be remembered.) Sometimes, perhaps most often, the trouble arises because a locution which is perfectly appropriate in writing of one level of formality (see pages 199–203) or of one tone is not appropriate to the level or tone of the paper in which you have used it. (This may occur, notice, if the phrasing is either overformal or too informal: On occasion *eschatology* can be as badly out of place as *catterwampus*.)

It is scarcely possible to say of a given phrase or word, "This may only be used in writing of such-and-such a level." Yet it can and must be said that the locutions in a given piece of writing should be appropriate to the topic, tone, and level of the piece as a whole. And it can be said of many of the phrases in this glossary that they tend characteristically to appear in writing of one sort rather than of another. Here and there, consequently, phrases are labeled to call your attention to the responses they may evoke, even though the intention is not flatly to prohibit their usage, but rather to warn you that they must be used judiciously.

The labels employed must be understood. *Nonstandard:* "not used by the educated writer except to secure special effects, as in dialogue"; *dialectal:* "used regionally, but not standard, not in general use"; *conversational:* "used in general educated speech, but rarely in writing, except of a highly informal, colloquial sort"; *informal:* "used in educated writing, but probably not on the most serious subjects or occasions"; *formal:* "used in educated writing on serious subjects or occasions."

Occasionally, you will find a word or phrase characterized as "acceptable," or "established," but with the added recommendation that it be avoided in college writing. This means that even though the dictionaries record the locution without any special label, many college instructors will disapprove of its use in papers prepared for college classes because they know that many readers object to the phrase and would be distracted by it. The wise writer will generally be conservative when faced with a choice. His purpose is to present his idea as clearly and as effectively as possible, not to disturb and distract his readers unnecessarily by his phrasing. If he knows that many readers will object to a locution, he will avoid it even though he himself is aware that the linguistic authorities have demonstrated its complete propriety.

Accept—except. *Accept* means "to take" or "receive." *Except* means "to exclude," "with the exception of."

> I accept your invitation.
> If I were inviting your guests, I would except Jim.
> All may come, except Jim.

Ad, exam, phone, photo. Such "clipped forms" are informal; many readers object to them unless the tone of the paper is clearly casual. Avoid in college writing.

A.D. *Anno Domini,* "in the year of Our Lord." Usually precedes a specific year date. Avoid with centuries. B.C., "before Christ," follows year or century.

Adapt—adopt. *Adapt* means "to make suitable." *Adopt* means "to take as one's own."

> He adapted the suggestion to suit his own plans.
> I will adopt your suggestion as it is.

Note: In the nouns of action made from these verbs, *adaptation* contains four syllables, *adoption* contains three.

Affect—effect. In student writing, *affect* is usually a verb meaning "to influence"; *effect* is usually a noun meaning "the result."

> Your words do not affect her.
> The effect of your words is negligible.

Note: Affect, verb, may mean "to adopt as an affectation."
Effect, verb, means "to bring to pass."

> He affects a Harvard accent.
> The law was inadequate to effect the desired change.

Aggravate—irritate. Formally, *aggravate* means "to intensify."

> His carelessness aggravated the seriousness of the disease.

Informally and conversationally, *aggravate* means "to irritate." Avoid this use in college writing.

Ain't. This once useful contraction for "am not" has been successfully banished by repeated strictures against it. It is not used by educated American writers.

Alibi. Formally, *alibi* (Latin for "elsewhere") means that one was elsewhere at the time some act was committed. Informally, *alibi* means simply "excuse."

All—all of. Either is acceptable, although *all* is somewhat more formal. *All of* is usual before a pronoun. "All of it."

All ready—already. Not interchangeable. Distinguish between "They are all (All of them are) ready" and "We have already (before this time) decided."

All right. *All right* is strongly preferred to *alright.*

All the farther. Dialectal for "as far as," as in "This is all the farther (as far as) I mean to go."

All together—altogether. Distinguish between "They are all (All of them are) together" and "You are altogether (entirely) too insistent."

Allude—refer. *Allude* means "to refer indirectly."

> In your speech you referred to Lee, but didn't you also allude to Jackson?

Almost—most. *Almost* is an adverb and is used before adjectives, verbs, or other adverbs. *Most* is an adjective and is used before nouns.

> Almost every person present agreed.
> Most people agreed.

Note: The *every* of *everyone, everybody,* and the *any* of *anyone,* etc., still retain enough adjective force to require the adverb *almost.*

> Almost everyone agreed.

A lot. See **Lot.**

Alright. See **All right.**

Altho. One of the simplified spellings never used in the carefully edited publications. It should be avoided because it distracts and often annoys the reader.

Although—though. Virtually interchangeable. The choice is largely a matter of sentence rhythm. *Although,* however, can be used only to introduce its clause. It is never inserted parenthetically.

Among—between. *Among,* strictly, is used of more than two, *between* of two. The distinction is weakening and *between* is becoming common in both situations. In college writing, the strict usage is usually preferred.

Amount—number. *Amount* refers to quantity, *number* to countable units in a group.

> Any amount of time.
> Any number of people.

And etc. *Et cetera* means "and other things." *And etc.,* is redundant. See also **Etc.**

Anybody else's. The standard form. Do not use the stilted *anybody's else.*

Anyway—anyways. *Anyway* is normally preferred, though *anyways* is possible in the sense of *anywise,* "in any manner."

Apt—liable—likely. *Apt* means "habitually tending," but chiefly means "suited," "to the point." *Liable* means "obligated to" or "exposed to the danger of." *Likely* means "of a nature to render possible."

> She is apt to get excited in a crisis.
> That was an apt remark.
> You are liable to fall if you climb too high.
> It is likely that he will come.

As—for—because—since. All of these conjunctions are used in rough synonymy with *because,* but avoid using them in a sentence which might be confusing, as in "As you were speaking (Because? While?), I slept briefly." Restrictive adverbial clauses use *because.* In formal writing, nonrestrictive, explanatory clauses use *for,* as in "Critical revision is important, for even Homer nods."

As . . . as—so . . . as. *As . . . as* is used in both affirmative and negative statements, but many still prefer *so . . . as* after a negative.

As if—as though. Virtually interchangeable.

As—like. In meticulous usage, *as* is usually a conjunction introducing a clause (containing a subject and a verb); *like* is a preposition taking a substantive object.

> Do not do as I do, do as I say.
> Do not act like me.

As, "in the role of," is a preposition: "He was employed as a reporter."

As—that. Use *that,* not *as,* to introduce noun clauses.

> UNACCEPTABLE: I don't know as I do.

As to. Redundant in such sentences as "I inquired as to whether he was ready."

At. Nonstandard and redundant in such sentences as "Where is he at?"

At about. Avoid this noncommittal phrase in such sentences as "He came at about five o'clock." (Which was it, at five or about five?)

Auto. A "clipped form" perhaps best avoided in college writing.

Awful. A counter word, meaning roughly "very bad." Do not overuse it. Strictly, it means "awe-inspiring."

Back of—in back of—behind. *In back of* is conversational. *Back of* or *behind* may be used without apology, although *behind* is somewhat more formal.

Bad—badly. *Bad* is an adjective; *badly* is an adverb. After such verbs as *look, feel, seem,* use the predicate adjective *bad,* as in "I feel bad."

Balance. Avoid this commercial term in the sense of "remainder," "rest of."

Because. See **As.**

Because. See **Reason is because.**

Being as—being that. Dialectal for *because.*

> AVOID: Being as (that) I'm already here, I'll stay.

Beside—besides. *Beside* is usually a preposition, meaning "by the side of."

> He sat beside the Prom Queen.

Besides is now chiefly an adverb, meaning "in addition."

> I'm too tired to go. Besides, I can't afford it.

Between—among. See **Among—between.**

Boy friend—girl friend. Informal. Many people object violently to these terms. They should be avoided even though there is no other easy way to express the concept.

Bring—take. *Bring* means "to carry with oneself to this point." *Take* means "to carry with oneself away from this point." Avoid the dialectal use of *bring* in both senses.

Broke. Slang for "bankrupt," "without money."

But—hardly—scarcely. These words, implying negation, are not used with an additional negative.

> NONSTANDARD: I haven't but a dime.
> NONSTANDARD: I didn't hardly hear you.
> NONSTANDARD: I haven't scarcely started.

But what. Dialectal.

Can—may. Strictly, *can* means "to be able"; *may* means "to have permission." Informally, *can* is used in both senses, but in college writing the distinction between the two might well be observed.

Can't hardly. See **But.**

Can't seem. Informal for "seem to be unable."

Character. Avoid in the sense of "person," as in, "This character spoke up and said . . ."

Claim. Often objectionable as a synonym for "say" or "assert," because it suggests a pugnacious contradiction of a prior assertion. Avoid for the sake of tactful phrasing.

Climactic—climatic. *Climactic* means "pertaining to climax." *Climatic* means "pertaining to climate."

Common—mutual. *Common* means "shared by others." *Mutual* means "sharing equally, jointly, and reciprocally."

> Common experiences
> Mutual obligations

Complected—complexioned. *Complexioned* is the standard adjective.

Considerable. Avoid *considerable* as a noun: "He did considerable." As an adjective, use it with *amount, degree, extent,* as in "It cost a considerable amount of money," not "It cost considerable money."

Contact. Informal in the sense of "to get into communication with." But even in informal writing many readers object to it violently.

Continual—continuous. *Continual* means "with prolonged and frequent recurrence." *Continuous* means "in an uninterrupted stream."

> My morning was ruined by continual interruptions.
> The distracting noise of the power mower was continuous throughout the class hour.

Could of. See **Have—of.**

Couple. Colloquial in the sense of "any two," as in "Give me a couple of days to decide." Standard at all levels in the sense of "an associated, especially a married, male and female pair."

Cute. A much overworked counter word. Find a more exact synonym, such as *attractive, charming, dainty, pretty.*

Date. Informal in the sense of "an appointment for a particular time" and "a social engagement with a person of the opposite sex."

Deal. A commercialism in the sense of "agreement," "arrangement": avoid. *A great deal* means "a great amount," not "a great number."

Definitely. An overworked counter word. Find a more exact synonym, or simply omit the word, unless you are using it necessarily and precisely in the sense of "clearly defined."

Different from—different than. *Different from* is preferred in American usage, but *different than* is common before a clause as object.

Dove—dived. *Dived* is the preferred past tense in American usage, but *dove* is an established alternative form.

Due to. Clearly established in the sense of "because" or "because of." Many readers, however, still strongly object to the use of *due* except as an adjective. *Due to* and especially *due to the fact that* often result in wordiness.

> AVOID: Due to illness, I missed the examination.
> AVOID: Due to the fact that I was ill, I missed the examination.
> PREFER: Because of illness, I missed the examination. Because I was ill, I missed the examination.
> RIGHT: My absence was due to illness.

Dumb. Informal for *stupid.*

Each other—one another. Virtually interchangeable.

Effect. See **Affect.**

Either—neither. *Either* and *neither* are singular and normally require singular verbs and pronouns. Used of two things. When more than two are involved, use *any—none.*

> Either (of two) was willing, but neither was chosen.
> Any of the class could have explained the problem, but none of them was called on.

Enthuse. Informal for "to make or become enthusiastic." Avoid *enthuse,* because many readers strongly object to it.

Equally as. Do not confuse *equally* with *as good* (etc.) *as.* In such a sentence as, "He was equally as prepared as she," the two constructions overlap.

He was as prepared as she.
They were equally prepared.

Etc.   *Etc.* is an abbreviation of the Latin *et cetera,* "and other things." Never write *and etc.* Never write *ect.* Avoid *etc.* in general writing. It weakens a series which by its nature is evidently not intended to be exhaustive.

> AVOID: He is very energetic, always swimming, riding, playing tennis, dancing, etc.

If you need to indicate that the series is not an exhaustive list, prefer "and so on," "and so forth," or "and the like."

Every so often.   Conversational for "every now and then."

Exam.   See **Ad.**

Except.   See **Accept.**

Expect—suppose.   *Expect* is informal in the sense of "suppose."

Famous—notorious.   *Famous* means "widely and favorably known." *Notorious* means "widely but unfavorably known."

Farther—further.   More or less interchangeable, but many writers use *farther* for "greater distance" and *further* for "additionally," and many readers are disturbed if these distinctions are ignored.

Feature.   Established as a verb in the sense of "to display conspicuously," but it has a flavor of theatrical or journalistic cant and probably should be avoided in college writing. Slang in the sense of "imagine," as in "Feature him in an apron!" Avoid.

Fellow.   Low informal in "Tom's her fellow." Informal (but not entirely complimentary) in the sense of "person": "He's a dependable fellow." Established for all levels, as an adjective or a noun, in the sense of "associate(d)": "fellow worker," "the Fellows of the Graduate Council."

Fewer—less.   *Fewer* refers to number; *less* refers to amount.

Fewer students, less noise.

Fine.   An overworked counter word in the sense of "superior," as in "a fine man." Select a more exact synonym.

Fix.   Informal in the sense of "repair," "arrange," as in "to fix a leaky faucet." Many regard it as slang, in the sense of "to settle or dispose of," as in "That fixed him," and in the sense of " a predicament," as in "He's really in a fix."

Folks. Conversational in the sense of "relatives," as in "Meet my folks." Avoid in the sense of "you people," as in "Watch closely, folks, while I demonstrate this indispensable carrot juicer."

For. See **As.**

Former—latter. Used of two: "the first mentioned," "the second mentioned."

Funny. Informal in the sense of "strange." Standard in the sense of "humorous," "amusing."

Gentleman—lady. Avoid *gentleman* and *lady* as genteelisms for *man* and *woman*. Never use the vulgar *gents*.

Get. *Get* has many slang and informal uses in addition to its formal use in the sense of "to obtain," "to receive." It might be well to consult the dictionary on the status of *get* in any dubious construction.

Girl friend. See **Boy friend.**

Good. *Good* is an adjective, not an adverb.

> NONSTANDARD: He writes real good.
> STANDARD: He writes very well.

But after such verbs as *look, feel, seem* the syntax often calls for a predicate adjective.

> INFORMAL: I feel good.
> FORMAL: I feel exuberant (or unconquerable, etc.)

Good and. Informal as an intensive.

> INFORMAL: I was good and tired.
> FORMAL: I was very tired.

Got—gotten. Both are established past participles of *to get. Have got to* is a common and emphatic informal synonym for *must*, as in, "I have got to do it." At more formal levels, "I must do it" would be preferred. To secure the same degree of emphasis at the formal level, a stronger synonym may be necessary, as "It is imperative that I do it." *Gotten* is obsolete in British usage, hence the occasional objection to it for formal writing.

Grand. An overworked counter word for *magnificent*, etc. Save it for use with nouns of superlative impressiveness.

Guess. Long established in the sense of "think," "suppose," "believe," but many readers object to it. Prefer a more exact word in college writing.

Guy. Low informal for "male person."

Hanged—hung. *Hung* is the normal past tense and past participle of *hang. Hanged,* however, is regularly used in reference to the execution or suicide of human beings.

Hardly. See **But.**

Have—of. Do not confuse the verb *have* (or its contracted form *'ve*) with the preposition *of.*

> WRONG: I should of known.
> INFORMAL: I should've known.
> FORMAL: I should have known.

Have got to. See **Got.**

Heap. Informal or jocular in the sense of "a considerable amount," as in, "It takes a heap of living to make a house a home."

Height—heighth. Do not add an extra and nonstandard *h* to *height.* The misspelling *heightH* presumably occurs in mistaken analogy with *length, breadth,* etc.

Human. Avoid *human* as a noun. Many readers object to it and prefer *human being.*

If—though—whether. *If* in the sense of "though" is acceptable at the informal level, as in "I approve, even if you don't." In clauses of doubt or uncertainy, *if* may be used in the sense of "whether," as in "I wonder if she meant what she said." If the alternatives are clear, *whether* is preferred, as in "I do not know whether to believe her or not."

Imply—infer. *Imply* means "to express or suggest indirectly." *Infer* means "to draw conclusions from the evidence."

> Your tone implies that you doubt my statement.
> I infer your doubt from the tone you use.

In—into. *In* means "being within an enclosure, etc." *Into* means "moving from outside to inside."

> He is in his seat.
> He walked into the room.

In back of. See **Back of.**

Individual. Avoid *individual* in the sense of "person," as in "He's an odd individual." It is properly used in the sense of "a distinct entity," "particular as opposed to general," as in "The state in

579

peacetime should respect the rights of the individual," or as an adjective, as in "He has a highly individual style."

In regards to.   Avoid. Say *in regard to,* or *about,* or *regarding.*

Inside of.   In the sense of "in," the *of* is redundant.

> He was inside the room.

In the sense of "within," "by the expiration of," *inside of* is informal.

> INFORMAL: He'll be here inside of an hour.
> FORMAL: He will be here within an hour (or, in less than an hour).

Intrigue.   Many readers strongly object to *intrigue* in the sense of "to arouse interest." You might well avoid it in college writing.

Irregardless.   A redundant vulgarism for *regardless.*

Is where—is when.   Avoid the "something is where" definition.

> AVOID: Security is where you don't have to worry about anything.
> PREFER: Security is freedom from anxiety.

Its—it's.   Do not confuse *its,* the possessive pronoun, with *it's,* the contraction of *it is* or *it has.*

Kind of—sort of.   Redundant or conversational as synonyms for *rather,* as in, "kind of tired." In the sense of "group," "class," as in "That kind of carelessness irritates me," the phrases are singular and require singular verbs. Plurals are formed normally, both the pronoun and the noun taking plural forms: "These kinds are . . ."

Lady.   See **Gentleman.**

Later—latter.   *Later* means "at a subsequent or a more advanced time," as in "John came at five; Jack came later." "Jack comes to class later every day." *Latter* means "the second of two things mentioned," as in "Of work and sleep, I prefer the latter." See also **Former—latter.**

Lay—lie.   *Lay* (*laid, laid*) always takes an object.

> Lay that pistol down.

Lie (*lay, lain*) takes no object.

> I lie down.
> The pistol lies where it fell.

Lead—led.   *Lead* is a metal, a noun. *Lead, led, led* are principal parts of the verb, *to lead.* Do not allow the similar pronunciation of *lead* the metal and *led* the verb to mislead you in spelling the latter.

Learn—teach. *Learn* means "to acquire knowledge." *Teach* means "to impart knowledge."

Leave—let. *Let,* proposing a course of action, is not interchangeable with *leave* in such a construction as "Let us arise and go now." In the sense of "to allow to be undisturbed," however, use either *let* or *leave,* depending on precisely what you mean. "Let me alone" suggests "Do not disturb me." "Leave me alone" suggests "Go away."

Let's. *Let's* is a contraction of *let us.* *Let's us,* consequently, is redundant. When *let's* is followed by an appositive, the appositive is in the objective case, as *us ('s)* is.

> Let us (you and me) go.
> Let's you and me go.

Less. See **Fewer.**
Liable. See **Apt.**
Lie. See **Lay.**
Like—as. See **As.**
Likely. See **Apt.**

Line. *Line* in the sense of "a department or kind of activity or business" is recorded by the dictionaries without comment, but many readers regard it as commercial slang, and it probably should be avoided in college writing. *Line,* as in "the Communist party line," is acceptable in all but very formal use. *Line* in the sense of "social technique" is slang. *Along the line of* is verbose.

> AVOID: His activities are along the line of banking.
> PREFER: He is a banker.

Loan—lend. *Loan* is a noun or a verb. *Lend* is a verb. The verb *lend* is more formal and is preferred by many readers.

Locate. Informal in the sense of "to recall" and in the sense of "to establish a residence."

Loose—lose. *Loose* means "to be unfastened" or "to unfasten."

> The dog is loose.
> Loose the dogs.

Lose means "to misplace."

> Don't lose my place in that book.

The pronunciations differ: *Loose* = lōōs; *lose* = lōōz.

Lot—lots. Colloquial in the sense of "a large amount." *A lot* is two words. Do not confuse with *allot*.

Lovely. An overworked counter word. Select a more exact adjective.

Mad. Colloquial in the sense of "angry."

Math. A slang, "clipped form" of *mathematics*.

Mean. Colloquial for *bad tempered, malicious, vicious*, etc.

Medium-media. *Medium* is singular, *mediums* and *media* are plural. Of the latter two, *media* is the more formal.

Mighty. A colloquial intensive, as in "a mighty big job."

Most. See **Almost**.

Must. The recent dictionaries disagree over the status of *must* as an adjective and a noun ("A must book." "This book is a must.") and many readers object to it; consequently it should probably be avoided in college writing.

Mutual. See **Common**.

Myself—me. Avoid the use of the reflective or intensive pronoun *myself* where the syntax calls for the personal pronoun *I* or *me*.

> AVOID: John and myself are responsible.
> AVOID: It was done by John and myself.

Nice. An overworked counter word signifying little more than vague approval. Select a more exact modifier. Even in its strict sense of "discriminating," it should be used with caution, unless you are certain no confusion could result.

None. Used as singular or as plural.

> None of them is present.
> None of them are present.

Not as—not so. See **As . . . as**.

Nowhere near. Informal for *not nearly*.

Nowheres. Dialectal for *nowhere*.

Number—amount. See **Amount**.

Of—have. See **Have—of**.

Off of. The *of* is redundant.

O.K. Conversational or informal.

Only. Place *only* as near to the word it modifies as possible, even though in conversational and informal use its position is highly fluid and confusion rarely results.

> CONVERSATIONAL AND INFORMAL: I only have a dime.
> FORMAL: I have only a dime.

Out loud. Informal. Formal: *aloud.*
Outside of. The *of* is usually redundant in the sense of "beyond."

> PREFER: His actions put him outside (or beyond) the pale.

Conversational in the sense of "except."

> CONVERSATIONAL: I've done nothing outside of a little reading.
> INFORMAL AND FORMAL: I've done nothing (but) except read a little.

Party. Dubious (and suggesting commercial cant) for *person.*
Passed—past. *Passed* is the normal past tense and past participle in verb forms. *Past* is normally an adjective or a noun.

> He passed the course.
> We have passed the middle of the twentieth century.
> Judge him by his past performance.
> The time for action is past.
> History is our interpretation of the past.

Per. Commercial cant.
Percent—per cent—percentage. *Percent* may be written as one word or as two. Use *percent* (or *per cent*) after a number; otherwise use *percentage.*

> He gets a 10 percent (or per cent) commission.
> He gets a fixed percentage of the net income.

Phone. See **Ad.**
Photo. See **Ad.**
Plan on. Conversational. Informal and formal: *plan to.*
Plenty. Avoid *plenty* as an adverb, as in "He was plenty tired."
Prof. College slang. Avoid it as an abbreviated title in addressing a letter, endorsing a paper, etc. Many professors object to it.
Proposition. Slang as a verb. A commercialism as a noun in the sense of "proposal."
Proved—proven. Both are past participles of *prove.*
Provided—provided that—providing. *Provided,* with *that* expressed in formal writing and implied when it is informally

omitted, is a conjunction meaning "on condition," "if." *Providing* may similarly be used as a conjunction, but many object to it in formal writing.

Put across—put in—put over. Conversational.

Raise—rise. *Raise* (*raised, raised*) always takes an object.

> Raise your hands.

Rise (*rose, risen*) takes no object.

> She rises reluctantly in the morning.

Raise—rear (children). Informally, *raise* is now more common in American usage. For strictly formal writing, *rear* is preferable.

Real—really. *Real* is a conversational intensifying adverb, as in "I was real pleased," but *really* (or in such constructions, *very*) is preferred in written English.

Reason is because. Frequently used, but violently disturbing to many readers. Prefer *reason is that.* Avoid particularly the wordy "The reason I did it is because. . . ." Say, "I did it because. . . ."

Reckon. Dialectal in the sense of "think," "suppose."

Regular. Informal in the sense of "complete," "genuine," as in "He's a regular fellow."

Right. Dialectal in the sense of "rather," "very," as in "We had a right nice time."

Rise. See **Raise.**

Run. Informal in the sense of "to manage," as in "He runs a restaurant."

Said—same—such. Avoid as pronouns. *Same* and *such,* however, are well established as pronominal adjective modifiers in such phrases as "the same thing," "until such time as."

Scarcely. See **But.**

Seldom ever. Illogical and confusing.

> AVOID: She is seldom ever on time.
> PREFER: She is seldom on time. She is never on time.

Self. Avoid in the sense of "the present writer or speaker," as in "I wish to reserve a table for self and party."

Set—sit. *Set* (*set, set*) always takes an object.

> Set the trunk over by the window.

Sit (sat, sat) takes no object.

> Sit there until the dean can speak to you.

Shape.   Conversational for *condition,* as in "After the exam, he was in bad shape."

Should of.   See **Have—of.**

Show.   Informal for *theatrical performance,* etc.

Show up.   Colloquial in the sense of "to expose" or "to appear."

Sick.   Slang in the sense of "disgusted." In the sense of "unwell," *sick* is well established in American usage.

Since.   See **As.**

Sit.   See **Set—sit.**

Situation.   An overused counter word in the sense of "the circumstances of the moment."

Size up.   Conversational in the sense of "to evaluate a person or a situation."

Slow—slowly.   Both forms are well established as adverbs. They are not, of course, interchangeable in all constructions.

So.   *So,* as a conjunctive adverb meaning "consequently" and as a subordinating conjunction meaning "so that," is grossly overused. Other connectives (*consequently, accordingly, therefore, as a result,* etc.) or further subordination of the *so* clause would often be more exact. *So* as an intensive ("I was so tired") is colloquial. In written English, where vocal emphasis cannot be given the word, it suggests an incomplete comparison ("I was so tired that . . . .")

So . . . as.   See **As . . . as.**

Some.   Informal or slang in the sense of "noteworthy," as in "That was some party last night."

Somebody else's.   See **Anybody else's.**

Sort.   See **Kind.**

Sure.   Conversational as an adverb. Use *surely* in college writing.

Suspect—suspicion.   *Suspect* and *suspicion* are both nouns.

> The suspect was arrested as soon as the suspicion of the police was supported by enough evidence.

Suspect alone may be used as a verb.

> AVOID: I didn't suspicion him at all.
> PREFER: I did not suspect him at all.

Swell.   Slang in the sense of "splendid."

Take.   See **Bring.**

Take in.   Conversational in the sense of "view," "attend," as in "Let's take in a show." Slang in the sense of "fool," "hoodwink," as in "You can fool some of the people, but you can't take me in."

Taxi.   A "clipped form" of *taxicab.* Well established for all but strictly formal usage, it is nevertheless objected to by readers who prefer *taxicab* without realizing that it itself is in origin a double clipping of *taximeter cabriolet.*

Terrible—terribly.   Overworked counter words meaning *difficult* or *very,* as in "a terrible job," "terribly tired." Best used in the sense of "dreadful," "dreadfully," "invoking terror," as in "a terrible storm," "terribly frightened."

Terrific.   Often used, as slang, to avoid the weakened counter word *terrible,* or merely as an intensive, as in "He's a terrific dancer." *Terrific* retains more of its root idea of "invoking terror" than *terrible* does.

Than—then.   *Than* is used in comparisons.

> He is taller than his father.

Then implies time, or means *consequently,* etc.

> We saw the flash and then heard the report.
> If you understand me, then, you will do as I say.

The two words do not sound alike, are not spelled alike, do not function in the same way. Do not confuse them.

That.   See **Which.**

That there—this here.   *There* and *here* are redundant. *That* means "the one over there." *This* means "the one over here." *That one there,* or *this one here,* however, are well established as emphatic locutions.

Tho.   One of the simplified spellings never used in the carefully edited publications. It should be avoided because it distracts and often annoys the reader.

Though.   See **If.**

Through.   *Through* is rather informal in the sense of "finished," as in "Are you through yet?" In college writing, *finished* will normally be preferred.

Thru.   One of the simplified spellings never used in the carefully edited publications. It should be avoided because it distracts and often annoys the reader.

Till—until. Virtually interchangeable. Never use the spelling *'til. Till* is not a contraction of *until*.

To—too—two. *To* is a preposition: "Give it to John." *Too* is an adverb: "John went, too." "He works too hard." *Two* is an adjective or a noun: "Two sides to an argument," "the number two." Avoid *too* as an intensive, as in "He is not too careful in his speech."

Toward—towards. Interchangeable, although *toward* tends to be preferred in American, *towards* in British usage.

Try and. *Try and* plus an infinitive is colloquial and low informal. *Try to* is preferred.

Unique. *Unique*, strictly, means "the only one of its kind." In the sense of "rare," "very unusual" it is informal. But because many readers find that usage objectionable, it should be avoided in college writing.

Used to. Do not omit the *d*. In origin, the phrase means "was accustomed to"; now often "formerly did." It is used only in the past tense.

Used to could. Vulgar for *used to be able to*.

Very. A standard intensive, sometimes unnecessarily used.

Wait for—wait on. *Wait for* means "to await."

> I will gladly wait for you.

Wait on means "to serve."

> I can't find a clerk to wait on me.

Wait on in both senses is informal.

Want in—want out. Dialectal. Use "want to get (or go or come) in or out."

Ways. Dialectal in such phrases as "come a long ways." As a combining form, as in *endways, sideways*, it is almost interchangeable with *-wise*. *-Ways* suggests extension in space; *-wise* suggests manner. (See also *-***Wise.**)

Well. See **Good.**

Where. *Where* in place of *that*, as in "I read in the paper where you had won a prize," is unacceptable in college writing.

Where—when. See **Is where—is when.**

Where at. The *at* is redundant.

Whether. See **If.**

Which. *Which* is used of nonpersons; *who* is used of persons; *that* is used of either: "The dog which, the place which, the man who, the man or dog or place that." *That,* however, is used only with restrictive modifiers.

While. See **As.**

While. Avoid *while* in place of *and* or *but* in such sentences as "I came as quickly as I could, while he dawdled." *While* suggests the duration of time.

> I came as quickly as I could while (during the time that) he dawdled.

Who. See **Which.**

Who's—whose. Do not confuse *who's,* the contraction of *who is* or *who has,* with *whose,* the possessive case of *who.*

> Who's going to the game?
> The man whose pocket you picked has complained.

Whose, informally, is often used as a possessive with nonpersons, in place of the formal *of which.*

-Wise. As an adverbial suffix, *-wise* has been used since Anglo-Saxon days to form adverbs of manner from substantives, as in *lengthwise, otherwise, clockwise,* but has long been obsolete for new formations. Its recent disinterment to form such adverbs as *time-wise* ("When do you expect to finish, time-wise?") seems deplorable to many readers. Avoid its use in college writing.

Wonder. In form, sentences with *wonder* as the verb are usually declarative. In purpose they are often interrogative. They are normally (and formally) closed with a period, but question marks are used in all but strictly formal writing if the interrogative note is strong.

> RIGHT: I wonder whether I should go.
> RIGHT: I wonder whether I should go?

Would have. Avoid the use of *would* phrases when the syntax requires the simple past tense.

> WRONG: If you would have asked, I could have told you.
> RIGHT: If you had asked, I could have told you.
> RIGHT: Had you asked, I could have told you.

Would of.   See **Have—of.**

Yes.   Avoid "the announcer's Yes." *Yes* is an affirmative adverb used to agree with what someone else has said. Its use in television commercials ("Yes, we all need Brand X Mange Cure now and then") does not need to be imitated.

You.   Beware of the indefinite and impersonal *you* because of its strongly personal flavor. It is often used in informal writing, however, when all readers could accept it personally.

> To write well, you must be prepared to rewrite.

In formal usage, *one* (often followed by *he*) is preferred.

> If one is to write well, he must be prepared to rewrite.

INDEX

INDEX